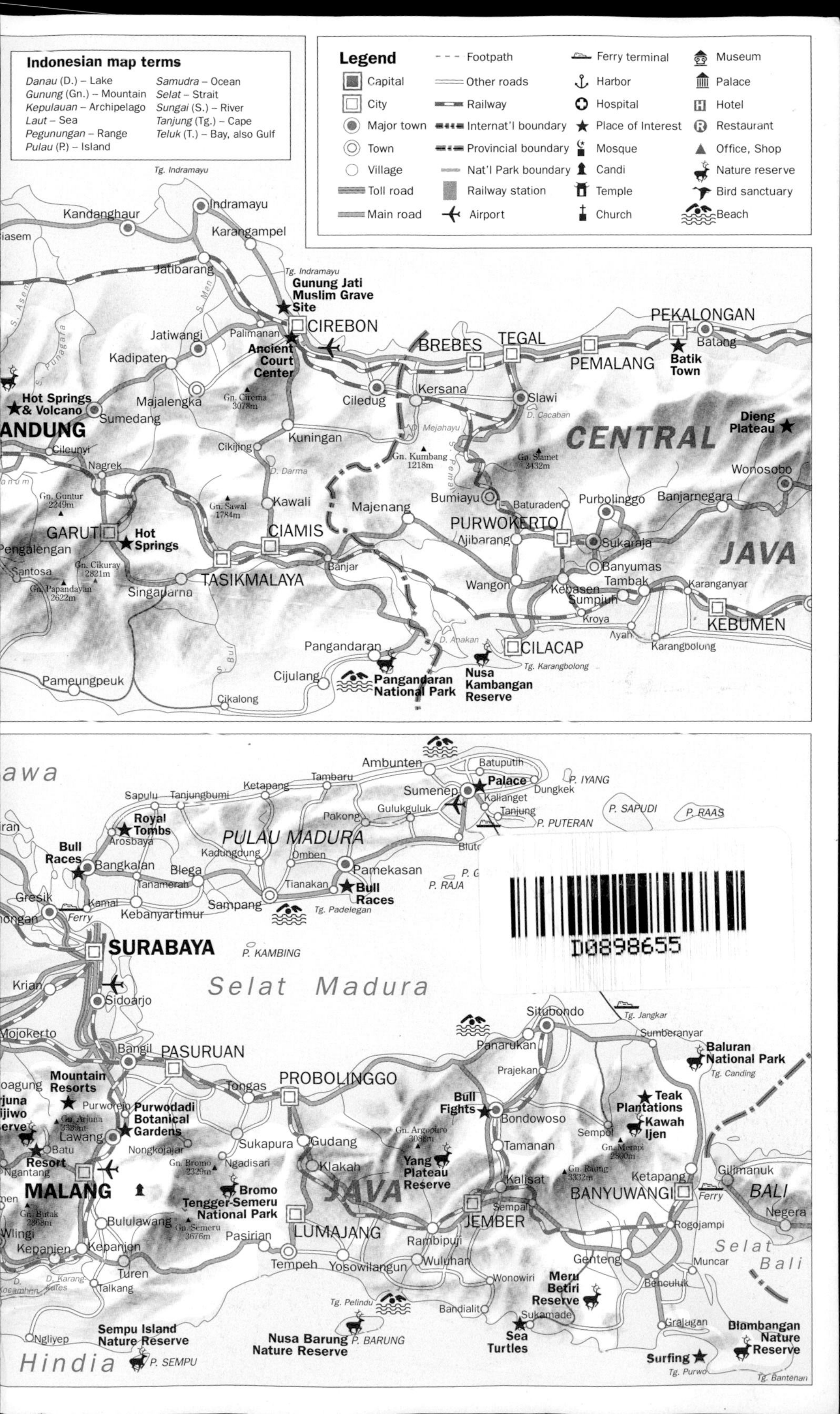
Indonesian map terms
Danau (D.) – Lake
Gunung (Gn.) – Mountain
Kepulauan – Archipelago
Laut – Sea
Pegunungan – Range
Pulau (P.) – Island
Samudra – Ocean
Selat – Strait
Sungai (S.) – River
Tanjung (Tg.) – Cape
Teluk (T.) – Bay, also Gulf
Legend
Capital
City
Major town
Town
Village
Toll road
Main road
Footpath
Other roads
Railway
Internat'l boundary
Provincial boundary
Nat'l Park boundary
Railway station
Airport
Ferry terminal
Harbor
Hospital
Place of Interest
Mosque
Candi
Temple
Church
Museum
Palace
Hotel
Restaurant
Office, Shop
Nature reserve
Bird sanctuary
Beach
Tg. Indramayu
Indramayu
Kandanghaur
Karangampel
Jatibarang
Gunung Jati Muslim Grave Site
CIREBON
Jatiwangi
Palimanan
Ancient Court Center
Kadipaten
Hot Springs & Volcano
Majalengka
Sumedang
ANDUNG
Gn. Ciremai 3078m
Ciledug
Kuningan
Cikijing
Cileunyi
Nagrek
D. Darma
Gn. Guntur 2249m
Gn. Sawal 1784m
Kawali
GARUT
Hot Springs
CIAMIS
Pengalengan
Santosa
Gn. Cikuray 2821m
Gn. Papandayan 2622m
TASIKMALAYA
Singaparna
Banjar
Majenang
BREBES
TEGAL
Kersana
D. Mejahayu
Gn. Kumbang 1218m
Slawi
D. Cacaban
Gn. Slamet 3432m
Bumiayu
Baturaden
PURWOKERTO
Ajibarang
Wangon
PEKALONGAN
Batang
PEMALANG
Batik Town
CENTRAL
JAVA
Dieng Plateau
Wonosobo
Purbolinggo
Banjarnegara
Sukaraja
Banyumas
Tambak
Kebasen
Sumpiuh
Karanganyar
Kroya
KEBUMEN
Ayah
Karangbolong
CILACAP
Tg. Karangbolong
D. Anakan
Pangandaran
Cijulang
Pangandaran National Park
Nusa Kambangan Reserve
Pameungpeuk
Cikalong
Jawa
Ambunten
Batuputih
Palace
Sumenep
Dungkek
P. IYANG
Kalianget
Tanjung
P. PUTERAN
P. SAPUDI
P. RAAS
Tambaru
Ketapang
Sapulu
Tanjungbumi
Royal Tombs
Arosbaya
Gulukguluk
Pakong
PULAU MADURA
Kadungdung
Omben
Bluto
Bull Races
Bangkalan
Blega
Tanamerah
Pamekasan
Tlanakan
P. RAJA
Gresik
Kamal
Ferry
Kebanyartimur
Sampang
Tg. Padelegan
SURABAYA
P. KAMBING
Selat Madura
Krian
Sidoarjo
Mojokerto
Bangil
PASURUAN
Mountain Resorts
Purwodadi
Purwodadi Botanical Gardens
Gn. Arjuna 3339m
Lawang
Batu
Resort
Ngantang
MALANG
Nongkojajar
Gn. Bromo 2329m
Ngadisari
Bromo Tengger-Semeru National Park
Gn. Semeru 3676m
Gn. Butak 2868m
Bululawang
Kepanjen
Turen
Talkang
D. Karangkates
Wlingi
Tongas
PROBOLINGGO
Sukapura
Gudang
Klakah
Pasirian
LUMAJANG
Tempeh
Yosowilangun
Gn. Argopuro 3088m
Yang Plateau Reserve
JAVA
Rambipuji
Wuluhan
Tg. Pelindu
Nusa Barung Nature Reserve
P. BARUNG
Bandialit
Sempu Island Nature Reserve
P. SEMPU
Ngliyep
Hindia
Situbondo
Tg. Jangkar
Panarukan
Prajekan
Bull Fights
Bondowoso
Tamanan
Kalisat
Sempal
JEMBER
Wonowiri
Meru Betiri Reserve
Sukamade
Sea Turtles
Sumberanyar
Baluran National Park
Tg. Canding
Teak Plantations
Kawah Ijen
Sempol
Gn. Merapi 2800m
Gn. Raung 3332m
Ketapang
BANYUWANGI
Gilimanuk
Ferry
BALI
Negera
Rogojampi
Genteng
Muncar
Benculuk
Selat Bali
Gralagan
Surfing
Tg. Purwo
Blambangan Nature Reserve
Tg. Bantenan
D0898655

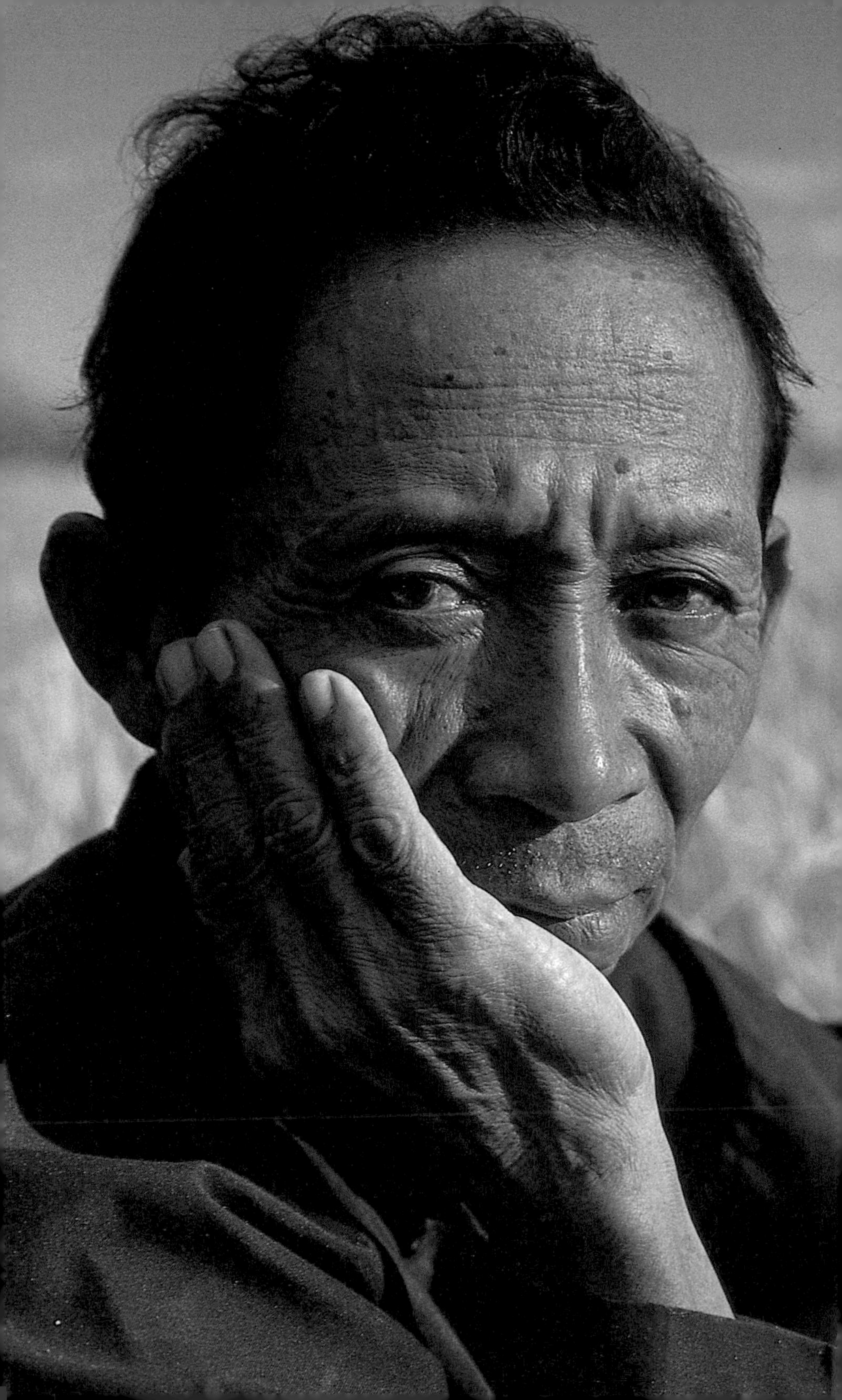

JAVA
Garden of the East

Edited by

ERIC OEY

PASSPORT BOOKS
a division of *NTC Publishing Group*
Lincolnwood, Illinois USA

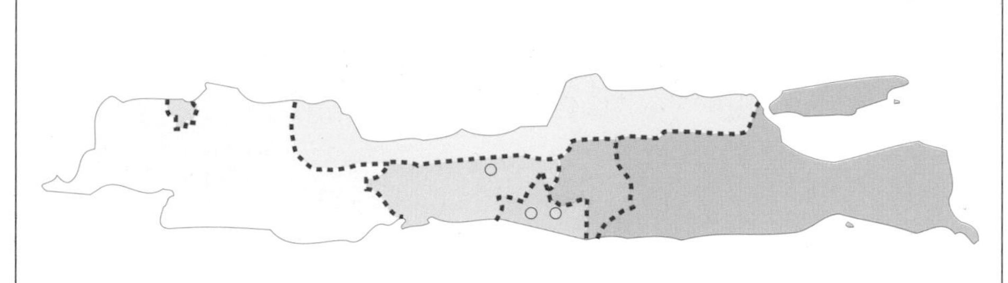

Administratively, Java has three provinces (West, Central, East) and two "Special Areas": Jakarta and Yogyakarta. This book contains chapters on Java's Antiquities, the old court city of Surakarta and the North Coast. The color coded bars at the top of each page are designed to help you quickly find the section you are looking for.

	West Java	Antiquities	The North Coast
Jakarta	Yogyakarta	Surakarta	East Java

This edition first published by Passport Books, a division of NTC Publishing Group, 4255 West Touhy Avenue, Lincolnwood (Chicago), Illinois 60646-1975 U.S.A. Originally published by Periplus Editions (HK) Ltd.

Printed in the Republic of Singapore

ISBN: 0-8442-9947-2

Publisher: Eric Oey
Design: Peter Ivey
Production: Mary Chia, Teresa Tan
Cartography: Kathy Wee,
Regina Wong and Violet Wong

Cover: Wayang Topeng mask dancer from Cirebon, West Java. Photo by Tara Sosrowardoyo.
Pages 4-5: Java's most famous sight—ninth-century Borobudur, with Mt. Merapi in the distance. Photo by Rio Helmi.
Pages 6-7: Rice harvest in Central Java, near Delenggu (Solo). Photo by Eric Oey.
Pages 8-9: Black sand dunes at Parangtritis, south of Yogyakarta. Photo by Fendi Siregar.
Frontispiece: A farmer-philosopher from the Cirebon area. Photo by Jez O'hare.

Contents

PART IV: *Yogyakarta*

PART V: *Antiquities*

PART VI: *Surakarta*

PART VII: *The North Coast*

PART VIII: *East Java*

On The Road

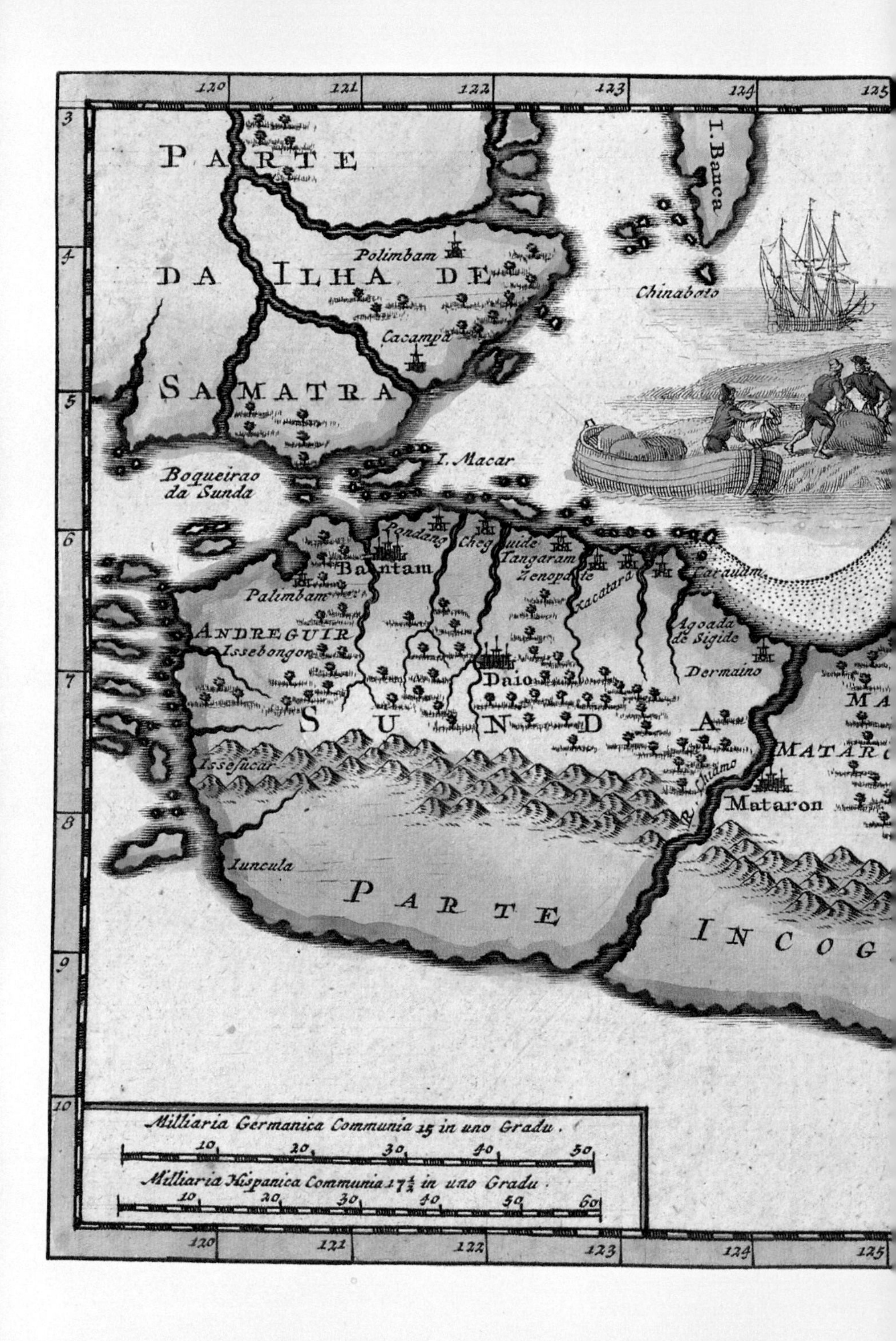

PARTE
DA ILHA DE
SAMATRA
I. Banca
Chinaboto
Polimbam
Cacampa
I. Macar
Boqueirao da Sunda
Pondang
Cheguide
Tangaram
Zenopate
Xacatara
Carauam
Bantam
Palimbam
Agoada de Sigide
ANDREGUIR
Issebongon
Dermaino
Daio
SUNDA
MATAR
Issesucar
Mataron
R. Chiamo
Iuncula
PARTE
INCOG
Milliaria Germanica Communia 15 in uno Gradu.
Milliaria Hispanica Communia 17½ in uno Gradu.

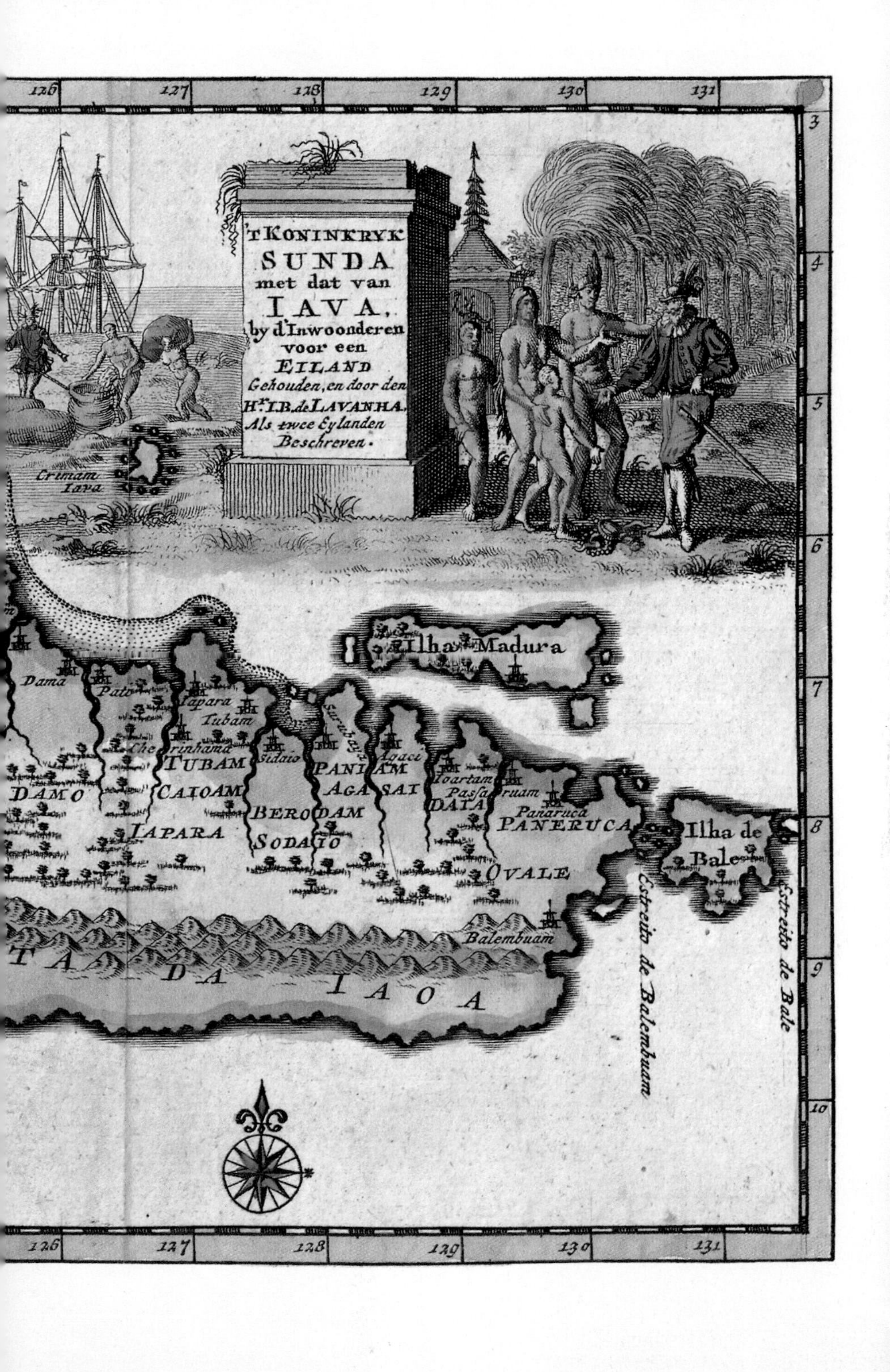

'T KONINKRYK
SUNDA
met dat van
IAVA,
by d'Inwoonderen
voor een
EILAND
Gehouden, en door den
Hr. I.B. de LAVANHA,
Als twee Eylanden
Beschreven.
Crimam Iava
Ilha Madura
Dama
Pato
Iapara
Tubam
TUBAM
CAIOAM
DAMO
IAPARA
BERODAM
SODAIO
PANIAM
AGA SAI
DATA
Agaci
Ioartam
Passaruam
Panaruca
PANERUCA
OVALE
Balembuam
Ilha de Bale
Estreito de Balembuam
Estreito de Bale
DA IAOA
126
127
128
129
130
131

PART I

Indonesia's Island of Eden

Java is truly extraordinary. Everyone who visits this fertile volcanic island seems to come away favorably impressed. From the earliest Buddhist pilgrims who stopped here in ancient times on the way from China to India, right up to the "Java-Bali" package tourists of today, who peer through the misted windows of air-conditioned coaches. Many have described Java as the most habitable and also the most hospitable place in all of Asia—a veritable tropical paradise where all manner of flora and fauna flourish in abundance, and where people seem to have a natural knack for making you feel welcome.

Java actually has one of the longest records of human habitation of any place on earth. It was here that million-year-old remains of one of man's earliest ancestors were first discovered a century ago—the infamous "Java Man" (*Homo erectus*) fossils that provided the first, controversial evidence of Darwin's "missing link."

For eons, the island was blanketed in a luxuriant mantle of tropical forest hosting an exotic assortment of wildlife. Violent volcanic eruptions periodically spread nutrient-rich deposits across the land, while the sculpted volcanic slopes provided ideal terrain for irrigated cultivation. Heavy monsoon rains, bubbling mountain springs and months of uninterrupted sunshine produced a bounty of grains, fruits and forest products.

In 1861, the great English naturalist Alfred Russel Wallace marvelled at the island's natural fertility: "Taking it as a whole, and surveying it from every point of view, Java is probably the very finest and most interesting tropical island in the world."

The Javanese have taken full advantage of such blessings, and their historical record is a long and illustrious one. Their great Hindu-Buddhist and Islamic kingdoms left a wealth of architectural wonders—most notably Borobudur, the world's largest Buddhist monument. Today Java is the political, commercial and population center of Indonesia—the world's fifth largest nation—and supports over 115 million people on a land area the size of England or New York State.

Ironically, the island that was a major source of agricultural wealth during the last century (providing half of the world's coffee, much of its rubber and sugar, and 90 percent of its quinine) is now overwhelmingly poor and rural. Three quarters of the inhabitants live in the countryside; about 55 percent making a living from agriculture. Though living standards are improving, as much as a third of the rural population finds it difficult to meet minimum nutritional needs.

Perhaps the most dramatic change of the last century has been the expansion of Java's cities. Jakarta—once a tiny, sweltering port surrounded by coastal swamps—had one-twentieth of its present population 50 years ago. And there are many other large cities. Bandung in West Java is an important intellectual and educational center. Yogya and Solo in Central Java maintain elements of their erstwhile courtly charm. Semarang on the north coast seems to be managing the transition to its new role as a center for light manufacturing with considerable equanimity. By comparison, Surabaya in East Java (the second largest city on Java) seems to have lost some of its soul amidst the smokestacks and traffic congestion that mark its rapid progress toward industrialization.

The pace of modernization on Java is rapidly quickening. Factories, highways and housing estates are growing up all around the major cities, and for better or for worse it is here that the future of Java (and therefore of Indonesia) is being defined.

—Eric Oey and Robert Hefner

Overleaf: *Early 18th century Dutch map, from which it is clear that only the north coastal ports of Java were well known.* **Opposite:** *The lush landscapes of Central Java. Photo by Luca Tettoni.*

GEOGRAPHY

Tropical Island of Superlatives

The island of Java is incredibly beautiful. From the air, it appears as a patchquilt of verdant rice fields interspersed by village settlements, palm groves and stands of rubber, teak and sugar cane. The bright green vegetation contrasts vividly with rich, red-brown soils, and everywhere the landscapes are dominated by soaring, blue-grey volcanoes whose inverted cones are balding on top, forested in the middle and blanketed by rice terraces below. Water trickles over tidy bunds and fields through a vast network of man-made channels, finally reaching broad, silt-laden rivers that meander to the sea.

This is the most fertile, the most productive, and also the most densely populated island in the world. With over 115 million people living in an area the size of England or New York State, the average population density is an amazing 850 persons per square kilometer (2000 per square mile). And although there are four cities with over a million inhabitants, and many more with over 100,000, the island is still predominantly rural. Java constitutes just 7 percent of Indonesia's total land mass, yet supports over 60 percent of the nation's huge population.

Many areas in the mountains and along the isolated southern shore are in fact still rather sparsely populated. Several of the island's densely packed agricultural zones, on the other hand, support more than twice the island average. In the fertile crescent around Yogyakarta in Central Java, for example, rural densities soar to an unbelievable 2000 per square kilometer (5000 per square mile), with the majority still making a living from traditional wet-rice cultivation, practiced under the most labor-intensive conditions found anywhere on earth.

Not all Java possesses such luxuriance, however. The low hills along the south coast, and several areas on the north coast, are formed over non-volcanic rocks which lack this inherent fertility. Limestone regions in Central and East Java are especially barren, and the plains along the north coast may be deeply flooded during the wet season yet parched in the dry season.

Volcanic 'Ring of Fire'

Volcanoes are the very essence of Java. They have molded the landscape and provided the

ALAIN COMPOST

basis for Java's rich soils. Frequent outpourings of nutrient-rich lava and ash are washed by heavy rains down across the foothills and plains, providing a continuous renewal of the land. For centuries, farmers have diverted these rich waters into their fields, planting two or even three crops a year.

The volcanoes form an irregular line running the entire length of the island—one of the most active segments in the circum-Pacific "Ring of Fire" that marks the boundary of drifting continental plates. Java lies at

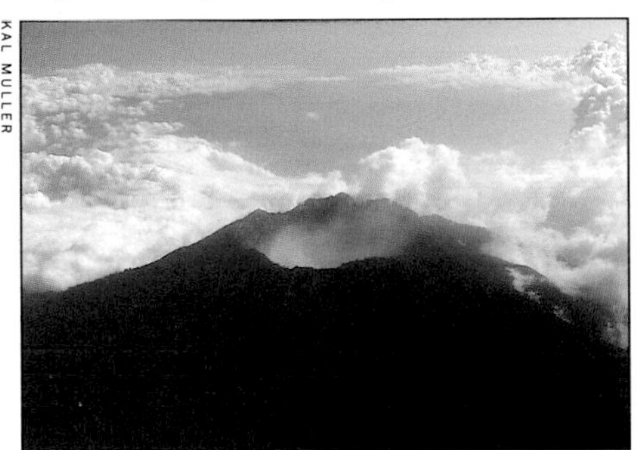

KAL MULLER

the southern extremity of one of these plates, which during the Ice Ages formed a huge sub-continent encompassing all of Java, Bali, Borneo, Sumatra, Malaya and the intervening area that now lies submerged beneath the shallow Java Sea. Java became an island at several stages in the past, most recently about 15,000 years ago when the seas rose with the last melting of the Pleistocene ice.

The Java Sea to the north of the island is in fact extremely shallow—less than 200 meters (650 ft) at its deepest point. The Java Trench to the south, on the other hand, drops precipitously to 7,000 meters (23,000 ft). This trench marks a zone of violent subduction where the Indo-Australian plate is sliding northward beneath the Sunda plate.

Two longitudinal folds along the line of impact between these two colliding continental plates form Java's basic "foundation"—a northerly and a southerly line of hills, with a trough running in between them. It is through this trough that the island's volcanoes have thrust dramatically upward. The volcanoes, which are andesitic or basaltic in composition, are more tightly packed in the west, where they create a tangled complex of upland plateaus and valleys. To the east, they are more widely spaced, creating a series of gradually sloping valleys that are perfectly suited to rice field terracing.

While many peaks date back to the Tertiary era and have long since weathered

AMIR SIDHARTA

and lost recognizable form, others are very young. Java and Bali together have 37 volcanoes officially listed, of which 23 have been active since 1600. There are 13 that have erupted in the last 25 years and another 6 are currently dormant.

The highest peak is Mt. Semeru at 3,676 meters (12,060 feet), which sends forth intermittent puffs of smoke. The most famous volcano is Krakatau in the Sunda Strait separating Java from Sumatra, whose cataclysmic eruption in 1883 set up tidal waves that reportedly killed 36,000 people.

Mt. Merapi (literally "Flaming Mountain") to the north of Yogyakarta erupts most frequently, but Mt. Kelud near Blitar is the most violent. Kelud's 1966 eruption killed over 200 people, but with improved early warning systems, a recent eruption in February 1990 resulted in a death toll of only 31.

The unpredictability of Java's volcanoes is well-illustrated by the eruption of Mt. Galunggung in West Java in 1982, which occurred after the volcano had lain dormant for centuries. The surrounding area was devastated—blanketed in grey ash that accumulated locally to over a meter in depth. Two jumbo jets en route from Singapore to Australia were nearly brought down by the dust clouds, while cars as far away as Bogor had to use headlamps in broad daylight.

In this tectonically active zone there are frequent earthquakes, though usually not very severe. There were major quakes in 1903, 1937 and 1943—the first was the largest recorded, measuring 8.1 on the Richter Scale. The main center of tectonic activity lies off the south coast, and the cities of the north rarely experience more than mild tremors.

With their potential for devastation, volca-

Opposite: *A sulphurous lake in the Dieng Plateau.* **Above, left and right:** *Java's highly destructive volcanoes are also, paradoxically, the source of the island's extraordinary fecundity.*

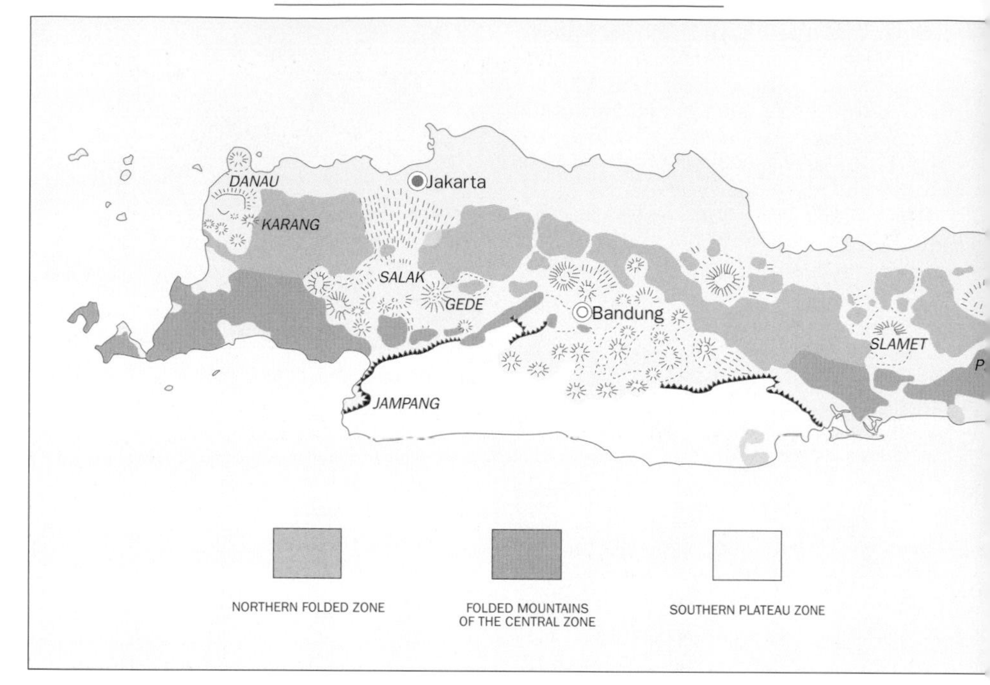

noes are a mixed blessing, yet as the dust settles after each eruption, land-hungry farmers move back into the area to redevelop the fertile soils. In some areas the dangers are more subtle—as, for example, the clouds of odorless poisonous gas that sometimes waft across the Dieng Plateau. Yet the Javanese often seek a livelihood in the very jaws of volcanic death, as in the quarries of fresh sulphur formed by hissing fumaroles in the crater of Mt. Ijen—Java's easternmost peak.

Striking regional contrasts

In stark contrast to the lush, green volcanic foothills of the island, the limestone karsts that line the northeastern and southern shores—forming the Rembang Plateau and the island of Madura in the east, as well as the Gunung Sewu range in the south—present an appearance more reminiscent of Mediterranean countries than of the tropics.

Here the soils are shallow and rainwater quickly seeps through sink-holes into the soluble rock below, so that the landscape becomes barren in the dry season. The heavy, dark grey clays of these regions crack deeply when dry, but become sticky and intractable when wet.

The remaining hills of southern Java are formed over older, volcanic and folded sedimentary rocks, and are reminiscent of Indonesia's outer islands. The soils are acid and leached, and will not support sustained cropping without substantial fertilizer inputs. This terrain is better suited to tree crops; tea and rubber are grown widely, and oil palms have been planted in West Java.

The mountains are never far from the sea, and few of the rivers on Java achieve significant size as a result. The two largest rivers on the island—the Bengawan Solo and the Brantas—have been diverted by volcanic activity. Both arise near the south coast of Java but wind around and between several peaks, finally debouching into the sea near Surabaya. Rather similar is the Citarum River in West Java, which flows out of the former lakebed around Bandung through a series of gorges and the Jatiluhur Reservoir before emptying into the sea at Cape Krawang, east of Jakarta.

The flat alluvial plains of the north coast are extensively cultivated with rice wherever water drainage can be managed. Toward the sea, the swampy rice fields merge into fish ponds. Most mangroves of the north have recently been converted into lucrative prawn farms (*tambak*), and there are extensive salt pans in the dry areas on the coasts around Surabaya, Rembang and on Madura.

Hot and wet climate

The weather of Java is hot and humid, with only minor seasonal variation. Maximum temperature in the lowlands is about 34°C (93°F) on a sunny day, and 30°C (86°F) on a

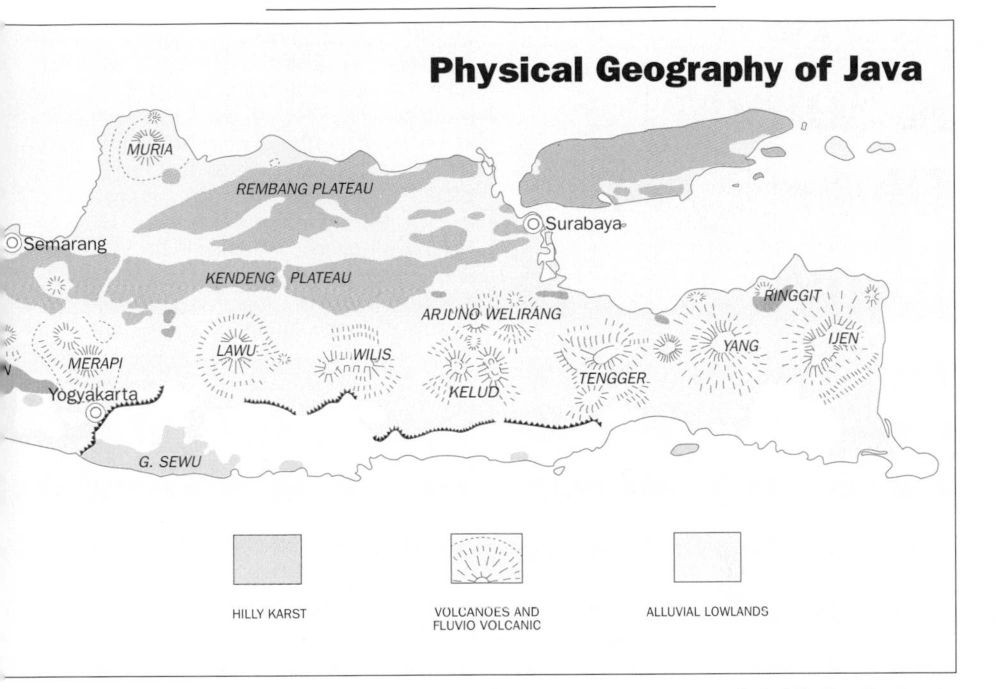

cloudy day. Due to the presence of nearby seas, the highest temperature ever recorded on Java is only 36°C (97°F). Night minima are constant at about 22°C (72°F) on the coast. With such constancy of both temperature and day-length (Java lies only 800 kilometers/480 miles south of the equator), Indonesians measure their seasons by rice and fruit crops and the arrival of the annual monsoonal rains.

Temperatures drop markedly with altitude, at the rate of about 1°C (1.8°F) for each 200 meters (650 feet). In the highland resort of Puncak south of Jakarta, at an altitude of 900 meters (3000 feet), temperatures range between 17° and 26° C (63° and 79°F). On mountain peaks, they range from 4° to 14°C (39° to 57°F) during the day, and frosts can occur at night above 1500 meters—a fact that should be taken into account by overnight visitors to Mt. Bromo in East Java.

Parts of Java are very wet. The slopes of Mt. Slamet in Central Java receive over 7000 mm (275 inches) of rainfall each year, and most of Java's hillsides receive 3-4000 mm (115-160 inches). Few places in the world receive as much rainfall as this.

By contrast, the average rainfall along the north coast and in the lowlands of East Java is only about 1500 mm (60 inches) per year. The driest spot is Asembagus at the island's easternmost extremity, which receives less than 900 mm (36 inches)—still more than most temperate areas. Rainfall distribution is extremely complex, being profoundly influenced by topography and exposure, and it is not unusual for average annual rainfall to increase twofold over a distance of only 20 kilometers due to purely local factors.

Much of the rain falls in short but very intense thunderbursts—and rainfalls of 50-100 mm (2-4 inches) in a single storm are not unusual. Bogor in West Java holds the record as the most thundery town in the world, with over 320 days on which thunder has been heard in a single year. Java is spared the fury of tropical cyclones and tornadoes, although thunder squalls are occasionally quite fierce.

The wet northwesterly monsoon arrives in January and February, with cloudy and wet winds flowing toward a low pressure zone over northern Australia. The northwestern coasts exposed to this wind experience a daily drenching that may average 15 to 20 mm (0.6-0.8 inches).

From July to September, the dry southeast monsoon blows up from the Australian desert, bringing with it somewhat cooler temperatures and drier air. The eastern and southern coasts of Java are very dry and clear at this time, though the west and north coasts rarely feel the benefit of these tempering breezes. Yogyakarta and Bali, in particular, experience deliciously cool and fresh nights during these months.

— Derek Holmes

FLORA AND FAUNA

A Surprising Diversity of Native Wildlife

The large, western islands of the Indonesian Archipelago—Sumatra, Java and Borneo—are home to some of the richest and most diverse flora and fauna in the world. These islands were attached to one another and to the Asian mainland at various times in the past, and many species are common to all of them. It is quite surprising, therefore, that Java itself has so many species not found on any of the surrounding islands.

Even more surprising, given the island's high population density, is the fact that several mammals only recently extinct on Sumatra —such as the leopard and the Javan rhino—still survive on Java. Indeed, the scattered pockets of wildlife that remain on this island are evidence of an extraordinary biological richness that is now, sadly, somewhat depleted but still well worth the effort to explore.

Even in the most densely populated cities, in fact, there are mongooses, snakes (including pythons), lizards and civet cats, not to mention myriad forms of insect life—some more irritating than others. And most visitors are amazed to find that within only a day's journey of Jakarta, one can visit half a dozen national parks and reserves and see one of the few remaining tracts of primary forest on Java. Here indeed are many of the 5,000 plant species, 100 species of snakes and over 300 colorful bird species found on the island.

Traveling the length of Java from one end to the other, moreover, one experiences a notable change in vegetation—from the very humid, species-rich rainforests of West Java to the deciduous forests and dry savannah grasslands of the East. Java actually straddles the boundary between two quite different climatic zones—the perennially moist equatorial region of Sumatra, Kalimantan and Malaya to the north, and the more arid islands of Nusa Tenggara to the southeast. In contrast to both, Java has both a distinct wet season (January-March) and a prolonged dry season (July-October). As one moves eastward, the climate becomes markedly drier, with fewer mammals and birds inhabiting environments more spacious than in the west.

The humid climate of West Java, for example, is ideally suited to orchids and tree ferns, and except in the dry season there are few other flowers to be seen until you reach the eastern part of the island.

KAL MULLER

ERIC OEY

The ever-present water buffalo is the most common domestic animal—commonly seen ploughing the rice fields, or being herded in procession by small boys. All other grazing animals are kept tethered and have their fodder brought to them, because land is too precious here to be given up to pasture.

Chicken farming is also common in Java, and the scrawny *kampung* (village farmyard) chickens which run suicidally in front of oncoming traffic are descendants of proud jungle fowl native to the region. These birds still bear the characteristics of their ancestors—long legs and very little meat (though the Javanese insist they are more tasty than factory chickens). They lay small eggs, and large numbers of cockerels are kept in the hopes of breeding a champion fighter. Visitors will also see flocks of small brown ducks waddling around the rice fields looking for frogs and snails. These too are kept mainly for eggs—duck eggs are a popular delicacy.

An agricultural cornucopia

An astounding 63 percent of all land on Java is cultivated, compared to only 10 to 20 percent on other Indonesian islands. A third of this is irrigated farmland worked by smallholders who may or may not own their own plots—while another 7 percent is under cultivation by large estates growing tea, rubber, oil palm, cacao and teak.

At least 55 percent of the population of Java are farmers, and by far the most important crop is rice. Irrigated rice fields or *sawah* in fact occupy 24 percent of Java's total land area. Other crops of importance, such as maize, soybeans, peanuts, cassava and potatoes, are grown on dry fields, but rice is the staple food and beautifully engineered rice terraces and irrigation systems are a characteristic feature of the landscape.

As you travel through Java, bear in mind that some of these terraces and irrigation networks are over 2,000 years old, and all have been painstakingly constructed by hand using very simple tools—a feat made possible only through close cooperation among village farmers. The land is still largely tilled, weeded and harvested by hand, although some draft animals—such as oxen and water buffalo—are also used.

Most farmers' plots on Java are too small to make machinery worthwhile, and yet surprisingly at least two rice crops a year can be grown. Indeed, triple-cropping is even possible in some areas, although this is currently banned by the government in order to control the spread of pests. Even so, the application of improved water management techniques, high-yield rice strains and chemical

ERIC OEY

Left: *A common sight in Java—water buffaloes enjoying a bath in flooded rice paddies after a day of plowing.* **Above:** *Tea pickers on a plantation in West Java.* **Right:** *A rice harvest in Central Java.*

fertilizers on Java and Bali has enabled Indonesia to achieve self-sufficiency in rice in recent years, despite the periodic ravages of floods, droughts, rats and insects.

Marginal land is still being opened up, and new terraces carved out of land which was, until recently, primary forest. This means that the centuries-old process of deforestation is now nearly complete. Less than 10 percent of the island's original forests remain intact; a century ago, the hills just outside of Jakarta were still thickly forested.

Those having read Wallace's *The Malay Archipelago* will be amazed to find that only 100 years ago Wallace could report that a child had been killed by a tiger at Mojoagung near Mojokerto, now one of the most densely populated rural areas in East Java. The little forest that is left on Java consists mainly of residual mountain tracts. The original forests were equatorial rainforests in the west, but became increasingly deciduous eastwards, with a form of fire-climax monsoon savannah found in the driest areas.

Parks and nature reserves

For the conservation of natural ecosystems, it is very fortunate therefore that the lowland rainforests in Ujung Kulon National Park and Meru-Betiri Game Reserve, and the savannah forests of Baluran National Park, are now protected, as they are vitally important for the conservation of Java's bio-diversity.

Less than 150 km (90 mi) from the center of Jakarta, on Java's westernmost tip at Ujung Kulon National Park, is the island's last refuge for the crocodile. More importantly, it is also the sole remaining haunt of the Javan rhino—one of the rarest mammals on earth. Only about 60 individuals survive, and as they are bashful creatures you have to be lucky or dedicated—or both—to catch sight of one. You are much more likely to see the *banteng*, a species of wild cattle which are also shy but numerous.

From the Ujung Kulon Park, you can sail to Anak Krakatau in the middle of the Sunda Straits separating Java from Sumatra. There you will be able to experience firsthand the amazing regeneration of plant life on the devastated slopes of the Krakatau volcano.

An hour's drive south of Jakarta lies Bogor, with its world-famous Botanic Gardens (Kebon Raya), which were established at the beginning of the 19th century. The gardens hold an excellent collection of tropical plants—spice trees, rainforest species and palms of all size and shape—as well as the venerable "ancestor" of all oil palms in Southeast Asia, brought from South America in the last century. This is also an important haven for bird life.

Above Bogor, take a trip up through the tea plantations of Puncak into the Parahyangan ("Abode of the Gods") highlands. In this area, still quite heavily forested in parts

ALAIN COMPOST

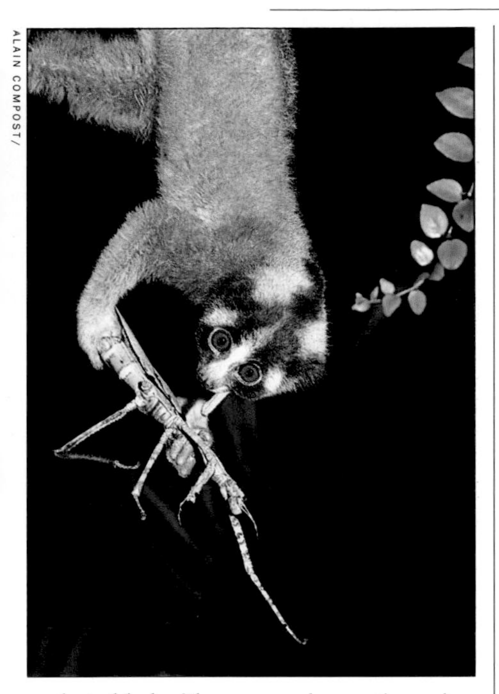

ALAIN COMPOST/

and studded with more or less active volcanoes, you can climb to the summits of several volcanoes, look down into hissing craters and cool off under magnificent waterfalls.

Gunung Halimun Reserve, only six hours from Jakarta, still has some primary forest, and despite being surrounded by tea and clove plantations contains a wide variety of primates—some rare, like the Javan Gibbon, the Javan Leaf Monkey and the Silvered Leaf Monkey. Some of these monkeys can also be seen during the five-hour climb to the crater of Gunung Gede. Start from the montane botanic gardens at Cibodas, and on the way up you will pass magnificent tree ferns, many species of begonia, and amazing epiphytes growing on trees. This is also a good place to see a fair number of birds—look out for the Javan Scops Owl, which has not been sighted for several years.

Gunung Gede has meadows below the crater with an amazing alpine flora, including many species closely related to some found in the Swiss Alps. There are giant Javan Edelweiss, gentians and St. John's Wort, as well as wild raspberries and strawberries.

Along the central volcanic spine of West Java you will travel through some of the most spectacular scenery in Indonesia—glorious mountain peaks and rushing cataracts. Along the south coast lies the resort and nature reserve of Pangandaran. This is perhaps the most accessible of all reserves on Java, even though it is about nine hours by bus from Jakarta. There are many different birds and monkeys, and in the cleared areas deer and *banteng* can be seen. There are also wonderful beaches, and a boat trip through the lagoon is well worth the time.

Around Central and East Java there are a number of reserves. Many, however, are rather inaccessible unless you have your own four-wheel drive transport and are prepared to walk long distances carrying food and bedding, though this can be very enjoyable.

Around the eastern tip of Java are a number of reserves which are easy to reach from Bali. Banyuwangi Selatan is a surfer's paradise; Mt. Ijen is a steaming crater where sulphur is mined; Meru Betiri is where the last sightings of the Javan Tiger were made several years ago, and where giant sea turtles lay their eggs on the beach at night. The easiest of all these reserves to visit, however, is Baluran, where the climate is almost East African and the landscape similar. Here it is easier to see the animals, especially in the dry season because they come to the water holes near the guest house. This is another good place to see *banteng*, jungle fowl and peacocks in their native habitat.

—Cécile Lomer

ALAIN COMPOST

Left: *One of only about 60 remaining Javan rhinos in the Ujung Kulon National Park.* **Above:** *A slow loris eating an insect.* **Right:** *A black langur.*

BIRDWATCHING

Endemic and Endangered Species

Indonesia has over 1500 distinct bird species, giving it the richest avifauna in Asia and one of the richest in the world. This is because the archipelago extends across three major faunal regions—Sundaland (comprising Sumatra, Borneo, Java and Bali) in the west, Sahulland (New Guinea and Australia) in the east and Wallacea (the transitional zone comprising Sulawesi, Maluku and Nusa Tenggara) in between.

Java's avifauna is the product of its recent geological history. The island lies at the southern extremity of the ancient Sunda subcontinent, and its birds thus have affinities with those of Sumatra, Borneo and the Malay Peninsula. During the Pleistocene era, land stretched continuously from Java to the Asian mainland, allowing bird populations to intermingle, but since the Ice Ages Java has been isolated for a long enough time to evolve endemic species in several families. The avifaunas of other Sunda regions have more in common with each other than with Java.

Conversely, Java has several species which it shares with mainland Southeast Asia, but which are absent in Sumatra, Borneo and Malaya. These are savannah birds that must have moved south across the sub-continental landmass millennia ago, taking advantage of the monsoonal climate and enormous, seasonally flooded river valleys that existed at that time. As the coastlines receded, these birds became isolated in Java's drier zone, but were unable to survive in the intervening rainforest areas.

Java is a favorable place to familiarize oneself with regional bird genera before embarking on the intricacies of identification in Sumatra and Borneo. For example, there are only 3 species of hornbills and 3 malkohas here, compared to 9 and 6 respectively in Sumatra. Similarly, there are 11 bulbuls and 19 babblers, compared to Sumatra's 27 and 42.

First impressions of bird life may be disappointing, as few birds are seen in the cities and open countryside. This is true throughout Southeast Asia, because native birds are forest dwellers. There are, however, three main habitats in which the visitor can expect to encounter most of Java's birds: wetlands, lowland forests and mountains.

Endemic species

Java has about 325 breeding species—substantially fewer than the 400 to 440 found on the neighboring islands of Borneo and Sumatra. Yet Java (with Bali) has 29 endemics. A similar number is found on Borneo, whereas mainland Sumatra has only 13. Sulawesi, by contrast, has over 65.

One of the island's endemic species has become extinct in recent decades: the Javan Wattled Lapwing (*Vanellus macropterus*), which once inhabited grassy swards in the plains. Recent searches in its former haunts have been without success. Another endemic, the Javan Hawk-Eagle (*Spizaetus bartelsi*), is also endangered, although it can still be seen in the Mount Gede-Pangrango and Meru-Betiri reserves.

Another conspicuous endemic is the Black-winged Starling (*Sturnus melanopterus*), a white bird of open country with black primaries and bare yellow skin around the eye—heavily trapped for the bird trade and rare in West Java.

A fourth endemic is the Javan Kingfisher (*Halcyon javensis*), a large, noisy open-coun-

ALAIN COMPOST

try bird, wild and difficult to see. No less than three of Java's six barbets (*Megalaima* sp.) are endemic.

Two endemic owls are noteworthy. The Javan Barred Owlet (*Glaucidium castanopterum*), which inhabits woodlands, is quite common in the wilder regions. It repeatedly sings a series of haunting notes at dusk and dawn. By contrast, the Javan Scops Owl (*Otus angelinae*) is confined to the montane forests of West Java and is habitually silent—its calls have never been described.

ALAIN COMPOST

Waterfowl

Java is very rich in large waterbirds. There are major colonies on Pulau Dua (Banten), Pulau Rambut (northwest of Jakarta) and in some ten sites in the Brantas and Solo deltas near Surabaya. The total number of breeding pairs in these 12 colonies exceeds 30,000, including various species of egrets and herons, and large numbers of Night Herons (*Nycticorax nycticorax*) and Little Black Cormorants (*Phalacrocorax sulcirostris*). A few Glossy Ibis (*Plegadis falcinellus*) and Black-headed Ibis (*Threskiornis melanocephalus*) are present, while Pulau Rambut has a few nests of the endangered Milky Stork (*Ibis cinereus*). These occasionally feed in swamps close to Jakarta's airport, giving visitors the rare chance to see an endangered species immediately upon arrival in the country.

Lowland forest species

The most threatened habitat in Java is the lowland rainforest, and the few remaining forest reserves are extremely important. Here you will see forest birds such as the lowland woodpeckers, barbets, bulbuls and babblers. All three hornbills, now generally rare in Java, are still common here, notably the Rhinoceros Hornbill (*Buceros rhinoceros*) and the Wreathed Hornbill (*Rhyticeros undulatus*). The smaller Pied Hornbill (*Anthracoceros coronatus*) is not confined to forests

ALAIN COMPOST

and occurs more widely. At Ujung Kulon, parties of Green Peafowl (*Pavo muticus*) feed on open pastures. The Green Peafowl is also common at Baluran in East Java—an excellent venue for the birder.

Montane forest birds

Many forests scattered throughout the mountains offer exceptionally good bird-watching. Visitors to the Gede-Pangrango Reserve in southwest Java can view the majority of montane forest birds quite readily, including several endemic species. Obtrusive in the mountains are the noisy Chestnut-backed Scimitar Babbler (*Pomatorhinus montanus*), the endemic Red-tailed Fantail Flycatcher (*Rhipidura phoenicurus*) and the endemic Javan Partridge (*Arborophila javanica*). Two species of barbet, both endemic, can be heard calling for much of the day: the Brown-throated (*Megalaima corvina*) and Blue-crowned (*M. armillaris*) Barbets. Mountain birds tend to be active until the daytime clouds descend, and bird-watching here is a cool and extremely rewarding pastime.

With extensive deforestation, more birds might be expected to have become extinct. Loss of habitat is not the only threat, however; illegal trapping continues to decimate the populations of such popular cage birds as the Banded Pitta (*Pitta guajana*), the White-rumped Shama (*Copsychus malabaricus*), the Straw-crowned Bulbul (*Pycnonotus zeylanicus*) and the Talking Myna or Grackle (*Gracula religiosa*). The combination of trapping, intensive agriculture and constant disturbance has now ensured that many in Java will never experience the pleasure of bird song as they go about their daily lives.

— *Derek Holmes*

Opposite: *A Blue-throated Bee-eater in Ujung Kulon National Park.* **Above, left:** *A stork-billed Kingfisher eating a shrimp, also in Ujung Kulon.* **Above, right:** *A Lineated Barbet.*

PREHISTORY

'Java Man' and Later Migrations

Java formed the remote southeastern rim of continental Asia for as much as 90 percent of the time after the first humans arrived, about a million years ago. Due to a lowering of sea levels, early humans were able to colonize Java by land very early on, and indeed the famous "Java Man" fossils discovered here a century ago by Eugene Dubois were among the very first pieces of evidence confirming Darwin's evolutionary theories.

For many millennia, Java and Bali marked the migratory endpoint for large placental mammals such as cattle, deer, elephants and tigers that are typical of the Asian mainland but are not found on the eastern islands of Indonesia. Along with these species, early humans were prevented from moving farther to the east by deep straits separating Borneo and Bali from Sulawesi and Lombok. These straits, in existence long before humans appeared on the scene, were only crossed following the innovation of rafts, which probably occurred around 50,000 years ago and subsequently allowed a fairly rapid human diaspora across the islands of eastern Indonesia and the Philippines to New Guinea, the Bismarck Archipelago and Australia.

Earliest humans on Java

The first humans to reach Java were members of the species *Homo erectus*, an ancestor of modern humans whose fossilized remains have been found in ancient volcanic, riverine and lakebed deposits in the basin of the Solo River in Central Java.

The most important of these localities is Sangiran, where parts of many fossilized skulls have been found in a sequence of geological deposits dating between one million and 500,000 years ago. These older remains are popularly referred to as "Java Man," while those from Sambungmacan and Ngandong are known as "Solo Man" and are much younger—possibly around 100,000 years old. The large gap separating them poses serious problems, and renders a detailed understanding of human evolution in Java very elusive.

Muscular and beetle-browed, *Homo erectus* was nevertheless bipedal (upright and two-legged) like ourselves, and only slightly shorter in stature. Brain size was about two-thirds of the modern average, while jaws,

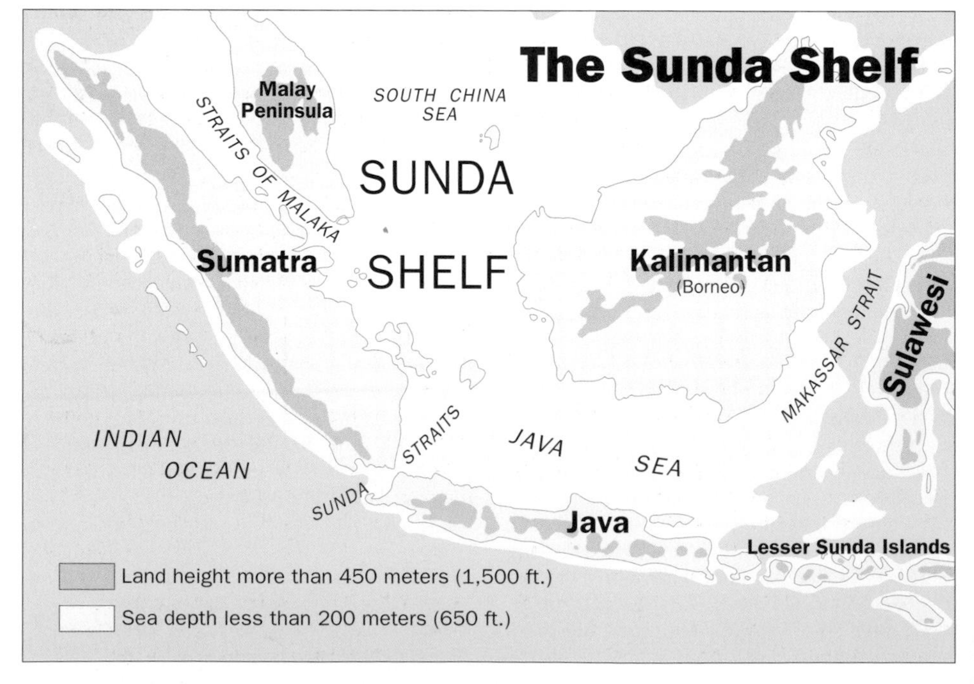

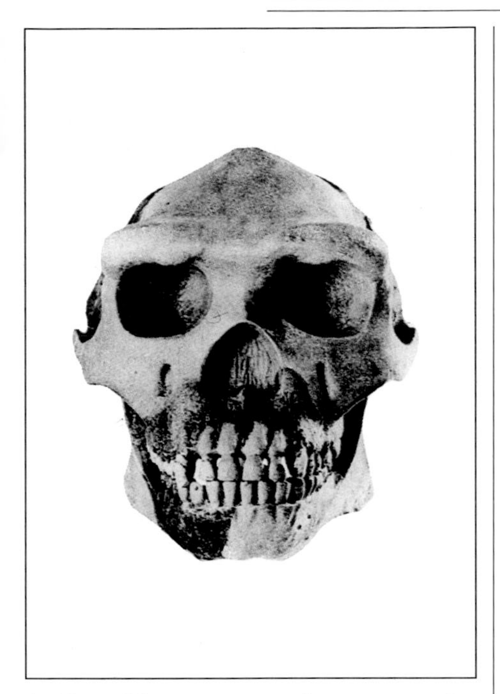

teeth and faces were much more massive than those of modern humans.

Virtually all authorities agree that *Homo erectus* evolved in Africa and spread from there into Eurasia. Many also regard Javan *Homo erectus* as a line that eventually became extinct and was completely replaced by a later migration of modern humans, who also evolved in Africa.

Skeptics, however, ask if this rather ignominious fate for Java Man, following a million years of documented local evolution, is really believable. Many paleoanthropologists in China and Southeast Asia believe that there was a continous local evolution from *Homo erectus* to modern humans in Asia that paralleled a similar evolution in Africa, and it has to be admitted that the case for *erectus* extinction in Java or anywhere else in Asia is by no means watertight.

Whatever the ultimate verdict on *Homo erectus*, it appears that modern humans of Australoid physical appearanc—ancestral to modern Australian Aborigines and Melanesian—had spread throughout Southeast Asia and the western Pacific by about 30,000 years ago. Their remains have been discovered in caves in the Philippines and Sarawak, and skulls from Wajak in eastern Java seem to provide evidence of their presence here as well. Some aspects of modern Javanese physique may indeed trace back to this time, though in general the modern-day Javanese are descendants of an entirely distinct group who arrived here much later from the north.

Arrival of the Javanese

The biological and cultural roots of the present-day Javanese go back to the period around 4-5000 years ago when agricultural peoples settled the island from the north, thus commencing a Neolithic agricultural phase in Java. The modern Javanese are basically a Southern Mongoloid population having close biological affinities with other East and Southeast Asians who live to their north. They speak languages belonging to the huge Austronesian family, which includes almost all indigenous languages of Island Southeast Asia—including Indonesia, the Philippines and the Pacific.

The Austronesians were the great seafarers of ancient Asia, and as a result their language family was the most widespread in the world before the colonial era—extending from Madagascar in the west to the eastern Pacific islands. The first Austronesian settlers in Java must have found an outstandingly fertile and suitable environment for their rice crops, and we may suppose that Java was among the most densely populated regions in Southeast Asia from this time onwards.

Unfortunately, Java still has no detailed Neolithic archaeological record, and we must fall back on information from other areas to put the last 2000 years B.C. into perspective. Many of the superb stone axes and adzes found in Java may indeed date from this period, but the archaeological picture for the island only comes into focus about 2000 years ago, when bronze casting and iron smelting arrived together with the massive bronze drums of Vietnamese (Dongson) origin.

These drums, with their elaborate surface decorations of boats, raised-floor houses, animals, birds, and human warriors are testimony to an active Southeast Asian trade that was soon to attract the attention of civilizations in India and China. Indian pottery dating from the first and second centuries A.D. has now been found in western Java and northern Bali, heralding a new era of Hindu-Buddhist civilization. But behind this great flowering of Indianized civilization lay an Austronesian heritage dating back several millennia which is still of fundamental importance today.

— *Peter Bellwood*

Overleaf: *Detail of a relief from 9th century Borobudur, greatest of Java's ancient monuments.* **Above:** *Fossilized skull of "Java Man."*

CLASSICAL HISTORY

Java's Ancient 'Indianized' Kingdoms

Javanese history—in the sense of locally-produced written records—begins in the 5th century A.D., with seven brief stone inscriptions found near present-day Jakarta and Bogor. These commemorate a kingdom known as Tarumanegara, whose capital probably lay along the course of the Citarum River, some distance up from the coast. Several of the inscriptions were produced by a certain King Purnavarman who lived around A.D. 450, but most other traces of the kingdom have long since vanished.

The people of Tarumanegara were probably Sundanese. The Javanese living in the center of the island only began to produce similar inscriptions and large stone monuments some two centuries later. These ancient peoples are nevertheless linked by a shared fascination with the art, literature and philosophy of India—a fascination shared also by a number of powerful kingdoms in Sumatra, Burma and Cambodia. All of these early states drew heavily upon pre-existing local traditions of religion and government as well, and each of the ancient civilizations they created thus represents a unique synthesis of Indian and autochthonous elements.

Early historical notices

The earliest indigenous record of central Javanese civilization is an inscription found on the northern slope of Mt. Merbabu, at a site called Tuk Mas. Though its exact age is unknown, the script leads us to believe that it dates from the late 7th century.

The names and something of the history of Java before this time can nonetheless be discovered in records from other countries. *Yavadvipa* ("Barley Island") is mentioned in a version of the Indian *Ramayana* epic which may date back to the 3rd century B.C. Java is described here as rich in grain and gold. Probably by this time Indonesian merchants were already sailing to India, bringing forest products such as camphor, *gharu* wood and sandalwood, and spices such as cloves, nutmegs and pepper.

In the late first century A.D. an Alexandrian geographer, Claudius Ptolemaeus, wrote a geography of the Indian Ocean. His manuscript was no doubt copied many times in later centuries, but the earliest extant text mentions *Iabadiou*—a Greek transcription of

Yavadvipa. Thus it is possible that news of Java had reached the Mediterranean by the time of the early Roman Empire.

In the first centuries A.D., the volume of trade between Southeast Asia, India and China increased dramatically, and ports along the coasts of Java were strategically positioned to prosper from this development. The first evidence that foreigners were visiting Java dates from the early 5th century. In 413, a Chinese Buddhist monk named Faxian voyaged from Sri Lanka to China, stopping in Java en route. A certain Prince Gunavarman of Kashmir traveled the same route in the opposite direction a few years later. Gunavarman was on his way to China to visit the court of the Liu Song emperor Wen Di, the first Chinese ruler to have close relations with Southeast Asian kingdoms. In A.D. 449 the emperor sent envoys to bestow recognition on three rulers in Indonesia, one of whom ruled a kingdom in Java known to the Chinese as *He-luo-dan*. The ruler reciprocated with numerous missions to China between A.D. 430 and 452. Though it is not certain, *He-luo-dan* may have been Tarumanegara.

Thereafter, numerous references to Javanese kingdoms are to be found in Chinese records. A kingdom from the interior of Java known as *Dan-dan* began sending missions to China in A.D. 530, and a Chinese pilgrim, Yijing, reported that *Dan-dan* still existed around 695. East of *Dan-dan* lay another kingdom, *Po-li*, which was in contact with China between 473 and 630.

Perhaps the most important Javanese kingdom known to the Chinese in this period was *He-ling*. It came into contact with China in 640, and missions continued until 818, after which the Chinese referred to the principal kingdom in Java as *She-po*. *He-ling* was probably in central Java. A 7th century Chinese source (the *Tung-dien*) records that there were salt wells in the country. According to Tang dynasty reports, *He-ling* was "exceedingly rich." Its trade products included tortoise shell, yellow and white gold, rhinoceros and elephants. The country was surrounded by 28 vassal states and its government had 32 ministers. These numbers are perhaps based on the significance in Javanese thought of the number four and its multiples.

He-ling bridges the gap between prehistory and history in central Java, for thereafter we have fragmentary records left by the Javanese themselves. It is important to note, however, that according to Chinese sources *Dan-dan* was Hindu whereas *He-ling* was Buddhist. The later history of *He-ling* coincides with the period of great Buddhist monuments in central Java, notably the remarkable stupa known as Borobudur.

A tale of two dynasties

Javanese inscriptions from this period suggest that by 832 a ruling dynasty which espoused Hinduism had absorbed a previous line of Buddhist kings. These two dynasties were known as the Sanjaya and the Sailendra, King Sanjaya being the first central Javanese ruler whose name has come down to us. He left an inscription in 732 on a small hill now called Gunung Wukir—west of present-day Yogyakarta and just 10 km (6 mi) from the spot where Borobudur was later built. He also caused a *lingga* or phallic representation of Siva to be set up here, in a country which he called Kunjarakunja. This may have corresponded to the Kedu Plain, bounded to the east and north by volcanoes and to the south by the Indian Ocean.

A later inscription from the plain says Sanjaya was a prince of Mataram—a name which came to denote the paramount kingdom of central Java. His descendants contin-

Opposite: *A river boulder inscribed with the name and oversized footprints of King Purnavarman, 5th century ruler of Tarumanegara in west Java.*
Above: *A copper cast from the Kedu Plain, probably the* bodhisattva *Avalokitesvara Padmapani.*

ued to use Sanjaya's name, but his successor, Panangkaran, became a vassal of another Javanese line of kings known as the Sailendra, who were adherents of Buddhism. By 778 several important Buddhist temples were erected on the Prambanan Plain southeast of Mt. Merapi, beginning with Candi Kalasan.

The Sailendra (the name literally means "kings of the mountain") continued to exercise supreme authority over Mataram until about 832. In that year a Sailendra queen married a Sanjaya king, and the latter family seems to have quickly become the dominant ruling house in Java once again. A member of the Sailendra family, Balaputra, later rebelled against the Sanjayas but was defeated and fled to Sumatra where he became ruler of Buddhist Srivijaya, Mataram's mightiest foe.

Ancient Javanese society

Historical sources suggest that society in ancient Mataram was prosperous, with agriculture and trade both well developed. The number of ancient temples and the amount of skilled labor devoted to their production show that the economy produced enough food to support many people who were not full-time farmers, and also that the population must have been quite dense. Inscriptions mention a wide variety of occupations and a broad range of goods that were traded.

The structure of government does not appear to have been highly centralized or authoritarian. In addition to rivalry between the Sanjaya and Sailendra lines, frequent competition for position and power arose within the ruling families.

The status of women was high; in several instances queens held supreme authority, and women could become village heads. Many temples were consecrated to female deities such as Tara, a female *bodhisattva*, or Durga, a female aspect of Siva. The goddess Sri was also highly honored.

We do not know much about the everyday life of the common man. No large cities have been discovered and people probably lived mostly in agrarian villages, among which were interspersed a few royal complexes where tribute was collected and redistributed, and where religious and craft specialists lived together with a large staff which served the elite. No permanent military forces existed. In times of war, the nobles subject to a paramount ruler mobilized their able-bodied men. Large-scale warfare seems to have been rare, in any case.

Transportation was easiest by river. The Bengawan Solo and Progo Rivers were important waterways. Ferries existed to assist overland travelers across rivers, but even in the 16th century roads were not well developed in Java. Many specialized types of watercraft existed in Dutch colonial times, which were probably already used in earlier periods. Reliefs on Borobudur display both

MARCELLO TRANCHINI

small boats and large sea-going vessels with such skill that the sculptors must have been quite familiar with them.

Foreigners were restricted to quarters in the seaports, and few were allowed inland. In later times the dichotomy between hinterland (*pedalaman*) and coastal (*pasisir*) society in Java has been important in religious, economic and political spheres. Perhaps this situation traces back to early historic times. The major monuments of ancient Java are clustered in the south-central part of the island, where the densest agrarian populations are found today. The people of the north coast were more exposed to external influences, and depended more on commerce and fishing for their livelihood.

Although the rulers promoted organized religion in the form of Hindu and Buddhist rituals, the majority of the population may have retained traditional beliefs and practices. We cannot directly study those pre-existing beliefs, but it is likely that they included the worship of ancestors who were perceived not as individuals but as souls who rejoined a greater entity upon death. Ancestors were probably associated with high places such as mountain peaks.

Buddhism's appeal was limited compared to that of Hinduism. Archaeological remains of Buddhist shrines are fewer than Hindu ones, and less widely distributed. Buddhism's main support may have come from a relatively small elite, whereas Hinduism was more readily incorporated into the daily rites of the majority of the population.

It must be emphasized that the forms which Buddhism and Hinduism took in Java were not the same as in India. There was no hostility between the two, unlike in India, apparently because there was no caste system of the type assumed by Brahmanical Hinduism. Thus Buddhism did not pose a threat to a particular stratum of society. The majority of the population may not have perceived any significant difference between the two, and in later centuries the two religions achieved a sort of synthesis wherein rulers worshipped a deity known as Siva-Buddha.

The nature of ancient Indian religious practices, writing systems, vocabulary and artistic motifs found in Java makes it clear that these were all transmuted into Javanese forms. Certainly there was strong sympathy and respect in Java for things Indian, but Javanese civilization was not due simply to Indian tutelage. The Javanese had been acquainted with Indian culture for a thousand years before monuments and writing appeared in central Java, and Javanese identi-

Above: *A famous panel from Borobudur. Although it is not the intended meaning, the scene may perhaps be interpreted somewhat freely to depict the arrival of foreign (possibly Indian) merchants on Indonesian soil in ancient times.*

ERIC OEY

ty was well preserved in the civilization which then took shape.

Mysterious move to east Java

After 919 no more inscriptions or monuments were produced in central Java for a period of several centuries, and the center of the kingdom mysteriously moved to the east. No one knows why this happened. Speculations have ranged from volcanic eruptions to epidemics to an invasion from Srivijaya, but no definite answer has been discovered, nor is there any indication in Javanese historical records.

Civilization had already made its mark on east Java before A.D. 929, when a ruler named Sindok set up a palace somewhere southwest of Surabaya in the Brantas River valley. Before that time, east Java had formed a peripheral part of the kingdoms of the Kedu and Prambanan plains, and the early architecture and sculpture of the east seems as a provincial reflection of the distant central area. After 929, kingdoms flourished in east Java and this area then stood alone as the center of Javanese culture for several centuries.

Sindok was a very active ruler, and archaeologists have discovered many inscriptions which record his decrees. He left such a powerful impression on the minds of the Javanese that for the next 300 years all rulers claimed him as their ancestor. Sindok was succeeded by his daughter. His great-granddaughter married a king of Bali, and much of the Javanese influence in Balinese culture is thought to be due to this connection.

In the late 10th century the east Javanese kingdom was strong enough to invade Sumatra, according to Chinese records. Then in 1016 a rebellion broke out and the capital was destroyed. The 16-year-old crown prince, Airlangga—son of Balinese King Udayana by Sindok's great-granddaughter—retreated to a hermitage on a mountain. Four years later he became the ruler of a small coastal kingdom near Surabaya. By the time he was 30, Airlangga felt strong enough to begin a campaign to reconquer his ancestral domains, and by the time of his death in 1049, he had recovered the position of paramount ruler which he claimed by inheritance.

According to tradition, Airlangga divided his kingdom into two realms upon his death. In fact clusters of archaeological remains are found in the two areas which he is said to have demarcated: the Malang region south of Surabaya (called Janggala) and the southwest Brantas Valley near Kediri (called Panjalu). The Kediri area is rich in inscriptions dating from the 150 years following Airlangga's death, indicating that a thriving kingdom existed here, but the history of the Malang region is practically blank. Chinese records describe Java as one of the most prosperous countries at this time, but few if any temples or other archaeological remains can be dated to this period.

In 1222 a man named Angrok somehow acquired power over the Malang area, then overthrew the king of Kediri and officially unified Airlangga's old kingdom. Angrok is traditionly depicted as a commoner who rose to the throne by assassination and brute force. His new kingdom became known as Singasari—after the site where Angrok built his palace, just north of modern-day Malang.

Singasari's history is marked by continued turbulence—assassinations occurred regularly. Several of the most beautiful temples in east Java, such as Kidal, are memorial shrines dedicated to rulers who were murdered. Nevertheless Singasari grew so powerful that by 1275 it had acquired suzerainty over major population centers on Sumatra and the Malay Peninsula as well as Java.

The last ruler of Singasari, Kertanegara, was responsible for Singasari's territorial

Opposite: *The beautiful Prajnaparamita statue from 13th-century Singasari, now in the Jakarta museum.* **Right:** *Relief from Sukuh, one of the last temples to be built before Islam swept Java.*

expansion and had himself commemorated in the form of a massive Buddha statue which still stands in the middle of Surabaya (known locally as Joko Dolog—the "fat boy"). In 1289 he felt sure enough of himself to mutilate the face of a Chinese envoy sent by Kublai Khan, demanding that he go to China and submit to the Mongol ruler in person. Kertanagara met a violent death, trying to put down a surprise attack on his palace in 1292.

A large Mongol fleet arrived in Java the next year to punish Kertanagara, only to find that he was already dead. Their troops became embroiled in a civil war between rival claimants to the throne, ironically allying themselves with Kertanagara's son-in-law, Prince Vijaya. Vijaya succeeded in defeating his rival from Kediri with Mongol help, and then forced the Mongols to depart without bringing him back to China to pay tribute.

The 'golden age' of Majapahit

Vijaya founded a new kingdom named Majapahit ("Bitter Gourd") which became the most powerful in Indonesian history. An early European traveler, Odoric of Pordenone, visited Majapahit in 1321 and marvelled at its palace. The capital at Trowulan became a center of art and culture, and was the largest city to form in Indonesia before the colonial era. Two names of importance stand out in the history of Majapahit: Hayam Wuruk, who ruled from 1350-1389, and Gajah Mada, who served as prime minister from 1331-1364. During Hayam Wuruk's reign, Majapahit claimed suzerainty over an area larger than modern Indonesia.

Majapahit's golden age did not last long after Hayam Wuruk's death. By the early 15th century, internal conflicts had broken out between political rivals. Ancient Javanese kingdoms never seem to have developed a stable mode of royal succession, and this prevented the development of a permanent power center. During the 15th century, Islam became another source of instability.

According to Javanese tradition, the kingdom fell in 1478 in a holy war launched by the Muslim ruler of Demak, a port on Java's north coast. This version of events is apocryphal, for we know that a vestige of the old kingdom, still calling itself Majapahit, existed when Portuguese traders arrived in 1511.

The date 1478 is nevertheless symbolic of sweeping changes which were taking place in Java due to a combination of religious, economic and demographic factors. Islamization did not occur instantaneously; rather the process of religious change occupied much of the 16th century and occurred under the eyes of early European observers. Still, it is true that by 1500 the course of development which ancient Javanese civilization had followed for a thousand years had changed, and it now embarked on a new direction.

—John Miksic

AMIR SIDHARTA

16TH-18TH CENTURIES

The Rise of Islam and the Dutch

In the 16th century, following the decline of Majapahit, no single power managed to achieve political dominance of Java. The north coast was characterized by a cluster of small trading polities of which the most prominent was the Islamic sultanate of Demak. Though Muslims had been present on the north coast for centuries, and there were Javanese converts in the heartland of Majapahit at least from the 1360s, it was only in this period that Islam became the religion of Javanese rulers.

The process of 'Islamization'

In the first half of the 16th century Demak's power grew, a development associated with the figure of Sunan Gunung Jati—one of the nine *walis* or venerated apostles of Islam on Java. Sunan Gunung Jati was also involved in the foundation of two sultanates in northwest Java—Banten and Cirebon. Demak's political influence extended as far away as south Kalimantan, but an unsuccesful attempt to conquer the Hinduized kingdom of Blambangan in east Java brought about its demise in 1546. Nevertheless, Demak still occupies a special place in Javanese lore, and the mosque in Demak is Java's holiest pilgrimage point. It is even believed that going seven times to Demak is equivalent to making the pilgrimage to Mecca.

The town of Giri, near Gresik in East Java was founded by another of the *wali,* Sunan Giri, and was a center for the propagation of Islam to Lombok, Sulawesi, Kalimantan, the Moluccas and Ternate.

The civilization of the north coast, known as the *pasisir*, maintained old Javanese traditions but combined these with a new literature and theater of Persian and Arabic origin—the heroic Amir Hamzah cycle and the story of Yusup (Joseph), for instance.

After the demise of Demak, the sultanates of Banten and Cirebon continued to flourish. Banten was a wealthy pepper-growing and trading port in the 16th and 17th centuries, and remains of its affluence can be seen today in the 16th century Masjid Agung mosque (the minaret was reputedly designed by a Chinese Muslim), in the ruins of the Surasowan and Kaibon palaces, and in its old Chinese temple (*klenteng*). Cirebon, whose name is said to derive from a word meaning

"mixture," does indeed display a fascinating blend of architectural styles—Majapahit, Islamic, Chinese (see the ruins of the 17th-18th century Gua Sunyaragi, and the *wadasan* rock motifs on other buildings), and even Dutch—its buildings were quite often ornamented with Dutch tiles. Sunan Gunung Jati is buried in a royal cemetery 5 kms north of Cirebon, and his grave, like those of the other *wali* (e.g. Sunan Muria, buried on Mt. Muria near Kudus) is a place of pilgrimage. Giri and Kudus on the north coast and Tembayat in central Java continued as small states ruled by the descendants of *wali* until being extinguished by the rising power of Mataram in the hinterland.

It would be wrong to assume that all Javanese have had an equally positive attitude to the Islamization of Java, however. Many have argued that the coming of Islam brought tensions and divisions into Javanese society, and today an influential group claims that there is a distinctive "Javanese religion" which should receive the same recognition as Islam. Devout Muslims, known as *santri*, counter that the adherents of this "Javanese religion" are lax and superstitious Muslims.

Historical interpretations of the period of Islamization have been recently complicated by the publication of controversial evidence that some of the *wali* and rulers of Demak were actually Muslim Chinese. This has aroused outrage among leaders of the *santri* community, to whom the Chinese are associated with usury, opium, pork eating and other practices prohibited by Islam. There is no doubt, however, that there was a very strong Chinese input to the *pasisir* in this period, as may be seen both in the architecture and in the old *klentengs* along the coast—notably the Sam Po or "Gedung Batu" complex at Semarang, with its syncretism of Chinese and Javanese cult figures.

The wars for Java, 1630-1800

Two powers which were to contest the sovereignty of Java arrived on the scene almost simultaneously in the early 17th century. The inland kingdom of Mataram was founded by Senapati, whose grave at Kota Gede near Yogyakarta is still a place of pilgrimage. Under Mataram's best-remembered ruler, Agung (r. 1613-1646), the kingdom expanded rapidly—conquering Tuban, Gresik, Surabaya and Pasuruan in an attempt to dominate the trade of the coast. Agung also introduced the Javanese Islamic calendar and obtained from Mecca the title of sultan. He is buried in the highest, most revered spot in the royal graveyard of Imogiri, 20 kms (12.5 mi) to the south of Yogyakarta.

The second power to arrive in Java at this

Left: *The mosque at Jepara, with its characteristic Hindu-Javanese* meru *roof.* **Above:** *An Arab trader arrives in the Indies.* **Right:** *A* seninan *tournament.*

time was the Dutch, who organized the Dutch East India Company (VOC) in 1602 and established a trading post on the northwest coast of Java at Banten in 1603. From 1611 they also had a post in the nearby port of Jayakarta or Jakarta, ruled by a vassal of Banten. In 1619 the Dutch took over and renamed this town Batavia, building fortifications according to the latest European designs. Agung launched unsuccessful attacks on Batavia in 1628 and 1629—considerable military feats that were to be the first and last direct confrontation between Mataram and the Dutch. From then on, the Company fought on the side of a warring rival in one of Mataram's many wars of succession.

Such a war began in 1671 with a revolt at the end of the reign of Agung's successor, Mangkurat I, who was hostile to Islam. The rebellion was led by Islamic leaders and a Madurese prince, Trunajaya. The Dutch helped to suppress the rebellion and to enthrone Mangkurat II. He shifted the capital of Mataram to Kartasura, whose ruins can be seen to the west of present-day Solo.

There was further warfare in the 1680s involving Surapati, an escaped Balinese slave who had been involved in a Dutch campaign to dethrone the sultan of Banten, but had subsequently changed sides and joined the sultan and an anti-Dutch Islamic party. A Dutch East India Company expedition was sent to Kartasura to extradite him, but ended in the death of its leader (the famous Captain François Tack) and many of his men in a battle where Surapati received covert support from Mangkurat II. Surapati subsequently set up an independent principality in east Java at Pasuruan, where he was finally killed in the Dutch expedition of 1706-7. His sons continued to lead resistance here, however, and Surapati remains a celebrated figure in the popular Javanese theater.

Warfare continued throughout much of the first half of the 18th century. The First Javanese War of Succession began in 1704 and ended in the dethronement of Mangkurat III in favor of his uncle, who became Pakubuwana I with VOC support. In return Pakubuwana ceded to the Dutch the whole Priangan region of west Java, as well as Cirebon and the eastern half of Madura. Surabaya rebelled at the end of his reign, and another succession dispute broke out when he died in 1719.

In 1740, a major conflict originated not in Mataram, but in Batavia. The city had a substantial population of Chinese tradesmen, artisans, small traders and commercial agriculturalists specializing in sugar and its by-product, *arak* (a distilled spirit consumed locally and also exported). The Dutch population and government came to regard this growing group as a threat, and began to deport Chinese to their post in Ceylon. Tensions escalated, leading to a revolt and

subsequent massacre of thousands of Chinese prisoners. From Batavia the revolt spread along the north coast of Java and into Kartasura, where the ruler, Pakubuwana II, decided to join forces with the Chinese. This ended with the sack of Kartasura and the cession to the Dutch of the entire north coast to a depth of 600 *roods* (just over 2.5 kms) from the sea, and all of Java east of Pasuruan.

Afterwards the Chinese of Batavia, who had previously lived throughout the city, were ordered to live in a single settlement (the Kampung Cina, present-day Glodok) outside and to the southwest of the city walls. The Company also acquired for a fixed payment the right to collect tolls throughout Mataram, a monopoly which, like a number of others (e.g. the right to run markets and deal in opium), was then leased out to Chinese operators. Finally, the war also led to the eventual establishment of a new capital at Surakarta (Solo).

Yet another war of succession ensued, leading ultimately to the partition of Mataram in 1755 into two major courts—Surakarta and Yogyakarta—and the creation in 1757 of a minor principality, the Mangkunegaran, dependent on Surakarta. In 1812, another minor principality, the Pakualaman, dependent on Yogyakarta, was created. One of the most remarkable features of the new palace constructed at this time in Yogyakarta is the huge Taman Sari water garden complex. The site was dedicated to the mystic union of the sultans with the Goddess of the South Seas, Kangjeng Ratu Kidul—a divinity still much venerated in Java today.

From 1767-1777 the VOC fought a long and bitter campaign to conquer the eastern part of Java which had already been ceded in theory to the Company. This resulted in the demise of the last Hinduized kingdom on Java, Blambangan (finally destroyed by Sultan Agung) and the depopulation of large areas of the east.

From the late 18th century onwards there was great literary activity on Java, especially at the Surakarta court, home of the Yasadipura family of poets. These authors embraced both Hindu-Javanese and Islamic heritages and produced many new and original works.

Women also seem to have played an important role in the literary and cultural life of the court, and it was customary for rulers to maintain a militia of young women who not only accompanied them on ceremonial occasions on horseback and *en travestie*, but were selected for their beauty and accomplishment as dancers and musicians.

—*Ann Kumar*

Top left: *Van Linschoten, whose* Itinerario *(1595), guided the first Dutch expeditions to the Indies.* **Left:** *J. P. Coen, architect of Dutch empire in the East.* **Above:** *The first Dutch fleet is repulsed by forces of the prince of Banten (1596).*

19TH CENTURY

The Dutch Colonial Period in Java

Following decades of decline, the Dutch East India Company was finally dissolved in 1799, and the world-wide conflict of the Napolconic wars soon reached Java. In 1806, Napoleon put his brother Louis on the Dutch throne, which led to the appointment in 1808 of Napoleonic Marshal Daendels to govern Java.

Daendels pushed through many military works for the defense of Java, among them a great post road running the length of the island from Anyer to Panarukan, which revolutionized travel. But his successor lost Java to the British, and young Thomas Stamford Raffles, later founder of Singapore, became Lieutenant-Governor from 1811-1815.

Like Daendels, Raffles was not particularly sympathetic to the Javanese rulers and nobles (*priyayi*), and in 1813 he abolished the sultanate of Banten and annexed its territory. The sultans of Cirebon were then similarly reduced to the status of government pensioners. Raffles also attempted to move away from the forced agricultural system of the Dutch toward a more modern taxation system, effecting the first comprehensive census of Java's population for this purpose. He took measures against slavery, and he also produced the first great work of western scholarship about the island and its people—his monumental *The History of Java* (1817).

A last great war, the Java War of 1825-30, broke out following a period of political instability and economic hardship in the sultanate of Yogyakarta. Daendels and Raffles had not only annexed parts of the sultan's territory, they had even deposed him, and, in the case of Raffles, had plundered the palace library and treasury. Drastic alterations in the terms under which land was leased to Javanese aristocrats impoverished the aristocracy, and the operation of toll gates by Chinese using armed force to extract extortionate payments impoverished the peasantry.

The Java War was led by Diponegoro, a charismatic prince of Yogyakarta who was a devout but very "Javanese" Muslim (recording in his autobiography how the goddess Ratu Kidul appeared to him). Thanks to the amount of popular support he received and the guerrilla tactics employed, the war went on for five years, ending with the duplicitous arrest of Diponegoro under a flag of truce and his exile to Sulawesi, where he died in 1855. After the Java War more than 90 percent of Java was under Dutch rule, as compared to about 60 percent in 1808.

The 'Cultivation System'

With the introduction of a new "Cultivation System" (*Cultuurstelsel*) in 1830, the colonial government resumed the VOC's old role as "sole agent" with a monopoly on buying and selling tropical cash crops—notably coffee and sugar, but also indigo, tea, quinine and others. This required the use of forced labor organized by the Javanese *priyayi*—the Regents (*bupati*) and their subordinates —who could also exact labor for their own purposes.

Later in the century, the *priyayi* class gradually became more of a native bureaucracy. They also set social norms to a considerable extent: even Dutch civil servants were expected to know Javanese dancing until quite late in the century, and were not reluctant to adopt Javanese appurtenances of rank, such as parasol bearers and the foot-kiss.

On the other side of the coin, virtually no effort was made to bring European education

or civilization to the Javanese. Government efforts toward the populace were aimed mainly at preventing any further outbreaks, principally by driving a wedge between the aristocracy and Islamic leaders. Princes were no longer able to lead major rebellions, but after 1860 "law and order" became an increasing problem—with *kecu* (robber) bands prevalent in central Java, while much of Banten remained a no-man's land.

During this period the four central Javanese courts developed in different ways. The Mangkunegaran specialized in dance (which one can still see today in its magnificent *pendopo* audience pavilion), literature and horsemanship, while the Pakualaman was characterized by literary interests and a social conscience that was to take its members on divergent paths early in the 20th century. Vestiges of the old military culture of the courts lived on in mounted tournaments, and in the spectacular tiger-buffalo fights, held as late as the second half of the 19th century.

Among the peasantry there was considerable population growth, though the exact rate is debatable depending upon what factor of error is attributed to Raffles' census. Due to the requirements of the Cultivation System in taking land and manpower out of food production and into the production of export crops, serious famines occurred in Cirebon in 1843 and in central Java in 1848-50, when a quarter of a million people died.

Humanitarian criticism of the Cultivation System, notably in the famous Dutch novel *Max Havelaar* (1859), was joined by that of private entrepreneurs, particularly in the sugar industry, who wished the government to abdicate in their favor. Limited changes slowly began in 1870, and in 1885 some compulsory labor services were abolished.

From 1885 to 1900 tremendous profits were generated in a private Dutch sector in Java modernized by the introduction of the telegraph (from 1856), inland post (from 1866), railways (mostly post 1870), and telephone (from 1882). But there was impoverishment of the Javanese peasants, with less work available for lower wages and a population growth that outstripped rice production, leading to the consumption of more corn and cassava. There was also a religious revival in the second half of the 19th century, which is perhaps traceable to the rebuilding of the Demak mosque in 1842, and many more Javanese made the pilgrimage to Mecca after about 1870, a journey which was greatly facilitated by the opening of the Suez canal.

— *Ann Kumar*

Opposite: *Dutch officials often adopted Javanese appurtenances of rank, such as the parasol.*
Above: *A Dutch tobacco factory in Java.*
Overleaf: *A Saturday night dinner dance in Bandung's fashionable Homann Hotel, ca. 1920. Photo courtesy of Antiquariaat Acanthus, Utrecht.*

EARLY 20TH CENTURY

Great Social and Political Upheavals

Two developments—declining economic conditions among the peasantry and increasing "fanaticism," as the government termed the Islamic religious revival—led to colonial policy changes at the end of the 19th century. In 1899 C. Th. van Deventer published his influential article "A Debt of Honor" which argued that the Dutch government had extracted 187 million guilders from the Indies and should repay it. In 1901 P. Brooshoft's brochure, "The Ethical Trend in Colonial Policy," provided a name for the new policy—the "Ethical Policy." These publications and an enquiry into the "diminished welfare" of the Javanese led to new initiatives—clinics and agricultural extension programs, representative bodies from the village level up, and the development of a more extensive educational system, notably the "Dutch-native" schools using Dutch as the medium of instruction when pupils reached a certain level.

Education and Islam

The colonial government had not previously encouraged the use of Dutch by Indonesians, and Malay was the "official" language of communication. One of the few regents in turn-of-the-century Java who spoke Dutch, the Regent of Jepara, had a daughter named Kartini whose letters open a window into the previously closed world of aristocratic (*priyayi*) women on Java and the effects of seclusion, rigid hierarchy and polygamy. Kartini also records instances in which young educated Javanese were put down in no uncertain terms for daring to use the language of their masters.

Now, however, Dutch experts such as C.C. Snouck Hurgronje argued that the only way to stem the advance of Islam was to develop a positive attachment to European (i.e. Dutch) civilization among the leaders of the native communities and to give them a greater role in administration.

In fact the demand for education came as much or more from the Javanese themselves. Before her premature death, Kartini wrote an article called "Educate the Javanese!" and set up her own school within the household of her Regent husband. She herself had experienced the frustration of being given a taste of European education (in itself unheard-of for Javanese girls) and then being refused

permission to continue it after the age of puberty. Kartini's pioneering spirit is honored in Indonesia today on Kartini Day.

A high male *priyayi*, Raden Mas Suwardi Surjaningrat (who later took the name of Ki Adjar Dewantara), succeeded in doing what Kartini could not—study overseas. Ironically, he did this after being exiled from Java as one of the founders of the Indies Party (founded in 1912 with mixed Dutch, Eurasian and Javanese leadership) which shocked the colonial government by demanding complete independence from the Netherlands.

Though far from uncritical of Western education—which he regarded as promoting materialism, individualism and intellectualism at the expense of social values—Ki Adjar Dewantara was influenced by revisionist educators such as Montessori, Frobel and Dalton. He founded the idealistic Taman Siswa school system, with its strong emphasis on Javanese culture and self-directed learning, which is still in existence today.

A very different moral and educational philosophy underlay another educational system founded at this time by modernist Muslims. The Muhammadiyah schools largely followed the government curriculum with only the addition of special "religious education" classes, in sharp contrast to the religious orientation of the mosque schools. This school system also operates today.

Nationalist stirrings

A new nationalist movement centered on Java arose during the early decades of this century, stimulated by the new schools that both introduced western ideas and provided meeting places for students from many parts of the archipelago. The island's first modern organization, however, was quintessentially Javanese in character. Budi Utomo, founded in 1908 to educate *priyayi* Javanese in Western learning and their own culture, drew its members (numbering about 10,000 in 1909) largely from the ranks of the civil service and white-collar professions.

Sarekat Islam (Islamic Union), which was to be the first mass movement in the Netherlands East Indies (not just in Java), had very different roots. It grew out of an association of Muslim Javanese traders founded in 1909 in central Java to counter severe competition from the Chinese. After the outbreak of anti-Chinese violence and a subsequent government clamp-down, however, the association revised its strategy and re-established itself on a more general basis in 1912 as Sarekat Islam.

Despite the middle-class, *priyayi* composition of its leadership it attracted a broad base

Opposite: *A traditional Javanese* pesantren *or Quranic school.* **Above:** *The* dokter djawa *medical school in Batavia early in this century.*

of support. In 1919 the organization claimed two million members, a figure which may be exaggerated but indicates its wide appeal. Many of these were peasants who had previously had no outlet for their grievances, and who identified themselves with Islam as much as a statement of ethnic identity as a religious commitment. In 1919, in an atmosphere of great unrest on Java, when sugar plantations were being set ablaze by angry peasants, a few small, localized disturbances attributed to Sarekat Islam brought on government repression and the organization lost many of its members.

The second great "international" ideology to develop popular leadership in the Indies was Marxism or socialism, which made its appearance in Semarang not long after the founding of Sarekat Islam and soon began to work within that organization. A socialist wing developed within Sarekat Islam, some of whose leading figures were Javanese aristocrats (one of them, Suryopranoto, was the elder brother of Ki Adjar Dewantara) while others were railway employees. It forged an alliance with the devoutly Muslim Sarekat Islam members in condemning capitalism, though the latter group wished to confine this to foreign capitalism. But the alliance broke down and the socialists were forced out of Sarekat Islam in 1921.

The organization which became the Indonesian Communist Party (PKI: Partai Komunis Indonesia) had by this time already been set up, and competed with Sarekat Islam in supporting the trade union movement which was in its infancy in Java. A strike of employees in the government pawnshop system in January 1922 led to the arrest and exile of both Sarekat Islam and PKI leaders, however, and harsh government measures stifled both opposition groups. Sarekat Islam was thereafter increasingly beset by internal quarrels and financial problems, while the better organized PKI continued to expand.

Sukarno and the PNI

Sarekat Islam and the PKI were both based on supra-national ideologies and had definite reservations about nationalism as a principle. A specifically secular-nationalist organization, the Indonesian National Party (PNI, Partai Nasional Indonesia) was established in 1927. Its leadership came from the Dutch-educated elite. Hatta and Sjahrir (both from the Minangkabau area of Sumatra) received their higher education in the Netherlands, and it was in student associations there that the term "Indonesia" was first used.

Sukarno, a Javanese and the most famous of the PNI leaders, received his tertiary education at the Bandung Engineering College founded in 1919 by private capital to overcome a shortage of engineers from Europe. Other such institutions were slow to arrive. In 1924 a law college was set up, followed by

a medical college in 1926. The three were amalgamated and others added to form the University of Batavia (now University of Indonesia) during the Second World War.

Students in these institutions played a critical role in the definition of Indonesian nationalism. In October 1928 at a youth conference in Batavia they avowed in an "Oath of the Youth" (*Sumpah Pemuda*) to recognize a single fatherland (Indonesia), a single nation (the Indonesian nation), and one language of unity (Bahasa Indonesia).

After this time it was impossible for any political organization not to advocate complete independence and the creation of a united Indonesian nation-state. But progress towards this goal was to be very difficult, with a colonial government in full retreat from the ideals of the Ethical Policy and convinced that education simply made people discontented.

The leadership of the PNI were not agreed on the best tactics to pursue in the wake of the failure of armed rebellion. Hatta and Sjahrir favored organizational work (developing cooperatives, trade unions, schools, free legal service for peasants, etc.) rather than "talking." Sukarno however felt that dialogue was important, particularly for his strategy of uniting nationalists, Muslims and Marxists into a single mass movement, which he saw as the only way Indonesia could achieve independence.

Neither side had much chance to put their strategy into effect. Sukarno was imprisoned from 1929 to January 1932 and again arrested and exiled from August 1933, and Hatta and Sjahrir from 1934, all three till the end of Dutch rule. The 1930s were not only a time of great political repression, they were also a time of great economic hardship. The Depression hit the Indies harder and lasted longer than elsewhere, with its catastrophic effects on agricultural prices. Coolies were dismissed from plantations and workers from processing mills, returning to villages which could not absorb them, since the proportion of landless on Java was approaching 40 percent. Taxation was not reduced for some years and diet, already below minimal Western standards, became still worse with an increase in the consumption of low-nutrition foods like cassava.

Between 1931 and 1936, 158 million guilders in gold left the colony for the Netherlands, mainly through government-owned pawnshops, as people sold whatever they could to survive. From 1936-7, there was some recovery, but this was more in the outer islands than on Java.

— *Ann Kumar*

Opposite: *Surabaya's "Red Bridge" (Jembatan Merah) ca. 1900.* **Above:** *Bandung's "Indo-European" Gedung Sate building, completed in 1920. The area is now one of fashionable residences.*

WAR AND REVOLUTION

The Struggle for Survival and Freedom

Following the Pearl Harbor attack in December 1941, the Japanese conquered virtually all of Southeast Asia within a few months. By March 1942 they had taken Burma, Malaya and Indonesia, and the only remaining resistance was in Luzon. While the appearance of Japan as a formidable military power had been anticipated by well-informed Indonesians like Sjahrir, to most Indonesians the disappearance of Dutch colonial rule meant a total revision of their view of the world.

The previously unassailable European rulers were gone, and with them their language, culture and economic structure. Bahasa Indonesia, not Japanese, replaced Dutch. Export crops were abandoned for commodities of strategic importance (tin, bauxite, rubber, oil and rice). There was runaway inflation and a breakdown of road, rail and sea transport. Administration was military-dominated, and the Kempeitai (secret police) were universally feared.

The *romusha* system of forced labor on such projects as the Burma-Thailand railway brought enormous horror. With rice requisitioning at pitiful prices, malnutrition was rampant and there was an unprecedented ratio of deaths to births. Epidemics broke out, people were falling dead on the streets from starvation or disease and beggars appeared throughout the cities.

Japanese wartime policies

Unlike the Dutch, the Japanese sought not to eliminate political activity but to harness it for the war effort. Thus they brought in political leaders at least for social control and propaganda work, if not for actual decision-making. Many of those who became involved in political and military organizations set up by the Japanese were young people, to whom the Japanese made a special appeal.

The Japanese adjusted their policies to the strength of pre-war nationalist movements, so that they envisaged self-government as a more distant development in Indonesia than in, for instance, Burma. Within Indonesia, political participation was to be greater in Java than in the other islands. Indonesia's nationalist leaders—notably Hatta, Sjahrir and Sukarno—were all released from detention, putting them under great pressure to cooperate. Hatta and Sukarno did so, participating prominently in affairs of state, while Sjahrir lived a retired life in contact with semi-underground youth groups.

Hatta and Sukarno were involved in organizations such as the Djawa Hokokai (Java Support Group), established in 1944 when the war effort was going badly. Although its Indonesian leaders had no power of independent action, they did have, for the first time, a vast communications and propaganda apparatus—parades, rallies, military demonstrations, radio broadcasts, films and theatrical shows—which allowed them to reach millions of Indonesians. After the war, the voice and oratory of Sukarno were known throughout the nation to an extent unparalleled by any previous historical figure. The Japanese also brought a number of Muslim groups together in a single organization, Masyumi.

The Japanese policy of popular involvement in the war effort also led to the creation of indigenous military forces, notably PETA ("Defenders of the Fatherland"), a force of about 100 trained battalions, and Heiho, an auxiliary corps in the Japanese army. These predated any unified civilian organization to wield political control. The Japanese also set up a committee to guide Indonesia towards independence in May 1945.

The independence proclamation

In the momentous month of August 1945, Hiroshima was bombed on the 6th and the Emperor surrendered on the 15th. Indonesia's independence was proclaimed on the 17th by Sukarno and Hatta, under pressure from youth groups who insisted that it should be proclaimed in the name of the Indonesian people alone. The red-and-white national flag of Indonesia was first officially flown on August 17th, Indonesia's Independence Day.

Indonesian independence was seen by the allies as a sham—the attempt of a small group of "collaborators" to maintain themselves in power without popular support or legitimacy. Allied forces moved into Indonesia with the intention of restoring Dutch

Right: *The "Proklamasi Kemerdekaan" of August 17th, 1945, read by Sukarno with Hatta at right.*

rule over their former colony. By the time they arrived in Java and Sumatra however, the new Republic of Indonesia had established some sort of government machinery and had considerable support, albeit of a poorly organized nature, especially among young people. There was a Republican army, formed of many small fighting groups who remained after the disbanding of PETA by the Japanese. Japanese weapons had also found their way into Indonesian hands, despite an agreement prohibiting this.

When British troops arrived in Surabaya at the end of October, they were attacked by soldiers and youth groups, and had to fly Sukarno, Hatta and Sjahrir into the city to ask that the British be spared. Even so, Brigadier Mallaby was shot, and after Sukarno's appeal had allowed the British to evacuate 6,000 Dutch internees and to land Indian troops, they decided to punish Surabaya in an attack which united all Indonesians against them.

The new Republican governor of East Java announced that the city would resist to the last, and the British were staggered by the strength of that resistance. With air strikes and naval bombardments, it took three days to take two-thirds of the city, but the fighting went on for three weeks, showing the world how strong the support for independence actually was. November 10 is now commemorated as Heroes' Day (*Hari Pahlawan*) in honor of those who fell. Surabaya was also famous for the pro-republican radio broadcasts of Ktut Tantri ("Surabaya Sue")—a British woman long resident in Bali who supported the cause.

By the Linggajati Agreement of November 1946, the Republic (Java and Sumatra) was required to cooperate with the Dutch in a new Indonesian federation. There was much opposition to this on the part of both Indonesians and the Dutch, and the latter launched a military offensive in July of 1947, taking the major cities and road networks in east and west Java, where they set up regional states. Their conquests were ratified by the Renville Agreement of January 1948—a humiliation the Indonesian side accepted due to American pressure.

On the December 18, 1948, the Dutch launched a full-scale military attack which captured the Republican capital of Yogyakarta. Republican leadership then passed to the military and to guerrilla fighters. However, this further resort to violence by the Dutch alienated international opinion—significantly that of the United States, which suspended Marshall Aid to the Netherlands.

A year later, on December 27, 1949, the Netherlands officially transferred sovereignty to a federal Indonesian state, excluding West New Guinea. By August 1950, all the federated states had ceded their powers to a unitary Republic of Indonesia.

— Ann Kumar

SINCE INDEPENDENCE

From 'Guided Democracy' to a 'New Order'

After the departure of the Dutch, Indonesia's leaders were faced with the herculean task of building a system of parliamentary democracy in a multi-racial, multi-ideological nation that had been devastated by the Depression and by a decade of occupation and war—a nation then having one of Asia's lowest literacy rates (about 6.5 percent) and a tiny elite with little or no experience in government.

Under these circumstances, the survival of Indonesia at all is almost a miracle, as centripetal forces within the fragile young state soon threatened to tear it apart, with violent dissent coming from the left and from Muslim factions. When the constitution was drawn up in 1945, the final form of the new state was based on the so-called Pancasila or "Five Principles": 1. Nationalism; 2. Internationalism or humanitarianism; 3. Representative government by consultation and consensus; 4. Social welfare/justice; and, 5. Belief in God.

Muslim dissatisfaction quickly led to a series of revolts. A Javanese mystic, S.M. Kartosuwirjo, proclaimed an Islamic state (Darul Islam) in West Java in 1948-9, and was subsequently joined by Muslims in south Sulawesi and Aceh. On Java, the Darul Islam rebellion continued until 1965.

Economic and political breakdown

Meanwhile the economy was still in the hands of oligopolistic western firms, mainly Dutch. Insofar as there was a local bourgeoisie, it was made up of Chinese who had little political representation. Politics was dominated by western-educated Indonesians from Javanese *priyayi* families, with strong links to a civil service that was highly politicized, as was the large, heterogeneous army.

There were no fewer than seven cabinets between 1949 and 1957, none lasting as long as two years, and the economic climate and army-civilian relations deteriorated after 1952. Prior to the 1955 elections there was acrimonious debate, especially concerning the relative merits of Pancasila and Islam, and the subsequent election results were not auspicious for stable government. The PNI and Masyumi gained 57 seats each; another Muslim party, the Nahdatul Ulama, had 45 seats, and the communist party (PKI) had 39 seats. There were then 25 other minor par-

ties with between 1 and 8 seats.

Alarming developments outside Java followed in 1956-7, with military seizures of power in the rich exporting island of Sumatra and in eastern Indonesia. There was, of course, great concern both about ideological divisions within the government and about its inability to make its writ run throughout Indonesia's territory, even in areas of nearby West Java under Darul Islam, let alone in more distant regions.

President Sukarno, who had so far taken a low-key role, now took action. In a 1956 speech entitled "Let us Bury the Parties," Sukarno had already suggested the cause of the problems. He now proposed moving away from parties as the basis of political representation to "functional groups," such as women, workers, youth, peasants and the army, working together within a framework he called "Guided Democracy."

Sukarno's balancing act

Sukarno made these proposals at a time when Indonesia's very existence seemed threatened, with leading politicians, notably from Masyumi, joining military dissidents in declaring an alternative government in West Sumatra. But whereas in 1957 the rebels faced a party-based government and a hesitant central army command, by the end of 1958 Sukarno and the army dominated the scene, with presidential decrees to cut back party representation and a state of emergency giving the army sweeping powers.

The confiscation of Dutch estates and other property provided economic resources, particularly to the army. On the ideological front, Sukarno united the three main streams in Indonesian politics—Nationalism, Religion and Communism—while cracking down on those who refused to cooperate.

During Guided Democracy, the PKI expanded greatly, and some observers have seen Sukarno as moving increasingly to the left. Others, however, say that while Sukarno appropriated communist rhetoric, he gave them little actual role in government. Sukarno's main targets were external. He led an ultimately successful campaign for the transfer of West New Guinea (now Irian Jaya) to Indonesia from 1957 to 1962, and a campaign to "crush Malaysia" after its inception in 1963. The other "partner" in Guided Democracy, the army, was hostile to communism, and unlike the PKI was moving in the direction of centralization, rationalization and ideological unity.

Economic conditions deteriorated dramatically during Guided Democracy due to the government's use of deficit financing and to a decline in productivity under unsettled conditions. The standard of living of middle-class Javanese, especially public servants, dropped sharply, with runaway inflation during the early 1960s.

The 'year of living dangerously'

The PKI's strategy was to push for land-reform on overcrowded Java. In areas such as Klaten, for instance, there was serious conflict in 1964 between very poor and very rich peasants. Similar clashes (involving stabbing, kidnapping, arson and armed fighting) between Muslim landowners and PKI supporters took place in Banyuwangi, Jember, Jombang, Kediri, Sidoarjo and Bangil, despite Sukarno's attempts to quell the situation.

Generally the PKI got the worst of it. On the other hand, it was rumored that the communists were shortly to receive arms from China. The question of how long Sukarno, in failing health, could prevent the development of far greater violence, dominated the Jakarta rumor circuit in 1965—a year that Sukarno himself dubbed *tahun vivere pericoloso*, "the year of living dangerously."

Events came to a head early on October 1st, when six senior generals, including the army commander Lieutenant-General Yani, were abducted and murdered, and a radio broadcast announced a takeover by another army officer, Lieutenant-Colonel Untung, who claimed to have acted to pre-empt a coup by a CIA-sponsored "council of generals."

The tangled history of the Untung coup has been variously interpreted. All agree that two parties were involved: an army group, and at least part of the PKI. Opinions differ on the questions of which of the two groups began the coup; whether it was really in response to a planned CIA-sponsored coup, and the extent of Sukarno's role in all of this.

It seems unlikely that the full truth will emerge in the foreseeable future, if ever. But the results of the short-lived coup, soon crushed by General Suharto, are clearer—it was the end of Sukarno's long tightrope act, though he was eased from power gradually, not being stripped of all powers until March 1967. It was also definitely the end of the PKI—as an estimated half million alleged supporters were killed, mainly in central and

Opposite: *President Sukarno and Vice-President Hatta with the first cabinet (1950).*

east Java and Bali. And the hegemony of the army was firmly established, in partnership with Muslims, students, and intellectuals disaffected with Guided Democracy.

Suharto's 'New Order'

Where the years from 1942-1965 were full of war, rebellion and aggressive propagation of ideologies, the years since then have been very quiet by comparison. Suharto's personal style is that of a traditional Javanese ruler, reserved and impassive, in contrast to Sukarno's extravagant populism.

Coming to power in alliance with Muslims, Suharto decided to allow the founding of a new Muslim party (Partai Muslimin Indonesia), excluding much of the old leadership. In a March 1968 session of parliament, he increased the armed forces' representation from 43 to 75. Suharto was then appointed full (as opposed to acting) President for 5 years and it was agreed that elections should be held in 1971—by which time the government had decided to develop Golkar, a federation of "functional groups" going back to the Guided Democracy period, as an alternative to the parties. With the full weight of the bureaucracy and army behind it, Golkar has achieved more than 60 percent of the vote in all elections since 1971.

After the 1971 election, the remaining political parties were forced to amalgamate into two superparties: the Development Unity Party (PPP) and the Indonesian Democracy Party (PDI). Not surprisingly, both have been rent by factionalism, and much of the political conflict under the New Order stems from the disillusionment of Muslims, as in the debates over a new marriage bill in 1973. Muslims have been executed for terrorist acts such as hijackings, and there were Islamic riots in Tanjung Priok near Jakarta in 1984.

Islam is more prominent in Java today than in previous decades—in the number, opulence and increased congregations of the mosques, the number of people actually performing the five daily prayers, the dramatic increase in the number of young women wearing Islamic dress, in the *kiblat* (direction of Mecca) indicators found in hotels, and the widespread appeal of popular Islamic music like Rhoma Irama's *dangdut* group.

The great majority of Indonesians, meanwhile, has benefitted substantially from the New Order's social and economic development programs. Per capita income has risen dramatically, to US$550 in 1990, with an average annual growth rate of 4.6 percent over the past 20 years—higher than in Malaysia or Thailand. The number of Javanese living in poverty, as measured by minimum standards

Above: *Presidential power was officially transferred to General Suharto on March 11, 1967.* **Right:** *Agricultural development has been a top priority of the "New Order" government.*

of caloric intake, housing, clothing, health and education, has dropped both in absolute terms and also as a percentage of population—from 40 percent (32.4 million) in 1976 to 17 percent (19.5 million) in 1987. Infant mortality rates have been halved, and the percentage of children attending primary school has doubled to over 90 percent. Most surprisingly, the world's most densely-populated island has become self-sufficient in rice, the staple crop, as production has risen from 17.9 million tons in 1979 to 27 million in 1987 through the introduction of "green revolution" rice strains and cultivation techniques.

Much of this progress was fueled during the 1970s by a huge boom in oil prices. Indonesia was and still is the fifth-largest producer in OPEC, despite the default in 1975 and subsequent restructuring of Pertamina, the state oil company, due to mismanagement and reckless borrowing. The 1980s, however, brought a long and severe recession, beginning in 1982, and a steep drop in oil prices in 1986—both of which forced the government to drastically re-think their strategy. Abandoning a policy of import substitution, high tariff barriers and heavy regulation of capital and licenses, the government after 1985 sought to encourage investment by relaxing restrictions on foreign investment, abolishing tariffs and reducing red-tape.

The result has been a rapid surge of growth going into the 1990s. Foreign investments have soared from US$1.4 billion in 1987 to $4.7 billion in 1989, and so have exports of manufactured goods—rising from US$3.9 billion in 1982 to $13.5 billion in 1989. Growth in the industrial sector is expected to continue at a brisk 8-10 percent rate during the coming years, as Indonesia is increasingly seen as the "final frontier" for manufacturers from Japan, Korea, Taiwan, Hong Kong and Singapore in search of cheap labor and un-tapped markets. The largest investments have been in textiles, shoes, food processing and wood products.

Critics have argued that these developments have made Indonesia too dependent on foreign capital, and that the disparity between haves and have-nots has grown. A frequent target is Indonesia's Chinese minority, who dominate the nation's private domestic capital and who have benefitted most from the recent boom. Meanwhile, 2.3 million young people join the workforce (which now has 40 percent unemployment) each year and the greatest challenge facing the New Order is to provide jobs and higher living standards. By the year 2010, Java's population will have topped 150 million, and the only way to provide adequate food, housing, health care and education is seen to be through rapid industrialization. Faced with this prospect, one can only wonder if the island's physical resources will be able to withstand such an assault.

— Ann Kumar

ERIC OEY

PEOPLES

Java's Five Regional Cultures

In contrast to other areas of Indonesia and despite its huge population, the island of Java is relatively homogeneous in its ethnic composition. Only two ethnic groups are actually native to the island: the Javanese and the Sundanese. A third group, the Madurese, inhabit the neighboring island of Madura and have migrated to East Java in large numbers since the 18th century. The Javanese are by far the dominant group, accounting for about two-thirds of the island's total population, while the Sundanese and Madurese comprise another 20 and 10 percent respectively. The nearby islands of Sumatra and Borneo, by contrast, have far fewer people but a much broader spectrum of ethnic groups.

Ethnicity, of course, is only one aspect of cultural variation, and in fact Java possesses great regional and social diversity. Travelers and scholars have long recognized four major cultural areas on the island: the *kejawen* or Javanese heartland, the north coast or *pasisir* region, the Sunda lands of West Java, and the eastern salient, also known as Blambangan. The island of Madura, lying to the northeast of Java, comprises a fifth region with close cultural ties to the neighboring coasts of Java.

The *Kejawen* heartland

The best known of Java's cultural areas is the so-called *kejawen* or Javanese heartland of Central and East Java. This area's language, arts and etiquette are regarded as the most refined and exemplary on the island. This is the home of Java's surviving aristocracy, and it remains the region from which the majority of Indonesia's generals, political leaders and business people have come.

The *kejawen* territory stretches from Banyumas in the west to Blitar in the east—encompassing the richest and most densely inhabited agricultural lands in all of Indonesia. The clusters of volcanic mountains which define the topography are widely spaced here, creating broad, well-watered basins ideally suited to wet-rice agriculture. It is no coincidence that this region hosted the island's most distinguished ancient kingdoms. The major 18th-century palaces of Yogyakarta and Surakarta lie at the center of the *kejawen* region, giving an aristocratic flavor to the local arts, language and culture.

Etiquette and personal bearing are softer

ERIC OEY

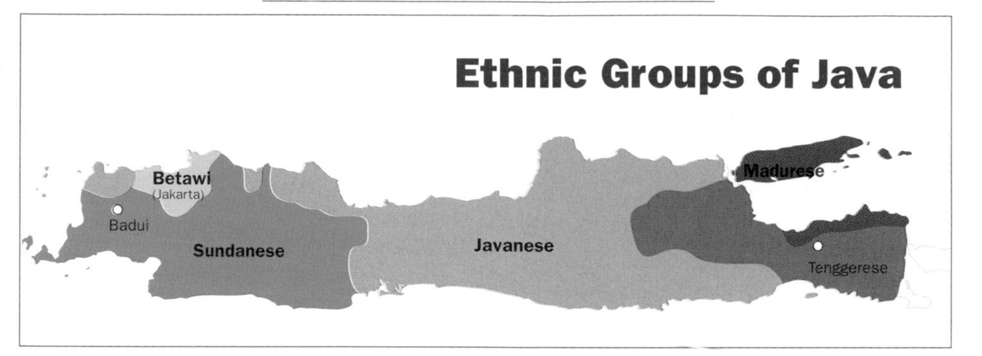

and more reserved. Textile patterns are similarly restrained, emphasizing sober earth tones like *soga* brown and indigo. Not surprisingly, given its courtly heritage, *kejawen* people tend to be acutely preoccupied with issues of status and rank, expressed in elaborate language levels that encode such differences in vocabulary and usage (see "Language and Literature").

Kejawen religious practices are varied. As elsewhere on Java, the majority is Muslim, but the Islamic community is split between orthodox practitioners who emphasize prayer, Quranic study and Islamic holy days, and "Javanist" Muslims who stress mysticism, local rites, and distinctly Javanese customs (*adat*). Tensions between the two have sometimes resulted in conflicts, and as a result some *kejawen* Muslims have become Christians or Hindus. In some Central Javanese towns, in fact, Christians comprise up to 20 percent of the local population.

Maritime *pasisir* Javanese

A distinctive *pasisir* culture dominates the long north coastal plain of Java, stretching from Cirebon in the west to Surabaya and Pasuruan in the east. Although they are ethnically and linguistically Javanese, the inhabitants of this region have a good deal in common with the Malay-speaking traders and seafarers of other coastal areas in the archipelago, with whom they have interacted for centuries. The *pasisir* is more thoroughly Islamic, and the people here are more direct and less reserved.

Kejawen inlanders tend to regard *pasisir* Javanese as somewhat coarse and aggressive. The soft features, round faces and languid expression prized by inland Javanese give way on the coast to a higher proportion of curly hair and sharp features that display their mixed Javanese, Malay, Arab and outer island ancestry. Clothing styles differ too. *Pasisir* batik is an explosion of bright reds, greens, blues and yellows.

Pasisir society is, at least by temperament, urban and bourgeois—in contrast to the rural and feudal character of the *kejawen*. As the Dutch improved Java's transport infrastructure in the 19th century, *pasisir* entrepreneurs fanned out into the hinterland, establishing businesses and introducing inland Javanese to more orthodox variants of Islam. With them, too, they brought the *pasisir* preference for drumming rather than gamelan, Quranic reading rather than *wayang*, and *silat* martial arts rather than Indian-influenced courtly dances.

Sundanese of West Java

The Sundanese who inhabit the western highlands of Java are the island's second largest ethnic group, and their language is more closely related to Malay or Minang than to Javanese. From the Javanese, however, they have borrowed the system of language levels denoting rank and respect, as well as many forms of *kejawen* dance, literature, gamelan music and shadow play theater.

Sundanese culture is different, however, in two important respects—it is more conspicuously Islamic, and its system of status hierarchy is much less rigid. The inland Sunda area is hilly and was, until the last century, thickly forested and sparsely inhabited. The Sundanese traditionally lived in small, isolated hamlets and engaged in dry-field (*ladang*) agriculture. The dispersion of the population made control by the native courts difficult, and as a result, the Sundanese maintained a more independent mien.

Though court cultures thrived here in ancient times, they apparently lacked the resources to construct the sort of magnificent religious monuments that are found in East and Central Java. When the interior was

Opposite: *Java is overwhelmingly young; over half of the population is under the age of 18.*

opened for coffee, tea and cinchona (quinine) cultivation in the 19th century, the highlands took on the air of a frontier society, further reinforcing the individualistic temperament of the Sundanese people. The strong influence of Islam is apparent in the Sundanese shadow play, which draws more heavily on Islamic folklore than on the Indian epics depicted in Central Javanese *wayang*.

It should be noted that one small segment of the Sundanese population—the Badui of the southwestern highlands—has remained aloof from Islam to this day. The religion of the Badui preserves a mixture of pre-Islamic polytheism and Hindu liturgy. Though they are sometimes referred to as a separate ethnic group, the Badui are actually peasant Sundanese who cling to the pre-Islamic ways of their ancestors.

ERIC OEY

Blambangan: the rugged east

The far eastern tip of Java—beginning just west of Malang and stretching to the straits opposite Bali, is known as the "eastern salient"—also, historically, as Blambangan, in honor of the ancient Hindu-Javanese kingdom once based here. This is the most rugged and culturally varied of Java's regions, and is also the least familiar to most foreign visitors.

After the fall of Hindu-Buddhist Majapahit in the 16th century, the eastern salient never came under the control of Muslim Javanese kingdoms. Despite repeated attacks by Muslim armies, the small Hindu principality of Blambangan (whose capital lay just to the south of present-day Banyuwangi) maintained its independence until the late 18th century. Following its conquest, the indigenous people of the region, known as Osing, were Islamized but nonetheless preserved a dialect, aesthetic tradition and body of custom distinct from the rest of Java.

A purer, though largely peasant variant of this same indigenous East Javanese culture is found among the population of the Tengger highlands around Mts. Bromo and Semeru. The Tenggerese remained non-Islamic even after the fall of Blambangan, and although Muslim armies periodically raided their territories to take slaves, this remote mountain area was never effectively controlled. Even today, 500 years after the fall of Hindu-Buddhist Majapahit, Tengger priests recite prayers to Siva, Brahma and Visnu. Unlike the Balinese, however, they have been isolated from courtly centers of Hinduism, and thus preserve none of the great literature of ancient Java. Like the Badui, the Tenggerese nonetheless provide fascinating populist echoes of pre-Islamic ways.

The warfare that pitted Muslim armies from Central Java against the Tengger and Blambangan severely depleted the eastern salient's native population. By the beginning of the 19th century, most settlements lay in ruins, and the Dutch colonial government then encouraged the migration of laborers to work the coffee and sugar estates they established throughout the area. Central Javanese settled along the southern coast in Malang and Lumajang, while the north coast was largely settled by Madurese migrants.

The Madurese

Madurese society bears the clear imprint of the maritime Malay world of western Indonesia. The island of Madura is hilly and arid, with severely eroded topsoils. Agriculture is difficult and the population is extremely poor. In the face of this, the Madurese early on turned to the sea and to maritime trade. Some Madurese also worked as mercenaries for Javanese kings, or later, for the Dutch. Though the Javanese regard the Madurese as their social inferiors, they readily concede their superiority in martial skills and greatly fear their "hot-headedness." The Madurese refute these deprecatory remarks by insisting they are braver than the Javanese, and better Muslims.

The migration of Madurese to Java was

pioneered by religious teachers who built communities centered around Muslim religious schools (*pesantren*). The results of this migration are seen today in everything from women's dress to the strength of Islamic parties in the national elections.

New lines of differentiation

Together, these five areas—*kejawen*, *pasisir*, Sunda, Blambangan and Madura—map out Java's traditional cultural regions. The boundaries between them were never impermeable, however, and the migrations of recent centuries have insured that elements of each tradition are now found all over Java.

Within each area, moreover, there is significant variation. Throughout Java, for example, uplanders tend to be more direct than lowlanders, whom they regard as rather snobbish. Lowlanders by contrast, view hill people as uncultured country bumpkins. Aristocrats tend to be more mystical, traders more orthodox, and peasants more syncretistic in their religious beliefs.

In fact, the contrast between the urban middle class and the rural population today presents a more striking line of social differentiation than ethnicity. Although comprising only about 25 percent of the island's population, urban dwellers stand at the forefront of cultural change. A new "Indonesian culture" is emerging based on mass education and mass media, and with few exceptions, urban middle class Javanese, Sundanese and Madurese are today less concerned with gamelans and *wayang* than they are with cars, televisions and pop music.

In this respect, modern Java is quite different from Bali, where middle class urbanites actively support the traditional arts and religion. Such traditionalism wins little praise in Java, and the finest examples of traditional Javanese culture are often now to be found in remote inland villages. Peasants, not the urban wealthy, are the sponsors of mask (*topeng*) dances and shadow plays. Many urbanites have never even seen such performances except on television.

Despite the regional and ethnic differences, which in any case often seem rather subtle to first-time foreign visitors, all of Java's people seem to share certain basic social characteristics. Foremost among them is an engaging sociability. Amusement is found here not in retiring to some isolated spot at far remove from the madding crowd, but in the bustle and intensity of human contact. The Javanese even have a word for it, *ramé*, which connotes an atmosphere of laughter and conviviality that always occurs when a crowd gathers on Java.

In colonial times, European psychologists were struck by the rarity of clinical depression among this island's people. The Javanese seem very much at home in almost every situation—bubbly and cheerful as long as they are surrounded by people—and individuals seemed to respond to personal trauma by throwing themselves right back into the rhythm of society.

Foreign visitors obsessed with the need to keep to a tight schedule often feel themselves overwhelmed by the heat, the crowds, or the poverty of Java. They may do well, however, to keep in mind this simple truth—Java's beauty lies not just in its arts, its landscapes or its antiquities, but also in the smiles and tremendous warmth of its people. In hotels and railway stations it may at times be difficult to appreciate this, and in remote areas the attention lavished on foreign travelers may become positively oppressive. But as with the tropical heat, the point is to relax and engage your environment on its own terms. When you do so, you will feel an incredible human vitality that is perhaps the most lasting wonder of this fascinating island.

—Robert Hefner

ERIC OEY

Opposite: *An aristocrat from the Surakarta court, in Central Java.* **Above:** *A simple peasant girl harvesting rice fields along the north coast.*

ERIC OEY

JAVANESENESS

Equanimity, Etiquette and Self-Control

For the Javanese, an infant is an endearing but emotionally fragile being—said to be *durung jawa*, "not yet Javanese." To be Javanese on the other hand is not only to be adult, but to have achieved the proper degree of emotional self-control, balance, bearing and grace that in the Javanese scheme of things distinguishes them from animals, infants, the mentally impaired and most foreigners.

On becoming Javanese

The learning of Javaneseness begins from the first days of a child's life. The Javanese regard a baby as vulnerable to starts and sudden shocks (*kaget*), while its own impulses and desires are too strong for it to direct and understand. The infant's well-being is a matter for spiritual as well as physical concern: a startled child may be so weakened that its soul is penetrated by one of the malicious spirits who hover around during the infant's first months. The child may be protected by rituals to purify and strengthen it, until eventually it is strong enough to withstand these menacing forces.

In the meantime, the infant is enveloped in a gentle, loving world of caregivers. During its first year, a Javanese child is in almost constant physical contact with the mother or other adult kin. It is never left alone while awake and is never left to cry; at the first sign of distress, it is nursed and entertained—bounced, rocked, or otherwise distracted until it recovers its good mood. At nap time, it may be swaddled in a soft blanket that is not firmly tied. Should it protest, the swaddling is immediately removed.

At night the baby sleeps by its mother, beginning a pattern of "social sleeping" that continues throughout early life. If the infant awakes during the night, it is cleaned, nursed and rocked back to sleep. During the day it nurses when it pleases, and in general experiences a life of loving indulgence.

As the child begins at one or two years of age to produce its first utterances, the mother calmly begins teaching respectful behavior. For example, if the child reaches out with a left hand to receive a gift, the mother gently but firmly replaces this with the right. In interactions with elder siblings or adults, the mother provides the child with the proper kin terms required in respectful speech. At other times, especially in the presence of the father, the mother speaks for the child, sprinkling the right mix of respectful vocabulary into the bewildered child's speech. Javanese "baby talk" is made up of honorific terms, and children may even be addressed in refined speech in an effort to familiarize them with these forms. Through these and other exercises, the child is taught that its own impulses are to be mistrusted and that proper social interaction requires a mastery of one's emotions, and of elaborate expressions of respect.

The language of respect

Language training, which takes place mostly within the family, is an important part of becoming Javanese. As the child approaches the age of four or five, the father becomes rather more reserved and distant, and the mother and other adults focus on him as an object of respect—prompting the child with proper speech terms and reminding it not to use the straightforward vocabulary it learned during its early years.

The child must now begin to master the formal speech of high Javanese (*krama*). The father's role thus introduces the child to the demands of the public world. The mother remains a source of solace and support, but from this time on the father becomes more reserved and emotionally aloof—not a stern disciplinarian, but a reminder of the strict etiquette required in Javanese social life.

Only a few other languages—notably Korean, Japanese and Samoan—are as preoccupied as Javanese with the vocabulary of respect. Javanese is divided into three different "levels," each distinguished by its own vocabulary, affixes, sentence elaboration and etiquette. *Ngoko* or "low Javanese" is the language of early socialization—simple, unrefined, and therefore appropriate only for intimate or informal relations or for use by people of equal social standing. Since, in general, Javanese view humans as inherently unequal, in adulthood one speaks *ngoko* only with immediate family members and friends.

Opposite: *Javanese body language—the* sembah *performed before members of the royal family.*

Krama is more elegant and refined—suitable for addressing people of high social standing. *Madya* or "middle Javanese" is a less refined variant of *krama* used by peasants, the urban working class, and others in circumstances in which *krama* would sound overly stiff and pretentious.

No interaction is linguistically neutral in Java. During every encounter, speakers must assess their relative social standing and determine the vocabulary that is appropriate to the relationship. In some well-defined social situations—students with teachers, peasants with government officials, homeowners with servants—the exact contours of the relationship and its appropriate speech style may be crystal clear. In many interactions, however, the precise relationship is ambiguous. As a result of this uncertainty, there is in Java an obsessive preoccupation with social status and a considerable anxiety about how this is to be defined.

When strangers first meet, much of their initial conversation is obliquely concerned with defining each person's social standing, and determining just what measure of respect he or she is due. Invariably the conversation begins with a large proportion of high Javanese or Indonesian, then slowly descends to the level each speaker feels comfortable to give and to receive. Where there is disagreement about their relative social standing, the conversation may be cut short, as each speaker retreats into silence rather than compromise his social standing.

Modesty and moderation

Through these and other social exercises, "well-bred" Javanese come to mistrust spontaneity in interaction. More generally, they learn to refrain from an exuberant expression of their emotions. It is largely for this reason that they stress modesty in sexuality and other sensual pleasures, such as eating. This pattern of self-control is not one of emotional repression—as a Westerner might expect—it is instead a gentle modulation of self and emotion in personal comportment. Grace and bearing is the key to inner equanimity and proper social interaction.

Contrary to the stiffness Westerners associate with formal etiquette, this Javanese emphasis on social grace still allows for a clear and vibrant expression of personal warmth. Indeed, for the Javanese, one's public bearing is a more accurate index of one's inner worth than what Westerners would regard as the "inner self." It is useful for foreign visitors to keep this in mind, as it helps one to appreciate the seriousness with which Javanese take small gestures of respect and the maintenance of social appearances.

These same values are reflected and reinforced in the traditional Javanese arts. The shadow play and the *wayang wong* theater are both extended variations on Javanese themes of status, social etiquette and spiritual power. Many of these same values receive philosophical elaboration in the mystical tradition known as *kebatinan*. Popular among the better-educated urban middle class, *kebatinan* is a mystical regimen that emphasizes emotional self-control and the flattening of desire. This is achieved through fasting, sleeplessness, meditation, and other exercises drawn

from the Indian mystical tradition, both Muslim and Hindu. Quite unlike in India, however, Javanese *kebatinan* is not other-worldly in its focus. In fact, its mastery of affect is regarded as an instrument for the acquisition of spiritual power—the pay-off of which is health, wealth and worldly influence.

Role models

There are individual variations in the art of "being Javanese." Javanese women, for example, are less preoccupied with status than men. Their role as mothers—and the positive value placed on that role—means that their lives center on relationships with an intimacy that transcends the formal reserve of public life. In other domains, too, women are allowed to act with a directness forbidden to men of similar standing. In markets, for example, women haggle over prices without fear of compromising their dignity. Some men view this as evidence of women's venality—a quality they link to spiritual inferiority. Women laugh and shrug off such characterizations, and tend to regard men as rather stiff and overly sensitive.

In most Javanese families, women in fact assume the primary responsibility for household finances and play a critical role in family decisions. Whereas in external affairs they acknowledge the husband's authority, this authority can be compromised if the man meddles too directly in family matters. As a result the husband remains aloof, and his

day-to-day influence is usually less than his wife's. His is an idealized authority—not a hands-on, practical one. His wife holds the purse strings and makes day-to-day decisions.

Devout *santri* Muslims tend to diverge from these Javanese norms. In activities like mosque worship, for example, they place great emphasis on the equality of (male) worshippers before Allah, and in social greetings and conversations they tend to be less formal or emotionally reserved than other Javanese. Many modernist Muslims view traditional Javanese culture as backward and undemocratic, and many urban middle-class Javanese see Islam, rather than traditional Javanese values, as the most solid foundation upon which to build a national culture.

Java's peasantry—still over half of the population—has always occupied the lowest rung on Java's social ladder, and its attitude toward traditional values has been similarly ambivalent. Throughout history, there have been peasant rebellions calling for the upending of the existing social order. In pre-modern times, most of these either ended in failure or eventually resulted in the founding of a new dynasty grounded on principles of social hierarchy similar to the old.

In the modern era, however, nationalism and the establishment of the Indonesian nation have greatly changed the peasant's lot. The old hierarchies have become less relevant, and less of the fatalism or resignation that once characterized the rural population remains. The democratization of education has not meant equality of opportunity by any means, but it has created a revolution in popular aspirations. New agricultural and commercial enterprises have upended traditional village arrangements, and have allowed a portion of the rural population to achieve what is, by Javanese standards, remarkable wealth. The horizons of peasants in even the most remote mountain villages have expanded enormously, and a quiet revolution is reshaping popular Javanese identity.

Many peasant children today go on to high school; a small percentage even to university. The influence of modern media is evident in everything from dress to entertainment to consumption. Today, for example, an affluent peasant family is as likely to invest in a truck or a stereo as in a ritual festival. Such seemingly mundane changes reflect a far-reaching transformation. Status is still a preoccupation, but there is a new mobility.

It is a common mistake to conclude from all this that Javanese culture is under assault from "Western" values. Nothing could be further from the truth. The Javanese have a very strong sense of themselves and actually very little idea what it means to be Western. With its ancient civilization and rich cultural inheritance to draw upon, Java is practically a world unto itself. Though beset by serious social and economic problems, the people of Java possess an uncommon charity and keen sense of humor that have allowed them to survive difficult circumstances in the past. Hopefully these same traits will continue to serve them just as well in a better future.

—*Nancy and Robert Hefner*

Opposite and above: *The aristocratic ideal in Java involves a mastery of personal affect.*

RELIGION

A Gentle Blend of Islam and *Adat*

Visitors to Java are invariably struck by the great variety of religious practices observed on the island. In the central square (*alun-alun*) of most towns, graceful church spires stand alongside silver-domed mosques whose loudspeakers blare out the call to prayer five times each day. Not far away, usually near the central market, a brightly-decorated Chinese temple (*klenteng*) is filled with images of Buddha and a heavenly host of other deities. At road intersections throughout Java the observant visitor will notice small flower offerings (*sajen*) set out to appease spirits who might otherwise cause mischief. And at remote mountain shrines, crowds of pilgrims flock to the graves of holy men whose spirits provide assistance in everything from romance to business.

The picture is a complex one. Although the island's most famous antiquities, Borobudur and Prambanan, were the product of an ancient Hindu-Buddhist civilization, today the vast majority of Javanese are Muslims. Indeed, as government brochures proudly proclaim, Indonesia is the world's largest Islamic nation, and there are in fact more Muslims living on tropical Java than in any Middle Eastern country.

This basic fact is complicated, however, by the prominence of several religious minorities and a very great variation within the Muslim community itself. About 12 percent of Java's people are Christians, Buddhists or Hindus. Even among the remaining 88 percent who are Muslims there is wide variation in practice and belief.

Some Javanese Muslims would just as soon meditate motionless in a pond or burn incense and present offerings to the spirits of saintly ancestors as enter a mosque to perform the *salat* (the prayer required of Muslims five times each day). Disputes between strict *santri* Muslims and "Javanist" Muslims who prefer native customs (*adat*) over orthodox piety have been a recurrent theme in this island's history. An overriding native tolerance, meanwhile, has resulted in a gentle blending of beliefs that is the hallmark of religion on Java today.

Mystical devotion

A strong mystical vein runs through Javanese culture. Whatever their faith, the Javanese

KAL MULLER

display a deeply spiritual attitude toward reality. The anthropologist Clifford Geertz once said he believed Java was the only place in the world where one could approach almost any peasant in the fields, inquire as to the ultimate nature of reality, and receive an extended and deeply mystical commentary on the nature of Allah and being.

Javanese Islam has been tempered by this mystical sensibility since the very beginning. The "nine saints" (*wali songo*) who according to popular Javanese belief spread Islam

JILL GOCHER

throughout the island in the 15th century are said to have been adept at magic and meditation—they could make themselves invisible, appear in two places at once, and magically deflect the daggers of their enemies.

In modern Java, there are still many masters of the occult arts (*dukun*), whose specialties range from massage and midwivery to magic and exorcism. Though Javanese today express scepticism about the abilities of individual specialists, most believe that magic is real and that some practice it with great effect. Meditative traditions emphasizing fasting, sleeplessness and other ascetic rites are also common, though equally controversial.

Many Muslims reject such practices, insisting that the only proper avenue to Allah is through ritual acts sanctioned by the Quran. They regard mysticism practiced outside the framework of orthodox devotion with suspicion. As in India (whence Javanese Islam arrived), such disagreements have racked the Muslim community for centuries. One of the original Islamic apostles to Java, Seh Siti Jenar, was immolated for his revelation of the mystical truth that Allah and the individual are one. This belief is still popular in Java, and is used to justify inward-oriented asceticism and to downplay the importance of mosque prayer or the annual fast.

Islam and the imperial cult

This tension between mysticism and ortho-

ERIC OEY

doxy was strongly manifested in Central Java's Muslim courts. Through their long history, the sultans saw themselves as defenders of the faith—forbidding non-Muslims from residing within the palace walls, sending delegations and gifts to Mecca, and using Islam as a rallying cry against European invaders. Yet like the Muslim kings of north India (from whom they borrowed many of their ideas), they also put great emphasis on mystical devotion and sought to restrict the development of a powerful and independent Arabian-style clergy.

Javanese rulers went on to create an imperial cult in which the king, not the clergy, was the ultimate authority on Islamic matters. The sultan was "Allah's representative on earth." Royal cemeteries and mosques in Java were regarded as holy shrines on a par with sacred sites in Arabia, and seven pilgrimages to them were deemed equivalent to one pilgrimage to Mecca.

Despite their heterodoxy, the courts played a key role in the Islamization of Java. In the 16th and 17th centuries they oversaw the destruction of Hindu-Buddhist monasteries and temples, and in their place erected mosques, Muslim schools and pilgrimage sites. Thrice a year the sultan sponsored huge religious festivals at the palace to celebrate holy days like the birth of the prophet Muhammad. He also required male subjects to undergo circumcision, symbolic of their entrance into the community of Islam.

At the same time, however, these rulers continued much of the pomp and ceremony of the earlier Hindu-Buddhist courts. On Muslim holy days, the court presented rice-mountain offerings (*gunungan*) to the four guardian spirits of the island at the same time that it gave worship to Allah. And each year

Opposite: *Jakarta's Istiqlal Mosque.*
Above: *Islamic schools. There are more Muslims on Java than in any Middle Eastern country.*

the sultan was supposed to have sexual intercourse with his ocean-spirit wife, Ratu Kidul, the goddess of the southern seas. The marriage of the sultan and the queen spirit guaranteed the fertility of the land and the prosperity of the realm. Though some aristocrats regard it as repugnantly polytheistic (*shirk*), the cult of the goddess continues. Each year, representatives from the Yogya and Surakarta palaces approach the southern shores with offerings of food and clothing, thus renewing the ruler's ties to the ocean queen.

Popular worship—the *slametan*

Until recently, much of Java's peasantry practiced rites of spirit invocation similar to those of the courts. In inland Java, especially, the guardian spirit shrine (*danyang*) and not the mosque was the village's ritual center. Each year, the protection of the spirit was secured through offerings of incense and food in a rite of "village purification" (*resik dusun*).

Just as the court and the village had regular rites of purification and protection, the household was and still is secured through periodic ritual offerings. Pregnancy, the birth of a child, the first cutting of an infant's hair, circumcision, marriage, and death all inspire a flurry of ritual activity. Personal growth and life passage are spiritual, as much as biological realities. Their safe progress is insured through the simplest and most popular of Javanese religious rites—the *slametan*.

A Javanese variation on the universal communion meal, the *slametan* brings together male neighbors and relatives for a quiet religious feast. Cooked foods are set on a mat in the center of the room, incense is lit, and a prayer is intoned in which local saints, guardian spirits and Allah may be addressed. After the prayer, guests take a few perfunctory bites of food, then usually pack up the remainder to share with their family at home, thus "spreading the blessing" to others.

With its emphasis on mystical communion, spiritual sharing, and calm restraint, the *slametan* brilliantly expresses the core Javanese value of social harmony (*rukun*). Through this and other aspects of popular religion, Javanese culture succeeded in giving Islam a distinctly Javanese face.

Islamic reform

The northern and western coasts of Java were always more closely connected to the Islamic maritime culture than to the central Javanese courts. Beginning 600 years ago, these ports assimilated Muslim traders from Sumatra, India, Persia, Arabia and even China. Visitors to cities like Semarang, Surabaya, Pasuruan and others along the north coast will note the striking presence of Islamic institutions and dress styles here.

Dutch colonialism contributed to the decline of Javanist traditions and the rise of orthodox Islam. As Europeans undermined

the autonomy of the traditional rulers in the 19th century, they provoked a crisis of identity. For some, the solution was to reject the courts and identify more strongly with the new tradition of international Islam.

The decline of the courts coincided with a rapid expansion in the number of Javanese making the pilgrimage to Mecca—a development facilitated by the advent of European steamships traveling to the Suez canal. By the beginning of the 20th century, calls for religious orthodoxy were heard throughout

ERIC OEY

Java, as reformers sought to bring Javanese Islam in line with modern teachings emanating from the Middle East.

Reformist demands were controversial, even among devout Muslims. Long-standing traditions of prayer, mysticism, aesthetics and female comportment that many people on Java had heretofore regarded as compatible with Islam were suddenly denounced by purists since they deviated from Middle Eastern norms.

The reformist movement eventually provoked a counter-reaction. Although still considering themselves good Muslims, many Javanese became adamantly opposed to the elimination of what they regarded as traditional Javanese custom from their practices. Affirming their allegiance to "Javanese Islam" they went on to reject the demand for "Arab" Islamic orthodoxy.

Religious pluralization

This religious controversy gave rise to other developments. At the turn of this century, a few Javanese began converting to Christianity. The trickle turned into a flood after independence, when Protestants successfully demonstrated their autonomy from European churches. In doing so, they made conversion to Christianity attractive for a small but influential "modernist" minority. Since 1965-66, a smaller number of Javanese have also converted to Balinese Hinduism.

ERIC OEY

In the 20th century, tensions between Javanist and orthodox Islam developed into a full-blown schism, pluralizing Javanese religion to a degree never before seen. This continues today, though the influence of reformist Muslims continues to grow too. Since 1965-66, the New Order government has vigorously defended pluralism and imposed strict limits on religious extremism. Atheism is forbidden, since it is identified with a now discredited communism, and all Indonesians are required to profess one of five officially sanctioned religions—Islam, Protestantism, Catholicism, Hinduism or Buddhism. Muslim organizations are in turn required to affirm their allegiance to the idea that Indonesia is a multi-confessional society, and to relinquish the idea of an Islamic state.

The government's effort to depoliticize religion and promote pluralism has not dampened the influence of Islam in public life. The changes that have swept the Muslim world since the early 1970s have been felt in Java, and in recent years growing numbers of middle-class urbanites have turned to Islam for spiritual refuge from the ills of modern life and western liberalism. On campuses and in big cities, it is now common to see modern, well-educated women dressed in the *jilbab*, their heads covered by scarves and their ankles and arms fully clothed. Mosques and Muslim schools, meanwhile, are more crowded than ever. Still, the vast majority continue to practice an Islam marked by tolerance and moderation, and tinged with the mysticism of their forebears. Though they may differ in their individual beliefs, this mysticism infuses the sensibilities of all Javanese, thereby providing a certain unity within the great diversity of religious practices on the island.

— *Robert Hefner*

Opposite and above: *The Sekaten festival held at the Solo palace on Muhammad's birthday incorporates earlier Hindu and indigenous elements.*

THE JAVANESE CALENDAR

Traditional Ritual and Market Cycle

The traditional Javanese calendar is a wonderful piece of chronometric syncretism combining Hindu-Javanese, Islamic and indigenous elements. Though it has now fallen into disuse for everyday purposes, many ceremonies and performances are still essentially based on the calendar. Visitors interested in seeing village *wayang* performances and major court ceremonies should be aware of it and make an effort to schedule their visits accordingly.

Just as in Bali, two interlocking time-keeping cycles were traditionally employed on Java—in this case the indigenous, 210-day *pawukon* "year" and the 354-day lunar year of the Islamic calendar. Neither of these is adjusted to fit solar or sidereal cycles, so their relationship with the Gregorian calendar is constantly changing.

The *pawukon* cycle

The basic components of the 210-day *pawukon* cycle are two different weeks—a seven-day week (*wuku*) and a five-day one (*pasaran*). The days of the seven-day *wuku* week now have names that derive from Arabic and Portugese—Senen, Selasa, Rebo, Kemis, Jumuwah, Sabtu and Minggu (or Ngahad)—though prior to the 17th century, as in Bali, each of the days was known by a Sanskrit-derived name. Thirty of these *wuku* weeks form a complete cycle; each of the 30 weeks was given a distinct name corresponding to an elaborate ritual cycle in ancient times. Nowadays this cycle of weeks is used only in divination.

The names of the *pasaran* days, by contrast, are purely Javanese: Kliwon, Legi, Paing, Pon and Wage. The five-day cycle was formerly used to fix the movement of rotating markets (*pasar*) from one village to the next on a weekly circuit. In many cities, one still finds markets or areas with names like Pasar Kliwon, Pasar Legi, Pasar Pon, etc.—even though the markets, if they still exist, are now active all week long.

These two cycles run concurrently, going in and out of phase with one another. For example, a given Tuesday (Selasa) may fall on Kliwon in the five-day cycle, but the following Tuesday will fall not on Kliwon but Paing. Any given pairing of days from the two cycles recurs every 7 x 5 = 35 days.

This "month" made up of 35 paired days from the two cycles is an intimate part of Javanese life. Some combinations, such as Selasa Kliwon and Jumuwah Kliwon, are believed to be inherently auspicious. Most, however, have a more personal significance. The combination of days on which a person was born—his or her *wetonan*—is a sort of personal holy day.

Traditional Javanese will mark their *wetonan* every 35 days by fasting or visiting a local shrine. Prominent and wealthy citizens may invite their friends and family to share a ceremonial meal, while a prosperous businessman or performer may sponsor entertainments. For example, Solo's best-known *dalang* (*wayang* puppeteer)—Ki H. Anom Suroto—celebrates his *wetonan* every 35 days on the eve of Rebo Legi with a *wayang kulit* performance at his home.

When is Rebo (Wednesday) Legi? Every fifth Wednesday, of course, but which Wednesdays? The easiest way to find out is to buy a traditional Javanese calendar with the *pasaran* days marked on it. It is also possible (though tedious) to count backwards or forwards from given dates. Since 19 December 1990 is a Rebo Legi, 30 January 1991 will be, too. But don't forget that the Javanese day starts at sunset. The eve (*malam*) of Rebo Legi is not Wednesday night, but the previous night.

The Javanese Muslim calendar

In 1633, Sultan Agung changed the existing Hindu-Javanese *saka* calendar over to the present Islamic one. As a result, many of the old court ceremonies and holy days were shifted to coincide with important Islamic holy days. Thus, for example, the Sekaten harvest fair and festival—an ancient custom which probably pre-dates even the Hindu-Buddhist presence on Java, but later incorporated the Indian *lingga* and *yoni* fertility symbols made of food—was moved so as to fall on the birthday of the Prophet.

The Muslim lunar year consists of 354

Right: *Detail from a 19th century Javanese calendar showing the 5* pasaran *market days.*

days (eleven fewer than the Western or Gregorian year), which are divided into twelve months of 29 or 30 days each. This means that major Javanese holidays and ceremonies reckoned by the lunar calendar occur eleven days earlier each year by comparison to the Gregorian calendar. As an approximate reference for calculation, the following dates may be of use (remember to subtract 11 days for each subsequent year):

10 June 1994 Satu Sura, occasion of the Kirab Pusaka in which the Solonese courts bring out their sacred regalia to be ritually washed and carried in a very slow, stately circumambulation of the palaces and the town. Hundreds of courtiers take part in these midnight processions, witnessed by teeming, yet totally silent crowds. In Solo, a sacred albino water buffalo leads the march and local farmers fight to scoop up bits of its faeces to be used as magically-charged fertilizer. In Yogya there is no procession, but offerings to Kangjeng Loro Kidul—goddess of the south sea and patronness of Java's rulers—are brought to the shore and ritually cast adrift at Parangkusumo

25 July 1994 15 Sapar, occasion of the Ongkowiyu festival in Jatinom (a small village located about an hour away from Solo in Central Java). The festival is held in commemoration of Kyai Gribig, a local religious teacher. *Apem*, specially prepared rice cakes, are thrown from the tops of high towers to the crowds below. Those who are fortunate enough to catch one are assured of good luck and prosperity.

19 August 1994 12 Maulud (or Mulud), the anniversary of the birth of Muhammad and the occasion of the Sekaten festival in both Yogya and Solo. For one week before the climactic day (*garebeg*), an amusement park springs up on the north *alun-alun* complete with haunted house. For several hours each day, the palace's ancient Sekaten gamelans play in front of the royal mosque. On the final day, two *gunungan* ("mountains" of rice cakes and vegetables) are carried in procession to the mosque to be blessed, and are afterwards torn apart by a frantic mob of people who wish to partake of the magically potent offering. A similar festival, called Panjang Jimat, is held in Cirebon.

Visitors on a tight schedule should know that the Solonese and Yogyanese court celebrations are held a day later than they should be according to the Islamic calendar. This discrepancy dates from 1936, when the courts—in a gesture of defiance against reformist Islam—refused to acknowledge an obscure Islamic leap year that occurs only every 120 years. The royal houses thus celebrate holidays such as Satu Sura a day later than is indicated in calendars sold for general use. This fact is not widely recognized even in Central Java.

—Marc Perlman and Joan Suyenaga

LANGUAGE & LITERATURE

An Elaborate Hierarchy of Speech Levels

Java, though relatively small in size, is an island of considerable linguistic diversity. Sundanese, Jakartan Malay (Betawi), Madurese and Javanese are the four major indigenous languages. All of them belong to the huge Malayo-Polynesian (now known as "Austronesian") language family, but are as different from one another as, for example, English, French, German and Spanish.

In addition to these four, Dutch and English, several Chinese dialects, and numerous languages from neighboring Indonesian islands are spoken in enclaves. Overlaying them all is the national language, Bahasa Indonesia (a variant of Malay)—the language of government, media and education.

In Central and East Java, the language heard most frequently is Javanese—the mother tongue of some 80 million Javanese, Indonesia's largest ethnic group. Most Javanese also speak Indonesian as a second language, and in towns and cities individuals will often address each other first in this language, slipping into Javanese as they become more familiar. Indonesian is thus considered appropriate for more formal occasions, including any communication with outsiders, as it is direct and neutral—free of the complex status distinctions found in Javanese.

Javanese, conversely, remains the language of choice for informal and intimate communication, but is less well suited to contexts that are modern and urban. Indeed, conversations in Javanese concerning politics, economics or any other "modern" subject frequently slip in and out of Indonesian, thus creating a hybrid *gado-gado* (mixed salad) language that moves easily between expressive Javanese verbs and adjectives and the Indonesian technical vocabulary (much of it derived from Dutch and English) used to describe the contemporary world.

Expressions of social status

The most notable aspect of Javanese—and what keeps it from being considered "modern" by even the Javanese themselves—is that every utterance expresses a social status distinction between the person speaking and the person being addressed. This is achieved through intonation, vocabulary, honorific pronouns and word morphology (suffixes, prefixes and infixes), that together produce a series of distinct levels within the language ranging from very familiar (spoken only between intimates or to social inferiors) to very formal (spoken only among court officials within the palace precincts).

Conversations among individuals of high but equal status are carried out in a very respectful mode of speech called *basa* or *krama*. At this level, word choice is very limited, as are the topics that can be covered; language grows less specific and more constrained as it becomes more refined.

In conversations between individuals of differing status, the social inferior uses high *krama* expressions, while his superior speaks down to him in the crasser *madya* or *ngoko* idioms. In fact, there are numerous intermediate levels, and these are deftly juggled and interchanged during the course of a conversation so as to express even finer status distinctions between the speakers and the persons spoken of. Even for a Javanese, this can create confusion, especially when one is unsure of another's status or unfamiliar with the niceties of refined *krama* speech.

In view of all this, it is no wonder that progressive, Western-educated Indonesian activists (many of them ethnic Javanese) who debated the language question in the early days of the nationalist movement chose Malay as the national language, even though almost half of the population speak Javanese as their mother tongue.

To a degree, the "feudal" overtones of Javanese are fading, as fewer people bother to master the high *krama* speech style. Some intellectuals, moreover, make a point of speaking only the most familiar or *ngoko* level of the language, and more and more Javanese simply employ the ever expanding *lingua franca* of Indonesian.

An ancient literary tradition

Javanese literature is as complex as the language itself. The oral traditions remain strong in many forms, in both city and village. Folk expressions and wisdom, popular sciences of numerology and divination, popular tales of history and adventure, and above all the vast repertoire of the ever-popular

ERIC OEY

shadow puppet theater (*wayang kulit* or *ringgit wacucal*), with its many offshoots, all enjoy a good deal of currency, though there has been erosion in recent decades due to mass education and mass media.

By contrast, the traditional courtly literature, composed in complex meters for vocal performance, has had a much sadder fate. The wealthy courts that once supported the composition and transmission of such works have been in decline for over two centuries, and with their eclipse the arts they supported have had to find external popular or institutional support in order to survive.

While the same is true of other Javanese performing arts, the difference is that no new audiences have developed for the traditional romances and mystical treatises once patronized by kings. As a result, Javanese literature in its traditional forms has all but ceased to be produced, and the number of literati who still can consult the texts of earlier periods is tiny and rapidly diminishing.

Part of the reason that the traditional literature is disappearing is that it is composed in a highly idiosyncratic literary dialect of Javanese never found outside the written text—a dialect that is even farther removed from everyday Javanese speech than is Shakespearean English from the contemporary idioms of middle America.

These texts therefore cannot be understood without special literary training. A further complication is the fact that traditional works were rarely published, but were transmitted in manuscript form, with each reader copying the texts that he wished to collect. Most of the copying, of course, was restricted to the palaces, which maintained productive scriptoria into the 20th century.

Manuscript copies were made in the native Javanese script, a complex syllabary of Indic derivation containing over 60 characters. Knowledge of this script has today almost vanished, since the printing of Javanese has been carried out almost exclusively in Latin script in recent decades. Few young people today can read the Javanese alphabet with any fluency.

At the same time, however, a modern Javanese literature has developed in the 20th century, influenced less by traditional forms than by modern Indonesian literature (which in turn took much of its inspiration from Western fiction). The short story is the most popular genre, but short novels, poetry and personal essays are also known. The principal vehicle for the transmission of these works is the modern print media, particularly several weekly magazines published in Central and East Java.

— *Tim Behrend*

Above: *Evidence of Java's lively oral traditions—a* tembang *singer weaves tales of chivalry, love and political intrigue set in the historical past.*

GAMELAN MUSIC

'Moonlight and Flowing Water'

The diversity of traditional musical forms on Java is staggering. Best known of these is the gamelan (from the Javanese word *gamel* meaning "handle" or "hammer")—a large ensemble composed of metallophones, drums, flutes and other instruments—whose wondrous music is "pure and mysterious, like moonlight, and always changing, like flowing water" in the words of Dutch musicologist Leonard Huizinga.

Regional musical styles cluster around the old traditional courts and district capitals, each displaying local characteristics in performance and repertoire. Cities lying a relatively short distance from one another—such as Bandung, Sumedang and Cirebon in West Java—often display very distinctive styles of musical performance.

Three major regional styles are acknowledged: those of West, Central and East Java, and the three are sufficiently distinct from one another to make appreciation across their boundaries difficult. Several elements are nonetheless common to all or most of these musical forms.

The instruments

Certain instruments are found throughout the island. The most famous of these are the large bronze gongs which have been a specialty of Java since ancient times. The English word "gong" indeed derives from Javanese, and nearly every traditional ensemble on Java incorporates them. Some employ only a few as time markers or to play ostinatos, while others have scores of gongs of varying sizes and shapes used to sound a whole range of elements, including melodies.

Xylophone-like instruments with bronze keys are also widely used—these are in fact the instruments most commonly associated with the gamelan. Here again, they come in many shapes and sizes—their dimensions, number of keys, types of resonators and beaters varying widely within a particular ensemble type as well as between regions.

Hand drums are employed in most ensembles and come in many sizes. Bamboo flutes are also common, as are bowed lutes (usually with two strings) and multi-stringed zithers in the shape of a box. In rural areas, the sliding bamboo rattle (*angklung*) and an oboe-like wind instrument are prevalent.

ERIC OEY

Each gamelan set possesses a unique visual and sonic identity. Although Central Javanese instruments are tuned to two different scales (neither of which corresponds to Western tuning), these are not standardized and no two ensembles are tuned exactly alike. Furthermore, the wooden cases and ornamentation of each set are unique. Instruments cannot therefore be interchanged, as they would neither look nor sound compatible. Consequently, gamelan musicians do not own their instruments but gather to play where an ensemble is housed—at a rich person's house, a community hall, a theater, office building or school.

Due to their unique character, gamelan sets are often given a personal name preceded by the honorific title Kyai, meaning "Venerable One." Some particularly old and beautiful sets are believed to have powerful spirits that reside in the large gongs, and are treated with great respect.

A complex fabric of sound

Musical notation is rarely used, nor is there a conductor. Individual pieces, called *gending*, form part of a vast aural tradition and may be performed in different ways depending on the context and the performers.

Each instrument and vocal part plays a distinctive role in the overall musical fabric. Instruments with large and medium-sized metal keys, for instance, carry the melodic outline of the piece. The larger, suspended gongs, played by three or four musicians, create a repeating cycle of beats that mark off phrases of a consistent length. Several instruments elaborate the melodic core of the *gending*, and the drummer usually regulates the flow of the music—his rhythms providing a central beat around which the rest of the players orient themselves.

The complex, filled-in fabric of a gamelan performance thus results from a clear "stratification" of the instruments and their respective parts. Musicians do not exactly memorize the parts for a paritcular piece; instead they learn a vocabulary of patterns for their instrument, which can be applied to various musical situations. As a result, a performance by a gamelan ensemble can be quite spontaneous while at the same time involving almost no free "improvisation" in the Western sense of the term.

Left: *The sacred Sekaten gamelan of Solo, played only in the week before Muhammad's birthday.*
Right: *Large bronze Javanese gongs.*

Communal aspects of performance

Music making is intimately connected with religious and life-cycle celebrations within the community. Village purification (*sedekah bumi* in West Java; *resik desa* in Central and East Java) and wedding ceremonies are often accompanied by music.

Javanese music is thoroughly integrated with the other Javanese performing arts of dance, theater, puppet shows and even martial arts. In fact, music is most commonly heard as an accompaniment to these and concert halls or other venues solely for the performance of music do not exist.

Commercial theater troupes with live music play before paying audiences in the larger cities—the best known of these are the East Javanese *ludruk* and the Central Javanese *wayang orang* and *ketoprak*—but such companies are struggling today. An increasing number of dance and puppet performances are arranged for tourists, and local governments are organizing festivals and performing arts competitions. Commercial cassettes of traditional music are also having a big impact, altering the way people learn about the arts and sometimes even replacing live performers. Yet most Javanese still consider live gamelan performances, dance and theater to be the only appropriate accompaniment for traditional celebrations.

— *Roger Vetter*

EVERHARD DIJKSTRA

DANCE AND DRAMA

Dazzling Refinement and Grace

The rapid flick of a scarf, the delicate turn of a wrist, the seamless shuffle of bare feet across a polished floor and the glints of light reflected from a bejewelled headdress as a dancer slowly shifts her gaze—such are the images of Javanese dance that linger long after the performance is over. So powerful is the spell cast by this ancient and highly refined art form that it is often only after the performance is over that we begin to wonder what we have seen.

A vocabulary of movements

Despite the diversity of dance forms and wide range of performance venues—from a simple village ceremony to a crowded fair to an elegant palace *pendopo*—certain elements are common to all Javanese dance genres.

The still torso and emphasis on the attitude of the neck, wrists, hands and ankles certainly tempts comparisons of Javanese dance with the dance traditions of other Southeast Asian countries like Thailand and Cambodia, as well as with the *wayang kulit,* or shadow puppet theater. The dancer's body moves from side to side on a single plane, giving it a two-dimensional quality which suggests the shadow play, although this association can be overstressed. What seems puppet-like to us—the rigid torso, the angular limbs—also reflects the influence ancient Indian dance movements and of deeply-rooted Javanese cultural ideals.

Dance movement in any culture is a kinetic expression of cultural and aesthetic values and Javanese dance is no exception. The Javanese place a very high value on emotional control, social deference and avoidance of conflict. This is mirrored in their body movements, and is even more accentuated in the dance. A refined Javanese is marked by refined movements: torso contained, limbs moving within a circumscribed space in a delicate and peripheral way, not imposing or visceral. The facial expression must be pleasant but impassive and the movements smooth, controlled and fluid—never sharp, abrupt or rushed.

It is no wonder, then, that the study of dance by young Javanese is considered as much a social training as a training in performance art. Not only does a refined Javanese move in a refined manner, but training in

such movement creates a more refined Javanese. According to dance master Sasmintamardawa of Yogyakarta, "Learning the dance has a deep effect upon one's everyday behavior."

The highly articulated head, foot, and hand movements demonstrate the Javanese penchant for ornamentation and their obsession with detail. The elaborate hand gestures may once have told a story, as they do in other courtly Southeast Asian dance forms. They have long since lost any specific lexical meaning, however, although the gestures do occasionally imitate specific actions.

Ideal character types

Javanese dance, like the gamelan music which accompanies it, is highly structured and very modular. Motifs are based on eight count phrases and are carefully coordinated within the structure of the music. Each dance genre has a prescribed sectional structure. Whether a simple gesture or a complete choreography, the possibilities for individual expression are very limited.

Instead, what is expressed in this and most traditional dance and theater forms is an incredibly wide spectrum of character types, who inhabit a mythical world of monkeys, kings and ogres. A dance drama may tell a story inspired by the *Ramayana* or *Mahabharata* epics, a quest by the folk hero Panji (traditionally performed with masks), an adventure from the *Menak* stories, or a historical romance from one of the Javanese *babad* (royal chronicle) traditions. Whatever the story is, many of the same character types appear again and again, and certain principles of character typing always apply.

As in the *wayang kulit*, a character's type as well as his or her specific identity is immediately made evident in a dance drama through costume, movement quality and stylized speech patterns. Using varying types of accents and ornamentation, a dancer may be transformed into any number of characters.

There are three major categories of Javanese characters—female, refined male, and strong male. The female style uses a small, narrow space with continuous, delicately accented movements and limited ornamentation. The refined male style is similar to the female style in movement quality, but uses a low, broad stance. The strong male style utilizes a high, broad space with leg lifts, strong accents, and a wider range of ornamentation.

Within each main style there are many subtypes, corresponding to the different personalities portrayed—humble and refined, proud and forthright, coarse and quick-tempered—and also to the specific characters

Opposite and below: *Bedoyo Semang and Beksan Taruna Jaya, two court dances in the Yogyakarta* keraton. *Late 19th century photos by Céphas.*

ERIC OEY

being played, such as Prince Arjuna, Hanuman the white monkey, the god Indra, etc. Beyond telling a story, a dance drama is an orchestration of character types with which all Javanese are intimately familiar. Much of the enjoyment of such performances derives from an appreciation of an individual dancer's ability to become a particular character.

Courtly dances

In the *bedoyo* and *srimpi* court dances, a corps of female dancers moves in unison. Considered the very model of courtly refinement, the *bedoyo* is a sacred dance performed for kings. In fact, the *bedoyo* dancers form part of the royal retinue and represent the *shakti* or female component of kingly power—which is generally associated with Loro Kidul, the volatile and mythic goddess of the south seas and putative power behind the throne.

The *bedoyo* tradition is steeped in ritual and mysticism. The dance is a slow, stately one in which nine young women slip in and out of carefully prescribed formations. The dancers strive to lose their identity, seeming to move as one. It is said that at the annual performance of the sacred Bedoyo Ketawang in the Solo court, Ratu Kidul appears as a shimmering tenth dancer, and afterwards retires with the ruler to his bedchamber.

In *srimpi*, four dancers move in unison in graceful mirrored pairs. Formerly performed only by princesses of the ruling family, the *srimpi* dancers portray dueling Amazons who dodge and feint with deliberate grace, wielding dainty bows and daggers. Though less shrouded in mystery than the *bedoyo*, the *srimpi* dancers exemplify the refined, female end of the refined-coarse, male-female continuum of Javanese prototypes.

Solo dances

Solo dances are also frequently performed. Interestingly, they all depict either a lovesick male or a coquettish female, and all have episodes in which the dancer struts and grooms. Two solo female dances are the *golek* and *gambyong*. Both have roots in the *teledek* or wandering singer-dancer tradition, formerly associated with prostitution and also with rural agricultural rites. At one time, *golek* was considered too flirtatious to be danced at court by a female and was only performed by males.

Gambir Anom and Klana Alus are refined male dances from Surakarta and Yogyakarta, respectively. Gambir Anom is frequently performed by a female—a common practice in Surakarta style. The refined male style in both Yogyakarta and Surakarta is a subtle blend of masculine and feminine qualities.

Gatutkaca Gandrung and Klana Topeng are the strong male counterparts in this genre. The former features the popular character from the *Mahabharata*, Gatutkaca, who becomes *gandrung* or lovesick. The latter fea-

KAL MULLER

ERIC OEY

tures evil King Klana from the Panji cycle, who wears a *topeng* or mask with red face, large bulging eyes, long nose and large mustache—denoting a character who is quick to anger, coarse and proud.

Continuity and change

Traditionally taught in the courts or the villages, Javanese dance is now studied in private schools and at the national dance academies (STSI—the Indonesian Academy of Performing Arts). Court dances formerly taught within the palace precincts are now studied by all—even by foreigners, many of whom come to Central Java and stay on for years to perfect their technique.

Despite all this, teaching methods have changed very little. Dances are learned almost through osmosis. There is no formal instruction, the dance is not taught in sections, and movements are not broken into separate parts. The pupils learn by imitating the teacher, with an occasional correction by a dance assistant, and endless repetition.

Dance and dramatic traditions are changing rapidly now. The Ramayana Ballet at Prambanan—a huge performance with a cast of over 200 developed at the urging of a tour operator in the early 1960s—has signalled a significant departure from traditional aesthetics and has had a great impact. Traditionally meant to be viewed at close range in order to appreciate the detail and subtlety of costuming, movement and dialogue, at Prambanan the dancers are tiny figures moving on a huge open-air stage. Though the dancers dress and move in the traditional way, the dialogue has been deleted and the dance streamlined to more closely follow the storyline. Specially choreographed tourist performances are today a major source of income for many dancers.

Other changes are also evident. Although still slow and languid, dances have been shortened to suit modern schedules. Choreographies incorporating dance styles from many parts of Indonesia are now common, contrasting with the fierce regionalism once prevalent. More literal choreographies are being created, such as dances depicting planting or weaving.

This process of adaptation is nothing new. *Golek*, for instance, was created only in the early 20th century, and most dance dramas assumed their present shape at about this time also. Even a dance form as steeped in ritual as the *bedoyo* has had a long history of change and adaptation to courtly tastes since at least the mid-18th century.

— *Valerie Mau Vetter*

Above and far left: *The martial male and graceful female dance styles of the Yogyakarta palace.*
Left: *A dance rehearsal in the Yogya* keraton. *Traditional court dances are now taught in several private schools outside of the palaces.*

WAYANG KULIT

A World of Haunting Beauty

Every visitor to Java is struck by the haunting beauty of the Javanese *wayang kulit*. As it has for centuries, the tinkling bronze gamelan today beckons young and old on balmy, tropical evenings all over Java to witness the shadows of ancient heroes and heroines flickering across a white cotton screen.

The Javanese shadow play is, above all, a storytelling medium. The stories may be historical, religious, political or didactic in nature, but in every performance the puppet master (*dalang*) weaves an intricate narrative web out of numerous strands drawn from the rich oral traditions of Java. While many puppet theater forms are found on the island—variously employing puppets made of animal hide, round or flat wooden puppets or painted scrolls—the *wayang kulit* or flat "leather shadow" play (also known as *wayang purwa* or "ancient shadow") has always been the most revered and the most popular.

Scholars postulate various origins for the *wayang*, but most believe it springs from ancient rites associated with ancestor worship. As performed today, it probably represents a fusion of indigenous folk ceremonies with courtly performances from India. Although the basic plots trace their roots to the Indian *Ramayana* and *Mahabharata* epics, the narratives performed in Java frequently have no counterparts in India and are not found in any Sanskrit texts. The proud and distant Indian characters, meanwhile, have here been repainted in softer, more familiar Javanese hues.

Thus King Yudistira, eldest of the five Pandawa brothers from the *Mahabharata,* is so pure that the Javanese say his blood runs white. Powerful Bima, the second Pandawa hero, here becomes a mystical savior, scorning all but his true inner teacher. Handsome Arjuna, middle of the five Pandawa heroes, is known in Java as much for his prowess in the bedchamber as on the battlefield.

The *dalang*

The skill of the Javanese *dalang* is formidable. He or she handles all the puppets, presents 40 or 50 different voices of characters appearing in each nine-hour play, cues the musicians, sings and chants, raps on a wooden chest to punctuate the dialogue, and clashes bronze plates with one foot during the furi-

ERIC OEY

ous battle scenes (some say the latter marks a *dalang*'s true skill)—all the while composing the narrative and gauging its impact upon the audience.

Puppeteers master hundreds of tales so they can enact whichever story is requested by a family commissioning the performance. Certain *dalangs* are known for their clever dialogue, others for their skill and grace at manipulating the puppets, still others for their action-packed fight scenes, their deep mystical knowledge, or their biting and earthy wit. A good *dalang* caters to his audience—drawing clever parallels during the evening's narrative with events in the community or peccadillos of the hosts, often to great humorous effect.

Every performance is accompanied by a gamelan orchestra and one or more female singers or *pesinden*. Sometimes the singers are married to the puppeteer or the musicians—and they are often known for their beauty as well as their voice, so that young men come specifically to ogle them. In a typical performance, the *dalang* pokes fun at the musicians and the singers and weaves daily events into the tale to keep them lively and laughing into the wee hours of the morning.

Puppet masters study the tradition over a period of many years. In the past, it was common for aspiring young men to apprentice themselves to famous puppeteers. The ability to become a *dalang* is believed to be in one's blood, and the skill is often passed from generation to generation in a particular family.

Dalangs learn mainly by imitation, using their eyes and ears and practicing on their own rather than receiving any formal instruction. They also undertake mystical exercises to enable them to enchant audiences and to develop the mental and spiritual stamina necessary to withstand the strenuous all-night performances. These may include midnight circumambulations of the town at auspicious times, meditating in graveyards or cool mountain streams, fasting or retreating to a cave or a room for several days on end. Asceticism is believed to create strength and power—two qualities essential to protect puppeteers and their families from the forces of black magic that may be invoked in a performance featuring gods and demons, and may even be used by a jealous competitor to undermine a successful *dalang*.

Javanese believe that the charisma and power gained by a *dalang* through such exercises is shared with the audience during performances. The music is also believed to keep harmful spirits away, and staying up late into the night is a sign of spiritual strength in Java. There is even a genre of stories used specifically for exorcistic purposes. Arising

Opposite: Wayang *puppets seem to come alive in the hands of an experienced* dalang. **Below:** *One of Java's best known* dalangs, *Ki Anom Suroto.*

ERIC OEY

ERIC OEY

from a layer of the tradition strongly connected with spirit belief and magic, these stories recount the exorcism of ogres.

Shadow play performances have been held in connection with Javanese religious ceremonies and life-cycle rites for centuries. Weddings, births, circumcisions, funerals and the fulfillment of a vow are all considered suitable cause for the hiring of a performance. In addition, performances are occasionally held to cleanse a household or village and protect it from future harm. In the past, *dalangs* were often called to court for palace ceremonies; today performances are often held in conjunction with national and religious holidays.

Communal knowledge and lore

The shadow theater was an important means of organizing knowledge in a society that traditionally depended greatly on oral storytelling for the preservation and propagation of information. The *wayang* tradition represents the accumulated body of Javanese history, genealogy, ethics and religious lore. It teaches mysticism, etiquette and proper language usage, and sometimes offers specific advice to the sponsor. Today *wayang* performances are even used to promote government programs like birth control.

The *wayang* is also a mirror in which the Javanese see themselves. The characters provide idealized role models, behavioral norms and even physical stereotypes—running the gamut from refined to rude, large to small, delicate to grotesque. All of the characters are immediately recognizable by certain key attributes, and Javanese lore suggests that the extreme stylization of the puppets is due to Islamic proscriptions against representing the human body. Certainly many of the puppets that the Javanese view as handsome heroes appear quite the opposite to most Westerners. The best loved puppets—the clown-servant Semar and his three sons—in fact have the oddest shapes. The rotund, hermaphroditic Semar is said to represent the Javanese folk, known both for his coarse humor and his wisdom.

The puppets are produced through a time-consuming process in which water buffalo hide is first scraped, stretched and dried, then delicately cut and painted. Hundreds of tiny holes are painstakingly carved into the hide to cast decorative patterns onto the screen, and gold paint or gold leaf are often added. In the Javanese palaces the puppets are considered to be sacred heirlooms and are taken out and aired every 35 days.

Wayang in the modern world

The shadow theater has been nurtured in both the courts and villages of Java. During the early decades of the 20th century, however, the palaces opened schools for *dalangs* to "upgrade" and refine their skills in accor-

AMIR SIDHARTA

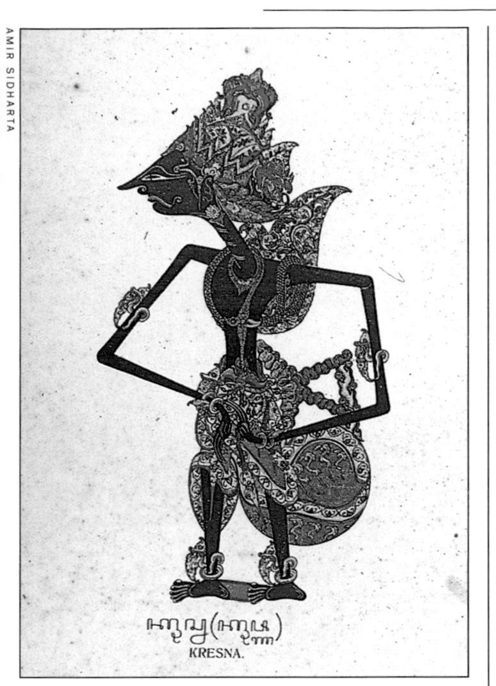

dance with the aristocratic tastes of the Javanese elite. *Wayang* traditions shaped in the Solonese courts during the 1920s then became the standard against which other performances were measured, and it was not until the 1950s that *dalangs* once again felt free to return to the less refined village traditions of earlier days.

Children used to follow their fathers and mothers to performances night after night in the days before modern schooling had spread throughout the Javanese countryside.

Young *dalangs* today increasingly learn their craft in the classroom. For example, there is both a high school and a college of traditional performing arts in Solo which aspiring young puppeteers attend, in addition to courses sponsored by the palaces. In the classroom, teachers emphasize the accurate reproduction of fixed texts and the technical aspects of performance. Though many academy-trained *dalangs* are highly accomplished, it is interesting to note that when the schools themselves sponsor a *wayang* performance they normally hire a puppeteer from a distant village who may have poor technical skills, but whose tales are "alive" with humor and activity in a way the academy performances are not.

In the villages, the *wayang* tradition continues to absorb new material and to recast it into old molds. Restraints on form and characterization are loosening in response to the massive social changes of recent decades. Additions such as flashing disco lights, motorcyclists and female puppets wearing pants are among the "modern" touches seen in village performances. Decried by purists, such changes assure that the *wayang* remains meaningful to contemporary audiences, and in many ways the stories and stereotypes have not changed.

The story of Javanese shadow theater in the 20th century has centered around government efforts to preserve the aesthetic standards of the tradition while maintaining its appeal as a popular art. Javanese villagers do not see the shadow theater in danger of dying out—they only wish they had more money to sponsor performances. The *wayang* is thus thriving in certain circles, but it is not the *wayang* of the courts or the government schools. New styles which reject the school standards forced upon the tradition in the 1920s and 1930s are becoming popular, stimulated by *dalangs* who delight in breaking established conventions. As a result, performances are once again attracting the multitudes reported by European scholars of the *wayang* in the 19th century.

— *Laurie Sears*

Above, left: *A shadow play performance in the Gedung Batu Chinese temple in Semarang.*
Above and right: *Puppets are fashioned of buffalo hide that is delicately carved and then painted.*

RIO HELMI

JAMU

Traditional Javanese Herbal Tonics

The "woman with the bottles" is a familiar sight throughout Java—frequently seen wandering village backlanes and city streets bearing bottles of garishly-colored liquids slung over her shoulder in a long scarf, or *selendang*. She is a purveyor of the traditional Javanese herbal tonic known as *jamu*.

Usually, these medicinal drinks are prepared at home by the vendor and then sold door to door—served up in glasses which she carries with her in a bucket of water. Her clients do not know the composition of the drinks, nor do they order specific mixtures, as these are generic tonics intended to alleviate a variety of minor ailments, such as colds, headaches and fatigue.

Many Indonesians also prepare their own *jamu* at home for specific complaints, obtaining recipes and ingredients from friends or a local shop. Most village women are familiar with the composition and preparation of a wide range of potions and ointments. The *materia medica* employed consist mainly of vegetable substances collected from their gardens and nearby fields, supplemented with dried ingredients bought from a shop. Approximately 150 different plants are used—everything from eucalyptus oil and tamarind, to acacia and ginger. Spices and sweeteners such as cinnamon, fennel, mint and palm sugar are often added for flavor, as the mixtures tend to be rather bitter.

The use of mineral and animal products, on the other hand, is relatively unimportant—normally comprising additives such as salt, chalk, ashes, oils and eggs—though certain special recipes may prescribe ingredients like sulphur, sulphate of copper, or even powdered animal skins, tails and testicles.

The modern jamu industry

Around 1930, the production of factory-made *jamu* was begun. This change evolved largely as a response to the increased importation of Western patent medicines. Factory products were perceived as more modern, easy to use and efficacious than the traditional home preparations.

Initially, this production was confined to *jamu bubuk* or "powdered *jamu,*" but beginning with the period following the Second World War, the *jamu* industry rapidly modernized. Soon, a broad range of *jamu* medications was developed to counteract virtually every conceivable malady. The assortment of these so-called "modern" *jamu* preparations available on the market today includes not only the standard powdered concoctions, but also a bewildering range of pills, tablets, capsules, creams and cosmetics.

Packaged *jamu* has become a multi-million dollar industry in Indonesia, with over 350 factories now reportedly producing better than 5 million dosages a day. Some of the better-known brands, such as Air Mancur, Nyonya Meneer, Cap Jago, Mustika Ratu and others, vie fiercely with one another for market share, while a great deal of money is spent on advertising.

The evocative names given to their wares —Tresnasih ("Love"), Sorga ("Heaven"), Dewi Kecantikan ("Goddess of Beauty") and Sek Hot ("Hot Sex")—give an indication of the prevalent marketing strategy. Many are aimed less at healing than at assuring the satisfaction of the opposite sex.

The industry developed unregulated until 1963, when the Indonesian government

ALAIN COMPOST

stepped in and placed restrictions on what could be sold as *jamu*—now defined as "indigenous Indonesian medicine" (*obat asli Indonesia*). While on the one hand this represented a recognition of *jamu* as an integral part of Indonesian society and identity and an attempt to establish minimum standards of quality, on the other hand it involved limitations on the ingredients that could be used. Since that time *jamu* may only contain traditional and natural ingredients—thus discouraging research and development into new formulas which might combine the benefits of traditional with modern medications.

Traditional therapeutics

Jamu preparations are taken for an incredibly wide spectrum of disorders in Indonesia, but roughly speaking there are four areas where they are considered most effective—against minor ailments, against febrile skin diseases (like measles, chickenpox and mumps), for the improvement of sexual performance, and to alleviate a variety of female reproductive problems encountered in menstruation, pregnancy and postpartum.

Jamu mixtures are thought to fall into several broad categories associated with popular principles of health and sickness. A major distinction is that between "hot" and "cold," though other characteristics such as bitter, sour and sweet are thought to be therapeutically significant as well. These qualities refer not to the taste of the particular medication, but to its effects upon the body. These designations are related to a similar categorization of physical disorders. Some examples of "hot" ingredients are ginger, galangal and pepper, while "cold" substances include coconut milk, betel nut and tamarind.

Madurese women who wish to become pregnant drink "cooling" herbal mixtures to enhance their fertility. A woman who has become pregnant will resume drinking the "hot" herbal drinks—to which coconut oil and other "slippery" ingredients may be added to facilitate delivery. After giving birth, a woman is washed with water containing kitchen hearth ashes, then rubbed with a combination of special ointments—one "hot" for the lower part of her body, the other "cold" and fragrant for the upper part. The hot ointment is believed to aid the expulsion of "dirty" blood (lochia), while the cold ointment is supposed to stimulate lactation.

These treatments of bathing and rubbing are continued for about 40 days, and are supplemented by massage and the administration of a variety of *jamu* beverages—thus demonstrating the great complexity of traditional healing practices in the region.

— *Roy Jordaan*

ALAIN COMPOST

Above: *A* jamu *seller.* **Opposite and right:** *Factory-produced packets of* jamu. *The one at right features a well-known Indonesian body-builder.*

Konica FILM

PART II

Introducing Jakarta

Founded on the site of the ancient pepper trading port of Sunda Kelapa more than four and a half centuries ago, the city of Jakarta is a vibrant commercial center drawing together peoples from all over the vast Indonesian archipelago. Today it is the sprawling and rapidly growing capital of the world's fifth largest nation—a crowded metropolis of more than 9 million inhabitants, with a dynamic economy and a fast-paced lifestyle.

In the 15th century, Sunda Kelapa was an important coastal outpost for the inland kingdom of Pajajaran, competing for a share of the regional spice trade with a host of other riverine ports lining the strategic Malacca and Sunda straits.

In 1527, the port was conquered by the joint Islamic forces of Banten and Demak and re-named Jayakarta—"City of Victory." It was to this town that Portuguese spice merchants (who had earlier called at Sunda Kelapa in 1522) came and began a trading association with the West that was to dominate the history of the area for the next four centuries.

Birth of a colonial capital

The Portuguese were followed by the Dutch at the end of the 16th century, who with faster ships and better organization soon took the lead in the spice trade and forced out all other rivals. In 1618, the Dutch moved their regional base from nearby Banten to Jayakarta. Then, under the leadership of an aggressive and determined envoy of the VOC, Jan Pieterszoon Coen, they forcibly proceeded to take possession of the town they called "Jacatra."

At first the local ruler, Prince Wijayakrama, accepted the Dutch. But he soon became suspicious of their intentions and enlisted the help of a passing British fleet and forces from neighboring Banten to expel them.

A prolonged seige followed, during which a handful of Dutch defenders were badly outnumbered and out-gunned, but were never actually forced to relinquish their tiny fortress due to mutual suspicions on the part of the three attacking parties. Eventually Coen arrived with reinforcements from the eastern islands, broke the siege and leveled the town and palace of Jayakarta. He immediately began enlarging the Dutch fortress, which during the siege had been dubbed "Batavia" in honor of early Germanic tribes which settled Holland. It was by this name that the city was to be known throughout almost 350 years of Dutch colonial rule.

Coen established Batavia as the administrative and military hub of a vast and powerful trading empire that extended from the Cape of Africa across the Indian Ocean to the eastern Indonesian archipelago, with northern outposts in Formosa (Taiwan) and Japan.

Attacks on the city in 1628 and 1629 by Sultan Agung of the powerful Central Javanese kingdom of Mataram were repelled, but the fighting destroyed much of Batavia. Coen died of cholera during the second Mataram siege and was replaced as Governor-General by Jacques Specx, who rebuilt the town according to a plan conceived by Coen.

Like his predecessor, Specx enlisted the active help of Chinese traders, granting them the right to levy taxes for the use of facilities they constructed. Batavia prospered—becoming known as the "Queen of the East" on account of its economic might.

During the next two centuries, the fortunes of Batavia first waxed and then waned along with those of the VOC. Throughout the 17th century, a lucrative monopoly in eastern spices buoyed the city's economy. But in the 18th century, the Company's trading activities increasingly suffered from drastic fluctuations in prices, while the high cost of maintaining a military presence in faraway cor-

Overleaf: *The sprawling metropolitan area. Photo by Kal Muller.* **Opposite:** *Jakarta's "money mile," Jl. Jend. Sudirman. Photo by Alain Compost.*

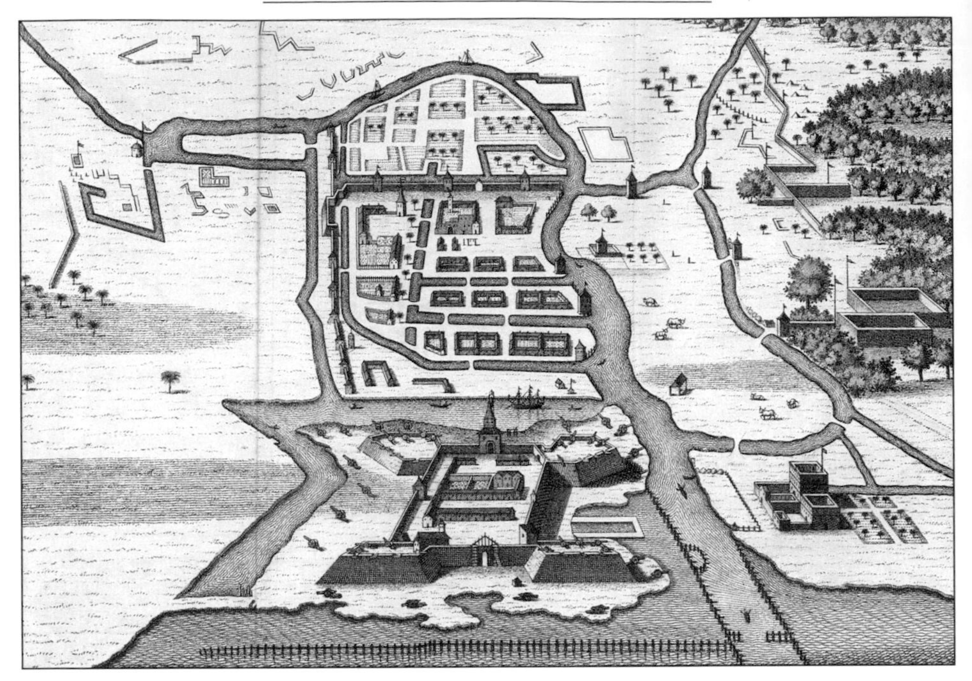

ners of the empire was compounded by rampant corruption within the VOC ranks.

Declining economic fortunes were mirrored by deteriorating physical conditions within the city itself. The fine canals Coen had designed to make Batavia an Eastern version of Amsterdam were unsuited to the tropics. Sluggish and dirty, they soon silted up and became a breeding ground for mosquitoes and vermin. The solid but airless Dutch buildings became infested with rats, plaster rotted and peeled in the damp heat, and epidemics of cholera, typhoid, dysentery and malaria decimated the town's population.

In 1740, fear of an uprising by the Chinese, who then formed the principal source of trade goods and labor in the town, ignited a massacre that crippled Batavia economically for some time, touching off a period of slow but steady decline. Years of mismanagement and expensive wars resulted finally in the bankruptcy of the VOC, and at the turn of the 19th century the Dutch government took over the former VOC territories.

A new city arises

Under Governor-General Daendals (1808-1810), the old fortress and town around the harbor were demolished. A new city center was begun in the more salubrious southern districts, where broad, tree-lined boulevards and handsome civic buildings in neo-classical style laid the foundation for modern Jakarta.

In 1811 Batavia once again came under attack, this time from the British. Following a plan by the brilliant young Thomas Stamford Raffles, British troops invaded Java and ousted a joint Dutch-French administration that ruled during the Napoleonic period.

Raffles' administration lasted only until 1816, when control of the Indies was handed back to the Dutch. But during his brief tenure as lieutenant governor, Raffles introduced many reforms and promoted the study of science and culture in the capital. Raffles' most enduring legacy, however, was to be his subsequent founding of Singapore—a rival port that quickly displaced Batavia as the premier trading center in Southeast Asia.

Batavia prospered once again after the institution in 1830 of the "Cultivation System" of forced labor that generated millions of guilders in profits for the Dutch. Canals and roads were rebuilt, civic buildings increased in number and leafy residential suburbs appeared in Menteng, Cikini and the surrounding areas, so that Batavia once again experienced a "Golden Age"—this time earning the sobriquet of "Pearl of the Orient."

The city thus entered the 20th century as a small but prosperous colonial capital with only about 300,000 residents. It underwent a process of rapid modernization in the 1930s with the introduction of gas lighting, tramways and automobiles, and became the focus for a new class of young, Dutch-educated

Indonesians who began to sow the seeds of nationalism and independence.

In 1942, the Japanese invaded and Batavia was renamed Jakarta, becoming overnight an occupied capital beset by food shortages and outbreaks of violence, resulting in the rapid destruction of the Dutch colonial infrastructure as well as many of the buildings erected by the Europeans.

Years of crisis and a 'New Order'

The post-war Sukarno era left an indelible stamp on the face of modern Jakarta. While struggling to rule a nation torn by factionalism and bereft of the colonial administration that had held it together since the days of the VOC, Sukarno dreamed of a capital that would embody the surging spirit of *Merdeka* ("freedom"). He commissioned grand parks, broad ceremonial boulevards, dramatic sculptures and monuments—creating a new "theater state" that masked many of the very real problems besetting the city.

During this period Jakarta was rapidly filling up with hundreds of thousands of migrants who came to the big city in search of a better life. The shantytowns, poverty and desperation of the early 1960s, hauntingly depicted in the novel *Twilight in Djakarta* by Mochtar Lubis, represent another low point in the history of a city that had once experienced the height of European elegance.

After the catastrophic events of 1965, General Suharto replaced Sukarno as President of the Republic and a new era of development dawned in the nation's capital. Under the so-called "New Order" government, plans were implemented for the resuscitation of the economy and long-term renewal of the capital, with a new emphasis on the welfare of city inhabitants and the overhaul of an inefficient, corruption-riddled bureaucracy.

The city has entered a dynamic period of development. Office towers and construction cranes dominate the skyline. An increasingly enlightened civic administration is undertaking sanitation programs, instituting training courses for unskilled workers and overhauling its own lumbering bureaucracy.

Jakarta is still beset by problems typical of Third World capitals, where rapid-yield investment in business and industry take precedence over basic infrastructure and support systems. But Jakarta is also vibrant, energetic and colorful. For those who develop more than a passing acquaintance with it, the city is touched with all the excitement and magic of the Indonesian nation. Indeed, for the millions who call it home, Jakarta is *Ibu Kota*—the "mother city" of Indonesia.

—Janet Boileau

Opposite: *The fortress and town of Batavia as it looked in 1629.* **Above:** *The 18th century canals and Dutch-style houses made the city look like an Eastern version of Amsterdam.*

SIGHTS OF JAKARTA

Historical Tour of the Capital

Historically, Jakarta developed from north to south, and the best way to explore the city's sights is in their proper chronological order. Take in each area in a series of half-day excursions, starting with the old harbor in the north. Move south through the VOC or Dutch East India Company precincts (Kota) and the Chinatown district (Glodok), ending up in the newer Medan Merdeka (Freedom Square) area and the new satellite suburbs.

The old harbor

The Dutch colonial city of Batavia grew up around the ancient spice-trading harbor known as **Sunda Kelapa**, located at the northern end of Jakarta where the Ciliwung River meets the sea. The East India Company erected a trading outpost here on the east bank of the Ciliwung, fortifying it with thick masonry walls and 15 large bastions.

LUCA INVERNIZZI TETTONI

Today you can climb up the old **Uitkijk** or lookout tower on Jalan Pakin for an overview of the entire area. The tower was erected in 1839 on the Culemborg bastion—site of the former customs house (*pabean*) of Sunda Kelapa. It served as a lookout for ships, and later as a meteorological station.

To the north and across the river from the tower lies the old port, in continuous use since at least the 12th century. The Dutch first built a wharf here in the early 17th century; it was re-built and extended in 1817. Scores of *pinisi* schooners still dock here daily—it's a wonderful place to witness one of the world's last major commercial sailing fleets. Sun-darkened stevedores run up and down wobbly planks loading and unloading sacks, crates, cables, drums and timber. These handsome, hand-built boats lined up gunwale-to-gunwale are one of Jakarta's most picturesque sights. Adventurous types can negotiate passage to other islands—ten days to Sulawesi with favorable winds.

Just north of the lookout on the west side of the river stands **Museum Bahari**, a maritime museum located in an old warehouse that was built by the VOC in 1652. It once housed a vast hoard of trading goods—pepper, cloves, nutmeg, coffee, tea, copper, tin and bales of Indian cloth. It is a fine building, musty with creaking floorboards that echo the footfalls of seamen and merchants of centuries past. Several models of traditional Indonesian sailing craft provide a glimpse of the nation's seafaring heritage.

Just in front of the museum stands the only remaining section of the massive city wall that once ringed Batavia. It runs west from here to the Zeeburg bastion. Of the 15 bastions surrounding the original fortress, the four main ones were lozenge-shaped and named after precious stones, earning Batavia the nickname "Kota Intan" (Diamond City).

Behind the museum is **Pasar Ikan**, a large fish market. The market is hard on the nose, particularly as the day heats up, but surrounding it is a veritable rabbit warren of tiny shops crammed to the gunnels with seashells, ships chandlery, kitchenwares, fishing nets, stuffed turtles, model ships, shoes and sealing wax. A colorful cast of traders, babies, beggars and chess players carry on here as they have for centuries.

The area immediately to the south and east of the harbor was the center of the walled city known as **Kota** and still contains several relics of the Dutch East India Company days. Between Kali Besar and Jl.

ERIC OEY

Kakap stand the old VOC shipyards. The 18th-century wharf was closed in 1809 due to unsanitary conditions, but the dilapidated yard and handsome building are still in use today. Four old warehouses on Jl. Tongkol ("Tuna Street") are also still in use, but entry is restricted to army personnel.

Walking south along Jl. Nelayan Timur, you pass an old Dutch drawbridge that looks like it was transplanted from Holland—the so-called "Chicken Market Bridge" (*Hoenderpasarbrug*) which spans the north end of Kali Besar. Constructed about 200 years ago, it was restored during the 1970s but has again fallen into disrepair.

South and west of the bridge at Jl. Kali Besar Barat 11 stands the home of Governor-General van Imhoff, dating from around 1730. Known as Toko Merah ("Red House"), it has fine Chinese woodwork characteristic of 18th-century Batavian houses. Three doors to the south stands another house from the same period, now the offices of the Standard Chartered Bank. Both may be visited during normal office hours.

Fatahillah Square

The administrative center of old Batavia was situated some distance away from the noise and bustle of the port, around a square now known as **Taman Fatahillah**. The city founders built here a splendid city hall (*Stadhuis*) whence a vast Asian trading empire was controlled. The square and the buildings surrounding it were restored during the mid-1970s as part of a large-scale conservation of Jakarta's historic sites, and the colonial administrative buildings were then converted into museums.

The *stadhuis* or city hall on the south side of the square has become the **Museum Fatahillah** (Jakarta History Museum)—37 rooms filled with old maps, antiques and memorabilia, mostly from the Dutch period. Opulently appointed rooms now recreate the atmosphere of the VOC period.

The *stadhuis* was actually rebuilt three times, and the current structure dates from 1710. It had a long and checkered career as a law court, administrative center and prison. Prisoners were kept in dungeons under the front portico, often partially submerged in filthy water.

Indonesians say you cannot know the Javanese until you know the *wayang*. A huge collection from throughout Indonesia is on display in the **Wayang Museum** on the western side of Fatahillah Square, at Jl. Pintu Besar Utara 27. A church once stood on this site, and the tombstones of early Dutch notables are still preserved at the back.

On the eastern side of Taman Fatahillah,

Opposite: *The old harbor of Sunda Kelapa.*
Above: *The 18th c.* stadhuis *or city hall, now the Jakarta History Museum (Museum Fatahillah).*

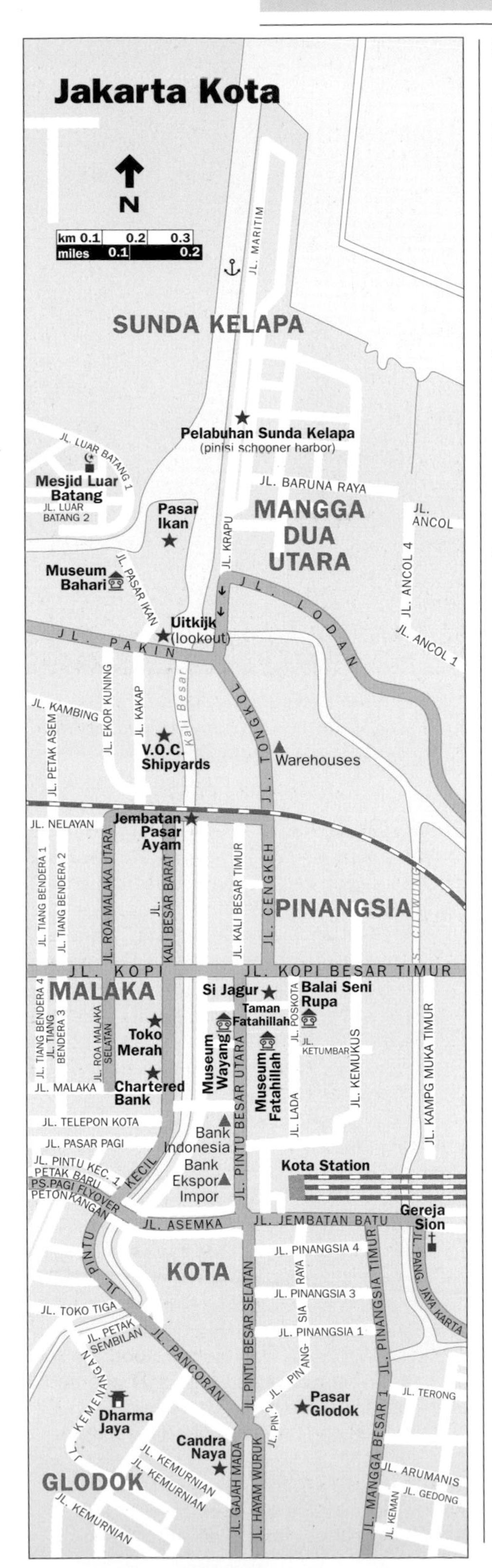

in the neo-classical Hall of Justice dating from 1870, is the **Fine Arts Museum** (Balai Seni Rupa). It houses a superb collection of rare porcelain assembled by the late Vice President Adam Malik, and modern paintings by well-known Indonesian artists.

Next door to the Fatahillah Restaurant and Art Shop on the north side of the square is Si Jagur—a Portuguese cannon brought to Batavia from Malacca in 1641. A large fist protrudes from the butt, making what for Indonesians is an obscene gesture, and childless women often come to sit on the cannon's barrel in the hopes of becoming pregnant.

The area immediately to the south of Fatahillah was almost totally reconstructed during the 19th and early 20th centuries. One notable exception is the **Gereja Sion** or "Black Portuguese Church" on Jl. Pangeran Jayakarta east of the Kota train station. It was built in 1695 for the *mardijkers*—a community of Portuguese-Indian mestizos brought to Batavia as slaves in the 17th century and later freed. It is the oldest remaining church in Jakarta and still has the original pews, copper chandeliers, and a fine canopied pulpit.

Jakarta's Chinatown

The Chinese have always played an important role in Jakarta's economy. After some 5,000 died in a bloody massacre in 1740, they were relocated just outside the fortress walls, to an area just south of the old city now known as **Glodok**.

Public use of the Chinese script is discouraged in Indonesia, so the signboards that give a distinctive character to Chinatowns elsewhere are here absent. But Chinese architecture is still in evidence along a maze of narrow streets behind Glodok Plaza, filled with hawkers, foodstalls and small shops.

The Dharma Jaya temple on Jl. Petak Sembilan was one of the earliest centers of worship for the Batavian Chinese—founded around 1650 and dedicated to the Buddhist goddess of mercy, Kuan Yin. Nearby at Jl. Gajah Mada 88 is Candra Naya, the former home of So Bing Kong—a merchant who was appointed *kapitan* or headman of the Chinese community. He mediated between the Batavian Chinese and three VOC governors. His tomb is in a house on Gang Taruna.

Many Batavian Chinese converted to Islam prior to the 20th century, and there are several old Chinese mosques in the area. South of the former National Archives on Jl. Hayam Wuruk is the Kebun Jeruk mosque built in 1786, a curious mixture of Islamic and

Chinese influences. There is another 18th-century Chinese mosque, Mesjid Krukut, on Jl. Kebahagiaan off Jl. Gajah Mada.

During the 18th century, many wealthy VOC officials moved out of the old fortress area and developed large plantations to the south. They built lavish Dutch-style manor houses along what is now Jl. Gajah Mada and Jl. Hayam Wuruk.

The only remaining mansion from this period until recently housed the **National Archives** (Arsip Nasional). This lovely house on Jl. Gajah Mada was built as a country home in 1760 by Rainier de Klerk before he became Governor-General. Now engulfed by the city, it was restored in 1925.

The area just south of here is known as **Harmonie** after Southeast Asia's largest club, completed during the tenure of Raffles in 1815. The Harmonie Club was the premier meeting place for the wealthy and powerful in colonial times, but its fine building was demolished in 1985 to make way for a new traffic interchange.

Across the road on the corner is a building that once housed a fashionable French couturier known as Oger Frères; now it is a travel agency. This intersection was in fact the epicenter of the elegant and wealthy new European town center that developed in the 19th century. A statue of Hermes stands on the balustrade of the bridge here, a forlorn reminder of the district's former splendor.

KAL MULLER

Little Mercury peers whimsically over rush hour traffic, his globe ignominiously painted as a World Cup football.

Freedom Square

Medan Merdeka or "Freedom Square" is an expansive, open field lying at the heart of Jakarta, bordered on four sides by broad boulevards and government buildings that form the nation's administrative nucleus. Originally used as a military training ground and a field for cattle-grazing, in the 19th century it became Koningsplein (King's Square), the symbolic center of Dutch Batavia.

In the 1960s the square was the site of mass rallies at the height of Sukarno's anti-imperialist nation-building rhetoric. Its centerpiece is **Monas** (short for "Monumen Nasional"), a towering obelisk commissioned by Sukarno to commemorate the soaring spirit of Indonesian nationalism.

As Jakarta's most conspicuous landmark and unofficial symbol, Monas appears on the covers of maps, guidebooks, souvenir placemats and key rings. It rises to a height of 137 meters (445 ft) and is topped by an illuminated bronze flame sheathed in 35 kgs of gold.

Monas is visible from many parts of the city, providing a central point of orientation.

Above: *Jakarta's best known landmark, the National Monument (Monas), with a statue of Prince Diponegoro in front.* **Left:** *Istiqlal Mosque.*

ERIC OEY

The view of Jakarta from the top, reached by elevator, is exhilarating on a clear day. Housed in the base of the monument is a museum with 48 dioramas depicting scenes from Indonesian history.

From Monas, it is a short walk to the **National Museum** on the western side of the square. This is the oldest and best museum in Indonesia, containing fascinating stone, bronze and ceramic collections. The building itself is in need of restoration and reorganization and many displays are poorly marked, yet there are some real treasures to be found. Indeed the world famous skulls of Java Man are here, as are famous sculptures and inscriptions from Indonesia's classical period, so it is best to take a guided tour. The Ganesha Society conducts them in several languages in the mornings.

The most interesting displays are the treasure and bronze rooms on the second floor. There are also exquisite Asian, Persian and European ceramics on display at the rear of the ground floor.

Adjoining one another on the northern side of Merdeka Square are two imposing presidential palaces. The **Istana Negara**, which faces north onto Jl. Veteran, was erected as a private residence in the late 1700s by a Dutch businessman and is now used for important state functions. It served for a time as the official residence of the Dutch Governors-General, until the larger Koningsplein Palace was constructed in 1879. The latter faces southward onto the square, and was renamed **Istana Merdeka** when Indonesia achieved independence. It is the official residence of the president, but President Suharto prefers to occupy his more modest home in Menteng.

East Asia's largest mosque

East of the palaces on Jl. Veteran is **Mesjid Istiqlal**, East Asia's largest mosque. Officially opened in 1978, the enormous marble edifice stands on the site of the Noordwijk Fort, which was torn down during the post independence anti-colonial fervor.

Although the vast majority of Indonesians are Muslims, the state ideology embraces all religions. Significant Christian communities exist, especially in the eastern parts of the archipelago. Striking evidence of this religious heterogeneity is found in the presence of several churches just near Istiqlal. Behind it rises the black spires of the neo-gothic **Catholic Cathedral** on Jl. Katedral, built in 1901. And to the south on the corner of Jl. Pejambon, opposite Gambir railway station, is the **Immanuel Church**—a curious but appealing mixture of Greco-Roman and classical European theater architecture. After its completion in 1835 by Dutch Protestants of

Above: *Looking south along Jl. Thamrin, the heart of Jakarta's modern banking and office district.*

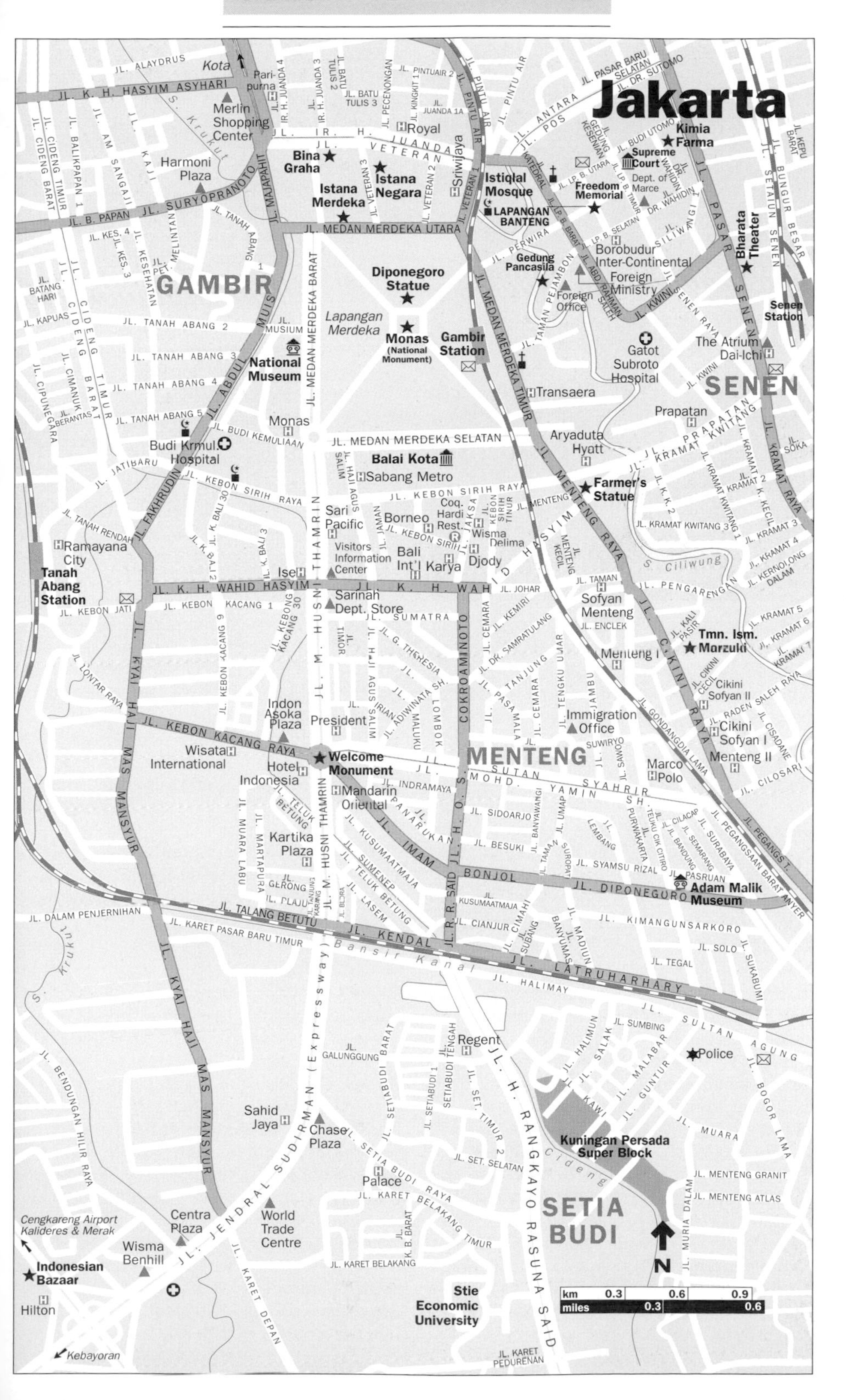
Jakarta
GAMBIR
SENEN
MENTENG
SETIA BUDI
Kota
Merlin Shopping Center
Harmoni Plaza
Bina Graha
Istana Merdeka
Istana Negara
Royal
Sriwijaya
Istiqlal Mosque
LAPANGAN BANTENG
Kimia Farma
Supreme Court
Dept. of Marce
Freedom Memorial
Gedung Pancasila
Borobudur Inter-Continental
Foreign Ministry
Foreign Office
Bharata Theater
Senen Station
The Atrium Dai-Ichi
Gatot Subroto Hospital
Diponegoro Statue
Lapangan Merdeka
Monas (National Monument)
Gambir Station
National Museum
Transaera
Prapatan
Aryaduta Hyatt
Monas
Budi Krmul Hospital
Balai Kota
Sabang Metro
Farmer's Statue
Sari Pacific
Borneo
Coq. Hardi Rest.
Wisma Delima
Ramayana City
Tanah Abang Station
Visitors Information Center
Bali Int'l
Karya
Djody
Ise
Sarinah Dept. Store
Sofyan Menteng
Tmn. Ism. Marzuki
Menteng I
Cikini Sofyan II
Cikini Sofyan I
Menteng II
Immigration Office
Indon Asoka Plaza
President
Wisata International
Welcome Monument
Hotel Indonesia
Mandarin Oriental
Marco Polo
Kartika Plaza
Adam Malik Museum
Bansir Kanal
Regent
Police
Sahid Jaya
Chase Plaza
Kuningan Persada Super Block
Palace
Centra Plaza
World Trade Centre
Wisma Benhill
Cengkareng Airport Kalideres & Merak
Indonesian Bazaar
Hilton
Kebayoran
Stie Economic University
JL. K. H. HASYIM ASYHARI
JL. SURYOPRANOTO
JL. MEDAN MERDEKA UTARA
JL. MEDAN MERDEKA BARAT
JL. MEDAN MERDEKA SELATAN
JL. MEDAN MERDEKA TIMUR
JL. ABDUL MUIS
JL. FAKHRUDIN
JL. K. H. WAHID HASYIM
JL. M. HUSNI THAMRIN
JL. KEBON SIRIH RAYA
JL. KEBON KACANG RAYA
JL. KYAI HAJI MAS MANSYUR
JL. MENTENG RAYA
JL. CIKINI RAYA
JL. PASAR SENEN
JL. KRAMAT RAYA
JL. IMAM BONJOL
JL. DIPONEGORO
JL. H. O. S. COKROAMINOTO
JL. R. SAID
JL. TALANG BETUTU
JL. KENDAL
JL. LATRUHARHARY
JL. JENDRAL SUDIRMAN (Expressway)
JL. H. RANGKAYO RASUNA SAID
JL. SETIA BUDI RAYA
JL. SULTAN AGUNG
km 0.3 0.6 0.9
miles 0.3 0.6
N

Batavia it was known as Willemskerk; the present name dates from 1948. Further south on Jl. Prapatan opposite the Hyatt Hotel is the Anglican All Saints Church. Built in 1829, it has beautiful hand-painted glass windows.

The field between the cathedral and the Hotel Borobudur is called **Lapangan Banteng** (Cattle Square). The grimacing statue at the center—a muscled figure breaking his chains of bondage—was erected by Sukarno in 1963 to commemmorate the "liberation" of Irian Jaya from the Dutch.

In colonial times the square was known as Waterlooplein and was the site of a magnificent governors' mansion. Nothing is left of it now, but a second palace begun by Daendels in 1809 still stands to the east of the square. It now houses the Department of Finance—the oldest government building still in use. Next to it stands the Supreme Court or Mahkamah Agung building, dating from 1848.

On Jl. Taman Pejambon nearby is the so-called **Gedung Pancasila**—a mansion built in the 1830s. After President Sukarno's "Birth of Pancasila" speech here in 1945, the building was declared a national monument.

North of Lapangan Banteng on the corner of Jl. Pos and Jl. Kesenian stands the old colonial Schouwberg Playhouse, now known as **Gedung Kesenian**. Built in 1821, it was restored and reopened in 1987 as a stylish performing arts hall. Just across the canal from here lies **Pasar Baru** ("New Market") shopping district, a bustling maze of alleys lined with shops selling everything from textiles to computers.

Leafy, laid-back **Menteng** is a large residential and diplomatic district composed of colonial mansions and posh new villas, located to the south of Freedom Square. A thick canopy of angsana trees shades streets lined with fine colonial houses—some restored, some in sad disrepair, many containing hidden gardens and other delights. Jl. Diponegoro, which bisects Menteng, is the finest address in town; most of the bungalows here are occupied by high government officials, foreign embassies and diplomats.

At the east end of Diponegoro, a left turn brings you onto **Jalan Surabaya**, known for its fascinating flea market. The many stalls overflow with trinkets and treasures, but exercise caution when purchasing "antiques." They are more likely modern imitations, but charming just the same (and cheap!).

Sights of suburbia

Jl. Jend. Sudirman, the busy boulevard rushing south from Menteng, is Jakarta's "money mile," lined with gleaming, steel-and-glass towers housing banks and corporate offices. Another grimacing statue, this one bearing something that resemples a flaming hotplate and nicknamed the "Pizza Man," marks the southern end of Jl. Sudirman. Here begins **Kebayoran Baru**, Jakarta's huge satellite suburb, centering around the bustling Blok M shopping complex.

New suburban development has moved further south to **Pondok Indah**, an enclave of lavish villas. The *nouveaux riches* have here transformed rice paddies into palatial estates and plush country clubs. Just beyond, in Pasar Minggu, about 15 km (9 mi) from the city center, is **Ragunan Zoo**, where tropical animals are displayed amid exotic foliage. Pleasant for picnics or just a stroll, the zoo is open daily from 7 am to 5 pm but gets crowded on weekends.

Another Sunday magnet for the masses is **Taman Mini Indonesia Indah**, just off the Jagorawi toll road in south Jakarta. This 160-hectare (395-acre) park provides a vicarious tour of the architecture and cultures of the vast Indonesian archipelago. Start at Keong Mas, shaped like a giant golden snail, where there is a spectacular cinematic journey through Indonesia on an Omnimax screen. The park also has a museum, an orchid garden and a bird park with walk-in aviary.

—Janet Boileau

LIVING IN JAKARTA

A Taste of Life in the 'Big Durian'

Some say Jakarta is a great place to live but a lousy place to visit. Indeed, the occasional T-shirt declares: "I spent two days in Jakarta and lived." Of course this is a strictly subjective point of view, held by unadventurous souls who disapprove of such things as littering, smoking, speeding, jaywalking and other petty vices. Living here no doubt requires patience and a finely-honed sense of the absurd, but also has its rewards.

Foreigners working for multinational companies in Jakarta find themselves surrounded by legions of servants and chauffeured cars. They shop at Kem Chicks supermarket, where even the fried rice is pre-packaged for the microwave. The mysterious East this is not, but for many it is a bourgeois dream come true—though with some nightmarish elements.

Jakarta's inefficiencies are legendary, and are getting harder to take because they sneak up on you. In an impoverished or remote area you are psychologically prepared for hardship. But in Jakarta it is possible to wake up in an air-conditioned room, take a hot shower, breakfast on muesli and yogurt, watch the CNN news—then spend 90 minutes trying to phone across town.

The telephone is as essential in Jakarta as a keen sense of humor. Making a proper connection on the city's antiquated exchanges can be like trying to win the weekly lottery. Dial tones are an elusive commodity during peak hours (all morning). Dialing invites varying results—rarely the intended one. Even when you do get through, the party you are speaking to is likely to abruptly vanish in mid-sentence. Third parties suddenly interrupt, curtly demanding "Who are you?"

Thus it is little wonder that Jakartans prefer personal contacts. Unfortunately, getting to one opens up a new world of frustrations. Walking is not recommended. Sidewalks are the domain of rubble, streetside vendors and open sewers—which can turn a short stroll into an obstacle course of black holes and sizzling grease. The alternative is to travel by car, but this too has its drawbacks.

Traffic replaces the weather as the great conversational fall-back in Jakarta. Everyone talks about it. This can become monotonous because the traffic is either heavy or impossible—frequently both. But at least it is possible to blame someone.

Generally, everyone blames everyone else. The government blames car owners, saying there are too many of them. Car owners claim it is the government's fault for not building enough roads.

All in all, Jakartans probably face about as many frustations as those who live in other large capital cities—no more, no less. Expatriates who weather the first year here often find it difficult to leave.

Jakarta's blend of the bitter and the sweet is reflected in the city's many nicknames. Some have called it the "Big Mango," the "City of Drains" or "Queen of the East" (perhaps with reference to the sizeable gay population). Most appropriate of all is undoubtedly the "Big Durian." People either love or hate this delicious, but foul-smelling fruit—and by the same token few Jakartans, locals or expatriates, are ambivalent about their city.

— *Janet Boileau*

KAL MULLER

Opposite: *A Jakarta fashion show.* **Right:** *Letting it all hang out at the famous Tanamur disco.*

PULAU SERIBU

Jakarta's Paradise Islands

Pulau Seribu literally means "Thousand Islands" but this mini-archipelago actually consists of fewer than 200 coral atolls (the count alters with the tides) strewn to the north of Jakarta in the calm and shallow Java Sea. As an idyllic island getaway from the overheated atmosphere of the city, Pulau Seribu has been popular since VOC times. Here you can swim from one palm-fringed shore to another, visit neighbors for a sundowner in your swimsuit, barbecue fresh fish, and dance barefoot in cool, powdery sands beneath the moon. The main resort islands are three hours from Jakarta by ferry, one hour by speedboat, or 20 minutes by plane. Several have been developed with up-scale hotels, but most retain an alluring simplicity.

The historic inner islands

The islands closest to Jakarta were used by the Dutch during VOC times and are of some historical interest. **Pulau Onrust** lies just offshore—only half an hour from Ancol Marina by ferry. This is where Batavia's founder, J.P. Coen, marshalled his forces for the final assault on Jayakarta in 1619. A shipyard was later built here—which included a small fort, hospital, church and artillery store—and Dutch vessels put in for repairs after the long haul from Europe. A model can be seen in the Museum Bahari (see "Jakarta Sights").

Nearby **Kelor**, **Kahyangan** and **Damar** also have historic VOC maritime links. **Pulau Bidadari** ("Heavenly Nymph Island"), once the sight of a fort and a lepers' hospital, has now been turned into a resort with bungalows and a restaurant. One of the earliest residents of Jakarta to appreciate these islands was the Dutch Governor-General Camphuis. In 1685 he constructed a Japanese-style villa on Pulau Damar amidst gardens stocked with rare animals and plants.

Outer island resorts

The outer resort islands require an overnight trip or longer. During the week you will have them to yourself and many of the resorts offer reduced rates. Weekends can be crowded but there is so much sand and sea, it is still possible to find a quiet spot.

Nearly all of the islands are fringed with coral reefs, and there is good snorkeling off **Putri**, **Genteng** and **Opak Besar**. Serious

Pulau Seribu

P. DUA BARAT
P. DUA TIMUR
P. PANCALING KECIL
P. PANCALING BESAR
P. JAGUNG
P. GOSONG RANGAT
P. SEBARU
P. ANTUK
KEPULAUAN KELAPA
P. SABTU
P. MALINJU
P. SEPA
P. PANJANG
P. PAPA THEO (TONDAN TIMUR)
P. PELANGI (TONDAN BARAT)
N
P. GENTENG
P. BIRA
P. KELAPA
km 5 10 15
miles 5 10
P. PUTRI
P. OPAK BESAR
P. OPAK KECIL
P. KOTOK
KEPULAUAN PANGGANG
P. SIMPUL
P. PANGGANG
P. LANG
Laut Jawa
P. TIDUNG BESAR
P. AYER
KEPULAUAN TIDUNG
P. TIDUNG KECIL
P. PAYUNG
P. TIKUS
P. PARI
KEPULAUAN UNTUNG JAWA
P. LANCANG BESAR
P. LANCANG KECIL
P. BOKOR
P. DAMAR BESAR
P. LAKI
Bird Sanctuary
P. RAMBUT
P. UNTUNG JAWA
Tg. Kait
Karangserang
Tg. Pasir
P. ONRUST
P. KAHYANGAN
P. NYAMUK
P. KELOR
Kramat
Tanjung Pasir
P. BIDADARI
P. NYAMUK KECIL (P. NIRWANA)
Mauk
Sukarno-Hatta International Airport
Teluk Naga
Teluk Jakarta
Tg. Priok
Ancol
JAKARTA

divers should note, however, that Pulau Seribu offers only a fraction of the underwater riches that can be found elsewhere in Indonesia. The islands' beauty and their proximity to Jakarta are their main attraction, and well worth a trip if time is short.

Novice snorkelers must beware of stings, abrasions, cuts and sunburn. Cover arms and legs while diving or snorkeling. A lycra bodysuit is ideal, but a T-shirt and lightweight pants will do. Never touch coral or sea creatures; several varieties are poisonous.

The reefs have already suffered from the human invasion; souvenir hunting is damaging their fragile ecology. Marine life includes turtles, moray and garden eels, rays, pelagic and reef fish, nudibranches, anemones, giant clams, sea fans, soft and hard corals. Reef sharks are more curious than aggressive. Dolphins and flying fish can often be seen during the boat trip from Jakarta.

Up-market resorts have gone up on **Pantara Timur** and **Pantara Barat**. Built in cooperation with Japan Air Lines, they are favored by tourists who feel closer to nature in a marbled bathroom.

More moderately priced and popular are Pulau Pelangi and Pulau Putri, both operated by Pulau Seribu Paradise. **Pulau Putri** offers cottages and family bungalows, simply furnished, with and without air-conditioning, as well as a restaurant and a bar. A dive shop offers tank fills and equipment rentals. Sailboats and sailboards can also be hired.

Pulau Pelangi is a larger resort with fancy, air-conditioned cottages, tennis courts and a popular restaurant built out over the water. Shops at these and other places only sell basic necessities such as toothpaste, sunscreen and souvenir T-shirts, so bring along your own snacks and supplies.

Pulau Sepa has simple cottages with Indonesian-style bathrooms shared between two semi-detached rooms, a dive shop, a restaurant/bar and nice beaches.

Papa Theo is billed as a dive camp but is actually a pristine island hideaway that can be enjoyed by non-divers as well. Comfortable, clean huts provide a bed on the floor covered with a crisp clean sheet and a simple splash bath; that's it. The generator shuts down soon after dark; then night breezes, starlight and the sound of breaking wavelets filter through the palm thatch walls. Hurricane lamps and candles illuminate the restaurant; it serves very fresh fish and Indonesian food.

Pulau Ayer, with cottages on stilts in the sea, and **Pulau Laki** are family resorts closer in to Jakarta, but the water is not as clean as the islands further out.

—Janet Boileau

KAL MULLER

Left: *A small fishing boat glides over the calm Java Sea at dawn.* **Right:** *Aerial view of one of the many coral atolls in the Pulau Seribu group that has been turned into an up-scale tourist resort.*

PART III

Introducing West Java

With more than 35 million inhabitants and covering roughly the western third of the island (an area slightly larger than Holland, 46,300 sq. km. excluding Jakarta), West Java is not only Indonesia's most populous province, but also its most productive—yielding more agricultural products and manufactured goods than any other part of the country.

Huge factory complexes ring the cities of Bandung and Jakarta, producing everything from textiles to computers. More than half of all electricity produced in Indonesia is consumed here, and Indonesia's only aircraft factory and atomic reactor are both found in the provincial capital of Bandung, along with a prestigious engineering institute (ITB).

But ask Indonesians about West Java and they will tell you first of all that this is the homeland of the proud and staunchly Islamic Sundanese people. More than three-fourths of West Java's inhabitants are Sundanese. They speak a language different from the Javanese, Madurese or Jakarta Malay spoken on the rest of the island, and have developed their own sophisticated cultural and artistic traditions—including some of the most intricate drumming heard anywhere in the traditional world. Ancient Sundanese kingdoms flourished in West Java from at least the 5th century, but left few stone monuments due to the isolation and sparse population of the region in former times.

West Java is noticeably more mountainous than the rest of the island. The volcanic peaks of the region are here tightly packed, producing a fragmented series of narrow upland valleys and plateaus that are difficult of access. Until it was drained in the last century, the north coastal fringe was extremely swampy and inhospitable. As a result, it was the remote but fertile and well-watered river valleys of the central highlands—stretching from what is now Bogor in the west through present-day Cianjur and Bandung to Ciamis in the east—that were settled and cultivated in ancient times. This area, known as the Priangan or Parahyangan—the "Abode of the Gods" of Sundanese lore—is a vast stretch of uplands that until recently was inhabited by fewer than a million Sundanese.

This mode of existence changed dramatically in the 19th century. Between 1808 and 1811, a post road (the *Grote Postweg*) was cut through the highlands by the Dutch, linking the Bandung area with Cirebon and Batavia on the coast. European planters quickly moved in, opening up huge estates of coffee, tea, rubber, cinchona and indigo worked by forced labor. The Parahyangan soon became the vital cornerstone of the colonial economy, supplying more than half of the world's coffee and fully 90 percent of the world's quinine by the turn of the century.

The coastal areas, meanwhile, followed a very different line of development. Although not particularly favorable for agriculture, the estuaries of major rivers provided access into the highlands and served as trading areas from very early times. Ports such as Banten and Sunda Kelapa (now Jakarta) also lay on the vital sea lanes connecting the Indian Ocean with the South China Sea. During the heyday of the spice trade, western Java and southern Sumatra became major pepper-producing areas controlled by Banten—then one of the busiest ports in the world. All of these harbor towns were Islamized in the early 16th century, then came under Dutch influence in the 17th. When the coastal areas were opened up for rice cultivation in the 18th and 19th centuries, they were settled by Javanese and Sundanese migrants. As a result, the coasts today are home to a rich admixture of cultures.

— *Eric Oey*

Overleaf: *Ram fighting, a popular Sundanese pasttime. Photo by Kal Muller.* **Opposite:** *The beauty of fair-skinned Sundanese women is legendary in Indonesia. Photo by Alain Compost.*

WEST COAST

The 'Quick Escape' From Jakarta

The jaunt to Java's west coast, only 120 km (72 mi) and three hours from Jakarta by car or bus, can be tremendously therapeutic after the heat and congestion of the capital. Few people realize how much there is to see and do here. Along the way you can stop and explore the ruins at Banten, and still be sipping cocktails on the beach by late afternoon. Spend several days here relaxing on idyllic, palm-fringed shores and making excursions to nearby Krakatau or to the highland Badui villages. About a week is needed to visit the remote Ujung Kulon National Park at Java's westernmost tip.

Leaving Jakarta is easier now with the new Jakarta-Tangerang toll road in place, which will eventually reach all the way to Merak on the coast. Tangerang, 30 km (18 mi) west of Jakarta, is an industrial town with textile and rubber factories.

On the coast 28 km (17 mi) north of Tangerang lies the Tjoe Soe Kong Chinese temple at Tanjung Kait, reached by a narrow, dusty road via Mauk. Built 200 years ago by Chinese merchants, it is visited on weekends by those who come to seek the blessings of the temple's deities—gods of the water and land. Tidal waves created by the Krakatau eruption in 1883 devasted these shores, but left the temple intact. There is a tiny fishing harbor nearby where boats can be hired to visit Pulau Laki, about 10 km (6 mi) offshore.

Another 70 km (42 mi) to the west lies Serang, the turning-off point for Banten (see following section). After Serang, you'll encounter the huge Krakatau Steel Mill complex at Cilegon. Here the road forks—the main road to the north bringing you to the bustling Sumatra ferry terminal at Merak.

A smaller road leads left to a sandy shore and the village of Anyer, 12 km (7 mi) farther down the coast. This is the western terminus of the old trans-Java post road. The beach here is now packed with hotels, many quite luxurious (see "West Coast Practicalities"). The beach at Anyer has a rocky bottom and isn't that great for swimming, however. Carita, 30 km (18 mi) farther south, has a better one. The coast in between is incredibly scenic—white sand and swaying palms, with the ominous, smoking cone of Anak Krakatau looming omnipresently on the horizon.

— Arya Subijakto

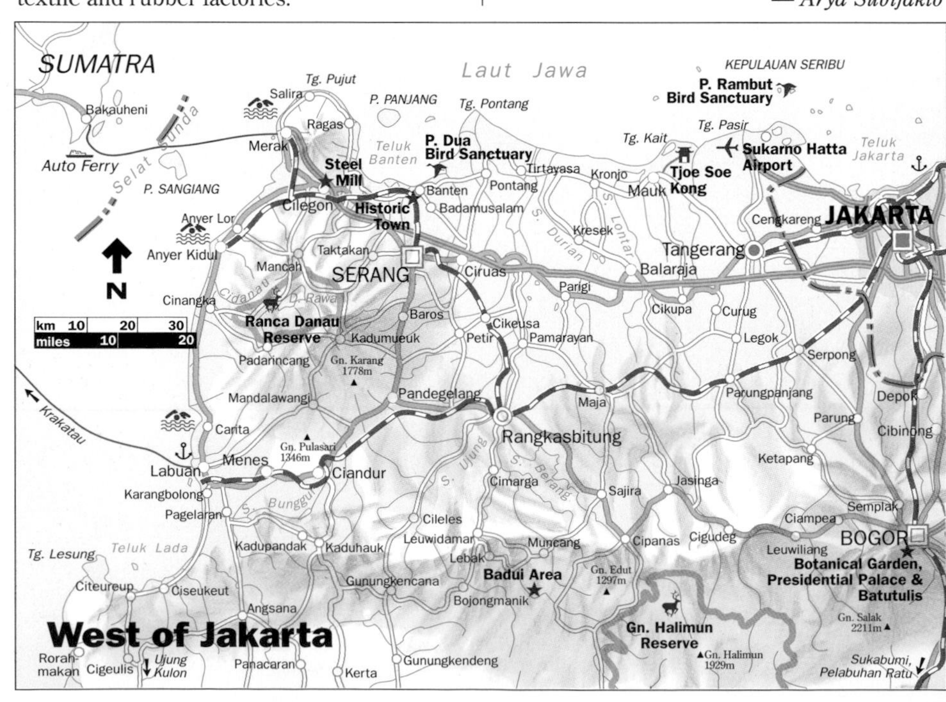

BANTEN

Old Pepper Port on Java's Western Tip

The port of Banten, located 80 km (50 mi) to the west of Jakarta on Java's northwestern shore, was the largest and most important spice trading entrepôt in all of Southeast Asia during the 16th and early 17th centuries—rivaling even Amsterdam in size and importance in its heyday. Today it is a tiny fishing village that does not even appear on most maps, but several of the ancient ruins have been excavated, and this small town is a fascinating place to visit.

Asia's premier trading port

As early as AD 1300 Banten was the site of a seaport belonging to the ancient kingdom of Sunda, whose capital, Pajajaran, lay in the interior near present-day Bogor. When the Portuguese arrived here at the beginning of the 16th century, Sunda was still Buddhist. A commonality of interest led the Portuguese and the ruler of Pajajaran to forge an alliance against the encroaching forces of Islam; this alliance won the Portuguese permission to build a fort at Sunda Kelapa (now Jakarta). The agreement was commemorated by a stone pillar carved in Portuguese called a *padrao*. Rediscovered in 1918, it now resides in the Fatahillah History Museum of Jakarta.

The Portuguese did not move quickly enough, however. A Muslim army from Demak invaded Sunda in 1525 and quickly subdued the ports, though the inland capital was not conquered until 1578. Banten (which the Portuguese spelled Bantam) was chosen as the capital of a new Islamic trading kingdom, and soon became the principal spice trading port on Java.

Banten's proximity to the strategic Sunda Strait separating Java and Sumatra was an important factor in its development. After Malacca fell to the Portuguese in 1511, Muslim merchants avoided the Malacca Straits, sailing instead down Sumatra's west coast and through the Sunda Strait to Java, where they held their traditional rendezvous with Chinese merchants bringing cloth and porcelain, and Indonesians who provided spices such as pepper, nutmeg and cloves.

Banten grew rapidly. By the end of the

Below: *Banten's bronze cannon, Ki Amuk, is said to convey spiritual power upon all who embrace it. Behind are visible the mosque and its minaret.*

KAL MULLER

16th century it was the largest city in Southeast Asia and one of the most famous ports in the world. When the first English and Dutch fleets arrived in the East at the close of the 16th century, Banten was their first stop. According to Dutch estimates of the time, Banten's population then equalled that of Amsterdam.

Splendid walled city

The city was at this time surrounded by a massive defensive wall. All foreigners lived outside the wall in special quarters: Muslims to the east, non-Muslims to the west. The city had a river on either side, with another flowing directly through the middle. Much of the traffic within the city was effected by water rather than by land.

In the center of the city lay an open field, called the *alun-alun,* where numerous activities of importance were conducted, including royal council meetings, law court sessions and public displays. In the morning a market was held here. On Mondays, jousting tournaments (*seninan*) were held in which the nobility took part. The king gave audience in a raised, roofed platform on the southern edge of the *alun-alun* in front of the royal palace. On the north side, the king's royal barges were kept in a special shed, beside a canal.

The British and Dutch were welcomed and allowed to establish trading offices and warehouses at Banten. Dutch monopolistic aims soon led them to quarrel with Banten's authorities, and they subsequently moved to Jayakarta.

For the next 30 years the Dutch blockaded Banten, causing its commerce to suffer. The city experienced a revival under Sultan Agung, who ruled from 1651 to 1682. Agung hired British and other foreigners to man his trading fleet, and constructed irrigation systems to increase local rice production. In 1682, however, Agung fought with his son Haji over policy toward the Dutch. Besieged in his palace, Haji offered the Dutch concessions in return for military assistance. After bitter fighting, Agung found himself in prison, and the Dutch were in possession of Banten and its Sumatran dependencies.

Banten remained a royal capital and a trading center under Dutch supervision until 1810. The last sultan voluntarily abdicated in 1815 under British occupation. Banten's fortunes rapidly waned until it was no more than a congeries of fishing and farming villages.

Antiquities of Banten

The first site which visitors come to, on the side of the narrow road leading into Banten, is the Kaibon Palace. This partially-restored complex was used by the mother of one of the Banten sultans. The palace was once reached from the coast by canals, which now are almost completely dried up.

Driving into the village and veering off to

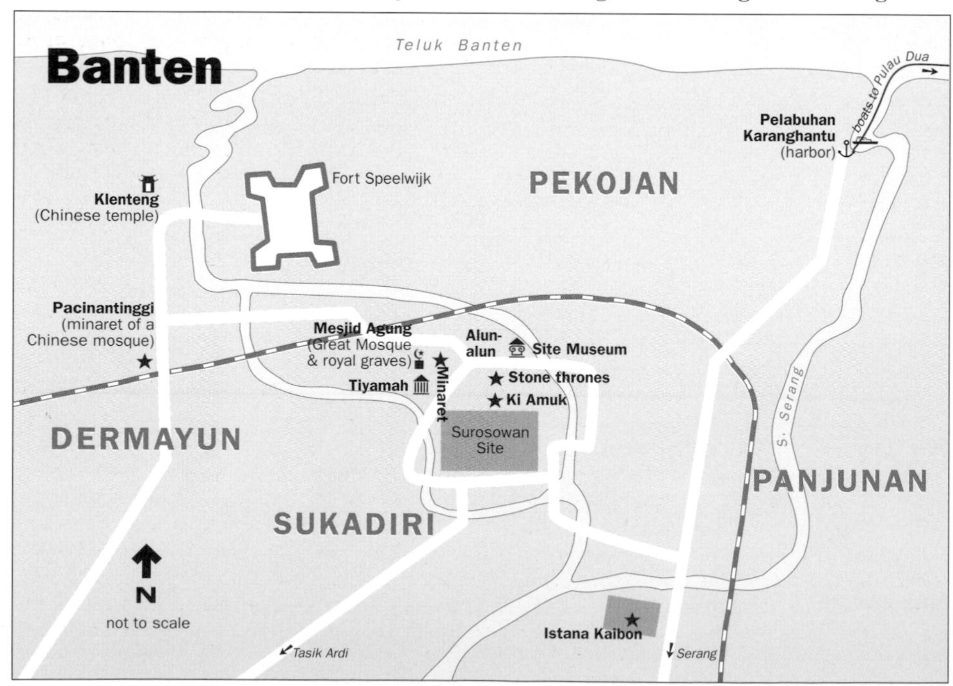

the left, the old *alun-alun* or square which still defines the center of Banten (now called Banten Lama or "Old Banten") swings into view. On the west side stands a major landmark, the Mesjid Agung or "Great Mosque," with a 5-tiered roof that is typical of early Javanese mosques. Next to it is a tall octagonal minaret, built in the mid-16th century, with an entrance displaying motifs taken from pre-Islamic architecture, such as stairways ending in volutes and winged figures above the doors. Inside is a spiral staircase by which visitors may ascend to two balconies at the top which provide an excellent view over the entire site. Royal graves lie in the mosque and its courtyard. A small donation will be welcomed by the watchman.

A building resembling a Dutch-style mansion on the south side of the mosque was built in the 1670s by a renegade Dutch artisan, Jan Lucaszoon Cardeel, who became Sultan Haji's friend. Called the Tiyamah, it was used for religious meetings.

A large bronze cannon, named Ki Amuk, sits at the southeast corner of the square. The gun bears Arabic inscriptions on medallions near the touchhole, and a sunburst motif around the muzzle, reminiscent of a pre-Islamic symbol used by the Majapahit kingdom of East Java.

Two stone thrones are located on the east side of the square. One is said to have been brought from Pajajaran when the kingdom was defeated in 1578; the other is connected with the Banten rulers.

A site museum stands a few meters east of the square. It contains exhibits on Banten's history and archaeology, including artifacts excavated at the site of the former palace. The director, Halwany Michrob, enjoys discussing the site's history with visitors when his duties permit. In the museum's courtyard are remains of an iron-working smithy excavated when the museum was built.

The palace (Surosowan) is surrounded by a high brick wall, of which portions have been excavated. Remains include foundations of pavilions, one of which was called Rara Denok and stood over a pool. It is said to have been the royal treasury. A bathing place at the south side has been partially restored.

Water was brought to the baths by means of an aqueduct leading from an artificial reservoir, Tasik Ardi, about 2 km to the south. Tasik Ardi was built by Sultan Agung, who had a pleasure pavilion on an island in its center. Remains of two brick structures, perhaps filtration tanks (*pengindelan*), can

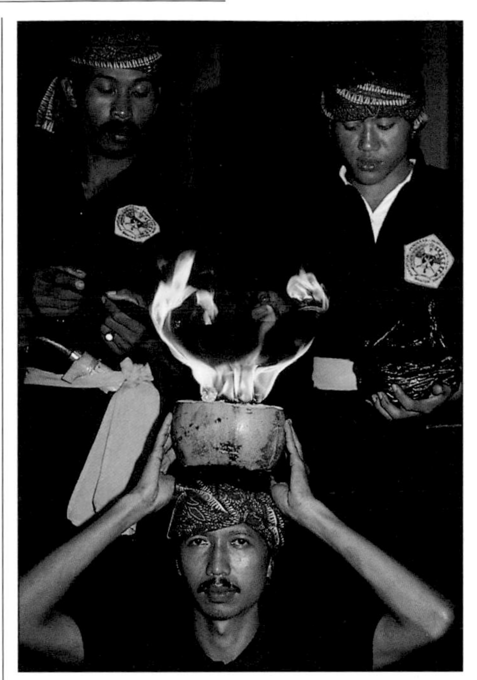

still be seen along the aqueduct's route.

Fort Speelwijk stands at the former river mouth. The coastline has since moved several hundred meters out to sea; the new land is used for fishponds. A large Chinese temple across the river is popular with Indonesian Chinese, who come here in great numbers on the birthday of the principal deity, the goddess of mercy, Kuan Yin. Further south is the restored minaret of a mosque once used by Chinese Muslims.

To the northeast is a small fishing harbor, Karanghantu, where the Serang River empties into the sea. From here boats can be chartered to nearby islands. One of them, Pulau Dua, is a major stopping point for migratory birds, and during the breeding season as many as 50,000 egrets, ibis, teals, mynas, starlings, kingfishers, cormorants, pelicans, herons, sea eagles and other species can be seen here. Situated about one km to the east of Banten, Pulau Dua can be reached by walking across mudflats during low tide.

—John Miksic

Above: *The Banten area is famed for its* debus *players, groups of Islamic ascetics who practice martial arts and perform gruesome feats of self-immolation. These include eating glass, immersing their hands in boiling oil and skewering themselves with metal stakes. It is said that meditation and spiritual devotion allow them to survive such ordeals without suffering bodily harm.*

ALAIN COMPOST

KRAKATAU

The Day the World Exploded

Head west of Java, not east. The famous film *Krakatoa, East of Java* is as shaky in its geography as the volcano it describes. There have been greater volcanic explosions in recorded history—the eruption of Tambora on Sumbawa in 1815 was five times as destructive—but perhaps only Vesuvius conjures up the same images of incalculable subterranean forces as Krakatau.

The name comes from an old Sanskrit word, *karkata*, meaning "crab" (perhaps referring to the shape of the atolls once formed by the volcano's caldera). It lies in the middle of the Sunda Strait, right on the unstable "elbow" where the range of volcanic mountains forming Sumatra turns abruptly eastward to form Java. Ancient Javanese chronicles tell of a mountain here called Kapi, which in about A.D. 416 "burst into pieces with a tremendous roar and sank into the depths of the earth, and the water of the sea rose and inundated the land." Whether Kapi was Krakatau we shall never know, but geologists have shown that at least one massive eruption of Krakatau took place in premodern times.

Prelude

At the end of the 19th century, Krakatau was a fertile and pleasant island, though one which had been long been deserted by human inhabitants. Tropical jungle clothed the slopes of its three peaks—Rakata (830 m/2722 ft), Danan and Perbuatan. This was the spot where European mariners once filled their larders with giant sea turtles, as well as the occasional supplies of pepper and rice which they purchased from small villages along the shores.

The eruption of Krakatau was not unheralded. Beginning in early June, 1883, tremors shook the town of Anyer on the west coast of Java for several days. By the middle of June, puffs of steam and ash were visible above the cone of Perbuatan. But on an island where the earth regularly trembles, and dozens of volcanoes frequently emit smoke, few would be likely to take special notice of such commonplace activity.

By the end of June, however, Krakatau presented a fearsome sight. Two columns of steam rose from the island, which was now blanketed with grey ash, and only the bare trunks of large trees remained of the once-luxuriant jungle. The waters surrounding the island churned and heaved, while here and there floated carpets of pumice so thick a man could walk on them. A party of sightseers from Batavia reported a "fiery purple glow, appearing for a short while every five to ten minutes, from which a fire rain fell."

Climax

This overture to one of nature's greatest known cataclysms lasted for two months. Finally, early in the afternoon of August 26th, 1883, Krakatau exploded with a series of roars heard from Rangoon, Burma to Perth, Australia. A pillar of ash and pumice towered 26 km (16 mi) into the sky. Rock and dust rained over the surrounding region, forming a blanket cloud which turned day into night for 150 km (90 miles) in every direction. Ash from the eruption gradually spread throughout the atmosphere, creating spectacular sun-

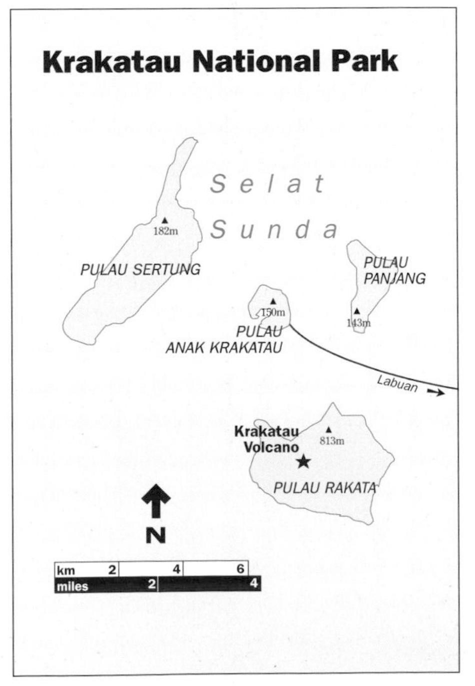

Left: *A minor blast, in 1981, from one of the world's most famous volcanoes.*

sets across the world for two years.

The finale came the following morning, when a gaping maw in the earth's crust—hollowed out by the expulsion of 18 cubic km of ash and rock—collapsed on itself. The sea rushed in and began to boil immediately upon contact with the molten rock, throwing up tsunamis (tidal waves) 10 meters (33 ft) high. The waves could still be detected a day and a half later when they finally rolled against the coast of France.

The devastation near Krakatau was of incredible proportion. The little coastal towns of Anyer and Merak were obliterated. No one knows the exact toll of the explosion in human lives, though a common figure cited is 35,000. Eyewitnesses described a wall of water "taller than a palm tree" sweeping away all in its path. In Teluk Betung on Sumatra, the funnel effect of a narrow bay lifted the waves to a height of 30 meters (100 ft), carrying a Dutch gunboat more than two kilometers inland.

When the waves had subsided and the dust dispersed, three quarters of Krakatau was gone. The peak of Rakata was still close to its original height, but its northern half had disappeared, sliced off as if by a knife, leaving a sheer cliff hurtling 300 m (1000 ft) to the sea below. Two islands, Panjang and Sertung, had been totally re-shaped, while debris from the eruption merged to form islands farther away.

Krakatau and its vicinity remained in a state of geological flux for some time. The new islands disappeared within a few years, but volcanic activity continued below the surface, and in January, 1928 the rim of a new crater arose close to where the vent of Perbuatan had first erupted. Since then, Anak Krakatau ("Child of Krakatau"), has continued to grow, and now stands 150 m (500 ft) high. This "baby island" gives scientists a fascinating opportunity to observe the colonization of plant and animal species on new soil.

Visiting Krakatau

To see Krakatau you need only travel along the palm-fringed western coast of Java. As long as the air is clear, the old peak of Rakata will be visible on the horizon, a low symmetrical cone about 40 km (25 mi) offshore. A journey to Anak Krakatau, however, requires a sturdy boat and stamina for the 8-hour return journey. On a calm day, the crossing is idyllic. Dolphins leap ahead of the bow while flying fish skim the waves. On a windy day, however, it's best to stay on shore.

JILL GOCHER

Visitors land at the island's southern corner, where pine-like casuarinas, hardy colonizers of the shoreline, offer welcome shade. Walk north along the beach until the vegetation thins out, then strike uphill. The succulent plants of the shore quickly give way to clumps of tough grass, but even these only survive on the first few hundred meters.

The slope looks gentle but the going is tough. The fine, black volcanic sand, hot under the tropical sun, gives way underfoot, causing the trekker to slide backwards with each step. Twenty or thirty minutes brings you to the crest of a ridge—the outer edge of Anak Krakatau's crater. From here the view is spectacular. The smouldering cone is in front and a dark skirt of recent lava flows on either side, while behind you the slope you have just climbed spreads out like a fan, delicately edged with young, green vegetation and fringed with a line of surf. The older islands of Rakata, Sertung and Panjang hover in a circle like ladies-in-waiting.

The truly enthusiastic can go further, down into a scorchingly hot valley where giant misshapen lumps of lava lie as they fell from the sky, and up a rocky path on the other side past sulphur fumaroles to the edge of the inner crater. The view is no better from here, but there is an awe-inspiring sensation in standing next to a void that leads straight into the underworld.

—Robert Cribb

THE BADUI

Preservers of Archaic Pre-Islamic Ways

The Badui are a reclusive group of some 3000 people living in the remote Kendeng mountains south of Lebak. "Badui" is a term used by outsiders; the people refer to themselves as *urang Kanekes* (people of Kanekes), and claim to be the original pre-Islamic inhabitants of the Sunda highlands.

Their language is an archaic dialect of the Sundanese language spoken by the majority ethnic group who live all around them, and in this and other respects they greatly resemble the Tenggerese of East Java. Both minorities claim a common heritage with the surrounding populations, but have rejected the Islamic faith in favor of earlier religious traditions. Unlike the Tenggerese, however, the Badui also cling to traditional dress and house styles, and until recently have resisted efforts to introduce schools into their territory.

The Badui territory comprises about 35 settlements. Three are located in what is called the "inner territory," from which outsiders are barred. The remaining villages are part of the "outer Badui" region. Today the outer Badui residents travel regularly to nearby towns; some even market their produce in Jakarta. Nonetheless, the distinction between inner and outer remains. Residents of the inner villages are accorded higher status than the outer, and it is from the inner region that members of the religious elite are drawn.

Each outer village is associated with, and subordinate to, an inner village. A council of elders in the inner villages makes decisions that affect the Badui community as a whole. Individuals violating the codes of the inner Badui can be exiled to the outer villages.

The Badui pantheon is a mélange of ancestral and territorial spirits and deities with Hindu names. This, together with aspects of village settlement and ritual life, suggests that before the destruction of the Pajajaran kingdom by Muslim armies in 1578, the Badui may have formed part of a Hindu priesthood who lived among the peasantry in a clerical arrangement known as *mandala* or "holy mountain" communities. If this is so, the Badui are in fact closely related to the Tenggerese of East Java, who are descended from a popular Sivaite clergy. Religious texts preserved by Tengger priests confirm their Sivaite identity.

One of the greatest enigmas of both the Tengger and the Badui is how such minorities have survived the Islamization of Java's courts. Their geographical isolation has been cited as the principal reason, but this seems less of a factor than attitudes within the courts themselves. While they destroyed pre-existing Hindu-Buddhist temples and monastic communities, the early Muslim potentates of Sunda and Java appear to have spared a few remote bearers of pre-Islamic ways. Indeed, in both Sunda and Java these non-Muslim peoples were regarded as an important source of magical power—capable of mediating with supernatural forces less accessible through the court's Islamic media.

While this served the Badui (and Tengger) well in earlier times, it carries less weight today, as they face the most severe challenge in their history—the inevitable countercurrent of the modern world.

— *Robert Hefner*

CANA IRFAN

Above, left: *Scrambling across loose volcanic scree atop Anak Krakatau.* **Right:** *The Badui eschew the modern world and bar outsiders.*

ALAIN COMPOST

UJUNG KULON PARK

Java in the Time Before History Began

Standing atop the National Monument in Jakarta today, it is hard to imagine Java as it was just a few centuries ago—a landscape of dense tropical jungle dissected by crystal rivers flowing from distant mountains to a pale blue sea. This Java, the Java of a time before intensive human settlement, has disappeared from most of the island. Only in the isolated National Park of Ujung Kulon—one of Java's most exciting destinations for the nature lover—can the visitor get a feeling for the days when Java was one of the most lush and beautiful islands in the world.

Ujung Kulon (the name means "western tip") is barely part of Java. From the nearby port of Labuhan, and even from the peak of nearby Anak Krakatau, it lies hidden over the horizon—a low, wooded peninsula connected tenuously to the mainland by a narrow, swampy isthmus. Only at the peninsula's far western end does the land rise abruptly, reaching a height of 240 m (800 ft) before plunging through turbulent waves into the vast Indian Ocean.

Mousedeer island

Most visitors to Ujung Kulon stay at the visitor center on the island of Peucang, named after the elusive mousedeer occasionally seen in the thick shrub. Wildlife comes to your door here: meter-long monitor lizards or *biawak*—smaller cousins of the Komodo dragon—lurk in the undergrowth and emerge just after human mealtimes to scavenge for leftovers, their long tongues flicking as they follow the scent of discarded chicken bones. Bold grey macaques sit on the lawn in family groups waiting for scraps, occasionally venturing closer to seize a banana or a pair of glasses from an unsuspecting diner. Don't let this boldness raise your eyebrows: raised eyebrows is macaque body language for a challenge, and you are likely to find a large male advancing aggressively towards you with bared teeth.

Peucang itself is interesting for short walks. The track across the island to Karangcopong Point takes only one hour or so, and leads past tall trees with spectacular buttress roots twining in sinuous panels which stretch up to several meters from the trunk. Despite their appearance, these roots do not help to keep the tree upright, but rather allow the roots to absorb oxygen not available in the quickly rotting humus of the jungle floor.

Listen out, too, for the steady, whistling wingbeats of hornbills as they pass overhead, especially around dusk. These magnificent birds feed on the fruit of the forest canopy and can be seen in almost any part of the park. Occasionally, too, *rusa* deer can be sighted near the track on Peucang, waiting perfectly still for intruders to pass. If you get up before breakfast and follow the path a few hundred meters, you may be rewarded with a glimpse of a rare Java squirrel.

Across to the mainland

Delightful though it is, Peucang is just the jumping-off point for adventures on the mainland. Perhaps the best way to start is with the short boat trip across to the Ciujung-

ALAIN COMPOST

Left: *Containing one of the last remaining stands of virgin rainforest left on Java, Ujung Kulon Park is a treasure trove of biological wonders.*
Right: *A monitor lizard, cousin of the famous Komodo "dragon," on Peucang Island.*

kulon feeding ground—an unexpecteldy broad pasture set in the middle of the jungle a few hundred meters from the coast.

Open areas like this are found in several parts of the reserve; they are probably a legacy of fires set by hunters at the beginning of this century.

Early morning is the best time to climb the viewing tower at the edge of the pasture and to watch the shy herd of grazing *banteng* cattle; you may see a black or deep-red bull presiding over a group of delicate fawn females and calves identified by a distinctive white disc on their rumps. Occasionally, too, red jungle fowl and the rare green peafowl appear at the forest margins.

From Ciujungkulon a rough path leads westward along the coast to the headland called Tanjung Layar, or "Sail Point." Here one can stand beneath the old lighthouse and watch heavy freighters and tankers breasting the waves of the Indian Ocean as they emerge from the placid Sunda Strait. This was the promontory known to the Dutch mariners of yore as Java's First Point, the first sight of land after the long voyage from the Cape of Africa, and a sign that the journey to Batavia was almost over.

A morning's visit to the feeding ground and Tanjung Layar leaves time for an afternoon with mask and snorkel in the warm coral waters next to the jetty on Peucang.

For the more robust, a trek across the peninsula to the south coast is not to be missed. The path starts from the feeding ground and leads up the valley of the Ciujungkulon. This is the real jungle, and you have to sharpen your senses and watch your feet. There is no mistaking the roughly dug patches where wild pigs have scratched for edible roots, but also check the muddy areas at each of the steep creek crossings for the footprints of leopards and fishing cats. Ujung Kulon's tiger population, sadly, is now extinct. Experts believe that they probably died out in the 1960s or 70s after disease had decimated the deer population which was their main source of food.

Stop and listen. The jungle is full of sounds: the harsh cry of peacocks, the staccato hammering of woodpeckers, the croaking of frogs, the near-deafening roar of thousands of cicadas, and the whining crescendo of squadrons of approaching mosquitoes.

The south coast, when you reach it, is an abrupt jolt. Ragged waves crash onto a shore of uplifted stone blocks and the air is cool and full of spray. It is a wild place and leaves you in no doubt why the Javanese saw it as the realm of a powerful magical ruler, Kangjeng Ratu Kidul, Queen of the South Seas. Swimming is not advised.

Rhinos and crocodiles

Ujung Kulon is best known for its most elusive inhabitant, the Javanese rhinoceros.

ALAIN COMPOST

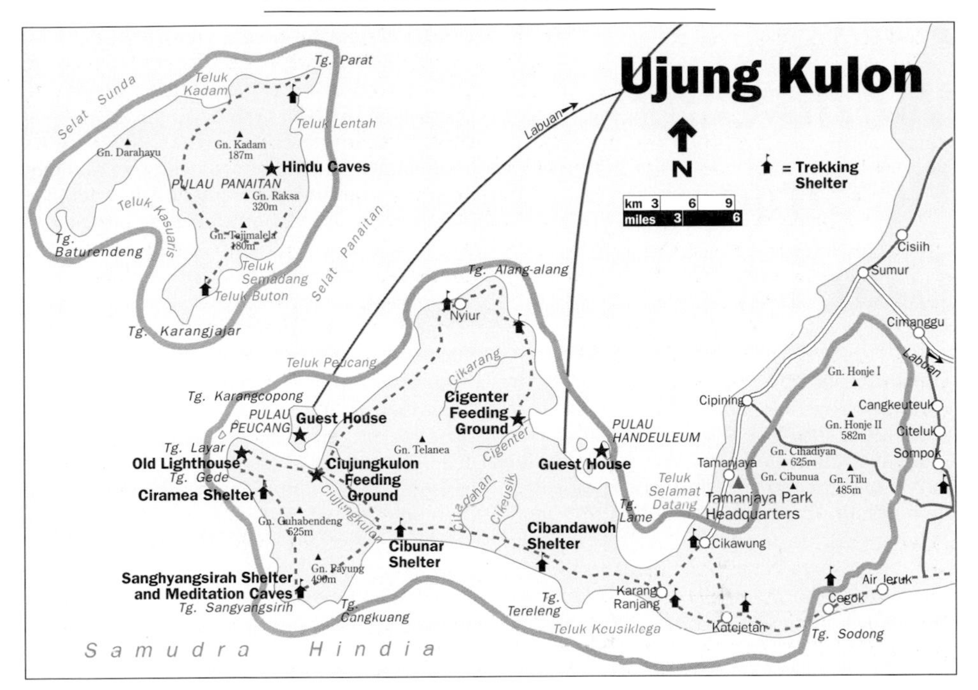

Once abundant in the lowland forests of Java, it is now found nowhere but the thick jungles of Ujung Kulon. Those who know the park say that perhaps 50 or 60 survive. Many of the rangers have seen rhino only once or twice. They patrol the national park constantly to keep out poachers attracted by the enormous price which rhinoceros horn fetches on the black markets of Hong Kong, Singapore and Taiwan—the Chinese believe the horn (which is actually made of matted hair) to possess aphrodesiacal powers.

The rangers can often help locate recent rhinoceros footprints. The sight of the deep dinner-plate sized impressions in the mud often persuades visitors that footprints are close enough. If you do happen across a rhino, the advice from experts is to climb a tree high enough to avoid their surprisingly sharp teeth.

One of the best places to find rhino footprints is near the Cigenter feeding ground on the eastern side of the peninsula. Cigenter is well worth a visit in any case, for it is the home of hundreds of bee-eaters—small, brightly colored birds which nest in concealed burrows in the sun-baked soil of the feeding ground. They burst from the ground in an flapping explosion of blue and gold as intruders approach.

It is sometimes possible, if falling vegetation has not blocked the stream, to take a canoe ride along the Cigenter River—one of the largest streams in the park—to a beautiful set of limestone terraces over which the river cascades. This river is home to numbers of crocodiles. If this is an objection, a rough track well away from the water's edge can be followed instead.

For visitors with more time, there is a fascinating (though demanding) walk along the northern coast of the peninsula from Cigenter all the way around to Ciujungkulon. Most noticeably in the Nyiur area along this route, an ancient coral reef just behind the beach forms a natural dam, creating a swampy terrain rich in birdlife. The offshore island of Panaitan, too, has very basic facilities for visitors, and the rangers there can take you to caves in the interior where old Hindu relics have been found.

To return, you may take a seldom-used track from the lighthouse at Tanjung Layar which leads around the western tip of the peninsula, along the south coast and eventually back to park headquarters at Tamanjaya—about 42 km (25 mi). The path from the lighthouse in the other direction is slightly shorter (32 km/19 mi), cutting across the peninsula before joining the south coast stretch. To fully enjoy the park, you should allow yourself at least four days, plus two full days to get there and back from Jakarta.

—Robert Cribb

Opposite: *Banteng cattle grazing at Cigenter.*

BOGOR

World-Class Botanic Gardens

The small but rapidly growing city of Bogor (pop. 300,000) lies just 60 km (35 mi) due south of Jakarta, only an hour by road or rail. Situated at the foot of Mt. Salak at an altitude of 260 meters (860 ft), Bogor is noticeably cooler than the coast, providing quick and welcome respite from the sweltering heat and chaos of Jakarta. This was the picturesque spot where Dutch Governor-General van Imhoff had a private retreat constructed in 1745—a place which he named Buitenzorg, meaning "free of cares."

Bogor is famous for many things, but most of all for its world-class botanic gardens, situated just behind the stunning 19th-century presidential palace. The town also boasts record-breaking rainfall figures (300 thunderstorms have been recorded in a single year!), two important stone inscriptions and one of Java's few remaining *gamelan* foundries.

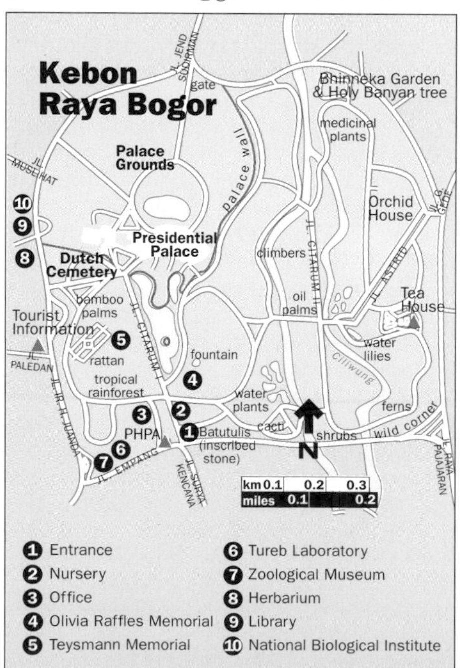

Residence of ancient kings

One of Indonesia's earliest known kingdoms was probably based in the vicinity of Bogor—the 5th-century Hindu-Javanese state of Tarumanegara. We know of it from a number of stone inscriptions found in the vicinity, including one particularly striking one that is still *in situ* at Ciampea, 15 km (9 mi) west of the city—a riverbed boulder inscribed with several lines of Indic script and two oversized footprints supposedly belonging to world-conquering King Purnavarman.

A replica of the stone is on display in the Fatahillah History Museum in Jakarta, and the name of the kingdom seems to be echoed in the name of the Citarum River which passes from the Bandung basin to the coast some distance east of Bogor. Because of the inscriptions discovered here, historians have concluded that this was at one time the site of Tarumanegara's capital—an easily defensible spot giving access to the fertile hinterlands as well as to the nearby trading ports bordering the Sunda Straits.

A later *batutulis* (*batu* = "stone," *tulis* = "writing") is found in Bogor itself on Jl. Batutulis, about 2 km south and west of the botanic gardens off Jl. Bondongan. This inscription records the ascendancy in 1533 of King Surawisesa of Pajajaran—a powerful Hindu king who was variously a vassal and rival to East Java's great Majapahit rulers.

As with most ancient Sundanese sites, architectural remains are nonexistent. All that we have are the inscriptions. This leads historians to conjecture that palaces and temples must have been built of wood, or else, as was the case elsewhere, that stones used for buildings were carried off later to build houses and goat pens.

The sacred inscriptions, meanwhile, continue to be worshipped. Sukarno built a house across from the Bogor *batutulis* so as to partake of its alleged mystical powers. He even requested to be buried here, a wish that was not granted.

The town as it is known today grew up around the country home van Imhoff built and soon became popular with the Dutch due to the unhealthy living conditions in Batavia (now Jakarta). Raffles occupied the house while ruling Java from 1811-1816. From 1870 until 1942, the rebuilt and expanded palace became the primary residence of the Dutch Governors-General of the East Indies.

Since independence, Istana Bogor has been one of five official homes of the Indone-

LUCA INVERNIZZI TETTONI

sian president. President Suharto declines to use it, but Sukarno spent a good deal of time here and his spirit is said to inhabit the place, amidst a large and notoriously risqué art collection (the more voluptuous works are kept prudently out of sight). A herd of spotted deer, imported from Holland as a source of venison to be served at grand official banquets, now serve as ambulatory decoration on the 24-hectare (95-acre) grounds.

Biological treasures

Bogor's pride, and one of the world's great biological treasure troves, is the Kebon Raya botanic gardens. Though Raffles is said to have laid out a small garden here with the help of botanists from London's famous Kew Gardens, the Kebon Raya was officially established by the Dutch in 1817 under the directorship of C.G.C. Reinwardt, and he and subsequent generations of botanists performed the herculean feat of assembling over 15,000 species of tropical plants from around the world. Within the carefully laid-out 87 hectares are over 400 palm species, 5,000 trees and an orchid house with 3,000 varieties. On uncrowded weekdays, it is delightful to stroll around the lawns, pools and tree-shaded paths within the park. Sundays, however, are to be avoided, as the park is deluged with visitors.

Kebon Raya actually has five branches in Java, Sumatra and Bali—the largest of which is the important Cibodas Park just to the southeast of Bogor (see following section). The gardens were designed to serve as a research institute—a function which continues today. Institut Pertanian Bogor, Indonesia's leading agricultural institute on the east side of the gardens, works to develop new strains of rice and other important crops.

Near the entrance to the gardens is a zoological museum with an immense collection (300,000 specimens) of land and sea creatures from throughout Indonesia. The museum also boasts a fine library, the skeleton of a blue whale, and the last rhino (stuffed) found on the Bandung plateau.

Near the park entrance is the main office for Indonesia's Forestry Protection and Nature Preservation Department (PHPA). You may obtain permits here to visit any wildlife refuge in Indonesia, though they may also be obtained at local field offices.

From the Ramayana movie theater take a *bemo* toward Cihampus and Pak Sukarna's Bengkel Gong gamelan foundry at Jl. Pancasan 17. Here you will see red-hot bronze disks pounded into large sonorous gongs. At Pak Karna's house across the street you can order an instrument or an entire orchestra, as well as a variety of *wayang golek* puppets.

— *Roggie Cale*

Above: *Istana Bogor, constructed in 1856, the official residence of the Dutch Governors-General.*

SOUTH FROM BOGOR

Puncak Pass and the South Coast

To the south of Bogor rises a towering volcanic massif containing some of the most beautiful scenery on Java. The highest peaks, Mts. Gede (2,958 m/9,615 ft) and Pangrango (3,019 m/9,810 ft) stand side by side 40 km (25 mi) to the southeast of Bogor. Together with Mt. Salak (2,211 m/7,185 ft), they have created a broad alluvial fan with rivers spreading down to the coast in several directions. One of the largest rivers, the Ciliwung, has carved a valley into the northern slope of Mt. Pangrango, and it was here, at the beginning of the 19th century, that a narrow, winding road was built across the 1,450 meter (4,750 ft) pass known as Puncak (which literally means "the summit"). Today the cool and spectacularly scenic area traversed by this road is a popular weekend resort.

Tea plantations blanket the upper reaches of the pass, while villages just below it supply Jakarta's kitchens with fresh fruits and vegetables. Today, innumerable hotels and private bungalows scatter throughout the hillsides. The weekend traffic is pure terror.

The nights here are invigorating, especially during the rainy season, with temperatures averaging 20-22° C (68-72° F). There are splendid views of the plains below on a clear day, and lovely hikes through terraced ricefields and dense forests. The road itself is lined with small restaurants and fruit stalls.

Coming up from Jakarta, you pass a number of hotels long before reaching the higher elevations. The villages of Tugu and Cisarua have a good range of accommodations and eateries. Numerous scenic country walks around Cisarua lead to picnic grounds and small waterfalls. There is also a new African-style "Safari Park" (**Taman Safari**) in which lions, tigers, zebras and giraffes graze in open spaces and stare at passing motorists. A campground, forest recreation area and caravan park are being added, which will bring Taman Safari's total area up to 168 hectares.

Near the top of the pass, the highway enters the Gunung Mas tea estate, which is open to visitors. Also in the estate is the **Telaga Warna** "Colored Lake." This large pond is tucked into a mountain niche 500 meters (1600 ft) below the Rindu Alam Restaurant. Walk behind the fruit stands on the east side of the highway and bring a lunch. Dancing light refracts on the water's

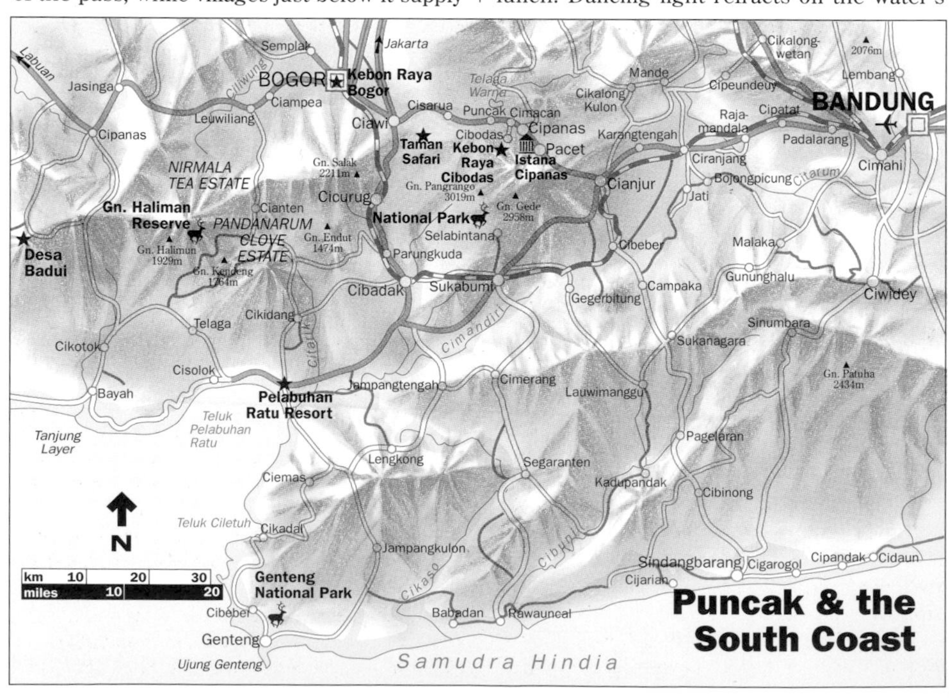

ALAIN COMPOST

surface, providing visual entertainment.

Cibodas and Cipanas

Once over the summit, the road descends through more resorts. In Pacet, 7 km (4 mi) beyond the pass, there is a poorly marked road to the right leading up to the **Kebon Raya Cibodas**—a high-altitude branch of the Bogor Botanic Gardens. These 60 hectares (150 acres) were laid out in 1852 for the study of temperate and montane flora from around the world, and pioneering work done here on cinchona (quinine) and coffee made Java the world's largest supplier of these commodities by the late 19th century.

Assembling Cibodas' collection of over 5,000 specimens, most of them from abroad, was an even greater undertaking than the larger gardens at Bogor. There are pools, quiet walks, flowing streams and great views of the volcanoes on a clear day. The park includes virgin native jungle—the starting point for hikes to Mts. Gede and Pangrango. (See "Gede and Pangrango" page 135.)

A few kilometers further east along the main highway is the town of **Cipanas** (meaning "hot waters"), site of a natural hot spring whose sulphurous waters are claimed to cure skin diseases and relieve rheumatism. The town is also a center for vegetable gardens supplying Jakarta's markets.

Also in Cipanas is the **Presidential Summer Palace**, Istana Cipanas. This colonial mansion, built in 1750, sits on a large manicured estate fronting the highway and is now rarely used. The grounds extend into the jungle and contain their own hot spring.

Mt. Halimun

There are several other, less commonly visited hill stations and nature reserves in southwest Java which are well served by a major road that passes south and east of Bogor via Sukabumi. The mountains here are an eerie wilderness of sharp peaks, narrow valleys and thick jungle shrouded in frequent mists and rain. Local people speak of them as a place of dangerous spirits, and perhaps for this reason they contain the largest tract of untouched forest in Java. Just before Cibadak, at Parungkuda, is a side road leading west to the Pandanarum Clove Estate and the Nirmala Tea Estate, situated in the midst of Java's least known reserve.

Botanists have only begun to explore the wealth of Mt. Halimun (1929 m/6327 ft), whose name literally means "misty mountain"—though Indonesia's powerful logging interests had seen enough of its tall *meranti* and *rasamala* trees to pencil in the area for future exploitation. Halimun, however, has been saved, as in 1987 plans were finalized to

Above: *Just below Puncak Pass the road winds through the manicured Gunung Mas Tea Estate. Mt. Salak may be seen in the distance.*

KAL MULLER

include it within the Gede-Pangrango National Park.

Visiting Halimun is difficult; much of this 36,000-hectare (89,000-acre) park consists of steep terrain lying above 1200 m (3900 ft). Roads into the Nirmala Tea Estate are often impassable after a rain. It may be possible to stay in the estate's guest house, but food is a problem and walking tracks in the park are few. The local staff are not familiar enough with the region to offer detailed advice.

Even from the road, however, Halimun's rich life is visible: brilliant black-and-scarlet Sunda Minivets, Racket-tailed Drongos with their spectacular long-tail feathers, several species of woodpecker and the rare Java Laughing Thrush. Early in the morning one can hear the loud singing calls of endangered Javan gibbons announcing their territories. Leopard and mousedeer are also found, though you will be lucky to see them.

Sukabumi and Selabintana

South of Mts. Gede and Pangrango, the Cimandiri River flows into the Indian Ocean. High in this valley lies the small, placid Sundanese hill town of Sukabumi. This region records the largest number of earthquakes and tremors anywhere in Indonesia, and was devastated in 1972 by a major quake that killed 2,500 people.

Sukabumi itself is of no special interest, but 7 km (4 miles) to the north lies a compact hill resort and recreation area called Selabintana. The road to Selabintana climbs up a crease between the slopes of the two towering volcanoes and ends on the 36-hectare grounds of the Hotel Selabintana. A number of other hotels, villas and restaurants line the road, making this a refreshing alternative to Puncak's heavy traffic and crush of weekend visitors. Trails reach the mountain peaks via a local PHPA post further up at Situgunung, but climbers should get a park entry permit first at Cibodas.

Surf-wracked southern coast

From a turn-off at Cibadak, 17 km (10 mi) west of Sukabumi, a side road to the south follows the Cimandiri River valley to the coast and a large horseshoe bay measuring 20 km (12 mi) across. The area, including the bay and a picturesque fishing village near the river's mouth, are called **Pelabuhan Ratu** ("Queen's Harbor") in honor of the goddess of the south sea, Ratu Kidul. According to local legend, she is a distraught woman who

ERIC OEY

threw herself into the sea at Karang Hawu, about 14 km (8.5 mi) to the west. There an ancient lava flow cuts the beach into jagged pools. This is a popular picnicking spot on weekends and foodstalls perch on the hillside along the road to Cisolok.

Pelabuhan Ratu lies 145 km (87 miles) and only about four hours south of Jakarta by car—a busy holiday beach resort on the weekends. The black sand beach is broad and inviting, but the riptides can be very treacherous and they claim a number of victims every year. Swimming is generally discouraged, and bathers are warned against wearing green, as this is Ratu Kidul's favorite color—local belief attributes drownings to her malevolent spirit. Once a year in early April, fishermen appease Ratu Kidul by sacrificing a buffalo and spreading flowers on the water. This so-called Pesta Nelayan ("Fisherman's Festival") also occasions sporting contests and cultural performances.

The coastline here is ruggedly beautiful. To the east and west cliffs drop to the ocean, and the road down from Cibadak is shaded here and there by the silver-green leaves of rubber trees. A newly surfaced and very scenic road connects the resort with Cisolok and on to Serang in the west. Heading south along a rough track from here, the traveler eventually reaches the turtle-spawning beaches at Ujung Genteng.

—Roggie Cale and Robert Cribb

MTS. GEDE & PANGRANGO

Exhilarating Ascent to the Summit

A trail beginning just next to the main gate of the Cibodas Gardens (see previous section) forms the principal entrance to Mt. Gede-Pangrango National Park. This is the oldest park in Indonesia (declared in 1889), and it encompasses some 15,000 hectares (37,050 acres) on the upper slopes of the two volcanoes—sheltering a unique tropical alpine flora and some of the finest remaining stands of native montane forest on Java. By the parking lot, the local PHPA office issues permits and route maps to hikers. Rain and high winds make the park unsafe between December and April and the gates are then closed, but at other times of the year you need only register to be allowed in. This office also oversees Mt. Halimun Reserve to the west.

During the May-October dry season you can make the exhilarating climb to the summit of Mt. Gede (a 6- to 7-hour climb) or Mt. Pangrango (7 to 8 hours). Bring sturdy shoes and warm clothing. Temperatures at the peak approach freezing, and frosts are common in the meadows below.

Waterfalls and hot springs

The path climbs quickly, and you may have to scramble over fallen trees blocking the way, but you are quickly in the midst of the jungle. Because trees are so often blown down, this is a bright, open jungle. Iridescent blue dragonflies hover near mountain streams and "flying" lizards glide from tree to tree on bright orange membrane-wings. High in the trees sit troops of crested leaf monkeys, their black crests erect and their long tails hanging straight down.

Best for the day visitor is the 90-minute walk to **Cibeureum waterfall**, where three separate streams plunge over a cliff. This is a good place to picnic as you watch huge green Arjuna butterflies sipping salty mud at the water's edge.

For the more energetic the main path winds higher to a hot spring which bursts from the jungle floor to wash down over the track. The Sundanese say that the sulphurous water is good for the skin, and it comes from the ground at 60° C (140° F).

To go higher involves hiring a guide and camping out overnight. Bring warm clothing; the near-freezing temperatures of these mountains can make you miserable. There is a shelter about 4 hours up at Kandang Badak ("Rhino Stable"), a saddle at 2,400 m (7,800 ft) between the two peaks. Or, you can camp further up at the 2,800 m (9,200 ft) high *alun-alun* meadow just below Mt. Gede, famous for its Javan edelweiss (*Anaphalis javanica*).

Plan to reach the summit of Gede just before dawn, when the air is most likely to be clear and you may have the chance, like Thomas Stamford Raffles, who climbed the mountain in 1815, to stand above the sheer cliffs of Gede's hissing crater and scan the coasts of western Java from north to south, with Krakatau and Sumatra in the distance. Java suddenly seems very remote.

You can also make the climb from the highland resort of Selabintana near Sukabumi, but you must first get a *surat jalan* (hiking pass) at Cibodas.

—Robert Cribb and Roggie Cale

TAMNI A. GANIE / SUARA ALAM

Opposite, left: *The palm-fringed southern shore.* **Opposite, right:** *The fish market at Pelabuhan Ratu, known especially for its delicious fresh tuna.* **Right:** *Javan edelweiss in the* alun-alun *or meadow just below Mt. Gede's summit.*

BANDUNG

The Most 'European' of Java's Cities

With a population of over 2 million (reaching to 4 million when the surrounding towns are taken into account), Bandung is Indonesia's third-largest metropolis. This is the administrative and commercial capital of West Java, largely laid out around 1920 by Dutch urban planners as the first "modern" city in the Indies, and still today perhaps the most "European" of all Indonesian towns.

Lying 187 km (120 mi) southeast of Jakarta in the midst of the lovely Priangan highlands, Bandung enjoys a surprisingly mild climate, with temperatures averaging a pleasant 22.5° C (72.5° F). Partly as a result, most residents reckon that this must be the most liveable spot on the island, even if rain falls on an average of 144 days in the year (mostly between November and April).

The city is situated on a high plateau at an altitude of 768 meters (2,500 feet), surrounded on all sides by brooding volcanoes and lofty mountain ridges. A number of rushing rivers have carved deep gorges through these uplands, converging in the Citarum River which drains the basin and empties into the Java Sea east of Jakarta at Karawang.

Rice is farmed all around Bandung, while the mountain slopes are blanketed with plantations of tea, rubber, coffee and cinchona. The moderate climate favors dairy, vegetable and fruit farming; foodstuffs are processed here and Bandung is also a major industrial center, dominating the production of textiles in Indonesia. It is also the home of the nation's nascent high tech industries—including computer assembly factories and an aircraft manufacturing plant.

The city boasts many universities and academies, including the prestigious Institut Teknologi Bandung (ITB)—the oldest techincal institute in Indonesia. A center for monitoring Indonesia's volcanoes and a nuclear research station are also located here.

Bandung was founded only at the beginning of the 19th century, with the establishment of a tiny Dutch outpost. At this time the area was still heavily forested and sparsely populated. Patches of swampland here and there were remnants of a huge lake—the legendary Situ Hiang or "Lake of the Gods" that once covered the entire basin. Access was difficult, involving an arduous trip aboard boats, rafts and sedan chairs up the Citarum

and Cimanuk Rivers. In 1786, a horse track was cut into the plateau, and in 1789 the first coffee gardens were planted on the southern flanks of Tangkuban Perahu—the "Up-turned Boat" volcano that defines the northern edge of the basin.

The 'Paris of Java'

Between 1808 and 1810, reformist Governor-General Daendels constructed a post road that spanned the length of Java, connecting Batavia with central and east Java via the Priangan highlands of the west. He then ordered the Sundanese leaders of Tatar Ukur (as the Bandung area was then called) to move to a spot where this road (now Jl. Asia-Afrika) crossed the Cikapundung River.

The area remained sparsely inhabited, but during Raffles' tenure (1811-1815) some state lands were sold to private entrepreneurs, who cleared the forested slopes and planted coffee, tea and cinchona. Between 1831 and 1870, under the harsh "Cultivation System," some 823 million guilders in profits were sent back to Holland, about 75 percent of it deriving from the sale of coffee grown in this area.

With the end of the Cultivation System in 1870, the Priangan was further opened to private investors, and the number of plantations soon jumped to over 150. By 1902, there were 81 tea plantations operating here; by 1939 some 60 cinchona plantations in the area were producing 90 percent of the world's quinine.

While the surrounding slopes were thus cleared and cultivated by a growing class of wealthy *Preangerplanters*, the town remained a backwater. This began to change with the opening of a Batavia-to-Bandung rail link in 1884. The line was extended to Surabaya ten years later via Yogya and Solo, thus making Bandung an important stop on the trans-Java rail route. Bandung was still a small town-however; in 1896 the population stood at only 29,386 (1,250 of them Europeans), despite the fact that in 1864 Bandung had been designated the capital of the Priangan residency.

After 1918, construction of a "new town" to the northeast of the old business district began around what is now Gedung Sate and Dago. A fairground was opened in 1920, and an annual "Jaarbeurs" fair held during June and July featured exhibitions that attracted attention and many visitors from abroad. Due to meticulous urban planning and large profits generated by the local economy, Bandung developed into the most modern and most European of all cities in the Indies—billed by local civic boosters as the "Parijs van Java" on account of its gracious, tree-lined boulevards and fashionable shops and houses.

Jl. Braga was the epicenter of Bandung life in those days—the "foremost European

Overleaf: *Bandung Basin, with Mt. Malabar hovering behind.* **Below:** *The city's new European district in its colonial heyday, ca. 1920.*

ANTIQUARIAAT ACANTHUS, UTRECHT

shopping street in the Indies." Here one could buy a tailored suit, a drop-dead evening gown, a Swiss watch, an imported cigar and the latest Packard coupe. When the shops shuttered for the day, the sidestreets off Jl. Braga (an area called Margawati) opened, and planters who had worked hard all day could frolic till dawn in the bars and brothels.

The 1920s were Bandung's "Golden Age." A decision was made to move the colonial capital here in stages, and a number of large companies transferred their headquarters and factories to new premises in the city, which brought even more money into an already prosperous area. Bandung also became a major tourist destination, attracting some 200,000 visitors in 1941.

The city has now been largely eclipsed by Jakarta, though the Asia-Africa Conference, hosted here in 1955 by Sukarno and attended by such Third World luminaries as Nehru, Nassar, U Nu, Chou En-lai and Ho Chi Minh, gave the city a fleeting moment in the international limelight.

Like Jakarta, Bandung has experienced a massive influx of people from the countryside. From just 226,877 in 1941, the population swelled to over a million by 1960, and is now double that. This has put a severe strain on infrastructure and public services, while creating problems of pollution, traffic congestion and crime.

Bandung is now no longer the gracious "Paris of Java" of the pre-war era. Urban archaeologists can nevertheless glimpse here and there remnants of Bandung's faded glory. The Savoy Homann Hotel and the BPD Jawa Barat Building (at the corner of Jl. Braga and Jl. Naripan) are classic art-deco confections. The tree-lined neighborhoods of Jl. Juanda and Jl. Cipaganti are showcases of colonial suburban life. And the imposing Gedung Sate (literally "*sate* building," named for the resemblance of its spire to a skewer of meat) is a paragon of Indo-European architecture and one of the most striking buildings in all of Indonesia—now the headquarters of the West Java provincial government.

Bandung is also a cultural and intellectual center, though it assumed its present role as the center for Sundanese culture only at the end of the last century. Before that, Sundanese population and political power concentrated in Sumedang, Ciamis, Bogor and Cianjur. Once the regency shifted here from Cianjur in 1864, however, the Sundanese aristocracy followed, and the traditional arts have

flourished as a result.

Bandung now rivals Jakarta as the home of artists, writers and academics. The most daring new artistic and political movements germinate among Bandung's progressive student population. And the Siliwangi Division based here has always been regarded as Indonesia's most technically skilled and best disciplined army unit.

Last but not least, Sundanese women are, in the estimation of Indonesians, the most beautiful in the land. Because of the climate, they have a lighter complexion than other Indonesians, and because the Sundanese diet features raw vegetables, they reputedly possess especially soft skin. Bandung ladies are fashion smart and forward looking—and the city's nickname, Kota Kembang, ("City of Flowers") has always been more of a sly reference to Bandung's distaff attractions than to its shrubbery.

A 'nostalgic' look around Bandung

Tourists come to Bandung mainly to get away from the heat of Jakarta, and to have a nostalgic backward look at what remains of the city's colonial landmarks. A good start would be a stroll around the Jl. Asia-Afrika and Jl. Braga area in the center of town. This was the main shopping and tourist district of

Above: *Shops and two of Bandung's beauties.*
Right: *Gedung Sate (1920), a local landmark.*

colonial Bandung in its heyday. Gedung Merdeka ("Freedom Building"), at the northwest intersection of the streets, is where the 1955 Asia-Africa Conference was held. Formerly it was the Societeit Concordia, an elegant high society club, built in 1895. Inside is a museum displaying documents and photographs of the Bandung Conference.

To the east along Jalan Asia-Afrika on either side of the street stand two hotels dating to the 1930s, the art-deco Savoy Homann and the Preanger. In the other direction, across a bridge spanning the Cikapundung River, lies the town square or *alun-alun* that was the site of the original settlement at the beginning of the 19th century. To the northwest of here is the Pasar Baru market district, dominated by Chinese shops and traders.

Moving northwards along Jl. Braga from Jl. Asia-Afrika, you see many proud old Dutch shops, now rather decrepit and forlorn. On the left is the Majestic Cinema, built in the "Indo-European" style that was pioneered here in the early 1920s. Next to it is a building that formerly housed Au Bon Marché, a purveyor of *haute couture*. Across the street is a sidewalk cafe and department store called Braga Permai—site of the former Maison Bogerijen restaurant, where lecturers from the university gathered for lunch every Saturday at 1:00 pm, and where every Sunday evening wealthy planters would come to feast on French *haute cuisine* washed down with bubbly glasses of Veuve Cliquot champagne.

Continue your tour with a look at the European "new town" which lies 1 km to the northeast of Jl. Braga around Gedung Sate. Visit the **Geological Museum** on Jl. Diponegoro, where replicas of "Java Man" fossils from Central Java are on display. In the back is a cartographic department where detailed maps of Indonesia may be purchased.

From Gedung Sate, walk or ride up to the **Bandung Institute of Technology** (ITB) through leafy suburban streets lined by magnificent colonial houses. The extraordinary university buildings designed by Maclaine Pont, one of the first and most influential proponents of the "Indo-European" architectural style that attempted to fuse traditional Indonesian forms with modern Western techniques. The up-turned roofs of the buildings are modelled on traditional Batak and Minang houses, while the library is a spectacular honeycomb of wooden beams.

From ITB, continue up to the **Dago Tea House**, with its panoramic view over the city and nearby waterfall, just 2 kilometers from the Pajajaran University campus. Or, walk past the Bandung zoo to the Babakan Siliwangi Restaurant—a traditional Sundanese *pondok* consisting of pavilions raised on stilts above carp ponds. Both are within walking distance of the university, though the Tea House is a bit of a climb.

— *Roggie Cale, Eric Oey, Gottfried Roelcke*

BEST

THE SUNDANESE ARTS

An Exuberant Performance Tradition

Unlike many traditional music and drama forms in Java, the appeal of the Sundanese performing arts for foreign visitors is quite immediate. The lifelike movements of three-dimensional *wayang golek* puppets, the dynamism of *jaipongan* dance, and the sheer tunefulness and complex rhythms of Sundanese music—by turns boisterous and melancholy—are all readily enjoyable upon first acquaintance.

In the past, different performing arts were clearly associated with different sectors of Sundanese society. Thus *tembang Sunda* (sung poetry) and *gamelan degung* were for the aristocratic *bupati* or regents, while *gamelan slendro* and *ketuk tilu* (an erotic street dance) were enjoyed by the masses.

Since independence such distinctions have become blurred. Genres and styles are now mixed, and some are disappearing completely. Despite this, the traditional arts are still very much alive. Many young artists are avidly innovating, striving to renew the traditions and creating novel genres and combinations. Many are short-lived, while others—like the songs of Nano S., the *jaipongan* of Gugum Gumbira and the *wayang* of Asep Sunandar—enjoy a huge commercial success. Traditionalists are incensed by this, while others reflect that people will eventually tire of the fads and return once again to the traditional forms.

Unique musical genres

Gamelan degung is an ensemble found only in Sunda. It is tuned to a five-note scale known as *pelog degung* with intervals not unlike those of Western music (roughly G-F#-D-C-B, though every gamelan set is slightly different). There are relatively few instruments, but these are of wider range than a Javanese *gamelan*—spanning some three octaves. The ensemble includes a short, four-holed bamboo flute, the *suling degung*. The purely instrumental repertoire from the courts is now rarely played. Instead, the *degung* is used to accompany a female soloist (*pasinden* or *juru kawih*), or to play catchy instrumental arrangements.

Like *degung*, the *kacapi* (zither) is unique to Sunda. There are two types. The first and more "classical" is the boat-shaped *kacapi perahu*, with an elegantly curled prow and

stern. A large and a small *kacapi* combine with long, 6-holed *suling* to accompany the singing of traditional poetry or *tembang Sunda*. The vocal style is rich in timbre and ornament and heart-rendingly beautiful. This remains an elite form of entertainment.

Another type, the *kacapi kawih,* is somewhat less refined; basically it is a flat, rectangular box. It is used to accompany *kawih,* songs in a much lighter vocal style. The *kecapi kawih* is inexpensive and is often used by buskers, many of whom are blind.

Another instrumental form, *gamelan salendro,* resembles a small Javanese gamelan and is used to accompany *wayang* and dance. Nowadays a female vocalist singing *kawih* songs and a *kendang* drummer dominate the ensemble. *Gamelan salendro* groups never include a flute—instead, a *rebab* (two-stringed fiddle) is used to carry the melody.

Life-like *wayang golek*

The famous Sundanese rod puppet theater, or *wayang golek purwa,* is often performed in the open air during feasts (*hajat*) held to celebrate a wedding, birth or circumcision. The performance begins around 9:00 in the evening and lasts until just before dawn.

The puppeteer (*dalang*) sits cross-legged at the front of a covered stage, with gamelan players behind him. In addition to manipulating all the puppets, he provides dialogue, narration and mood songs, and directs the musicians through rhythmic and verbal cues.

The puppets have carved wooden heads mounted on rods passing through the body. These are stuck into banana tree trunks when the puppet is not being held. Jointed arms are moved with separate sticks. A skilled *dalang* can make the puppets dance, fight, breathe and express an extraordinary range of emotions with surprising realism.

The stories consist of episodes from the *Ramayana*, *Mahabharata* and *Arjuna Sastra Bahu* epics. The clowns provide slapstick relief and social commentary. The Sundanese favorite is red-faced Cepot, who often has a cigarette drooping from his mouth. Some younger *dalang* are even experimenting with grotesque puppets which bleed, vomit, spill brains or lose parts of their anatomy as well as move their foam-rubber faces.

Popular and classical dance

Since its advent in the late 1970s, the social dance known as *jaipongan* has been all the rage in Sunda. A direct descendant of *ketuk tilu,* a street entertainment formerly associated with prostitution, *jaipongan* is now sufficiently respectable to be performed at *hajat* and before tourists.

KAL MULLER

Its movements owe much to the indigenous martial art *penca silat*. Members of the audience are invited to join the dancers. Unlike *ketuk tilu*, it is accompanied by a complete *gamelan salendro*. This is drowned out by a singer and a loud, flamboyant drummer synchronizing the dance movements.

As opposed to these popular forms, classical Sundanese dance is known as *ibing keurseus* (literally "tutored dance"—reflecting the formal way it was taught to members of the upper classes). It is closely related to Central Javanese and Cirebon styles. *Tari wayang* depicts brief episodes from the *wayang* stories. The masked dance, *tari topeng*, derives from the Cirebon tradition.

Some *topeng* dances mimic the movement of *wayang golek*, with hands held at a stiff angle, and chest heaving like a *golek* puppet expressing anger. So-called *kreasi baru* ("new creations") are recent inventions which usually employ the traditional movements. They often depict animals and the like—for example, the *kupu-kupu* or "butterfly" dance and the *merak* or "peacock" dance.

— *Simon Cook*

Opposite: *A roving* ketuk tilu *troupe at the turn of the century.* **Above:** Angklung *instruments made of bamboo that resonate gently when shaken.*

THE PARAHYANGAN

Exploring the Lofty 'Abode of the Gods'

The highlands around Bandung are collectively known as the Priangan or Parahyangan (from *para*="many" and *hyang*="gods"), which roughly translates as "Abode of the Gods." This is the sacred Sundanese homeland—a tangled and once-isolated series of peaks and valleys stretching from Bogor in the west to Ciamis in the east.

Thousands of years ago a cataclysmic eruption of Mt. Tangkuban Perahu dammed the Citarum River, forming a vast lake measuring 50 km (30 mi) east to west and 30 km (20 mi) north to south. What is now Bandung's central square then lay under 30 meters (100 ft) of water. Two millennia later, an earthquake opened a crack in the side of the valley and allowed the lake to slowly drain, leaving behind fertile alluvial deposits and swampy ponds that have since been filled in. Ringing the valley is an array of dramatic volcanoes, many of them sputtering and bubbling with sulpherous hot springs, solfataras and fumaroles, and for most people the highlight of a visit to this region is an encounter with the primordial chthonic forces embodied in these mountains.

A 'drive-in' volcano

The old Dutch resort town of **Lembang**, 16 km (10 mi) north of Bandung, is the first stop on a trip up to the crater of Tangkuban Perahu ("Up-turned Boat") volcano that dominates the northern side of Bandung basin. Lembang lies at the foot of the volcano in the midst of a lush market garden area famous for its fruits, vegetables, flowers and dairy products. Fresh strawberries, zucchini, cabbage, avocadoes, corn and other produce are for sale in the market.

On the way into town, you pass the Grand Hotel—opened in 1926 and once the premier hostelry in these parts, with tennis courts, a large swimming pool, and spacious suites set around a central garden. With a climate even cooler than that of Bandung (elevation here is 1,400 m/4,550 ft), this was a favorite holiday spot for colonial city dwellers.

From Lembang, the road skirts the eastern flanks of the volcano past a turn-off to Maribaya (see below), passing through verdant tea plantations. After about 9 km (5.5 mi) you reach a gate marking the entrance to **Tangkuban Perahu Nature Reserve**, and a

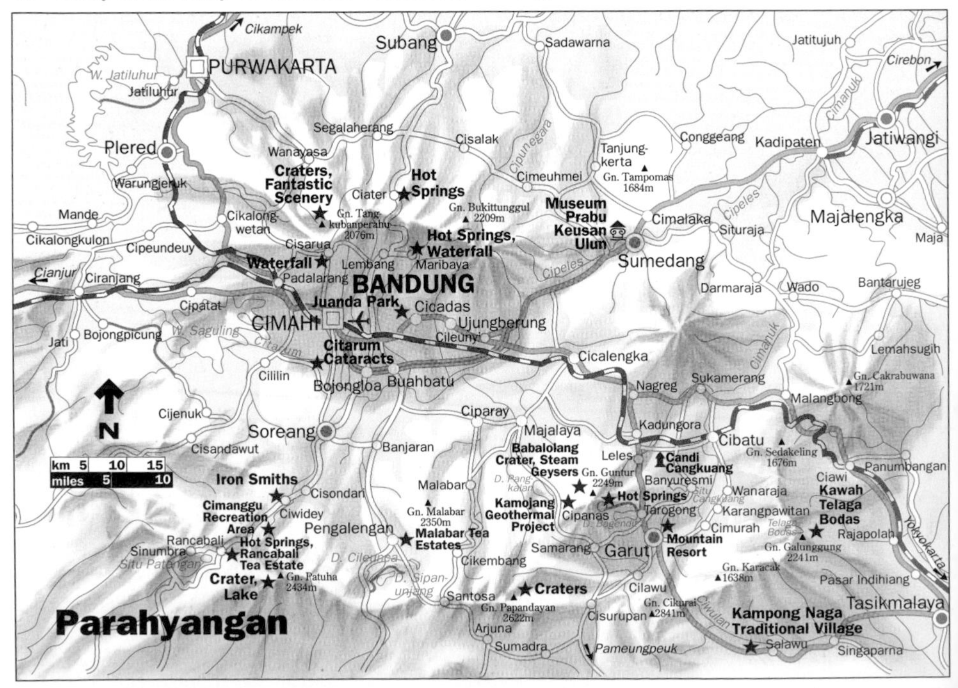

ERIC OEY

narrow but well-surfaced road winds 4 km (2.5 mi) right up to the crater's edge. This "drive-in" volcano is now a popular tourist spot—there are souvenir stands, restaurants and guides offering their services. In spite of all the hype, it is quite spectacular. There is a whole series of craters to walk around and even down into, where sulphurous steam gurgles out of muddy fissures in the earth. When the mountain mists roll in, as they generally do in the late morning or early afternoon, the entire area, with its jagged, brown-black ridges and stunted shrubbery, takes on an eerie, other-worldly atmosphere. Another way to explore this area (dry season only) is to hike up from the end of Jl. Jayagiri in Lembang—a distance of about 8 km (5 mi).

Seven km (4.2 mi) north, along the main road at **Ciater**, is a delightful spa fed by hot water from the springs that pour out of Tangkuban Perahu. Here there is good restaurant, several bungalows and two sizeable pools for soaking: one hot, the other hotter.

At **Maribaya**, 5 km (3 mi) east of Lembang, is a small park and landscaped garden built around a waterfall and hot spring. Bandungers descend here in hordes on weekends, effectively bringing the city to the country. The park has nature trails and restaurants—none of them very inspiring, but from here you can begin a superb 6-km (3.5 mi) walk down to the Dago Teahouse in Bandung. Start from the bigger waterfall at the back of the park and follow the Cikapundung River downstream. This trek takes you across two bridges and passes by the Goa Pakar caves, which were tunneled into the cliffs by Japanese soldiers during WW II. The hike takes a couple of hours, and is best accomplished in the late afternoon.

From Lembang, you can also take local minibuses to **Curug Cimahi**—a grotto waterfall with a lovely pool at the bottom of a deep gorge. Bring food and drink along for a relaxing tropical idyll.

Southwest of Bandung

The neighborhoods immediately to the west of the central market in **Ciwidey**, a small town 14 km (8.5 mi) southwest of Bandung, are home to the last community of ironsmiths (*pande*) in West Java. The smiths no longer smelt their own ore, but instead transform old car springs into useful implements such as knives, hoes and machetes, etc. Local carvers make handles and scabbards from wood and bone. The fancier products are sold in houses and small shops along the main village road.

Follow the Ciwidey River up the valley and into a forest reserve. At the top of the pass near the 42 km (25 mi) marker is **Cimanggu**, a small recreation area with water that is

Above: *The crater of Mt. Tangkuban Perahu lies in the midst of an area of great volcanic activity.*

piped down from nearby Mt. Patuha (2,434 m/9,130 ft) to two public soaking pools and a few private ones.

The road continues on from here into the Rancabali Tea Estate. In the midst of rolling hills blanketed with tea shrubs lies scenic **Situ Patengan**, a small lake that is reputedly the home of a local version of the Loch Ness monster. This area is excellent for picnics or short hikes (except on Sundays, when it is extremely crowded) and there is an incongruous old buddha carved into a cliff below a lakeside guest house.

Heading back toward Bandung, on the road between Soreang and Cimahi, stop at a cluster of brick factories by the side of the highway. From here you can walk down to

KAL MULLER

the **Citarum cataracts**, which is the largest waterfall by volume on Java. Villagers will point the way down to what they call "Curug Jompong." Not high, but thunderous and rough, it looks like the falls that Bogart and Hepburn went over in *The African Queen*.

Other excursions in this area include visits to the well-manicured Malabar Tea Estates around **Pengalengan**—where an endless sea of rolling, green hills spreads across the horizon—and to two nearby highland lakes, Cileunca and Sipanunjang. Pengalengan is reached from Bandung via the town of Banjaran along a good road which winds up and around Mt. Malabar (2,350 m/8,800 ft). From here you may also continue on to Mt. Papandayan (see below) via Santosa.

Historic Sumedang

The highway east of Bandung to Cirebon follows the route of the "Great Post Road" (Grote Postweg) built between 1808-1810 by order of "Iron Marshal" Willem Daendels. It winds down a narrow valley through a range of mountains drained by the Cipeles and Cimanuk Rivers which flow north and east to the Java Sea.

The upper stretch of this picturesque road was carved into the walls of a steep cliff at the cost of many lives. Workers hacking and hewing at the rock face fell sick of malaria and died. Defiantly, the prince of Sumedang, Kusumah Adinata, ordered his people to lay down their tools, forcing Daendels to call in Dutch troops to finish the job. To this day the area is known as Cadas Pangeran ("Prince's Gorge") and a commemorative marker here advertises the spot of the prince's confrontation with the Dutch.

The highway then descends into the small mountain village of Sumedang, 40 km (24 mi) east of Bandung. This delightful town lies flush against the encircling hillsides in a natural fortress that was the last capital of a powerful kingdom which reigned in West Java for a thousand years.

The Cipeles Valley was long an important Sundanese political center, lying on a major access route between the highlands and the coast. At the end of the 15th century, the Hindu kingdom of Sumedang-Larang was allied to Galuh (near present-day Ciamis). Under pressure from the newly Islamized sultanate of Cirebon, Galuh moved its capital to Pakuan (now Bogor) and established a state known as Pajajaran, ruled by the Siliwangi dynasty of kings. This, the last Hindu state in West Java, held dominion over all of the coast and the interior except for the coastal areas around Banten and Cirebon.

In 1578, Muslim raiders from Banten invaded Pajajaran and made off with the stone seat upon which its kings had been enthroned. Pakuan's nobles rescued the crown, however, and offered it and the other regalia to Prabu Geusan Ulun at Sumedang-Larang. Much to Banten's dismay, Geusan Ulun gathered the refugees of Pakuan under his wing and declared himself ruler of Pajajaran's former domain.

Geusan Ulun was the last fully-independent ruler in the Parahyangan; his successor pledged obeisance in 1620 to Sultan Agung, the powerful king of Mataram in central Java. Convoluted rivalries and treacheries among the rulers eventually led to an increase of Dutch influence in the area, and in 1706 the VOC effectively took control of West Java and began supervising the succession of rulers at Sumedang.

The glories of the Parahyangan's last kingdom are on display in the former residence of Sumedang's *bupati*, now housing the **Museum Prabu Geusan Ulun**. Consisting of five buildings on the south side of the town square, this is one of the finest museums in Java. The main building, Srimanganti, was built as a living quarters and audience hall in 1706. It houses the museum's offices and a library of over 3,000 volumes. The display here includes furniture, silverware, ceremonial garb, incunabula in various scripts and languages, royal umbrellas and other objects which once belonged to the household of the *bupati* and his family.

The neighboring building, known as Bumi Kaler, was built in 1850 during the reign of Pangeran Sugih, who was equally famed for his wealth and his generosity. A large part of the museum's collection dates from his era. Another structure, Gendeng, was built in 1950 to house the museum's incomparable arsenal of traditional Sundanese weaponry.

The museum's greatest treasures, however—the original gold crown and jewelry of Pajajaran's rulers, brought from Pakuan to Sumedang in 1578—are safely locked away in a tiny room in this building. Alongside these priceless Siliwangi relics are several *keris* with gold and diamond inlaid sheaths dating from the founding of Sumedang-Larang and the time of Geusan Ulun.

In 1973, former Jakarta mayor Ali Sadikin donated a small building to house the museum's collection of gamelan and to train dancers. And a royal rice storage barn on the grounds still performs its traditional function of distributing food to the needy. The museum is open to the public only on Sundays, but foreign visitors will be admitted on any morning except Friday. The special collection of jewelry and weaponry is exhibited only on Maulud, but the museum will try to accommodate those who send a written request at least one week in advance.

Mountain resort of Garut

Garut is a small town which lies 60 km (48 mi) to the southeast of Bandung, near the headwaters of the Cimanuk River. It is situated at the same elevation as Bandung, and is encircled by five perfectly-formed volcanoes. Agriculture is the major industry here—the area is famous for its citrus, tobacco, apple and tea crops.

This was one of the first areas in Java to be developed as a tourist destination, being touted in the 1920s as the "foremost mountain resort in Java." In the past few years Garut has attempted to regain this former status, and there is indeed plenty to see here. The ideal place to base oneself is **Cipanas**—a hot springs resort town located 6 km (3.5 mi) to the north of Garut in the foothills of Mt. Guntur. Because of the proximity of the springs, every hotel room in this town is equipped with a sunken pool with piped-in hot water The 2-km road up to Cipanas from Tarogong passes through terraced fish farms lined with coconut groves. Just above the

BEST

town, you can see a black lava flow on Mt. Guntur's flanks, which dates from an 1843 eruption.

Ten km (6 mi) north of Tarogong on the road toward Bandung, stop at Leles and walk or ride in a horse carriage the short distance to **Situ Cangkuang**, a shallow lake covered with water lilies. Located on what used to be an island in the lake is Candi Cangkuang, the only Hindu shrine in West Java, its Siva statue facing east toward the sunrise. It is thought that the temple may have been built by the early Sundanese kingdom of Galuh,

Opposite: *Steam rises from volcanic hot springs at Ciater.* **Above:** *Candi Cangkuang, the only Hindu-period stone monument in West Java.*

JILL GOCHER

though its exact date is uncertain.

Directly behind the shrine is the grave of Mbah Dalem Arif Muhammad, a 17th-century soldier of Mataram who raised six daughters and one son on the island. Arif's descendants are governed by a series of unusual traditions. The village may have only six houses (none with a square roof) and one prayer room. Only one household head may occupy each house, and daughters receive priority. No four-footed livestock are permitted, and visitors are banned on Wednesdays. Arif's descendents are not permitted to strike large gongs, only drums. A museum, open sporadically, displays early leather Korans from this unique hamlet.

The 'golden crater'

Garut is truly a trekker's paradise. From Cipanas itself, you can hike across to the Curug Citiis waterfall, then up to Babalolang crater at Guntur's summit, where spectacular steam geysers shoot up into the air. This trip lasts from dawn till dusk and requires a guide, food and water.

There is an almost endless number of other excursions. Kawah Telaga Bodas, a pale-green, sulphurous lake up on Mt. Galunggung, sits 24 km (14 mi) east of Garut via Wanaraja. To the northwest via Samarang, it is 23 km to Kawah Kamojang's geothermally driven power plant, surrounded by bubbling mud pools and screaming fumaroles. Inactive Mt. Cikurai, the tallest peak around Garut, is a perfectly symmetrical cone standing 2841 m (10,700 ft) high.

The area's star attraction, however, is undoubtedly the Golden Crater (Kawah Mas) of **Mt. Papandayan**, so named because of its bright-yellow sulphur deposits. Spectacularly active and exceptionally dangerous, the volcano's name appropriately means "forge" in Sundanese. It lies 36 km (23 mi) southwest of Garut, and is reached via a scenic road that winds up and around the volcano through the villages of Cisurupan, Sumadra and Arjuna (also reachable from Pengalengan via Santosa). A stroll amidst the misty, hissing mud pools of Papandayan is an unforgettable experience, but be careful: scalding mud and poisonous gases are a very real hazard here.

For a change of pace, head for the remote southern coast at Pameungpeuk. Buses from Garut make the slow, twisting 70-km (42-mi) run daily to the area, which offers pristine beaches and passable accommodations.

Leuweung Sancang Nature Reserve, home of unique flora as well as *banteng*, gibbons and crocodiles, is 40 km (24mi) east of Pameungpeuk. To visit, you must first get a PHPA permit in Bogor (Jl. Juanda 9, next to the Botanic Gardens).

— *Roggie Cale*

Above: *Sulphur deposits inside the "golden crater" of Mt. Papandayan.* **Right:** *Kampung Naga.*

BANDUNG TO YOGYA

Via the Scenic South Coast Route

Traveling between West and Central Java, one has to make the difficult choice between a northern and a southern route. The southern route is more direct and also more scenic—it passes through the eastern Parahyangan highlands and allows for a relaxing detour to the south coast beach resort and nature reserve at Pangandaran. But the north coast also has a great deal to offer in terms of historical sights and traditional textile crafts (see "Part VII: The North Coast"). Either way, some extra time spent on stopovers is richly rewarded.

Garut to Tasikmalaya

The splendidly scenic highway from Garut east to Tasikmalaya snakes through the mountains along the winding course of the Ciwulan River. Snug against the Ciwulan's banks lies tiny **Kampung Naga**, one of the most beautiful and most traditional villages in West Java. At Neglasari, near Salawu, a path known as Jl. Naga leads down a concrete stairway in the hillside. Turn left and follow the dirt path, staying on the same side of the river. It's about a 15-minute walk each way.

The 400-odd residents of Kampung Naga maintain one of the few villages built according to old Sundanese custom. Each of the 102 houses, as well as the mosque, are built on stilts along an east-west axis, using wood, bamboo and thatch. Terrace walls and walkways are fashioned from river rock, and the houses are laid out in neat rows, as in the traditional villages found in some remote outer island areas of Indonesia.

The people of Kampung Naga preserve many indigenous traditions. One of them is a monthly pilgrimage to the grave of the village founder, Sembah Dalem Singaparna, who lies buried atop a hill to the west. Weapons and heirlooms are ritually cleansed on the 12th of Maulud. Also in this month, the large Pedaran festival is held to honor the village ancestors.

Women hull their rice manually in the *lesung*—a wooden trough set in a small gazebo above the river. There is an elementary school nearby, but further education means moving into town and boarding. A surprising number of village girls become nurses. Window glass was introduced only in the 1960s, and electrification has been forestalled because the thatched roofs are a fire hazard.

JILL GOCHER

Much of the village was rebuilt after fundamentalist Muslims attacked the area in 1956, and a book written in Sanskrit containing an account of Kampung Naga's founding was unfortunately burned.

Tasikmalaya

The district capital of Tasikmalaya lies 121 km (73 mi) southeast of Bandung in the lovely Citanduy River valley. While the town itself is unappealing, it is a major center for various types of handicrafts fashioned from rattan, pandanus, bamboo and other natural materials. These are bent, carved and woven into baskets, floor mats, lampshades, hats, purses, home furnishings, umbrellas and souvenirs. There are a good number of shops in Tasikmalaya itself, but manufacture largely centers around the village of **Rajapolah**, 15 km (9 mi) to the north. The highway there is lined with shops doing both retail and wholesale trade.

A unique style of batik cloth is also produced in Tasik, which uses sprightly geometric designs executed in deep hues of wine red, indigo and mustard yellow. Finer pieces employ more elegant, cursive motifs and softer colors like teal and tangerine. For genuine Tasikmalaya batik go to Pak Ijon's home at Jl. Burujul I/39, a 2-minute walk from the main Simpang Lima intersection (a local landmark). This is strictly home industry for local consumption. Fine pieces must be specially ordered. Another Tasik specialty to look for here is embroidery—on everything from clothing to pillow cases and even batik shirts.

Intrepid trekkers who wish to climb **Mt. Galunggung** can go by city minibus to Pasar Indihiang just to the north of Tasik. Motorcycle riders (*ojek*) will then take you up as far as the village of Sinagar; from there it is a 2-hour walk to the top. Galunggung was a devil's cauldron from 1982-84—its eruption put out so much ash and smoke that it interfered with air traffic on Java.

Court center of Ciamis

Just 17 km (10.5 mi) east of Tasikmalaya lies the historic town of Ciamis, the site of what was once a powerful kingdom. About 12 km (7 mi) to the east is the tiny town of Bojong, which in the Sundanese language means "peninsula." Near here a rectangle of land is bounded on three sides by the confluence of the Citanduy and Cimuntur Rivers. The ancient Sundanese located a kingdom called Galuh at this easily defensible spot. Today it is known as **Karang Kamulyan**.

With a history dating back a thousand years, the area has now been transformed into a park and nature reserve. Wide paths link scattered ruins within 25 hectares (62 acres) covered by jungle and bamboo. Consisting mainly of stone foundations, the remains include a bathing facility, a cockfighting arena, a royal grave site and a mystic stone upon which queens gave birth to future

ALAIN COMPOST/SUARA ALAM

LUCA INVERNIZZI TETTONI

kings. Karang Kamulyan has a haunting "lost city" feel about it that gives a sense of ancient times on the island.

Another old Sundanese kingdom left an impressive mark in the mountains near Ciamis. Head 22 km (13 mi) north to Kawali, then 14 km (8 mi) west to Panjalu. In the 7th century, the residents of Galuh Panjalu flooded a small valley, making an exquisite 42-hectare (100-acre) mountain lake called **Situ Lengkong**. They built their capital on a 7.5 hectare (19-acre) island in the middle, which is now a nature reserve. Only royal graveyards remain, under a dense forest canopy. Rented boats will take you to the island or to go fishing (which is allowed, but you must release your catch).

From Ciamis, you say goodby to the Parahyangan highlands and head off in one of three possible directions. An excellent highway runs north to Cirebon through the small town of Kuningan, a center of traditional and mystical arts. Or you can board a train or bus on its way from Bandung to Yogya and other points in Central Java. Most visitors, however, detour south via Banjar to Pangandaran on Java's southern littoral.

South coast detour

Pangandaran is both a nature reserve and a beach resort—a 530-hectare (1310-acre) teardrop-shaped peninsula tethered to Java's south coast by a slender isthmus. Buses make the 55-km (33 mi) journey here from Banjar, a town on the Bandung-Yogya high way, ending up at the village of Pananjung. You can either walk or hop a *becak* from here to the isthmus (about 2 km), which is lined on both sides with white-sand beaches.

The beach on the eastern side of the isthmus is accessible from the main north-south thoroughfare, Jl. Kidang Pananjung, and is a base for the local fishing industry. There are also excellent accommodations here, and after a swim visitors can huddle in the shade of fishing *perahus* hauled up on the sand. The fish market at the southern end of the beach assures a bountiful supply of fresh, cheap seafood for local restaurants. Fishermen shoulder their catches to be weighed and sold. The marine harvest spread out on the concrete floor is astoundingly varied— rays, sharks, eels, turtles, lobsters, prawns, squid and countless species of fish.

Another main street, Jl. Pantai Barat, runs along the western side of the isthmus along a beach that is said to be the safest on Java's southern shore. A coral reef tempers the Indian Ocean's assaults and provides decent snorkeling, although there are a few well-marked danger spots. At sunset, flocks of fruit bats fly overhead to forage in the village.

Above: *The narrow isthmus connecting Pangandaran to the mainland has beaches on both sides.* **Opposite:** *The eruption of Galunggung in 1982.*

Many hotels and restaurants face this beautiful shoreline or lie tucked along sideroads connecting the two beaches, and Pangandaran has been developing slowly from a somnolent fishing village into a would-be Kuta. Domestic tourists swamp the place on holidays and weekends; at other times it can be rather forlornly deserted. There is a crafts center on the western beach where chartered buses disgorge groups of tourists, primarily from Bandung. In addition to typical Tasikmalaya products, there is a lively trade in souvenirs and jewelry made from seashells and coconuts.

Pananjung village has interesting overlays of Sundanese and Javanese culture. Music, language and arts from both ethnic groups co-mingle behind the *losmen*. After dusk, tourists can sometimes witness Sundanese *jaipongan* and *wayang golek*, or Javanese *wayang kulit* performances.

There is also a popular local performance called *sintren* wherein a young girl is incarcerated under a basket with her hands tied behind her. After 15 minutes she emerges, Houdini-like, dressed as a princess. The independent tourist information centers at Jl. Kidang Pananjung 107 and 203 may be able to provide up-to-date information on the *sintren*.

The villagers also revere Nyai Loro Kidul, the goddess of the south seas. Once a year local fishermen perform a ritual sacrifice to her, here called Hajat Laut.

Pangandaran Nature Reserve

The nature reserve covers the entire peninsula south of the isthmus, and consists of a raised central plateau (100 m/330 ft high) covered with dense secondary forest and teak plantations. Pangandaran owes its preservation to a colony of *banteng* cattle introduced by European hunters in 1921. These animals, close relatives of the domestic Javanese cow, produce a fine set of horns and exceptionally lean meat which is now exported in modest quantities to the discerning markets of Japan and Hongkong.

Some *banteng* are still found on the peninsula; If you get up early in the morning, you may be able to catch them grazing. As soon as the sun begins to get hot, they retreat into the jungle.

The game reserve set up to protect the *banteng* also preserved what is now the real jewel in Pangandaran's crown—the rare Rafflesia lotus. The Rafflesia is a strange parasite growing on jungle vines, which manifests itself as a giant (they can reach up to a meter across) malodorous flower. Sumatra's *Rafflesia arnoldi*—which smells like a five-day-old horse carcass—is the world's largest bloom. Pangandaran's species is smaller, about the size of a dinner plate, and is less offensively scented, but your local guide will still probably use his nose as much as his eyes in finding one for you.

There are two entrances to the reserve from the isthmus—one near the southern end of either beach. Maps are available at the the PPA office by the east beach entrance, where you also pay a small entrance fee to the reserve. Some areas are very remote, though, and it is foolish to tramp the deep jungles on your own. Private tourist offices can arrange a guide for 4- to 6-hour walking tours for around US$8. Ask for an older guide; the young ones are more interested in nightlife than wildlife. Be sure to wear a pair of sturdy shoes.

The peninsula seems much larger than its five square kilometers. Even the "Tourist Park" (Taman Wisata) near the entrance of the reserve, open to all without need for a PHPA permit, has plenty to explore. Limestone cliffs rear up unexpectedly, dotted with narrow, winding caves which lead, like true pirate caves, down to secluded beaches.

Looking for a mate? Try to find the spring called Cirengganis. According to legend, whosoever washes his or her face in the water as it flows from beneath the rock will soon find a partner. In one corner of the park are the remains of an ancient Hindu temple, complete with carved bull, which were left by the ancient rulers of Galuh. In another corner is a concrete bunker built by the Japanese as part of their coastal defenses during the Second World War. There is also a swimming hole at the top of a waterfall that plunges 50 meters (165 ft) over a cliff into the Indian Ocean below.

And everywhere there is wildlife: athletic squirrels, pugnacious grey macaques, patrician crested leaf monkeys, and gossamer-fine black and white butterflies—all this despite the apparently roaring trade in stuffed animals done by the stalls in Pangandaran itself.

West of Pananjung, there are several more isolated beaches. **Karang Tirta** is the closest. **Batu Hiu**, 18 km (11 km) distant, is famous for its spectacular sea cliffs. **Parigi** and **Batu Karas** are near Cijulang. These spots can be reached by local transport, or by rented bicycle or motorcycle.

A cruise on Java's 'Inland Sea'

When leaving Pangandaran, you can backtrack by local bus to Banjar to connect with eastbound buses and trains to Yogya. Or you can take the most enjoyable journey anywhere in Java—the ferry ride through Segara Anakan, the "inland sea" or strait separating Java from Nusa Kambangan Island. Take a local bus 15 km (9 mi) from Pananjung to Kalipucang and walk 5 minutes to the ferry dock. Here you board a 20-meter market boat bound for Cilacap, a 4-hour voyage. Boats leave in both directions at 7 and 8 am, and at 12 noon and 1 pm.

From Kalipucang, the ferry floats down the Citanduy River, then enters the Segara Anakan, skirting the north coast of Nusa Kambangan Island. Along the way, it stops at several riverbank landings and small villages to transfer passengers and cargo. This is a quiet world of mangrove swamps, dugout canoes, water birds and indecipherable river traffic signs.

Nusa Kambangan is a vast nature reserve with large stretches of virgin forest. Formerly a part of the Galuh kingdom, the island holds a number of historical remains. With PHPA approval, a few places in both Pangandaran and Cilacap now organize day trips to this wild island. At its eastern end you see the Bui Besi maximum security prison (Java's Alcatraz). The boat then turns north toward the Pertamina oil refinery and docks at Sleko. From here you can take a *becak* or a *bemo* to the Cilacap bus station, and thence on to Yogya (or to Dieng via Wonosobo).

— *Roggie Cale and Robert Cribb*

LUCA INVERNIZZI TETTONI

Above left: *A playful group of young bikers from Bandung, in Pangandaran for the holidays.*
Right: *The tiny, tear-drop shaped Pangandaran peninsula, now a scenic nature reserve.*

PART IV

Introducing Yogyakarta

Lying at the epicenter of a fertile crescent of ricelands that is overshadowed to the north by smouldering Mt. Merapi and bordered to the south by the churning Indian Ocean, the graceful old city of Yogyakarta or "Yogya" (pronounced JOG-ja) is, with Solo, one of only two traditional court centers remaining in Java's ancient hinterland.

Yogya is one of the most productive traditional agricultural areas on earth, with a rural population density that is among the world's highest. The province's 3.2 million people inhabit just 3,169 sq km, for an average density of over 1000 persons per sq km (2500 per sq mile). This is particularly striking since the great majority of buildings are single-story structures and most people live in small village hamlets scattered about the countryside, making a living from subsistence agriculture. In fact, fewer than 400,000 people inhabit the city itself.

Of ancient courts and kings

The Yogya area, traditionally known as Mataram, has been continuously settled for at least two millennia. The earliest-known kingdom is mentioned on a stone *linggam* dating from A.D. 732 and discovered at Canggal, just north of present-day Yogya. It describes a just and peaceful Sivaite king, Sanjaya, whose descendants ruled the area up until the early 10th century A.D.

A Mahayana Buddhist dynasty known as the Sailendra or Kings of the Mountain at this time also occupied the same region, and between them these families left a series of inspiring statements in stone—including the world-renowned monuments of Borobudur and Prambanan.

The Mataram region revived politically at the end of the 16th century with the establishment of a new and powerful Islamic kingdom. The son of a Majapahit prince from east Java, Panembahan Senopati, founded a simple settlement at Kota Gede in 1575 which attracted merchants and artisans, and soon flourished as a center for trade. In 1598, Senopati built a bathing pool, Umbul Pacethokan, over a large spring southwest of the village of Beringan—site of Yogya today.

The capital was moved south to Kerta in 1614 by Senopati's grandson, Sultan Agung. Agung was Mataram's greatest ruler, extending the domain to include most of central and east Java during his long reign (ca. 1613-46). Following his death, the capital was moved again several times to the east, first to Plered then to Kartasura.

Sultan Agung's grandson, Amangkurat II, began the construction of a retreat near Beringan but died before it was completed. His brother, who later became Pakubuwono I, finished it and changed the name to Ngayogya—a Javanized form of Ayodya, the idyllic kingdom of Prince Rama in the *Ramayana*. The present name, Ngayogyakarta Hadiningrat, embraces the associations with the Indian heroic epic and the expectations of peace (*karta*) and prosperity (*gya*).

A long and convoluted series of rebellions and wars of succession in the middle of the 18th century culminated in a Dutch-negotiated settlement between Pakubuwono III and his rebellious uncle, Prince Mangkubumi. This nine-year conflict ended with the unprecedented division of the kingdom into two separate but equal domains ruled by rival courts. Mangkubumi was granted half of the realm and assumed the title of Sultan Hamengkubuwono I, establishing himself in a new capital at Yogyakarta.

Founding a new capital

Hamengkubuwono I was an extraordinarily dynamic and creative leader. He selected the site for his new palace carefully, choosing a

Overleaf: *Mt. Merapi, Java's most active volcano.*
Opposite: *A talented court dancer from Yogya's* keraton. *Both photos by Kal Muller.*

spot at the southern foot of Merapi that was rich in historical associations—close by the ancient Mataram monuments as well as the earlier courts of Senopati and Sultan Agung.

The *keraton* he built at Yogya symbolically represented the hub of his new kingdom. The southern approach to the palace was planted with fruit and flowering trees that suggested the growth of a human embryo from conception to birth, while the processional leading north from the *keraton* (now Jalan Malioboro) was planned as a ritual path to clear one's thoughts in preparation for union with the Creator—symbolized by the Tugu monument at the northern end.

Besides being a master builder, Hamengkubuwono I was a successful military strategist and a decisive leader. His death in 1792 ushered in another turbulent period, as conflicts between his sons and grandsons erupted into disputes involving the Dutch and English colonial powers. In an attempt to introduce a stabilizing element into the local scene, the English granted one of Hamengkubuwono II's half-brothers, Prince Notokusumo, an independent principality and the title of Sri Paduka Paku Alam I in 1813.

Court intrigues and rebellions did not subside, however, and land disputes became increasingly volatile—culminating in the devastating Java War of 1825-30. A religiously-inspired and economically-fired rebellion led by charismatic Prince Diponegoro of the Yogya royal house spread quickly throughout central Java. The rebellion resulted in about 15,000 military casualties, but it is estimated that as many as 200,000 others died from famine and disease—as much as 10 percent of the central Java's population at this time.

In 1830, the war-weary Diponegoro was tricked, captured and sent into exile, and from this time onward the court's attention became inwardly-focused on the arts, on ritual displays of status, and on managing the huge inputs of labor required to work the Dutch sugar estates. The population in rural villages, meanwhile, soared about eight-fold during the 19th century, transforming entirely the ecology of the region.

In the early 1900s, Yogya was the scene of several important social movements. In 1908, a group of young, Dutch-educated idealists founded the Boedi Oetomo group. Four years later, K.H.A. Dahlan founded the Muhammadiyah organization, devoted to promoting modern Islamic education and health services. In 1922, Ki Ajar Dewantara founded the Taman Siswa schools in Yogya, and the First Indonesian Women's Congress, with representatives from 30 member groups, was held here in 1928.

Revolutionary fervor

The coronation in 1940 of 27-year-old Sultan Hamengkubuwono IX was a significant event-not only for Yogya but for all of Indonesia.

Educated at Leiden in Holland but deeply conscious of his Javanese heritage, the young sultan was a reformer who provided crucial support for the independence movement during the darkest days of the revolution.

Shortly after the proclamation of independence on August 17, 1945, Hamengkubuwono IX and Pakualam VIII declared their support for the new republic. In early 1946, the capital was secretly shifted from Jakarta to Yogya, and the sultan's personal treasury was used to help support the new government. The Dutch did not dare depose the sultan, and their attempts to recruit him to their side by offers to set him up as the head of a new pan-Javanese state were rejected during a six-month Dutch occupation in 1949. Throughout this time, the sultan kept in personal contact with republican guerilla forces based in the outlying villages.

In recognition of the sultan's invaluable support during the revolution, his domain was granted special provincial status, becoming known the Special Region of Yogyakarta (Daerah Istimewa Yogyakarta), in which he, as governor, and the Pakualam VIII, as vice governor, serve life-time terms and report directly to the central government (and not to the governor of Central Java).

City of education and culture

Yogya is today a city of great diversity. Proud of its Javanese cultural heritage, it has attracted large numbers of painters, dancers and writers, both Indonesian and foreign, and the arts flourish here. As the city where the Taman Siswa and the Islamic Muhammadiyah schools were founded, Yogya is now also a city of students. The city is home to more than 40 academies and university-level institutions, including Gajah Mada University, which was founded during the revolution and is now one of the largest and most prestigious universities in the nation.

Founded in a spirit of rebellion more than two centuries ago, Yogya is simultaneously a traditional Javanese city and a stronghold of youthful and innovative thinking. Here the graceful serenity of the *keraton* lies just steps away from a batik painters' market where outlandish new creations are on display. Computer shops line the city streets, and satellite dishes bristle skyward from homes in the fashionable residential suburbs. An independence day celebration in Yogya may begin with a classical *golek* dance, followed up by groups of teenage disco dancers. Everything, from the ancient to the modern, is accepted easily and naturally, and is quickly assimilated into the rich and complex fabric of Yogyakarta's heterogeneous heritage.

— Joan Suyenaga

Opposite: *A tiger "fight" in Yogya's main square.* **Below:** *Sultan Hamengkubuwono VIII with the Dutch Resident of Yogya.*

THE HAMENGKUBUWONOS

Yogya's Popular Line of Sultans

Unlike many former Indonesian rulers who have retreated to their palaces or plunged into the world of commerce and industry, the Hamengkubuwono ruling family of Yogya has managed to forge a new and dynamic role for itself in modern Indonesia—a role based on public service and a deep concern for the commonweal. In the process, they have not only retained the great respect and loyalty historically accorded them by their own Yogyanese subjects, but have also developed a nationwide following. Much of this is due to the unusual energy and talent of the late Hamengkubuwono IX (r. 1940-1989).

From its founding in 1755, Yogya's rulers have been quick to adapt to new situations. Hamengkubuwono I (r. 1755-92) was a dynamic military commander who fought the Dutch and his own ruling family to a standstill through nine years of war, then negotiated to receive half of the Mataram kingdom with Dutch blessings as the price of a peace settlement. As an innovative city planner and builder throughout the remaining 37 years of his reign, he carefully selected a site for his new kingdom and then constructed not only an elegant palace, but a unique pleasure garden surrounded by a vast, artificial lake (Taman Sari). Both complexes are imbued with a symbolism and a powerful aura which the centuries have not obscured.

MUNSYI AHMAD

Following Hamengkubuwono I's death, the throne fell to one of his sons, an intelligent but arrogant ruler whose reign was marred by intrigues. Hamengkubuwono II had the unique misfortune of being deposed three times (once by the Dutch and twice by the British), and exiled twice—once to Penang and once to Ambon—only to be restored to the throne each time. He was also an extremely prolific father; his two queens and 31 concubines bore him 80 children.

Hamengkubuwono III inherited neither his grandfather's great authority, nor his father's arrogance, and during his tenure an unfavorable agreement with the British under Raffles led to unrest among the Yogya nobility. The ascendency to the throne of his 13-year-old son, Hamengkubuwono IV, in 1814 brought on a flurry of court intrigues, and poisoning was the suspected cause of the young ruler's untimely death in 1822.

A three-year-old son succeeded him under the tutelage of a Dutch-appointed committee, which included one of the young Sultan's uncles, Prince Diponegoro. Land disputes and religious zeal led Diponegoro into a bloody 5-year rebellion against the Dutch and his own family between 1825-1830.

Thereafter, Yogya lived in peace under the reign of four successive sultans, all of whom became wealthy patrons of the arts. Like most of Asia's traditional rulers at this time, the sultans hob-nobbed with foreign dignitaries and styled themselves after the manner of European royalty.

A "Golden Age" of courtly dance and drama was ushered in by Hamengkubuwono VIII during the 1920s and 1930s. Much of the sizeable court income from sugar estates was lavished upon massive performances lasting many days and featuring casts of hundreds, but a part of it was also devoted to providing a Western education for his children.

Left and right: *Yogyakarta's newest sultan, Hamengkubuwono X, on his coronation day (March 7, 1989).*

The young Prince Dorodjatun, who was to become the next sultan, was sent to live with Dutch families from the age of four, and attended Dutch schools in Yogya, Semarang and Bandung. Upon graduation, he was sent to Holland where, after nine years of study, he reached the final stage of his doctoral studies at Leiden University.

Because of the unstable situation in Europe and his father's failing health, Dorodjatun was called back to Yogya in 1939. On arriving in Batavia, he was informed of the Sultan's intentions to name him as crown prince. The Sultan's health took a turn for the worse on the trip home, however, and it is said that when they alit from the train a thunderbolt suddenly struck the city from clear, blue skies—an ominous note in the eyes of the Javanese. Hamengkubuwono VIII died the following day.

Fluent in Dutch and conversant in Western political and economic matters, the young sultan-to-be prudently negotiated the terms of his rule with the colonial government for six months before agreeing to ascend the throne. In his coronation speech (in Dutch), he proudly declared: "Although I have a Western education, I am first and foremost a Javanese."

Practical and quick to act, Hamengkubuwono IX assumed responsibility for the day-to-day administration of his realm in extremely difficult times. Through three and a half years of wartime occupation (1942-45) he steadfastly refused Japanese requests to send Yogyanese laborers abroad to an almost certain death, insisting that they were needed at home to construct an irrigation canal linking the Progo and Opak Rivers. Frequent visits incognito to the villages, meanwhile, kept him in touch with the peasants and their deteriorating living conditions.

His support of the new Indonesian republic proved crucial to its survival through four long years of revolution, and his strength and quiet integrity helped steer the young nation thereafter through several decades of social upheaval and economic hardship. He held several ministerial posts, even serving a term as Vice President under Suharto, all the while maintaining an active role as Yogya's sultan. Under his rule, palace rituals were simplified but not abolished, and several new dances were added to the palace repertoire.

Five months after his death, on March 7 1989, his eldest son was crowned Hamengkubuwono X amidst much pomp and ceremony. The young sultan has inherited not only his father's throne but also some of his charisma and common sense. Chairman of the local Chamber of Commerce and a member of the national legislature, the new sultan is a popular figure who is very much aware of his dual role as preserver of Yogya's traditional culture and pioneer of the city's future.

—Joan Suyenaga

MUNSYI AHMAD

KERATON CEREMONIES

Royal Pomp and Ritual Offerings

The *keraton* ceremonial cycle has been greatly scaled back in post-independence Indonesia, but many of the elaborate rituals nevertheless continue to be practiced. For the Javanese of today, as in the past, they consitute living proof of the divinity of the Sultan and the influence of his court. All are determined according to the traditional calendar (see "The Javanese Calendar").

Symbols of power

The palace heirlooms (*pusaka*), imbued with a distinctive spirit and power, serve to legitimize the reign of the ruler. They are ritually cleansed with holy water and flower (mostly rose) petals once a year. Three ceremonies are held between 10 am and 12 noon on Tuesday or Friday Kliwon during the month of Suro, the first month of the Javanese calendar. The first ceremony is closed to the public and takes place within the palace, where the Sultan cleans the sacred kris, spears and flags. Next, the royal coaches in the Rotowijayan stables are washed with holy water and flowers. The latter ceremony is open to the public and there is a mad scramble for the water which drips from the coaches, as this and the flower petals are thought to possess mystical powers. Finally, at the royal cemetery at Imogiri, large pitchers containing holy water are emptied, cleaned and filled again. This attracts a crowd as the water from these pitchers is also highly prized.

Sekaten

In pre-Islamic Majapahit, Javanese princes conducted an annual harvest feast called Asmaweddha which lasted for six days. On the seventh day, the princes meditated in state temples and asked for the blessings of the gods for the continued fertility of the soils and prosperity of the realm. This ceremony was later incorporated into celebrations surrounding the birthday of the prophet Muhammad by the Islamic kingdom of Demak, and Sultan Agung (r. 1613-1646) is credited with introducing gamelan performances to the celebrations to attract crowds in the interest of propagating Islam.

The festivities begin a full month before the actual Sekaten week, with a nightly fair featuring local crafts and folk performances held in the city's northern square (*alun-alun*

MUNSYI AHMAD

lor). At 11 pm on the first day of Sekaten week, (the eve of Mulud 6), the two sacred Sekaten gamelan are carried with great ceremony from the palace and placed in raised pavilions in the courtyard of the royal mosque bordering the square. Each set has a name. Kyai Gunturmadu, said to have originated with the Demak empire (late 15th century) and obtained from the Solo *keraton* after the partitioning of the realm in 1755, is placed in the southern building, while Kyai Nogowilogo, commissioned by Hamengkubuwono I, occupies the northern pavilion.

MUNSYI AHMAD

The gamelans are played alternately from morning to evening (except Thursday afternoon through Friday morning) for the next six days. The music begins solemnly as enormous buffalo-horn beaters crash on ancient bronze keys, imperceptibly building to a furious climax before fading to a single gong beat. Villagers gather in droves to listen to the music, which is regarded as spiritually powerful. At midnight on the eve of Mulud 12, the instruments are carried back to the palace and thousands of spectators fill the square to witness this late night procession.

Grebeg Mulud

The Sekaten festival culminates with the Grebeg Mulud procession—in which food offerings in the shape of mountains symbolizing male and female fertility are brought from the *keraton* to the mosque. Two days before Grebeg, a simple ceremony is held in the south Kemagangan courtyard to begin preparation of food used in the offerings. The ceremony, Tumplak Wajik, begins at 4 pm and takes its name from the snacks made from glutinous rice (*wajik*) which are used in the construction of the mountains. Rhythms pounded out on large rice pounders (*lesung*) create charming melodies.

At sunrise on Mulud 12, the faithful congregate in fields throughout the city for morning prayers. The Grebeg procession begins at 8 am when ten palace guard units, each outfitted in special, brightly colored garb (striped black-and-white jackets or red coats; Napoleonic or stove-pipe hats worn over traditional Javanese headdresses with leather earrings), march out of the palace armed with lances, bows, arrows, swords and rifles, bearing flags and playing their own fife-and-drum music. They pass through the Siti Hinggil and Pagelaran onto the north square, then turn west at the two sacred banyan trees to enter the royal mosque.

MUNSYI AHMAD

Behind them are the *gunungan*—mounds of rice cakes, green beans, chili peppers, peanuts and eggs. Once every eight years a special smoking mountain is also presented. At the mosque, the offerings are blessed with Islamic prayers and then eagerly dismantled by spectators who scramble for bits and pieces of the food, which are regarded as sacred amulets capable of warding off disaster and illness.

For a good view of the processional, enter the Pagelaran area at the northern end of the *keraton* (tickets are available at the Pracimasono office) or wait at the Kemandungan (Keben) courtyard, which is not as crowded as the north square.

On the night of Mulud 12, an all-night *wayang kulit* performance is held in the south Kemagangan courtyard or at the Pagelaran. This is called Bedol Songsong ("to extract the umbrella"), referring to the act of retracting the symbol of royal presence (the umbrella)—signaling that something has

Opposite: *Kyai Garudoyekso, a carriage produced in Holland in 1861 for Hamengkubuwono VI and used only in the coronation procession. A number of old royal carriages of European manufacture may be seen in the* keraton's *Rotowijayan stables.*
Above, left: *Court regalia carried in procession.*
Above, right: *Because of their appearance, dwarves and albinos are believed to have special powers, thus they form part of the royal retinue.*

come to an end. This performance is open to the public.

Ramadan

The end of the Ramadan fasting month (*poso*) is celebrated on a much larger scale in Indonesia than in other Islamic countries. It is a joyous occasion when families gather, neighbors visit and everyone asks for mutual forgivenesses for wrongs and slights of the past year. On the evening before Syawal 1, children carrying torches and paper lanterns parade from their neighborhood mosques to nearby fields. At sunrise, there is a massive prayer gathering in the fields, and the Grebeg Poso (similar to the Grebeg Mulud above) procession takes place that morning. A Bedol Songsong *wayang kulit* performance is then held in the evening at the south Kemagangan courtyard.

Day of ritual sacrifice

A holy day known as Idul Adha or Idul Korban commemorates Abraham's profession of faith and willingness to sacrifice his son to God. Goats, sheep and cattle donated by devout Muslims are ceremonially sacrificed at neighborhood mosques and the meat is distributed to the needy. A children's torch parade is conducted on the eve of Besar 10, and the Grebeg Besar procession from the palace to the mosque is held in the morning.

Honoring the protective spirits

On the anniversary of the sultan's coronation according to the Javanese calendar, offerings of food, clothing, holy water and flower petals together with clippings of the sultan's nails and hair are delivered to the protective spirits of the kingdom in their abodes— Ratu Kidul at Parangkusumo on the south coast, and the spirits of Mt. Merapi and Mt. Lawu in their craters. Once every eight years, offerings are also brought to a spot near the river at Dlepih, Wonogiri, where Panembahan Senopati is said to have received a divine message that he and his descendents would rule Java.

The offerings leave the *keraton* at 8 am. The most accessible of these ceremonies is the one at Parangkusumo beach, just next to Parangtritis and only a short distance south of Yogya, where part of the offerings (the nail and hair clippings and flower petals) are buried in an enclosed area on the beach. It is said that Panembahan Senopati emerged from Kangjeng Ratu Kidul's underwater palace here after spending three days and three nights with her in matrimonial bliss.

The other offerings are tied to bamboo rafts, weighted down with stones and released into the sea by court retainers. These are immediately snatched up by eager hands, to be used as sacred amulets.

—*Joan Suyenaga*

RATU KIDUL

Goddess of the Southern Seas

High cliffs along the southern coast of Java plunge dramatically into the Indian Ocean, where a raging surf and violent currents give evidence of awesome natural forces at work. This is believed to be the realm of the powerful queen of the spirits, Kangjeng Ratu Kidul—who serves as wife and patroness to Java's Mataram rulers.

As told in the 19th century *Babad Tanah Jawi* chronicle, an orphaned prince of the Pajajaran kingdom, Raden Joko Suruh, met a hermit who instructed him to found the powerful Majapahit kingdom in east Java. Joko Suruh realized that the hermit was actually a beautiful young woman and fell in love with her, but his advances were refused, as unbeknownst to him she was in fact his great aunt, Ratna Suwida, who had retreated to meditate in the hills when she was still young. She would soon go to the south coast of Java and become ruler of the spirits, she told the prince, and when Joko Suruh's descendents established a kingdom near Mt. Merapi by the southern coast, she would marry each of the rulers in turn.

Generations later, Panembahan Senopati, founder of the second Mataram kingdom, retreated to the southern shore to concentrate his energies in preparation for a military campaign against the north coast kingdoms. His meditations attracted Kangjeng Ratu Kidul and she promised to aid him. For three days and nights he studied the secrets of war and government and the intricacies of love in her underwater palace, finally emerging from the sea at Parangkusumo, south of present-day Yogya. Since then, Ratu Kidul has reportedly been in communion with all of Senopati's ruling descendents, and offerings are brought to her at this spot each year by representatives of both the Solo and Yogya palaces (see "Keraton Ceremonies").

The founder of Yogya's ruling house, Hamengkubuwono I, constructed an intricate fortress and pleasure garden complex consisting of sunken pools and underwater passageways surrounded by a vast, man-made lake which is supposed to replicate Ratu Kidul's watery realm. A unique sunken chamber known as the *sumur gumuling* ("circular well"), located in the Taman Sari complex, is believed to be the place where the Sultan annually renewed his contact with the goddess—in a replica of her underwater palace.

The most sacred dance in the Surakarta palace, the Bedoyo Ketawang, is performed once a year on the anniversary of the ruler's coronation. Nine dancers in formal Javanese wedding attire invite Ratu Kidul to come and wed the Susuhunan, and it is said that she then magically appears as a shimmering tenth figure on the dance floor. The Yogyanese counterpart of this dance, the Bedoyo Semang, is no longer performed.

Along the south coast near Cilacap where birds' nests are situated precariously on the steep sea cliffs, gatherers restrict their activities to specific months, offering a buffalo head to the queen before proceeding with their tasks. Recently, screenings of a popular movie about Ratu Kidul in Cilacap were cancelled following unseasonal rain and winds which coincided with the movie's showing. In West Java, the luxurious Samudra Beach Hotel at Pelabuhan Ratu ("Queen's Harbor") reserves a room on the top floor for the goddess. Those who wish to meet with her may do so here through an intermediary who presents the requisite offerings.

Although the popular belief is that she is eternally young and beautiful, the late Sultan Hamengkubuwono IX acknowledged that she ages with the moon, and is young only at the beginning of each lunar month. Her favorite color is green, particularly a pale yellow-green known as *gadung melati*. Her ministers, Nyai Roro Kidul and Mbok Roro Kidul often recruit drowning victims as subjects in their underwater kingdom.

Her presence, marked by a sudden gust of wind that slowed to a breeze and left behind a powerful fragrance was felt and noted at the coronation of Sultan Hamengkubuwono X in 1989 not only by members of the royal family but by many others in attendance. It appears that Kangjeng Ratu Kidul has not deserted the Yogyanese royal house.

—*Joan Suyenaga*

Opposite: *Pangeran Senopati, founder of Java's Islamic Mataram dynasty, accompanies Ratu Kidul to her underwater palace. She promises to marry and protect each of his successors in turn.*

THE KERATON

Miniature Model of the Cosmos

The Yogya *keraton* or palace, designed and built in stages between 1756 and 1790 by Yogya's founder, Sultan Hamengkubuwono I, is a splendid example of traditional Javanese court architecture. Conceived not only as the royal residence but as the focal point for the entire kingdom, the *keraton* is carefully constructed to form a model of the Javanese cosmos in miniature. Each gateway, each pavilion, each courtyard, tree and field has a specific symbolic meaning, and it was thought that by structuring the *keraton* in this way, the court and kingdom could be harmonized with the divine forces of the universe—thereby ensuring the ruler's continued success.

Ancient Hindu-Javanese conceptions of the cosmos were based largely on Indian cosmological models, and these continued largely unchanged into later Islamic times. In this scheme of things, the sacred mountain (Mahameru) stood at the very center of the universe as a kind of Mt. Olympus where the gods resided, surrounded by an elaborate series of concentric seas and continents.

In traditional Javanese palaces, the sacred mountain is represented by a spacious central courtyard (the Pelataran Kedaton) containing a spacious pavilion (*pendopo*) that is open on all sides and has a high, peaked *joglo* roof overhead. A storeroom for the royal heirlooms stands behind the pavilion.

To both the north and south of this courtyard, symmetrically arranged, lie a succession of spacious walls and high gateways, smaller courtyards, a raised platform, another large pavilion, and an open field (*alun-alun*) planted with two banyan trees in the center. The gates and elevated buildings in this plan represent continents while the courtyards and fields symbolize the oceans.

It is along this all-important north-south axis that all court ceremonies take place. Processions to celebrate coronations, marriages and other significant events move northward (in the direction of the mountains), while funeral processions pass through the southern gates (seaward, to the abode of the ancestors).

The northern pavilions

Approaching the *keraton* from the town one first encounters a magnificent audience pavilion facing onto the broad and grassy north-

ERIC OEY

ern square (*alun-alun lor*). This is the Pagelaran, where formerly the sultan's ministers and troops assembled. The 64 posts supporting the roof symbolize perfection (8 x 8—the age of the prophet Muhammad when he died). Currently it is used for musical and theatrical performances during the Sekaten festival. (see "Keraton Ceremonies").

To the left and right of the Pagelaran are smaller pavilions where court officials sat during royal audiences. Now they house displays of elaborate clothing worn by princes and princesses on ceremonial occasions.

Behind the pavilions is a flight of steps leading to a platform known as the Siti Hinggil or "Elevated Ground." Royal coronations are held here. A small structure ornamented with gold leaf in the middle of the platform is the site of the sultan's throne, the Bangsal Manguntur Tangkil. Within this pavilion is another building, Bangsal Witono, where the court regalia and royal heirlooms are placed when the sultan holds court.

All of these buildings are open to visitors. The ticket office is in the Pracimasono just west of the Pagelaran—a compound which once served as a dormitory for Dutch troops and now houses the office of the palace guards and a school for *wayang* puppeteers known as Habiranda. (Open daily 8 am to 1 pm, Fri until 11 am. A small admission fee includes a guided tour.)

Entering the palace

To enter the *keraton* proper, walk or drive around the western side until you see a large clock (seldom correct), and pass through a gateway into the shaded outer courtyard known as North Kemandungan or Keben (because of the *keben* trees planted here). Once inside, the heat and clamor of city streets become a cool and welcome hush. The broad courtyard, once carpeted with black sand from the southern shore and now covered with cement, is shaded by spreading trees overhead. A palpable sense of serenity is reinforced by the buildings' elegant lines, painted in muted tones of green and yellow, and by the deliberate, restrained manners of the palace retainers.

In the center of the yard stands a small *pendopo* with a stone throne where the Sultan once sentenced lawbreakers. A small building to the left of the main gateway leading

Overleaf: *An elaborate chronogram decorates this pavilion in the central courtyard.* **Left:** *The main entrance to the Pelataran Kedaton.*

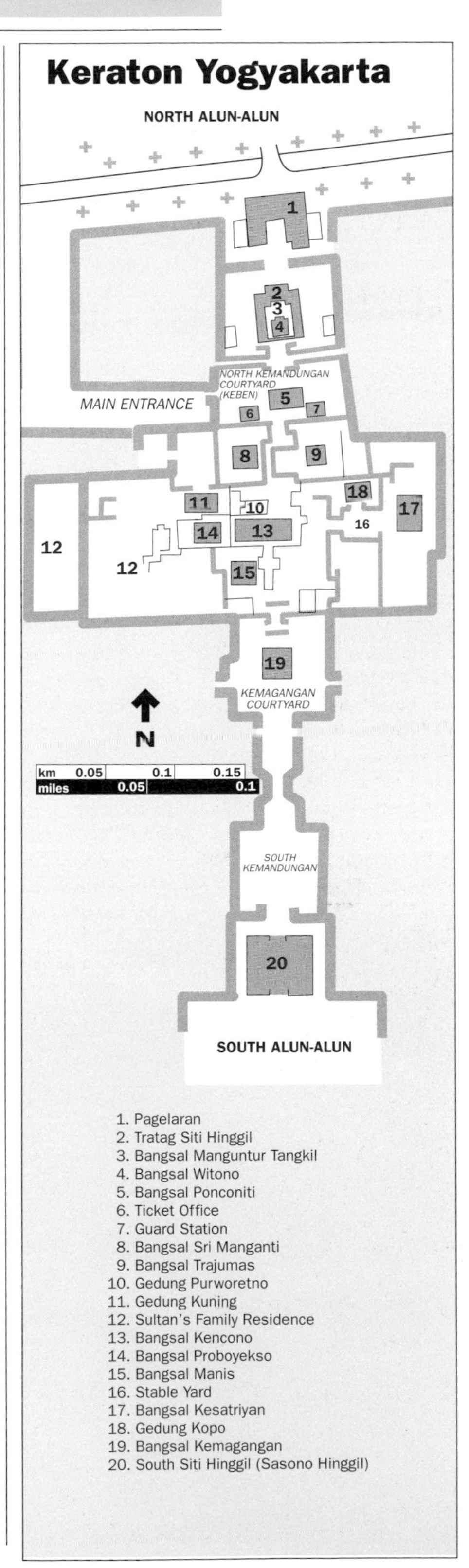

into the palace is for guards who alternate on half-hour watches. To the right of the gateway is the ticket office, where you must first register and pay a small entrance fee and are then assigned a personal guide who accompanies you into the palace.

Just behind and blocking the main entryway is an enormous wall. As in Bali, this *baturana* barrier is designed to keep out evil spirits, who seem to have difficulty turning corners and can only travel in straight lines.

Inside, two small pavilions stand in a tidy courtyard planted with fruit trees. On the western side is the Bangsal Sri Manganti, where the Sultan receives guests. Dance performances are presented here on Sundays. To the east is the Bangsal Trajumas pavilion where wedding palanquins, cosmetics tables, and a tray in the shape of a tiny house for the presentation of gifts are on display.

Grimacing silver giants stand guard on either side of the gateway from here leading into the central Pelataran Kedaton or "Royal Courtyard." These are heavenly guardian beings modeled after the huge *dwarapala* figures seated by the entrance to the ancient Candi Sewu complex outside of Yogya.

Engraved on a *baturana* at this entrance is the coat-of-arms of the Yogya ruling family. In the center are the Sultan's initials written in Javanese script: *ha* and *ba*. Above is a winged crown which formerly had nine feathers on either side, symbolic of Hamengkubuwono IX's reign. Hamengkubuwono X, has added one feather to each wing and placed the number 10 in Javanese script at the bottom.

Immediately inside the main courtyard on the right is the Gedung Purworetno, the Sultan's private office. Behind this is the Gedung Kuning which serves as his private residence. The gallery here contains 19th century European furnishings of the sort that were once very fashionable on Java—ornate mirrors, marble side tables and crystal chandeliers. The *kantil* tree in the corner, with its fragrant white flowers, is considered sacred.

To the left of the entrance is a small music pavilion in European style with charming stained-glass panels decorated with violins, trumpets and drums. Palace musicians once played European music here, and struck up the national anthems of visiting dignitaries as they arrived to attend royal functions.

The 'Golden Throne Pavilion'

The splendid Bangsal Kencono or "Golden Throne Pavilion" dominates the courtyard with its tall, peaked *joglo* roof that represents the sacred Mt. Meru at the center of the universe. The roof is supported by four massive teak pillars whose decorations provide an excellent example of Javanese syncretism—a red Hindu pattern, gold Buddhist lotus petals at the base, and Arabic calligraphy with the opening passage of the Quran: "There is only one God, and his name is Allah."

KAL MULLER

MUNSYI AHMAD

Behind the throne hall, through glass walls, lies the Bangsal Proboyekso where the sacred *pusaka* or regalia are stored. The Bangsal Kencono and Bangsal Proboyekso together form the core of the palace and are the only buildings in it to face eastward—the direction of power and the rising sun.

Two small pavilions face the Bangsal Kencono. To the south is a long banquet hall with glass windows and a marble floor. A golden snake and a giant's head with leeches in its hair on the side symbolize the Javanese year 1853 (A.D. 1925) when this hall was last restored.

Rooms lining the southern and eastern sides of the courtyard serve a variety of functions. One is where tea is prepared daily for the sultan at 7, 11 and 4, and a mid-morning procession of elderly female retainers bearing tea trays under royal umbrellas can be observed emerging from here each day. Another room, the aptly-named Sarangboyo or "Nest of Danger" is where alcoholic drinks are prepared. Still other rooms house the royal treasury and gamelan instruments.

An arched passageway to the east leads into another small yard which formerly served as the royal stables. A larger courtyard behind this, the Kasatriyan, was once the residence of the crown prince but is now used for dance rehearsals. Galleries on the south and east side of the courtyard display portraits of the royal family through nine generations. A small museum and souvenir shop at the north end occupies the Gedung Kopo, formerly a storage space for equestrian paraphernalia. On display are replicas of the regalia and lavish gifts presented to the sultans by state visitors—including crystal lamps, medallions and porcelain vases.

Throughout the palace, court retainers sit or stand silently. The men, dressed in dark blue striped jackets and batik skirts, with the front pleat neatly folded, guard the entrances and gateways. The women, bare-shouldered, are swathed in batiks with sober, earth-tone patterns. These 1,400 retainers serve here primarily for the prestige, peace of mind and spiritual protection which are believed to derive from physical proximity to the sultan. Advancement in the ranks of the service is very slow, based on age and years of service, and wages are nominal.

Many Javanese still believe fervently in the mystical powers of the palace and the sultan. Open to tourists since 1968, the *keraton* receives hundreds of visitors daily, including bus loads of Indonesian tourists on Sundays. Respectful dress is required and no hats may be worn inside the *keraton*, which is open from 8 am to 1 pm daily, and Fridays until 11 am. A small admission charge includes a guided tour. Gamelan rehearsals are held on Mondays and Wednesdays from 10 am to 12 noon; dance performances from 11 am to 12:30 pm each Sunday, except for the last Sunday of the month, when a *wayang kulit* demonstration is put on instead. The palace collection of *wayang kulit* puppets is aired every Thursday.

The royal stables

Before leaving the area, have a look at the royal carriages on display in the Rotowijayan stables at the southwest corner of the main square (between the square and the entrance to the palace). Many were made in Europe and presented to the sultans by Dutch patrons. Among them are Nyai Jimat, a coach made in England and used by Hamengkubuwono III (1812-1814), and Kyai Garudoyekso—an elaborate carriage made in the Netherlands in 1861 and used by Hamengkubuwono VI and his successors in coronation processions. Kyai Rotopraloyo is a special carriage used to bear the sultan's coffin to the royal cemetery at Imogiri, and Kangjeng Kyai Cekatak is an old saddle and harness inset with diamonds and sewn with gold and silver thread that belonged to Hamengkubuwono I. Opening hours are the same as for the *keraton*.

—*Joan Suyenaga*

Opposite: *Tea is brought to the sultan from a special room facing onto the central courtyard, where it is prepared for him three times daily.* **Above:** *A detail showing fine European-style cast-iron work on the* keraton *pillars. European and Chinese architectural elements and furnishings are evidence of court's great cultural eclecticism during the 19th and early 20th century.*

THE OLD CITY

Within the Fortress Walls

A massive fortification of sand and limestone, five meters high and four meters across, was erected by the crown prince of Yogya (later Hamengkubuwono II) all around the palace in 1785. Much of this wall remains intact today, tracing a square one kilometer on each side around the oldest parts of the city. It was formerly surrounded by a broad moat, and is so thick that the Sultan is said to have conducted tours of inspection riding along the top of it in his carriage.

Broad bastions mounted with cannons stood at each of the four corners (all but one is still intact) and five arched tunnels (*plengkung*) provided access through the wall into the city. Each was provided with a bridge across the moat and had a thick wooden door that was opened during the day but closed at 8 pm each night upon a signal from the *keraton*. Of these, the southern gate known as Nirbaya (or Gading) is in the best condition today, with stairs leading up on both sides of it. The wooden tower on top is for sounding sirens signalling the beginning and end of the day's fast during Ramadan. The sultan is forbidden to pass through this southern gateway except when his funeral cortège is en route to Imogiri, the royal cemetery.

These walls, together with the area enclosed by them, are known as the *beteng* (literally: "fortress"), and this is a fascinating district to explore on foot. The narrow alleyways are lined with white-washed walls and gateways giving access to aristocratic mansions constructed along the same lines as the palace itself. The highlight of any exploration of this area is a visit to the ruins of the royal pleasure garden known as Taman Sari.

The northern square

Begin at the large, grassy northern square (*alun-alun lor*), which until 1928 was not planted with grass but filled with black sand. It was formerly forbidden to walk here, and those who passed by could not use umbrellas or footwear, as both were reserved for use by the sultan.

There are 62 banyan trees around the square; the six in the square itself all have names and the two in the middle are considered sacred. At the southeastern corner of the square is a cage, now empty, once used to hold tigers that were pitted against buffaloes

for royal entertainment (the buffalo almost always won).

Presently the *alun-alun* is used for soccer matches, physical education classes and kite flying. At night, *martabak* pancakes are thrown like pizzas then filled with an egg and meat batter by vendors who line the northeastern corner, while grilled corn-on-the-cob is available along the eastern side.

To the west of the *alun-alun* stands the Grand Mosque (Mesjid Ageng). Built in 1773 by order of Hamengkubuwono I, it has a multi-tiered roof capped by a Hindu-Javanese spire or *lingga*. The main prayer hall is simple and open; on either side of the front courtyard are small buildings where the sacred gamelans are played during Sekaten week (see "Keraton Ceremonies").

Sono Budoyo Museum

At the northwest corner of the square is the Sono Budoyo Museum. Founded by the Java Institute, an organization composed mainly of Dutchmen devoted to the study and appreciation of Javanese culture, it was inaugurated by Hamengkubuwono VIII in 1935.

The main building is constructed in the traditional Javanese style. Two gamelan sets—one, ornately carved, from the Cirebon palace, and another from the Yogyakarta palace—are housed in the front pavilion. A shallow verandah leads from here into the museum proper.

A *patanen* greets the visitor upon entrance to the exhibit rooms. This room, traditionally forming the heart of the Javanese home, is devoted to Dewi Sri, goddess of rice and fertility, and is decorated as a bridal bedchamber with two *loro blunyo* (bridal couple) figures placed in front. The permanent exhibit also features an excellent collection of ancient bronze bells, a variety of *wayang* puppets and masks from Java, Sunda, Bali and Madura, an exquisitely carved teak partition from Jepara, and excellent Balinese woodcarvings and paintings. A room for special exhibitions and an extensive library are modern additions behind the complex.

The 'Water Castle'

Southwest of the keraton is the remarkable Taman Sari complex, known during Dutch colonial times as the "Water Castle" because of an imposing structure, now in ruins, that once stood at the center of a huge, man-made lake. To reach Taman Sari from the *keraton* entrance/exit, walk due west and turn south (left) at the intersection with Jl. Ngasem, then left again (east) at the Ngasem market and follow the road as it curves around to the right (south). The main entrance is here, reached by turning in at the third opening in the high wall on the right.

In 1758, Hamengkubuwono I began work on this elaborate retreat that included not only an impressive two-story masonry mansion built on an elevated mound and surrounded by an artificial lake, but also underground and underwater tunnels, sunken bathing pools, secluded meditational chambers, and 18 lavish gardens planted with flowers, vegetables and fruit trees. The pools were fed by a large, clear spring which Panembahan Senopati, founder of the modern Mataram line, is said to have used as a bathing spot (Umbul Pacethokan) in 1598.

The architect of the water palace was R.T. Mangundipuro, lord of Madiun, and construction was supervised by K.P.H. Notokusumo, who later became Prince Pakualam I. The name Taman Sari means "fragrant gardens," referring to the flower and fruit trees that exuded a delicious fragrance which permeated the entire complex.

The present entrance is at the end of a broad driveway once lined with mango and other fruit trees. Just to the left of it stands a "single-pillared" mosque. Although built in the traditional Javanese *pendopo* style, it has only one central pillar instead of the usual four. The stone block supporting the pillar was taken from the ruins of the former reception hall of Kerta, the early 17th-century palace of Sultan Agung.

Two small buildings lie at the foot of a massive stone gateway decorated with *naga* snakes leading into Taman Sari; the northern one presently serves as the ticket office. Stop and pay a small admission fee here, and if you like, hire one of the "guides" who offer their services and are in fact quite helpful in leading you around the maze-like complex, though many of their explanations are of dubious accuracy. The gateway beyond leads into an octagonal courtyard with four small buildings in which the sultan and his wives relaxed and enjoyed the large flowering plants which adorned the yard.

Through a gateway and down a flight of

Opposite: *The Taman Sari complex as it originally appeared, at the end of the 18th century. All around it was an artificial lake; access to the "castle" was by means of ingenious underwater passageways with small towers placed at regular intervals providing light and ventilation.*

ERIC OEY

stairs is a high walled compound containing three bathing pools—the Umbul Binangun where the sultan and his wives bathed and relaxed in privacy. The two larger pools were for the wives and concubines, and are separated from a third smaller one by a three-story tower containing a bedchamber whence the sultan could oversee the activity in the two female pools. The third pool on the other side, reserved exclusively for the sultan and his chosen partner, is fed by the original Umbul Pacethokan spring.

A room at the northern end of the women's pools is referred to as the "Tea Room" and was presumably used for the preparation of refreshments. Stairs on the west side lead into another octagonal courtyard bordered on the far end by the Gapura Agung—an imposing gateway decorated with reliefs of birds gathering pollen from flowers, a chronogram symbolizing the year 1691 (the year of Taman Sari's completion). A broad terrace on the second level of the gateway overlooks what was once the main entrance to the complex on the west side, an area now densely populated. All around the courtyard are large pots which were once planted with flowers and fruit trees.

The royal sleeping quarters

A path leads south from the western courtyard under an arched staircase and through a quiet neighborhood to a dark, U-shaped complex known as the Pasareyan Dalem Ledoksari—the sultan's sleeping quarters. Couches in the central room had water running beneath them and are strewn with flowers, as the place is regarded as sacred and is still used as a meditation chamber.

Popular belief has it that a secret passageway led from here to the palace or even to the south coast. A kitchen, a tailor's pavilion, a storage house and two more pools for servants, as well as a spice tree orchard and a vegetable garden, all formerly filled this area. However, they have now been overtaken by *kampung* houses.

The 'coiled well'

Returning along the path through the courtyard and continuing past it to the north, one enters the area that was once covered by a large artificial lake (*segaran*) that drew water from the Winongo River via a canal. In the midst of this area are the ruins of a large mansion, and to one side, hidden amidst the rubble, is a dark stairway leading via an underground (formerly underwater) passageway into the most marvelous of all the ingenious structures at Taman Sari—the Sumur Gumuling or "Coiled Well." One emerges at the end of the passageway into the bottom of a remarkable circular atrium that is partially open to the sky above, with galleries on two levels all around.

At the bottom of the atrium in the center

is a small pool, said to have formerly been a well. Four arched staircases extend upward from the sides, forming a tiny platform suspended in mid-air above the well. From here, a single flight of steps ascends gracefully to the upper gallery, where the open archways face the atrium and whose windows formerly looked out just above the surface of the surrounding lake.

Small alcoves on the west side of both the upper and lower galleries suggest that this building was once used as a mosque, but popular stories have gamelan music being played on the lower gallery while dances were performed in the upper. There are also suggestions of Hindu influence, as Hamengkubuwono I clearly identified himself with the god Visnu and his statue was traditionally placed above a well. Also, it is said that *keris* blades were found beneath the central platform over the well.

In all likelihood, however, this curious structure was designed as a meditational retreat mirroring the design of the underwater palace of Kangjeng Ratu Kidul, the Goddess of the South Seas to whom all Mataram rulers were greatly devoted and from whom they are said to derive great powers. Perhaps this was even the chamber where the sultan renewed his annual connubial relations with the goddess. The passageway leading to the well once continued to the western edge of the artificial lake, but it has now collapsed.

The 'Portuguese' fortress

The high ground in the midst of the lake, with its imposing Gedung Kenongo mansion, was once an island reached by two underwater passageways. The mansion is said to have been designed by a "Portuguese" architect from Batavia, and though there is no evidence of this it was obviously strongly influenced by European designs, perhaps by representations of country manors found on Dutch porcelains. Although the original stairways of the building have long since collapsed, one can scramble up the newly installed staircase to view the second floor (the original wooden floor is missing) and the panorama from the rooftop.

The underwater passageways connecting the mansion with the pleasure pools and gardens were ventilated and lighted by small towers projecting above the surface of the lake. A portion of one of the tunnels has been restored; to the east of it lay one of three royal barge landings around the lake. From the end of the restored passageway, a turn to the south brings you back to where you started at the eastern entrance.

Obviously intended as a pleasure retreat, the Taman Sari complex was also likely planned as a defensive position in the event of an attack. It took 11 years to complete and was abandoned shortly after Hamengkubuwono I died, partly because the elaborate hydraulic works were so difficult to maintain. The gardens were neglected and the buildings suffered some damage during the Java War of 1825-1830. An earthquake in 1867 caused further damage, and although an effort at restoration was made in the early 1970s, only the central pools have been completely rebuilt.

The Pasareyan and Sumur Gumuling are probably best left as dim, moss-covered mysteries. Although its glory and grandeur was short-lived, even in shambles, Taman Sari remains a tribute to the ingenuity and imagination of its creator, Hamengkubuwono I.

Batik painters' colony

Hundreds of families have taken up residence amidst the ruins of the Water Castle,

KAL MULLER

Above, left: *The Umbul Binangun pools where the sultan and his wives relaxed in privacy. Atop the central tower is the sultan's bedchamber; behind it is another, smaller pool for his private use.* **Right:** *The "coiled well" and its unique atrium.*

and because of the large numbers of tourists who pass through here, many have taken to producing batik paintings. The style of paintings produced changes with the demand. Once dominated by scenes from the *Ramayana* and misty landscapes, one now finds charming animals, vivid "primitive" portraits and wild abstracts.

The more creative and successful artists soon leave the area to set up studios elsewhere, but many retain their ties to a neighborhood artists' cooperative that has organized successful group exhibits in Yogya, Jakarta and Malang. Most of the work found here is not very original—but there are always exceptions. Choose carefully and bargain hard.

At the northern end of the Water Castle and the batik painter's colony lies the large Ngasem market. A regular daily market, Ngasem has an annex specializing in birds and animals, where champion song doves can sell for up to $60,000. Also sold are homing pigeons, parakeets, parrots, macaws, cockatoos and other exotic tropical birds as well as dogs, cats, rabbits, and fighting cocks. Stalls outside offer a variety of intricate bamboo birdcages.

The southern alun-alun

The southern *alun-alun* at the foot of the *keraton* and just to the east of Taman Sari is a mirror image of the northern square, somewhat smaller and planted with fruit trees along the edges.

Four banyan trees stand in the square itself—two in the center, and two at the southern gate. The royal elephants, which were once housed in a stable on the west side of the field, have been moved to the zoo, and the moat here has been filled.

At the north end of the square stands the Sasono Hinggil Dwi Abad pavilion erected in 1955 to commemorate the 200th anniversary of the *keraton* on the site of the ruined Siti Hinggil. Community events are often held here, including a monthly all-night *wayang kulit* performance and a Christmas eve mass which uses a gamelan orchestra in place of an organ.

Formerly filled with sand and used for military drills and tiger matches, the grassy field is now used for sporting events and bird singing contests.

Those interested in the unexplainable may want to try walking blindfolded at night from the north end of the field to the south, passing between the two banyan trees in the center. The trees have persistently defended their turf for years, and potential intruders are said to invariably veer off to the right or left as they approach the trees.

KAL MULLER

The portion of the old city lying to the east of the *keraton* originally was reserved for the residence, gardens and mosque (Mesjid Selo) of the Crown Prince (later Hamengkubuwono II) and of his son, Prince Mangkurat. The only remaining building from this period is the small mosque, built in 1784 and still in use.

Smaller compounds, once princely residences, scatter about the western half of the old city. These were once restricted to royal family members and court retainers, but the rules have been relaxed and the area is now densely populated with extended families of the descendents of court retainers, newcomers and students. Foreigners, however, are still forbidden to formally reside within the walls of the old city.

Besides the batik found all around the Taman Sari compound there are stores in this area specializing in traditional Javanese dress and dance costumes (Tjokrosuharto, Sawojajar, Toko Jawa and DSO).

—Joan Suyenaga

Above: *Bird-lovers had best avoid the Pasar Burung market just behind the Water Castle.* **Right:** *One of Maliboro's bustling side-streets.*

JALAN MALIOBORO

A Stroll Down Yogyakarta's 'Main Street'

The ceremonial boulevard extending 2.3 km (1.5 mi) north from the *keraton* was part of Hamengkubuwono I's original design for his new capital. This was the route taken by the royal cortège on important occasions. The city of Yogya has since grown up around it, and the street—now known as Jalan Malioboro (though the name actually changes several times along its length)—still has a special significance for most city residents. Indeed, each new city administration has seen fit to give the street a complete "facelift" soon after coming into office. Ironically, traffic now moves one-way (north to south), counter to Hamengkubuwono I's intended path of meditation, beginning at Siti Hinggil and moving north to the Tugu Monument.

Colonial landmarks

Heading north from the *alun-alun*, one passes through a large, open gateway with guard posts (*pangurakan*) on either side that mark the outer limits of the *keraton* area. The gate opens onto a major intersection surrounded by colonial buildings, including the central Post Office on the southeast corner (built in 1910), Bank Negara Indonesia 1946 on the southwest corner (built in 1923 to house a Dutch bank and insurance company) and the former society club on the northwest corner (built in 1912 and partially bombed in 1946), which currently functions as a theater and exhibition hall (Gedung Senisono) where open-air Saturday night concerts, drama and poetry readings are held.

A monument on the northeast corner commemorates the guerilla attack of revolutionary forces fighting the Dutch on March 1, 1949. Behind it stands the old Vredenberg Fort, built by Hamengkubuwono I for the Dutch between 1756-1787. It once housed 500 Dutch troops and included barracks, officers' quarters, a hospital, a warehouse and a jail. In a new twist on the beating of swords into plowshares, Vredenburg has recently undergone renovation and is now a museum known as Benteng Budaya, literally "Fortress of Culture." The old barracks have been transformed into spacious air-conditioned galleries with dioramas depicting key moments in the struggle for independence.

Opposite the fort-museum is the elegant State Guest House, surrounded by a magnifi-

KAL MULLER

cently manicured lawn planted with fruit trees and ornamented with Hindu-Javanese statues. Built in 1823 as the Dutch Resident's mansion and rebuilt in 1869 after an earthquake, it served as the Presidential Palace when Yogya was capital of the republic for several years during the revolution.

The Margo Mulyo Congregation Reformed Church, inaugurated in 1830 and located just north of the Guest House, is the oldest church in the city.

Beringharjo market

Yogya's central market place was established north of the *keraton* during the reign of Hamengkubuwono I. The present building, the size of a city block, was constructed in 1925, and Sultan Hamengkubuwono IX then dubbed the market Beringharjo in commemoration of the "beautiful *bering* tree" forest which stood here when the city was founded. Undergoing major reconstruction in 1991-92, it will reopen as the Beringharjo Center.

Entering the crowded, dimly-lit market from the street you move into quite a different world. Tropical fruits are piled high under paper umbrellas near the entrance. Stacks of clothing, batik (new and used), colorful *lurik* and other fabrics are displayed along the narrow aisles. *Keris* repairers and tailors ply their trades in stalls half enclosed by darkness, and an amazing array of food stuffs is found—pungent meats and fish, fresh carrots and potatoes, leafy spinach and mountains of bright-red chili peppers. Other stalls contain heaps of bamboo baskets and stacks of second-hand miscellany such as motor parts, records, lamps and hardwares.

ERIC OEY

The market is teeming with surprises; the joy here is in exploring the dim corners pierced by occasional beams of sunlight from the rafters. Beware of mud holes, pickpockets and "guides" who attach themselves to you in the hopes of finagling a commission on everything you purchase. Although a few batik stalls have posted fixed prices, bargaining is the order of the day.

What's in a name?

Folk etymology is a popular pasttime in Java, and a lively debate has grown around the origin of the name of Yogyakarta's busiest street. The long-held opinion that the street was named after the Duke of Marlborough during the English occupation of Java between 1811 and 1816 is highly unlikely. A root in the Sanskrit phrase *malya bhara*, meaning "bearing garlands of flowers," has also been contested, as the phrase appears in neither Sanskrit nor Old Javanese texts. A proposal is that the name is a deformation of the Dutch *mergelburg* (equivalent to the English "marlborough"), meaning "fortress walls made of limestone" and referring to the *beteng* walls surrounding the palace area.

Whatever the etymology, it is certain that the name, which became popular only after 1945, is of foreign derivation, as traditionally the Javanese do not name streets, only areas. The practice of granting street names (and changing them every few blocks) is a recent development in Indonesia.

The southern portion of Malioboro, from the post office up to the first major intersection, is officially called Jl. Ahmad Yani in rememberance of one of the martyrs of the revolution. This section houses gold jewelry, batik and snack shops—while clothing, electronic, fabric, and curio stores line the thoroughfare north of the intersection up to the railway tracks. It is this section of the street that is officially called Malioboro.

The broad sidewalks here are lined with an array of street vendors, hawkers and artisans offering souvenirs, personalized rubber stamps, painted leather wallets, watercolor miniatures, clothing, fruit, books (a few in English), sandals, bags, posters, potions, lottery predictions and bamboo bird whistles. Prices are fixed in many of the stores and a few of the street stalls (notably for clothing), otherwise bargaining is necessary.

As a major thoroughfare with slow lanes for *becaks* and bicycles defined by planter-lined islands, Malioboro has far more traffic than it is built to handle, and crossing the street demands patience, daring and a good sense of timing. After 9 pm the stores close, the vendors pack up and late night food stalls roll mats out on the sidewalk for business. Known as *lesehan* ("relaxing on the floor"), these stalls are a Yogya hallmark, offering *gudeg*, fried chicken, fried pigeon and rice dishes cooked over makeshift gas burners.

About midway up Malioboro on the east side (just south of the helpful Tourist Information Office), is an imposing gateway leading into the Kepatihan. Once the residence of Patih (minister) Danurejo, this complex of pavilions and courtyards now houses municipal offices. Performances are often held in the main pavilion.

Further north, on the same side of the street, is the Gedung Dewan Perwakilan Rakyat Daerah, the home of the regional legislature. The building originally served as the meeting place for Dutch theosophists, then later housed the legislative body of the new republic. It has a spacious lawn with a statue of General Sudirman, one of the leaders of the guerilla campaign (1948-49) against the Dutch. Beyond this is the Garuda Hotel, and across the street south of the train station is the Pasar Kembang ("flower market") area that was formerly a red-light district. Now, it has grown into a center for budget accommodations and eateries, the narrow lanes filled with tiny shops, hotels and restaurants.

North of the tracks

Built by the Dutch in 1886, the old Tugu Railway Station has served Yogya since the days when a trip from Jakarta (then Batavia) to Surabaya took two days. Across the tracks to the north Jl. Malioboro changes names to Jl. P. Mangkubumi. It is lined on both sides by hotels, offices, restaurants and shops.

The Tugu monument at the northern end of Jl. Mangkubumi was constructed to mark the founding of Yogya in 1755. It is said that Kyai Jogo, the serpent spirit who once resided in the *bering* forest which was cleared when the city was founded, now occupies the monument.

— *Joan Suyenaga*

Opposite: *The Tugu monument marking the northern end of the Malioboro-Mangkubumi processional boulevard.*

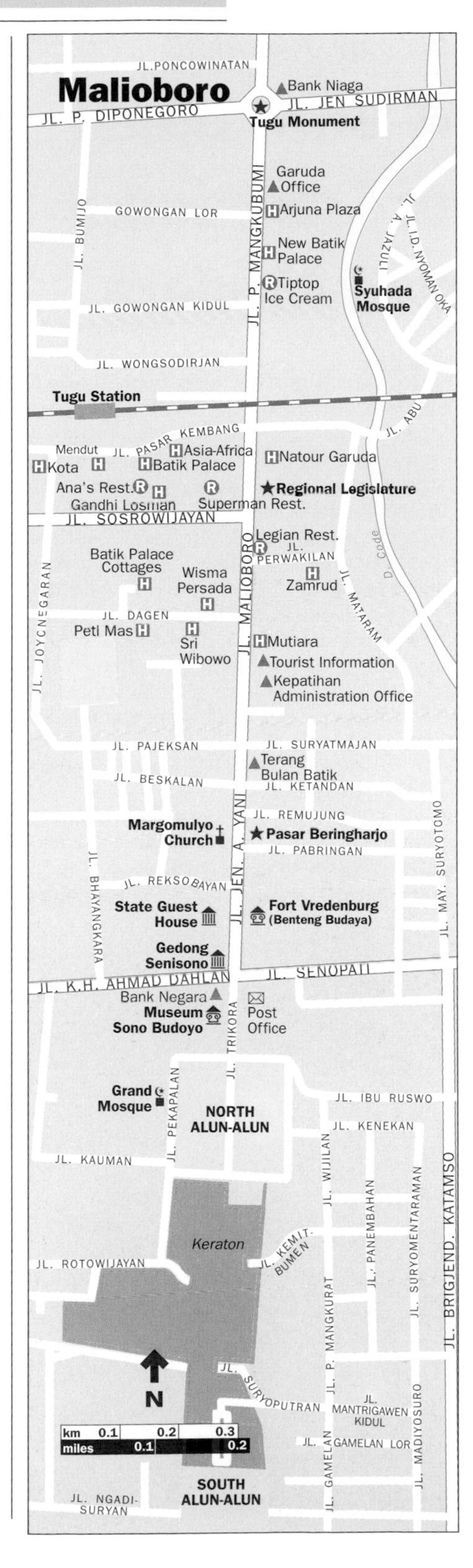

CITY OF THE ARTS

A Vital Blend of Traditional and Modern

Palace patronage (and more recently tourism) has nurtured the traditional arts in Yogya. In this age of mass entertainments, a *wayang kulit* performance still draws a crowd here, gamelan music can be heard wafting through the streets on any quiet evening, and the most popular local television show is a weekly *ketoprak* (folk drama) featuring amateur as well as professional troupes.

Yogya shares its billing as a center for traditional Javanese court culture with neighboring Solo, and subtle distinctions have been cultivated ever since the Mataram kingdom was split in 1755. The term *mataraman* refers to the style of music, dance, drama and costume characteristic of Yogya (in contrast to Solo). In general, Yogyanese music and dance is more vigorous than its Solonese counterpart and the instruments themselves tend to be larger and more numerous.

Court dances

Hamengkubuwono I, in founding his new court, created a dance style that was strongly militaristic in flavor. He is attributed with creating the marathon Beksan Lawung, a dance for 40 male dancers that lasts five hours. The *wayang wong* dance dramas staged during his reign depicted a war between two of Arjuna's sons—performances that may be regarded as statements of legitimization of the new kingdom. Even the *bedoyo* and *srimpi* female dances of Yogya have a militaristic touch, lyrically enacting battles in supremely graceful slow motion.

A livelier dance genre, the *golek*—depicting a young girl enjoying her newly discovered womanhood—has its roots in popular social dancing and was cultivated in aristocratic circles before it was accepted fully as part of the *keraton* repetoire after about 1954. Usually performed by a single dancer, its catchy rhythms and coquettish movements have made this a popular genre that is taught widely throughout Yogya. The dance's male counterpart, the Klana Topeng masked dance is equally popular.

Dance continued to evolve at court even after real political power ceased to exist, and the palace devoted great energy and resources to the arts. Until 1918, these dances were the preserve of the sultan and were not for public consumption. However, during the

KAL MULLER

reign of Hamengkubuwono VII, a dance organization called Kridha Beksa Wirama was established outside the palace walls at Dalem Tejokusuman with the sultan's permission. Although the students were mainly culled from the nobility, an important step had been taken in opening the palace arts to a wider public. As a model for the many dance organizations which followed, it has made a valuable contribution to the healthy state of traditional Yogyanese dance.

The golden age of performing arts in Yogya occurred during the reign of Hamengkubuwono VIII, who acted as empresario for lavish dance drama productions in the *kераton*. These performances ran for three or four days, lasted from 6 am until sunset, and involved 300-400 dancers. Dance costumes were elaborated to imitate carved *wayang kulit* figures, and props and animal costumes were added. The young female warrior sitting proudly astride a towering *garuda* bird, its wings spread in flight, has become one of the lasting images of Yogyanese dance.

Dance education

A number of private dance schools now operate in the city, most of them with palace connections. Choreographies in the schools have been adapted to changing tastes, but have remained true to the classic tradition. It is these dances which are being taught now in villages throughout the region. By reaching out to the villages, the court tradition has endured and even been strengthened.

Two formal educational bodies also contribute to the strength and status of the traditional arts today. Established in 1961, the SMKI offers courses in gamelan music (*karawitan*), dance and traditional puppetry at a campus in the southwest corner of the city. A university-level dance academy, ASTI, was established in 1963 and is now part of the Indonesian Art Institute (ISI). Its campus is at Bulaksumur, next to Gajah Mada University, though new facilities are being prepared to the south of the city. Semi-annual recitals (usually in July and December) offer re-creations of long-neglected classical dances and modern Javanese versions of Western ones.

The Padepokan Seni ("Art Colony") of Bagong Kussudiharjo, batik artist and choreographer, and the Institut Kesenian (Art Institute) under the tutelage of Wisnu Wardhana both focus on new dance creations using traditional movements. Bagong's six-month workshops are held in a cozy, palm-shaded compound south of the city. His

KAL MULLER

choreographies combine regional styles, notably Javanese, Sundanese and Balinese, with modern (Martha Graham) movements.

Modern dance forms

The popular *sendratari* (an acronym for *seni-drama-tari*, "art-dance-drama") has evolved out of attempts to make traditional dance dramas more accessible to non-Javanese audiences. Verbal dialogue is replaced with hand gestures and facial expressions, movements from other regional dances are incorporated, and the emphasis is on dynamic movements and quick story progression.

Unlike the traditional *wayang wong*, which usually takes its story line from the *Mahabharata*, *sendratari* often enact tales from the *Ramayana*. The most spectacular performance is held beneath the full moon at Prambanan (May–October), where scenes from the ancient temple reliefs are brought to life on an enormous stage with a cast of hundreds. A new indoor theater here lacks the temple as backdrop, but is equipped with a new computerized lighting system. Featuring groups from schools and villages, performances are staged throughout the year.

Having replaced the palaces as principal

Opposite: *The Yogya style of dance is dynamic and vigorous by classical Javanese standards.*
Above: *Yogyanese* wayang golek *puppets enact tales from the Arabic-influenced Menak cycle.*

ERIC OEY

patron of the arts, the government's Education and Culture Ministry began sponsoring art festivals in the late 1970s. The extremely popular *sendratari* festival is usually held in October at the Kepatihan pavilion.

Puppets and popular drama

While courtly dance and drama have recently moved from the *keraton* to the villages, *wayang kulit* has always been essentially a popular art form. Rising costs have reduced the frequency of performances, but radio and the availability of cassette recordings may have actually increased the accessibility of *wayang* to the average Javanese. Subtle differences in puppets, characterizations and musical accompaniment may be elusive to the uninitiated, but the magic of shadows flickering and dancing to the glistening tones of the gamelan is universally captivating.

In 1925, the *keraton* opened a school for *dalang*, Habiranda, in the Pracimasono building, just west of the Pagelaran pavilion bordering the north square. Habiranda's students include university students, farmers and *becak* drivers, all of whom pay nominal fees. Twice a year, on the evening following Grebeg Puasa and Grebeg Maulud, the *keraton* stages a public *wayang kulit* performance in the south Kemagangan courtyard.

The *wayang golek* rod puppet theater is mildly popular in Yogya. Whereas in West Java *Mahabharata* stories are enacted, the Central Javanese *wayang golek* repetoire is drawn from the Arabic-influenced Menak stories (though local shows for tourists often stage *Ramayana* tales instead). The puppets sport black jackets (as opposed to the triangular bib-vests of Sundanese puppets) and have long, oval faces (to be distinguished from Cirebon *wayang golek* puppets, which have flat, triangular faces). Most are produced in the village of Sentolo, west of the city. Although simply constructed, in the hands of an experienced *dalang* they gracefully flick their long scarfs, dance, breathe, ride horses and fight with great vigor.

By far the most popular theatrical form in Yogya is *ketoprak*, a folk melodrama which traces its roots to a rural game in which folk stories are improvised to the accompaniment of music produced by pounding rice husking logs. At the turn of the century the game moved to the city, and groups quickly appeared in many neighborhoods. The sound of the pounding—*prak, prak*—gives it its name, and *ketoprak* has moved to the stage, with gamelan replacing the pounding logs.

The repetoire has expanded to include not only folktales, but historical legends and Javanese versions of the European classics such as Cinderella and Romeo and Juliet. The dialogue is in Javanese and is improvised, though there is now a tendency toward written scripts. Professional troupes are few, but almost every *kampung* can rustle up enough people for a performance (usually during the National Day celebrations in August).

Modern art in Yogya

During the early days of the republic, between 1946-49, Yogya became the home of talented avant garde artists caught up in the revolutionary ferment of the times. Their overriding theme was social realism as an expression of a new national consciousness. After independence, styles diversified and became less political, sometimes degenerating into pure ego-centrism and self-indulgence, but during the mid-50s, fully two-thirds of Indonesia's professional painters still lived and worked in Yogya—among them Affandi, Hendra, Rusli and Saptohudoyo.

The focus of Indonesian art shifted to Jakarta during the 1960s, but many artists are still active in Yogya, particularly in the mediums of oil painting, primitive sculpture (incorporating motifs from Kalimantan, Sumatra and Irian) and collage.

Affandi was Indonesia's most famous modern artist. Born in Cirebon in 1908, he

KAL MULLER

was actively painting portraits, usually finished in one-hour sittings, up until his death at the age of 81 in 1990. His house-studio-gallery (Jl. Urip Sumoharjo 167) rests on stilts above a river and is topped by an uplifted roof in the shape of a banana leaf. He said this reminded him of a time when, as a young, struggling artist, he was forced to seek refuge from the rain under banana trees. Affandi's private collection of about 100 works (including many intriguing self-portraits), as well as that of his daughter Kartika, fill two galleries that are open to visitors.

An Indonesian Academy of Fine Arts (ASRI) was founded in 1950 by several highly respected artists. As part of the Indonesian Institute of the Arts (ISI), it is now one of the top art institutes in the country. Course offerings include sculpture, painting, graphic arts, commercial and industrial art, symbolic and decorative painting, interior design and traditional stone sculpture.

Batik

Yogya is of couse also famous as a center for traditional textile production, particularly batik. As with the performing arts, distinctions have developed between Yogyanese and Solonese fabrics, in designs as well as production techniques. Identical names sometimes refer to slightly different patterns in the two cities. In Yogya, the basic colors are brown, indigo and white. Whereas Solonese patterns tend to be more floral, the Yogyanese prefer more geometric designs.

The Batik Research Center (Balai Penelitian Batik) at Jl. Kusumanegara 2, was opened in the early 1960s in an effort to revive the suffering batik industry. Research into traditional methods of wax and dye application proceeds here alongside experimentation into new dyes and techniques, many of them more complicated than the traditional ones. The center offers intensive, personalized courses in batik methods, ranging from one week to three months, as well as technical guidance and assistance to individuals and home industries. Interested parties may tour the premises, although a guide is not always available.

Yogya has also stood at the forefront of the batik-painting boom. In the early 1960s, artists such as Soelarjo, Bagong Kussudiardjo, Kuswadji Kawindrasusanto, Bambang Oetoro, Soemihardjo and Amri Yahya began experimenting with traditional motifs and applying them to pictures. This initiative has taken hold amongst the young artists of the city, and batik-painting studios have sprouted in every corner of Yogya. In the short span of twenty years, batik has made the transition from applied to fine art.

—*Joan Suyenaga*

Opposite and above: *The craft for which Yogya is undoubtedly best known— its batik textiles.*

YOGYA SIDETRIPS

Sputtering Peaks and Raging Seas

Nature's statements in this densely populated part of Java—whether in the form of smouldering volcanoes, jagged limestone cliffs or violently pounding surf—are unquestionably powerful. Gunung Merapi (literally, "Mountain of Fire"), just to the north of Yogya, is Java's most active volcano—a towering behemoth that periodically spews clouds of smoke and ash. The overnight climb to the summit is strenuous and dangerous, but is one of the island's most spectacular sights.

Along the southern coast, shallow waters near the shore drop suddenly into a deep undersea trench, creating a strong undertow. Although dangerous for swimming, the numerous beaches to the south of Yogya, many with dramatic black sand dunes, are scenic and alluring. Parangtritis is the closest to town, and a visit here may be combined with stops at Kota Gede and Imogiri.

Kaliurang

For a break from the punishing tropical heat, race up to the quiet highland resort of Kaliurang, 24 km (15 mi) to the north of Yogya and only half an hour by car on a good road. Refreshingly cool, it lies 900 meters above sea level on the southern slopes of Mt. Merapi. Although the weather is unpredictable, the panoramas offered on a clear day are breathtaking, and there are numerous hikes around the outskirts of town. One can easily spend several days here relaxing, swimming and exploring.

There are two swimming pools in Kaliurang, Tlogo Putri and Tlogo Nirmolo. The former is at the end of the bus/minibus route from Yogya, next to rows of food and fruit stalls offering stalks of delicious bananas. From here a path leads into a pleasant, wooded park featuring a small waterfall and three paths for the hiker.

The first is a short hike up Pronojiwo Hill. The second is a 2.5 km hike to the Plawangan seismological station, where the activity of Merapi is monitored and the view of the mountain and the lowlands can be spectacular. The third and most difficult is the arduous trek to the crater of Merapi, which should be undertaken only in the company of an experienced guide (see below). Tlogo Nirmolo and another park are at the other end of the trail to Plawangan, which circles

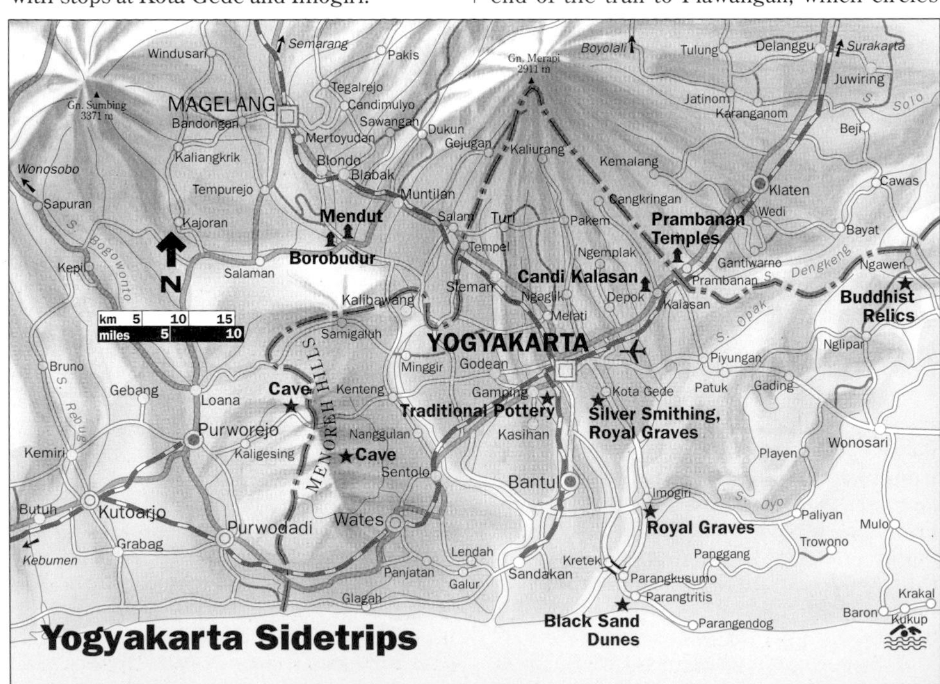

ERIC OEY

up and around the slope.

Accommodations are easy enough to find in Kaliurang. Popular among Western budget travelers is Vogel's Homestay; the owner, Mr. Awuy, organizes treks up Mt. Merapi every night in the dry season. To get here, take the Baker bus from the back of the shopping center just east of the main post office in Yogya, or a minibus from the Terban sub-terminal. Buses and vans return to Yogya regularly from the Tlogo Putri parking lot in Kaliurang.

Climbing Mount Merapi

The arduous climb to the summit of Merapi is the ultimate experience in this part of Java—though only for the adventurous and physically fit. It can be tackled either from Kaliurang (difficult: not for first-timers) or from the village of Selo (easier), which sits on the saddle between Merapi and Merbabu and can be reached from Muntilan or Boyolali along a winding and spectacularly scenic road.

The volcano is one of the most active in the world. Six observation posts (including the one at Plawangan, near Kaliurang) are situated on its slopes to monitor the volcano and warn residents of impending danger. An eruption in A.D. 1006 partially buried Borobudur in ash. The most destructive eruption of this century occured in 1930, when 1300 human lives were claimed and more than 2000 head of livestock lost.

Although there are occasional lava flows, most of the damage is not caused by lava, but by ash, black sand, boiling mud and boulders which slide off the steep slopes and are washed down by rivers at high speeds through fertile farm land and residential areas, resulting in soil erosion and damage to houses, dams, canals, bridges, roads and irrigation systems. Muntilan, to the west of the volcano, is particularly exposed to danger. Respect for the mountain's awesome power is given in the form of annual offerings (*labuhan*) brought from the palace on the anniversary of the sultan's coronation.

Sunrise at the crater's rim is a reward well worth the effort, providing 360 degree panoramic views unlike any in the world. Arrayed across the horizon are a series of dramatic volcanic peaks—Merbabu just to the north, Sumbing, Sundoro and Slamet to the west and Lawu to the east. The Java Sea is visible far to the north and the Indian Ocean to the south.

The safest approach to the summit is from its northern flank. Take the Yogya-Magelang bus and get off at Blabak, then transfer to a minibus heading up to Selo, where you can spend the night. Register here at the observation post (*pos pengawasan*) and arrange for

Above: *View of Merapi from Kaliurang, about half an hour from Yogya. There are two approaches to the summit—from the north (Selo) and the south (Kaliurang). The climb from Selo is much easier.*

a guide to lead you up to the summit before dawn. As the path markers above the treeline are confusing, be sure the guide is experienced. Several tourist services offer guided treks from Selo. Check with the Tourist Information Center on Malioboro, Kartika Trekking Service or Gypsy Adventure Tours (see Yogya Practicalities for details).

The approach to the crater from Kaliurang is long (6-7 hours), dangerous and best taken in the company of an experienced guide, unless you are a seasoned volcano climber. Christian Awuy of Vogel's Homestay gives a daily information session at 7 pm (except Saturdays) to prepare trekkers. Christian only climbs in emergencies: he is the leader of the rescue team. The hike doesn't actually start until 1 am. This brings you to the crater rim for sunrise, heading back down the mountain by 8 am before clouds envelop the summit and visibility drops to zero. It is truly a climb, so go prepared with a light (torch or flashlight), warm clothing, water, food and sturdy shoes.

Kota Gede

Founded in 1575 by Panembahan Senopati, the town of Kota Gede (pronounced Ge-DAY) just to the southeast of Yogya grew into a flourishing trading center which attracted merchants and craftsmen and served as the first capital of the Mataram kingdom until 1614, when Sultan Agung moved it to Kerta. Kota Gede is a maze of narrow streets lined with tiny silversmith shops and moss-covered, mozaic-tiled houses, once the homes of wealthy Arab and Dutch merchants.

The royal cemetery of Kota Gede, a site of serene ancient grandeur, is one-half km behind the marketplace (turn right after the market). Two huge banyan trees, said to date from the early days of the Mataram kingdom, guard the entrance to the complex, which includes an ancient mosque, royal graves and two courtyards with spring-fed pools.

Javanese dress is required to enter the cemetery itself, and can be hired at the registration post. There are 81 graves here, including Senopati's, his parents' (Ki Ageng Pamanahan and Nyi Ageng Pamanahan), and his son's (Ingkang Sinuwun Sedo Ing Krapyak). Sultan Hamengkubuwono II is buried in the Bangsal Praboyekso, the large building in the northwest corner of the courtyard, and Ki Ageng Mangir's grave is partially inside the building and partially outside (he was Senopati's rebellious son-in-law).

Javanese pilgrims visit the graves (principally Senopati's) to burn incense, scatter flower petals over the tomb and ask for blessings of wealth, health and good fortune. The cemetery can be visited on Mon and Thurs 10 -12 and Fri 1 -3.

One of the pools is home to a large yellow tortoise, Kyai Dudo, and numerous catfish, one of which is named Kyai Reges. The latter's head and tail, it is said, are intact, but its body is skeletal and only becomes visible to those whose prayers will be answered. The rectangular nails of the original building, which was destroyed by a fire in 1900, bring good fortune to the finder. Small donations are appreciated.

To get there, take a *becak* or *andong* from the bus terminal on Jl. Veteran, veer south on Jl. Pramuka and take the left turn on Jl. Tegalgandu to the marketplace. Turn right after the market—the cemetery complex is on the right.

Royal graves at Imogiri

The royal cemetery at Imogiri was constructed by Sultan Agung in 1645 on the western face of the "Thousand Mountains" (Gunung Sewu)—a range of jagged limestone peaks lining the southern coast of Java. Resting on a hill 17 km (10 mi) southeast of Yogya, Imogiri ("Mountain of Mist"), remains a focal point for Javanese ancestor worship. A path from the parking area in back of the quiet village leads up a broad staircase to the cemetery's mosque. From here the pilgrim jour-

KAL MULLER

neys up 345 (some count 360) stairs to the tombs. (If your count of the stairs going up matches your count coming down, it is said your prayers will be fulfilled.)

At the top of the stairs are four large water pitchers—from west to east, Kyai Darumurti (from the Srivijaya empire), Kyai Danumoyo (from Aceh), Kyai Mendung (from Turkey), and Nyai Siyem (from Thailand). These are emptied, cleaned and filled again once a year during the Javanese month of Suro. The water kept in these pitchers is considered to possess high medicinal and fortuitous value.

Sultan Agung's tomb is the highest within the walled-in complex entered via a series of ancient Hindu-style gateways. This is a popular pilgrimage point for Javanese—the tombstone lies in the center of a small chamber with white cloth draped around the walls, and the acrid sweetness of burning incense and rose petals permeates the place. As at the royal cemetary at Kota Gede, traditional Javanese dress (which can be rented at the entrance) is required to enter. One of 70 court retainers from the Yogya and Solo palaces is in constant attendance and will individually take requests for blessings and pass them on to the honored deceased as visitors kneel and pray.

Almost all of Sultan Agung's descendents are buried here also—the Pakubuwono kings of Solo on the western side and the Hamengkubuwono rulers of Yogya in the compounds to the east. The main burial houses have marble floors and house the graves three or four rulers and their relatives. Hamengkubuwono IX, who died in 1988, is buried in the compound farthest to the east. The many graves surrounding the central chambers are those of royal relatives.

Visitors may climb the stairs and circumambulate the complex (a walk around the compound takes about ten minutes and offers a panoramic view of the surrounding countryside, sweeping down to the southern coast) at any time. The tombs, however, are open only on Mon 10 -1 and Fri 1:30 -4, and are closed during the Puasa fasting month. Donations are appreciated. No photographs may be taken within the burial grounds. To get there, take the Jalur (Route) 5 ABADI bus from the Umbulharjo bus terminal and get off at the village of Imogiri, then walk a short distance (veer off to the left) to the parking area and steps to the entrance.

The mystical southern coast

Jagged cliffs meet stormy seas over a glistening black sand beach called **Parangtritis**, 28 km (17 mi) south of Yogya. With its raging surf, salty sea-breeze, star-lit nights and ever-shifting, silvery-black dunes, Parangtritis

Opposite: *A Kota Gede silversmith at work.*
Above: *Funeral services at Imogiri for the mother of Surakarta's Susuhunan (1983).*

ERIC OEY

opens itself to myths, mystics and meditation. The area is filled with beaches, caves, lakes, paths and gravesites, each with its own story. Backed by steep hills and overlooking a wild surf, the sand whispers tales of royal rendezvous, meditating hermits and lost lives.

Makeshift shelters line the beach so that one can sit in the shade (for a minimal charge) on this otherwise scorching beach while contemplating the sea. Currents and undertow are very strong and swimming is dangerous.

This is the domain of Kangjeng Ratu Kidul, Queen of the Southern Ocean, and she is not hesitant in claiming new retainers for her underwater court. She is attracted to the color green, particularly the yellow-green shade called *gadung melati*, and Javanese avoid wearing the color when visiting the shore. Eating stalls and simple accommodations line the beach.

According to local legends, Panembahan Senopati spent three days and three nights in the underwater palace of Ratu Kidul, where he was instructed in and mastered the principles of government and the art of love. The beautiful goddess became his wife, and pledged herself to all his descendants in turn, and she is said to be the power behind the thrones in all the Yogya and Solo palaces.

The spot where Senopati emerged from the queen's underwater palace is enclosed by a white stone wall at **Parangkusumo**, 1 km west of Parangtritis. Ceremonial offerings are presented to Ratu Kidul here by the Sultan of Yogya, and many Javanese come to ask for aid, guidance and blessings. Requests may be made at any time, but most appropriately on Thursday nights, particularly the eve of Friday Kliwon.

Just east of Parangkusumo are the hot water springs of **Parangwedang**. A nominal fee is charged for a 15 minute bath (dip- and-pour *mandi* style) in these reputedly rejuvenating waters.

In the hills behind the beaches are former hermitages and gravesites of legendary figures known for their meditative efforts and supernatural achievements: Syeh Belabelu, Syeh Maulana Mahribi, Kyai Barat Tigo, Panembahan Selaning, and Pangeran Dipokusumo. All are pilgrimage sites for Javanese who have special requests to make.

Even if you have no unfulfilled wishes, the spectacular views from the hilltops makes the hike up well worth the exertion. Paths lead east to the Gambirowati Plateau and over to the edge of limestone cliffs with caves opening out over the ocean, accessible only by rope ladder. One of these was the meditation chamber of a charismatic prince of Yogya, Diponegoro, who led a bloody campaign against the Dutch between 1825-30.

Further east is **Parangendog**, where the sand pebbles are egg-shaped (*endog* in Javanese). Here, a complex of bungalows are

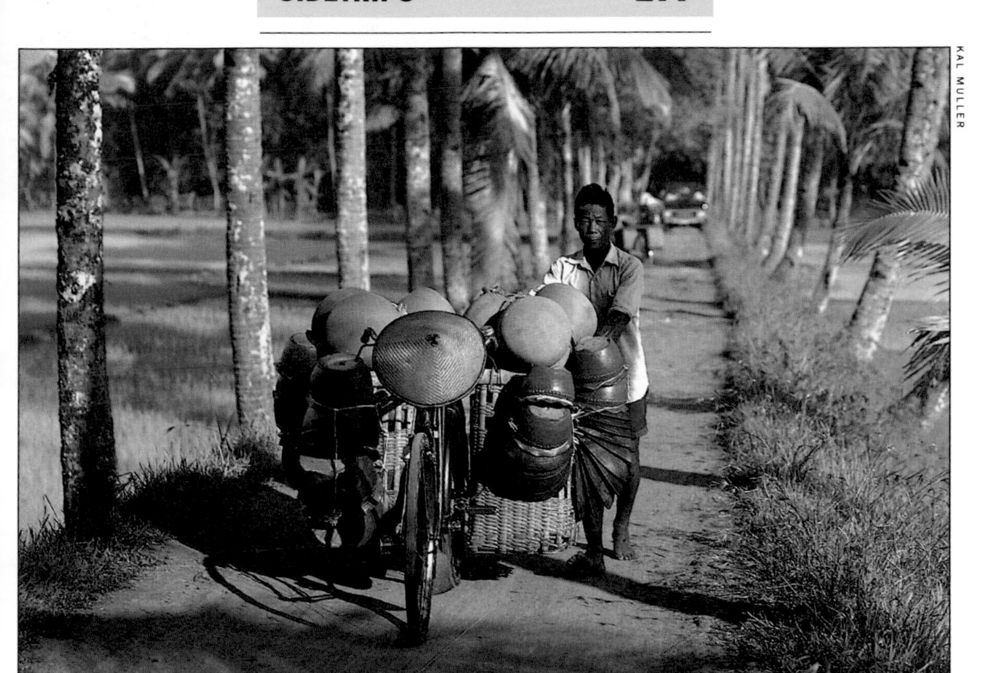
KAL MULLER

available for rent; huts that offer basic, comfortable accommodations without the trappings of modernity (no air-con, telephone, TV, etc.). Take the Jatayu bus from the Yogya bus terminal. Rp600 includes the entrance fee in the beach area.

Secluded beaches

An excursion to the secluded beaches of Baron, Kukup and Krakal—60 km (37 mi) to the southeast of Yogya—offers both the harsh drama of the southern mountains (Gunung Kidul) and the refreshing sea breezes of the southern ocean.

The road to **Baron** winds through one of the driest and poorest areas in Central Java. Lush terraced fields give way to barren limestone hills that centuries ago lay submerged below the sea. Here, an occasional stubby tree dots a landscape where only cassava and maize grow, and villagers must walk for miles to fetch fresh water.

Finally, the violent surf and rough coast come into view. **Kukup** and **Krakal** lie 1 and 6 km to the east of Baron, respectively. To get there, take the minibus to Wonosari from Yogya's Rejowinangun terminal, then transfer to another minibus or *andong*. Head back to Yogya by 4 pm, as there are only simple accommodations in the area. A taxi costs $40 round-trip.

Thirty kms south of Yogya, by minibus via Bantul, is **Samas**, another scorching black sand beach with raging surf. Swimming is dangerous. No overnight accommodations and only a few simple food stalls. To get there, board a white "Abadi" bus marked "Samas" at the north end of Jl. Bantul (just by the southwesternmost corner of the outer *beteng* wall).

Glagah is yet another expansive black sand beach lying to the southwest of Yogya, with new recreational park that is still not completely landscaped. Shaded areas along calm inlets offer pleasant picnic spots; a misty stretch of low surf provides the setting for fantastic sunsets. Swimming here is dangerous, as usual. There are a few eating stalls, but no accommodations. The bamboo contraptions along the edges of the inlets are fish traps with nets.

To get to Glagah, take a white "Abadi" bus marked "Glagah-Congot" from the southwest corner of the *beteng*. You can also get there by car heading west from Yogyakarta along Jl. Wates toward Purworejo, then turning south at the 39 km marker. About 2 km down the road you will see the entrance to the beach area; be prepared to pay a small entrance fee.

—*Joan Suyenaga*

Opposite: *The surf-swept, black-sand beach at Parangtritis is a place of mystics and meditators.* **Above:** *The small villages and districts around the city of Yogya represent a whole different side of urban/suburban life than most tourists see.*

FURTHER EXPLORATIONS

Palaces, Dragons and Caves

The number of interesting places to visit and things to do in and around the Yogya area is literally limitless. Below are some suggestions for those who have already seen the major sights and wish to spend a bit more time exploring off the beaten tourist track.

Other city sights

Just by the first main intersection east of the central post office stands a large, brightly painted **Chinese temple**, Cetiya Buddha Prabha. Simple, folksy *wayang kulit* performances—sponsored by temple members to give thanks for the fulfillment of a prayer—are often held on the front terrace.

Continuing east about 1 km, one comes to the **Biology Museum** (Jl. Sultan Agung 22). Owned and run by the Gajah Mada University's Biology Department, the museum features dioramas of native flora and fauna in their natural habitat. Open Mon-Thurs 8-1, Fri 8-11, Sat and Sun 8-12; Rp150.

Just around the corner (turn right) is the former residence of General Sudirman, the first commander of the Indonesian Army. The house is now a revolution museum, **Sasmita Loka Pangeran Jenderal Sudirman** (Jl. Bintaran Wetan). On display are documents, weapons (some home-made), photos and other memorabilia, including the litter used to carry the general—who suffered from a debilitating lung disease—while commanding the troops. Open Mon-Thurs 8-1, Sat 8-12.

Pakualaman palace

Further east on Jl. Sultan Agung, on the north side of the street, is the Pakualaman, residence of Prince Pakualam VIII, current Governor of Yogyakarta. The Pakualaman was established in 1813 by Raffles during his tenure as Lieutenant-Governor of Java. He awarded autonomous status and a fiefdom to Prince Notokusumo (Pakualam I), in order to counter-balance the power of his older brother, Sultan Hamengkubuwono II.

Unlike the Yogya *keraton*, the Pakualaman faces south (as do all princely residences) and has an open field (*alun-alun*) only in front. The main *pendopo*, Bangsal Sewotomo, stands serenely behind a circular driveway. Gamelan concerts are held here every Sunday Pon on the birthday of the current Prince Pakualam VIII. Attendance (open to the public at no charge) provides ample proof of the acoustic perfection of the structure.

Bordering the pavilion is a quaint cottage that seems as if it belongs in the Swiss Alps. A radio station and various offices inhabit rooms lining the courtyard. The buildings are not open to the public, but a small museum in the southeast corner has ceremonial umbrellas, weapons, flags, banners, royal carriages, gamelan sets and guard outfits. Open Mon, Thurs 10-1.

Gembira Loka Zoo

Much further east, at the end of Jl. Kusumanegara, is the Gembira Loka Zoo. Opened in 1956, its 22 hectares (54 acres) encompass a botanical garden, an orchid nursery, an artificial lake for boating, a children's park with a tunnel running down a hill, foot bridges across the Gajahwong River—and, of course, around 470 animals and birds.

Notable among them are the Komodo "dragons" or monitor lizards (*Varanus komodoensis*) found only on several tiny islands in the Lesser Sundas. This is thought to be the oldest living species of lizard, hailing back some 60 million years. They are enormous, growing to 3.5 meters (11.5 ft) long and weighing up to 130 kg (300 lb). Also present are shy tapirs from Sumatra and scaly anteaters (*Manis javanicus*), as well as *anoa* dwarf buffaloes from Sulawesi and the royal elephant couple, Kyai Rebo and Nyai Rebo.

One of the tigers here was captured some years ago on the campus of Gajah Mada University after wandering down from the slopes of Mt. Merapi. The orangutans, gibbons and newly acquired hippopotamus are all popular favorites. It's best not to go on Sundays, when the zoo is flooded with local visitors. Open daily 8-5. Admission: Rp300.

Prince Diponegoro's home

Nestling in the ricefields at the northwest corner of Yogya (on Jl. H.O.S. Cokroaminoto) is Sasono Wirotomo, the site of Prince Diponegoro's home. The eldest son of Hamengkubuwono III, Diponegoro arose from the economic and political turmoil of the early 1800s to lead a messianic campaign against the colonial rulers and his own ruling family from 1825-30. Today he is venerated as a national hero.

The stately, renovated *pendopo* houses a gamelan and the northern wall is decorated with reliefs of the Java War. A small museum displays Diponegoro's *keris* and lances, which are strewn with flowers—a sign that they are still held to possess spiritual powers. A hole in a brick wall is said to be where Diponegoro escaped from the Dutch to go into hiding and lead the revolt. Admission is by appointment only (tel: 3068). By bicycle, *becak* or *andong,* ride west from the central post office across the bridge, turn right on Jl. HOS Cokroaminoto and ride up to the monument. City buses #1 and #2 pass the site.

Gajah Mada University

Gajah Mada University is one of the largest educational institutions in the country. Founded in 1949 through the merger of several schools in Yogya, Solo and Klaten, the university operated for many years in the Siti Hinggil and Pagelaran pavilions of the *kera-ton*. Since then, Gajah Mada has moved to its own sprawling campus at Bulaksumur and Sekip at the northern edge of the city, land granted by Hamengkubuwono IX. It now boasts an enrollment of 24,000.

Folksy earthenwares

All of the folk ceramics and earthenwares in Yogya comes from the village of **Kasongan** just to the south of the city. Head down Jl. Bantul and turn west (right) at the 6.5 km marker. Follow the road for about 1 km and you'll find yourself in the midst of clay horses, elephants, *naga* snake-dragons, dogs, frogs, piggy-banks, sphinxes, dolls, Chinese-inspired vases, masks and pots. Special orders take a week to ten days. Packing services are provided. Take Aspada Bus C or the ABAADI Bus 2/N from the bus terminal or from the top of Jl. Bantul and walk into the village from the main street.

Sights west of Yogya

During the Javanese month of Sapar, a ritual sacrifice of two larger-than-life dolls made from sticky rice and decorated as a traditional bridal couple is made at the foot of the limestone hills at **Gamping** near Sleman, 6 km (4 mi) west of Yogya, on the road to Wates. The ceremony, which dates back to 1756, is a thanksgiving for the divine protection of the spirits of the mountain. A parade of folk dancers, costumed beasts and spirits, offerings, palace guards, gamelans and royal heirlooms stretches from the village center to the hills where the *bekakak* dolls are slaughtered. The "blood" of the dolls (red palm syrup) is considered auspicious. Ask the Tourist Information Center in Yogya for the date.

Nestled high in the Menoreh hills, 35 km (21 mi) west of Yogya, is **Gua Kiskendo** cave, where vast terraced gardens overlook breathtaking panoramas of the Progo River. The cave, tucked under an enormous banyan tree, is where the mythical monkey kings of the *Ramayana*, Subali and Sugriwo, battled the demon king Maesosuro and his prime minister, Lembusuro. The story is carved in relief into the limestone hills near the cave mouth. A cement stairway leads down into a dank world of stalactites, stalagmites, mountain springs, a natural platform (said to be the battlesite), and a hole in the cave roof that opens up to the sky.

One may enter the cave only if the caretaker is there to unlock the bamboo gateway Sunday is perhaps the best t7ime to find someone here. Take the road west toward Wates and turn right at Sentolo, in the direction of Muntilan. Follow the signs that lead 17 km (10 mi) up into the hills. The last 4 km are fairly steep, and public transport at Girimulyo village can be hired for the final leg.

Sendangsono, the Javanese Lourdes, is the object of a pilgrimages by thousands of Catholics during the month of May. It is located 32 km (20 mi) northwest of Yogya, further north along the road between Sentolo and Muntilan in the Menoreh mountains. The natural mountain spring water at this site is believed to be holy. A statue of the Virgin Mary is enshrined in a niche shaded by an enormous banyan tree, at the spot where she is said to have made an appearance. Pilgrims may take a 3.5 km (2 mi) hike to the Promasan Church from Banjaroya village on the Sentolo-Muntilan road, then follow a 1.5 km (1 mi) pilgrims' path which leads up to the complex. It is also possible to drive in from the village Bendo, near Kalibawang.

West of the Menoreh range, about 750 meters (2450 ft) above sea level, is an impressive cave known as **Seplawan**. Descending 18 meters (60 ft) underground, the main cave is at least 700 meters (2275 ft) deep. The cool, tropical rainforest here and majesty of the cave contrast sharply with the atmosphere of the city. Take a city bus to Purworejo and transfer to a minibus to the village of Donorejo, in Kaligesing sub-district.

—Joan Suyenaga

PART V

Antiquities of Central Java

Hundreds of ancient stone monuments lie scattered about the rugged volcanic landscapes of Central Java. These extraordinary remains date from the early classical period of Javanese civilization, beginning in the first part of the 8th century A.D. and ending rather abruptly soon after A.D. 900. Building activity in this period was even more intensive than the figures alone suggest, as most of the temples were constructed within a few fairly limited areas in the short span of about 80 years between A.D. 780 and 860.

Many of the sites have vanished since their existence was first noted by European observers in the 19th century. On the other hand, more new ones are being unearthed every year. What we see today is of course but fragmentary evidence of a civilization which existed for many centuries, but which created these elegant works of art in a brief but intense burst of activity.

The monuments are also of great interest for what they tell us about early Javanese society. Unlike other hearths of civilization such as Sumer, Harappa, Pagan and China which are situated in flat, featureless river valleys on the Asian mainland, the ancient Javanese inhabited a stunning and lush volcanic terrain—building temples at elevations of up to 2,000 meters (6,500 ft) on a tropical island hundreds of miles from the mainland. Java does not have the harsh climate and seasonal changes of a continental land mass. This gentle physical environment may be partially responsible for the serenity which these carved stones display.

Stone was only used by the ancient Javanese to build temples. No traces of palaces or other secular buildings have been identified, and these must have been built of wood. Palaces are portrayed on Borobudur, but we do not know the extent to which they are accurate depictions of real structures as opposed to fantasies which existed only in the imagination of the sculptor.

The enigmatic Ratu Boko, lying on a hill overlooking the Prambanan Plain, is the best candidate for a site which was designed for secular as well as religious activities. We have no remains of dwellings, nor have any village sites or towns been discovered. Unlike most other centers of ancient civilization, we still lack a detailed context into which to fit the temples of ancient Javanese.

Many artifacts have been unearthed in close proximity to the temples, some of them of a mundane nature. These are almost exclusively earthenware pottery—a medium to which Javanese craftsmen did not devote great artistry. Skilled workers expended much more of their energy on producing metal objects—utensils of bronze, and jewelry of silver and gold. Most of these metal objects were made for religious purposes. Some Chinese porcelain was imported, but not in great quantities.

Most of the everyday objects with which ordinary Javanese would have come in contact were made of organic materials such as wood, bamboo, rattan and vegetable fibers which do not survive a tropical climate for a millennium.

We should perhaps feel grateful, nevertheless, that of all the expressions of ancient Javanese material culture, it is the glorious stone monuments that have been spared, for these appear to have been important cultural focal points. Because we lack other sources of historical information, we must try to use the stone works to recreate as best we can the world of those who created the temples. Viewing the monuments today, we hope to gain an understanding of how these people saw themselves and their work.

— *John Miksic*

Overleaf: *Borobudur's intriguingly intricate form was designed to appeal to the intellect rather than the emotions.* **Opposite:** *The Loro Jonggrang temple at Prambanan. Photos by Luca Tettoni.*

BOROBUDUR

A Pilgrim's Progress to Enlightenment

Borobudur stands on a small hill above the fertile Kedu Plain, 42 km (26 mi) to the west of Yogyakarta, surveying a vast sea of verdant rice fields and coconut groves bounded on all sides by lofty peaks. To the north and east, a majestic procession of volcanoes soars to heights of more than 3,000 meters (10,000 ft); to the south a jagged array of limestone cliffs marches across the horizon, crowned by 1,000-meter (3,000-ft) spurs.

At first sight, the monument itself does not, perhaps, seem as impressive as one might have been led to expect. It does not, for example, soar up into the air, nor does it possess a massive, awe-inspiring profile. Borobudur was designed to appeal to the intellect rather than the emotions, and it appears from a distance as a rather squat, grey mass of stone of rather intriguing intricacy. Indeed, it is only after retracing the long and arduous route of the ancient pilgrim—past 1460 exquisitely-carved stone relief panels set in galleries along the four lower levels, arriving finally at the spectacular upper terraces representing the pure knowledge and enlightenment of the Buddha—that one comes to fully appreciate the extraordinary power and beauty of this, the world's largest Buddhist monument.

Discovery, decay and restoration

The first description of Borobudur appeared in T.S. Raffles' *The History of Java* (1817). Although Raffles is commonly said to have "discovered" the temple, it was not completely buried at this time, as contemporary drawings show, though the galleries were filled with soil and large trees were growing upon it. Javanese living in nearby Yogyakarta were well aware of its existence.

The work of uncovering the stones was begun by a Dutch military engineer, H.C. Cornelius, who was deputed by Raffles to investigate the monument. This work was not pursued intensively, and in 1872 some of the galleries were still covered with dirt. The first measures to conserve the temple were taken in 1874, when van Kinsbergen filled in sunken areas with sand to help water drain away. A major restoration was then undertaken between 1907 and 1911 by a team under Theodor van Erp, who filled in more depressions with concrete and completely recon-

structed the upper round terraces and the collapsed stupas upon them using many new stones.

The monument continued to deteriorate, however. The worst problem was the gradual sagging of floors and tilting of walls, many of which were in danger of falling over. The cause of the problem was rainwater seeping through the stones and undermining the natural hill upon which the monument rests. International appeals resulted in a thorough restoration undertaken between 1975-1984, with sponsorship from UNESCO but majority funding from the Indonesian government. The intricate galleries with their lovely relief panels were then taken apart piece by piece, and altogether over a million stones were individually cleaned, treated and replaced on a new foundation of reinforced concrete.

Architectural history

Borobudur was not designed and built according to a single plan, but instead evolved through at least five different phases of construction over a period of more than 50 years. It was probably begun in about A.D. 780; the last phase of renovation took place between A.D. 835 and 850. Substantial changes were made in the original layout for technical as well as symbolic reasons. Each phase influenced the later ones, and this complicated architectural history makes it even more difficult for us today to unravel the monument's complex symbolism. Borobudur does not in fact embody a single overall concept; its form is the result of an elaborate interplay among many disparate elements, each with its own concepts and messages.

As the temple was being taken apart during the recent restoration, archaeologists got the first detailed view of its internal structure. From this it was possible to compile a detailed history of the five phases of the temple's construction.

In the first phase a smaller building three terraces high was erected, on which another structure was later begun but then destroyed. It seems that the building was initially designed as a stepped pyramid—a shape which may betray the influence of non-Buddhist beliefs, either from Hinduism or some form of indigenous mountain cult. There were no balustrades, so that one could look directly at the inner walls of the terraces from below.

In the second phase, Borobudur's foundation was widened and made higher, so that the stairways had to be redesigned. Now it had five square terraces and a round structure was begun at the top.

In the third stage more thorough changes

Opposite: *Borobudur just after its "discovery" in 1815, based on a sketch by H.C. Cornelius.*
Above: *The collapsed stupas before the 1907-1911 restoration by van Erp, who is shown here.*

were made. The round structure was taken apart and a new set of three round terraces and stupas built. Thus the monument was radically redesigned in the third phase. The entire upper area, and the overall form which we see now then began to appear.

The fourth and fifth periods entailed minor alterations, including the addition of new reliefs and changes in the stairways and archways. The symbolism of the monument remained the same; the changes were largely decorative.

Traces of the various phases can be seen today: a relief from an earlier stage is partially obscured by a door frame from the last period, and part of the round upper terrace from the second phase is exposed in the side of a staircase cut through it in the third phase.

When it was completed, Borobudur may in fact have seemed rather more impressive than it does now. The top was then crowned by a tall, multi-tiered spire symbolizing the Buddhist *cattra* or parasol found on stupas in other Buddhist countries. The *cattra* is now destroyed; it was shattered by lightning.

It seems that Javanese Buddhist concepts changed and became more complex around A.D. 800, and that the structure of Borobudur was altered largely to harmonize with these new ideas. No one knows precisely what these were. It is sufficient for visitors to be aware as they tour the monument that much (though not all) of what they see has resulted from efforts by the monument's planners to erect a building expressing concepts about the nature of an invisible world with which they were trying to make contact.

Form and symbolism

Borobudur is not a temple at all in the sense that it has no cave-like inner sanctuary such as most Javanese temples contain. This tells us that it was designed not to worship a particular deity or person; rather we find that Borobudur was intended to foster a very unique form of personal spiritual education.

No inscriptions have been found around the temple which might illuminate its form and function. Surprisingly, only one possible ancient reference to the temple has been identified—a phrase in an inscription dated A.D. 842 which suggests that Borobudur may originally have been called *Bhumisambhara bhudara*, "Mountain of the Accumulation of Merits of [ten] States [of the Bodhisattva]."

The Javanese of the early 9th century practiced a version of Buddhism belonging to the Mahayana ("Greater Vehicle"). They believed not only in the moral value of Gautama Buddha's teachings, but also in the existence of a large number of supernatural beings known as *bodhisattvas* who could help devotees attain their goal of Nirvana.

There was great diversity within Mahayana Buddhism. It seems that around A.D. 800, Buddhist ideas in Central Java under-

KAL MULLER

LUCA INVERNIZZI TETTONI

went a significant change and that many Buddhist temples were redesigned at this time. The men who converted the pre-Buddhist structure at Borobudur into a Buddhist monument were followers of a school of Tantric thought in which *mandalas*, sacred diagrams, played an important part in rituals used to initiate people into higher levels of spiritual awareness and power.

Borobudur's horizontal plan is in fact a great *mandala*—a fact which becomes evident when the monument is seen from the air. It consists of six concentric outer terraces, each roughly square in shape, with three almost circular terraces above them. A large dome, the principal stupa, stands at the center.

Yet another aspect of Borobudur's symbolism is that it portrays a mountain. The square terraces represent the slopes and the many buddha images in their niches resemble hermits in mountain caves. According to Javanese thought, mountain peaks and hermitage caves are places where contact with sources of ultimate truth and supernatural power may be made. As pilgrims approach and ascend such mountains, they are subjected to physical and mental experiences from which they may draw lessons about themselves and their place in the world. The symbolic mountain which the terraces of Borobudur represents supplies these experiences through the medium of stories sculpted in stone.

The narrative reliefs

The scenes portrayed on Borobudur were probably meant to be viewed by lay pilgrims in the company of priestly teachers. Remains of a monastic complex were uncovered southwest of the monument in 1975. Foundations of another complex which may have been a monastery were found on the same hill as Borobudur to the northwest.

It is customary today to divide the monument from bottom to top into three categories or stages which correspond to the three stages in Buddhist thought on the way to ultimate salvation and Nirvana. Whether the builders of Borobudur recognized these distinctions we have no way of knowing.

According to this scheme, the lowest category is the *Kamadhatu*, or "Realm of Desire." This represents the state of man before he acquired a knowledge of morality, before the teachings of the Buddha became known. The reliefs which illustrate this state were originally sculpted on the foot of Borobudur's first level—now hidden—and depict a text called the *Mahakarmavibhangga*. They show the

Opposite: *From the ground Borobudur appears as a small mountain.* **Above:** *Brahma and a group of gods pay homage to Gautama; a panel from the Life of Buddha reliefs in the first gallery.* **Overleaf:** *Horizontal plan of Borobudur, showing that it forms a* mandala, *a sacred Tantric diagram.*

5m

LUCA INVERNIZZI TETTONI

operation of the laws of cause and effect, which in a Buddhist context includes punishments for various sins.

The *Mahakarmavibhangga* reliefs, numbering 160 panels, had to be covered up during a later phase of Borobudur's construction by the addition of a new and broader base. This occurred around A.D. 800, when the weight of the upper levels became too great and the original foundation began to topple. These reliefs were discovered by accident in 1885, and a complete photographic record was made in 1890-91. Four panels at the southeast corner were left exposed following the recent restoration.

The second stage is known as *Rupadhatu*, the "Realm of Forms"—the period in which man was becoming more enlightened concerning the meaning of life, the need to sacrifice oneself for others and the ultimate reward for right behavior, which was the escape from rebirth. This realm is thought to be represented in the four straight-sided galleries which contain narrative reliefs along both inner and outer walls.

These narratives begin in the middle of the east side of the temple and run clockwise around the monument. Thus to follow the stories, start at the eastern stairway and turn to the left, keeping the monument always to your right. Such a circumambulation or *pradaksina* formed a major part of Buddhist worship. By following the stories one thus accumulates merit simply by the act of walking. There are four series of panels on the first level, followed by two series on each of the three subsequent levels. In order to follow them all in sequence, therefore, one must walk around the monument ten times—a total distance of almost 5 km (3 mi).

Entering the gallery on the first level, two series of reliefs are visible on on the inner wall of the balustrade to the left, an upper and a lower one. These depict episodes from the *jataka* tales, a collection of stories regarding lives of Buddha before he became a human.

To one's right, on the main wall of the first gallery, are two more series of reliefs. Those in the upper series are the most significant, and are devoted to the life story of the historical buddha, Sakyamuni, who lived in the 6th century B.C. The narrative follows an ancient text known as the *Lalitavistara*, "The Unfolding of the Play."

The first panel in this series shows Buddha in heaven. In the next scene, he informs the assembled deities that he will be born as a human. The next 5 panels concern activities in heaven. In panel 8 we see Queen Maya, Buddha's future mother, with her husband King Suddhodana in the palace. This is followed by Queen Maya in her pavilion; then a group of gods in a heavenly palace (the text at this point concerns the decision of the gods to accompany Buddha on his descent). Homage is paid to Buddha, and the next reliefs depict his descent to earth in the form of a white elephant; the queen discussing her dream about the elephant; and various episodes leading to Queen Maya's journey to the Lumbini Park in preparation for Buddha's birth, which takes place in panel 28.

This sequence is followed by other familiar episodes in the life of Buddha: the archery tournament (panel 49), Buddha's encounter with old age (56), sickness (57), death (58) and a monk (59). Panel 65 shows Gautama's escape from his father's palace; in 67 he cuts off his hair; in 94 he is attacked by the demon Mara, and in 95 he is tempted by Mara's daughters. Panel 96 shows Buddha's enlightenment; in 115 he crosses the Ganges; relief 120 shows the first sermon in the Deer Park at Benares. Now we have returned to our original starting point at the eastern stairway, and here the story ends.

The lower reliefs on the main wall depict more *jataka* tales. The first shows a prince who married a nymph. In panel 16 nymphs are taking water from a pool; in 19 the prince and his spouse are serenaded.

On the next terrace begins a new story which takes up most of the rest of the reliefs. This is the *Gandavyuha*, the account of a merchant by the name of Sudhana who made a pilgrimage in search of spiritual knowledge. The *Gandavyuha* material occupies almost 500 panels, many of which are quite similar. They represent Sudhana and the various teachers whom he encounters on his pilgrimage, each of whom offers him guidance. The object of this series was to instruct and edify rather than entertain; the reliefs tend to be repetitive, and the last set of panels on the fourth terrace illustrates the *Bhadracari*, a sequel to the *Gandhavyuha*.

You will notice that set atop the five balustrade walls defining the four relief galleries are 432 buddha statues set into niches. The hand posture or *mudra* of buddhas on each side of the monument is different, except for the top level, where a fifth *mudra* is shown on all four sides.

These *mudras* and their directions correspond to a system of *dhyani* buddhas, each with a specific name. The buddha of the east is known as Aksobhya; on the south is Ratnasambhava; on the west Amitabha, and on the north, Amoghasidda. The buddha positioned on the top wall, Vairocana, is the guardian of the center or zenith.

The 'Realm of Formlessness'

The third and highest realm of Borobudur is called *Arupadhatu*, the "Realm of Formlessness." This term is applied to the three upper terraces of the monument, with their stupas enclosing buddha images. It is thought that upon reaching this level, having received the instruction of various teachers portrayed on the lower galleries, the pilgrim was no longer in need of external guidance.

All that remained was to complete the last steps of the journey at one's own pace. The pilgrim now understood that the pictures below, like everything else in the visible world, were illusory.

The visitor who reaches the uppermost levels of the monument experiences a startling physical transition that is one of the greatest marvels of Borobudur. While in the galleries below, one is completely cut off from the outside world except for a view of the sky and the tips of nearby mountains, which seem as mere echoes of the temple's spires. One's attention focuses instead upon the fine details of the bas reliefs, only a few of which can be seen at a time.

Finally, upon reaching the round terraces, one enters into a large, open space giving expansive views out across the Kedu Plain. The architects undoubtedly sought to create this sensation to represent the pilgrim's newly expanded view of the world.

Set atop these terraces are 72 stupas surrounding a massive central stupa, 9.9 meters (32 ft) in diameter. The smaller stupas have a lattice structure which makes it possible to see buddha images set inside them All of these buddhas display a *mudra* posture symbolizing Sakyamuni's first sermon. You may see people clustering around a stupa just to the right of the eastern stairway; according to popular belief, whosoever touches this statue will obtain good fortune.

The massive stupa at the center of the monument has no openings, but is not solid; there are two hollow chambers at its center, one above the other. When the Dutch Resident of Kedu cleared vegetation from the temple in 1842, it was found that these chambers had been broken into, probably by men searching for treasure. An unfinished buddha image was found in one of them; it now rests on a base beneath a tree about 100 meters to the west of the temple.

—*John Miksic*

Opposite: *In contrast to the enclosed galleries on the lower levels of Borobudur, the round upper terraces open out on all sides, offering panoramic views of the surrounding Kedu Plain.*

THE KEDU PLAIN

Monuments in the Vicinity of Borobudur

The Kedu Plain to the west of Yogya is covered in a thick blanket of volcanic ash washed down from Merapi's slopes. The plain is deeply incised by the Elo and Progo Rivers, which join and flow south from here into the Indian Ocean. A number of smaller ruins have been found around Borobudur, of Hindu as well as Buddhist origin.

Candi Mendut

Mendut is a Mahayana Buddhist temple, 2.9 km (1.8 mi) east of Borobudur, that was discovered in 1834. It first appeared as a mere heap of stones, but when some of these were removed it was found that large sections of the temple walls remained intact, sheltering three magnificent Buddhist statues.

Mendut was the first ancient ruin in Indonesia to be restored. During the dismantling, which began in 1897, traces of a brick structure were found beneath it which may have belonged to an earlier Hindu sanctuary. The temple we see now was built during the reign of King Indra, between about A.D. 784 and 792; slight modifications were later made, in the middle of the 9th century.

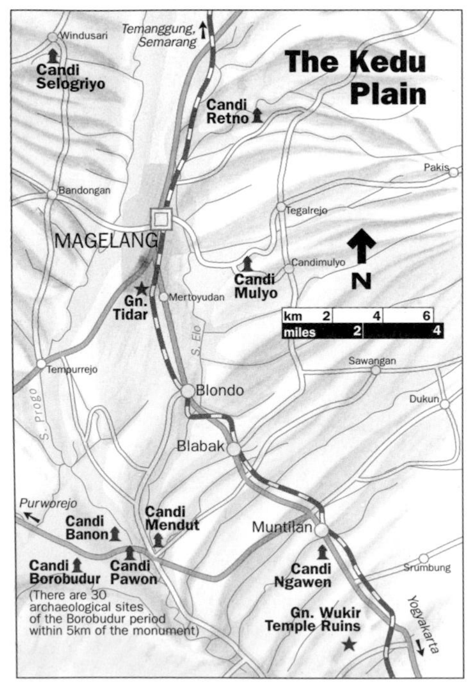

The restoration could not be completed, however, because stones that once formed the tall central stupa, 26.5 meters (86 ft) high, were missing. At some time in the past an avalanche of volcanic mud may have struck Mendut with enough force to sweep away the stones or smash them to bits. They may also have been removed by local residents for use as building materials.

Large decorative panels on the outer walls of the sanctuary portray *bodhisattvas* (including Manjusri and Samantabhadra), recognizable by the parasols sheltering them. On the rear is a large figure depicting Avalokitesvara; another carrying a sword is Khagarbha. In the center of the south wall is a goddess who arises from a lotus in a lake formed by Avalokitesvara's tear.

The temple base contains 30 panels, some with decorative conches and jewels, others with reliefs depicting moralistic fables. One concerns a clever monkey caught by a crocodile who wanted to devour his heart; the monkey convinces the reptile that his heart is actually a mango in a tree and so is carried to safety. The crocodile is stylized; from its mouth a lotus protrudes.

The stairway to the northwest is in an unusual position (most Javanese temples open to the east or west). The walls of the stairway bear more reliefs; on the north side, to the left in the second row, is a brahmin who rescues a crab which subsequently returns the favor by helping him evade a wicked snake and a bird. In the lower right panel, a tortoise is carried through the air by two geese while clinging to a stick. The tortoise thoughtlessly criticizes the geese and plunges to his death.

Inside the entrance are more reliefs. On either side are *kalpataru,* or wishing trees, and *kinnara*—heavenly beings with the head of a human and the body of a bird. These are followed by a man and a woman, Hariti and Atavaka or Alavika, who by nature were fond of eating children. Buddha converts them into protectors and guardian spirits.

Inside the temple are three of the largest and best-preserved statues in Java. In the center is Sakyamuni, the historical Buddha. He is flanked by an image representing either Manjusri or Vajrapani to his left and Avalokitesvara, with an image of Buddha in

LUCA INVERNIZZI TETTONI

his headdress, to his right. These three form a triumvirate of *bodhisattvas,* termed Garbhadhatu; according to the Old Javanese *Sang Hyang Kamahayanikan* text they represent "ultimate reality" (*advaya*). From them issued the five Tathagata or *dhyani* buddhas, also called Vajradhatu. Four niches in the walls, now empty, may have once contained images of the four deities who, together with Sakyamuni, formed the Vajradhatu.

The central figure holds his hands in the *dharmacakra mudra*, setting the wheel of the law in motion. The wheel between two deer in relief on the plinth symbolizes the first sermon in the Deer Park at Benares.

Candi Pawon

On a direct line between Mendut and Borobudur, near the confluence of the Elo and Progo Rivers, lies a small temple sometimes called Brajanalan. It may have been constructed around the same time as Mendut, in the late 8th century. It was restored in 1903 but the shape has been criticized as inaccurate, particularly the roof. It has unusually small windows and relief decorations of bearded men dispensing torrents of riches, *kalpataru*. This may have been a sanctuary for Kuvera, god of wealth. The name Pawon derives from the Javanese word for "ash," reflecting a belief that it was a cremation temple. There is no specific evidence to support this idea.

Candi Canggal

The next oldest antiquity which may be visited in Central Java is Candi Canggal, on a hill called Gunung Wukir to the east of Borobudur. To reach this site, take the road which leads from Yogyakarta to Borobudur, turn off to the left (west) just before a slope covered by a recent Chinese graveyard. Proceed down this road for a few kms then turn right and follow a village road until the end. Park in the village and walk across the paddy fields for about 200 meters to the top of a low hill.

An inscription found here commemorates the erection of a *lingga* by King Sanjaya, who claimed to rule Java and is the first Central Javanese ruler whose name has come down to us. The inscription's date is expressed in the chronogram *cruti-indrya-rasa* (654 Çaka = AD 732). The inscription has been taken to Jakarta, but ruins of several temples can be seen on the broad summit of this hill, from which one has a pleasant view across the plain. Little restoration has been done on the structures, which include a main sanctuary and several smaller buildings. A large *yoni* or base for a *lingga* remains there, and may have been intended for the *lingga* to which Sanjaya referred.

—*John Miksic*

Above: *Three larger than live-size* bodhisattvas *in Candi Mendut, 2.9 km to the east of Borobudur.*

THE DIENG PLATEAU

Misty Abode of the Deified Ancestors

The oldest temples in Central Java stand on an isolated plateau 2,000 meters (6,500 ft) above sea level, about halfway between the north coast and the southern-central hinterland. An early 19th-century visitor estimated that the remains of at least 400 structures were then visible here; only 8 now remain. These are relatively small and unimpressive, and their interest to the casual visitor lies more in the extraordinary setting in which they are found than in the temples themselves.

The name of the plateau comes from the Old Javanese honorific *di-hyang* which was applied to deified ancestors. It lies within the old caldera of a volcano, enclosed by steep mountain walls. Intense volcanic activity is in evidence all around—brightly-colored sulphur springs and lakes, bubbling mudholes and screaming fumeroles. Poisonous gases are sometimes emitted in an area that is well-marked to keep people away. Thick mists swirl into the valley, creating constantly shifting patterns of light. One can easily understand why the ancient Javanese considered this to be the seat of supernatural powers. Modern visitors are equally enthralled by the unearthly natural beauty of Dieng; many find its atmosphere rather spooky.

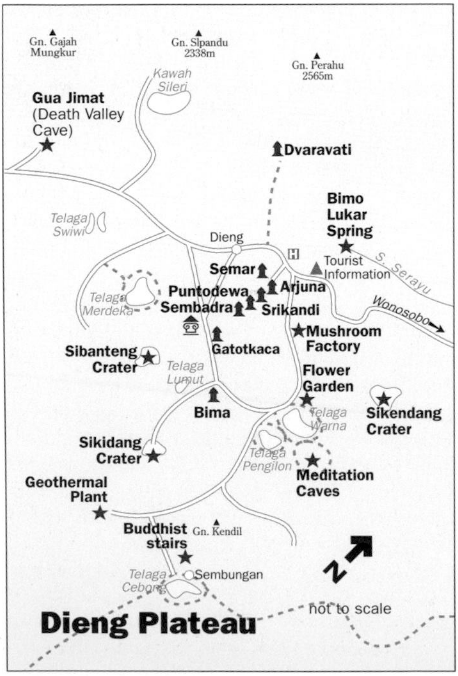

The Arjuna group

Five temples cluster at the northern end of the valley, where the road from Wonosobo enters. The largest is called Candi Arjuna. In front of it (to the west) stands Candi Semar; to its south is Candi Srikandi. These date from between the late 7th century and about A.D. 730. Next to them, to the south, are Puntadewa and Sembadra, which are slightly younger (built between 730 and 780).

Candi Arjuna was consecrated to Siva. The sanctuary contains no cult object; perhaps it originally housed a statue which was ceremonially bathed, the water flowing out through a spout on the temple's north side. There are small niches on the interior wall, probably intended for lamps. The body is plain except for the *kala-makara* ornaments above the niches.

Candi Semar probably housed a statue of Siva's vehicle, the bull Nandi. Similar small shrines once stood in front of Srikandi and Puntadewa, though only the foundations now remain.

Candi Srikandi bears reliefs of three deities on its outer walls: Visnu on the north, Siva on the east, and Brahma on the south. This is quite different from later Hindu temples in Java; where Agastya is on the south, Durga on the north and Ganesa on the side opposite the entrance (which may be east or west). The roof is badly damaged but the body bears additional motifs, such as an incense burner and a water vessel or *kendi*.

The third temple, **Candi Puntodewa**, once had a raised foot around it, but this has disappeared. Near this temple, fragments of a Dongson bronze drum were discovered. Such drums were important in late prehistory and have not been found elsewhere in connection with temples of the classical era.

Candi Sembadra differs from the other temples in that it has no foot. The entrance is decorated with a *kala* motif, but the usual *makara* is absent.

Right: *The Dieng temples are Java's earliest Hindu monuments, and it is likely that this area was already considered sacred in pre-Hindu times.*

Other ancient remains

A temple called **Candi Dvaravati** stands 850 meters north of the Arjuna complex, on a hillside above the Kali Tulis River. The main building has been restored; the *lingga* found in the interior indicates the temple's dedication to Siva. Another *candi*, **Parikesit**, once stood 150 meters to the southwest, but no traces now remain.

Candi Gatotkaca lies on the west side of the valley and is nearly identical to Dvaravati. Another temple once stood to the south of it, but only the foundation remains. Across the road is a small museum where statuary and pieces of the temples are stored.

Many foundations are scattered about the northern part of the valley. Some were probably meant to support wooden buildings that may have served as living quarters for priests, who remained permanently on the plateau, and for pilgrims from the lowlands.

An ancient drainage ditch more than 3 meters (10 ft) deep was constructed to conduct water out of the valley via the northwest corner. It was partly open and partly covered, with shafts at intervals for maintenance. When Europeans first visited in the early 19th century, this channel was out of order and a great swamp covered with forests concealed the temples. The lake in the center of the valley is a remnant of that swamp.

Candi Bima, at the south end of the valley, is unique in all Java. It was built according to a model commonly used in Orissa in northeast India, and was later remodeled, perhaps in order to adapt it for Buddhist use. The upper levels are divided into three tiers, from which sculpted faces gaze outward. The temple stands on an octagonal base facing east, in contrast to most temples at Dieng, which face west.

East of Candi Bima is a lake called **Telaga Warna** ("Colored Lake"), the water of which is tinged with brilliant colors by underwater sulphur vents. A peninsula projects into the lake from the south shore and contains a number of meditational caves. An inscription dated A.D. 1210 has been found here, one of the few from Central Java in this period.

Two different types of remains are found near the point where the road enters the plateau on the east. A hundred meters north of the modern split gate which marks the entrance is a stream with a bathing place containing ancient stone spouts and other remains. This site is known as **Bimo Lukar**.

Just on the other side of the entrance, south of the main road, is a large stone retaining wall. The function of this wall, which is built against the mountainside and equipped with steps, is unknown. It is possible that another structure once stood on the flat space above it, from where enjoys an excellent view of the valley .

—*John Miksic*

ERIC OEY

PRAMBANAN PLAIN

The 'Slender Maiden' and other Marvels

The Prambanan Plain east of Yogyakarta contains the greatest single concentration of ancient sites in Indonesia. Many lie within sight of the main highway connecting Yogya with Solo, suggesting that a road may have existed here already in the 8th century. Colin Mackenzie, a surveyor who accompanied Raffles during the British invasion of Java in 1811, came upon the ruins of the magnificent Loro Jonggrang temple by chance during a journey along this route.

Many more sites, about 50 in all, were later discovered in the vicinity, indicating that this must have been a densely populated area in ancient times. The ancient plain now lies buried beneath several meters of volcanic debris, and no doubt many more sites lie beneath this blanket of sand and gravel awaiting the archaeologist's spade.

Sites covered in this section can be divided into three areas: those along the road from Yogya to Prambanan, those around the town of Prambanan itself, and those lying on the Siva Plateau, a limestone ridge south of the Prambanan Plain.

Candi Sambisari

The first site encountered during a trip east from Yogya along the main road is Sambisari, which probably dates from between A.D. 812 and 838. The temple was discovered in 1966 when a farmer hoeing his field struck a stone which turned out to be the top of the temple, the base of which lay buried under 6.5 meters (21 ft) of earth. This is the largest temple to have been found buried intact in Java. To reach it, turn left at the 12.5 km marker and proceed north for 2.5 km.

Sambisari was built on a raised terrace, probably near a river. Periodic avalanches of volcanic ash seem to have progressively covered the building. More structures may be buried nearby; a wall was accidentally discovered 100 meters to the east when a ditch was dug to drain water from the site. For the moment, the expense of excavating huge volumes of dirt prevents further investigation of this possibility.

The temple complex consists of a main sanctuary and three subsidiary ones. It was dedicated to Siva; the central temple still contains its *lingga* and *yoni*. The temple has no foot, so that the niches on the outside are

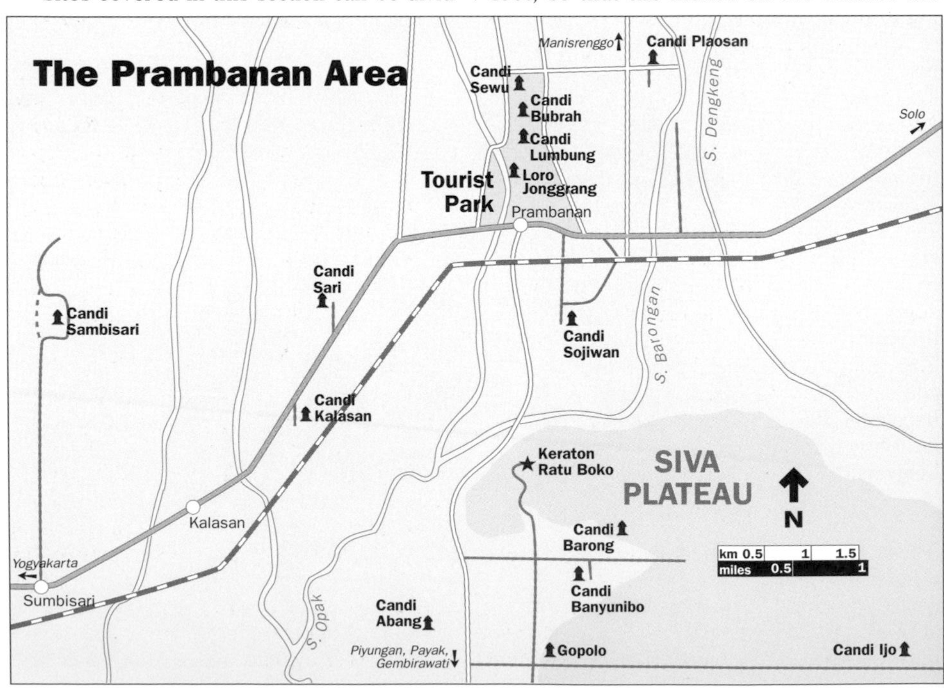

very low, just above the floor. Twelve stones project up from the pavement around the temple body—probably bases for wooden pillars supporting a roof that sheltered the central sanctuary.

The temple's statuary is nearly complete. In exterior niches we find the standard configuration of Durga to the north, Agastya to the south and Ganesa to the east. Niches on either side of the doorway once contained the two door guardians, Mahakala and Nandiswara, but these have been stolen.

The subsidiary temples consisted of stone bases with wooden superstructures. Two of them still contain pedestals for images. Eight small stone pillars resembling *linggas* were placed at the corners and midpoints of the temple grounds. These were installed during ceremonies conducted to lay out the temple.

Candi Kalasan

The next site is Candi Kalasan, an important temple on the south (right-hand) side of the road. A sanctuary was first built on this site in A.D. 778, but later renovations enclosed it. Restorers in 1927-1928 left a part of the earlier structure exposed on the west side, just above the foundation. The restoration could only be partially completed because important parts of the structure were missing.

Several patches of the original white plaster which once covered Kalasan's exterior have been preserved. This is the best surviving example of the type of covering that was once found on most Javanese temples, including Borobudur. The temple's decoration is also quite beautiful, particularly the great *kala* head over the south door, the *kalamakaras* surmounted by temple outlines over the niches, and the vases and flowers in panels on the sides.

The temple contains one large and three small chambers. The main room is entered from the east; inside is an altar which once supported the temple's main image. This is thought to have been a large bronze statue of Tara. Each of the subsidiary chambers once contained three statues. Other buildings, perhaps monasteries, formerly stood in the vicinity. Stones lying about the courtyard have been collected from these sites.

Candi Sari

A few hundred meters east of Kalasan, down a lane on the opposite (north) side of the road, one reaches another Buddhist sanctuary, known as Candi Sari. This temple is very different—it is rectangular and has two stories, each containing three rooms, separated by a wooden floor which has vanished. The main entrance is to the east. It was restored in 1929-1930; originally it was probably accompanied by subsidiary structures, but only a few stones remain. The temple would have been surrounded by a broad foot where worshippers performed their *pradaksina* circumambulations to gain merit, but this has also disappeared.

The exterior walls are decorated with exceptionally beautiful figures. There are sensuous female deities, probably Tara (some in dance posture), as well as male *bodhisattvas* and *naga* kings (many playing musical instruments), and *kinnara*. Windows allow shafts of light into the interior, where statues once stood but have now completely vanished. The niches for them are well preserved, surmounted by stern *kala* heads.

The Loro Jonggrang complex

The major Prambanan area temples begin just across a bridge over the sacred Opak River. The main site here is the so-called Loro Jonggrang complex, generally considered to be Java's most elegant and awe-inspiring *candi*, noted for the graceful proportions of its 47-meter (152-ft) central Siva temple. An

LEIDEN UNIVERSITY LIBRARY

Above: *The voluptuous statue of Durga which stands in the northern chamber of the main Siva sanctuary at Prambanan.*

RIO HELMI

inscription housed in the National Museum in Jakarta records that the complex was completed in 856 to mark the victory of a Hindu king, Rakai Pikatan, over his Buddhist rival.

The temple name literally means "Slender Maiden" and derives from a local legend. It is said that King Boko's son, Bandung Bondowoso, desired to marry the daughter of a ruler at Prambanan, but she resisted by setting him the impossible task of building a thousand temples in a single night. He nearly accomplished this feat with the help of gnomes, but she then ordered her maidens to begin pounding rice—an activity which Javanese women normally conduct at dawn. This caused the roosters to begin crowing and the gnomes, fearing that they would be caught abroad in daylight, fled and left the last temple unfinished. Bandung Bondowoso thereupon cursed Loro Jonggrang, turning her into the voluptuous statue of Durga which now stands in the northern chamber of the main Siva temple.

The work of restoration was begun in 1930-33 and continues today. The central Siva temple was completed in 1953, the Brahma temple to the south of it in 1987, and it is expected that the Visnu temple to the north will be completed in the early to mid-1990s. Two temples in the second or outer courtyard have also been restored.

The complex is dedicated to Siva. The temples stand on man-made terraces on three levels. The two lower levels once supported 224 practically identical temples; the top level contains the main Siva, Brahma and Visnu temples, opposite which are shrines for Siva's vehicle, the bull Nandi, and two other statues.

The main sanctuary appears even taller than it is due to the skillful use of architectural techniques to exaggerate the vertical perspective. To the left of the main stairway is a small shrine; this stands at the central point in the complex, and was probably used to appease the chthonic spirits of the place.

Climbing the main staircase on the east side of the temple, one arrives at a terrace enclosed by a wall. On the outside of this wall, seen from below, are niches containing groups of three heavenly beings interspersed by dancers and musicians. All these decorations are meant to denote that the temple itself is a *meru* or abode of gods, as these are the things which the ancient Javanese expected to see in heaven. The dancers signify the role of Siva as Nataraja, the "Lord of the Dance" who dances at the end of each era to destroy the world so that it may be recreated.

The *Ramayana* reliefs

One of Prambanan's main attractions is the series of beautiful narrative reliefs illustrating the *Ramayana* epic that runs along the inside of the low wall around the walkways of the Siva and Brahma temples. The series begins on the Siva temple to the left of the eastern stairway, proceeds clockwise around this temple, and concludes on the south side of the Brahma temple.

In the first panel, Visnu is upon a serpent with Garuda behind him, and sacrifices are being made to him. The next panels show the palace of Rama's father, Rama's victory over the demons, his marriage to Sita, and the preparations for his coronation, which are then thwarted by one of the king's consorts. Rama, together with his brother Laksmana and Sita, go into exile and experience various adventures. Sita is later kidnapped by the demon Rawana and a long battle ensues to free her, with the help of a monkey army. Guides at the temple will recount the story for you, panel by panel.

Opposite the *Ramayana* reliefs, on the main wall of the temple, are 24 relief sculptures of deities representing the guardians of the compass directions. The temple itself has four interior chambers housing statues of Siva, Agastya, Ganesa and Durga.

The *Ramayana* story is continued on the

KAL MULLER

Brahma temple, which stands to the south of the main Siva sanctuary. Here are scenes from the battle between Rama and Rawana, and the aftermath when Rama and Sita are reunited. A statue of Brahma stands in the temple's single interior chamber.

The large northern temple is dedicated to Visnu and houses a statue of him. Its terrace wall bears reliefs illustrating legends about Visnu's incarnation as Krishna.

Sewu and Plaosan

Two important Buddhist complexes, Sewu and Plaosan, lie very close to here. About 500 meters to the north, Candi Sewu is older than Loro Jonggrang and underwent several modifications during its lifetime. Like the latter, it consists of a main sanctuary surrounded by many subsidiary temples, in this case 240 (though the name literally means "1000 temples"). This symmetrical configuration seeks to generate harmony in the kingdom by creating a replica of the world in miniature, just as the *keratons* of Yogya and Solo do now.

The Sewu complex is being restored; it is famous for its large, well-made and well-preserved guardian statues, as well as for its subsidiary temples with relief carvings, one of which has been completely restored. The fierce *dwarapala* guardians have often been copied; replicas stand by the main entrance to the central courtyard of the Yogya palace.

Candi Plaosan is another large Buddhist complex which has been partially restored. The main group consists of two large structures similar in form to Candi Sari. This is called Plaosan Lor (north) to distinguish it from Plaosan Kidul (south), a smaller complex 100 meters (325 ft) away.

Surprisingly, Buddhist Plaosan Lor was probably built between A.D. 835 and 860, during the reign of the Hindu king, Rakai Pikatan, whose principal monument, Loro Jonggrang, was dedicated to Siva. He was married to a Buddhist queen, and religious tolerance was such in ancient Java that he contributed financial support for the construction of a temple for his wife's religion. This is one indication of the harmonious relationship that existed between Hinduism and Buddhism in classical Indonesia, in contrast to the situation which existed in India.

The main temple that has been restored originally contained three groups of three statues on the lower level, with perhaps more statues on the upper level. The floor was made of wood and has disappeared, although a base for the steps can still be seen in the south chamber. The central statues have all disappeared; they were probably bronze bud-

Opposite: *The restored Brahma and Siva temples in the Loro Jonggrang complex.* **Above:** *A panel from the famous* Ramayana *reliefs. While hunting in the forest, Rama spots and chases a golden deer, who is actually the evil Rawana in disguise.*

LUCA INVERNIZZI TETTONI

dha images. The flanking *bodhisattvas* are still in place, and reliefs on the walls of the side chambers depict people in worshipful attitudes; these were probably temple donors. One, on the south wall of the north chamber, wears a Khmer headdress.

The ruins of a second temple essentially identical to the one just described stand to the north. Both buildings have courtyards enclosed by walls, beyond which are guardian statues. Remains of an encircling moat have been recently uncovered.

These two rectangular buildings were once surrounded by a dense forest of 116 stupas and 58 small temples. One example of each of them has been reconstructed. Short inscriptions were carved into the foundations of many of these, and have provided much valuable information for historians.

North of the two stone buildings is the foundation of a very different type of structure. It consists of a large stone pavement, square in shape, with protruding stones that once supported wooden pillars. Stone statues, badly defaced, line the entire east side and part of the north and south sides. Originally a wooden roof sheltered them.

Sojiwan and Ratu Boko

Another Buddhist temple, Candi Sojiwan, lies 2 km (1.2 mi) to the south of Loro Jonggrang. Restoration work here is in the early stages. Some interesting reliefs can be seen around the foundation depicting scenes from various *jataka* stories. Archaeologists have also discovered many well-preserved Chinese Tang ceramics at this site.

Sojiwan lies at the foot of the Siva Plateau, a steep-sided line of limestone ridges that borders the Prambanan Plain to the south, forming a prominent backdrop to Loro Jonggrang and a striking sight for visitors arriving at Yogya's Adisucipto airport. Ancient Javanese architects chose these heights as the setting for several structures. The most interesting is referred to by the Javanese as Keraton Ratu Boko ("King Boko's Palace"), a reference to the legend described above which gives Loro Jonggrang its name.

The ruins attributed to Ratu Boko fall into three separate clusters. The first which the visitor encounters in walking up from the parking area is an impressive gateway on two levels, with remains of elaborate stone facings. East of the gateway is a flat area covered now in rice fields. No traces of ancient structures have been found here; the popular term for this area, *alun-alun*, underlines its resemblance to the open square found in front of traditional Javanese palaces.

From the northern edge of this field one has impressive views of the Prambanan and Yogyakarta Plains, Mt. Merapi to the north, the Menoreh Hills to the west, and the Indian Ocean to the south. Near the northwest corner of the plateau is a large, square stone structure, the top of which is accessible by a staircase on the west side. In the center is a large, square depression. Its function is unknown; it is popularly regarded as a place for ancient cremations.

The second cluster of ruins is reached by following a path to the southwest corner of the *alun-alun*, then turning left between a line of houses which are actually built on stones taken from the ancient structures. After about 50 meters the path turns to the right and crosses a stone foundation, which once supported a wooden structure. The way continues down a slope, then turns east and climbs back upward; after a few hundred more meters one sees a stone enclosure with gateways to the north, west and south. Inside is another foundation consisting of two parts connected by a narrow, bridge-like walkway. Slightly raised circles formerly supported ancient wooden pillars and a very broad roof.

Leaving the enclosure through the south doorway one comes upon an area where more stone floors and pavilions once stood; their outlines are being gradually revealed by

LUCA INVERNIZZI TETTONI

archaeological excavations. To the east, just beyond the enclosure wall, is a long, low stone foundation for another wooden building. Standing upon this platform, one can gaze down upon a complex of artificial pools carved into the limestone. Several rectangular pools may be seen to the north, and a second group of circular pools to the south. These still provide local villagers with an important source of water for washing and bathing.

Beyond the pool area is a terrace with a number of ruins, referred to by villagers as the *keputren* or women's quarters. When the southerly of the two foundations was being cleared in 1987, a base for a *lingga* was discovered in the center of the floor, marking this as a Siva sanctuary. In the same year, pieces of a Buddhist stupa came to light nearby, and a number of inscriptions found here refer to a Buddhist monastery and the consecration of Sivaitic *linggas*.

A third cluster of remains lies several hundred meters north of the first enclosure. Here are two man-made meditation caves, the roofs of which have collapsed, as well as a square pool with a niche and a stairway hewn from the limestone. This area was the quarry from which stones were obtained.

Neither the uses for these clusters nor the relations between them are clear. Theories range from a palace to a religious center to a fort. The site was perhaps first occupied during the late 8th century when Buddhism was dominant, but by the mid-9th century was perhaps appropriated by Hindus.

Other sites

Many other structures once stood at the western foot of the limestone escarpment and atop its crest. Just west of the foot of the plateau's northwest tip is Watugudik, marked by enormous stone pillar bases and bricks. Southeast of Ratu Boko's "palace" stands Banyunibo, originally part of a much larger Buddhist site, now completely restored. On the hill above it stands Candi Barong, and nearby is Dawungsari where the foundations of very large stupas are being excavated.

South of Ratu Boko's palace, on the next road leading up the ridge, are the remains of Gopolo and Candi Ijo. Further south one passes Candi Abang, standing on a separate hillock west of the road from Prambanan to Piyungan. South of Piyungan lies Payak, the best-preserved bathing place in Central Java.

Much further south, only 2 km from the ocean, is Gembirawati, two stone terraces with facings and a staircase. This site is of great archaeological interest despite its simple form because it probably dates from the 15th century.

— *John Miksic*

Opposite: *A figure, perhaps a* bodhisattva, *adorns one of the subsidiary temples at Candi Sewu.* **Above:** *The huge gateway at Ratu Boko.*

PART VI

Introducing Surakarta

The regal city of Surakarta, popularly known as Solo (pronounced SAW-law), straddles the banks of the mighty Bengawan Solo River, just 60 km (38 mi) to the east of Yogya. The Mataram court was transferred here in 1745 by Pakubuwana II following the sacking of his palace at nearby Kartasura, and since that time Solo has assiduously cultivated its reputation as a city of aristocratic refinement—of exquisite manners, elegant speech and great artistic accomplishment.

Two of Java's greatest poets, Yasadipura and Ronggowarsito, lived here, and since the beginning of the 19th century many Europeans have come to the city to study traditional Javanese literature. As early as 1832 the Dutch opened a Javanese language institute in Solo; one of Indonesia's first museums was founded here in 1890, followed in 1930 by an institute for the study of Javanese culture, *Panti Budoyo*.

The Solonese style of dance, gamelan music and *wayang kulit* puppetry is immediately recognized by Javanese connoisseurs on account of its subtlety and elegance. Ethereal, fluent and supple, this style has become popular throughout Indonesia—even making inroads in rival Yogyakarta, which prides itself on its own artistic traditions. Solo is also famous as a center for batik production. Although traditional hand-crafted batik has lost ground in recent years to machine-printed fabrics, there are still three major batik factories in the city and dozens of smaller ones. As with all its artistic products, Solo batik has a very distinctive look.

Solo is known as "the city that never sleeps"—its *warung* foodstalls and *kaki lima* foodcarts operate virtually around the clock. Certain dishes are even associated with times of the day—*soto* (soup) in the morning, *sate* in the evening, *nasi liwet* (rice cooked in coconut cream) at night and *bubur* (rice porridge) in the pre-dawn hours.

Last but not least, Solo is known for the beauty of its women, as described in the well-known *kroncong* song, *Putri Solo* ("The Solo Girl"): *The Solo girl is quite a flirt—with jasmine in her hair she takes your breath away.*

The town has a population of over half a million today, with a density comparable to that of Brooklyn. It seems even more crowded than this, however, as there are no high-rise buildings. But then, the Javanese are a gregarious people; *mangan ora mangan nek kumpul* ("Company is more important than food") as they are fond of saying.

War and rebellion

Solo's role as a royal capital traces back to the Islamic kingdom of Mataram that flourished near present-day Yogyakarta in the 17th century. Under Sultan Agung (r. 1613-46) it conquered most of Central and East Java, and for the next 100 years the dynasty ruled as the undisputed power in the area. The court moved several times as the result of wars and intrigues, finally settling at Kartasura, 12 km (7 mi) west of Solo, in 1680.

In 1740, a massacre of Chinese in Batavia resulted in a long and complex series of battles that soon engulfed Central Java. Chinese who escaped the massacre fled here, where they besieged Dutch outposts and received assistance from Pakubuwana II (r. 1726-49). The Dutch responded by allying themselves with the ambitious ruler of Madura, Cakraningrat IV, who promptly invaded and sacked Kartasura in 1742.

Restored to his throne by the Dutch, Pakubuwana II was forced to grant them considerable territory and influence. In 1743 he abandoned Kartasura and erected a new

Overleaf: *The annual Kirab Pusaka festival, in which the court regalia are ritually cleansed and carried in a stately midnight procession around the* keraton. **Opposite:** *The Sekaten festival, held annually on Muhammad's birthday in the Javanese month of Maulud. Both photos by Eric Oey.*

palace at the village of Solo, which he then renamed Surakarta.

Why was Solo chosen as the site for the new court? Perhaps its location on the banks of Java's longest river, the Bengawan Solo, was a major consideration. Until the 19th century, river travel was far easier and quicker than travel by land, and although it is now silted up and impassable, the Solo River at this time provided access all the way to the coast near Surabaya.

Traditional stories about the founding of Surakarta stress the miraculous way in which the site was chosen. Neither the king nor his Dutch advisors considered the swampy town, it is said, until certain divine portents pointed to it. Even then, the swamps could be cleared only after the spring which fed them had been stanched through divine intervention.

A kingdom divided

Pakubuwana II's descendants have ruled in Surakarta for over two centuries, but not as undisputed overlords of the Mataram realm. Two members of the royal family—the king's brother, Mangkubumi, and his nephew, Raden Mas Said—refused to accept Pakubuwana II's capitulation to Dutch demands. Convinced of their own right to rule, they refused to join him in Surakarta.

Subsequent battles between Mangkubumi and the combined forces of Pakubuwana and the Dutch resulted in a stalemate. In the end, Mangkubumi was given half the kingdom and built a new palace in Yogyakarta. Raden Mas Said remained in rebellion for some time, but was finally appeased by a grant of 4,000 households carved from Pakubuwana's domain. In 1757, he ended his rebellion and founded a "junior" line of Solonese nobility, taking the name of Mangkunegara I (r. 1757-95). He built his own palace in the north of Solo; the city's main thoroughfare, Jl. Slamet Riyadi, today marks the boundary of his former desmene.

The *Pax neerlandica* which followed lasted (apart from the Java War of 1825-30) up to the Japanese invasion, leaving Javanese aristocrats without battles in which to demonstrate their martial virtues of courage and loyalty. As the knightly ethic became less relevant, connoisseurship in the arts gradually replaced it as the distinguishing mark of nobility. The ideal aristocrat became one who appeciated the arts, sponsored them, and even practiced them if possible.

Pakubuwana IV (r. 1788-1820), for example, authored a classic Javanese homiletic poem, was an amateur *dalang,* and had several splendid gamelan sets cast for him. His successor, Pakubuwana V (r. 1820-1823) supervised the compilation of the *Serat Centini*, a verse romance incorporating encyclopaedic descriptions of all things Javanese, from medicine to music. (The king is said to have personally contributed many sexually explicit passages to the final draft.) Mangkunegara IV (r. 1853-1881) was a particularly prolific author, and is credited with producing the best-known of all Javanese poems, the *Wedatama*. In it, he warns his readers against those who deem themselves to be strict Muslims, and praises the traditional mystical strain in Javanese Islam.

The last emperor

The definitive history of Surakarta has yet to be written, but it would certainly contain a colorful cast of characters. Besides Javanese, Chinese, Arabs and Indians, there were Dutch administrators and Theosophists, the occasional Turk or American—even a former Prussian mercenary employed in the palace to oversee the janitorial staff.

Of the Pakubuwana rulers, the Solonese recall Pakubuwana X (r. 1893-1939) with special reverence. The initials "PB X" can still be

Above: *The young Pakubuwana X with Dutch Resident de Vogel.* **Right:** *The same ruler, with wife and children, several decades later.*

seen around the city on ornamental archways and on the stained-glass tower in front of the palace Pagelaran. Like his predecessors, Pakubuwana X commanded no real army, and did not even have a free hand in appointing his own *patih* (prime minister). Yet he was tremendously popular, and nettled the Dutch through a series of royal progresses in which he was lionized by his people as if he were in fact the island's true ruler.

Pakubuwana X is remembered today not so much for the many buildings, schools, mosques and hospitals that were established during his long reign, but for the great mystical power he is said to have possessed. His speech was putatively *mandi*—magically potent; a word of displeasure from him, it is said, could kill instantly. He is also the last ruler of Surakarta to have lived in true royal splendor. In 1930 there were 5,000 attendants at his court, including wives, children, concubines and servants. The expense of maintaining this household and of staging the spectacular ceremonies required by the traditional calendar was a source of constant irritation to the Dutch. When Pakubuwana X died in 1939, the government deprived his son and successor of the last vestiges of autonomy, and cut the palace budget by 50 percent.

Dawn of a new era

At the beginning of the 20th century, nationalist sentiments brewed in Surakarta. Boedi Oetomo, the first Indonesian nationalist organization, was founded here in 1908, and its leadership was almost exclusively Solonese after 1914. Indonesia's first mass political party, Sarekat Islam, was re-formed in Solo in 1912 and unrest mounted throughout the 1920s as strikes, arson and bombings, were answered by jail sentences and exile for the leaders.

It thus came as a great shock that a lightning blitzkrieg by the Japanese in 1942 could so easily dislodge the Dutch. After three long years of suffering under the rationing, confiscations and forced labor of the occupation, the Solonese had to suffer through four more years of revolution (1945-1949). When it was clear that the Dutch forces could be resisted no longer, the city's radio transmitter was dismantled and carried to the hills, where it was used to broadcast bulletins to the resistance. The exquisite *pendopo* of the Kepatihan, the municipal administration in Solo (now SMKI, the High School of the Performing Arts), was burned to the ground rather than be allowed to fall into Dutch hands.

When peace was restored, the Solonese chose to leave behind their feudal past, merging with the province of Central Java of the new Republic of Indonesia. They have not, however, abandoned their cultural heritage, and Solo remains a proud and conservative stronghold of Javanese arts and traditions.

— *Marc Perlman*

SIGHTS OF SOLO

Java's 'Other' Illustrious Court City

Few foreign visitors make their way to Solo, at least by comparison with the huge numbers who visit the rival royal town of Yogya, just 60 km (38 mi) away and only 2 hours by car or bus. Though sharing a common heritage and a similar layout, the two cities are actually quite different. Surakarta is considered (by the Solonese, of course) to be the more refined and more aristocratic—after all, the Surakarta palace can rightfully claim to be the elder and more legitimate royal house of Central Java. Solo today is also quieter than Yogya and more of a commercial town.

A visit here is well worthwhile, even if on a quick day-trip to tour Solo's two palaces. At the very least, the journey puts Yogya into some kind of perspective. Several days are of course needed to explore the city, and these can profitably be spent poking around fascinating old markets, shops and side streets.

ERIC OEY

The Kasunanan palace

In Javanese cosmology, the ruler is God's earthly "shadow"—a divine figure who sits motionless at the center of the universe. In fact the name *Pakubuwana* (as the king or Sunan of Surakarta is known) literally implies that he is a "nail" or "spike" around which the cosmos revolves. The Sunan's traditional palace or *keraton* thus forms a kind of hub or "anchor" for the kingdom.

Keraton Surakarta—also called the Kasunanan or "place of the Sunan"—was relocated to Solo from Kartasura in 1745. According to legend, emissaries of Pakubuwana II were led here by the beautiful and powerful goddess of the south seas, Kangjeng Ratu Kidul. Solo at this time was unsuited for the construction of a palace because of swamps and lakes which, it is claimed, were drained only with Ratu Kidul's assistance.

The move to the new *keraton* on February 17, 1745 was a grand and momentous occassion. The procession was preceded by two sacred banyan trees that now stand in the middle of the northern *alun-alun,* representative of the court's stability. These were followed by a succession of troops, horses, elephants and palanquins bearing the precious *pusaka* heirlooms—the *keris*, lances and other regalia in which the divine power of the royal line is thought to reside.

The *keraton* is aligned along a north-south axis. The northern gate is where all ceremonial processions begin, and where visitors are received. Tradition forbids the Sunan from entering or leaving by the southern gate, the Gapura Gading, except when his earthly remains are borne aloft to the cemetery at Imogiri after his death.

Entering the palace precincts from the northern *alun-alun* square, you first pass by a huge pavilion, known as the **Pagelaran**, where the king, seated on high, formerly held audience before the assembled populace. This ceased after independence, when the court lost all formal trappings of power; today the building remains unused.

Continuing around to the south, one passes through a massive gate, the Gapura Brajanala, and enters the **Baluwarti** district (the name is from the Portuguese *baluarte*, meaning bulwark)—a huge walled fortress surrounding the *keraton* proper. This neighborhood, measuring some 700 x 500 meters, formerly housed the king's servants and officers. The names of its sub-districts (Carangan, Wirengan, Tamtaman, etc.) refer to units

of the royal guards stationed there. Baluwarti was also home of the *abdidalem palawija*, the dwarfs and albinos whose strange appearance was ascribed to magical influences, and who resided near the king to augment his supernatural powers. Residency inside the fortress was once reserved for royalty and palace retainers, and a large proportion of the residents here are still aristocrats and officers of the court.

One enters the palace proper through a small door to the left of the main entrance. The main door is used only on ceremonial occasions, whereas the door to the right is reserved for the royal family. Visitors are required to wear a *samir* or red and gold ribbon around the neck as a mark of respect, and to remove their shoes.

Inside this gate are two small pavilions or *pendopo*. The one on the left is where military officials formerly gathered; the one on the right was for civilians. The latter is now used for monthly *klenengan gamelan* concerts.

Visitors next pass through yet another gate into the inner *keraton* courtyard, passing before a huge mirror whose inscription invites the visitor to examine his soul before being received by the king. Immediately inside stands a huge, phallic-looking tower whose eight faces are said to represent the eight-fold path of the Buddhist religion. In fact, the structure rather resembles an old Dutch windmill without the vanes, and one suspects this may have played a part in the design. At the top of the tower is a room which none but the king and certain female servants may enter; it is here that the Sunan communes with the goddess Ratu Kidul on the anniversary of his coronation each year. In these royal trysts the divine power to rule Java, originally conferred upon the dynastic founder, Panembahan Senopati, is periodically renewed.

Around the tower spreads a vast and sandy, tree-filled courtyard. The black sand was brought from the southern shore, home of Ratu Kidul. To the right is a large, marbled *pendopo* where the ruler receives honored guests. This is attached to the *dalem* or royal chambers where the king resides. On the south side is the *keputren*, an area reserved for the Sunan's daughters and wives (the present Sunan has six). The only man allowed to enter this area is the king himself. To the left of the courtyard is a museum displaying the *pusaka* and paintings of the previous Sunans.

Many inner *keraton* structures are of recent construction, the result of an extensive restoration following a disastrous fire in

ERIC OEY

Opposite: *The reigning Susuhunan, Pakubuwana XI, on the anniversary of his coronation (Tingalan Jumenengan) in 1983.* **Above:** *The captain of the* keraton *guard.* **Right:** *Palace retainers with parasols, which constitute a mark of rank. Yellow ones are traditionally reserved for royalty.*

January of 1985 that destroyed more than half of the buildings, including the grand *pendopo* and the *dalem*. While electrical wiring was officially blamed, many Javanese believe that the neglect of court rituals aroused the anger of Ratu Kidul, and the restoration was duly followed by elaborate ceremonies of purification.

The royal mosque

Back outside the *keraton*, return to the *alun-alun lor* or northern square, which is empty except for a pair of sacred "fenced" banyan trees (*waringin kurung*) at the center. Tradition has it that these were carried wrapped in silk at the head of the great procession when Pakubuwana II moved his court here from Kartasura in 1746. Each tree has a name: Kyai Jayadaru stands to the east; Kyai Dewadaru to the west. In times past, only the king was allowed to walk between them. More recently, Javanese soldiers used the leaves of these trees to make protective amulets during the revolution.

On the west side of the main square stands the **Mesjid Ageng**—the Grand or Royal Mosque. Built in 1750 by Pakubuwana III and enlarged and improved by various Sunans since, this enormous structure sits in a compound measuring some 3.5 hectares. The mosque is in the form of an enclosed *pendopo* with traditional *joglo* roof—more Javanese, architecturally, than Middle Eastern. Ties with the *keraton* are still strong, as many court ceremonies and festivals, such as Sekaten, still take place here.

Two structures on either side of the main gate are reserved for the annual sounding of the royal gamelan orchestras during Sekaten week. Tradition states that these instruments were played here to attract converts to Islam —something that is strictly forbidden in Middle Eastern mosques. At the back of the mosque is a *pesantren* or Quranic school, and also a small graveyard for lesser relatives of the Sunan. Visitors are welcome outside of prayer times, but are required to dress neatly, to remove their shoes, and to wash their hands, face and feet before entering.

Palace craftsmen

At the northern end of the *alun-alun* are two interesting workshops where *wayang kulit* puppets and gamelan instruments are produced. Both are operated by *keraton* officials according to a system of royal patronage that has existed for centuries but is now waning. Their duties include the repair, tuning and maintainance of the royal gamelans, as well as the airing, cleaning and propitiation of the palace *wayang* puppets.

Mas Sibhanta, who runs the *wayang* workshop, has five boys working under him and produces traditional puppets of the finest quality. He also produces fanciful new creations—an Australian visitor recently com-

KAL MULLER

missioned puppets of an Irish leprachaun and Ned Kelly, the Australian bandit/folk hero. In the gamelan workshop, instruments are made from iron or brass rather than the superior and more expensive bronze, which requires forging. A nice *rebab* can be purchased here for about $20, an inexpensive *gender* for under $100.

Java's busiest textile bazaar

West of the *alun-alun* and the mosque is **Pasar Klewer**—a three-story concrete block housing Java's biggest textile market. The textile trade has traditionally been dominated by Muslims, and many stall-holders are of Arab and Muslim Indian descent. The more successful among them often sport a white *peci*—the mark of one who has made the prestigious pilgrimage to Mecca. Petty traders and shopkeepers from all over Java come here to buy, and Pasar Klewer serves as a major wholesalers' emporium. Cloth of every imagineable description is for sale in aisle after aisle of tiny stalls piled high with woven and printed cottons, linens, synthetics, silks—and most of all with batik.

Much of the batik available here is of the cheaper *batik cap* variety, produced using copper stamps. Some stalls, however, specialize in the more expensive, hand-drawn *batik tulis* that is still worn by well-to-do Javanese on ritual occasions. Many tailors are found in the market, and you can have clothes made to measure in a day. For best results, bring an item of clothing along to be copied, buy your cloth and then bring it to the tailor.

The Mangkunegaran palace

Across Jl. Slamet Riyadi to the north of here, on the west bank of the Pepe River, lies **Pura Mangkunegaran**—Solo's other palace. Its existence within the Surakarta royal domain is the result of a Dutch-negotiated peace between rival claimants to the throne in the middle of the 18th century. The Mangkunegaran was founded by a dissident prince, Raden Mas Said, who was given a portion of the Sunan's fiefdom as the price of his submission to the latter's authority. Although independent, the Mangkunegaran pays nominal homage to the senior royal line. Strictly speaking, this is therefore not a *keraton* at all but a *pura*—the domicile of a nobleman.

The Mangkunegaran faces southward in the direction of the Kasunanan *keraton*, thus symbolizing its junior rank. It is set in the midst of a huge compound measuring some 10,000 square meters, with lush gardens and European fountains. The vast *pendopo* (until recently the largest in Java) stands at the center, with the *dalem* or residence of Prince

Opposite: *The northern entrance to the Kasunanan palace.* **Above:** *The main gateway leading to the Royal Mosque, decorated with Arabic calligraphy.*

Mangkunegara and his family behind. Like the *keraton*, its design is rich with cosmological significance.

The grand *pendopo* houses four royal gamelan sets—only one of which, Kyai Kanyut Mesem, is for everyday use (dance lessons, concerts and such). The others possess special properties which restrict their use to specific ritual occasions.

Decorating the roof of the *pendopo* are brightly colored patches designed to repel specific evils—yellow against fatigue, blue against illness, black against hunger, green against frustration, white against lust, orange against fear, red against evil, purple against wicked thoughts. These colors are also associated with signs of the Javanese zodiac, and are flanked by weapons of the Hindu gods.

Behind the *pendopo* is a door leading to the Paringgitan—where *wayang kulit* performances are staged, and where the palace's dazzling regalia and private art collection are displayed—beautiful *keris* blades, sacred *wayang* puppets, paintings, medals, gifts from foreigners, and an odd assortment of ancient gold coins, jewelry and chastity belts.

Behind this lies the *dalem* or living quarters, parts of which are open to visitors. There is a small, neatly laid-out garden filled with caged parrots and song-birds, and visitors are even permitted to view the luxurious royal bathroom—a tiled affair with a large sunken tub.

While the Mangkunegaran ranks below the *keraton* in terms of status, financially it has been far more successful. Originally involved in managing sugar plantations in the 19th century, the family has since become developed a wide range of business interests, including a tourist hotel adjacent to the palace itself. As a result, the Mangkunegaran exudes an air of vigorous prosperity and is meticulously maintained. The palace actively courts tourists, often allowing groups to dine here in the open air and enjoy a royal dance performance.

Solo's flea market

Just south of Pura Mangkunegaran, on the eastern side of Jl. Diponegoro, lies the small but fascinating **Pasar Triwindu** flea market. The land upon which it stands actually belongs to the palace—the market was set up to commemorate the 24th anniversary of Mangkunegara VII's reign (the number 24 in Javanese represents three important *windu* or 8-year cycles), and the family has resisted proposals to modernize or redevelop it.

Anything and everything is for sale here, as long as it's old or at least used. The front stalls sell masks, paintings, photos, statuettes, *wayang* puppets, old coins and curios of all sorts. Many bargains are to be had if you are good at haggling, but be aware that most of the "antiques" were produced a couple of weeks before. At the back of the market, several stalls sell musical instruments alongside old car and motorcycle parts.

An interesting sort of cooperative system exists among the stallkeepers. Each puts Rp10.000 per year into a pool, from which he may then borrow to improve his stall or to purchase stock.

The Sriwedari area

To the west of Triwindu, on the south side of Jl. Slamet Riyadi, lies the huge Sriwedari amusement park—full of rides, bumper cars and food stalls, but also housing a theater with nightly *wayang orang* performances and an arena for concerts and popular spectacles. Sriwedari is liveliest during the fasting month of Ramadan, when a large fair called Maleman takes place here.

Just next to Sriwedari stands the Radya Pustaka museum, founded in 1890 by the *keraton* and the Dutch colonial government. Its original aim was to bring rarified *keraton* culture to the people; it originally boasted a school for classical dance, music, literature and shadow puppetry.

After independence, the museum's funding was cut and it lay dormant for many years. Today it has been revived as a small but fairly well-endowed museum—with displays of Javanese, Balinese and Thai puppets, weapons and intricate models of the *keraton* and the royal cemetery at Imogiri. The library contains a fascinating collection of old books, most in Dutch or Javanese.

Just to the north of here, at Jl. Dr. Cipto Mangunkusumo 15, is an art gallery displaying the work of Pak Dullah, an incredibly prolific Solonese painter. Much of his work depicts scenes from the revolution in the "social realism" style popular here during the 1950s—Dutch soldiers tearing the clothes from a peasant woman, shooting and bayoneting children, and so on. His work was much admired and collected by President Sukarno, and a number of his paintings hang in the presidential palace in Bogor. Pak Dullah is still alive and active and paints in a workshop above the gallery.

The central market

The area of town to the north and west of the main square was the European quarter in colonial times—site of the Dutch administrative offices, churches, theaters and clubs. To the northeast lay the Chinese district, centering around what is now **Pasar Gede**—the vast central market.

Every day villagers pour in from the countryside to sell their produce here. On the first level are vegetables, fruits, rice, coffee, dried fish, clothes and manufactured goods. Upstairs are the meats and some stalls selling frogs, live crabs, eels and even tortoises—the latter used mainly for soup. Hot, crowded and cramped, this market is the domain of women. Javanese men find bargaining and a concern for money degrading, and prefer to leave such matters to their wives, along with all chores relating to the household and family finances.

The Pasar Gede area is also still Solo's Chinese quarter, and across the road stands the brightly-painted Tri-Dharma temple, emblazoned with gold-leaf Chinese characters. Joss sticks burn inside, and the interior is filled with Taoist symbols and Buddhist icons. Tri-Dharma, the "three religions," refers to the syncretic mixture of Buddhist, Taoist and Confucian beliefs that are practiced here.

The caretaker is a woman in her fifties who has something of a reputation as a healer and a clairvoyant, and many Javanese also come to consult her on a wide range of matters. Representing the fifth generation of a family which has run this temple for more than 100 years, she worries that none of her children will follow her. Operating a temple, she says, is regarded as old-fashioned these days, and today's youth are not much interested in such matters.

Solo has plenty of other surprises. Out near the race course in Manahan, next to an eerie tree-filled cemetery, is Pasar Depok, Solo's bird market. All manner of feathered creatures are offered here for sale—parrots, doves, canaries, jungle fowl, owls and even the occasional eagle.

The Javanese value a bird's song more than its appearance—a specially bred, but ordinary-looking chicken may sell for $500 because of its crowing, whereas a beautiful parrot might go for only $10. A song bird is regarded as one of the five essential possessions of a Javanese knight—the others being a house, a *keris*, a horse and a wife.

The market is arranged around a central courtyard filled with stalls selling bird food and dominated by a huge old banyan tree. Next to it is a small enclosure where offerings are made to the *danyang* or spirit of the place, usually on Thursday evenings.

—Tim Kortschak

Opposite: *Pura Mangkunegaran, princely home of Surakarta's junior ruling line.*

THE ARTS IN SOLO

The Height of Aristocratic Elegance

While traditional *karawitan* music and its associated performing arts can be seen and heard throughout the island, the Javanese themselves feel that it is in the old royal principalities of Solo and Yogya where they have been given their highest and most refined expression. The reasons for this are rooted in Javanese history. Especially after the Great Java War of 1825-30, the Dutch ruled Java through a native aristocracy stripped of political power but made to serve a useful symbolic (and also economic) function. Lacking other outlets for their great wealth and energy, these former rulers surrounded themselves with grand displays of royal pomp and circumstance in which music, dance, and *wayang* played a substantial role.

Deep-seated traditional rivalries, and a struggle for status among the courts and their ruling families, were thereafter largely played out upon the stage rather than upon the battlefield. Talented musicians, dancers and *dalangs* were recruited from outlying villages, while their individual styles were refined and to some extent standardized to conform with court tastes, under the guidance of palace teachers. The rulers vied with one another in producing ever grander and more arcane theatrical productions, culminating in the massive *wayang orang* productions of the early part of this century, in which a cast of hundreds would perform different episodes of a tale nightly for days at a time.

The Mangkunegaran and Kasunanan styles of Surakarta developed in slightly different directions, partly as the result of a deliberate attempt by the junior Mangkunegaran to distance itself from the Kasunanan, and partly because of different sources that each court drew upon. It is said, for example, that the Mangkunegaran dance bears a greater similarity to Yogya's proud martial style than to the graceful, flowing style of the Surakarta *keraton*—the result of Mangkunegara VII's marriage to a Yogyanese princess, who brought her dance teachers with her.

ERIC OEY

Music as court ritual

Though their status has changed greatly since independence, the courts are still artistic centers. Live gamelan concerts are broadcast over the radio from each court once or twice a month, and both palaces occasionally send dance troupes on foreign tours.

Music in the courts was not traditionally regarded as mere entertainment, but instead formed an integral part of palace rituals. Even now, gamelan concerts are performed every 35 days to mark the *tingalan* or "birthday" of the Sunan and Mangkunegara. Music played at these events tends to be of the most classical and elaborate kind. According to Javanese tradition, the playing of music on such occasions placates the *danyang* or territorial spirit that inhabits the palace. Many Javanese believe that the fire which swept the Kasunanan *keraton* in 1985 was due to a neglect of such rituals.

Ceremonies occur in the palaces on a daily basis. There are also grander rituals which occur at regular intervals during the year—of which Sekaten is probably the largest. In the week preceding the prophet Muhammad's birthday, two sacred gamelan

Left: *Bedoyo Ketawang, the most sacred of Solonese court dances.* **Right:** *The royal Sekaten gamelan, played annually in the Mesjid Ageng.*

sets are carried in a huge procession from the palace to the royal mosque. The square is a riot of color and activity at this time—a large fair packed with booths and rides draws thousands of villagers from the surrounding countryside.

For six days leading up to the main Sekaten event, a set repertoire is played on these gamelan from dawn to dusk, and listening to them is said to have a beneficial effect on one's spiritual and physical being. The music is in fact powerfully austere—spare and stark compared to the gentle, wafting strains of ordinary *karawitan*.

Sacred and mystical dances

The art forms most intimately linked with the courts, though, are the *bedoyo* and *srimpi* dances. Until very recently these could not be performed outside the palaces, and young girls who performed them were required to be virgins of aristocratic birth. Dance performances were sometimes exchanged between courts as royal "gifts" but the dances were never taught to outsiders, as they were regarded as magically powerful possessions of the ruler.

The most important and most sacred of all court dances is the Bedoyo Ketawang, which depicts the courtship of the founder of the Mataram dynasty, Panembahan Senopati, with the goddess of the south sea, Kangjeng Ratu Kidul. This dance is performed annually in the great central *pendopo* of the palace on the anniversary of the Sunan's coronation, and it reaffirms the alliance of the ruling house with the powerful goddess. The dance is slow and graceful, performed by nine young women who are only permitted to rehearse every 35 days, on Selasa Kliwon.

While the actual performance is open to invited guests only, the Bedoyo Ketawang rehearsals can be witnessed if you happen to be present on Selasa Kliwon; simply apply at the palace in traditional Javanese dress. Both palaces, particularly the Mangkunegaran, are quite interested in revenue from tourist performances, and regularly stage concerts and shorter, more accessible dances for the public. These usually take place in the morning or in the evening, although exact days and times vary.

The performing arts academy

Other traditional art centers do exist outside the palaces. The most important of these is STSI (Sekolah Tinggi Seni Indonesia), the government performing arts academy of Solo, located next to the new university campus in Kentingan to the northeast of the city.

The orientation of STSI is very different from that of the courts. While much of the inspiration comes from traditional court dance and *karawitan*, the academy aims to develop secular Indonesian art forms that can stand alone, without reference to the

ERIC OEY

palaces and their elaborate rituals. Students are encouraged to draw on a wide variety of sources, and the music and dance of regions outside of Central Java are also taught.

In the academy's large *pendopo*, for example, students can often be seen rehearsing Balinese dances and Sundanese music, and guest performers and teachers are often brought in, occasionally from overseas. Experimental dance and music have been in vogue for some time, with the attempt usually being to blend traditional forms with modern or foreign ones. Gamelan music is often played in strange and unusual ways; recent compositions have incorporated the Australian aboriginal *didgereedoo*, tape recordings of frogs, and the sound of breaking glass.

Modern dance compositions also portray unusual themes—space landings, village life and madness are some recent examples—and these are frequently very abstract in nature, very much influenced by modern dance in the West. Performances are staged regularly as part of student examinations, usually at night, and are open to the public.

New *wayang* forms

The academy has been instrumental in devising new *wayang kulit* forms. The traditional *wayang* performance starts in the evening and continues until dawn, being staged as part of a communal wedding, funeral or harvest celebration. At STSI it was felt that the length of the *wayang,* in particular, limits its appeal for modern urban audiences, and so shorter forms based on so-called *lakon padat* or "compact stories" have been developed.

These short performances sometimes last only half an hour, focusing on battles and seductions and ignoring the long discursive passages that mark the traditional *wayang*. Even more radical is the *wayang santosa*, which draws stories from the traditional repertoire, but makes a clean break in terms of presentation. Instead of a single *dalang* sitting stationary beneath an immobile light surrounded by gamelan players, the audience sees a huge screen illuminated by multicolored spotlights, behind which a number of people run and jump, wielding puppets which cast shadows against the screen. Different performers portray different voices, unlike the traditional *wayang* in which a single *dalang* gives life to all the characters. Although interesting and innovative, many of the new creations are regarded as shallow in comparison with the traditional *wayang*.

The Solonese in fact regard their *dalangs* very highly, and a good one can earn several million rupiah for a single night's performance. Different *dalangs* are known for different talents and qualities. Ki Anom Suroto is known for his rich singing voice, Ki Manteb Darsono for his puppet manipulation, and Ki Mujoko Joko Raharjo for his brilliant characterizations. Traditional performances take place all over Solo and in the surrounding villages, and there is never an admission fee. Invited guests sit in spaces provided and are served food while uninvited onlookers crowd around to watch the show.

Each month, Solo's most famous *dalang*, Anom Suroto, invites a different practitioner of his craft to perform in his house in Notodiningratan to celebrate his "birthday" according to the 35-day Javanese month. These performances are held every fifth Tuesday night (Rebo Legi). Pak Manteb out in his village near Tawangmangu does the same. Solo's government radio station (RRI) stages a *wayang* performance on the third Saturday of each month in its huge auditorium.

Popular dance and drama

Of the other traditional art forms in Solo, the most important is *wayang orang*, a theatrical drama whose stories and characters are taken from the shadow play. As a form of commercial entertainment, *wayang orang* has been declining for years, losing its audience to films and television. Solo's Sriwedari amusement park has of one of the last remaining *wayang orang* troupes that performs nightly, at 8 pm. The only other such troupe is in Semarang.

Ketoprak is another, far more popular, dramatic form. Decidedly "lowbrow" in comparison with *wayang orang*, it employs less music and dance, as the emphasis is on earthy comedy, "soap opera" melodrama, and action. *Ketoprak* seems to appeal to a less elevated audience too—both *ketoprak* theaters in Solo are in fairly rough parts of town. Budaya Jati is in the Gilingan district near the bus station, while Wahyu Budaya is by the southern *alun-alun* square.

Ketoprak acting is largely a hereditary profession, and players live in gypsy-like encampments near the theaters. The stories draw on a great variety of sources—Arabic and Chinese as well as Javanese history—with lots of fantasy thrown in. Wahyu Budaya even incorporates scenes espousing the benefits of patent medicines! Performances are at night.

Spectacles for the masses

At an even further remove from the palace arts is Solo's *kuda kepang* troupe, which performs most Sunday mornings at the zoo and whenever and wherever they can find an audience. Headed by a former *becak* driver who learned his trade in Ponorogo (Java's *kuda kepang* capital), the Solo troupe employs less "horse dancing" than in East Java. The dancers go into trance, are wrapped in cloth, whipped and then emerge unscathed. Some are young children who breathe fire and wield whips just as their parents do. This spectacle is accompanied by a four-piece gamelan which beats out a droning, hypnotic beat, increasing in tempo as the performers fall into trance.

Dangdut, the pan-Indonesian popular music of the working classes, also thrives in Solo. *Dangdut* is a sort of sweet, sexy blues style of singing, strongly influenced by Indian film music. Singers wear garish make-up and dress provocatively in ultra-mini skirts, writhing and jiggling before their largely male audiences. Respectable, middle-class Indonesians shudder at the sight (and sound) of *dangdut*—considering it the epitome of everything that is *kampungan* or "hick."

Kroncong, the pop music of the 1950s generation, is slightly more upmarket. A Portuguese influenced, jazzy style of music—good *kroncong* can be heard at the Puri Sari Kedai Kopi in Kentingan on Friday nights, while performances of both *dangdut* and *kroncong* often take place at Sriwedari on Saturday nights and in the *alun-alun* and all over Solo on special holidays.

— *Tim Kortschak*

Opposite: Wayang orang *at Sriwedari.*
Above: *High melodrama in a* ketoprak *play.*

SIDETRIPS FROM SOLO

Hill Resorts and Ancient Temples

As much as Solo has to offer in terms of history and culture, it is refreshing to get out to the surrounding villages. Some of the most interesting places in this area are located up on the slopes of nearby Mt. Lawu, around Tawangmangu and Sarangan, just 42 km (25 mi) and 56 km (34 mi) to the east, respectively. The air here is cool and refreshing and the views down across the plains spectacular.

Heading east from Solo, the traffic subsides considerably once you cross the broad and sluggish Bengawan Solo River. Soon after crossing the bridge, the main road turns off to the left and a smaller road heads straight up the mountain. Beyond the town of Karanganyar, you are presented with a broad expanse of verdant rice and sugar cane fields. From here the road climbs and the air freshens, while the views get better and better.

Beyond Karangpandan, a statue of Semar guards a small hilltop to the left of the road. There is a library and meditation room here owned by a well-to-do Jakartan. Further along is the Inri Center for meditation and *kebatinan* (spiritual power), a small temple called Candi Menggung, and a hot spring at Pablengan. After that the road twists and climbs steeply; buses crawl up the mountain belching black clouds of diesel exhaust, while others race down again at breakneck speeds.

Cool mountain air

Upon first arriving at **Tawangmangu** (elevation 1,050 m/3,415 ft) you may wonder if this is really a resort after all—the bustling market and bus terminal resemble those in any other Javanese town. Further up the road, however, is a strip of hotels lining either side of the street, catering mainly to the great numbers of Solonese who fill the place to capacity on weekends and holidays. During the week the resort is rather deserted, and this is the best time to visit.

The Tawangmangu area is famous for its produce, and inviting stands selling fresh fruits and vegetables are everywhere. The best thing about the place, however, especially after the sweltering lowlands, is that you can hike around in the surrounding hills and enjoy the views and the fresh air.

The Grojogan Sewu waterfall and park is the major "sight" here—reached by taking a left at the sign about halfway through town.

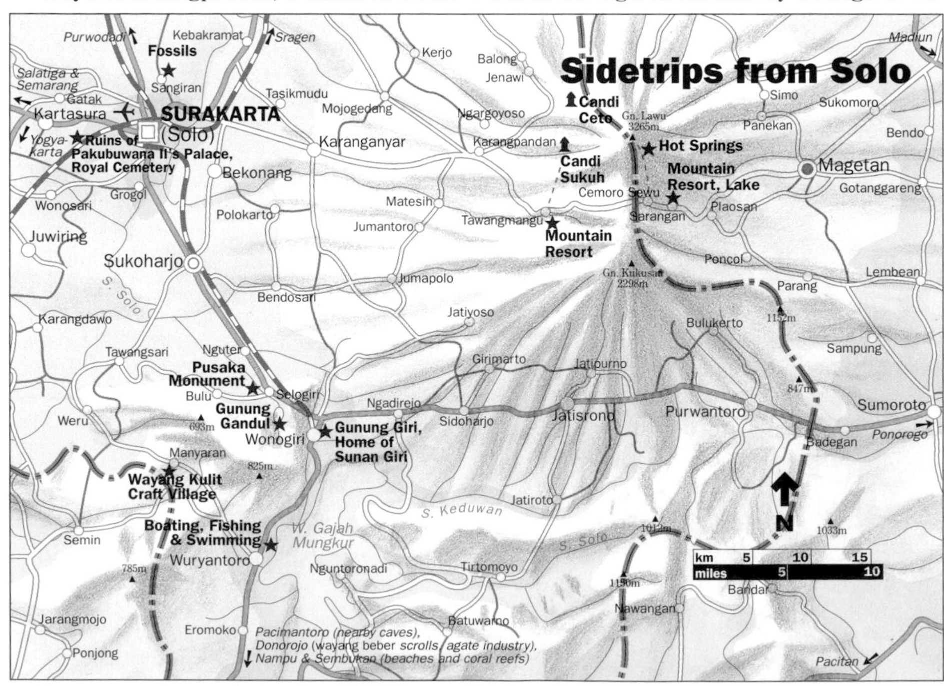

The entrance is marked by a cluster of *warungs* and fruit stands, but once you pay an entrance fee and descend the stone steps, the serenity of the place takes over.

It is cool and quiet during the week. There are small pavilions and benches scattered about the area, perfect for sitting, reading or picnicking. It's all rather romantic—one of the few places in Indonesia where mixed couples may frequently be seen holding hands. The forest is home to a sizeable population of monkeys. They're fairly shy and polite, but be careful with your belongings nonetheless. You can learn Indonesian tree names from plaques marking the various species, enjoy the cool spray from an 80-meter (260 ft) fall, stroll along the paths and swim in one of two pools—a childrens' pool with a slide and frog fountain, or an adult pool below. The water is cold, there may be teenagers splashing about, but the place is magical—a cascading stream, waterfall in the distance, sunlight filtering through towering trees, birds calling and a lush, green setting. Bring a picnic or eat at the stalls below. The park closes at 4:30 pm.

There is plenty more to do in Tawangmangu. You can walk or rent a horse to Gua Maria ("Maria Cave"—turn right off the main road at the lower end of Tawangmangu; it's 2-3 km away), browse through the Horticultural Garden, with its exhibits of medicinal plants, or hike the lovely cobbled path that winds through scenic farmlands to Candi Sukuh (See "Sukuh and Ceto"). Horses are for rent for $3 an hour. You can also pay to enter the Tawangmangu Baru campgrounds near the top of the town to picnic and swim in their pool.

Sarangan's scenic lake

The lovely mountain resort of Sarangan (elevation 1,287 m/4,185 ft) is just 14 km (8.5 mi) past Tawangmangu, and is even more picturesque and more up-scale than the latter—catering to wealthy Indonesians and foreigners. To reach it, continue along the main road out of Tawangmangu leading up and over Mt. Lawu. Private villas dot these hills, including one belonging to the late President Sukarno, which now looks a bit dilapidated. The views of the volcano are spectacular, as are the geometric patterns produced by terraced fields blanketing the steep slopes. Farmers tote huge sacks of produce up and down the hills; cabbage and carrots are the major crops.

Eventually farmland gives way to forest and, crossing a bridge, you enter East Java. On the right are food stalls; across from them on the left is a trail leading up Mt. Lawu. After a few more kilometers there is another sign for "Gunung Lawu" on the left—this is the more commonly used route up the moun-

Below: *The road leading east out of Solo up to the hill resorts of Tawangmangu and Sarangan.*

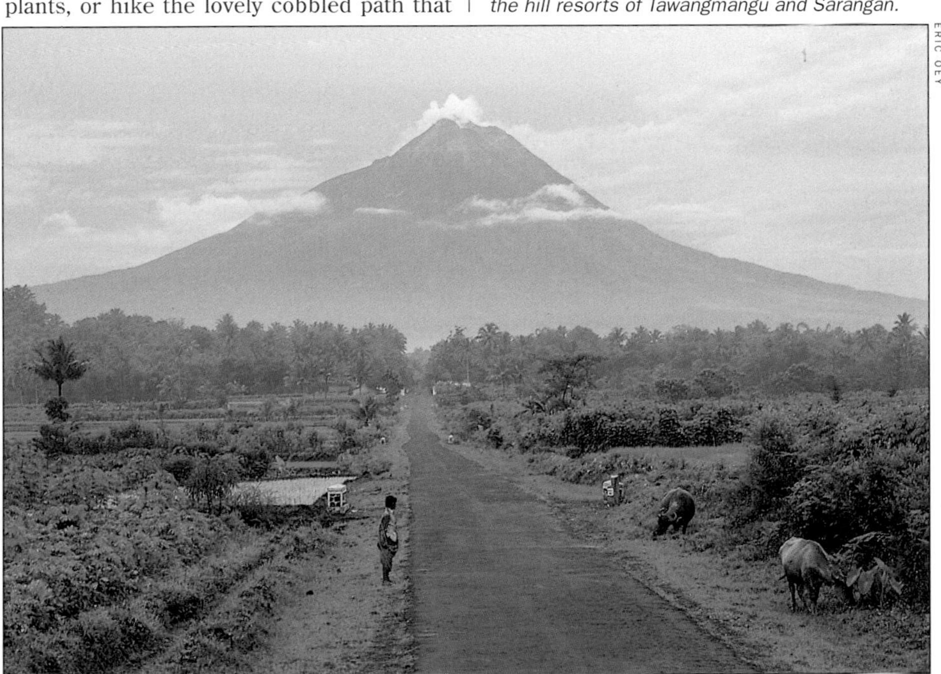

ERIC OEY

tain (see below). Even if you aren't planning to scale the peak it's a peaceful place to stop for a while and perhaps take a short hike.

Sarangan itself is a relaxing resort town with a lot to offer. A scenic crater lake, Telaga Pasir, lies at the center of it, with mountains stretching up one side and slopes reaching down the other to Magetan and Madiun. You can swim, fish and hike or hire a canoe, boat or "water *becak*" for a jaunt around the lake. You can also rent a horse for a ride around the town, or hike to one of several waterfalls in the area.

Air Terjun Mojoseni is about a mile away (you will see the entrance off the main road as you come into Sarangan). On the other side of the lake are two more waterfalls. The smaller one, Sarang Sari, is about a kilometer away; the larger one, Ngadilojo, is 3 km (1.8 mi) distant.

Climbing Mt. Lawu

The most common route leading up Mt. Lawu (3,265 m/10,611 ft) begins 5 kms (3 mi) from Sarangan in Cemoro Sewu. This well-maintained stone path, marked by a small sign across from the TV relay station, is 6.5 km (4 mi) long. It takes about 4 hours to make the climb, and 2 hours for the descent. A trek can be organized in Sarangan; cost is around $20. Ask for Pak Terima by the lake.

There are hot springs on the way up, and if you climb at night, you can catch the fabulous sunrise from the top. It can get very cold though, so bring warm clothes, food and water. There are several shelters along the way if you need to rest.

During school holiday periods, you'll be joined by scores of young Indonesians, since this is a favorite outing. Another route up begins next to the bridge that marks the Central Java/East Java border, but this trail is much longer—about 12 km (7.5 mi).

Climbers should comply with regulations requiring them to report to the official at the entrance to the trail; this is for your own safety. The walk to the summit area takes about 4.5 hours for a person of average fitness. The vertical climb from Cemoro Sewu to the peak is about 1,000 meters (3,300 ft). It is advisable to take a guide from Sarangan or Tawangmangu; hotels and guest houses can provide one for you.

There are ancient stone terrace complexes around the summit at Hargo Dalem, Hargo Tiling, Hargo Dumilah, and Pasar Dieng. Metal shelters have been erected at several locations, where people may spend the night. Indonesians commonly begin the climb before dawn, arrive at the summit in the early morning, spend a few hours exploring the summit area, and then descend in the early afternoon. Of course, this is quite a strenuous hike, and should not be attempted except by those who are in good physical condition.

Home of 'Java Man'

The short trip out to **Sangiran**, 15 km (9 mi) north of Solo, is an excursion back in time. The area first became famous in 1936 when a team headed by Berlin-born paleontologist, G.H.R. von Koenigswald, unearthed a fossilized "Java Man" or *Homo erectus* jawbone here. Other such fossils had been discovered by Dubois in 1891 farther to the east down the Solo River, but the ones at Sangiran are much older, dating back a million years or more—proof that *Homo erectus* existed in Java about as early as in Africa.

The Sangiran area is rich in fossils of all types. These are in fact often discovered lying loose in the fields following a heavy rain. The reason is that soft sedimentary soils have here been up-lifted to form a dome, whose top has then eroded by the elements, exposing many layers beneath.

The Sangiran Site Museum is a simple, one-room affair. In the central case are replicas of skull fragments and jawbones of Java Man (the originals are stored in Bandung). Lining the far wall, a life-sized diorama depicts how these prehistoric men might have lived. Other cases house fossil shells and animal bones, including enormous 4-meter tusks from a mastodon which must have measured 11 m (33 ft) head to tail. The fossils range in age from 1,200,000 to 500,000 years. Artifacts from prehistoric settlements round out the collection, and upstairs is a viewing room overlooking the valley. The museum is open from 7-5 daily.

It is fascinating to think that man's ancestors lived here hundreds of thousands of years ago. Ask the guard to point out the spot down the road where landslides continue to expose fossils, mainly seashells. Local residents are only too keen to sell them to you, but be prepared to bargain and take their claims of authenticity with a grain of salt. Though some of the fossils are genuine, collecting and selling fossils is illegal, and some of the residents have turned to making stone replicas for a living.

South from Surakarta

If you love the outdoors, spend a day or two exploring the lakes and caves around **Wonogiri**, 32 km (19 mi) south of Solo. Along the way one passes the villages of Sukoharjo and Nguter, with rice fields all around and mountains on the horizon.

At **Selogiri**, 6 km (3.5 mi) before Wonogiri, there is a black stone monument in which the sacred royal heirlooms (*pusaka*) of the Mangkunegaran court are kept. Most of the time there is not much of interest here, but on the first day of the Javanese month of Sura, members of the court show up in traditional dress and take the heirlooms to the Gajah Mungkur reservoir, where they are ritually bathed.

Next stop is **Gunung Gandul**, 2.5 km (1.5 mi) west of Wonogiri, a beautiful spot for hiking and camping. Look for a small sign marking the turnoff on the right side of the road as you near Wonogiri. The road is rocky so you might have to walk much of the way in.

A little further on, a sign on the left points the way to **Gunung Giri**, home of Sunan Giri, one of the nine Muslim apostles who are thought to have spread Islam on Java. The place is considered sacred by the Javanese, many of whom travel here to pray on the eve of certain special days of the month (Selasa Kliwon and Jumat Kliwon).

The main attraction of the Wonogiri area, however, is the huge (83 sq km) **Gajah Mungkur Reservoir** formed by a dam across the Bengawan Solo near its source. To make room for it, 51 villages and 60,000 residents had to be relocated through transmigration. The reservoir lies 6 km (3.5 mi) southwest of Wonogiri on the main road, and you have a panoramic view of it as you crest the top of a small hill on the way in.

Most visitors head straight to Gajah Mungkur Park (also known as Giri Sendang Sari), open 7-6 daily. There's a swimming pool, a children's zoo and a picnic area and you can charter a motor boat for about $4 for a trip around the lake. Many come here just to fish. Special floating ponds a short distance from the park make it easy—get a boat to ferry you across. You can rent fishing gear and eat at the floating "cafe."

Continuing south along a bumpy but bearable road you have the lake on your left and mountain slopes and fields on your right. **Goa Ngantap**, a subterranean cavern with gray stalagmites and stalactites and the echoing sound of dripping water, lies 50 km (30 mi) to the south, past the towns of Wuryantoro, Eromoko and Pracimantoro. At the latter, turn east until you come to Giribelah, then continue through the intersection. The road twists and turns up through beautiful forests, with rocky cliffs on either side. Lit only by natural light from the mouth, the cavern itself has a primordial feel about it, and local resi-

Opposite: *Sarangan's scenic crater lake.*

dents like to bathe inside in the cool darkness when no one is around. There are other caves in the area, such as Gua Platar.

Some 60 km (35 mi) south of Wonogiri lie unspoiled beaches and coral reefs at **Nampu** and **Sembukan**. There are plans to develop the area as a tourist resort in the near future. Ask at the tourist office in Solo or at the Gajah Mungkur dam for directions.

Wonogiri is also famous for its handicrafts, especially *wayang*. Many *dalangs* and musicians come from this area. The most famous village in all of Java for high quality puppets is tiny **Manyaran**, about 20 km (12 mi) south and west of Wonogiri. All the work is done on a cooperative basis, overseen by the village head, Pak Sukar Hadiprayitno. The best quality pieces, with gold leaf details, cost $100 and have to be specially ordered several weeks or even months in advance.

The old *keraton* at Kartasura

History buffs will want to explore the area west of Surakarta, where two pre-18th-century palaces were located. An unpretentious patch of rice fields in the village of **Pajang**, near an intersection on Jl. Joko Tingkir, mark the site where the dynasty's first ruler is said to have constructed his palace in the late 16th century. Not a trace remains of it now, but farther down this road is an interesting old cemetery. Nearby it is another cemetery for Chinese Muslims who served as craftsmen in the Kartasura palace.

There is much more to see at **Kartasura**, 11 km (6.5 mi) west of Solo. Follow an unmarked road south of the town's market until you come to massive, moss-covered walls. This is Pakubuwana II's old palace, site of the powerful Mataram court from 1680 up until 1742. The walls are 3 meters (10 ft) high and over a meter thick, yet did not prevent the palace from being sacked, thus necessitating the move to Surakarta.

Signs at the gateway identify the site. At the main pavilion (*pendopo*) you may find a caretaker who can explain the history of the place to you in Indonesian. The grounds are now used as a cemetery for people of low royal birth. On holidays such as Lebaran, aristocratic families come to honor their ancestors by strewing red and white roses over the tops of gravestones, lighting incense and praying. Such visits are only fleeting though; the tombstones then resume their quiet repose under the dappled shadows of gnarled frangipani branches.

While the wooden palace buildings have vanished , you can see several stone relics left behind when the *keraton* moved, and which are still revered. You can also walk all around the wall. Don't be surprised, however, if the caretakers—wizened old men—and women and local children follow you around and ask to have their photos taken.

—Peter Hadley and Jennifer Thom

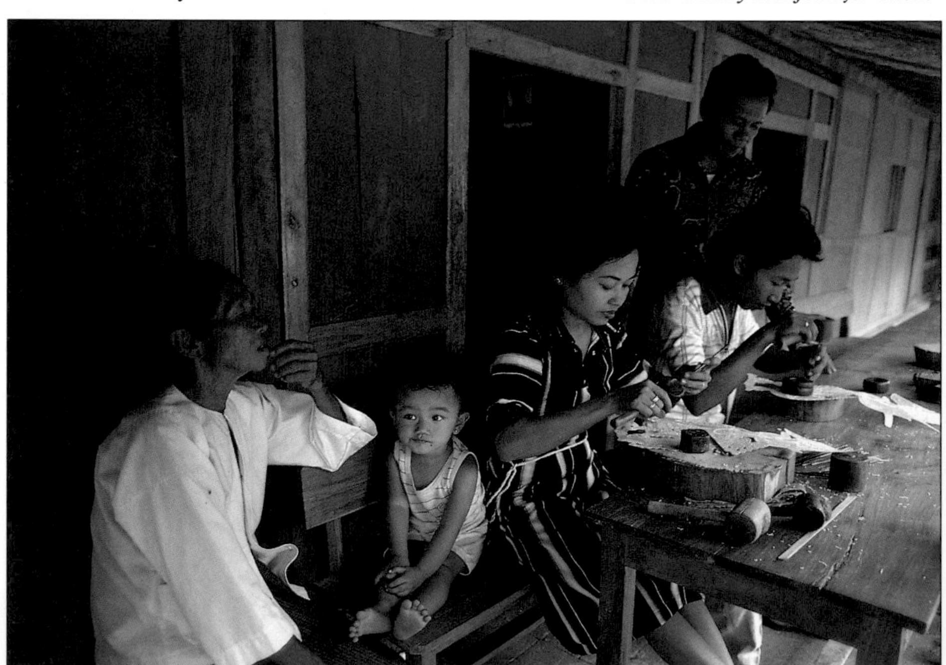

ERIC OEY

SUKUH AND CETO

Enigmatic Temples High on Mt. Lawu

During the 15th century, several temples were constructed high on the slopes of Mt. Lawu, right on the border between East and Central Java. By this time, Javanese religion and art had diverged far from the Indian precepts that exerted significant influence during the 8th-10th centuries, and a new and idiosyncratic style had developed.

This region on the northwest slopes of Mt. Lawu was the last major center of temple-building in Java before the Javanese courts were converted to Islam in the 16th century. Because the temples are so distinctive, and because we possess few records of Javanese beliefs and ceremonies during the 15th century, it is difficult to interpret the significance of much of what we see on the antiquities of this period. They are nonetheless extremely beautiful and fascinating to visit.

Candi Sukuh

The largest and most complex of these mountain sanctuaries is Candi Sukuh, situated at an elevation of 910 meters (2,960 ft); reached by taking a turn-off to the left at Karangpandan on the road up to Tawangmangu. A number of inscriptions dating from the period A.D. 1416-1459 have been found here.

The main structure at Sukuh is shaped like no other building in ancient Indonesia—a flat-topped pyramid much resembling a Mayan monument. A stone stairway conducts the visitor through the side of the pyramid to its summit. We do not know what this unique shape was meant to symbolize. If it represents a mountain, as seems likely, we are still left with the question of why this shape replaced pre-existing forms of ancient Javanese temple design.

The main building gives no indication of having supported any wooden structure. The only object recovered from its summit was a tall *lingga* bearing an inscription, which is now in the Jakarta museum. This may once have stood on the platform over the stairway on the west side of the temple. Stone altars, three in the form of enormous turtles, stand around the pyramid's western foot.

The central pyramid is set at the rear of the highest of three terraces. Originally worshippers would have gained access to the site through a gateway at the edge of the western or lowest terrace. To the left side of the gate's exterior is a carving of a monster devouring a man, birds in a tree, and a dog. This can be interpreted as a chronogram representing A.D. 1437, the probable date of the temple's consecration. On the floor of this entrance is a realistic relief of male and female genitals. Genetalia are also graphically portrayed on several statues from the site, another respect in which Candi Sukuh is unique among classical Javanese monuments.

Unique bas reliefs

Disconnected fragments of narrative reliefs lie on the lower terraces, while a greater concentration of sculptures lies around the altars on the upper terrace west of the pyramid. On the south side, the first object one now passes upon entering the temple grounds is a large relief in three sections. The left side represents a deity as a squatting *keris* smith

ERIC OEY

Left: *Producing* wayang *puppets in Manyaran.*
Right: *Candi Sukuh, whose unusual pyramidal form, reliefs and sexual symbolism seem dedicated to a cult of Bima as spiritual saviour.*

AMIR SIDHARTA

hammering a blade on an anvil with his fist; in the background are the various tools of his trade. The same deity is portrayed on the right side as the operator of a traditional Indonesian piston-bellows. He is Bima, an incarnation of Siva who became the focus of a Javanese cult in the 15th century, filling the role of a savior figure. The center is occupied by an elephant, perhaps Siva's elephant-headed son Ganesa, carrying an animal. Blacksmiths and especially *keris* makers have been highly respected in Indonesia, but what relationship this scene bore to the ceremonies once conducted at Candi Sukuh is unknown.

To the right of the entrance to the pyramid is a cubical structure carved with two horizontal rows of reliefs. Their meaning is unclear, but they are reminiscent of the Sudamala story. Today offerings are often placed in the opening on the west side of the cube in honor of Kyai Sukuh, the temple's spirit.

On the far left side of the terrace is a platform with a pylon-like tower, the lower section of which is carved with a design known as a *kalamarga*—a *kala* head at the top of an archway which terminates in two horned animals representing deer. Inside the arch are images of Bima on the right and Batara Guru (both are aspects of Siva, the supreme deity) on the left, standing upon a two-headed serpent. Beneath them are two hermits.

Beside this *kalamarga* is a spout connected to a channel which runs behind the pylon and then in the same direction above a series of reliefs. Many parts of this relief are now lined up along the north edge of the terrace. They depict the Sudamala legend, which is a popular subject of modern Balinese dance performances. One of the reliefs bears a date corresponding to A.D. 1449. The upper part of the pylon is decorated with reliefs depicting the Garudeya legend concerning Garuda's search for the elixir of immortality with which to free his mother from slavery.

If one follows the path which leads south and downhill from Candi Sukuh, after about 1 km the village of Planggatan is reached. Just beyond the southeast corner of the village are the ruins of a small 15th-century shrine with some narrative reliefs.

Candi Ceto

Candi Ceto is located about 5 km (3 mi) north and 500 meters (1630 ft) above Candi Sukuh. Dates found inscribed here include A.D. 1468, 1472 and 1475. The layout of the temple is similar to Sukuh, but comprises many more terraces (14). As at Candi Sukuh, the main deity portrayed is Bima. On a lower terrace were found fragments of narrative reliefs in poor condition, no longer in situ, and a large number of small stone turtles.

The most interesting remain is a complicated figure composed of stones laid flat on the ground. At the western end is a large *lingga* like that found at Sukuh, lying horizontally and pointing due west. At its base is a composition representing a tortoise on the back of a huge bat. On the tortoise's back are a number of sea creatures oriented in various compass directions.

During the 1970s a new gateway was built and new structures were added to the upper terraces, including stone walls and floors. There are also pavilions built of wood and sugar-palm thatch, and a stone pyramid roughly similar in outline to the main building at Candi Sukuh.

About 50 meters farther up the slope are a bathing place with several recent statues, and a wooden shrine. For several years in the late 1970s the site was used by a group of people of high political status who came to meditate in the belief that supernatural power was inherent here. They have ceased to visit the place, but local residents continue to leave offerings at the uppermost shrine.

Antiquities atop Mt. Lawu

Some of the most interesting ruins in Java are found in rather remote locations nearby. At the very summit of Lawu—which stands over 3,000 meters (9,750 ft) above sea level—and on the surface of a plateau about 100 meters (330 ft) beneath it, are at least 10 terrace and stone wall complexes. No complete survey of the ruins has ever been published. The largest, called Hargo Dalem, has a lower terrace approximately 100 meters (330 ft) long and 20 meters (65 ft) wide. Above it are progressively smaller terraces surmounted by a stone-walled enclosure within which a wooden shrine of recent construction stands.

STEVE TEO

AMIR SIDHARTA

It is not possible for us to determine the exact dates of these complexes. They are likely to belong either to the late prehistoric period—about 1,500-2,000 years ago, just before the widespread adoption of Hinduism and Buddhism—or to the early post-classic period which began about 500 years ago when some Central Javanese resisted conversion to Islam.

The sites are still frequently visited by pilgrims who come here to meditate in seclusion. On the eve of the Javanese new year (1 Suro) as many as 2000 people may ascend to conduct traditional rituals. The Indonesian government does not recognize such practices, but permits them to be conducted under the term of *aliran kepercayaan* or "currents of belief."

—John Miksic

Opposite: *Relief depicting a scene from the Sudamala story, in which the hero Bima destroys his enemies. The background inscription contains a chronogram corresponding to* A.D. *1439.*
Left: *Bima and Batara Guru standing on a two-headed serpent inside of a* kalamarga *arch.*
Above: *Stone mosaics from Ceto depicting a bat carrying a turtle, a triangle with sea creatures inside and a large phallus with spheres at the tip.*

PART VII

Introducing the North Coast

The long northern or *pasisir* coast of Java shows the island in an entirely different light. The towering volcanoes of the interior here constitute a distant backdrop rather than a demanding presence, and it is instead the calm and expansive Java Sea—its waves lapping across a low and muddy shoreline punctuated by lazy, silt-laden rivers—which defines the region and gives it a unique, maritime flavor.

The *pasisir* (meaning "edge" or "fringe") coastal ports were important stopovers on international trade routes for many centuries. From around A.D. 1400 up to about 1800, this was in fact the most favored of all coastal areas in the tropical "lands below the wind" to which merchants and seafarers from abroad had resorted since ancient times.

To understand this development, one must realize that winds bringing ships from India and China alternate biannually, blowing steadily for four or five months in a northeasterly direction, then swinging around to blow the other way for a similar period.

Merchants thus had to sojourn for a period of months somewhere along the coasts of Sumatra, Malaya or Java while waiting for the winds to change before returning home. In the interim, goods could be exchanged and personal contacts developed, and this natural rhythm of the winds and the seas was one which regulated long-distance trade and imparted special importance to harbors bordering the Java Sea during pre-modern times.

Java itself of course possessed a special advantage—its fertile hinterland produced great surpluses of food, notably rice. Many other areas, especially the spice-producing eastern islands, were unsuitable for rice cultivation and their inhabitants were keen to exchange their products for rice and manufactured good brought by traders.

Very little is known about the area during classical times. Several names have come down to us, and port settlements existed here, but there are few remains and the greatest concentration of people and power clearly lay inland during this period.

This changed dramatically in later centuries, when the *pasisir* ports became the focus of a thriving international trade driven by spices. Put in very simple terms—Indian textiles, Chinese silks and ceramics, and European silver and gold were all brought to Java to be exchanged for Indonesian spices, with a large share of the profits accruing to local rulers and traders. The *pasisir* ports thus outgrew their earlier role as mere coastal outposts of inland Javanese empires, and around A.D. 1500 they emerged as powerful, cosmopolitan city-states in their own right.

The key players in this development were Islamic traders from the Middle East, India Sumatra and China. Together with influential local families they forged a new and heterogeneous Islamic culture that first absorbed and then conquered the old Hindu-Javanese civilization of the hinterland.

The powerful and wealthy city-states of this period—Demak, Jepara, Kudus, Tuban, Gresik, Surabaya, Pasuruan, Cirebon, Banten and others—were eventually to succumb to the inland Mataram armies of Sultan Agung (r. 1613-46) and to the monopolistic policies of the Dutch. A handful later developed into modern commercial centers, but most have faded into obscurity. Today they are somnolent backwater towns—physically the product of a century of colonial rule and several decades of post-war urban development.

Few tourists venture this way as a result; however with a bit of imagination these ancient towns can come alive with all the mystery of an age when they carried on an active trade with half the civilized world.

— *Eric Oey*

Overleaf: *A Wadas Singa ("Rocks with lions") royal batik from Cirebon. Photo by Amir Sidharta.* **Opposite:** *A Cirebonese boy at his ritual circumcision ceremony. Photo by Jill Gocher.*

CIREBON

Java's Oldest Surviving Court Center

Cirebon is the first major port encountered along the coast east of Jakarta—an unassuming commercial town of 225,000 inhabitants that has the distinction of being the only of the island's 16th century Islamic city-states to have survived until the present day with its palaces and royal families intact. Indeed, these are the oldest surviving courts on the island—founded some three centuries before Yogya or Solo. Without a doubt, this is one of the most interesting places on Java to visit—yet it is seldom seen by foreigners because it lies off the main tourist routes.

Cirebon's location is a strategic one. During Hindu times, this was the principal port of the powerful Sundanese kingdom of Galuh, whose capital lay to the south in the fertile Citanduy River valley around present-day Ciamis. The port also gave access to the Cimanuk River leading up via Sumedang to the Bandung basin. As the West Javan coast was marshy and inhospitable, Cirebon—together with Sunda Kelapa (Jakarta) and Banten in the far west—formed the principal points of access into the rich highlands.

Today Cirebon is a crossroads where the busy coastal highway meets the Bandung trunk route. Its harbor is a supply depot for oil rigs in the Java Sea, and is also well known for its abundant catches of delectable fish and crustaceans. *Cirebon* in fact translates as "Shrimp River," and the town has adopted the sobriquet Kota Udang ("Prawn City"), though according to historical records the name derives from the word *caruban*, meaning "mixing" or "mingling"—a testament to Cirebon's highly heterogeneous heritage.

An ancient maritime state

Though Cirebon's roots reach far back into the Hindu-Javanese past, it was the coming of Islam that was to elevate the city to the status of a major power. Cirebon may in fact have been the first Islamic city-state on Java—antedating Gresik and Demak—as local chronicles speak of a prince of Galuh-Pajajaran, a certain Cakrabuana, who became harbormaster of Cirebon then converted to Islam and ceased sending tribute, successfully fending off attacks from the Hindu capital. This may have taken place early in the 15th century, as the throne pavilion in front of the Kesepuhan palace bears the date A.D. 1425.

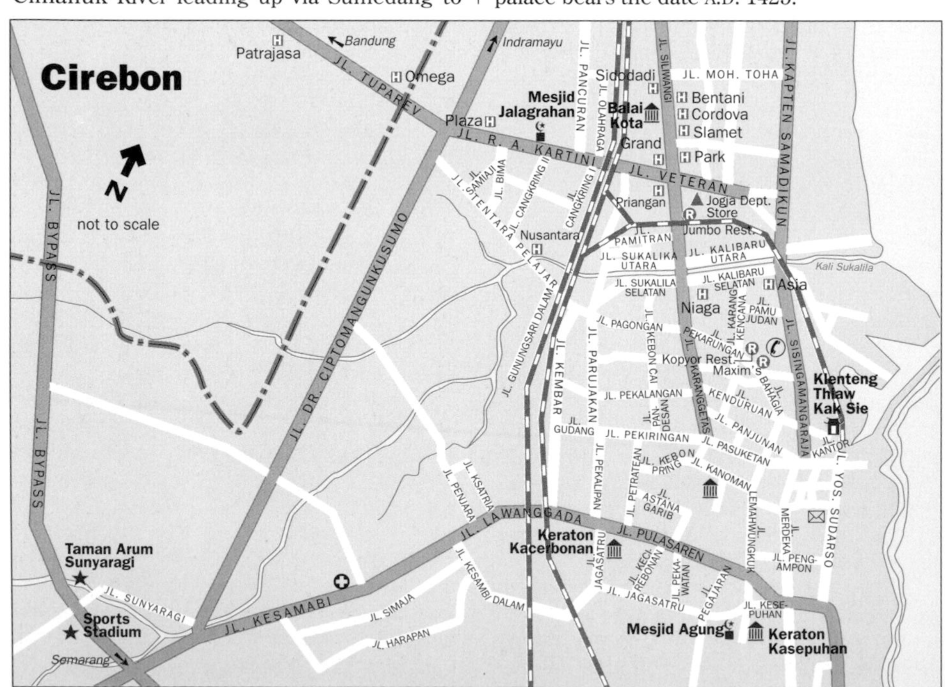

It is however with the powerful figure of Sunan Gunung Jati—one of the nine *walis* or saints who spread Islam on Java a century later—that Cirebon's rise to greatness is most closely associated. As legend has it, he was the son of a Middle Eastern sultan by Cakrabuana's younger sister, who went on a pilgrimage to Mecca with her brother. The boy was born in Sumatra, but on his arrival in Cirebon was immediately placed upon the throne. He proceeded to rebuild the palace and to develop a formidable reputation as one of the foremost holy men of his time.

During the 16th century—the "Golden Age" of Islamic maritime states on Java—Gunung Jati allied himself with powerful Demak and proceeded to conquer the Hindu ports of Sunda Kelapa and Banten at Java's western tip. He died in 1568, and his grave to the north of Cirebon is today an important pilgrimage point for devout Javanese and Sundanese Muslims.

The 17th century saw the rise of another Islamic power on Java—the inland kingdom of Mataram. While all other coastal states and their ruling families faded from view before the onslaught of Sultan Agung's Central Javanese forces, it seems that skillful marriage diplomacy and their position as venerated religious leaders allowed the Cirebon rulers to survive as vassals of Mataram. Sultan Agung took a Cirebonese princess as his principal wife, and all Mataram rulers have thus had blood ties to this coastal city.

In 1678, according to court chronicles, the kingdom was peacefully sub-divided and new palaces were erected by three of the Cirebon princes. At about this time, however, the entire coast was ceded to the Dutch by the Mataram ruler as payment of a war indemnity. The newly-installed Cirebon sultans were then required to sign contracts granting monopoly rights to the VOC over imports and exports, but in return were allowed to retain their domains and privileges.

The next century of colonial rule was a period of great hardships. Major epidemics and famines during the 18th century decimated Cirebon's population; roving brigands looted the outlying areas, while rapacious Dutch officials lined their pockets at the expense of the peasantry. Thousands died of disease and starvation, while many more were sold into slavery. It is said that a certain Resident van Hogendorp earned over 100,000 rixdollars per year during his tenure in Cirebon, so that the ship carrying his booty back to Holland sank from too heavy a load.

At the beginning of the 19th century a new colonial administration was installed and the kingdom was further sub-divided, so that today there are five separate royal households. However, in 1809 Cirebon's sultans

Below: *Cirebon's Kesepuhan palace, with its distinctive* wadasan *or rock motif decorations.*

AMIR SIDHARTA

DANA IRFAN

were stripped of their titles and granted a salary of 18,000 rixdollars per year. Thereafter, like the rulers of Yogya and Solo, they retreated to their palaces and devoted themselves to cultural pursuits—patronizing the arts and styling themselves after the manner of Central Javanese royalty. A new European quarter, meanwhile, grew up to the north of town, and for the most part Cirebon looks today like other medium-size Javanese cities.

Early palace architecture

As the oldest-remaining Islamic court center on Java, it is interesting and perhaps rather ironic that Cirebon possesses the finest surviving examples of earlier Hindu-period court architecture. The forecourt (*siti inggil*) pavilions of Cirebon's Kesepuhan and Kanoman *keratons* retain a design typical of 13th and 14th century East Javanese palaces—known to us from temple reliefs on the Singasari and Majapahit sanctuaries.

As in the Yogya and Solo palaces (and in Balinese state temples), this plan identifies the central pavilion of the complex with the sacred Mount Meru at the center of the universe, surrounded by concentric seas and continents. Only the foundations of these structures were originally of brick or stone, the posts and roofs being made of wood and thatch. Later palaces incorporated mortar, tiles and cast-iron, together with European and Middle Eastern design elements like archways and windows.

Cirebon's two major palaces display aspects of earlier as well as later architectural styles. The **Keraton Kesepuhan** ("Palace of the Elder Brother") stands on the site of the original 15th century Pakungwati palace, facing northward onto an old town square in the southeastern part of Cirebon. It is said to have been built in 1677-8, although the main structures may be later than this; in any case the palace was extensively restored in 1928.

It is in fact the gate and the Siti Inggil pavilions facing onto the square at the front of the palace that are most archaic. The red-brick entryway is in the form of an East Javanese-style *candi bentar* split gate of the type found mainly in Bali today. The low retaining wall around it, constructed without mortar by rubbing and sticking the bricks together with water, is inset with Ming ceramics. A large moat once ran around the complex, created by diverting a nearby river. Access was by means of a drawbridge.

Just inside the gate are former guard posts —tiny pavilions with peaked *joglo* roofs. The larger pavilions behind were for royal audiences, meetings of the law court, religious convocations and state rituals, as well as for the gamelan ensembles that normally accompanied official gatherings. The posts supporting the open pavilions are gracefully formed and often elaborately carved. These and the general layout of the Siti Inggil are its most distinctive aspects—as close as we can come today to an ancient Hindu-Javanese palace.

To the east of the Siti Inggil a part of the original Pakungwati palace lies in ruins. Here are the foundations of a meditational complex and a royal pool fed by sacred wells. During the Panjang Jimat festival held every year on Muhammad's birthday (12 Maulud on the Javanese calendar), young people come to bathe in the well water as it is believed this will assure them of obtaining a spouse.

A shady driveway leads from the Siti Inggil back to the main palace compound. The front portal is a curious structure—a pillared archway, essentially European in design, decorated with ornate *wadasan* rock motifs characteristic of this royal house. This motif is said to imitate the form of limestone hills to the south of the city, and to represent meditational grottoes from which spiritual power is derived. It also resembles Chinese representations of the *qi* or cosmic energy emanating from the person of the ruler. Two poised lions, symbols of the court, grace the garden in front.

The hall immediately behind is a reception area, Javanese in its form but with 18th century European-style furnishings. Directly behind are two more halls, used for ritual occasions, and to the east of them lie the royal residence chambers. Farther in back is a pleasure garden containing a pond with a "floating" pavilion in the middle and replicas of sacred mountains at the southern edges of the cosmos. Ask to be shown the small audience pavilion (*paseban*) on the west side of the rear Pringgodani hall; its intricately carved roof and supporting pillars are remnants of the original Pakungwati palace.

Before leaving the palace have a look in the Gedong Singa or "Lion's Stable" facing onto the front driveway. The so-called Singa Barong carriage stored here (said to date from 1549) combines all Javanese mythological creatures—*garuda*, horse, lion and elephant—into one. On state occasions the sultan rode in it in grand style, drawn by a team of albino oxen. Also displayed are palanquins and weapons, and across the garden is a small museum with musical instruments and *seni debus* instruments of self-immolation.

Other Cirebon sights

Next have a look at the **Mesjid Agung** or "Grand Mosque" on the western side of the old town square. Its two-tiered *meru* roof is a holdover from Hindu temples of the pre-Islamic era. A red-brick wall all around the compound has nine gates, symbolic of the *wali songo* or nine Islamic saints.

According to *keraton* tradition, this mosque was completed in A.D. 1500, which would make it the oldest on Java. Certainly it is the most striking. The roof is supported, in traditional Javanese style, by four huge pillars (*soko guru*). As with the Demak mosque, one pillar is said to have been made in a single night by Sunan Kalijaga, who pressed together chips left by carvers of the other three. The massive roof is an elaborate inter-locking matrix of wooden beams, while the lovely *mimbar* or pulpit is of solid teak, with Hindu-Javanese *kala-makara* decorations. Portals of carved sandstone are adorned with graceful mandalas, while a huge drum (*bedug*) used to call the faithful to prayer has a name, Sang Guru Mangir.

Cirebon's other major palace (remember—there are five in all) is called the **Keraton Kanoman** or "Palace of the Younger Brother." It is within walking distance of the mosque, just in back of a bustling market (Pasar Kanoman). It was founded at about the same time as the Kesepuhan and is similar in terms of layout, if on a smaller scale. A noticeable difference is that the Siti Inggil pavilions at the front are constructed in a more "modern" style—solid brick and plaster archways, studded with Chinese plates. The museum is worth a visit, for a look at the Paksi Naga Liman carriage that is a spitting image of the one in the Kesepuhan palace.

Nearby, too, is the **Keraton Kacirebonan**, founded early in the 19th century as a branch of the Kanoman. It is smaller and more modern than the latter. Also in this vicinity are two 17th century landmarks: an old mosque, **Mesjid Panjunan** on Jl. Panjunan ("potter's street"), and one of the oldest Chinese temples on Java, **Kelenteng Thiaw Kak Sie** on Jl. Pasuketan. The latter is dedicated to the goddess of mercy, Kuan Yin, and has frescoes depicting punishments in the ten courts of the hell in the main hall. In the back is a cast-iron anchor said to have come from the imperial Ming fleet of eunuch Admiral Zhenghe, who called at these ports in the early 15th century. It may actually have come from a later VOC ship, however.

Those with an interest in architectural eccentricities should pay a visit to **Taman Arum Sunyaragi**, a fanciful royal pleasure

Opposite: *The Grebeg or Panjang Jimat festival. Trays of food are brought from the palace, then blessed and distributed to the faithful.*

ERIC OEY

garden-cum-fortress 4.5 km (2.8 mi) southwest of the city center. Completed in 1703, it is near a river and was originally surrounded by a moat, containing bathing pools and meditation chambers for the sultan and his wives. Because it was easily fortified, it became the site of an insurrection against the Dutch in 1787 during a period of great oppression, and again during the Java War of 1825-30.

Largely destroyed in these battles, the complex was restored in 1853 by a Chinese architect in the employ of the Sultan Sepuh, who transformed it into a maze of celestial Taoist grottoes such as one sees in Beijing's Forbidden City. Narrow stairways wind over jagged nooks and crannies, leading to tiny chambers and sometimes nowhere at all. The whole place has now been transformed into a park that probably bears little resemblance to the original. While in this area, drive south in the direction of Kuningan, to the top of a ridge whence you have a panoramic view of Cirebon and the coast.

Grave of Gunung Jati

The most famous of Cirebon's sights is the **Astana Gunung Jati** or grave of Gunung Jati, located about 5 km (3 mi) north of town along the coast. A small hill stands 25 m (80 ft) above the ocean's edge here, covered with teak trees—the "teak mountain" (that is what "Gunung Jati" means) from which the great 16th century warrior-saint takes his name. Indeed this seems to have been the site of the original Hindu harbor settlement of Caruban that attracted an Islamic teacher known as Syeh Datuk Kahfi in the 15th century, and soon became a hotbed of Islamic conversions. There are graves in the complex dating back to A.D. 1418, and pilgrims come from all over Java to partake of the holy aura of the place.

Atop the hill, which is to the right of the road as one approaches from Cirebon, is the grave of Syeh Datuk Kahfi. A stone staircase ascends to the the summit past ancient crumbling walls, and from here one has an expansive view of the sea. The other important graves, including those of Sunan Gunung Jati and the royal families of Cirebon, are on another hill (Bukit Sembung) across the road to the west. There is a parking area here surrounded by shops selling souvenirs, amulets, empty bottles for holy water and softdrinks, and you are instantly swarmed by persistent vendors and "guides." Pay a small fee at the *candi bentar* gate into the complex and leave the vendors behind.

The important inner grave compounds are on a hill in the back of the complex, but are closed except on festive occasions or by special permission of the sultan. Nevertheless the pavilions and the mosque among the outer compounds give a good impression of the antiquity of the place. As in the Cirebon palaces, carved wooden beams support open

JILL GOCHER

JILL GOCHER

pavilions, and Dutch and Chinese plates are set into the masonry walls.

Pilgrims deluge the place every 35 days, on Thursday Kliwon according to the Javanese calendar, as well as on Muhammad's birthday. The site is staffed by 108 *kraman* or "elders" who are all said to be descendants of a ship's crew who were wrecked here in the 16th century under the command of a trader from Jepara, Adipati Keling. They were assigned by Gunung Jati to become caretakers of the royal graves. Nautical terminology is still in use among them—for example their duties are assigned like watches on a ship.

The arts of Cirebon

All too little is known about the fascinating artistic traditions of the Cirebon area except that this is one of Java's most active regions for folk crafts and performing arts. As in Bali, the passing of palace patronage in this century have not diminished the activities of village artisans. Indeed, village craftsmen and performers seem to have found new outlets for their productions, even as those in the city have turned to other, more lucrative pursuits.

There is evidence that the artisan villages to the west and north of Cirebon—Plered, Trusmi, Plumbon, Kalimanan, Arjawinangun, Susukan, Gegesik and others—were organized in the 17th century along the lines of Sufi *tariqats* or guilds, each devoted to a single craft. There is still a good deal of specialization. For example, Trusmi is known for its batik, Plered for its rattan work, Gegesik for its glass-painting and *topeng* dancing.

Cirebon is perhaps best known, along with neighboring Indramayu, for its distinctive batiks. Bold and striking patterns, along with the use of characteristic *soga* browns, indigo blues, "Turkish" reds and smooth creme or ivory yellows, give the fabrics an unmistakable look. The two most famous patterns are the brown, black and creme Wadas Singa (rock caves flanked by Kesepuhan lions) and the Mega Mendung "rain clouds" motif—brilliant, shimmering tones of red, blue, violet and gold. Unlike the batiks of other areas, the Cirebon style has a painted effect in which the fabric is treated almost like a canvas.

The mecca for batik in these parts is the studio of Ibu Masina, in the village of **Trusmi**, 12 km (7 mi) to the west of Cirebon. Turn off the main road in Weru at the sign and follow a narrow lane to the north; you will see the factory and showroom after about 500 m (1,600 ft) on the right. Since the early 1970s, Ibu Masina has been reviving the traditional Cirebon patterns, employing craftsmen from this and neighboring Kalitengah village.

— *Eric Oey and Onghokham*

Opposite, top: *The unusual grottoes of the Taman Arum Sunyaragi royal pleasure garden complex.* **Opposite, below:** *The grave of Sunan Gunung Jati.* **Above:** *A village* wayang topeng *performance.*

PEKALONGAN

Home of Java's Finest Batik Fabrics

The road east from Cirebon is level and fast. Waves of heat shimmer off the pavement and caravans of trucks send up black plumes of smoke, while more agile vehicles play a daring game of leap-frog around them. Every few kilometers the road crosses a sluggish river. Just out of Cirebon, pull up at one of the bridges and walk down to see colorful fishing *perahus* tethered by the river banks—their rakish bows painted a rainbow of colors.

The town of **Brebes**, 59 km (37 mi) east of Cirebon, is Java's shallot capital; bales of tiny onions pile high by the roadside. **Tegal**, 13 km (8 mi) to the east, is a major crossroads—a good road leads south from here to the Bandung-Yogya highway and to Cilacap.

After about 130 km (81 mi) and 3 hours, you enter **Pekalongan**. Twin pillars in the shape of wax pens (*canting*) at the outskirts announce it as Kota Batik ("Batik City") —and indeed this otherwise unremarkable town once produced the finest and most sought-after batiks on Java. Sadly, recent decades have seen a dramatic decline in the batik trade, as machine-made fabrics have flooded the market, but for the connoisseur this is still an important pilgrimage point.

The distinctive *pasisir* style

In marked contrast to the sober and conservative batiks traditionally produced in Yogya and Solo, the batiks of the north coast display an exuberant coloring and an eclectic design sense. The reason is that batik making here developed into a huge industry dominated by Indo-European, Chinese and Arab entrepreneurs who catered for a variety of markets and tastes. During the heyday of batik production from about 1880 up to 1930, everyone in the islands wore this colorful cloth, and it was also exported to Malaya, Thailand, Ceylon, Burma and the Philippines.

Each of a dozen batik centers developed its own style, influenced as much by local dye recipes as by the demands of the clientele. Lasem batiks, for example, were known for their creamy backgrounds and tiny red animals; those of Demak and Kudus for their Arabic calligraphy. Silk batiks with Chinese phoenixes (*jilin*) from Rembang were considered magical, while Madura's deep reds are said to have been produced by mixing *mengkudu* root with palm sugar and chicken meat.

Pekalongan was known for its delicate floral motifs deriving from Chinese and Dutch ceramics. When chemical dyes became available, local batikers were among the first to make use of the new technology, and their cloths are distinguished by bright, often garish color combinations. Most of all, however, this was the home of several talented producers who elevated the batik art to new heights. Craftsmen like van Zuylen, Metzelaar, Oey, The, Simonet and Liem produced pieces of exquisite delicacy during the early decades of this century—batiks that can never be imitated due to the lost art of mixing natural dyes. Surviving pieces are worth thousands of dollars in good condition today.

On the batik trail

Start your tour at **Pasar Banjarsari**, the central market on Jl. Sultan Agung. At the back of this dimly-lit rabbit warren of stalls and corridors, vendors seated on stools or squatting on mats in elevated compartments pluck brightly-colored fabrics from neat stacks around them, deftly unraveling them before prospective buyers. The clients are mainly peasants from outlying villages, and maintain an air of studied indifference—pointing to defects in the cloth, shaking their heads in disapproval. This is all part of the haggling involved, however, and in the end a selection is made and the cloths are neatly wrapped in newspaper and bound with a rubber band.

Fabrics sold here span the lower to medium ranges only; for higher quality you must visit a shop or the home of a craftsman. Stalls at the market also sell batik implements (drying-racks, pots for heating wax, *cantings* and copper stamps), however, and *pelekats*—hand-woven cottons with simple checked patterns. The latter were introduced from the Pulicat region of India centuries ago, but have been woven in massive quantities here since the 1850s. It was perhaps largely due to a pre-existing trade in *pelekat*, in fact, that Pekalongan developed into Java's largest batik export center.

Emerging from the market, turn down Jl. Blimbing, the heart of the **Chinese quarter**. A small *mie bakso* stand in front of the Po An

Thian Chinese temple is a good place for a drink and a snack. The residents of this area once did a booming trade in agricultural products, advancing money to villagers and receiving their harvests in return. The grandchildren have opened food kiosks, a dental clinic and a computer repair shop.

Cross over Loji Bridge to visit the former **European quarter** to the north. Situated around a grassy square are the old Resident's mansion, the Post Office, the Reformed Church (1852), the Municipal Offices (Kotamadya) and the colonial clubhouse (Societeit Cercle). Behind them stands the VOC fort, constructed in 1753, now a prison. Gracious mansions, many now dilapidated, line the shady boulevards, and a pot-holed road leads several kms north to the port.

Double back across the bridge and turn left (east) onto Jl. Patiunus—past a primitive sawmill and a tea factory reeking of jasmine. This is the **Arab quarter**, containing several mosques and Islamic schools. It was also a center for batik, and one still sees the occasional *becak* piled high with cloth on its way to being waxed or dyed. Look down Jl. Surabaya, which has a quaint Middle-Eastern air about it, but continue on to Jl. Teratai 24 (past the intersection with Jl. H. Agus Salim)—a factory called Tobal Batik specializing in export garments. Ask to have a look at the process and the latest fashions.

Head south from here to the town square (*alun-alun*). An old moorish-style mosque, the Mesjid Al Jami, stands to the west. It formerly had a Javanese *meru* or multi-tiered roof but this was removed in the 1930s. Behind it to the east lies the Kauman or **Muslim quarter**, another batik-producing area. Heading west along Jl. Hayam Wuruk, you pass several batik shops, and across the bridge are others selling chemical dyes and waxes. Turn right (north) down a small lane next to the Sederhana Restaurant and ask for the home of Pak Achmad Yahya (Jl. Pesindon 221), a devout Muslim whose original creations have been featured in Vogue Magazine and on the walls of Jackie Kennedy's bathroom in New York.

Last but not least, to view the finest batik in the area, perhaps in the whole of Java, pay a visit to the famous workshop of **Oey Soe Tjoen** in Kedungwuni, 9 km (5.6 mi) south of Pekalongan. Here, in a modest home marked only by a small sign saying "Batik Art," you will witness women tediously applying tiny lines and dots of wax to fine cloth. It takes an experienced craftswoman a month to wax a single 2-meter length, and as this must be repeated for each color, 6-months will elapse before the piece is finally completed. The old master is dead, but his son and wife carry on the fine work.

— *Eric Summers*

Below: *A modern Oey Soe Tjoen floral bouquet.*

ERIC OEY

SEMARANG & VICINITY

Commercial Capital of Central Java

Good roads have long connected the coast with Java's fertile hinterland. In ancient times a number of routes led across the mountains from the Mataram region around present-day Yogya to tiny riverine settlements on the north shore—entrepôts where the produce of the interior could be exchanged for valuable metalwares, ceramics, jewelry, spices, textiles, aromatics, and exotic ritual and medicinal substances from abroad.

Travel was slow in those days. Rivers had to be forded and the roads turned to mush during the rainy season. Still, the journey from Mataram to the coast—a distance of 120 km (75 mi)—could be accomplished in just a few days, with nights spent en route in the cool highlands—site of holy shrines, hot springs and meditational retreats.

Today of course the same journey takes only 2 hours along a smooth, asphalted road. The tiny settlements have been replaced by large cities, however, and since the 18th century the premier port along these shores has been Semarang—now the provincial capital of Central Java and the island's fourth largest metropolis, with about 1.5 million inhabitants.

Rise of a colonial entrepôt

Semarang's early history is hazy. Javanese chronicles refer to the port by the Sanskritic name of Pragota (or Pergota), indicating that a Hindu-Javanese settlement perhaps existed here in earlier times. Geologists tell us that a ring of foothills in southwestern Semarang known as Bukit Bergota once enclosed a crescent-shaped cove at the mouth of the Semarang River. This is precisely the spot where Ming admiral Zhenghe is said to have stepped ashore early in the 15th century, site of the Gedung Batu temple today (see below).

In the late 15th century an Arab mullah took the local name of Ki Pandan Arang and founded an Islamic settlement in this place, recognizing powerful Demak as his overlord. His grave lies on Bergota Hill. In this period Semarang was an insignificant port, but it became increasingly important as the harbor of Demak silted up in the 17th century. In 1678 the Dutch demanded and were ceded Semarang by the Mataram ruler; in 1708 they moved their headquarters here from Jepara.

The Dutch outpost was besieged by 3,500 Chinese rebels from Batavia in 1741, abetted

by about 20,000 troops from the Mataram court. Miraculously, the tiny VOC contingent was able to hold out until reinforcements arrived, and Dutch control of the area was not threatened thereafter. Ruins of the 18th century VOC fortress lie behind the Poncol train station on Jl. Imam Bonjol.

During the 19th century, Semarang developed into a prosperous commercial center, spurred on by the construction of all-weather roads leading south along either side of the Merapi-Merbabu massif. The plains and hills around Semarang itself were also cleared for cultivation, and by the latter part of the 19th century copious quantities of sugar, rice, coffee and other commodities were flowing through the harbor—one of the few on this coast to make the transition to steam shipping. Light industry followed, and in its heyday at the turn of this century, Semarang rivalled Batavia (Jakarta) and Surabaya in terms of wealth and size. Increasingly important today as a manufacturing center, it has fallen behind as an entrepôt port because it lacks a deep-water harbor.

The old city and Chinatown

Semarang is not a tourist town, though physically it is quite attractive because of steeply-rising hills to the south—the only place along the north shore where highlands approach the coast. Spend a day exploring the older areas of town, then head into the hills.

Start your tour with a look at the harbor, a smaller version of Jakarta's Sunda Kelapa and Surabaya's Kali Mas. Proceed south through the old European commercial district around Jl. Jend. Suprapto. The major landmark here, standing amidst 200-year-old warehouses and offices, is the copper-domed **Gereja Blenduk**, a Dutch church dating from 1753. To the west, across the river, lies Semarang's shopping and hotel district, but first make a detour south along Jl. Pekojan into the heart of the city's colorful **Chinatown** district.

Chinese merchants have contributed greatly to Semarang's success as a commercial hub. Best-known among them is Oei Tiong Ham, the "sugar king" who made a fortune from agricultural exports and control of the state opium monopoly at the turn of the century—becoming chief (*majoor*) of Semarang's Chinese community and owner of a vast business empire with interests in Singapore, Hong Kong, Shanghai, New York and London. His company has been called Asia's first multi-national corporation, and at the time of his death in 1924 he is said to have been worth 200 million Dutch guilders.

Today Semarang maintains a strong Chinese flavor, with the highest percentage of ethnic Chinese of any city in Indonesia. The maze of lanes tucked inside a bend in the

Below: *The odd "building of 1,000 doors" (Lawang Sewu) with the Tugu Muda in front.*

AMIR SIDHARTA

ERIC OEY

river at the end of Jl. Pekojan offers a fascinating glimpse of bustling shops and old "Nanyang" row-houses with carved doorways and latticed balconies.

The area also features a number of dimly-lit temples and clan houses. Just before the bridge on Jl. Pekojan, duck down a tiny lane to the right (Gang Lombok) and after a few paces you are at the entrance to **Tay Kak Sie**—Semarang's largest Chinese temple. The main deity here is the goddess of mercy, Kuan Yin, but in alcoves all around the complex are a host of other gods and saints.

The temple was constructed by craftsmen brought in from China in 1771-2, and over the years it has become a refuge for icons from many shrines in the region. A great many festival days are observed as a result, and even on normal days crowds flock here—buying sticks of fragrant incense at a counter by the entryway, then burning them at each of the altars in turn. Restaurants just outside offer delicious noodles and snacks.

Continue southward across the bridge and wander the narrow lanes between Gang Pinggir and Gang Warung, emerging finally on Jl. Wahid Hasyim to the west—Semarang's goldsmith street. Turn right (north) and you find yourself in front of the **Grand Mosque**, with its multi-tiered Javanese roof. In front of it is the former town square (*alun-alun*), which has now been taken over by **Pasar Johar**, Semarang's sprawling central market. This is a great place to browse, in stalls selling brasswares and bric-a-brac in addition to the usual foodstuffs and textiles.

Semarang's 'Champs Elysée'

West of Johar market is the busy intersection with **Jalan Pemuda**, Semarang's main shopping street. In colonial times this was called Jl. Bodjong—a broad, broom-swept boulevard bordered by leafy tamarind trees, shops and elegant villas. A Dutch writer at the turn of the century glowingly referred to it as the most fashionable street on Java—the island's "Champs Elysée."

To the north you will spot one of the few remaining hotels from that era, the Dibya Puri (rebuilt in 1913). Heading west (left) you encounter a number of other colonial landmarks. On the right is the Galendra Artshop, the former premises of bookseller and publisher G. Kolff. On the left is the venerable **Toko Oen** restaurant, opened in 1935 and still offering rib-sticking Dutch treats like *uitsmijter roastbief*, *paprika schnitzel* and *biefstuk compleet*—with potatoes and vegetables suitably swimming in butter. For dessert you can order ice cream (*vruchten sorbet*, *Oens symphoni*), cakes and cookies. Whirling ceiling fans, waiters in white suits and black caps, wicker chairs, linen tablecloths, long wooden display cases with glass cookie jars on top—all contribute to a fossilized *tempo doeloe* ("olden times") atmosphere. Beyond

Toko Oen is Mustika Mas, a former jeweler now selling handicrafts and antiques, and several stores selling batik.

At the very end of Jl. Pemuda, facing a fountain and the **Tugu Muda** obelisk commemorating youths who died here in the early days of the revolution, is the home of Resident Nicolaas Hartingh, built between 1754-61 (now a teacher's academy, displaying the letters APDN), and the "Indo-European" style offices of the former Netherlands Indies Train Co., dating from the 1920s. The latter has been dubbed Lawang Sewu (lit: "thousand doors") by the Javanese on account of its many outward-facing doorways.

The three-jeweled eunuch

Semarang's most famous sight lies just 1 km southwest of here: the **Gedung Batu** temple commemorating the visit of an envoy from the Ming court at the beginning of the 15th century. His name was Zhenghe (Cheng Ho), an imperial eunuch whose seven voyages to the coasts of Southeast Asia, India and eastern Africa were designed to re-establish trading and diplomatic links severed by wars of dynastic succession in China. Such a great corpus of legends grew up about his person, that he was later deified as the folk god Sam Po Kong or Sam Po Tay Jin—the "Three-Jeweled Grand Eunuch." Shrines honoring him are maintained by Chinese all along the coasts of Java, Sumatra and Malaya.

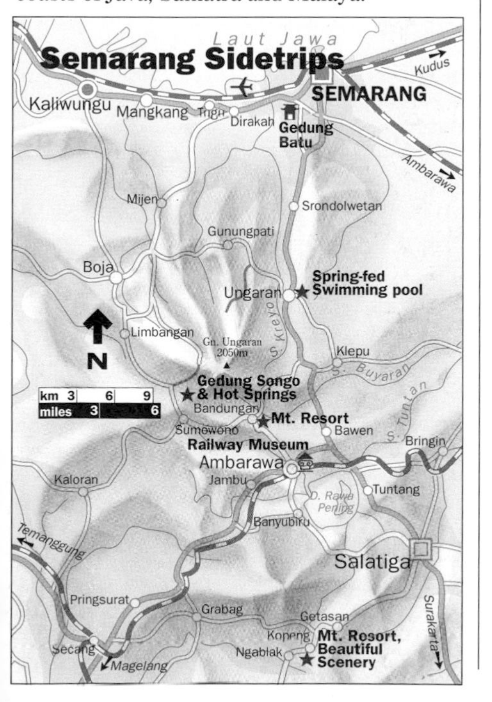

Zhenghe's huge fleets were the largest seen here in their day. The first comprised 27,800 men and 62 ships, the largest of which measured 132 meters (440 ft) by 54 meters (180 ft). It called here in 1406, and Zhenghe is said to have stepped ashore on the riverbank, and to have spent a night meditating in a cave, where the temple is now. Geologists confirm that this site was once a sheltered cove bordering the sea.

Perhaps because Zhenghe was a Muslim (from Yunnan), the Gedung Batu temple is considered sacred by Javanese Muslims as well as Chinese. It consists of several shrines clustered at the foot of a hill around a grotto containing an altar to Sam Po. To the left of the cave is an anchor said to have come from Zhenghe's ship (in fact it is a VOC anchor). To the right is the grave of Kyai Juru Mudi Dampoawang, the admiral's Muslim helmsman, while to the far right is a shrine dedicated to the temple's guardian spirit (*toapekong*). In front of these are pavilions used for offerings and performances on festival days.

The temple's anniversary falls on the 29th day of the 6th lunar month in the Chinese calendar, and in former times a colorful procession of deities was borne aloft in palanquins through the city streets, starting from the Tay Kak Sie temple at dawn and arriving at Gedung Batu by midday. They came to pay their respects to Sam Po, accompanied by musicians, trance mediums, lion and dragon dancers from all over Java. The spirit of Sam Po was called down to attend, and a horse was provided to serve as his mount. Today the participants travel here by bus and truck, and the ceremonies and entertainments are confined to the temple grounds. Thousands come from far and wide on this day to present offerings and incense to obtain the admiral's blessings.

Even on ordinary days, the temple is quite busy, as this is the most famous *klenteng* or Chinese temple on Java. Twice each month, moreover, on the eves of Friday Kliwon and Tuesday Kliwon by the Javanese calandar, Javanese and Chinese believers sleep by the grave of Kyai Juru Mudi Dampoawang to obtain his blessings.

The road south

There are other places to visit in Semarang, such as a provincial museum, a zoo and a "snake garden," but in any case before (or while) leaving the city, don't miss the view

Opposite: *A dragon dance at Gedung Batu.*

from **Candi** above the town (stop in at the Patra Jasa hotel) or from **Gombel** farther up (stop at the Sky Garden or Gombel Indah by the main highway). Enjoy a drink as you gaze out across the hazy lowlands to the Java Sea in the distance.

Four km (2.5 mi) south of Gombel is the **Nyonya Meneer** *jamu* (herbal medicine) plant. There is a museum offering a bit of history and showing some of the ingredients used; a guided tour of the factory is sometimes possible. Open Mon-Fri 10 am-3:30 pm.

About 8 km (5 mi) past Gombel on the left (opposite a new military complex) is the **Watu Gong** Buddhist monastery, founded by a man who studied agriculture at the University of California and then made a fortune growing vanilla and fruits. Later in life he became a monk, but after the age of 90 he doffed his saffron robes and married a young girl in the hopes of siring an heir. Now he has opened a small restaurant by the roadside.

A bit further up is the town of **Ungaran**, which has a spring-fed swimming pool (Tirto Agung) and a number of good restaurants. About 10 km (7.5 mi) past Ungaran, a small and scenic backroad leads up to Bandungan.

The main road forks in Bawen, 24 km (15 mi) past Ungaran. Left is to Salatiga and Surakarta. Right is to Ambarawa and Yogya. If you have time, however, an overnight in one of two lovely hill stations in this area—Kopeng or Bandungan—is highly recommended.

Only 4 km past Bawen on the Yogya road lies the tidy town of **Ambarawa**, where a Railway Museum has been set up to house steam engines dating from the "Golden Age" of rail travel. On exhibit are 21 German, Swiss and Dutch locomotives manufactured between 1891 and 1928. There is also an old cog railway running up to the nearby village of Bedono, 12 km (7 mi) away. The turn-of-the-century coaches and steam engine are in beautiful shape, and this is a memorable outing for railway buffs. Make bookings through the PJKA (state railway company) office at Jl. Thamrin 3, Semarang (tel: 24500), and bring a picnic lunch along.

Ambarawa is also the turn-off point for **Bandungan**, 7 km (4 mi) away—one of the most delightful highland resorts in Java. Lying at an altitude of 980 meters (3200 ft), on the southern slopes of Mt. Ungaran, it boasts good hotels and restaurants (see "Semarang Practicalities"), an early-morning flower market, a psychic healer named Ibu Imi who sells herbal medicines (near the Hotel Rawa Pening), a tofu factory (500 meters from the hotel on the left), and plenty of hikes with views down across Lake Rawa Pening to the volcanoes in the distance. The best is yet to come, though—just 6 km (4 mi) west are the spectacularly-sited Gedung Songo temples.

Ancient hilltop temples

The **Gedung Songo** (lit: "nine buildings")

ERIC OEY

are among the earliest antiquities in Java—direct successors of those found on the Dieng Plateau. Like the latter, they are set in high mountains in an area of volcanic activity, and are Hindu in character. The site however engenders a very different sensation. Whereas the Dieng temples are enclosed in a mist-enshrouded valley, the Gedung Songo are distributed over foothill slopes that provide breathtaking views across north-central Java. On a clear day, a line of volcanoes may be seen along the horizon—from Mt. Lawu in the east to Mt. Sumbing, Mt. Sundoro and the Dieng massif in the west.

These temples were built between A.D. 730 and 780, except for the first one encountered along the path leading up to the others, which may be 30 years younger. The name for the complex is not the original one, nor is it a literal count of the structures; the number 9 has numerological significance in Javanese culture. The temples are more or less evenly spaced between 100-200 meters (300-600 ft) apart on individual plateaus or ridges projecting horizontally from the mountain.

Temple 1, the youngest of the temples, stands alone, but the rest form groups similar to the Arjuna group at Dieng. The pathway from Temple 1 to Temple 2 preserves part of the original pavement from the 8th century.

The largest group of buildings clusters around Temple 3. On the main temple, dedicated to Siva, the statues of Nandiswara on the north and Mahakala on the south of the doorway are still in place. This Siva temple shows that Javanese Hindu iconography had reached its mature form at this time: Ganesa is placed on the wall opposite the door, Durga on the north, and Agastya on the south. This distribution is the earliest example of a pattern which was standard throughout the rest of the Central Javanese classical period.

In addition to the Siva and Nandi temples, Visnu was worshipped in a building to the left of the main sanctuary. In front of the main temple is also a smaller building similar to Candi Semar on the Dieng Plateau; the only other known example of this type of structure. Other such buildings, probably for housing statues of Nandi, stood in front of temples 2 and 6.

From Temple 3 the path leads down into a ravine in which are hot springs and sulphur jets. On the opposite side are the other temple groups, some partially restored, some still heaps of stone. Bring along food and drinks (and a swimsuit if you want to soak in the hot springs), get here for the sunrise if you can, and spend a day of hiking around some of the most glorious landscapes in all of Central Java.

— Onghokham and John Miksic

Opposite: *The 1902 cog railway locomotive at Ambarawa.* **Above:** *Temple 1 in the Gedung Songo group, with Merbabu and Merapi behind.*

EASTERN PASISIR

The Cradle of Javanese Islam

The eastern *pasisir* region—300 km (185 mi) of dry, barren coast lying between Semarang and Surabaya—hardly seems like part of Java. Except for the "hump" around Mt. Muria, this is a non-volcanic region formed over low limestone hills, whose porous and chalky soils provide a poor base for agriculture.

This range of hills—the Bukit Kapur—begins east of Semarang and extends to the tip of Madura, submerging beneath the Java Sea just long enough to form a narrow strait separating the two islands. As on Madura, little of economic value grows here apart from teak, peanuts and coconuts, and people along the strand turn their attention to the sea—salt-panning, fishing and trading for a living.

In earlier centuries this was a bustling maritime center. In fact, in the 15th and 16th centuries, shippers along this shore dominated the inter-island trade, controlling the sea lanes to the eastern "Spice Isles" and maintaining close relations with ports bordering the Java Sea and the Malacca Straits.

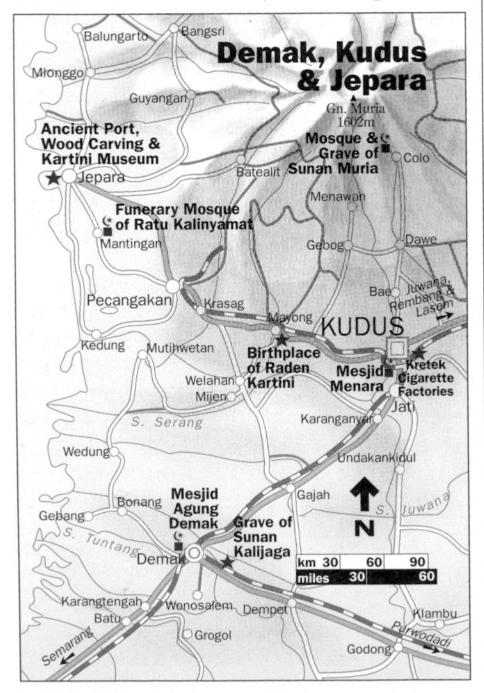

The common denominator in all of this was Islam, and foreign Muslim traders played a significant role. Many settled in the eastern *pasisir* ports and intermarried with local elites. The result was a new class of wealthy urbanites who combined foreign ways with local traditions, creating a cosmopolitan culture whose roots lay in the Middle East, India and China as well as in the ancient Hindu-Buddhist hinterland of Java.

The eastern *pasisir* was thus the birthplace of a new and uniquely Javanese form of Islam that was soon to transform the island's cultural landscape. According to tradition, this transformation was the work of nine Islamic saints—the legendary *wali songo*—who proselytized the new faith and assimilated it to Java's pre-existing social conditions.

Three powerful ports—Demak, Kudus and Jepara—rose to prominence in the early 16th century and conquered the weakened kingdoms of the interior. Their moment of glory was brief, however. A new Islamic kingdom in the center of the island returned the favor a century later, subjugating them and consigning their ruling families to oblivion.

Today the three towns can be visited in a long day-trip from Semarang. The journey is not for everyone, though—the mosques and graves lie scattered about, and are difficult to appreciate without an understanding of the history and art of the Islamic period.

Pilgrimage to the holy land

The history of Islam's ascendency on this coast is extremely shadowy, known mainly from later court chronicles that mix legends and local traditions with outright fabrications. All texts agree on one point however—a kingdom centered at **Demak**, 26 kms (16 mi) east of present-day Semarang—was the most powerful on Java during the first half of the 16th century, and was instrumental in bringing Islam to the rest of the island.

Though it now lies some distance inland as the result of heavy silting, Demak was formerly on the sea, and its rise to importance seems partly due to a ready supply of teakwood from nearby forests and the great skill of its shipwrights. The kingdom was founded at the end of the 15th century by a Chinese Muslim known to history as Raden Patah. His son (or perhaps younger brother), Raden Trenggana, took the throne around 1505 and proceeded to subjugate not only the inland

kingdom of Kediri/Majapahit, but all the major ports of the coast—from Banten and Sunda Kelapa in the west, to Surabaya and Pasuruan in the east. Trenggana was killed around 1546 during a military campaign, and Demak's hegemony did not outlive him.

Legendary accounts of Demak's rise and "Islamization" of the island stress the role of the court's spiritual advisor, Sunan Kalijaga. He is said to have used *wayang kulit* performances to teach the religion to the masses, and to have played gamelan music in the mosque to attract their attendance (something an orthodox Muslim would find quite blasphemous!). His grave lies in **Kadilangu**, 2 km (1 mi) southeast of Demak, and is visited by thousands of pilgrims each year.

Sunan Kalijaga is also credited with developing the Islamic court festivals of Grebeg and Sekaten, both of which incorporate elements of earlier Hindu-Buddhist court rites. These are today major events in the ritual calendars of the Yogya, Solo and Cirebon palaces. Grebeg is still celebrated in Demak: on the Muslim day of sacrifice, Idul Adha (10 Suro on the Javanese calendar), mountains of food are carried from the Kabupaten district offices to the mosque. After being blessed, the food morcels are eagerly snatched up for their putative talismanic powers.

Although this was Java's first great Islamic kingdom, great emphasis is placed upon its links with the earlier kingdom Majapahit in all traditional accounts. Raden Patah is conventionally described as the son of Majapahit's last king by a Chinese princess, while Sunan Kalijaga is said to be the son of a Majapahit nobleman. The palace gamelan, the royal *pendopo*, and the palace regalia are all similarly ascribed to the Majapahit court.

These links may seen also in Demak's **Grand Mosque**, which borders the square and is the town's only real sight. This is the holiest mosque on Java; seven pilgrimages here equal a single *haj* to Mecca. Its three-tiered roof is a *meru* or holy Hindu-Buddhist mountain, while the *pendopo* in front, with its ancient Hindu-Javanese style pillars, is said to have been brought from Majapahit following its conquest. The graves of Raden Patah and Raden Trenggana lie behind.

Otherwise the mosque is unremarkable, except for a tale about the four central pillars inside. As with the Cirebon mosque, Sunan Kalijaga is said to have fashioned one of them in a single night by pressing wood chips together with his bare hands. Steel bands enclose the pillar, but under the rafters the chips are said to be clearly visible.

Java's Jerusalem

Of all eastern *pasisir* towns, **Kudus**—25 kms (16 mi) northeast of Demak—is the most

Above: *The Kudus mosque, whose minaret and gates are said to date from pre Islamic times.*

interesting, and also the most prosperous. This is "Kota Kretek"—home of the hugely successful clove-flavored *kretek* cigarettes smoked by more than 50 million Indonesians. There are 25 producers in Kudus; Djarum is the largest (number 2 in Indonesia), employing 25,000 people in cavernous factories. (See following article, "Kretek.")

Of historical interest is the fact that Kudus is the only town on Java with an Arabic name, deriving from Al Quds—meaning "holy city" —the Muslim name for Jerusalem. The old mosque is called Al Manar or Al Aqsa—the name of Jerusalem's famous mosque—and the intended identification of Kudus with the ancient holy city of Palestine is thus quite unmistakable.

The Kudus mosque, **Mesjid Menara**, is unique in Java. All around and even inside the main building, which was rebuilt in 1933, are ancient red-brick structures whose design, if not the objects themselves, clearly derive from the Majapahit period. The most remarkable of these is the tall minaret, whose base is in the shape of an ancient *candi* or funerary monument. Set atop it in an open pavilion is a large drum (*bedug*) that is used, as in many older mosques on Java, to call the faithful to prayer instead of a muezzin. Elsewhere the *bedug* hangs under the eaves of a mosque's main veranda; here it is suspended in a tower like a Balinese *kulkul* or signal-drum used to warn of impending attack, fire or communal event.

In front of the minaret and around the compound are walls and gateways in the old *candi bentar* (split gate) and *ḳori agung* (main gate) styles. Inside the Mogul-style mosque, with its silvery onion-dome and concrete pillars, are two more old gateways—a smaller, inner one with relief panels on either side similar to those found at Mantingan, and an outer one that looks very much like the 14th-century Bajang Ratu gate at Trowulan. Other pre-Islamic touches are 8 *kala*-head water spouts in the ablution area and Ming porcelain plates set in the walls.

All of this gives the impression that the Kudus mosque has incorporated a pre-existing Hindu Javanese structure, and although this is likely we have no proof of it. The mosque itself has been rebuilt several times, so we have no idea what it originally looked like. The old gates, walls and minaret that appear so incongruous today may originally have blended more harmoniously with the main structure—which probably had a *meru* roof supported by large pillars, as in Cirebon and Demak. Still, the fact remains that no other mosque on Java is known to have had a drum-tower of this type, and the reference to Jerusalem does indeed suggest an ancient holy city of another faith appropriated by Islam. It is interesting also that the people of Kudus observe an old prohibition on the slaughter of cows, the sacred animal of the

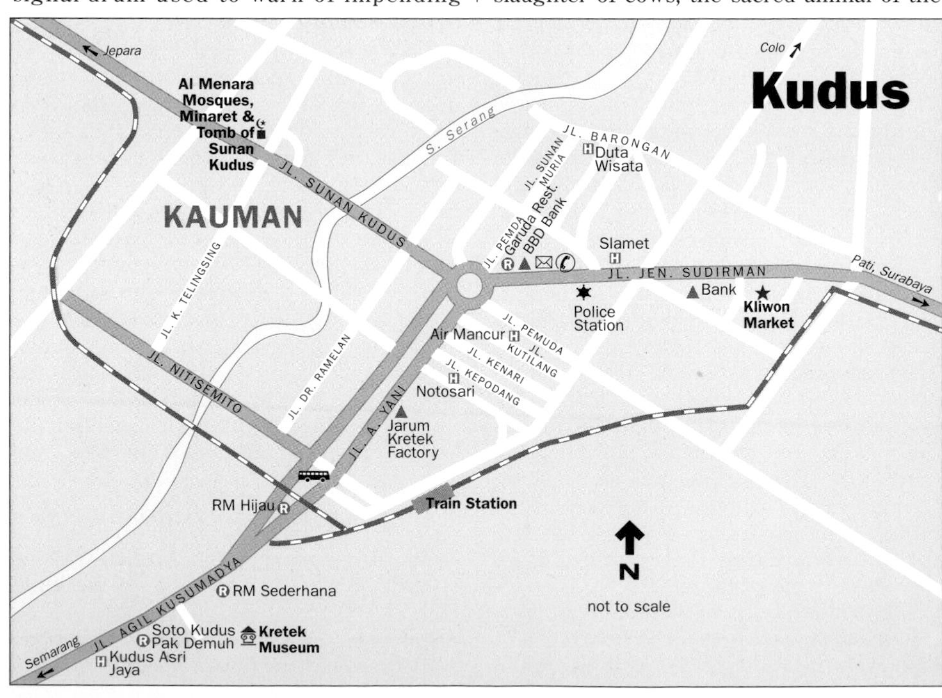

Hindus, so that beef has to be brought in from neighboring towns.

An inscription above the *mihrab*—a niche in the mosque indicating the direction to Mecca—says that it was founded by Ja'far Shodiq in 1549. He is apparently the venerated Sunan Kudus or *wali* of the place, who lies buried in an elaborately-carved mausoleum behind the mosque. Little is known about him or about the early history of the town. His Arabic name associates him with the founder of the Shiite school of Islam, while local traditions describe him as a great military leader and a forceful evangelist. Perhaps he was a general of the Demak armies.

After seeing the mosque, poke around the narrow lanes of the surrounding **Kauman district** in search of traditional carved houses. Kudus has always been an important craft center, and the older houses are constructed entirely of teak that is intricately carved from top to bottom with distinctive floral patterns still produced in nearby Jepara, though no longer in Kudus. The peaked gables are crowned with stylish terracotta finials in the shape of tridents, leaves and animals, and entire houses are now being purchased for fantastic prices, disassembled and brought to Jakarta, where they are incorporated into the homes of wealthy art collectors.

Kudus is also well known for its embroidery—still produced here, though no longer on the scale it was when brightly-colored lacey *kebaya* blouses were worn by every woman on Java with batik sarongs. Women in the towns now prefer dresses made of machine-printed fabrics, and the *sarung kebaya* is reserved for ceremonial occasions.

Handloomed fabrics are produced in the village of **Troso**, a few kilometers west of town on the road to Jepara. Many are imitations of Sumbanese and Balinese *ikats*, and amazing as it may seem Kudus actually exports Balinese-style weavings to Bali. Labor is cheaper here, and men do the work rather than women, which permits them to produce a broader fabric.

Quite a number of other old mosques and graves are found in and around the Kudus area, reinforcing its image as a ancient holy land. One in particular that is worth visiting is the grave of Sunan Muria up on the slopes of Mt. Muria near the village of **Colo**, 18 km (11 mi) north of Kudus. The name of this dormant volcano is yet another reference to Jerusalem—Moriah being the hilltop in the holy land that was leveled by Solomon to build a temple.

From the roadside just to the west of Colo, one climbs a long flight of stairs up to the shrine. The mosque is said to have been built by Sunan Muria, but has been renovated so that little of the original may be seen. It

Below: *A beautifully-carved teakwood house in the Kauman district of Kudus.*

FENDI SIREGAR

offers a commanding view of the area, however, and if you come on the night of Friday Paing or Thursday Legi you are surrounded by pilgrims who meditate and pray.

Town of woodcarvers

It hardly seems possible today but the sleepy town of **Jepara**, 33 km (20 mi) northwest of Kudus, sent large naval expeditions against Portuguese-held Malacca in 1513, 1551 and 1574. Mt. Muria was then separated from Java by an inland sea channel which flowed past Demak, Kudus, Pati and Juwana—so that Jepara lay in a strategic position on the west coast of an island. Facing the open sea, it had a deeper harbor than the other ports, that could accommodate larger ships.

The first powerful ruler of Jepara, Pati Unus, was the brother-in-law of Raden Trenggana, and seems to have ruled Demak for a time in his stead—ca. 1518-21. Following Trenggana's death in 1546, Queen Kalinyamat of Jepara took control of the Demak area, skillfully establishing alliances with Johor, Aceh, Banten and other ports near the Malacca Straits, thereby dominating the *pasisir* coast trade for several decades.

Her funerary mosque lies in the village of **Mantingan**, 8 km (5 mi) to the south of Jepara. It was founded in 1559 but was completely rebuilt in 1927. About 60 exquisitely-carved relief panels from the original mosque remain and have been set into the walls of the new one. These are round or oblong medallions that depict naturalistic scenes.

One, for example, shows a lovely lotus pond with a pavilion and spouting fountains, surrounded by a brick wall with a *candi bentar* gate. Another depicts towering mountains surrounded by forests. In yet another, leafy tendrils make up the figure of Hanuman, the monkey hero from the Ramayana. Orthodox Islam forbids the representation of humans and animals, and it seems that the carvers of these panels have resorted to this device to circumvent the prohibition.

A loose panel similar to the ones in the wall has a lotus pond on one side and a relief depicting Rama and Sita on the other, indicating that it may have come from an existing Hindu temple and was "recycled" for use in the mosque. An adjoining mausoleum contains the graves of the queen and her Chinese consort, Pangeran Hadiri.

The Mantingan reliefs are important early evidence of a carving style still practiced with great skill in this area today. In fact Jepara is Kota Ukir—"carving town"—where thousands of craftsmen are engaged in producing elaborately-carved wooden products ranging from furniture to decorative screens, to vases, ashtrays and chess sets. This style of carving is in great demand in Jakarta and other cities, because of its traditional associations with Javanese royalty. Though of course a range of motifs are now employed, many

still harken back to the delicate floral patterns seen at Mantingan.

It is not difficult to find carvings in the Jepara area as workshops line the streets of the town and many of the surrounding villages. In fact, the village of **Tegalsambi**, not far from the Mantingan mosque, specializes in fine relief panels.

The Jepara area is also famous as the birthplace of Raden Adjeng Kartini—daughter of a local aristocrat whose letters (written in Dutch, mainly to Dutch friends) at the turn of the century eloquently express a desire for greater freedom, education and respect for individual rights. She has been canonized as a national hero; a museum dedicated to her borders the Jepara town square, and the house of her birth lies just off the main road in **Mayong**, 12 km (7.5 mi) west of Kudus on the Jepara road.

Points east

The coast road east of Kudus is long, hot and not very rewarding, though there are a few high points. The sun-baked towns of **Juwana**, **Rembang** and **Lasem** lie within two hours of Kudus and have an almost Mediterranean feel about them. The coast here has been transformed into a vast network of solar salt pans that stretch as far as the eye can see and are laboriously worked as they have been for centuries. Old Chinese homes line the narrow alleys of these towns—their central courtyards enclosed by white-washed walls and massive wooden gates. Rembang and Lasem both have exquisite Chinese temples. Lasem in particular was once an important batik center, and a few producers are still active in the town today.

The town of **Tuban**, 88 km (55 mi) east of Lasem, was an important port for the ancient kingdoms of the Brantas Valley, mentioned as early as the 11th century in Chinese sources. It remained loyal to Majapahit until the kingdom's last days, and was conquered in 1527 by Demak. Today it is a poor backwater; the main sights are a large Chinese temple, and the mosque and holy grave of Sunan Bonang.

The surrounding area is barren and remote. About 25 kms (16 mi) to the west the interesting village of **Kerek** is one of the last places on Java where batik cloth is produced today in a completely traditional fashion. Even the cotton is locally grown, spun and woven, and one woman in the village is responsible for maintaining the sacred dying vats. Natural indigo blues and dark *soga* browns are still used, along with modern naphthol reds. The colors and patterns of fabrics worn by village women still designate the age and social status of the wearer, as they once did throughout Java.

The towns of **Paciran** and **Sedayu**, 30 kms (19 mi) and 55 km (34 mi) east of Tuban respectively, also have 16th century Islamic graves of a highly syncretic nature. The most interesting of these is the grave of Sunan Sendang, perched on a rocky outcropping by the village of **Sendang Duwur**, 3 km (2 mi) south of Paciran.

Two of the covered gateways here are elaborately carved and fitted with spreading Garuda wings as if they are ready to fly away. The one on the west side is quite extraordinary—richly decorated with plants, rocks, pavilions, nagas, deer and a *kala*-head much in the manner of a *gunungan* or "tree of life" from the *wayang kulit*. The style of carvings here enclosing the tomb are distinctively reminiscent of the Mantingan reliefs, and indeed a manuscript discovered in the village recounts that the mosque was a gift to Sunan Sendang from Queen Kalinyamat. The manuscript and a panel in the mosque both bear a date corresponding to A.D. 1561.

After Sedayu, the road heads past Gresik to Surabaya, and you are back to civilization.

— *Eric Oey*

AMIR SIDHARTA

Opposite: *A Chinese monk in Rembang.*
Above: *Sendang Duwur's unique "winged gate."*

KRETEK

Indonesia's Aromatic Smokes

Visitors to Indonesia often say that their most vivid memories of the country are not sights, but smells. Foremost among them is the sweet, acrid aroma of *kretek*—the ubiquitous clove-flavored Indonesian cigarette that crackles as it burns. The name is in fact onomatopoeic and means simply that—to crackle.

It is fitting that *kreteks* were invented and popularized here. After all, the clove is native to the eastern Indonesian islands of Maluku, which have exported the tiny buds for centuries. Once worth many times their weight in gold, cloves have been found in Egyptian tombs and were used at the ancient Han court of China as a breath-freshener.

No one knows when Indonesians began mixing the spice with tobacco, but *kretek* as an industry got started in the 1920s. At this time, an enterprising Kudus man named Nitisemito began wrapping his clove-tobacco mixture in cigarette papers rather than the usual dried corn husks. He promoted his product aggressively, offering free gifts for the empty packets, sponsoring sporting events and theatrical troupes—even producing a feature film and starting his own radio station. By the late 1920s, his Bal Tiga ("Three Circles") brand *kreteks* were the top-selling cigarettes in Indonesia, and his hometown of Kudus had become the nation's *kretek* capital.

Kretek statistics are quite astounding, as the industry now accounts for 90 percent of the tobacco market in a nation with over 60 million smokers. In 1990 alone, Indonesians puffed 140 billion *kretek* cigarettes worth $3.7 billion. A third of this money ended up with the central government in the form of taxes, accounting for 5 percent of the national budget—second only to oil revenues. The industry now employs 3.8 million people, about 2 percent of the population.

Ground cloves make up 30 to 45 percent of a *kretek* by weight, and clove consumption has sky-rocketed in recent decades along with *kretek* production. Three fourths of the world's cloves now go up in smoke every year—about 70 million kgs (154 million lbs) in 1990, three times more than in 1970. All of the cloves are grown domestically, and Indonesia is by far the world's largest producer and consumer of the spice, if no longer a major exporter.

What are the effects of smoking cloves? The active ingredient, eugenol, has strong anesthetic properties, and clove oil has long been used as a pain-killer by dentists. *Kretek* smoke gently numbs the throat and lungs, which addicts claim has a highly beneficial effect on their smokers' cough.

Medical tests of clove smoke have been inconclusive. Critics however are up in arms about the tar and nicotine levels in *kreteks*—commonly 3 to 4 times higher than popular Virginia smokes like Marlboro. This is due to the dark tobaccos and the long curing process used. *Kreteks* are banned in several countries for exceeding tar and nicotine limits.

Indonesians have a rather different complaint about *kreteks*. When smoked, improperly-dried clove nuggets have a nasty habit of jumping out like popcorn. The result is fiery embers that bore through your clothing. You can always tell a *kretek* smoker by the holes in his shirt, they say, and you need to stay alert when sitting next to one!

— *Eric Oey*

KAL MULLER

Right: *Kreteks rolled by hand in a Kudus factory.*

SOURCE: P.T. G.K. GOH OMETRACO

PART VIII

Introducing East Java

The fascinating province of East Java, extending from Mt. Lawu in the west all the way to the Bali Straits, is often treated by visitors as little more than a transit area between Yogya and Bali. Until recently it lacked facilities, and its sights were hard to reach except by hired car. In addition, the largest city—the venerable old port of Surabaya—is today a bustling commercial and industrial center that retains little of its colonial charm.

Yet East Java yields rich rewards to those willing to put in a bit of extra effort. This is Java's most diverse province, and it contains some of the island's most breathtaking scenery. From sleepy ports to thundering volcanoes, from ancient temples to vast wildlife reserves, East Java offers unparalleled opportunities to get off the beaten tourist track.

The province is marked by a stately procession of volcanic cones whose well-watered valleys have been cultivated for centuries. East Java's (and in fact Java's) highest peak, Mt. Semeru (3,676 m/11,980 ft), stands just 20 km (12.5 mi) from the coast—making this one of the steepest ascents from any shoreline in the world. Semeru is very active; an eruption in the early 1980s poured rivers of lava into the sea, blackening beaches with glittering cinder crystals.

East Java naturally falls into several distinct regions, each with its own flavor. The fertile Brantas River valley winds almost 360 degrees around the Arjuna/Butak/Kelud complex and actually forms an extension of the Central Javanese or *kejawen* heartland. For over 500 years, powerful Hindu-Buddhist kingdoms flourished along the Brantas; their remains are now found scattered throughout the river valley and in the surrounding highlands. These culminated in the 14th century empire of Majapahit, whose capital lay near modern-day Trowulan, about 40 km (25 mi) inland on one of the great river's tributaries.

After the collapse of Majapahit and the rise of Islamic Mataram in Central Java, Surabaya—in alliance with her neighbors—challenged the latter but suffered a horrible defeat at the hands of Sultan Agung's mighty army, which besieged and literally starved the city into submission between 1620-25. For the next hundred years, much of East Java became a no-man's land—sparsely populated and plagued by warfare and banditry.

As sustained population growth began in the mid-18th century, many Central Javanese emigrated to the rich plains of the East. Immigrants also arrived from the north coast and Madura—areas whose Muslim armies had earlier destroyed Majapahit and chased its vassals from the island.

The Tengger highlands north of Semeru, however, were never effectively subdued, and its 40,000 inhabitants today preserve some Hindu traditions of pre-Islamic Java. The Tengger-Semeru massif has been declared a reserve and is becoming a popular tourist stop. The huge Tengger caldera measures some 10 km (6 mi) across—a ring of steep walls rising 400 meters (1,300 ft) from a desolate "sea" of black volcanic sand. At the center rises a cluster of four smaller peaks, each 300-400 meters (1,000-1,300 ft) high. Bromo itself is a steaming heap of cinder and ash—one of the planet's most unusual sights.

Another huge volcanic complex forms the eastern tip of Java around Mt. Ijen. The latter is known for its sulphur deposits and bright-green crater lake. Around it are many remote reserves. Getting to them is difficult, but the rugged shoreline, set against a backdrop of majestic volcanoes, makes for some of the most ethereal and dramatic scenery in the world. It is well worth investing several days and some money in a hired car, preferably a 4-wheel-drive vehicle, to explore the region.

— *Robert Hefner*

Overleaf: *A scenic sideroad on the island of Madura. Photo by Amir Sidharta.* **Opposite:** *A Madurese fisherman. Photo by Alain Compost.*

SURABAYA

Sensuous and Lively 'City of Heroes'

As the burgeoning commercial and industrial region of Java, the island's north coast is anchored at its eastern end by Indonesia's second largest city, Surabaya. A blue-collar canton of 3 million people, the so-called "City of Heroes" has developed into the economic capital not only of East Java but of all of Eastern Indonesia. Its port, Tanjung Perak (meaning "silver promontory") is a crossroads of trade between the archipelago's eastern islands and points west—a role that Surabaya has in fact played for centuries.

Fueled by deregulatory measures introduced in the 1980s, Surabaya's industrial and service economy is booming. In the process, the city's notoriously shabby appearance is giving way to a richer, metropolitan look. It even seems poised to regain its former status as the premier center for commerce and industry in the archipelago—a position it held before WW II, but has since lost to Jakarta.

Surabaya does not have many pre-packaged tourist attractions. But it can be fun for travelers fascinated by the sensual side of urban life, and willing to dig beneath its surface. Unlike Jakarta, which is a catch-all of cultures from Indonesia and beyond, Surabaya's ethnic identity is Javanese. But unlike Solo and Yogya, the people of Surabaya are *pasisir* (coastal, marginal). Through its arteries runs a less syncretic, more orthodox strain of Islam known as *santri*. It has a faster pace and a more cosmopolitan outlook than the hinterland—cultivated through hundreds of years of contact with trading peoples from across the sea. Here there is little fascination with courtly life and etiquette; Surabaya is more commercial and more egalitarian.

Most residents belong to one of two ethnic groups: Javanese, born here or elsewhere on the island; or, Madurese, from the island just across the narrow strait. Up to a third of the population in fact traces its roots to Madura. And another seven percent are ethnic Chinese, with a sprinkling also of Arabs, Indians, Jews and Armenians.

People indigenous to the city are known in Javanese as *arèk Suroboyo*. They are frank, open, earthy and proud. To truly appreciate Surabaya, do as middle-class Surabayans do —take an evening stroll to a night market or shopping mall. Public places are great for people-watching and striking up acquaintances.

The shark and the crocodile

Local folk etymology relates that the name Surabaya derives from a story about a *sura* (a kind of shark) and a *baya* (crocodile) who had a fierce fight—the two entwine to form the letter *S* behind the Heroes' Monument on the city's coat of arms. Another possible origin for the name is the Javanese phrase *sura ing baya* which means "brave in the face of danger." This aptly describes the *arèk Suroboyo* who fiercely resisted the onslaught of Sultan Agung's troops at the beginning of the 17th century, as well as those who later touched off the revolution through their tough battle with Allied forces.

The exact date of Surabaya's founding is not known, but in the 1970s the municipal government designated May 31, 1293 as the big day. History records that as the moment when Raden Wijaya drove off Mongol-Chinese warriors and founded the powerful East Javanese kingdom of Majapahit.

The port evolved from early riverine settlements along the silty estuaries of the Brantas River. Perhaps that explains its Chinese name, Sishui—meaning "muddy water." Chinese records refer to it as the gateway to the mighty Brantas, the main route leading up into Java's interior.

During Majapahit's heyday in the 14th century, Surabaya remained of secondary importance to nearby ports like Tuban and Gresik, and it was even smaller than the port of Pasuruan until the first half of the 19th century. Its main claim to fame was its stubborn resistance to being swallowed up by Mataram, Madura and the VOC during the 17th and 18th centuries. Rebel leaders such as Trunojoyo (a maverick prince of Madura), Sawunggaling (a local hero), and Untung Surapati (a Balinese slave turned rebel) struck damaging blows against Mataram and the Dutch from bases in Surabaya.

Eventually the Dutch secured the city, but apart from the districts near the harbor where European, Chinese and other Asian traders lived, it was a typical Javanese *kampung* town of wooden and bamboo houses until the turn of the century. As with many cities in Java, it was only after about 1900 that Surabaya began to acquire a "colonial" appearance —large, masonry buildings bordering broad, tree-shaded avenues, often built uncomfortably close to the *kampungs* if not displacing them altogether. Even now it is common to hear people talk of "people of the avenues" and "people of the alleys."

ERIC OEY

The city center

Like Jakarta, Surabaya developed around its harbor and slowly expanded to the south. But a visit to Surabaya usually begins in the new commercial and administrative center around Jl. Tunjungan and Jl. Pemuda—a scaled-down but rapidly-developing version of Jakarta's Jl. Thamrin/Sudirman/Gatot Subroto strip.

Tunjungan's landmark is the old Oranje Hotel, now called Hotel Majapahit, site of the flag incident of September 1945 which sparked off revolutionary fervor in the city. In tandem with the Hotel Sarkies, diagonally across the street on Embong Malang, it creates a corner of a faded colonial glory flanked to the east, on Jl. Gentengkali, by the former *Das Deutsche Verein*—a private club now known as Balai Sahabat. The latter has a good Chinese restaurant, open to non-members. On certain evenings the meeting hall is used by Bethany Christian fundamentalists, comprising mainly businessmen and their families preaching the "theology of success."

Also on Jl. Gentengkali is Taman Budaya, a cultural center for art exhibits and performances. In the mornings, watch students rehearse traditional dances here. The complex served as the Regent (*bupati*) of Sura-

Left: *Looking down Jl. Tunjungan, Surabaya's bustling "main street."* **Above:** *Statue of Gov. Soerjo, with school children "on manoeuvers."*

baya's official residence and office until the 1970s, when the capital of the regency was moved to nearby Gresik.

Off Jl Pemuda to the south, on Jl. Dolog, is a statue of King Kertanagara in his incarnation as the Buddha Aksobhya. The statue bears the date A.D. 1289 at the base and was brought to Surabaya by the Dutch from the vicinity of Malang. Locally known as **Joko Dolog** ("fat boy"), it is still worshipped by Javanese syncretists.

Just to the east on Jl. Pemuda is **Grahadi**, official residence of East Java's governor—a mansion once used by colonial Residents. From the road you actually see the back of the structure; the front was built facing onto the canal in an era when travel by boat was still common. Across Jl. Pemuda from the mansion is a park with a statue of Governor Soerjo, East Java's first governor.

To the east of here, **Balai Pemuda** was built in 1907 as the Simpang Club. It has been turned into a luxury cinema complex and exhibition gallery of the Surabaya Arts Council. North of it in the middle of a traffic island stands a statue of General Sudirman—commander of Indonesia's revolutionary forces—and the Dutch-built City Hall, facing Taman Surya park. Nearby Zangrandi's Ice Cream parlor, with its colonial atmosphere, is a veritable institution in the city.

Further to the east down Jl. Pemuda is the 7-story **Delta Plaza**, reputedly one of Southeast Asia's largest shopping complexes. Across from it is Jl. Kayoon, where you can stroll along the river market, stop to eat at street stalls and buy flowers or semi-precious stones in gold and silver settings.

At night, Jl. Irian Barat further to the south across the river becomes a popular transvestite haunt. It is Indonesia's only government-designated strip for these *waria*, or "imitation women." Across the river, vegetable traders come out at night along Jl. Keputran ("princes' quarters"). Further south, where Keputran becomes Jl. Dinoyo, stands a Chinese temple where *wayang kulit* puppet performances are held on certain Thursday nights.

The old city

Surabaya's older quarters lie north of the Tunjungan-Pemuda-Kaliasin triangle. On Jl. Pahlawan stands another symbol of Surabaya, the **Heroes' Monument** (Tugu Pahlawan) built in the 1950s to commemmorate the bravery of Surabayan youths during the Battle of Surabaya. It is from this famous battle that Surabaya derives its epithet, "City of Heroes" (see following section). East of the square is the colonial Governor's Office; parts of it date from the 1930s.

From here, move back in time northwards along Jl. Veteran (formerly Jl. Niaga—the colonial buildings along either side date from the 1920s) to **Jembatan Merah**, the "Red Bridge" that stands at the center of the city's early 19th century colonial business district. The bridge has always been that color; a folk tale attributes it not to paint but to the blood shed during the legendary confrontation between the shark and the crocodile.

East of the bridge, Jl. Kembang Jepun ("Japanese flowers"), takes its name from former brothels that employed Japanese prostitutes (*karayuki-san*); it is now a business district and the heart of Surabaya's sprawling Chinatown. Just south of Kembang Jepun, on Jl. Slompretan, is the **Hok An Kiong** temple, built by Chinese merchants in the 18th century for Mazu, patron goddess of sailors.

Indonesia's only purely Confucian temple is on Jl. Kapasan, built in 1907. The Sunday services here resemble those in a Christian church, a syncretic influence that lingers from turn-of-the-century reforms instituted by Chinese pupils of Christian missionaries. Also in this area is the **Klenteng Dukuh** temple (Hok Tik Hian), where Fukienese hand-puppets (*potehi*) perform daily. Cross-acculturation is very much in evidence—as the puppeteers (who speak in Hokkien!) and the musicians are mostly Javanese, except for one old Chinese master. The parking attendant selling puppets is Madurese.

More striking evidence of the city's mingling of creeds and cultures is Jl. Panggung, where old two-story Chinese shops stand cheek by jowl with Muslim prayer houses. From here, follow the crowds to **Pasar Pabean**, an immense market where peddlers ply a centuries-old trade in farm produce, sea products, spices, perfumes and gems.

Continuing north, Jl. Kyai Mas Mansyur leads you back into Surabaya's colorful past, to the heart of the Arab Quarter. The Middle Eastern bazaar atmosphere here is palpable. A gateway graces tiny Jl. Ampel Suci, leading to **Mesjid Sunan Ampel**—the city's oldest mosque. A tomb in back belongs to the eponymous Sunan Ampel—one of the nine legendary holy men (*wali*) who brought Islam to Java in the 15th century.

The historic **Kali Mas** harbor lies just north of the Arab quarter. For centuries it has been visited by sailing ships from all over

ERIC OEY

the archipelago. Still seen here are the massive *pinisi* schooners from South Sulawesi. They dock at a 2-kilometer long wharf just east of Tanjung Perak, the modern port area that is closed to the public.

Back on Jl. Kapasan, a right turn at its eastern end into Jl. Kapasari leads to a flea-market that attracts swarms of people on Sunday mornings and afternoon. Continuing south, the road turns into Jl. Kusumabangsa, site of the THR Surabaya Mall, where the masses shop. It has indoor and outdoor theaters for traditional performing arts and not-so-traditional kitsch pop music. Next door is Taman Remaja Surabaya (Surabaya Youth Park), a non-stop night market and talent show. Of special interest on the outdoor stage is the Thursday night transvestite show. In their best falsettos they sing folk tunes to which young men attempt to dance.

The suburbs

Out at the eastern edge of the city, at the end of Jl. Kenjeran, lies the **Kenjeran Beach Amusement Park** (*Pantai Ria Kenjeran*). Not much of a beach, and the new amusement park has turned into a "love hotel," but the old park does offer some good seafood. It is set amidst Madurese fishing settlements where a popular pastime is pigeon racing; it's illegal but still goes on. Hire a boat for a cruise along the coast.

South and west of Kenjeran, past the new Surabaya Institute of Technology (ITS) campus, is a garish nouveau-riche suburb. The Indonesia-America Friendship Association gallery here has some worthwhile art exhibits at times. There are also good handicraft and textile collections at Toko Mirota.

At the southern end of Surabaya along Jl. Raya Darmo is a an elegant neighborhood developed by the Dutch early this century. Just opposite the entrance to the zoo, at Jl. Taman Mayangkera 6, is the **Mpu Tantular Museum** housing small but interesting historical and archaeological collections in the former residence of the Javaasche Bank agent. From the museum it is short walk to **Kebun Binatang**, one of Southeast Asia's oldest and largest zoos. Among its exhibits are somnolent Komodo dragons and Borneo river dolphins. Also in the Darmo area is the **Centre Culturel Français** on Jl. Darmokali; it has occasional art exhibits, films and musical performances.

The route back toward the city center along Jl. Diponegoro leads to a busy intersection at Jl. Girilaya. This street is notorious for a thriving brothel, locally known as Dolly's, after the madam who pioneered the district's sex industry in the 1960s. This red light district is a jarring blend of suburban homes, places of worship and brothels.

— Dédé Oetomo

Above: Pinisi *being off-loaded at Kali Mas.*

10 NOVEMBER 1945

Momentous Battle of Surabaya

Revolutionary Heroes' Day (November 10) is celebrated throughout Indonesia, but festivities in Surabaya are on a particularly grand scale. Colossal re-enactments are held, along with a parade of thousands from Mojokerto to Surabaya. People wear red and white, the national colors, and models don the latest 1945-style clothes in fashion shows.

The actual events of November 10, 1945 were an anticlimax to the Japanese surrender in early August, and the proclamation of independence on August 17th. But they were the culmination of injustices dating back to the last half of the 19th century.

American historian William Frederick notes that the increasing pace of development of Surabaya as a commercial center at that time displaced entire communities of people. And while the main streets of Surabaya were kept orderly and clean, no improvements were made to public facilities in the back-alley *kampungs,* so that living conditions deteriorated. The Dutch turned a blind eye to these problems and segregated themselves from the indigenous population. Only a strong police force protected the outnumbered Europeans from mounting resentment and threats of violence.

When news of independence finally came in 1945, the people of Surabaya took it coolly. But things heated up in early September when they learned that Allied forces would replace the Japanese. Released Dutch prisoners of war and internees also began returning to the city, acting as if nothing had changed. They ignored the fledgling Republican administration and reverted to their former colonial roles, sometimes with tacit help from the Japanese. This spawned ill feelings and suspicions among the *arèk Suroboyo.*

Their alarm heightened on September 16, when a group of British soldiers parachuted into the city and set up base in the Oranje Hotel on Tunjungan. The raising of the Dutch tri-color atop the hotel by a group of ultra-nationalistic Dutch and Eurasians was the last straw; a group of incensed Indonesian youths forced their way inside. One reached the flagpole and ripped the blue section of the Dutch flag away, transforming it into the Indonesian "Red and White." A Dutch leader was fatally wounded during the incident. Sensing retaliation, a group of *arèk Suroboyo*

decided to strike first.

In early October, vigilante youth groups began killing Japanese prisoners. Then they attacked and captured a number of Europeans and Eurasians; many were tortured and killed. The fledgling Republican leadership had a difficult time bringing these youths under control. The situation worsened on October 25th, when the British 49th Indian Infantry Brigade under Brigadier Mallaby landed. He and other leaders came to see Governor Soerjo to negotiate. They stormed out after being told the governor was engaged in a meeting.

A meeting finally took place the next day. Both sides agreed that Japanese troops would be disarmed and shipped out by the British. But towards evening small groups of British and Indian troops began seizing buildings in the business district and setting up command posts. Governor Soerjo and other Republican leaders immediately became suspicious of British intentions. Later that night, a British intelligence officer and a small group of soldiers forced the release of captured Dutch and Allied officers.

On October 27, a military plane from Jakarta dropped leaflets threatening action by Allied forces if there was resistance to the occupation of major cities. Mallaby seemed surprised by this, but could not convince Indonesian leaders in Surabaya that he knew nothing of it. Fighting broke out the next day, and Mallaby's relatively small brigade was overwhelmed by tens of thousands of young Surabayans armed only with bamboo spears. Europeans were indiscriminately butchered in the streets.

To defuse the situation, President Sukarno and Vice-President Hatta arrived in Surabaya on October 29. A ceasefire was drawn up, but neither Mallaby nor the Indonesians fully respected it. Only hours after Sukarno and Hatta flew back to Jakarta the next day, Mallaby and members of the liaison group were killed when his car exploded. The British convinced the Allied commander-in-chief for Southeast Asia, General Christison, to attack Surabaya unless Mallaby's murderers were handed over.

On November 4, the British 5th Division began moving into city in preparation for what would clearly be a vendetta operation. On November 9th, General Mansergh, the division commander, ordered Republican leaders to surrender by walking with their hands behind their heads down the main avenue by 18:00 hours that evening. All other Indonesians were to surrender their weapons or face British retribution at dawn.

ARSIP NASIONAL

Mansergh probably was well aware the Indonesian leaders could not afford to lose face by surrendering. The leaders contacted Jakarta but the President and Vice-President were out of town, so the Minister of Foreign Affairs gave his blessing to whatever action the people of Surabaya would take.

The bloody Battle of Surabaya lasted for three weeks. The city was virtually leveled by Allied sea, air and land attacks. Dutch soldiers ran amok, killing thousands of Indonesians at random. Ninety percent of the city's population fled to Sidoarjo, Mojokerto and other outlying towns.

The episode may have represented a technical victory for the Dutch but it was certainly a moral triumph for the Indonesians. It focussed international attention on their plight, and demonstrated to the world (as well as to themselves) that Indonesians were prepared to fight and die for independence.

Since that time, November 10th has gone done in Indonesian history as Heroes' Day, and a Heroes' Monument was erected in Surabaya in the early 1950s—and the "Heroes' City" had earned its nickname.

— Dédé Oetomo

Opposite: *Brigadier Mallaby and Gen. Sudirman attempt to calm a tense situation.* **Above:** *Bung Tomo, a fiery leader of the Surabayan forces.*

SURABAYA SIDETRIPS

Holy Graves and Mountain Springs

Surabaya and the surrounding area is not known for its tourist attractions. As with every other place on Java, however, serendipitous surprises await the adventuresome. Base yourself in the cool resort village of Tretes, an hour south of Surabaya, and make excursions to the historic town of Gresik, to the antiquities around Mt. Penanggungan and Trowulan (see "Antiquities of East Java"), and to the lovely waterfalls and peaks in the vicinity of Tretes itself—even to the east to the coastal towns of Pasuruan and Probolinggo on the way to Bromo and Bali.

Historic Gresik

The small town of Gresik lies near the coast about 25 km (15 mi) northwest of Surabaya. Today it is an insignificant backwater, and yet it was mentioned already in 15th century Chinese records as Ce Cun ("Dung Village") or Xin Cun ("New Village"). For a time after that it became an important Islamic trading port; today it displays an interesting mixture of cultures. The Sam Poo Tay Jien-Mbah Ratu Chinese temple on Jl. Demak (devoted to the Muslim Chinese eunuch admiral-cum-folk deity, Zhenghe) sits, oddly enough, on the site of old Muslim Javanese graves. Ladies of the night from nearby Bangunrejo come to have their fortune told, or to obtain spells to help them drum up more business.

Gresik's other main interests are its old houses, and the tombs of two more of Java's nine holy men *(wali)* of Islam—Sunan Giri (a disciple of Ampel) and Maulana Malik Ibrahim, a Persian Muslim missionary from Gujarat. The latter is buried with his family in Desa Candipuro in tombs dated 1419.

Sunan Giri's revered tomb is a popular pilgrimage site, located in an ancient Muslim heroes' cemetery on a hill guarded by two Hindu guardian statues in the town of **Giri**, 2 km (1.3 mi) south of Gresik. A final sight which should not be missed in the Gresik area is the Bat Cave (Goa Lawa), where thousands of flying foxes fill the air each evening.

Tretes

The mountain resort of **Tretes**, 60 km (35 mi) south of Surabaya, gives you a chance to escape the city heat and breathe fresh mountain air while hiking, swimming or horseback riding. From here you can scale Mts. Arjuna and Welirang; the cool and inviting Kakek Bodo waterfall is a shorter hike away.

Near Pandaan on the road to Tretes is **Candi Jawi**, a 14th-century temple built to enshrine King Kertanegara's ashes (see "Antiquities"). During the dry season, the **Candra Wilwatikta** amphitheater in Pandaan presents massive dance-dramas; the Javanese restaurant opposite is very good.

East of Surabaya

A coastal road winds east from Surabaya all the way to Banyuwangi, terminus for the brief ferry trip to Bali. Along the road, about 20 km (12 mi) to the east of Surabaya is **Bangil**, a town where Arab and Indian families specialize in goldsmithing.

Continuing eastward, another 15 km (9 mi) brings you to **Pasuruan**, onetime sugar capital of Java. Colonial houses built with sugar (and sometimes opium) money in the 19th century line the streets. *Pinisi* schooners from all over Indonesia dock at the town's tiny harbor. Pasuruan's renovated Grand Mosque is without a doubt one of Java's most beauti-

JEZ O HARE

BERENICE OEY

ful. At hawker stalls across the street you can sip ginger coffee and watch pilgrims from afar come to pay homage at the tomb of Kyai Hamid. This Islamic teacher and leader was the final arbiter in dogmatic disputes among Java's other Islamic leaders. While in Pasuruan you should also visit the Pohjentrek experimental mango orchard; eat all you want, but leave behind the pits.

About 17 km (10 mi) southeast of Pasuruan lie the **Banyubiru baths**, a natural spring pool and park, source of Pasuruan and Surabaya's drinking water. Along the way is **Umbulan**, another natural spring said to be connected to Banyubiru.

Try taking the alternate route to Mt. Bromo, from Pasuruan through Keboncandi, Pasrepan, Puspo, Tosari and Wonokitri. Keboncandi is famous for its large bananas, while Pasrepan is a paradise for durian aficionados. Cool, pleasant **Tosari** has the highest elevation of any town on Java and was the site of the best-known sanatorium on the island in Dutch times.

The Wonokitri side of the Bromo crater is a hang-gliding and hiking heaven. You can cross the sand-sea on foot or horseback to the Sukapura-Ngadisari side of the crater. Likewise, you can head for the southern side and the hamlet of **Dingklik**, where the majestic beauty of the Bromo-Semeru National Park unfolds from a vantage point atop Mt. Penanjakan (see "Visiting Bromo").

The road south from Pasaruan to Malang takes you through **Purwosari**, called Alkmaar by the Dutch, and hence Lekemar by the locals; stop here for a look at Bob's Antiques. Just beyond the town is **Purwodadi**, whose botanical gardens (specializing in dry-climate lowland vegetation, mainly from eastern Indonesia) are second only to those of Bogor. A trail at Purwodadi leads to the Gunung Baung Nature Reserve, where there is a breathtaking waterfall with a suspension bridge. From Purwodadi, drive or hike up to Nongkojajar, yet another route to Bromo.

About 40 km (24 mi) to the east of Pasuruan is **Probolinggo**, a town famous for its mangoes and grapes, and another launching point for trips to Bromo. Visit the harbor, or for an even better sea view, walk along the coastal road east of town.

There is a resort called Gunung Bentar 9 km (5.5 mi) east of Probolinggo. But if you're looking for more pristine beaches, take a boat 5 km (3 mi) north to tiny Gili Ketapang Island. Also worth a trip from Probolinggo are the recently discovered **Madakaripura Falls**, reputed to be a sort of fountain of youth; bathe in the pool under the falls to take off a few years. The Majapahit leader Gajah Mada is said to have meditated here.

— *Dédé Oetomo*

Above: *The delightfully cool hill resort of Tretes.*
Opposite: *Madakaripura Falls near Mt. Bromo.*

MADURA ISLAND

Java's Coarse but Colorful Neighbor

The dry, sun-baked island of Madura bears little resemblance to its luxuriant neighbor, Java, just across the Strait of Surabaya. The sun shines almost constantly, coloring Madura's tobacco leaves and cacti a rich green, burnishing its bare, white limestone rocks and salt pans.

Culturally, too, Madura is distinct from the mainland. The Madurese speak their own language. They are pious Muslims who show great respect for their island's religious leaders. In contrast to the Javanese (and also the Balinese), they are straightforward in their speech and actions. Indeed the Javanese look upon the Madurese as *kasar*—coarse and lacking in manners and refinement—and *panas*, easily offended and hot-tempered.

Few travelers go out of their way to visit Madura because it lacks natural attractions and facilities. Madura has never held great allure for foreign conquerors either; it was not included in Raffles' land rent system, nor in Van den Bosch's "Cultivation System", which had a tremendous impact on the agricultural economy of Java in the 19th century. As a result, the islanders still view westerners with curiosity—and often undue attention. To avoid becoming even more of a spectacle, visitors should dress and behave conservatively.

Characteristics of Culture

The Madurese are proud but have a keen sense of humor and enjoy the good things in life. Madurese women, renowned for their beauty, carry everything on their heads, often in enamelled green white basins or in huge bundles, even yellow and gold bananas that look as modish as a chic cocktail hat. Men fiercely protect the honor of their wives and daughters, yet boast about the sexual skills of Madurese women, who are noted throughout Indonesia for their ability to satisfy men. This may explain the plethora of traditional aphrodisiac tonics (*jamu*) found in many of Madura's roadside shops.

About 3 million Madurese live on the island, though many have been forced over the ages to seek their livelihood elsewhere due to the island's harsh conditions. Those who remain have had to scrape out an existence from their island's meager resources. They were and still are a tough, resilient and resourceful people.

ALAIN COMPOST

A troubled history

Up to the middle of the 19th century, the name Madura referred only to the western part of the island, comprising the present districts of Bangkalan and Sampang. The petty states of this area were first united under the prince of Arosbaya in the 15th century; they are recorded as being loyal vassals of the rulers of Majapahit.

In 1528, the son of the prince of Arosbaya became the first Madurese ruler to convert to Islam. He established a rigorous Islamic state in West Madura, which eventually stretched to East Madura. Since then, Islam has been the single most influential factor in Madurese politics.

Madura has always been deeply involved in Java's wars; indeed, princes of each island have constantly tried to subjugate or at least establish a foothold on the other.

In 1624, troops of Sultan Agung, ruler of the Central Javanese empire of Mataram, conquered Madura. In 1672, Mataram's hegemony was challenged by a revolt, led by the legendary Madurese prince, Trunojoyo. Backed by Makassar pirates, his troops drove out the Javanese and reduced the capital to ashes. Only with the help of the VOC was the revolt finally suppressed. In 1680, the island was divided in two: west Madura (Bangkalan and Sampang, under the Cakraningrat line), and east Madura (Sumenep, with Pamekasan).

Later, when the VOC again intervened in internal conflicts, Mataram had to cede several coastal districts, including east Madura, to the Dutch Company. Even after the Java War the Madurese princes were virtually independent allies of the Dutch colonial government, who used them to raise military contingents for their wars. Relations with the Madurese rulers were regulated by contracts—in exchange for maintaining their royal status, the rulers had to provide a certain amount of natural products, laborers and soldiers. Troops whom Madurese regents recruited for the Dutch fought as auxiliaries in the Java War, in western Sumatra and in Aceh, thus contributing their share to Dutch "pacification" of the archipelago.

The Madurese suffered severely under Japanese occupation during World War II, which devastated the island's already precarious economy. Many people starved, and many more were rounded up as forced laborers, never to be seen again.

Since independence, some concern has been shown for Madura's welfare. Due to the island's poor soils and limited natural resources, emigration continued. A positive consequence has been that, today, the culinary delights of Madurese *sate* and *soto* can

Opposite: *Fishing is a major source of livelihood.*
Above: *A pair of champion Madurese racing bulls are displayed by their proud owner.*

JILL GOCHER

be enjoyed throughout Java and beyond.

Visiting the island

The only way to get to Madura is by boat. Numerous ferries make the 30-minute trip between Surabaya's Tanjung Perak harbor and Kamal quay on Madura, where there is a marketplace and bus terminal, before getting to Bangkalan, the first main town on the island. Inexpensive "colt" minibuses hurtle along the uncrowded roads and riding with the locals costs only cents. Alternatively, they can be chartered for a tour around the island. Although only 30 minutes away from Java, Madura is still surprisingly traditional. Many of the old customs still exist. People who live in more remote villages still wear the traditional black cotton pants and jacket.

There are two major routes to Sumenep, Madura's easternmost town, and a trip across the island from one end to the other is not only a spacial journey but a cultural one as well. The people of the island make a sharp distinction between east and west Madurese: the latter are considered to be more refined. Wherever you are, though, it's a good idea to steer clear of conflicts and confrontations.

Most traffic follows the main highway east from Bangkalan through the regency towns of Sampang and Pamekasan near the southern coast. Another, smaller road leads north from Bangkalan and passes through tiny villages along the northern coast before cutting south to Sumenep. Travel on this road is less comfortable, due to poor surface conditions, but is more scenic and relaxed.

Charms of Madura's hills

Irrigated rice plains surround Bangkalan. From here, the highway climbs eastward winding through barren limestone hills—a hardscrabble area of small, rocky plots of land and ramshackle houses. After passing Blega and Torjun, the road enters dusty Sampang, then veers south to greet the coast, following it for about 20 km (12 mi). This is the domain of salt farmers and fishermen, the area's two most important industries. Large, floating bamboo structures (*bagan*) used for night fishing can be seen hovering over the water like spiders, their lamps transforming the Straits of Madura into a luminous Milky Way on a clear night.

Turning back into the interior, you pass through Pamekasan, a minor administrative town with several sub-provincial and local government offices, a cinema, a hotel, and several untidy but inexpensive *losmen*. Two routes lead from Pamekasan to Sumenep: a fast road along the south coast, and an interior side road through the Guluk-Guluk Valley where tobacco, Madura's main cash crop, is grown during the dry season.

Madurese tobacco is favored here over the sweet clove-flavored *kretek*. Tobacco also influences many aspects of social and cultural

AMIR SIDHARTA

life; earnings from its trade are not only invested in agriculture and fishing, but help build mosques, and finance religious institutions like *pesantren* (Islamic boarding schools) and pilgrimages to Mecca.

Batik and crafts

Madura is well known for its batik of various grades. Distinguished by its sombre rich, dark indigo blues, maroons and golds, the largely freehand drawn motifs are as exuberant and unrestrained as the people. It is quite common when wandering through walled villages in the north such as Tanjung Bumi and Jelaga Biru, to come across plain white cloth flapping in the breeze. This is material that has been prepared for batik.

In the shade of the late afternoon, women sit in their compounds drawing motifs of birds and flowers on the cloth. Other batik centers of Sumenep and Pamekasan in the south feature intricately designed batiks, still of the same sombre hues.

Madurese crafts are much sought after in other parts of Indonesia and abroad, especially the carved wooden furniture and chests with wheels. The rooster motif plays an important role in both the wood carvings and batiks.

Sumenep and surroundings

Sumenep is an urbanized crossroads; its regional market serves the surrounding countryside as well as the small islands east of Madura. Formerly its peasantry provided the rice, tamarind, taxes and labor for the upkeep of a large local court and nobility.

What remains of Sumenep's 18th-century prosperity (the Dutch claimed it resulted from "illegal" trade—meaning trade outside the VOC monopoly) can be seen in the keraton of Panembahan Sumolo and in the Masjid Jamik. The former was reputedly designed by a Chinese architect who settled here after the 1740 war, and the latter is also strikingly Chinese in appearance. Though small in number, there are pockets of Muslims of mixed Madurese and Chinese descent, particularly in the eastern part of the island.

The classical design of the gates of the royal graveyard and associated monuments at Asta Tinggi, 2 km west of Sumenep, show another aspect of the very mixed *pasisir* civilization of this period—a strong European influence in form and decoration.

A few miles southeast of Sumenep is Kalianget, a salt-industry center of considerable importance in colonial times, when a government-owned factory profited from the protection of a state monopoly. Today, the obsolete plant faces stiff competition from private salt-farmers. Along the road to the factory, stately residences that once housed fac-

Opposite: *Masjid Jamik mosque in Sumenep.*
Above: *Fishing* perahus *on the north coast.*

tory gentry now malinger in decay. Kalianget's harbor has ferries and boats linking Madura with Java and the islands off the eastern coast (Puteran, Sapudi, Raas and Kangean), the island of Masalembu, and even Kalimantan.

About 25 km (15 mi) from Sumenep, at the island's eastern tip, is the attractive fishing village of Dungkeh. The beach here is a base for beautifully decorated fishing boats. Do not walk barefoot in the sand, however, as there is no sanitation and the beach is a public latrine using the high-tide flush system.

The north coast

Madura's long north coast inspires visions of the Mediterranean. Driving along the coastal road, you look out over the turquoise Java Sea on one side, while limestone and cactus hedge the other. The powerful colors of the landscape reflect the heat, and at times take on a picture-postcard quality.

At the mouths of small rivers, which serve as natural harbors, are tiny fishing settlements. Natural conditions and local traditions determine the size of the villages and the fishing pattern. Sailing *perahu* of various sizes in the harbor and on the beach are used for different purposes: the smaller craft catch shrimp in shallow coastal waters, the larger (which can accommodate a crew of ten) fish sardines and mackerel in deeper waters.

Large ships often stay out for five to ten days at a time. Smaller boats meet them and return daily with the catches, which are sold to women traders waiting on the beach. Men in the area stick to fishing; outsiders come with their trucks to buy the fish in bulk.

Fishing is the focal point of life in these coastal villages, slowing only during the western monsoon from December through February, when high seas and strong winds make it too dangerous to go out. Full-time fishermen use the hiatus to repair their gear and relax; seasonal fishermen return to their inland villages to work the fields.

Fishing has not yet developed into a major industry in Madura, however. There are no canneries, and fish-processing remains a cottage industry. Fish-paste sold in glass jars is made at home; excess catches are salted and dried on bamboo racks. Some fresh fish finds its way to the Surabaya market through a network of fish traders but much of it is consumed locally or dried.

Before returning to the ferry, stop off in Arosbaya, the political center of west Madura during the 15th and 16th centuries. Located about 17 km (10 mi) north of Bangkalan on the northern route, Arosbaya has a royal graveyard containing the tomb of Ratu Ibu and other prominent members of the once-powerful Cakraningrat dynasty.

—Roy Jordaan/Anke Niehof/Ann Kumar

Below: *The royal burial chamber in Arosbaya.*

KERAPAN SAPI

An Exciting Day at the Ox Races

The action begins with a snort and the crack of a whip, and ends with a raucous crowd dodging for cover. During the brief moments in between, two yoke of brawny 600-kg oxen charge 100 meters (350 ft) across a grassy field, each dragging a sled manned by daredevil Ben Hur jockeys and reaching speeds of up to 50 kph (30 mph). This is Madura's most colorful and famous spectacle, known as *kerapan sapi*—the ox races.

Water buffalo are rarely found on Madura, where they would soon perish in the hot, dry climate. Instead, the more hardy Madurese ox is used for plowing—a powerful, light-brown skinned animal which, like its master, plays as hard as it works.

Given the central role played by the ox in rural Madura, it is easy to understand the general enthusiasm for bull racing. Oxen that show racing potential are exempted from the toughest work, and lead a pampered existence in comfortable stables. A champion brings great honor upon the owner and even his whole village. (There is a local saying to the effect that Madurese farmers treat their bulls better than their wives.)

Competition begins in August each year with a series of local village heats. These culminate with finals in Pamekasan in September, attracting droves of tourists and prompting festivities worthy of the Kentucky Derby.

The bulls hit town in the manner of visiting royalty, arrayed in colorful headdresses and sashes. There is tension in the air—and suspicion. Champion finalists are guarded against opponents, who have been known to cripple competitors by using poison, or even worse, black magic. The men caress, fawn over, and fortify their bulls with herbal drinks supplemented by eggs, beer and gin.

A red flag falls, and the animals charge furiously, goaded by a frenzied jockey armed with a spiked stick. With the high speed and short track, it is a miracle that the bulls can be stopped (usually) without crushing foolhardy spectators who crowd at the finish line.

Losing is a tragedy for the owners and for his entire village. Winners are heroes—feted, admired, and (best of all, from the bull's point of view) treated to a huge feast.

— *Roy Jordaan and Anke Niehof*

Below: *Racing for the finish line in Pamekasan.*

KAL MULLER

MALANG & ENVIRONS

A Colonial Town and Its Hill Retreats

Malang was a popular colonial retirement town, and its refreshing climate makes it a delightful place to visit. Situated 450 meters (1,450 ft) above the oppressive heat of the lowlands, the city is perched on a picturesque plateau ringed by volcanoes. Active Mt. Semeru dominates the eastern horizon, while to the northwest Mts. Anjasmoro, Arjuna and Panderman are dotted with resort hotels and recreation areas. Mt. Kawi, southwest of the city, is a mystic place that attracts pilgrims seeking their fortune.

The Dinoyo inscription dating from A.D. 760 indicates that an early kingdom existed here, and the Malang area contains many interesting antiquities (see "Antiquities of East Java"). But the modern city is a creation of the colonial era—its development fueled after 1870 by enterprising Europeans who set up coffee, rubbber and cacao plantations along-

side the government sugar estates. As the economy grew, more Dutch arrived—and in many ways Malang became an East Javanese version of Bandung. They built homes in the city and vacation bungalows in the hills of Batu, Selekta and Lawang.

Malang's *alun-alun* (town square) took shape in 1882 along the usual Javanese lines: bordered by a market, mosque, prison and local ruler's quarters. Colonial priorities dictated that it also have a home for the Dutch assistant resident, a Protestant church, and later a bank and a club. In 1914 a new municipal center was established across the Brantas River from the old one around a circular park. A new residential area also developed at this time in the city's northwest, where wide streets and tall shade trees are today a lingering legacy of the colonial era.

Since the war, the cigarette industry has fueled economic growth. P.T. Bentoel has a huge plant north of the city where dark, locally-grown tobacco is liberally spiked with cloves to make *kretek* cigarettes—many still rolled, trimmed and packed by hand.

Most visitors arrive from Surabaya—a 90 km (56 mi), 2-hr trip on a fast road. Along the way, 27 km (17 mi) north of Malang, you pass the **Purwodadi Botanic Gardens**, a branch of Bogor's Kebon Raya. These sprawl across the lower slopes of Mt. Arjuna and include the lovely Baung waterfall. About 18 km (11 mi) from Malang is **Lawang**, a town where the Dutch established a tuberculosis sanatorium and mental hospital. The town's imposing Hotel Niagara—said to be haunted and a perfect setting for a gothic romance—was built for a wealthy Chinese merchant in 1911 by a Brazilian architect named Pinitu.

Malang walking tour

Malang's size and climate make it ideal to see on foot—beginning with the **Balai Kota Malang** on Jl. Tugu, which houses municipal offices. From here you can look out across a circular park, with its shady mahogany trees. Originally it had a fountain at the center, but this was replaced by the present *tugu* monument after independence. Pink lotuses bloom in a pool at the base.

Turn into Jl. Mojopahit at the **Splendid Inn**. This former mansion was converted into a hotel in 1973. Now the bar is a favorite watering hole of the Malang Hash House Harriers. Continue down Jl. Mojopahit and look back at **Wisma IKIP** as you cross the Brantas River. This was formerly a hotel that towered over the river bank, a wooded area

ONG KIAN BIE/STUDIO MALANG

still frequented by bathers. *Kampung* houses crowd the incline on the other side of the bridge. At this point you have two options: a longer walk taking you through the market areas, or a short stroll up to the *alun-alun*.

For the long walk, turn right at the sign for **Pasar Senggol** and cross a small bridge. This market is active only at night, when hawkers sell foods such as *tahu campur, mie bakso* and *rujak cingur*. Next to it is the **Pasar Bunga**, or flower market—a terraced nursery on the river banks. Across Jl. Kahuripan is the Ayani Mosque, which has an interesting tiled dome. Turn left and cross the bridge to the intersection of Jl. Semeru and Jl. Basuki Rachmat, then left again onto Jl. Basuki Rachmat. Many colonial structures are still visible here above renovated storefronts; at the southern end look for a tobacco shop, Taman Tembakau, with old advertisments in the window. Continue past the telephone office around the corner to Toko Oen.

For the shorter walk, continue straight up Jl. Mojopahit toward the cathedral. You will emerge on Jl. Basuki Rachmat, a block north of the *alun-alun*. **Toko Oen** is just across the street. Opened by the father of the present owner, it looks just as it did when it opened in the late 1930s. Today the restaurant mainly attracts tourists, but Malang's matrons also crowd its bakery counters for fresh breads and cakes (closed Mondays).

After sampling some Dutch treats, cross the street to **Sarinah Department Store**, next to the Cathedral; on the second floor is a good selection of handicrafts from all over Indonesia. The building was formerly a Dutch club, the Concordia.

Walk along the west slide of the *alun-alun* for a look at the old Dutch Reformed church standing just a few doors from the town's main mosque. At the southwest corner of the square stands **Hotel Pelangi**, the former Palace Hotel—have a look at the Dutch tiles on the walls of its coffee shop. On the south side of the square is the central post office, a haven for food and toy vendors and fast-talking salesmen pitching patent medicines.

Malang's new commercial district lies to the southeast down **Jl. H. Agus Salim**. Both the Mitra Department Store and the adjacent Gajah Mada Plaza have well-stocked supermarkets. Next door, the Colonel's own Kentucky Fried Chicken is available at Malang Plaza, opposite a large *pendopo* belonging to the regional government. Further to the south, **Pasar Besar** is a rambling maze of stalls—a makeshift warren established after a fire destroyed the old market in the 1980s. Exploring it can be an adventure. Continue through Malang's Chinatown and turn left onto Jl. Ade Irma Suryani/Jl. Pasar Besar to visit the old En An Kiong temple.

Above: *Like Bandung, Malang is a highland city in the tropics with a very "European" ambience.*

AMIR SIDHARTA

Colonial suburbia

The northwest quarters of the city are best seen by *becak*. Catch one at the *alun-alun,* then direct your driver to **Jl. Kawi**. At the Jl. Arjuno intersection is the Webb Institute/ Bamboe Denn—an English school which has inexpensive accommodations. Here you can get information on hiking to Semeru and Bromo from Tumpeng (east of Malang), or trekking to the Lalijiwo Nature Reserve atop Mt. Arjuna from Lawang.

Continue down Jl. Kawi to The Wise Owl bookshop; it caters to expats and you can get foreign newspapers and magazines. It also has a good selection of English-language books on Indonesia. At the west end of Jl. Kawi is the Amsterdam restaurant, where you can dine in a garden setting.

Reboard your *becak* and tour **Jl. Ijen**—a posh residential boulevard lined with towering royal palms. Midway down the street, Japanese tanks guard the entrance to the Brawijaya Military Museum. Across from it is a musty library and opposite that a Batik Semar shop tucked into an old mansion.

Quiet, tree-canopied streets branch off on either side of Jl. Ijen. Some of the sturdy, pre-World War II colonial homes have been renovated—look for exotic contemporary statues, such as crouching peasants cutting grass on their lawns. The most conspicuous symbol of wealth, however, is the parabolic TV antenna. North and west of here are the campuses of Brawijaya University and IKIP Malang.

Hill resorts to the west

Just 20 km (12.5 mi) west of Malang are the former highland Dutch retreats of Batu and Selekta. Old colonial bungalows and new weekend villas here are now owned by the wealthy from Malang and Surabaya.

The main route northwest from Malang first passes through Dinoyo, which has a thriving ceramics industry producing everything from wall tiles to flower vases. Two recreation areas along this road, Togo Mas and Sengkaling, have pools and playgrounds and are best visited on quiet weekdays.

The turn off for **Selekta** is a bumpy road to the right that leads past nondescript storefronts before climbing past villas and remarkable poinsettia trees to the Selekta hotel and swimming pool complex, which lies beyond a large market. Once an exclusive European resort, the hotel nestles on a hillside offering expansive views and cool breezes. It has a large pool and a landscaped park that stretches up the mountainside.

AMIR SIDHARTA

More adventure lies farther along this road in the village of **Sumber Brantas**, at the headwaters of the great river. The pot-holed road winds past vegetable farms and wooded ravines quieted by cool mists. On the far side of the pass is the undeveloped Cangar hot springs, popular among Indonesian youths as a camping and swimming spot.

Back on the main road to **Batu**, a row of roadside stands on the outskirts of town sells locally-grown apples, oranges and melons for which the area is famous. The resort hotels are past Batu; here the new Amsterdam restaurant is a recommended stop.

West of Batu is the **Songgoriti** resort area. Near Candi Songgoriti are sulfurous hot springs and the Tirtanirwana recreation area of pools, playgrounds and a fishing pond. The highway winds sharply up Mt. Panderman past stands selling roasted corn on the cob. A statue of a cow marks the gateway to dairy country; turn left here for a panoramic view and a park with campground and picnic area. This road ends in a lush little gorge at the 60 meter (200 ft) Cuban Rondo waterfall.

Back on the main highway, the route continues west to the lowland cities of Pare and Kediri, past terraced rice paddies, the occa-

Above: *Malang's venerable Toko Oen restaurant.* **Right:** *The old colonial resort at Selekta.*

sional waterfall and thick, uninhabited forest. On the edge of the forest, 28 km (17.5 mi) from Malang, is the Dewi Sri swimming pool. From here the road descends to Ngantang and the Selorejo Reservoir (43 km/27 mi from Malang), popular for its water sports.

The south coast

Only 60 km (37 mi) from Malang are the windswept beaches of East Java's rugged south coast—isolated, desolate and beautiful. Most are accessible only by private vehicle, a 2-hr drive through poor farm villages over rough roads and limestone hills.

Ngliyep attracts the biggest crowds, especially on holidays such as Labuhan, which usually occurs in October. Although the water looks inviting, this and other beaches on the coast have hazardous currents and are dangerous. Javanese lore holds that Nyai Ratu Kidul is the spirit queen of these oceans; she is easily angered by the color green and swallows unwary swimmers with sudden waves.

The safest swimming is at **Sendangbiru**. Here you can hire a boat (bargain and fix a firm pick-up time for the return) across to **Sempu Island Nature Reserve**—reputedly the last home of the Javan tiger—which has sandy coves shaded by low trees. On the landward side of this 800 hectare island are warm, gentle waves and a view of Java's wooded shoreline.

Balekambang is another popular beach; it has a secluded bay with two small islands connected by footbridges. There is a Balinese temple on one of them where the Jalanidipuja ceremony takes place annually in March. A Javanese New Year ceremony called Suran is also held on this beach, usually in July.

All three beaches can be reached by car. Others such as Modangan and Tamban can only be reached by 4-wheel drive and on foot, using the coastal trails of fishermen.

About 36 km (22 mi) west of Malang lies mystical **Gunung Kawi**—which attracts pilgrims seeking a means of striking it rich. If you would like to try your luck, the most auspicious time for a visit is the eve of Jumat Legi, which occurs every 35 days on the traditional Javanese calendar.

The mountain is the site of the graves of Mbah Djugo and Mbah Iman Sudjono; little is known about them except that their spirits are powerful. Crystal chandeliers said to be gifts of gratitude from those whose wishes were fulfilled hang inside the carpeted building housing their graves. One story has it that a poor *kretek* producer received the inspiration for his company's name and trademark here, and subsequently became rich. Crowds sit amidst the dense and pungent smoke of incense, making their wishes known to the *juru kunci*—literally "keeper of the keys" or grave-master, and making offerings of flower petals.

—Jan Hostetler

STEVE TEO

ANTIQUITIES

Ancient Sites in the Brantas River Basin

The Brantas River has been a vital trade and communication route since the earliest periods of Java's recorded history. Hundreds of years before Islam took root in the 15th century, and long before the rise of the mighty Majapahit empire, Hindu-Buddhist kings were already diverting the waters of the Brantas to develop elaborate irrigation systems. For a period of several centuries thereafter they constructed numerous temples and monuments—remnants of which now stand all around the Brantas Valley.

The course of the river describes a nearly complete circle around a complex of active volcanoes that includes Mts. Arjuna, Kawi and Kelud. From its source above Malang, the Brantas flows south to a range of hills along the southern coast, westward until it meets the foot of Mt. Wilis, and then north and east—emptying into the Java Sea around Surabaya. Within this circle flourished important ancient civilizations, and the area is rich with archaeological sites dating from the the 8th to the 15th centuries—a "golden age" of Hindu-Javanese art and culture.

Political power shifted to East Java following the sudden decline of Central Java's Mataram kingdom in the early 10th century; a powerful ruler named Sindok then established a capital southwest of present-day Surabaya. Subsequently, Kediri in the western Brantas Valley briefly became the island's dominant kingdom in the early 11th century. By 1222, however, power again shifted to Singosari in the eastern Brantas basin. This move, however, was merely a prelude to the rise of the greatest kingdom of all, Majapahit, which developed in the northern part of the valley at the close of the 13th century.

In a series of day trips from Surabaya or Malang, the traveler can visit archaeological sites associated with these significant periods of Javanese history. A minimum of three days and nights are needed to make a complete circuit that includes the Malang and Batu-Selecta area and the more distant sites around Kediri and Blitar.

Penanggungan: the sacred peak

Mt. Penanggungan just to the south of Surabaya has a main peak surrounded by four smaller ones, and is therefore said to resemble the mythical Mt. Meru, revered by

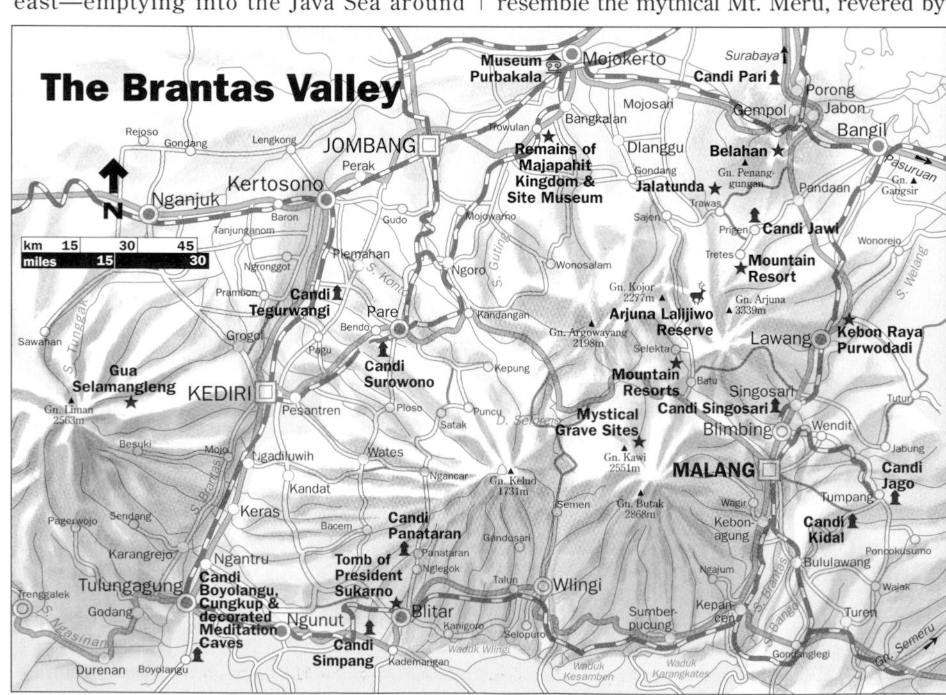

ERIC OEY

Hindus as the center of the universe and abode of the gods. For this reason, it became a popular destination for pilgrimages. Dozens of temples were erected on its slopes, connected by a route which began and ended at ceremonial bathing places on either side of the mountain's foot. Water from ancient channels still fills both of these bathing places.

Belahan, the eastern bathing spot, is reached via a rough side road which lies about 2 km (1 mi) south of Gempol. Turn off the main highway at a small sign until you reach Watukosek, then south to Kandangan.

Water spouts from the breasts of a beautiful stone statue of Visnu's consort, Laksmi, while a similar statue of Sri no longer functions. The pool, made of brick, was once larger and had more spouts and decorations. It was probably begun around A.D. 950, but was expanded in the 11th century when the ashes of one of Java's most revered kings, Airlangga, were interred here in 1049. A famous statue from this site depicting Airlangga as Visnu is now in the Mojokerto Museum. Nearby are the remains of a brick gateway.

The western pool, **Jalatunda**, lies 500 m (1,625 ft) above sea level near the village of Trawas. To reach this spot, you must take a long and bumpy road from Watukosek to Jedong via Ngoro. Built of stone, Jalatunda was constructed in 977; many beautiful carvings added in the 14th century and illustrating the Arjuna saga are now displayed in the National Museum in Jakarta, along with a spout in the form of Mt. Sumeru which once stood at the top center of the pool.

From Jalatunda the old pilgrimage trail may still be followed up the mountain to the summit (1,653 m/5,370 ft). The majority of the antiquities are located around the 1000-meter line. To reach them, you will need to camp at least one night here; the usual camping site is beside Candi Sinta. Bring your own camping equipment. The office of the archaeological service (Suaka Purbakala) in Trowulan should be notified. They can also recommend guides. Inquiries may also be made at Jalatunda.

The temples of Penanggungan are quite unusual. Not exactly buildings, they are stone-faced terraces five levels high, set against the slope of the mountain, with a stairway and the remains of three altars at the top. Several of the temples feature narrative relief carvings on the terrace facings. The principal temple sites are: Candi Carik, Lurah, Naga, Gajahmungkur, Wayang, Yudha and Kendalisodo. Nobody knows exactly how many there are, but there may be over 100. Most of them date from the 15th century.

Candi Jawi, near Prigen on the road to Tretes, is not far away and is easily reached by a good road turning off at Pandaan. This

Above: *The bathing place known as Belahan, at the eastern foot of Mt. Penanggungan.*

leads straight to the temple, which is located on the north (right-hand) side of the road. Candi Jawi was built in the late 13th century, remodeled in the 14th, and restored in the 20th. The temple was dedicated to a deity combining features of the Hindu god Siva with the Buddha, and is thought to have been the funerary temple of King Kertanegara. It is decorated with relief panels and surrounded by a moat and the remains of brick walls.

The Malang area

Singosari, 65 km (39 mi) south of Surabaya on the road to Malang, was the capital of a powerful kingdom between 1222 and 1292. The major site here is a partially-restored Hindu temple a short distance down a sideroad to the west side of modern Singosari town. In the courtyard is an interesting collection of statuary gathered from the area. A few hundred meters further west stand two huge guardian statues (*dwarapala*), all that remain of the ancient palace. There is a partially-restored stupa about 6 km (3.5 mi) away in a village called Sumberawan. To get there, take the road leading north from the temple, which then turns west; from there you must make a short, pleasant trek of several hundred meters across rice fields.

Candi Jago in Tumpang village sits just off the main road 6 km south of Singosari; to get there, turn left (east) at Blimbing. Built around 1280 and renovated in 1343, Jago was dedicated to a form of Tantric Buddhism and served as a funerary monument. Several statues stand in the courtyard, but the most beautiful are now in the National Museum. The temple has a long sequence of narrative reliefs carved in the so-called *wayang* style (two-dimensional, resembling shadow puppets) based on *Jataka* stories, the *Ramayana*, and other unidentified legends.

Candi Kidal, 11 km (7 mi) further along the same road, was built around 1260. The base is decorated with statues of the mythical Garuda bird on three sides. On the north he is carrying a goddess, perhaps Sri; on the east he holds a *kendi* or water jar, probably a reference to the story in which he had to find the elixir of immortality to ransom his mother from slavery; on the south side Garuda is carrying a snake.

Candi Badut, situated 3 km (2 mi) west of Malang, belongs to an even more ancient time. This temple, dedicated to Siva, was built in 760, during the earliest period of stone architecture in Java, but was drastically altered during the 13th century. To reach it, take the road to Dinoyo.

Travelers with more time to spare and a special interest in antiquities may wish to visit **Candi Pari**, located west of the Surabaya-Malang highway on a side road which branches off at Porong, just 1.5 km (1 mi) north of Gempol. This is a large but rather simply decorated brick temple dated 1371.

Two other temple sites lie off the main road east to Banyuwangi and Bali: **Gunung Gangsir**, 12 km (7 mi) east of Gempol, is also built of brick, but is distinguished by its beautifully modelled designs. The date of its construction is uncertain. **Candi Jabung**, 10 km (6 mi) east of Kraksaan, or about 90 km (54 km) east of Gempol, dates from 1354 and has recently been restored.

A bit further afield is **Candi Kedaton** (or Andong Biru) set on the slope of Mt. Malang. Take the side road from Gending to Tiris and continue along a narrow unpaved road, a total distance of 30 km (18 mi) from the main highway. Though small, Kedaton has interesting relief panels illustrating the story of Garuda's search for the elixir of immortality.

The Mojokerto route

Mojokerto is 30 km (19 mi) southwest of Surabaya. The **Museum Purbakala** at Jl. Ahmad Yani 14 is a modest structure containing many important ancient sculptures. The museum's centerpiece is the statue of Visnu riding Garuda from Belahan. In the same room are many stone panels carved with narrative reliefs from Candi Menak Jinggo at Trowulan. Other exhibits include funerary statues from the 14th and 15th centuries, inscriptions, carved stone bases for stone statues and wooden pillars, water spouts from bathing places, and terracottas.

Trowulan, 35 km (21 mi) from Surabaya

AMIR SIDHARTA

between Mojokerto and Jombang, was the site of Java's most powerful kingdom, Majapahit. Founded in the late 13th century, its famous *patih* or Prime Minister, Gajah Mada, claimed suzerainty over an area larger than modern Indonesia. Thus he was actually the first leader to establish the concept of a united Indonesia with an Indonesian identity. The **Trowulan Site Museum** has a large collection of objects collected from the area, including stone and terracotta statues, local earthenware pottery, and Chinese porcelain. The ancient city was extensive, and major monuments are scattered over an area of several square kilometers.

Most of Trowulan's sites are reached by the side road to Pakis which leads south from the main highway one kilometer from the museum in the direction of Mojokerto. The first site encountered along the road is a large (6.5 hectare/16 acre) artificial lake, **Kolam Segaran**, about 800 meters off the highway. The lake covers 6.5 ha and has been rebuilt with modern bricks.

A sideroad at the northwest corner of the lake leads east; 50 meters from the lake is the grave complex of **Puteri Cempo**, a princess who is credited with a leading role in the conversion of Java to Islam. Another grave simply called **Kubur Panjang** ("Long Grave") 250 meters further east has a stone inscription and bears the date 1281. The silver paint on the gravestone was added recently by locals. Turn south from Kubur Panjang, then east on another path to the ruins of **Candi Menak Jinggo**, another 250 meters away.

Returning to the reservoir, proceed south; the area's archaeological office is on the west, exactly 1 km from the highway. About 900 meters further down the main road is a large pavilion, the **Pendopo Agung**, on the

Opposite: *Late 13th-century Candi Jawi, with Mt. Penanggungan behind.* **Above:** *Jalatunda bathing pool.* **Left:** *One of the Singosari palace guardians.*

right (west). A small shed beside the pavilion houses many artifacts discovered when the pavilion was built in the 1970s. Another 325 meters beyond and down a side road on the right is the **Candi Kedaton** complex. This enigmatic group of structures includes a brick foundation for a temple and two wells (Sumur Upas, "Poison Well," and Sumur Kuno, "Ancient Well"), and a brick tunnel, Sanggar Pamelengan. This site may have been used for religious initiation rituals.

The last site on this road is a complex of Muslim graves at **Troloyo**, 2.8 km (1.5 mi) from the highway (550 meters beyond Candi Kedaton). These are the oldest known graves of Javanese Muslims. Dates and inscriptions are in Javanese and not Arabic.

Down a side road which branches off to the east just north of the Pendopo Agung are two significant sites. **Gapura Bajang Ratu**, a brick gateway 22 meters (72 ft) high decorated with narrative reliefs from the *Ramayana* and other stories, is 3.6 km (2.25 mi) from the highway. It is all that remains of a large walled compound. A recently restored bathing place, **Candi Tikus**, lies 550 meters further down the same road. It has *makara*-shaped stone spouts and a brick motif symbolizing Mt. Sumeru.

There are two other important sites off the main highway north of Museum Purbakala. **Gapura Wringin Lawang**, another gateway, stands 200 meters southeast of the highway 1.55 km (1 mi) from the Pakis junction in the direction of Surabaya. **Candi Brahu**, a brick temple and the largest standing structure remaining from Majapahit's capital, lies north of the main highway.

The Kediri-Blitar area

This region can be approached from either Malang (via Batu and Pare) or Jombang. A third route, the southern road from Malang to Blitar is narrow and winding. Kediri was the site of Java's most powerful kingdom during the 11th to 13th centuries, and its court produced several masterpieces of Javanese literature. Northeast of Kediri near Pare are two temples. **Candi Surowono** in Bloran, 2 km east of the highway to Kediri, has narrative reliefs carved in the early 14th century. Those on the lower section depict Tantri stories, while those on the top show scenes from the *Arjunawiwaha* (the nymphs are trying to seduce Arjuna as he meditates), *Sri Tanjung* (the story of a woman murdered for suspected infidelity), and *Bubuksa-Gagangaking* (two brothers, one Hindu, the other Buddhist, vie to see which can be more saintly).

Candi Tegurwangi stands 7 km (4 mi) from Pare. To reach it, turn right (west) at a fork 2 km from Pare (on the road to Kediri), then right again after about 4 km (2.5 mi). Narrative reliefs on the temple illustrate the *Sudamala* legend: The goddess Durga asks for Sadewa, one of the five Pandawa brothers

in the *Mahabharata*, as an offering in exchange for her help in fending off monsters that threatened them. Sadewa exorcises Durga's evil nature and turns her back into beautiful Dewi Uma, then marries a wise man's daughter.

An important artificial Buddhist meditation cave, **Gua Selamangleng**, lies on Klotok hill west of Kediri. The cave contains four or five chambers decorated with carvings of buddhas and scenes from *Jataka* tales. Two inscriptions in the cave date from different eras: one from the 12th century, the other from 1431.

There are a number of remains near Tulungagung, 35 km (21 mi) south of Kediri. Five km (3 mi) south of Tulungagung, is **Candi Boyolangu**, a cave containing the remains of a headless female statue, perhaps a *bodhisattva*. Nearby is **Cungkup**, a large brick structure with headless buddha statues but few other decorations. The most interesting remains are called **Gua Selamangleng** like those near Kediri, artificial meditation caves with reliefs, perhaps from the 10th century, illustrating the *Mahabharata* and *Arjunawiwaha*. Another decorated cave, **Gua Pasir**, lies 4 km (2.5 mi) past the main complex.

Blitar is about 35 km (21 mi) east of Tulungagung. On the southwest edge of the town, a road leads to the village of Bara and a river crossing guarded by a large image of Ganesa, the elephant-headed son of Siva and

LUCA INVERNIZZI TETTONI

LUCA INVERNIZZI TETTONI

overcomer of obstacles. Beyond the river are ruins of a small temple, **Candi Simpang**.

Blitar's most impressive remains are at **Candi Panataran** 10 km (6 mi) north on the road to Sumberwringin. There are seven major buildings and the foundations of many more. The first foreigner to describe it was Thomas Horsfield, an American friend of Raffles, in the early 19th century. The oldest inscription here is dated 1197, the latest 1454. Panataran was one of the most important sanctuaries in the kingdom of Majapahit; Gajah Mada visited it several times.

The large complex is divided into three courtyards. A giant statue guarding the entrance to the first is dated 1320. In this courtyard are two terraces, one dated 1375 and decorated with 80 narrative reliefs depicting the story of *Bubuksah-Gagangaking* and others not yet identified. A well-preserved temple with a statue of Ganesa inside is dated 1369. The main structure in the second courtyard is the **Naga Temple**, so called because it is decorated with serpents carved as if to entwine the building in their coils.

The site's largest temple is in the third courtyard. Its summit has disappeared, but the lower terraces bear reliefs from the *Ramayana* depicting many of the same scenes as Loro Jonggrang in Central Java, but executed in a different style. Beyond the eastern wall, at the southeast corner, is a stairway that leads to a bathing place decorated with narrative reliefs.

One modern site of interest is located between Panataran and Blitar: the grave of Sukarno, Indonesia's controversial first president. The elaborately-decorated site is now visited by many Indonesian pilgrims in the manner of a religious shrine.

—*John Miksic*

Opposite: *Arjuna (kneeling) grapples with Siva in a relief at Candi Surawono.* **Above and left:** *Ramayana reliefs on the main temple at Panataran.*

TENGGER HIGHLANDS

Desolate and Eery Volcanic Moonscapes

There is perhaps no other volcanic terrain in the world that can compare with East Java's spectacular Tengger region. At the center of this upland massif lies an ancient caldera measuring 10 km (6 mi) in diameter—sheer, grass-colored cliffs surrounding a black, windswept "sea of sand" (*laut pasir*). Four smaller peaks rise 300 to 400 meters (1,000 to 1,300 ft) from the center of this crater floor; three are green and lush with vegetation, while the fourth is a smouldering mound of cinder and ash that erupts every few years, veiling the surrounding countryside in nutrient-rich deposits. This is Bromo.

Java's highest peak, Mt. Semeru (3,676 m/12,060 ft), looms over this desolate lunar landscape just 20 km (12 mi) to the south. Its presence is so immediate you feel you could almost touch it from the northern lip of the Bromo caldera. An active volcano, Semeru erupted violently in 1983, wiping out two villages on its southern slopes.

Bromo's upheavals, by contrast, rarely amount to much more than a flurry of thunder and ash. Thus it is not surprising that the region's farmers view the latter somewhat ambivalently. Local myths affirm that Bromo is the home of the Tengger's most important guardian deity—an ancestral spirit named Joko Seger. He is thought to have given his life for the well-being of his descendants, when he was snatched from his parents' arms as they fled the angry volcano. Fittingly, he is seen as both a benevolent provider and a fearsome destroyer.

For the traveler, the journey to Bromo is an unforgettable experience that offers cool respite from the tropical heat and the urban bustle of the lowlands. Farmers have pushed their fields up the very steepest slopes, while an alpine flora of evergreen and eidelweiss blanket the mountain tops. Nighttime temperatures drop to within several degrees of freezing, while in the daytime the weather is refreshingly cool.

Hindu-Javanese survivors

The upper slopes of this highland massif are home to some 40,000 people—the Tengger Javanese—who are the only group on the island to have preserved a Hindu priesthood since the collapse of the Hindu-Buddhist kingdom of Majapahit about five centuries ago. After Islam swept Java in the early 16th century, Majapahit's aristocrats and priests took flight to the small Hindu principality of Blambangan at Java's far eastern tip, and to neighboring Bali. Many commoners, meanwhile, are said to have sought refuge in the Tengger highlands.

Though Bali remains Hindu to this day, Blambangan eventually fell to repeated attacks from Muslim armies and the Dutch, who took the unusual step of encouraging the Islamization of Blambangan's Hindus in the 1780s. They feared that its people would otherwise join forces with the Balinese to expel both the Dutch and the Muslim Javanese. This policy annihilated the last of the island's Hindu courts; so that only the Tengger Javanese in their remote highland stronghold have preserved Hindu ways.

In classical times, Javanese Hinduism was the noble religion of the courts. Among the Tengger's mountain peasants, however, cut off from the literature and visual arts of the courts, it gradually took the form of folk beliefs. In the 19th century even these were threatened with extinction, as Madurese and Javanese Muslims swarmed into the lower reaches of the Tengger highlands, bringing Islam to the area. Desperate to legitimize their faith, Tengger priests began incorporating Muslim prayers into their services.

The Kasodo festival

Somehow a small Hindu population survived, and in the 1960s and 70s the Tengger Javanese "rediscovered" their ties to Bali, sending schoolteacher emissaries to the neighboring island to learn from their Hindu brethren. By the 1980s, most villages had formally affiliated themselves with Hinduism, and a minority even continue to refer to their faith as *agama budha*—a general term used to refer to the Hindu-Buddhist religion of pre-Islamic Java.

While the liturgies of Tengger commoner priests (*resi pujangga*) recognize Siva as the supreme deity—with Brahma, Visnu, Mahadewa and Iswara as his associates—many Tengger traditions reflect local beliefs. This is evident in the ceremony held each year during the last month (Kasodo) of the Teng-

AMIR SIDHARTA

ger calendar, when the faithful make a ritual offering to Joko Seger at Bromo.

Thousands assemble in the sand flats beneath Mt. Bromo at midnight in the middle of this month, most bearing small offerings of vegetables, flowers, money, or even live chickens. The 28 priests of the Tengger region begin the rite by burning incense, annointing the assembled offerings, and invoking Siva and other guardian deities. The spirits' descent from the heavens brings blessings to all present. After the prayers, the throngs push their way up Mt. Bromo to throw the offerings into the caldera, ensuring their welfare in the coming year.

Rustic mountain ways

Contrary to some reports, the Tengger highlanders are not an archaic "lost tribe." They are ethnically Javanese and physically indistinguishable from their East Javanese neighbors. Although they are Hindus, there is no caste system; their kinship and social patterns are essentially the same as those of Javanese Muslims.

In some respects, however, the Tengger do differ. They speak a dialect related to that of the Osing Javanese of Blambangan—lacking the "levels" which require most Javanese to define their relative status when speaking to one another. While the Tengger are able to use this status-sensitive language when speaking to outsiders, among themselves they speak directly and democratically.

Other village traditions exhibit a similarly open and direct style. Visitors to a Tengger home are ushered directly to the kitchen hearth, something unthinkable for "normal" Javanese. Guests are invited to drink and, if they stay more than a few minutes, to eat—it is proper to have a few bites of food to indicate your appreciation of the gesture.

Houses in these highlands are made of sturdy pine rather than bamboo matting, and are painted bright white with blue-green trim. Population densities are high for a mountain region—300 to 400 per sq km (750-1000 per sq mi)—and yet the population is relatively well-off because the land is very fertile.

Since the 1960s, however, over-cultivation has resulted in disastrous erosion. The average plot size has also shrunk, and more farmers have thus shifted away from maize, their traditional staple, to crops like cabbages, potatoes and onions which fetch good prices in lowland markets. As in most of upland Java, this has further exacerbated problems of erosion, and soil degradation has reached epidemic proportions. The "tourist boom" now underway may actually bring economic relief to the region, allowing some people to move away from agriculture and thus reducing pressures on the land.

— *Robert Hefner*

Above: *The Bromo caldera seen from Penanjakan.*

VISITING BROMO

Trekking in the Tengger Region

There are three routes into the Tengger highlands. The first is easy; the others a bit more adventurous. All, however, feature some of the most enchanting terrain in all of Java.

The most common approach to the Bromo caldera is from the northeast via a road that leaves the main highway near Probolinggo and climbs 44 mountainous km (27 mi) up to Ngadisari, where there are hotels and other facilities (see "Bromo Practicalities"). Probolinggo itself is hot and uninteresting, and overnighting here is not recommended.

Another road runs south from Pasuruan up to Tosari and Wonokitri. From here, it's a longer climb up to the rim of the caldera, and the facilities are not as numerous as at Ngadisari, but it's less crowded with tourists and the views from this side are better.

Last but not least there is a steep track that runs up from Malang via Tumpang and Gubukklakah to Ngadas, a village in the forested region between Bromo and Semeru. There are no facilities here at all, but you can stay with villagers and this is a fabulous area for hiking. All three of these routes are in fact connected by trails, so you can go up one way and come down another.

Though most tourists race up and down in a day just to catch the sunrise, it's best to reserve at least two days for a visit, staying overnight in the mountains. This way you get to spend some time looking around. In fact, the sunset over Bromo, particularly in the dry season (May to October) when the cloud cover is not too thick, is equally impressive. Long-distance hiking or mountain climbing involves several more days and is only recommended during the dry season.

The Ngadisari route

From the turn-off at Ketapang, 5 km west of Probolinggo, the road winds through poor Madurese villages, peopled by the descendants of laborers who arrived in the 19th century to grow coffee for the Dutch. As this fiercely Muslim group settled in the area, local Hindus either converted to Islam or fled to the uplands.

About halfway up is **Sukapura**, an old hill station marking the boundary between the Madurese and Hindu Tengger settlements. It has moderately priced hotels and several *warungs*, and a hiking path offers pleasant

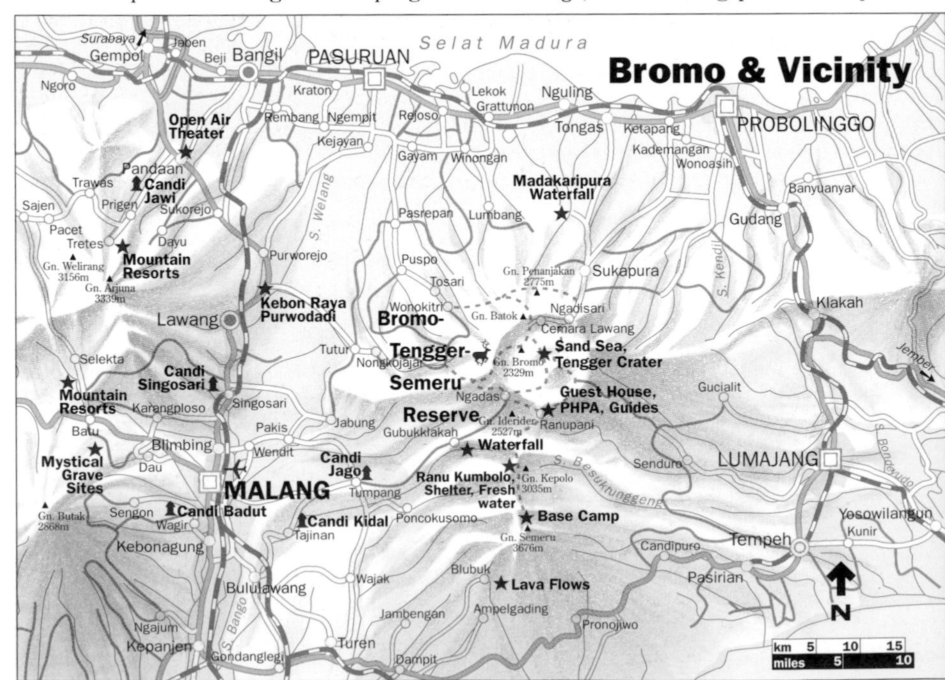

views. (Walk south from the town, then turn left/east toward the mountain wall for a vigorous uphill ascent). Most people, however, will want to continue on to Ngadisari and Cemara Lawang.

The night air in **Ngadisari** (altitude 1,950 meters/6,400 ft) is brisk, so pack some warm clothes and, most importantly, bring good walking shoes. On arrival, you will be taken to the local *hansip* (constabulary) and asked to pay a small fee. This is not a swindle; the money is for scout uniforms (the scouts help to receive guests), and to service tourist bathrooms. There are hotels in and around Ngadisari and along the road from Sukapura; you can also stay in villagers' homes.

Another, smaller village called **Cemara Lawang** ("Casuarina Gate") perches right on the rim of the caldera, 3 km (2 mi) above Ngadisari. Very basic accommodations are available, and for those who don't mind roughing it this is the place to stay. You can hike up in under an hour from Ngadisari or hire a jeep. Get there by late afternoon to see the sunset.

Traditionally, most visitors get up several hours before dawn and travel on horseback or on foot from Ngadisari or Cemara Lawang down into the caldera and across the sand sea in pitch blackness, arriving at the rim of Bromo in time to see the sunrise. Although the view from here is awesome, the view from Cemara Lawang itself is just as spectacular.

To be at Bromo for the sunrise (around 5 am), you should leave Ngadisari by 3 am, or Cemara Lawang by 4. If you are coming up from Probolinggo, leave before 2 am. Make all arrangements the night before if you are hiring a horse or a jeep, and buy some provisions—food and bottled water for the journey. During the main tourist season from July to September, and again around Christmas, you will usually be accompanied by 50-75 fellow pilgrims, but in the dark, desolate wastes of Bromo you will appreciate their company.

Descend to the sand sea from Cemara Lawang along the jeep track and follow the white-painted stones across to the volcano. It's a straight route, eerily silent and beautiful in the frigid night air, with the twinkling firmament overhead and just the outlines of jagged ridges visible around you on a clear, moonlit night. After about 2 km, you reach a small concrete podium, the *poten*, where each year Tengger priests make their offerings to Joko Seger, the spirit of Bromo. From here you begin your ascent, following a winding path over cinders and ash thrown out by the volcano. The mildly unpleasant but harmless odor of sulphur permeates the atmosphere.

A concrete stairway reaches from the base of Mt. Bromo 150 meters (490 ft) to the lip of the crater. Looking into its seething cauldron of bubbling water, ash and sulphur, it's easy to understand why the ancient Javan-

Below: *Sunrise from the rim of Mt. Bromo.*

ALAIN COMPOST

ese regarded this as the entrance to purgatory. An offering of a few rupiah will earn you the blessing of the volcano's spirit.

Celebrate the sunrise atop Bromo with food and drink (remember to bring provisions along and please carry your trash back with you). But don't be in too much of hurry to get back to the lowlands; there are other interesting excursions in the vicinity.

Hikes from Bromo

Just west of Bromo (to the right) rises Mt. Batok, a perfect cone with fluted ridges. According to Tengger legends, Batok was created from a coconut-shell used by the gods to excavate the area. For a vigorous hike (three to six hours, depending on the route), walk around Mt. Batok toward the outer caldera wall. Twenty minutes from Bromo you will reach the northwestern wall, which rises up even higher on this side than at Cemara Lawang. Dazzling sunlight reflects off the fir trees and grasses, and a broad jeep track winds up the cliff. Though steep, the hike up is well worth the effort.

As the path zig-zags up the wall face, you get ever more impressive views back to Bromo, Batok, and, far to the south, Mt. Semeru. At the top of the cliff—a vertical climb of 450 meters (1,500 ft)—you feel as if you are in an airplane, with the Tengger volcanoes lined up before you in a single, sweeping panorama.

STEVE TEO

JULIAN SIHOMBING

If you're tired at this point, turn back and return to Cemara Lawang by way of the sand sea—a two-hour walk. If you have the energy, however, another four-hour hike will bring you up and over the highest point on the caldera wall, to witness one of the finest scenes on Java. From the top of the trail you will see signs pointing north (right) to Penanjakan ("The Promontory"), 3 km (2 mi) and 700 meters (2,300 ft) further up. It's about 1.5 hours to the top, and the track then continues from here down to Ngadisari, another two hours on foot. Though steep, the path is safe and well marked, and will even accommodate 4-wheel drive vehicles during the dry season. In the rainy season the view may be clouded over, so check conditions before you go.

The view from Penanjakan is breathtaking. From this vantage point high above the Bromo crater, the full girth of Mt. Semeru is now visible 30 km (18 mi) to the south. Beyond lies Java's southern coast, 60 km (36 mi) away. To the north are Probolinggo and the island of Madura. Ancient Javanese Hindus believed this Penanjakan-Bromo-Semeru axis to be the center of the world; from Penanjakan you'll understand why. Continue north from here to Ngadisari; the path is safe and well marked.

The Tosari route

Another approach to Bromo, that is only a bit more difficult, involves traveling by local minibus or rented car from Pasuruan south to **Tosari** (44 kms/27 mi), whence you approach Bromo from the northwest rather than the northeast. Tosari was one of Java's most popular hill stations during Dutch colonial times, and though the old hostelries were destroyed during the revolution, new hotels are now being built here. For cheaper accommodations, you can also catch a local minibus or walk to **Wonokitri**, 3 km (2 mi) away. Along the way you'll see farmers bringing vegetables to market. The valleys are much narrower and deeper here than in Ngadisari, and the neatly cultivated hillsides are covered with brightly painted houses.

Wonokitri has won government awards for its development programs, and the cleanliness of the village is impressive. The local Balinese-style temple was one of the first to be built in the Tengger highlands in the 1970s, when the population "rediscovered" its religious ties with Hindu Bali.

It is a 14-km (8.5 mi) walk from Wonokitri up to Mt. Bromo through thick evergreen forests. If you want to catch the sunrise you will have to walk in the dark or hire a jeep for the climb. During the daytime, there is an impressive view of the northern coastline from the trail. On reaching the northwestern lip of the caldera, descend to the sand sea by the same track described above, or else climb up and over Penanjakan to Ngadisari.

Descent via Ngadas

The third and most difficult route to Bromo is actually better traveled in reverse—as an alternative descent from the caldera. After viewing Mt. Bromo, head east and south across the sand sea—away from Cemara Lawang and Batok. After about an hour the sand ends and you reach a lush valley of grass; at the southern end the trail gently ascends the caldera wall.

At the top is a sign directing you to the right (west) toward **Ngadas**, 2 km (1.2 mi) away. Here, you can experience rustic village life first-hand by staying overnight in a farmer's house (inquire with the village chief or *kepala desa*). There is a small *warung* opposite the chief's house where you can eat fried rice, and it is best to bring a sleeping bag if you plan to spend the night. This village feels as if it's in a time warp. There are interesting forest treks from here—notably the 8-km (4.8 mi) walk to **Ranupani** (due east, back past the caldera along a well-marked trail), where there are two small lakes for fishing or swimming.

Ngadas lacks amenities, water is scarce, and accommodations are primitive—thus you may want to proceed to the lowlands after a brief stop for a meal here. Minibuses depart in the early afternoon to Gubukklakah. You can also walk the route in 3 hours; the steep, 14-km track descends through temperate forests to subtropical jungles rich with wild boars and monkeys. The thick, pristine foliage provides a sense of what Java was like before most of its jungle was destroyed in the 19th century. From Gubukklakah minibuses are available to Tumpang, where you can change for Malang. Transportation is available into the late evening.

Climbing Mount Semeru

Java's highest peak, Mt. Semeru, offers spectacular climbing. Though the ascent does not require mountaineering gear, it is only for experienced hikers. You will need a warm sleeping bag, a guide and adequate supplies. Almost every year a lowland youth becomes separated from his party and dies of exposure after several nights in the mountains. Student guides are available through the Mahameru Mountain Climbing Club in Malang. You may also hire a man in Ranupani village for a two-day excursion. He will escort you to a point below the summit and wait there during your 4-hour ascent and return.

The trip takes 3 days altogether, and should not be attempted during the rainy season (December to March). Hire a driver in Malang (a 4-wheel drive vehicle if possible), or take public transport from Malang to Tumpang, Gubukklakah, Ngadas and Ranupani. There you can make arrangements to stay with the *kepala desa*; you will also have to register and get a permit for the climb.

The next morning, set out with your guide from Ranupani. The path is forested and extremely rugged. In the afternoon you will set up camp below the summit. Tents are not necessary, but you will need groundcloths. Don't try to make it up the mountain on the same day. Evening climbs up Semeru are extremely dangerous; evening winds blow deadly gases your way.

The ascent the next morning takes 2-3 hours. The last few hundred meters are difficult, as the path changes from dirt to loose volcanic scree. Standing near the summit, one can look into the Bromo caldera and beyond to the north coast. To the south, lava arms reach to the sea. To the east is Bali, a brilliant green and grey jewel set in the Indian Ocean; to the west Java stretches to the horizon. It is easy to understand why this peak is regarded as the abode of the gods—it is.

From here too, a plume of smoke rises from the volcano about every 90 seconds, accompanied by an earth-shaking rumble. Enjoy the view then head back to Ranupani. If you are using public transportion, book a minibus in advance for the descent.

— *Robert Hefner*

Opposite, below: *Mt. Batok's cone.* **Opposite, above:** *Racing across the desolate sand sea.*

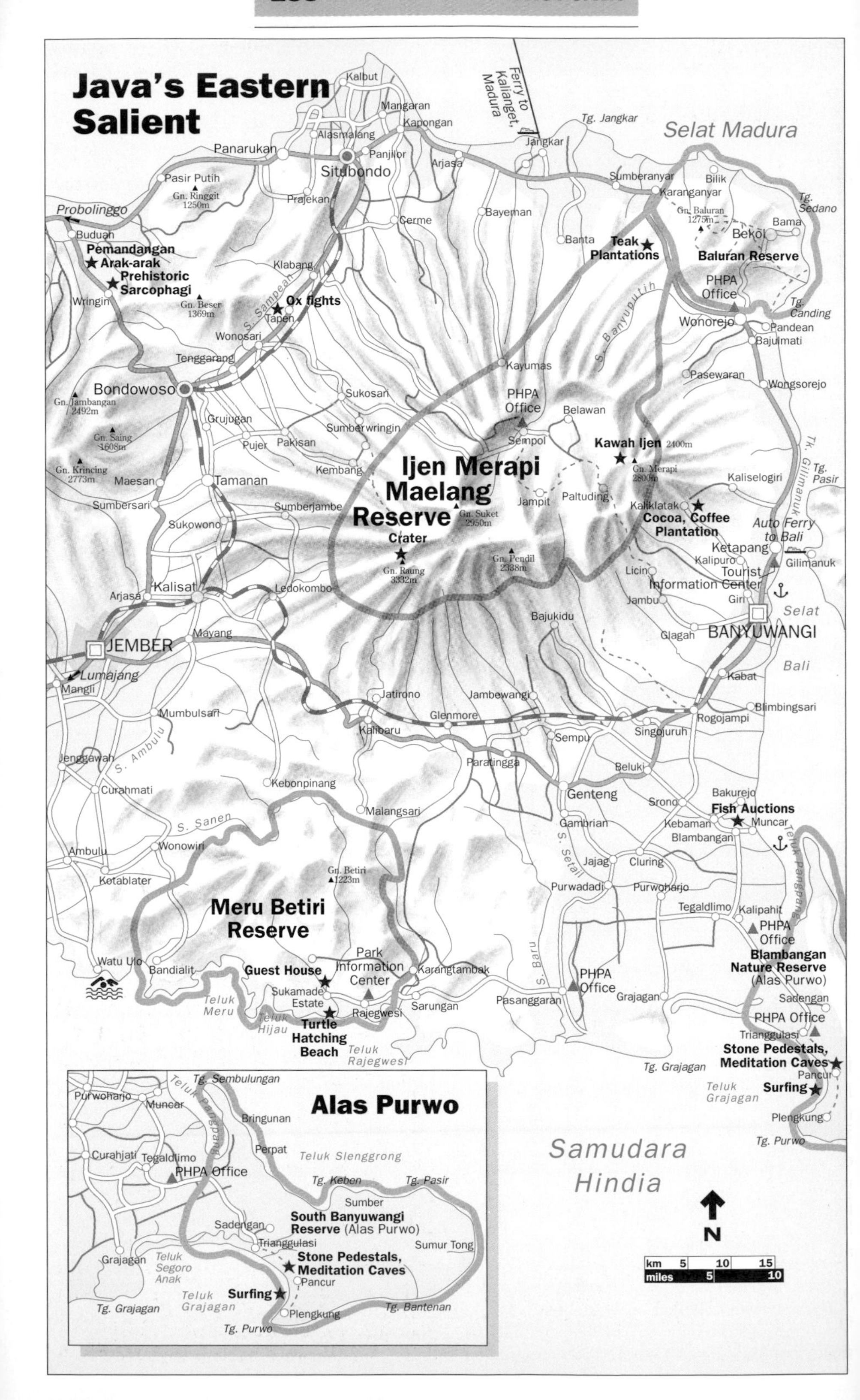
Java's Eastern Salient
Ijen Merapi Maelang Reserve
Meru Betiri Reserve
Baluran Reserve
Blambangan Nature Reserve (Alas Purwo)
Selat Madura
Samudara Hindia
Situbondo
Bondowoso
JEMBER
BANYUWANGI
Kawah Ijen 2400m
Ferry to Kalianget, Madura
Auto Ferry to Bali
Alas Purwo
South Banyuwangi Reserve (Alas Purwo)
Stone Pedestals, Meditation Caves
Surfing
km 5 10 15
miles 5 10

BLAMBANGAN

Excursions at the Eastern Edge of Java

The craggy, inhospitable terrain of Java's rugged eastern tip has never yielded easily to human habitation. Even today, this remote and sparsely populated region remains a challenging travel destination, though the difficulties are more than compensated by the area's exceptional natural beauty.

The eastern tip of Java was ruled in the 16th century by the island's last Hindu kingdom, Blambangan, whose capital was at Banyuwangi. Although attacked by the growing Muslim empire of Mataram in the early 17th century, Blambangan managed to survive as a tiny Hindu principality with alliances to neighboring Bali.

The Dutch largely ignored the area until the 18th century. Then, to counter the Balinese threat to the east, it recognised two Blambangan princes who converted to Islam and became the area's regents. A catastrophic eruption of Mt. Ijen in 1817, and a cholera epidemic depopulated much of the region.

Today Madurese migrants predominate in the northern part of the eastern salient, but there are still descendants of the Hindu Blambangan kingdom in the east and south, known as "Osing." The Javanese dialect spoken throughout the region is rather archaic and also shows a strong Madurese influence.

Geographically, the east is dominated by a number of sprawling plantations and five sizeable nature reserves: the Yang Plateau, Ijen, Baluran, Meru Betiri and Blambangan (Alas Purwo). The most famous sight in this area is the pale green Ijen crater lake at the top of Mt. Merapi in the Ijen range. While it is a hindrance to travel and communications, the region's underdeveloped infrastructure has proven to be a blessing in disguise, as the local ecosystem has been only minimally affected by human beings.

Because of terrain and transportation conditions in the eastern salient, it is advisable to allow at least a week—in fact two weeks are required for a comprehensive tour. Ideally, you should have your own vehicle, preferably a jeep; the alternative is long waits for buses, with dubious reliability over tough roads.

Bondowoso and Ijen

The coastal road leading east from Probolinggo is newly-repaved and fast, but plagued by heavy bus and truck traffic. About 24 km (15 mi) past Probolinggo on the right, between Pejarakan and Kraksaan, is Candi Jabung—a cylindrical Majapahit temple; note the magnificent Kala figures above the entrance.

The "White Sands" of Pasir Putih, located another 48 km (29 mi) to the east, are in reality a disappointing gray, and the place offers little of interest other than boat rentals to view what's left of the coral reef. *Sate Madura* is available at beachside stalls; accommodations are expensive and uncomfortable.

Bondowoso, a focal point for the region, lies 35 km (21 km) south of the coast via a wonderfully scenic, winding road that begins just past Besuki. Stop at Pemandangan Arak-arak to enjoy the view. At Wringin, midway along the road, some interesting prehistoric sarcophagi are still in situ.

Bondowoso is the best starting point for trips to the **Ijen Crater**. To go up the mountain, head northeast to Wonosari, then turn off toward Sukosari. From this point it is a two-hour drive up to Sempol, where you must check in with the PHPA office. From here,

AMIR SIDHARTA

Right: *Tough sulphur-carriers in the Ijen crater.*

continue on to Paltuding where the trek up to Kawah Ijen begins. Get water for the hike while you are at Sempol, and be sure you have a warm sweater or jacket with you.

Though only 3 km (1.8 mi), the climb is a strenuous 2.5 hours. Take heart, however, when you encounter sulphur quarry workers along the path carrying their bright yellow loads in baskets—they make the 35-km (20-mi) round trip from Jambu each day on foot.

At Pondok Kawah Ijen there is a dilapidated shelter—from here the crater is about an hour away. Cresting the crater's rim, you are presented with an awe-inspiring view of the lake below. You can descend to the edge of it and the sulphur quarry, but this takes several more hours to climb down and back.

South from Bondowoso, the road leads through **Jember** (33 km/20 mi), Java's main tobacco-growing area. The plantations in this region thrive on a lucrative trade with German tobacco importers in Bremen. This in turn has led to the growth of "agro-tourism" in the area—there is now even a lovely nine-hole golf course at Glantangan, 23 km (14 mi) south of Jember.

Continuing along the main road past Jember, turn south (left) at Mangli. This road winds through rugged hills past Ambulu to the south coast and the beautiful **Watu Ulo** ("Snake Stone") beach. You can catch an *ojek* (motorcycle taxi) from Mangli or Ambulu (50 cents) directly to the Hotel Wisnu Watu Ulo.

North to Baluran

Coming up from Bondowoso toward Situbondo you pass through **Tapen**, where ox fights are held every Saturday and Sunday. The people here are Madurese, and this is their favorite sport. They come from all over the region to watch the matches, which are governed by complicated rules that appear incomprehensible to outsiders; it's just as interesting though to watch the spectators.

Past Situbondo, the road east along the coast skirts the massif containing Mts. Merapi and Raung. The road dips through dusty teak forests and suddenly you are at the entrance to **Baluran National Park**. To enter you need a permit—obtained at the office by the entrance in Wonorejo; a donation of about $1 per person is appreciated.

Baluran is Java's driest corner, its 50,000-hectares (123,500 acres) lying in a rain shadow around the low eroded cone of an old volcano. There is nothing primordial about it. Although Baluran has been a game reserve since 1928, the countryside bears the scars of illegal timber-cutting, unsuccessful attempts at settlement, and military manoeuvres conducted in the 1970s. Since it was declared a park in 1980, however, the Parks Service has developed it into a haven for dry-country wildlife rare or absent elsewhere on Java.

To understand Baluran, look beneath your feet. The fine black soil is fertile enough, but

as it dries after the brief rains, it hardens, shrinks and cracks into hard, pebbly lumps, snapping young roots and trapping seeds that may have fallen into it. Only fast-growing grasses survive, and the northern part of the park is a vast treeless plain—an ideal habitat for deer, *banteng* cattle and feral buffalo.

Large game is the park's main attraction. At dawn and dusk, especially during the August to November dry season, you can spot the animals from the top of Bekol Hill making their way across the grassland from

ALAIN COMPOST

the shelter of surrounding trees to waterholes in the parched river beds.

The best way to see the park is to take a guide and venture out on the grassland yourself. The deer and *banteng* will keep their distance—bring binoculars and a long lens if you want photographs—but you may come upon a buffalo drowsing in its muddy wallow. Only the fortunate few catch a glimpse of the rare Javanese wild dog known as the *ajag*.

Tall *gebang* (*Corypha*) palms dot the grasslands. These reach 60 or more years of age before sprouting a spike of pale cream flowers up to 5 meters (16.5 ft) high, the world's largest known flower spike. Having flowered once, the tree dies, though the trunks stand like forgotten pillars for several more years.

Nearly 150 bird species have been recorded in Baluran. Look for the nests of weaver birds (*manyar*) in the thorn trees. Close to the forest margin you may see green peafowl, once exported to China and Europe for their feathers, and red-and-green jungle fowl—a racy cousin of the modern domestic chicken. Amongst the mangroves of the shoreline, metallic blue kingfishers dart in and out of the branches. If you are lucky, a family of crab-eating macaques may peer at you from the mangrove branches before resuming their own conversations.

While in Baluran, there are several interesting long walks you may take, including a fascinating circuit of the volcanic cone and a

KAL MULLER

walk southwards along the coast between mangroves and dry lowland forest to the little village of Pandean.

Unfortunately, the ecology of the park is now seriously threatened by the proliferation of a thorny African acacia. First noted in the late 1970s, the thornbush now covers large areas, forming impenetrable thickets which restrict the movement of both animals and visitors. Too firmly established now to be removed by cutting, the park authorities are hoping to eradicate the thornbushes by some form of biological control.

Simple accommodations for about a dozen visitors are available within the park, both at Bekol and on the coast at Bama. Bring food and a mosquito net. Alternatively, the comfortable Hotel Manyar, just south of the Bali ferry at Ketapang, is a convenient stopover point for both Baluran and Banyuwangi, though many visitors blink twice at the soft porn mural at its front entrance (the ancient Hindu hero Arjuna seducing a nymph), or so we are told.

By-roads from Bali

Banyuwangi is primarily a transit point between Java and Bali and need not detain you too long, although the town is rapidly gearing up for a tourism boom. This was the capital of Blambangan, the last Hindu kingdom on Java, but the kingdom was destroyed in the 18th century in a three-way tussle between Madurese pirates, Balinese rajas and VOC merchantmen. The town's fine mosque is worth a quick visit, as is the Chinese temple, Vihara Tan Tin Jin. The latter is dedicated to a Chinese architect of the Mengwi court on Bali who was commissioned to build the "floating" temple, Pura Taman Ayun. Legend has it that he completed the temple in a cloud

Opposite: *Sulphurous Kawah Ijen.* **Above, left:** *Picking coffee.* **Above, right:** *An old steam locomotive in a sugar plantation by the coast.*

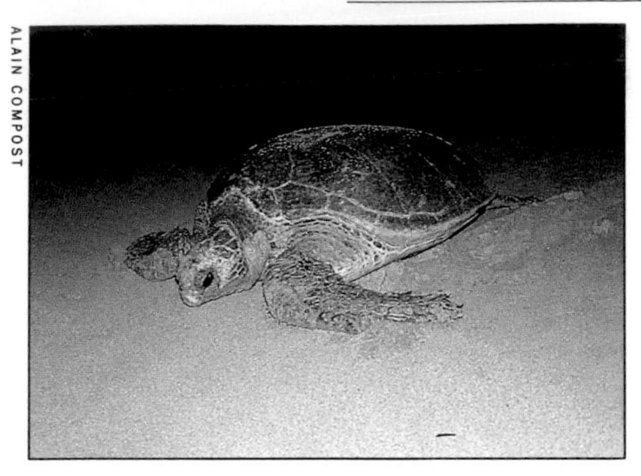

ALAIN COMPOST

burst of rain and lightening, but then had to flee for his life as the king feared his power.

In the hills above Banyuwangi, to the northwest, is **Kaliklatak**, a tranquil plantation producing coffee and cocoa. The plantation and its guesthouse are open to visitors.

Banyuwangi is a good base from which to visit two other nature reserves, South Banyuwangi and Meru Betiri, to the southeast and southwest. Both are reached by side roads off the main route through Genteng to Jember.

Heading for the South Banyuwangi Reserve, turn off at Beluki and stop at **Muncar**, famous for its festive fish auctions. Picturesque Madurese fishing *perahus* festooned in vibrant colors dock at its port, with pungent fish smells adding texture to the atmosphere.

South Banyuwangi Reserve

Alas Purwo ("Ancient Forest") as it is known locally, is Java's largest reserve—a peninsular appendage covering 43,420 ha (106,221 acres) that looks like a misshapen clubfoot. Here live peacocks, wild hen, wild boar, *banteng* and leopards among rare woods such as *ketapang*, *kepuh*, *asam*, *bogem*, *timongo* and *manggong* bamboo. The reserve is most renowned for its gigantic *sawo kecik* trees, which grow to a diameter of 1.5 m (4.5 ft).

Alas Purwo's game can be viewed throughout the year, as the land is dry. After obtaining a permit at the office beyond Tegaldlimo, head for Sadengan, 4 km (2.5 mi) away, and park. From here it's a pleasant walk along a marshy path to a watchtower from which grazing *banteng*, and the occasional deer and peacocks, can usually be seen.

From the Sadengan, drive to Trianggulasi, a 12-km (7-mi) white sand beach that stretches in a long crescent southward. From here it is a 5-km (3 mi) hike to Pancur, where stone pedestals are said to date from the 17th-century kingdom of the legendary Menak Jinggo. There are also meditational caves, Goa Putri and Goa Padepokan, which are still used today. At Plengkung, 7 km (4 mi) on, bamboo and thatch bungalows have been built for die-hard surfers in Grajagan Bay, reputed to have the world's best waves.

Meru Betiri Reserve

To get to Meru Betiri, take the main road west to Genteng, then turn south (left), squeezing your vehicle across a narrow bridge with concrete barricades designed to keep out anything bigger than a minibus. The road leads through pretty rice fields and past the occasional Hindu temple to Pasanggaran, where you must report to the PHPA office.

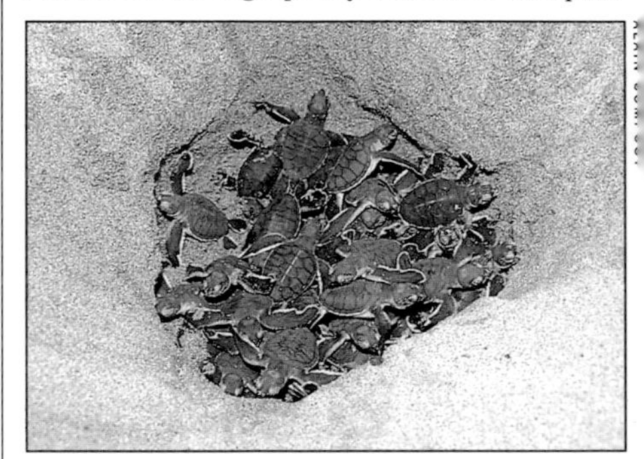

The time necessary to travel the final 35 km (21 mi) to **Sukamade**, in the heart of the park, will depend on your vehicle and the state of the road. It could take between one and three hours; in the wet season, however, you may not get past the first creek crossing. You will probably have to stop at frequent checkpoints along the road—these are part of the government's determined effort to stop poaching and illegal timber-cutting within reserves. Stop at the information center at Rajegwesi; from there the road winds over a long, steep hill before bringing you, bruised and relieved, to Sukamade.

Meru Betiri was declared a national park in 1982 to protect the last refuge of the Javan tiger. This magnificent animal once prowled lowland jungles everywhere in Java. Because it preyed on the wild pig which raided village gardens, it was valued as well as feared; some old men still claim to be *pawang* (familiars) of the tiger, able to call them at will.

Sadly, hunting and population pressures have now reduced the tiger community to a tiny, unsustainable number. The last investigation in 1988 discovered only a single animal, and its extinction is only a matter of time. Local people claim there are still many tigers in the hills around Sukamade, but the word they use for tiger (*macan*) is also used for leopards, which are still common.

Nonetheless, Meru Betiri is a naturalist's paradise. Magnificent hornbills nest in tall trees around the edges of the valley. The female, who incubates the eggs, is walled with mud into a hole in the trunk and kept alive by food brought by her mate, and by "aunts and uncles"—other hornbills without family responsibilities. Squirrels leap amongst the trees, and families of monkeys nod sagely to visitors who stroll past.

The low clouds which seem to hang constantly about the hills saturate Meru Betiri and sustain a rich plant life. Giant Rafflesia blooms are found in the hills, too far away unfortunately for a day trip.

An ideal jungle excursion is the full day's walk from beautiful Teluk Hijau (Green Bay) around the headland to Sukamade. The path leads past gloomy freshwater swamps, through untouched jungles festooned with lianas and across areas of secondary forest with tall bamboo and spiny rattans. The last part of the walk passes through the Sukamade estate, and you can refresh yourself here by sucking on the tart fruity beans of a freshly plucked cacao pod.

While at Meru Betiri, pay a visit to the turtle conservation station at Sukamade beach. The days when the station financed its operations by selling turtle eggs are fortunately long gone; the park now plays an important role in the conservation of one of Indonesia's few flourishing turtle beaches.

On most nights at least one turtle comes ashore at Sukamade. The giant carapace breaks the water at the sea's edge, and as the waves recede the mother-to-be begins her arduous climb to the top of the beach. Her flippers flail as she excavates a broad depression in the dry sand before delicately scooping a cylindrical egg chamber in the moist sand below. She may lay fifty to a hundred or more leathery white eggs the size of ping-pong balls before calling it a night, covering the hole and beating a retreat to the sea.

Conservation staff recover the eggs each morning and re-bury them in a fenced enclosure as a precaution against marauding civet cats, marking each new nest with a small cross, like a grave. Most beachings are by green turtles, also found in the Caribbean and eastern Australia, but occasionally an enormous leatherback makes an appearance, 300 kilos (660 lbs) of motherhood beneath a sharply ridged carapace.

The adventurous can go spotlighting at night in the jungle near Sukamade beach. Take a powerful flashlight and a guide. Giant owls, bush rats and squirrels are common, and you will see spiders' eyes, sharp pin-pricks of reflected light, under almost every leaf. This is your also best chance of seeing a leopard or the irascible Javan warty pig. Be careful; neither takes kindly to having its nocturnal activities disturbed.

In addition to the park itself, Sukamade also offers the chance to explore an old-style Javanese plantation. Cut-off by poor roads, the estate forms a self-contained community. Generations have lived out their entire lives here as employees of the estate.

Most visitors lodge in the simple but adequate quarters on the estate, where there is room for up to 30 people in 2-4 rooms. Meals are available, though what turns up on your plate each night will depend on how long it has been since the last supply truck arrived. Coffee, cacao, coconuts, cashews and rubber all grow here, and are processed in a simple factory at the jungle's edge. Ask the manager for a sample of *kopi luwak*, "civet cat coffee," a fragrant brew made only from beans that have passed through the alimentary tracts of wild civets. (Don't worry—the beans have been roasted before they reach you!)

— Robert Cribb and Amir Sidharta

ALAIN COMPOST

Opposite, left and right: *A green turtle lays its eggs in the sand at Meru Betiri, from which the young turtles later hatch.* **Right:** *Forested cliffs face out over the Indian Ocean at Meru Betiri.*

PASSPORT'S R

The idyllic "Island of the Gods" that has become a tourist mecca of near mythical proportions.
312 pages; 26 maps
ISBN 0-8442-9897-2
$17.95

Indonesia's most populous island, home of an ancient civilization, Java is today a microcosm of all that the archipelago has to offer.
400 pages; 40 maps
ISBN 0-8842-9947-2
$17.95

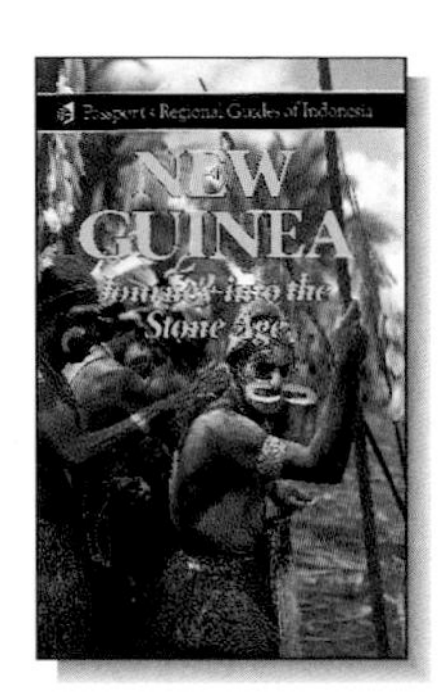

The ultimate travel adventure, remote stone-age tribes living in lush highland valleys on the world's second largest island.
208 pages; 17 maps
ISBN 0-8442-9898-0
$15.95

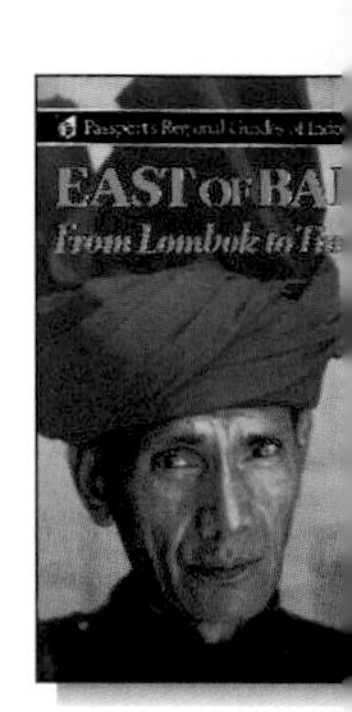

A diverse chain o islands stretching from Bali to Australia — inclu ing Lombok, Sumbawa, Komo Flores and Timor
312 pages; 26 m
ISBN 0-8442-994
$17.95

What the press says...

– *"If I could choose only one guidebook to take along, it would be [Passport] Java for its evocative color photographs, readable recounting of history and traditions, and up-to-the-minute travel information."*

– Travel and Leisure, USA.

Tropical beach resorts, colonial stations and bustling cities ec the era of the gr trading empires i the Malay penins and Singapore.
288 pages; 34 m
ISBN 0-8442-989
$17.95

·IONAL GUIDES

ıe fabled
'chipelago in
ıstern Indonesia
'hose cloves and
ıtmegs first lured
ıropeans to the
ıst.
›8 pages; 19 maps
BN 0-8442-9899-9
ı5.95

The most varied of Indonesia's major islands, this is the home of the sea-faring Bugis and the highland Toraja peoples.
288 pages; 26 maps
ISBN 0-8842-9906-5
$17.95

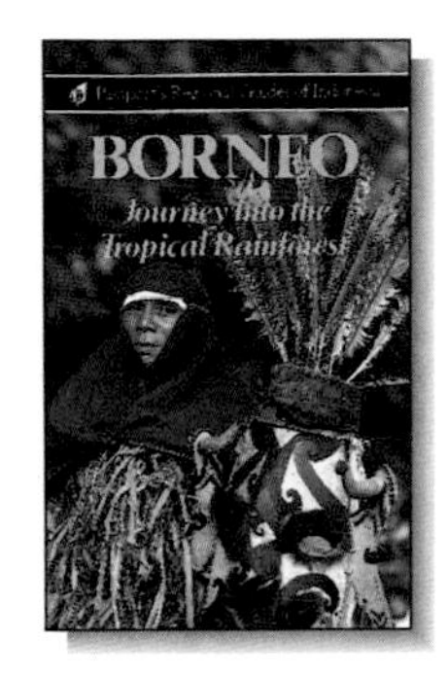

Dense rainforests, exotic wildlife and remote Dayak villages make for adventurous journeys up Borneo's mighty rivers.
224 pages; 20 maps
ISBN 0-8442-9904-9
$14.95

The world's fifth-largest island has been a crossroad on the trade routes between China and India for centuries.
344 pages; 32 maps
ISBN 0-8442-9907-3
$15.95

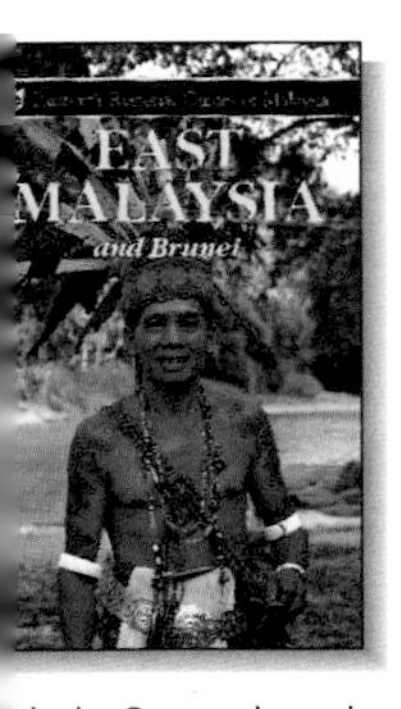

ıbah, Sarawak and
'unei form part of
ɔrneo. Rich
ıinforest wildlife,
ɔutheast Asia's
ghest mountain
ıd Dayak cultures
ı the world's third-
rgest island.
ɔ8 pages; 24 maps
BN 0-8442-9890-5
ı7.95

ORDERING PASSPORT GUIDES

NTC Publishing Group
4255 W. Touhy Avenue
Lincolnwood (Chicago)
Illinois 60646-1975

Order Toll-Free:
1-800-323-4900

Fax: 1-708-679-2494

RAVEL MAPS

DESTINATIONS

4-5 ISBN 0-945971-87-7 ISBN 0-945971-41-9 ISBN 0-945971-72-9 ISBN 962-593-031-0 ISBN 962-593-032-9

SIA

5-3 ISBN 0-945971-77-X ISBN 0-945971-76-1 ISBN 0-945971-98-2 ISBN 0-945971-78-8 ISBN 0-945971-79-6

THAILAND

6-X ISBN 0-945971-47-8 ISBN 0-945971-44-3 ISBN 0-945971-88-5 ISBN 0-945971-81-8 ISBN 0-945971-82-6

On The Road

KNOW BEFORE YOU GO, TRAVEL ADVISORY, PRACTICALITIES

The following On The Road sections contain all the practical knowledge you need for your journey. **Know Before You Go** provides all the non-transport information: facts about Indonesia, from the economy and health precautions to bathroom etiquette. It is followed by a handy language primer. **Travel Advisory** deals exclusively with transportation: getting to Indonesia and traveling in Java.

The **Practicalities** sections focus on each destination and have all the local details on transport, accommodation, dining, the arts, trekking, shopping and services, plus maps. These sections are split by area and correspond to Parts II to VIII in the first half of the guide. The easy-to-find margin tabs make cross-referencing simple and fast.

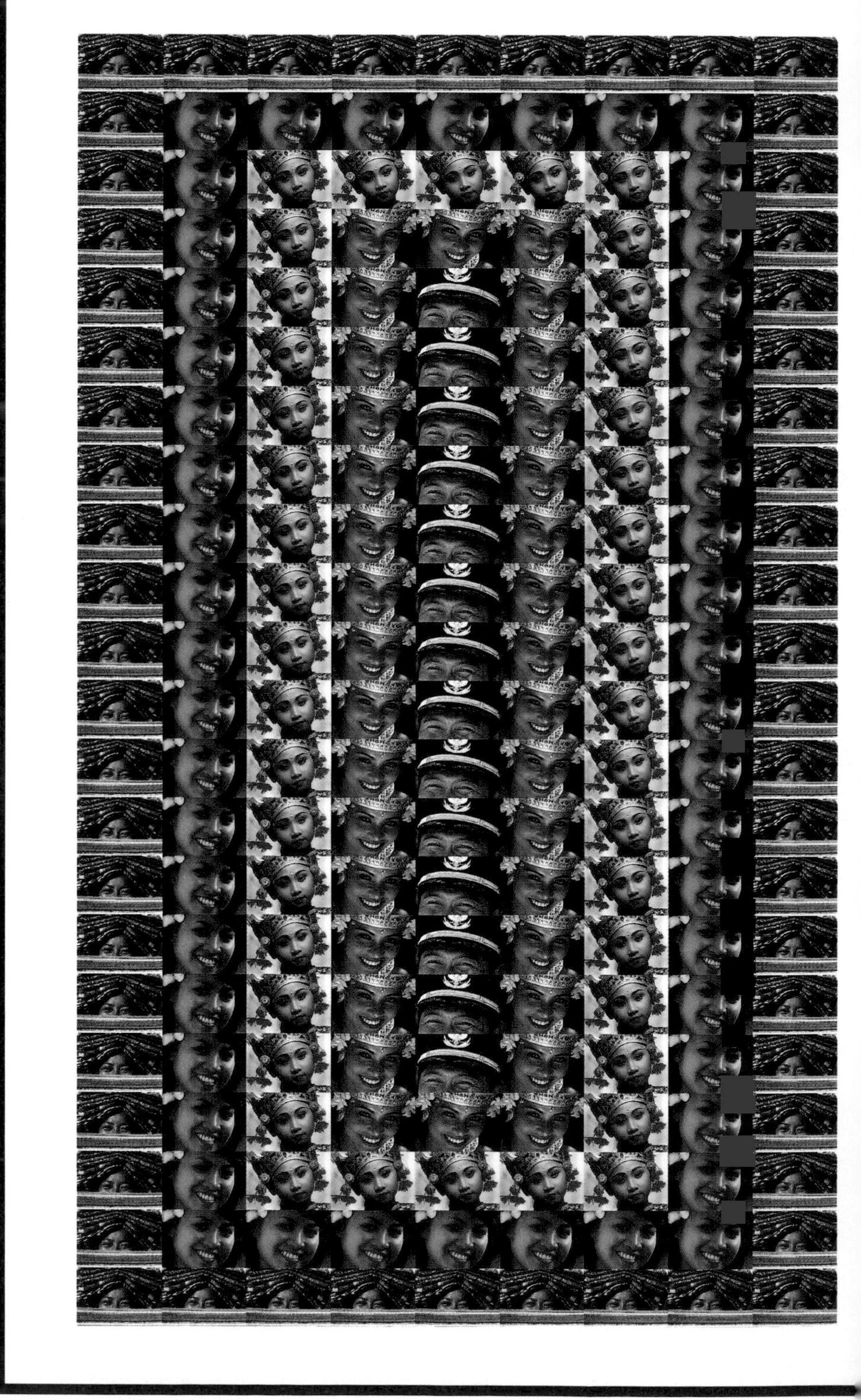

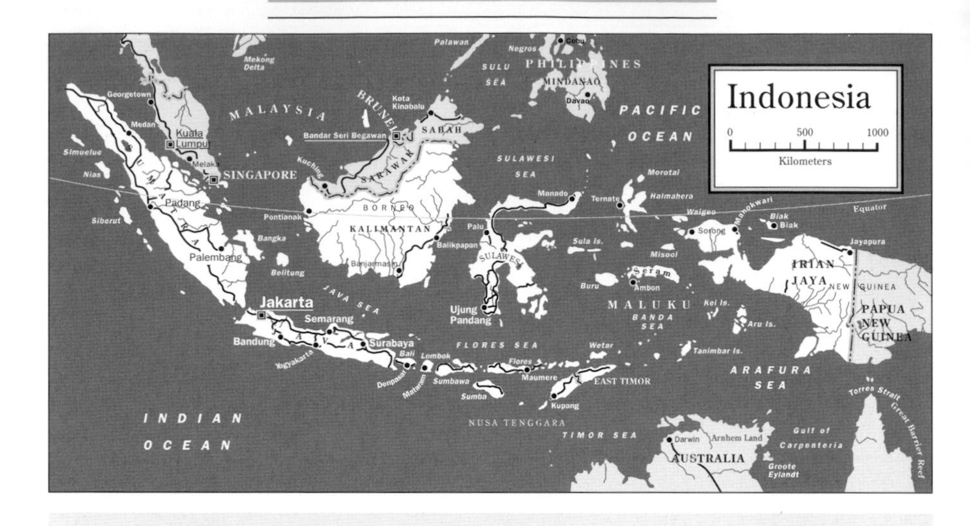

Indonesia At A Glance

The Republic of Indonesia is the world's fourth largest country, with 190 million people. The vast majority (88%) are Muslims, making this the world's largest Islamic country. More than 400 languages are spoken, but Bahasa Indonesia, a variant of Malay, is the national language.

The nation is a republic, headed by a strong President, with a 500-member legislature and a 1,500-member People's Consultative Assembly. There are 27 provinces and special territories. The capital is Jakarta, with 9 million people. The archipelago comprises just over 2 million square km of land. Of 18,508 islands, about 6,000 are named, and 1,000 permanently inhabited.

Indonesia's $120 billion gross national product (1993) comes from oil, textiles, lumber, mining, agriculture and manufacturing, and the country's largest trading partner is Japan. Per capita income is $605 (1993). Much of the population still makes a living through agriculture, chiefly rice. The unit of currency is the rupiah, which trades at approximately 2,150 to $1 (1994).

Historical overview. The Buddhist Sriwijaya empire, based in southeastern Sumatra, controlled parts of Western Indonesia from the 7th to the 13th centuries. The Hindu Majapahit kingdom, based in eastern Java, controlled even more from the 13th to the 16th centuries. Beginning in the mid-13th century, local rulers began converting to Islam.

In the early 17th century the Dutch East India Company (VOC) founded trading settlements and quickly wrested control of the Indies spice trade. The VOC was declared bankrupt in 1799, and a Dutch colonial government was established.

Anti-colonial uprisings began in the the early 20th century, when nationalism movements were founded by various Muslim, communist and student groups. Sukarno, a Dutch-educated nationalist, was jailed by the Dutch in 1930.

Early in 1942, the Dutch Indies were overrun by the Japanese army. Treatment by the occupiers was harsh. When Japan saw her fortunes waning toward the end of the war, Indonesian nationalists were encouraged to organize. On August 17, 1945, Sukarno proclaimed Indonesia's independence.

The Dutch sought a return to colonial rule after the war. Several years of fighting ensued between nationalists and the Dutch, and full independence was achieved in 1949.

During the 1950s and early 1960s, President Sukarno's government moved steadily to the left, alienating western governments and capital. In 1963, Indonesia took control of Irian Jaya, and began a period of confrontation with Malaysia.

On September 30, 1965 the army put down an attempted coup attributed to the communist PKI. Several hundred thousand people were killed as suspected communists.

In the following year, Sukarno drifted from power, and General Suharto became president in 1968. His administration has been friendly to western and Japanese investment, and the nation has enjoyed several decades of solid economic growth.

Know Before You Go

WHAT TO BRING ALONG

When packing, keep in mind that you will be in the tropics, but that it gets cold in the mountains. Generally, you will want to dress light and wear natural fibers that absorb perspiration. A heavy sweater is also a must, as are sturdy shoes.

Don't bring too much, as you'll be tempted by the great variety of inexpensive clothes available here. Most tourists find a Javanese batik cotton shirt more comfortable than what they brought along. If you visit a government office, men should wear long trousers, shoes and a shirt with collar. Women should wear a neat dress, covering knees and shoulders, and shoes.

For those wanting to travel light, a *sarong* bought on arrival in Indonesia ($5–10) is one of the most versatile items you could hope for. It serves as a wrap to get to the *mandi*, a beach towel, required dress for Balinese temples, pajamas, bed sheet, fast drying towel, etc.

Indonesians are renowned for their ability to sleep anytime, anywhere; so they are not likely to understand your desire for peace and quiet at night. Sponge rubber **earplugs**, available from pharmacies in the West, are great for aiding sleep on noisy journeys.

Tiny **padlocks** for use on luggage zippers are a handy deterrent to pilfering hands.

Also bring along some **pre-packaged alcohol towelettes** (swabs). These are handy for disinfecting your hands before eating, or after a trip to the *kamar kecil* (lavatory).

In most Indonesian department stores and supermarkets you can find western **toiletries**. **Contact lens** supplies for hard and soft lenses are available in major cities on Java, including Yogya and Solo. Gas permeable lens wearers should come well-stocked.

Dental floss and **tampons** are available in western style grocery stores like Gelael that are fast becoming common in Indonesian cities. **Sanitary napkins** are widely available. *Kondom* (**condoms**) are available at all *apotik* (pharmacies).

On your travels you will meet people who are kind and helpful, yet you may feel too embarrassed to give money. In this kind of situation a small gift (*oleh-oleh*) is appropriate. Fake designer watches from Singapore or Hong Kong selling for $5–$10 are a good idea (do tell them it's fake!). Chocolates, biscuits and pens or stationery from your hotel are also appreciated.

CLIMATE

The climate in this archipelago on the equator is tropical. In the lowlands, temperatures average between 21°C and 33°C, but in the mountains it can go as low as 5°C. Humidity varies but is always high, hovering between 60% and 100%.

The **rainy season** is normally November to April, with a peak around January/February, when it rains for several hours each day. The rain is predictable, however, and always stops for a time, when the sun may come out. Before it rains, the air gets very sticky. Afterwards it is refreshingly cool.

The **dry season**, April to September, is a better time to come, and especially June to August. This is the time to climb mountains or visit nature reserves; where wild bulls go in search of water and sea turtles lay eggs more often.

TIME ZONES

Indonesia has three time zones. Sumatra, Java, West and Central Kalimantan are on West Indonesia Time (Greenwich Mean Time +7 hours). Bali, South and East Kalimantan, Sulawesi and Nusa Tenggara are on Central Indonesia Time (GMT +8 hours). Maluku and Irian Jaya are on East Indonesia Time (GMT +9 hours).

MONEY AND BANKING

Prices quoted in this book are intended as a general indication. They are quoted in US dollars because the rupiah is being allowed to devalue slowly, so prices stated in US dollars are more likely to remain accurate.

Standard **currency** is the Indonesian rupiah: Notes come in 100, 500, 1,000, 5,000, 10,000, 20,000 and 50,000 denominations. Coins come in denominations of 500, 100, 50, 25, 10 and 5 rupiah. Unfortunately, the new coins are very similar in size, so look carefully.

Moneychangers and banks accepting foreign currency are found in most cities and towns. Banks are generally open 8:30 am to 1 pm, Monday to Friday and 8:30 to 11 am on Saturdays. Some banks however, open until 2 pm on weekdays and close on Saturdays. Gold shops usually bunch together in a specific area of town and change money at competitive rates during hours when banks are closed.

Moneychangers offer very similar rates and are open longer hours. The bank counters at major airports offer competitive rates. Bank lines in town can be long and slow; the best way around it is to arrive promptly at opening time.

Get a supply of Rp1,000 and Rp500 notes when you change money, as taxi drivers and vendors often claim to have no change for big bills. When traveling in the countryside, Rp100 notes are also useful.

Carrying **cash** (US$) can be a handy safety precaution as it is still exchangeable should you lose your passport, but it must be carefully stored and not crumpled: Indonesian banks only accept foreign currency that is crisp and clean.

Major **credit cards** are accepted in a wide variety of shops and hotels. But they often add a 3% surcharge for the privilege. Most cities have at least one bank at which cash advances can be made—look for Bank Duta, BCA and Danamon. Visa and MasterCard are the most frequently accepted foreign credit cards in Java.

There are no exchange controls and excess rupiahs can be freely reconverted at the airport on departure.

TAX, SERVICE AND TIPPING

Most larger hotels charge 21 percent tax and service on top of your bill. The same applies in big restaurants. Tipping is not a custom here, but it is of course appreciated for special services. Rp500 per bag is considered a good tip for roomboys and porters. Taxi drivers will want to round up to the nearest Rp500 or Rp1,000.

When tipping the driver of your rental car or a *pembantu* (housekeeper) of the house in which you've been a guest, fold the money and give it with the right hand only.

OFFICE HOURS

Government offices are officially open 8 am to 3 pm, but if you want to get anything done, be there by 11 am. On Fridays they close at 11:30 am and on Saturdays at 2 pm. In large cities most offices are open 9 am to 5 pm, and shops from 9 am to 9 pm. In smaller towns, including Yogya and Solo, shops close for a siesta at 1 pm and re-open at 6 pm.

MAIL

Indonesia's postal service is reliable, if not terribly fast. Post Offices (*kantor pos*) are usually busy and it is tedious lining up at one window for weighing, another window for stamps, etc. Hotels normally sell stamps and can post letters for you, or you can use private postal agents (*warpostel*) to avoid hassles.

Kilat express service is only slightly more expensive and much faster than normal mail. International *kilat* service gets postcards and letters to North America or Europe in 7 to 14 days from most cities. *Kilat khusus* (domestic special delivery) will get there overnight.

TELEPHONE AND FAX

Long distance phone calls, both within Indonesia and international, are handled by satellite. Domestic long distance calls can be dialed from most phones. To dial your own international calls, find an IDD phone, otherwise you must go via the operator which is far more expensive.

Smaller hotels often don't allow you to make long distance calls, so you have to go to the main telephone office (*kantor telepon*) or use a private postal and telephone service (*warpostel*). It can be difficult to get through during peak hours but the service in Indonesia now is quite good.

International calls via MCI, Sprint, ATT, and the like can be made from IDD phones using the code for your calling card company. Recently, special telephones have been installed in airports with pre-programmed buttons to connect you via these companies to various countries.

Faxes have become common, and can also be sent (or received) at *warpostel* offices.

ELECTRICITY

Most of Java has converted to 220 volts and 50 cycles, though a few places are still on the old 110 lines. Ask before you plug in if uncertain. Power failures are common in smaller cities and towns. Voltage can fluctuate considerably so use a stabilizer for computers and similar equipment. Plugs are of the European two-pronged variety.

TOURIST INFORMATION

The **Directorate General of Tourism** in Jakarta has brochures and maps on all Indonesian provinces: Jl Kramat Raya 81, Jakarta 10450. ☎ (021) 3103117; fax: (021) 3101146.

Local government tourism offices, Dinas Pariwisata, are generally only good for basic information. More useful assistance is often available from privately run (but government approved) Tourist Information Services. Be aware that many offices calling themselves "Tourist Information" are simply travel agents.

Overseas, you can contact the Indonesian embassy or consulate, or one of the following Indonesia Tourist Promotion Board offices:

Australia Garuda Indonesia Office, Level 4, 4 Bligh Street, Sydney, NSW 2000. ☎ (61) 2 232-6044; fax: (61) 2 233-2828.

UK, Ireland, Benelux and Scandinavia Indonesia Tourist Office, 3-4 Hanover Street, London W1R 9HH, UK. ☎ (44) 71 4930030; fax (44) 71 4931747.

The rest of Europe Indonesia Tourist Office,

Wiesenhuttenstrasse 17, D-6000 Frankfurt/Main, Germany. ☎ (069) 233-677; fax: (069) 230-840.

North America 3457 Wilshire Boulevard, Los Angeles, CA 90010-2203. ☎ (213) 387-2078; fax: (213) 380-4876.

Southeast Asia 10 Collyer Quay #15–07, Ocean Building, Singapore 0104. ☎ (65) 534-2837, 534-1795; fax: (65) 533-4287.

ETIQUETTE

The people of Java, and especially the Central Javanese, consider themselves the most refined, polite and cultivated of people. In the areas frequented by Europeans, many are familiar with the strange ways of Westerners but it is best to be aware of how certain aspects of your behavior will be viewed.

You will not be able to count on them to set you straight when you commit a *faux pas*. They are much more likely to stay silent or even reply *tidak apa apa* (no problem) if you ask if you did something wrong. So here are some points to keep in mind:

☛ The left hand is considered unclean as it is used for cleaning oneself in the bathroom. It is inappropriate in Java to use the left hand to pass food into your mouth, or to give or receive anything with it. When you do accidentally use your left hand it is appropriate to say *"ma'af, tangan kiri"* (please excuse my left hand).

☛ Don't cross your legs exposing the bottom of your foot to anyone.

☛ Don't pat people on the back or head. Go for the elbow instead.

☛ Pointing with the index finger is impolite. You will see the Javanese using their thumbs instead.

☛ If you are having a cigarette, offer one to all the men around you.

☛ Alcohol is frowned upon in Islam, so take a look around you and consider taking it easy.

☛ Hands on hips is a sign of superiority or anger.

☛ It is appropriate to drop your right hand and shoulder when passing closely in front of others.

☛ Blowing your nose in public is likely to gross everyone out within hearing distance.

☛ Take off your shoes when you enter someone's house. Often the host will stop you, but you should go through the motions until he does.

☛ Don't drink or eat until invited to, even after food and drinks have been placed in front of you. Sip your drink and don't finish it completely. Never take the last morsels from a common plate.

☛ You will often be invited to eat with the words *makan, makan* ("eat, eat") if you pass somebody who is eating. This is not really an invitation, but simply means "Excuse me as I eat."

☛ If someone prepares a meal or drink for you it is most impolite to refuse.

Some things from the West filter through to Indonesia more effectively than others and stories of "*free sek*" (free sex) made a deep and lasting impression in Indonesia. Expect this topic to appear in lists of questions you will be asked in your cultural exchanges. It is best to explain how things have changed since the 1960s and how we now are stuck with "*saf sek.*"

Also remember that Java is predominantly Muslim and it is startling for the Javanese to see women dress immodestly. Exposed backs, thighs and shoulders can cause quite a stir.

SECURITY

Java is a relatively safe place to travel and violent crime is almost unheard of, but pay close attention to your belongings, especially in big cities. Be sure that the door and windows of your hotel room are locked at night.

Use a small backpack or moneybelt for valuables: shoulderbags can be snatched. Bags have been snatched from the laps of tourists riding in *becak* in Yogyakarta, by thieves on motorbikes, so be vigilant.

Big hotels have **safety boxes** for valuables. If your hotel does not have such a facility, it is better to carry all the documents along with you. Make sure you have a photocopy of your passport, return plane ticket and travelers' check numbers and keep them separate from the originals.

Be especially wary on crowded buses and trains; this is where **pickpockets** lurk and they are very clever at slitting bags and extracting valuables without your noticing anything.

HEALTH

Before You Go

Check with your physician for the latest news on the need for malaria prophylaxis and recommended **vaccinations** before leaving home. Frequently considered vaccines are: Diptheria, Pertusis and Tetanus (DPT); Measles, Mumps and Rubella (MMR); and oral Polio vaccine. Gamma Globulin every four months for Hepatitis A is recommended. For longer stays many doctors recommend vaccination to protect against Hepatitis B requiring a series of shots over the course of 7 months. Vaccinations for smallpox and cholera are no longer required, except for visitors coming from infected areas. A cholera vaccination may be recommended but it is only 50% effective. Though **malaria** is almost non-existent on Java (Ujung Kulon National Park is the major exception), you may want to take along prophylactic medications anyway.

Find out the generic names for whatever prescription medications you are likely to need as most are available in Indonesia but not under the same brand names as they are known at home. Get copies of doctors' prescriptions for the medications you bring into Indonesia to avoid questions at the customs desk. Those who wear spectacles should bring along prescriptions.

Check your health insurance before coming, to make sure you are covered. Travel agents should be able to direct you to sources of travel insurance. These typically include coverage of a medical evacuation, if necessary, and a 24-hour worldwide phone number as well as some extras like luggage loss and trip cancellation.

Hygiene

This is a problem in Java. Very few places have running water or sewerage. Most water comes from wells, and raw sewerage goes right into the ground or into the rivers. Even treated tap water in the big cities is not potable and must be boiled.

Most cases of stomach complaints are attributable to your system not being used to the strange foods and stray bacteria. To make sure you do not get something more serious, take the following precautions:

☛ Don't drink unboiled water from a well, tap or *mandi* (bath tub). Brush your teeth with boiled or bottled water, not water from a tap or *mandi*.

☛ Plates, glasses and silverware are washed in unboiled water and need to be completely dry before use.

☛ Ice is not made from boiled water. It comes from water frozen in government regulated factories. Locals who are adamant about drinking only boiled water are, in general, not fearful of the purity of ice. However we advise you err on the side of caution and forgo it.

☛ Fruits and vegetables without skins pose a higher risk of contamination. To avoid contamination by food handlers, buy fruits in the market and peel them yourself.

☛ To *mandi* (bathe) two to three times a day is a great way to stay cool and fresh. But be sure to dry yourself off well and you may wish to apply a medicated body powder such as Purol to avoid the nastiness of skin fungus, especially during the rainy season from October to March.

Diarrhea

A likely traveling companion. In addition to the strange food and unfamiliar micro-fauna, diarrhea is often the result of attempting to accomplish too much in one day. Taking it easy can be an effective prevention. Ask around before leaving about what the latest and greatest of the many remedies are and bring some along. Imodium is locally available as are activated carbon tablets that will absorb the toxins giving you grief.

When it hits, it is usually self-limiting to two or three days. Relax, take it easy and drink lots of fluids, perhaps accompanied by rehydration salts such as Servidrat. Especially helpful is young coconut milk (*air kelapa mudah*) or tea. The former is especially pure and full of nutrients to keep up your strength until you can get back to a regular diet. Get it straight from the coconut without sugar, ice and color added. When you are ready, plain rice or *bubur* (rice porridge) is a good way to start. Avoid fried, spicy or heavy foods and dairy products for a while. After three days without relief, see a doctor.

Intestinal Parasites

It is estimated that 80 to 90 percent of all people on Java have intestinal parasites and these are easily passed on by food handlers. Prevention is difficult, short of fasting, when away from luxury hotel restaurants and even these are no guarantee. It's best to take care of parasites sooner rather than later, by routinely taking a dose of anti-parasite medicine such as Kombatrin (available at all *apotik*) once a month during your stay and again when you get on the plane home.

If you still have problems when you get back, even if only sporadic, have stool and blood tests. Left untreated, parasites can cause serious damage.

Cuts and Scrapes

Your skin will come into contact with more dirt and bacteria than it did back home, so wash your face and hands more often. Untreated bites or cuts can fester very quickly in the tropics, and staph infection is common. Cuts should be taken seriously and cleaned with an antiseptic such as Betadine solution available from any pharmacy (*apotik*). Once clean, antibiotic ointment (also available locally) should be applied and the cut kept covered. Repeat this ritual often. Areas of redness around the cut indicate infection and a doctor should be consulted. At the first sign of swelling it is advisable to take broad spectrum antibiotics to prevent a really nasty infection.

Mosquito-borne Diseases

Malaria is very rare in Java (Ujung Kulon National Park is an exception) and prophylactic medications have not been required in recent years, but check with your doctor before coming. Symptoms are fever, cough, muscle aches and diarrhea.

The other mosquito concern is **dengue fever**, spread by the afternoon-biting *Aedes aegypti*, especially at the beginning of the rainy season in November. The most effective prevention is not getting bitten (there is no prophylaxis for dengue). Dengue fever symptoms are headache, pain behind the eyes, high fever, muscle and joint pains and rash.

Portable nets (*kelambu*) provide protection at night when sleeping; you can buy these in most general stores for $5. They're a hassle to put up in hotel rooms but, upon request, your room will be sprayed for insects. Be sure this is done long before you are ready to sleep if you want to avoid the smell. You can also buy mosquito coils: light one before you go out for dinner to drive the critters away. Insect repellent is not widely available, but supermarkets do sell OFF!

AIDS & Hepatitis B

Surprise! **Safe sex** is also a good idea in Indonesia. AIDS is just beginning to surface with a number of documented HIV positive cases recently. Another consideration is Hepatitis B virus which affects liver function, and is only sometimes curable and can be deadly. The prevalence of Hepatitis B in Indonesia is the basis for international concern over the ominous possibilities for the spread of HIV virus, which is passed on in the same ways.

Medical Treatment

The Indonesian name for pharmacy is *apotik*; and a hospital is called *rumah sakit*. In smaller villages they only have government clinics, called *Puskesmas*, which are not equipped to deal with anything serious.

Fancier hotels often have doctors on call or can recommend one. Misuse of antibiotics is still a concern in Indonesia. They should only be used for bacterial diseases and then for at least 10 to 14 days to prevent developing antibiotic resistant strains of your affliction. Indonesians don't feel they've had their money's worth from a doctor ($5) without getting an injection or antibiotics. Be sure it's necessary. Ensure syringes have never been used before.

Even in the big cities outside of Jakarta, emergency care leaves much to be desired. Your best bet in the event of a life-threatening emergency or accident is to get on the first plane to Jakarta or Singapore. Contact your embassy or consulate by phone for assistance (see below). Medevac airlifts are very expensive ($26,000) and most embassies will recommend that you buy insurance to cover the cost of this when traveling extensively in Indonesia.

ACCOMMODATION

Indonesia has an extraordinary range of accommodation, much of it good value for money. Most cities have a number of hotels offering air-conditioned rooms with TV, minibar, hot water, swimming pool and the like costing $100 a night and up. While at the other end of the scale, you can stay in a $2-a-night *losmen* room with communal squat toilet (buy your own toilet paper), a tub of water with ladle for a bath, and a bunk with no towel or clean linen (bring your own). And there's just about everything in between: from decrepit colonial hill stations to luxurious new thatched-roof huts in the rice fields.

A whole hierarchy of lodgings and official terminology have been established by government decree. Theoretically, a "hotel" is an up-market establishment catering for businessmen, middle to upper class travelers and tourists. A star-rating (one to five stars) is applied according to the range of facilities. Smaller places with no stars and basic facilities are not referred to as hotels but as "*losmen*" (from the French "*logement*"), "*wisma*" ("guesthouse") or "*penginapan*" ("accommodation") and cater for the masses or for budget tourists.

Prices and quality vary enormously. In the major cities that don't have many tourists, such as Jakarta, Surabaya and Medan, there is little choice in the middle ranges and you have to either pay a lot or settle for a room in a *losmen*.

In areas where there are a lot of tourists, such as Bali and Yogya, you can get very comfortable and clean rooms with fan or air-conditioning for less than $20 a night. In small towns and remote areas, you don't have much choice and all accommodation tends to be very basic.

It's common to ask to see the room before checking in. Shop around before deciding, particularly if the hotel offers different rooms at different rates. Avoid carpeted rooms, especially without air-conditioning, as usually they are damp and this makes the room smell.

Advance bookings are necessary during peak tourist seasons (July to August and around Christmas and New Year). Popular resorts near big cities (like Puncak or Tretes) are always packed on weekends, and prices often double, so go during the week when it's cheaper and quieter.

In many hotels, discounts of 10–30% from published rates are to be had for the asking, particularly if you have a business card. Booking in advance through travel agencies can also result in a much lower rate. Larger hotels always add 21% tax and service to the bill.

Bathroom Etiquette

When staying in *losmen*, particularly when using communal facilities, don't climb in or drop your soap into the tub of water (*bak mandi*). This is for storing clean water. Scoop water over yourself with the ladle in your right hand and clean with your left.

If you wish to use the native paper-free cleaning method, after using the toilet, scoop water with your right hand and clean with the left.

This is the reason one only eats with the right hand—the left is regarded as unclean, for obvious reasons. Use soap and a fingernail brush (locals use a rock) for cleaning hands. Pre-packaged alcohol towelettes from home may make you feel happier about opting for this method.

Bring along your own towel and soap (although some places provide these if you ask).

Staying in Villages

Officially, the Indonesian government requires that foreign visitors spending the night report

11 *seblas*
12 *dua belas*
13 *tiga belas*
20 *dua puluh*
50 *lima puluh*
73 *tujuh puluh tiga*
100 *seratus*
600 *enam ratus*
1,000 *seribu*
3,000 *tiga ribu*
10,000 *sepuluh ribu*
1,000,000 *satu juta*
2,000,000 *dua juta*
half *setengah*
first *pertama*
second *kedua*
third *ketiga*
fourth *ke'empat*

Time

minute *menit*
hour *jam*
(also clock/watch)
day *hari*
week *minggu*
month *bulan*
year *tahun*
today *hari ini*
tomorrow *besok*
Sunday *Hari Minggu*
Monday *Hari Senin*
Tuesday *Hari Selasa*
Wednesday *Hari Rabu*
Thursday *Hari Kamis*
Friday *Hari Jum'at*
Saturday *Hari Sabtu*
later *nanti*
yesterday *kemarin*
What time is it? *Jam berapa?*
(It is) eight thirty. *Jam setengah sembilan*
(Literally: "half nine")
How many hours? *Berapa jam?*
When did you arrive? *Kapan datang?*
Four days ago. *Empat hari yang lalu.*
When are you leaving?
Kapan berangkat?
In a short while. *Sebentar lagi.*

Basic vocabulary

to be, have *ada*
to be able, can *bisa*
to buy *beli*
to know *tahu*
to get *dapat*
to need *perlu*
to want *mau*
to go *pergi*
to wait *tunggu*
at *di*
to *ke*
if *kalau*
near *dekat*
far *jauh*
empty *kosong*
correct *betul*
wrong *salah*
big *besar*
small *kecil*
pretty *cantik*
slow *pelan*
fast *cepat*
stop *berhenti*
old *tua, lama*
new *baru*
then *lalu, kemudian*
only *hanya, saja*
crowded, noisy *ramai*

Small talk

Where are you from? *Dari mana?*
I'm from the US. *Saya dari Amerika.*
How old are you? *Umurnya berapa?*
I'm 31 years old.
Umur saya tiga pulu satu tahun.
Are you married? *Sudah kawin belum?*
Yes, I am. *Yah, sudah.* Not yet. *Belum.*
Do you have children? *Sudah punya anak?*
What is your religion? *Agama apa?*
Where are you going? *Mau ke mana?*
I'm just taking a walk. *Jalan-jalan saja.*
Please come in. *Silahkan masuk.*
This food is delicious.
Makanan ini enak sekali.
You are very hospitable.
Anda sangat ramah tamah.

Hotels

Where's a losmen? *Di mana ada losmen?*
cheap losmen *losmen yang murah*
average losmen *losmen biasa*
very good hotel *hotel cukup baik*
Please take me to... *Tolong antar saya ke...*
Are there any empty rooms?
Ada kamar kosong?
Sorry there aren't any. *Ma'af, tidak ada.*
How much for one night?
Berapa untuk satu malam?
One room for two of us.
Dua orang, satu kamar.
I'd like to stay for 3 days.
Saya mau tinggal tiga hari.
hot water *air panas*
Here's the key to your room.
Ini kunci kamar.
Please call a taxi. *Tolong panggil taksi.*
Please wash these clothes.
Tolong cucikan pakaian ini.

Restaurants

Where's a good restaurant?
Di mana ada rumah makan yang baik?
Let's have lunch. *Mari kita makan siang.*
I want Indonesian food.
Saya mau makanan Indonesia.
I want coffee, not tea.
Saya mau kopi, bukan teh.
May I see the menu?
Boleh saya lihat daftar makanan?
I want to wash my hands.
Saya mau cuci tangan.
Where is the toilet? *Di mana kamar kecil?*
fish, squid, goat, beef
ikan, cumi, kambing, sapi
salty, sour, sweet, spicy
asin, asam, manis, pedas

Shopping

I don't understand. *Saya tidak mengerti.*
I can't speak Indonesian.
Saya tidak bisa bicara Bahasa Indonesia.
Please, speak slowly.
Tolong, berbicara lebih pelan.
I want to buy... *Saya mau beli...*
Where can I buy... *Di mana saya bisa beli...*
How much does this cost? *Berapa harga ini?*
2,500 Rupiah. *Dua ribu, lima ratus rupiah.*
That cannot be true! *Masa!*
That's still a bit expensive. *Masih agak mahal.*

Directions

north *utara*
south *selatan*
right *kanan*
near *dekat*
inside *di dalam*
west *barat*
east *timur*
left *kiri*
far *jauh*
outside *di luar*
I am looking for this address.
Saya cari alamat ini.
How far is it? *Berapa jauh dari sini?*

Travel Advisory

This advisory gives you an overview of the wide range of travel options available during your stay in Java. A comprehensive run-down of travel services enables you to plan your way around the island according to time and budget. More specific details for each area you will be visiting can be found in the relevant Practicalities sections.

Prices are in US dollars, unless otherwise stated. Prices and schedules are given as an indication only as they change frequently according to the season. Check with a travel agent prior to departure for the most up-to-date information.

In many ways, Indonesia is an easy place to get around. Indonesians are as a rule hospitable and good humored, and will always help a lost or confused traveler. The weather is warm, the pace of life relaxed, and the air is rich with the smells of clove cigarettes, the blessed durian fruit and countless other wonders.

On the other hand, the nation's transportation infrastructure does not move with the kind of speed and efficiency that western travelers expect, which often leads to frustration. It is best to adjust your pace to local conditions. There is nothing more pathetic than a tourist who has traveled half way around the world just to shout at some poor clerk at the airport counter.

The golden rule is: things will sort themselves out. Eventually. Be persistent, of course, but relax and keep your sense of humor. Before you explode, have a cup of sweet Java coffee, or a cool glass of *kelapa muda* (young coconut water). Things might look different.

GETTING TO INDONESIA

You can fly to Indonesia from just about anywhere. Most people traveling from Europe and the US arrive on direct flights to Jakarta, while those coming from Australia generally first go to Bali. The main international entry points are Sukarno-Hatta airport in Jakarta, Ngurah Rai airport in Bali, and Polonia airport in Medan, North Sumatra. There are now also flights between Singapore and Surabaya, in East Java, on Singapore Airlines (direct) and Garuda (via Jakarta).

Sukarno-Hatta airport is served by many international airlines, with over a dozen flights a day from Singapore alone. A cut-price alternative from Europe or the US may be to get a cheap flight to Singapore, and buy an onward discount ticket to Jakarta from there: the cost of these can be as low as $75 single, $150 return. A return ticket from Singapore to Bali with stops in Jakarta and Yogyakarta, good for a month, is available in Singapore for around $400. Buy through travel agents—check the *Straits Times* for details. Note: you need return or onward ticket to get a tourist visa on arrival.

Direct flights also connect Jakarta with many major cities in Asia and Europe. Air fares vary depending on the carrier, the season and the type of ticket purchased. A discount RT fare from the US or Europe costs from $850: about half that from Australia or East Asian capitals.

Air tickets from **Batam** and **Bintan** are less expensive, and these Indonesian islands just off the coast of Singapore can be reached via short ferry hops from Singapore's World Trade Centre. Tickets to Batam cost $12 single, $17 return, and to Bintan $32 single, $45 return.

Three daily jet flights from Batam to Jakarta via Merpati/Garuda and Sempati: $160. Two daily flights from Tanjung Pinang in Bintan to Jakarta via Merpati, Garuda and Sempati: $155. **Merpati** office in Batam ☎ (0778) 458864/458620. **Sempati** in Batam ☎ (0778) 455075/8. **Sempati** in Tanjung Pinang, Bintan ☎ (0771) 23780.

Airport tax for departing passengers is Rp17,000 for international routes and between Rp1,500 and Rp6,000 for domestic flights.

Having arrived in Indonesia, your choices for onward travel depend, as always, on time and money. Possibilities on Java range from boats, trains, hire cars, and chauffeur driven, to both slow and fast buses. Hiring a car or minibus with or without driver, is one of the most rewarding ways of getting around, if you can afford it.

Visas

Nationals of the following 36 countries do not need visas, and are granted visa-free entry for 60 days upon arrival (this is non-renewable). For other nationals, visas are required and must be obtained in advance from an Indonesian embassy or consulate.

Argentina	Iceland	Norway
Australia	Ireland	Philippines
Austria	Italy	Singapore
Belgium	Japan	South Korea

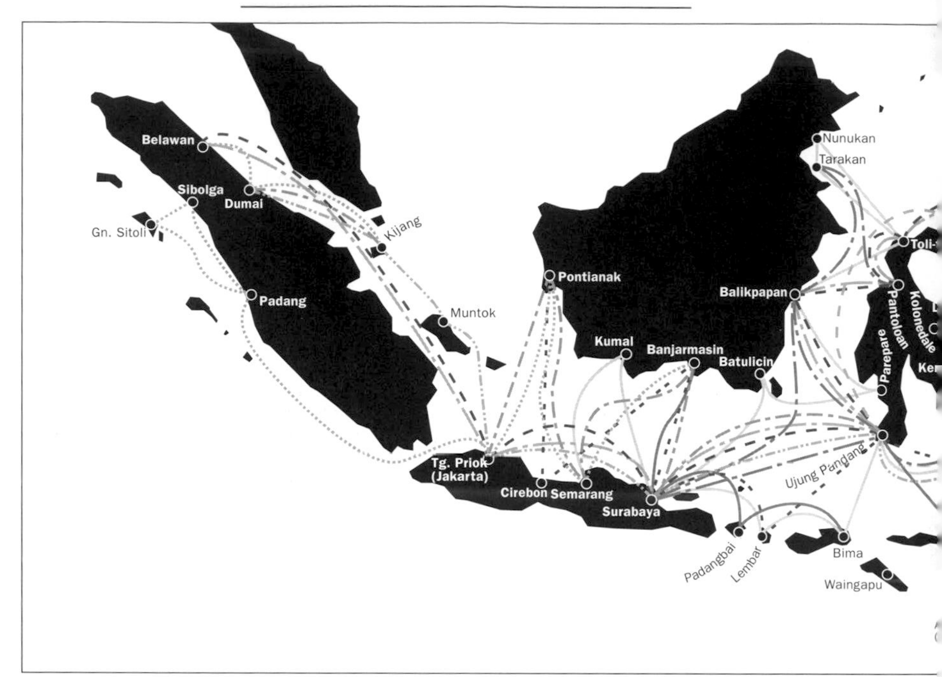

to Bali, if there is no space left on the flights, take a bus to Surakarta (Solo) and fly from there.

Garuda. Indonesia's flagship airline has been in business for 45 years. It serves all major cities in Indonesia and at least 28 international destinations. They fly only jets, mainly wide-bodies, and the service is reasonably good. Head office is at Jl Merdeka Selatan 13 ☎ (021) 2311801; fax: (021) 365986 with convenient sales counters in Hotel Indonesia, Hotel Borobudur and BDN Bldg., Jl Thamrin 5. After normal office hours, tickets can be purchased in a small Garuda office on the 3rd floor of Wisma Dharmala Sakti, Jl Sudirman 32 (open 24 hours).

Merpati. A Garuda subsidiary, with a huge network of domestic flights serving more than 160 airports throughout Indonesia. Merpati (literally "pigeon") flies smaller jets (DC-9s and F-28s) as well as turbo-props (F-27s, Twin-Otters and locally-made CN 212s and 235s).

Merpati is not known for its punctuality or its service, but the airline does at least connect towns and villages all across Indonesia, in some cases landing on grass airstrip in a highland village of only 100 people that would take days to reach by any other means. Consider yourself lucky that you can even fly to these places.

Merpati's standard baggage allowance is 20 kilos for economy class, but some of the smaller aircraft permit only 10 kilos (after which excess baggage charges of $1 per kilo apply).

Students (10–26 years old) receive a discount of 25% (show an international student ID card), and children between the ages of 2 and 10 pay 50% of the regular fare. Infants not occupying a seat pay 10% of the regular fare.

Main office: Jl Angkasa 2, Jakarta. ☎ (021) 4243608; fax: (021) 4246616.

Sempati. A new, privately-owned competitor on the scene, with quality service and a growing network inside and outside of Indonesia. Sempati flies new F-100s to several cities in Asia, such as Singapore, Kuala Lumpur, Bangkok, Hong Kong and Taipei. Domestically they fly between major cities such as Jakarta, Yogya, Surabaya and Denpasar. Head office: Ground floor terminal building, Halim Perdana Kusuma Airport, Jakarta.☎ (021) 8094407; fax: (021) 8094420.

Bouraq. A small, private company, flying mainly older planes linking secondary cities in Java, as well as Bali, Kalimantan, Nusa Tenggara, Sulawesi, and other destinations. Main office: Jl Angkasa 1–3, Jakarta. ☎ (021) 6595364; fax: 6008729.

Mandala. Operates a few prop planes to out-of-the-way airstrips in Kalimantan, Sumatra and Sulawesi. Main office: Jl Garuda 76, Jakarta. ☎ (021) 4249360; fax: 4249491.

NOTE: Travel agents often give cheaper fares than airline offices and are easily found. The best for ticketing are **Pacto** Jl Surabaya 8, Menteng, Jakarta ☎ 3487447 and **Vayatour** Chase Plaza, Jl Sudirman, Jakarta ☎ 5704119.

Sea Travel

There is four times as much sea in Indonesia as land, and for many centuries transportation among the islands has been principally by boat. Tiny ports are scattered all over the archipelago, and the only way to reach many areas is by sea.

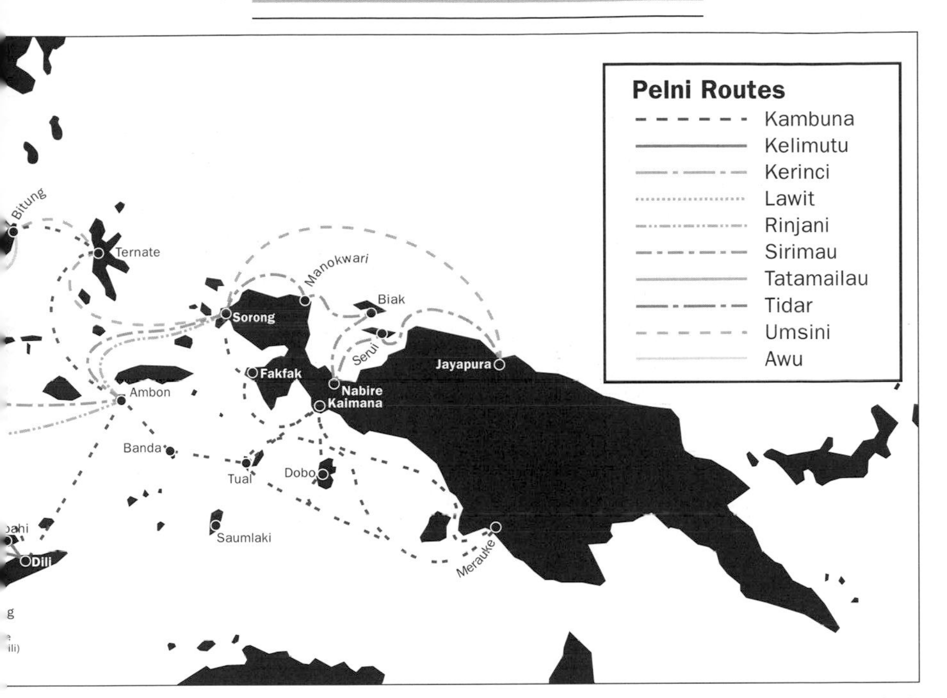

To travel by boat, you need plenty of time. Most ships are small, and are at the mercy of the sea and the seasons. Think of it as a romantic journey, and don't be in a hurry.

Pelni, the national passenger line, has 10 large ships criss-crossing the archipelago carrying up to 1,500 passengers each. These boats travel on fixed schedules and the first and second class cabins are comfortable.

There are a myriad of other options. Rusty old coastal steamers ply the eastern islands, stopping at tiny ports to pick up copra, seaweed and other cash crops and deliver commodities like metal wares, fuel and the occasional outboard motor. You can book deck passage on one of these ships in just about any harbor, for very little money. If you do, stock up on food—you will quickly tire of the rice and salt fish that the crew eat. Bring a waterproof tarpaulin and a bag to protect your gear. You can often rent bunks from the crew, to get a comfortable night's sleep.

Crowded overnight ferries connect smaller islands. Use your luggage to stake out a spot early, and bring a straw mat to lie on. It is usually best to stay on deck, where the fresh sea breezes keep your spirits up. Below deck tends to be noisy, verminous and smelly.

Small *perahu* can be rented in many areas for day trips upriver, around the coast, or to neighboring islands. These can be hired by the hour or by the trip, to take you snorkeling, sightseeing or birdwatching. Outboard motors are expensive in Indonesia, and tend to be small. Inspect any boat carefully before hiring it, as some craft are only marginally seaworthy. See if the boatman can rig up a canopy to block the blazing sun or the occasional cloudburst.

Pelni. Pelayaran Nasional Indonesia is the national shipping line, and their 70 ships go just about everywhere. Many of the older vessels look like floating trash cans, but the new German-built passenger ships are modern and comfortable. (See route map above for destinations served.)

Fares are fixed, and there are up to 5 classes, determining how many people share a cabin.

Head office: 5th floor, Jl Gajah Mada 14, Jakarta 10130. ☎ (21) 3844342/3844366; fax: (21) 3854130. Main ticket office: Jl Angkasa 18, Kemayoran ☎ 4211921. Open in the mornings.

Travel Overland

Road conditions in Indonesia have improved dramatically over the past years, but traffic has also increased and driving is a slow and hazardous affair.

Trucks and buses, minivans, swarms of motorcycles piled with goods or carrying a family of four, ox-drawn carts, bicycles and pedicabs (*becak*) and pedestrians of all ages, compete in what is at times a crazy battle for tarmac, where the biggest and fastest rule.

Rental cars and motorcycles are available in many major cities, and a number of different types of buses run cheap and regular services.

Indonesia only has 8,000 km of railroad track, all of it on Java, Madura and Sumatra and most of it dating from Dutch times. Only on Java is there a real system, running the length and breadth of the island.

PLANNING AN ITINERARY

The first thing to realize is that you can never cover the entire island even if you were to spend months here. Don't make yourself an impossibly tight schedule. Be aware that things happen slowly here, and adjust yourself to the pace. Better to spend more time in a few places and see them in a leisurely way, than to end up hot and bothered. You'll see *more* this way, not less.

If you have never been to Java before, there are a few "must sees"—Borobudur, Prambanan, the *kraton* and around Yogyakarta probably top the list—and these will easily fill several days. Those with more time, and an interest in arts and antiquities, should add the towns of Bandung, Cirebon, Solo and Malang to their list, for a three-week "grand tour."

Most tourists avoid Jakarta unless they have business there. Your plans really depend on how much time you have available. Those with only a week on Java would be advised to stay around the Yogyakarta area, while those with more time could consider a Java-Bali tour. Three weeks or more make tours of Bandung, East Java, the North Coast and Western Java possible.

If you are more interested in wildlife and the great outdoors, spend time in either West or East Java in addition to visiting Yogya. The trip to Krakatau and Ujung Kulon National Park at Java's western tip, combined with volcano hikes in the Puncak/Cipanas and Bandung areas, can fill a couple of weeks and provide some unforgettable scenery. The same can be said of the rugged and fascinating Tengger and Blambangan areas in East Java.

The North Coast is an entirely different sort of journey—some will be amazed by the intricate Chinese temples, others by the textiles and handicrafts produced here. In truth, just about every area on Java is interesting.

Wherever you are, keep in mind that the tropical heat takes its toll and you should avoid the midday sun. Get an early start, before the rays become punishing (the tropical light is beautiful at dawn). Retreat to a cool place after lunch and go out again in the afternoon and early evening, when it's much more pleasant.

TRAVELING AROUND JAVA

By Air

Air transport is considerably more costly but also much faster than land travel, on an island where the traffic and the trains crawl along at a snail's pace (average 40 kph/25 mph). Only problem is that you don't get to see very much from the air, though the glimpses of Java's majestic volcanoes can be truly spectacular. From Jakarta to Surabaya takes an hour by plane, for example, while the fastest bus or train will take at least 12 hours. Obviously, if time is limited, this is the only way to go—and by international standards it's quite cheap. For example: Jakarta to Surabaya $76. Jakarta to Yogya/Solo $53.

The following cities on Java are served by scheduled flights (see Practicalities for details):

Bandung	Cilacap	Cirebon
Jakarta	Malang	Semarang
Solo (Surakarta)	Surabaya	Yogyakarta

Jakarta is the hub for air traffic to all parts of Indonesia. Most major cities in the country are served by daily flights. The Jakarta-Semarang and Jakarta-Surabaya sectors are handled by hourly shuttle flights, with tickets sold at the airport on a first-come, first-served basis. There are also 3 or 4 flights daily from Jakarta to Yogyakarta and Yogyakarta to Bali.

By Train

Train travel is a great way to see Java and can be very cheap, depending on the class. The problem is that first class trains travel at night (you don't see much), and anything less than first class on long journeys is crowded, noisy, hot, and uncomfortable. Still, you can stretch your legs, walk through the train, sit on the back step and watch the tracks stream out from under you.

First class is good, but first class tickets do not always guarantee a seat when you get on the train. (In this case, see the station master for a hassle and eventual refund.) If your budget requires economy travel, purchase a second or third class ticket, spread a *sarong* out and sleep under the seats, not in the aisles, as vendors will tread or spill things on you.

Tickets normally have to be bought at the station on the day of departure (go early in the morning!) or in the case of night express trains, the day before. Note that in Jakarta you can also buy train tickets at several convenient agencies (see Jakarta Practicalities). During major Indonesian holiday periods, better forget it: take a plane or a bus or better still, stay put.

There are two basic rail routes across Java: a north coastal route running Jakarta-Cirebon-Semarang-Surabaya; and a southerly route Jakarta-Bandung-Yogyakarta-Surakarta-Surabaya. In addition, there are feeder lines running from the west coast to Jakarta, Semarang-Yogya and east of Surabaya (connecting with a ferry and bus to Bali at Banyuwangi).

Between major cities there is only a single line, dating from Dutch times, and delays are common as a result. Trains traveling in opposite directions have to wait for one another; if one is late or breaks down, the whole system is thrown out of whack, which happens often.

The two best trains on Java (air-conditioning, reclining seats, dining car) are the **Bima Express** (Jakarta-Surabaya via Yogya/Solo) and the **Mutiara Utara** (Jakarta-Surabaya via the north

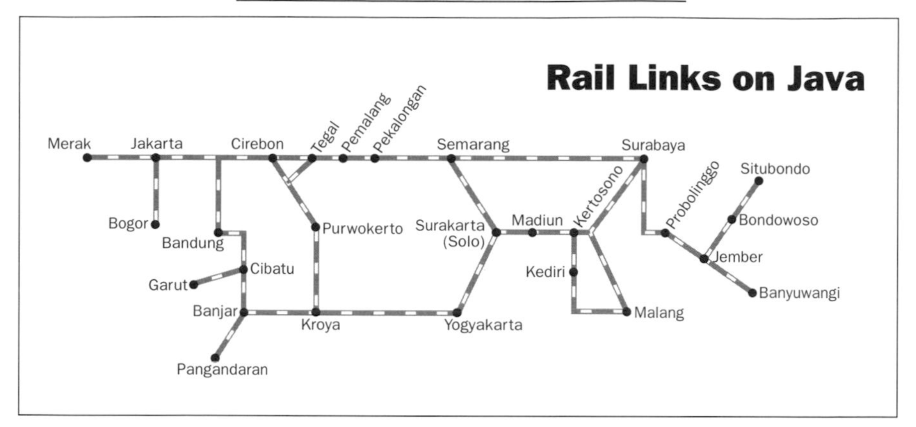

coast.) Both bypass Bandung, pulling out of Jakarta's Kota Station in the late afternoon (4 pm and 4:20 pm, respectively) heading east along the coast to Cirebon. The Bima then cuts south and pulls into Yogya/Solo in the middle of the night, while the Mutiara passes via Pekalongan and Semarang. The two theoretically meet in Surabaya early the next morning, but they are often late.

The most comfortable seats on the Bima Express are $30 for Eksekutiv A and $23 for Eksekutiv B, no matter where you get off or on.

The **Senja Utama** has AC cars and leaves from Jakarta's Gambir station at 6 pm every evening. These follow the same route as the Bima Express for slightly less money and you can choose between reclining seats or reserve a tiny berth in the sleeper car (*kuset*).

The Senja Utama is $24 for Eksekutiv and $16 for a sleeping berth.

If you are a train freak, definitely don't miss the Jakarta-Bandung **Parahyangan Express**, one of the most scenic rides around. (See Bandung Practicalities.) From Bandung to Yogya, there is also a slower 2nd or 3rd class train.

Trains also offer the cheapest transportation on Java, with Ekonomi tickets, sold according to distance traveled.

Night Express Buses—*bis malam*

The preferred mode of transportation for Indonesians, these buses operate only at night. Available in a wide variety of classes: from the public *patas* air-conditioned with reclining seats (crowded, run by the army) to the ultra-luxurious "Big Top" buses that run from Jakarta (these have seats like business class airline seats).

The better buses have a bathroom and arctic air-conditioning: the other reason you brought a sweater. The key to successful *bis malam* trips is sleep. Choose the best bus available as the price difference is usually not very great, and justifiable in that a good sleep is saving you a night's accommodation.

Most buses are fitted with televisions and show movies whether you want them or not, often followed by music. You are likely to be the only one who is annoyed by the volume, but a cheerful suggestion that the music be turned off (*dimatikan*) will at least get it turned down to the point where earplugs can block out the rest. The seats to avoid are in the very front and the very back. The back seats are raised up over the engine and don't recline, while front row seats give you too intimate a view of what the driver is doing.

There are also karaoke "sing-along" buses—for masochists and anthropologists only.

Buses leave from both ends of Java in late afternoon and cross midway in Central Java in the middle of the night. They stop en route at huge roadside cafeterias, and tickets often include a basic meal of rice and a bit of something. You can order more then pay the restaurant.

Tickets are sold at the bus terminal, or by agents, and there are usually a number of different buses going your way. Shop around, check out the seats, or the photos if the buses are not there yet, to see what you are getting.

Local Buses

The major advantages of these rattling buses is that they are extremely cheap, run every few minutes between major towns, and can be picked up at the terminals or any point along their routes. This is also their biggest disadvantage: they stop constantly.

If you depart from a terminal, find a seat near a window that opens. Try not to share this breeze with passengers behind you; they are likely to have a strong aversion to wind for fear of *masuk angin* (the wind which enters the body and causes a cold).

Seats in the rear offer a more spine-jarring ride than the front. The seats are very small, both in terms of leg room and width. You and your bag may take up (and be charged for) two seats. This is fair. But be sure you're not being overcharged for not knowing any better. The key is to know better. Ask someone what the proper fare is to your destination before getting on. A few words of Indonesian are indispensable to be able to ask for directions. People are generally very eager to help you.

Larger towns have city buses charging nominal fares, usually Rp300 (15¢). Flag them down wherever you see them. The catch is knowing which one to take as there are no maps or guides.

Express Minibuses—"travel" or "colt"

These come in two varieties: old and hot (sit by a window and keep it open) and the newer, much revered, L300 van with air-conditioning. Even the L300 gets a lot of engine heat, and at midday can still be sauna-like: especially if the air-conditioning is broken and the windows shut.

These 8 to 11 passenger vans connect major cities and deliver you right to your destination. They sometimes also pick you up. They usually travel during the day, though on longer routes (Semarang-Jakarta, for example) they travel at night like the *bis malam*. Express minibuses are slightly more expensive than the *bis malam* but more convenient and they save you a taxi or bus ride to your door.

Local Minibuses—*bemo*

These non air-conditioned vans ("colt" or "*bemo*") are the real workhorses of the transport network, going up and down even relatively impassable mountain tracks to deliver villagers and produce all over the island. Regular seats are supplemented by wooden benches, boosting the capacity of these sardine cans to 25. And there is *always* room for more. Take a seat up front with the driver whenever possible.

There are standard fares but these are flexible to account for how much room you and your bag are taking up. Ask someone before flagging one down if you are concerned by the potential Rp100 price gouging. Flag one down on any roadside. You can also charter one to most destinations. Just say "charter" and where you want to go, then bargain for the fare in advance.

Car Rentals

At first glance the unwritten driving rules of Indonesia seem like a maniacal free-for-all. It is only later that the subtle hierarchy (truck vs. car: you lose) and finesse (2-centimeter tolerances) become evident. This is as good a reason as any that self-drive car rentals are rare in Java. Sedans or taxis with drivers are available in Jakarta but are very expensive; they don't really like to go long distances, and you have to return them to your starting point. More for day trips or business clients. In Yogya now, however, there is one company offering self-drive cars with drop-offs possible in Bali (see Yogya Practicalities). To drive in Indonesia you need a valid international license. For car rental details, check Jakarta Practicalities.

Chartering a Car or Minibus

This can be the best way to see Java as you have the freedom to stop whenever things look interesting and the flexibility to try out some less traveled routes. This can also be an economical alternative if you can fill up a van. The minibus can take up to 7, but you need extra space if you are to be in it for a few days, so 5 passengers is generally maximum.

Some asking around will quickly give you an idea of where to hire a driver and what the local going rates are for a specific excursion or longer itinerary. A full day of driving one-way will cost from $50 to $80 and a five-day trip around $300. Much of this is for gas so distance traveled is a major factor and a less efficient vehicle like a jeep will cost more per day than a van. Most of the rest goes to the owner of the vehicle with a tiny percentage left for the driver.

It is understood that you will pay for the driver's meals and accommodation both while he is with you and on his journey back home. A tip of Rp5,000 per day is also appreciated if the driver is good.

The quality of both the driver and the vehicle will figure heavily in the enjoyability of your trip so don't be shy about checking both out before striking a deal. The air-conditioning should work well enough to overcome the midday heat and the vehicle should be clean and comfortable.

Your driver should be responsible and have a personality that won't grate on you in the long haul. If he knows about the area you will be seeing, and can speak some English, so much the better. Travel agents can also arrange such charters for you.

Stock up on water and snacks for you and your driver and head out early in the day.

TOURS AND TRAVEL AGENCIES

Organized tours are a good way to go if you don't want to bother arranging transport and lodgings on your own. Many companies offer "Java–Bali" bus tours which have itineraries of 5, 7, 10 or 14 days. Most tourists on them are Dutch. Other companies will organize customized minibus tours for fairly reasonable prices. This includes driver and guide as well as accommodation and petrol.

Contact the head offices in Jakarta on arrival, or write to them in advance. Most of the companies below, based in Jakarta, have branches all over Java and standards of service are quite high, as they are used to serving foreigners.

Musi Holiday Jl Cikini Raya 30 ☎ 322709.
Natrabu Jl H Agus Salim 29 A ☎ 322709.
Pacto Jl Surabaya 8 ☎ 348634.
Vayatour Jl Batutulis 38 ☎ 3800202.
Satriavi Jl Prapatan 32 ☎ 3803944.

—Sandra Hamid/Bob Cowherd

1 Jakarta PRACTICALITIES

INCLUDES PULAU SERIBU

Jakarta neatly falls into several distinct sightseeing areas. It takes time to get used to the suffocating tropical heat, so plan early-morning outings then spend midday sipping fruit juice at the poolside. Tours covering the main points of interest can be booked at any travel agent or major hotel. It is more rewarding, however, to simply explore independently.

Remember that museums and government offices close early. Late afternoon and evening are pleasant for shopping, and most stores stay open till 9 pm. The ideal way to get around is to hire a car or taxi. The novelty of riding in a *bajaj* (motorized ladybug-like three-wheeler) grows old fast.

Prices are quoted in US dollars, excluding tax & service (10–30 percent). Jakarta telephone code is 021. *See maps, pages 94, 97 & 106.*

ARRIVAL

By Air

Sukarno-Hatta International Airport, 12 km to the west of the city, is new, attractive and efficient. Terminal 2 handles all international flights as well as Garuda domestic flights. Other flights are handled by Terminal 1.

There are small restaurants and snack bars, moneychangers, information and left luggage counters in Terminal 2. Hotel rooms can also be booked at the **Indotel** counter near baggage claim. They offer discounts on 5-star and budget accommodation. Once in a while you can get an exceptional deal here, like a 5-star room for $60, transport included.

Quickest way into town (a 30–40 minute journey) is by taxi. The fare is about $10 to most hotels including surcharge and toll ($3). There are also AC airport DAMRI buses ($2) which serve five city depots, with stops along the way. These buses, however, do not leave the airport until they are full. Tell the driver your final destination and he will usually drop you off at the nearest point en route; you can then grab a cab.

When traveling to Sukarno-Hatta airport, allow 40 minutes in normal traffic and one to two hours during morning or evening rush hours.

See Travel Advisory for details of flights to/from Jakarta.

By Sea

The national shipping line (Pelni) has regular sailings from major ports in Indonesia to Jakarta's Tanjung Priok harbor, 18 km from downtown. A taxi into town costs around $5, or sweat it out on the No. 63 bus (Rp250) from Tanjung Priok terminal, 2 km from the main Pelni wharf. See Travel Advisory for further details.

Non-Pelni boats also take passengers; contact them at the Tanjung Priok harbor master's office. *Pinisi* schooners also offer a romantic mode of travel for adventurous types—bargain with a captain on the Sunda Kelapa wharf.

By Train

Jakarta's four major train stations are listed below according to the destinations they serve; be sure you know which one your train will depart from. Food and drinks can be purchased from numerous vendors along the way. See Travel Advisory for details of routes and map.

Gambir Jl Merdeka Timur ☎ 342777. Trains to and from points south and east, including Bandung and Bogor. Located right in town, within walking distance of some hotels. On arrival, insist that taxis use meters; many try to charge higher fixed fares.

Kota Jl Stasiun Kota 1 ☎ 677843. Night express (sleeper or coach) and local day trains to points east, including Yogya. Departure point for Bima II and Mutiara Utara night express to Surabaya and Banyuwangi, connecting with the ferry and bus to Bali.

Senen Jl Stasiun Senen ☎ 340078. Local trains to points east including Cirebon, Semarang and Solo.

Tanah Abang Jl Jatibaru ☎ 340048. Trains to points west, including ferry connection to Sumatra.

Onward bookings. Indonesian trains are often heavily booked; it is best to pay a small surcharge and book your ticket through Carnation Travel, Menteng, Jl Menteng Raya 24 ☎ 3844027 or Media Tour in Blok M, Kebayoran, Jl Melawai VIII/7, Blok M ☎ 7202680; fax: 7202689.

By Bus

Long distance buses, both AC (cheap) and non-AC (cheaper) operate from three major terminals on the fringes of the city. All can be reached by city bus or taxi.

Kampung Rambutan A new terminal east of the city, handles points south including Puncak, Bogor and Bandung. Designed to accommodate 1,500 vehicles.

Pulo Gadung Handles points east including Cire-

bon, Surabaya, Malang, Yogyakarta, Denpasar.
Kalideres Handles points west including Merak, Labuhan, and destinations in Sumatra.
NOTE: *Bis malam* (night bus) tickets to Surabaya, Bali, Yogyakarta, Malang, Palembang, can be booked by calling **Kramat Djati** ☎ 3865624, **Lorena** ☎ 353-662, or **Karina** ☎ 375662.

TOURIST INFORMATION

There are two tourist information centers in Jakarta:
Visitor Information Service, Arrival Hall Terminal A, Sukarno Hatta International Airport. ☎ 5507088.
Visitor Information Center, Jakarta Theatre Building, Jl MH Thamrin 9, Jakarta Pusat. ☎ 3154094, 364093, 3142067.

GETTING AROUND TOWN

Walking. The only people who walk more than 100 meters in Jakarta are tourists. It's hot, the pavement ruins your shoes, everyone stares at you, and there is usually an easier way to get there.
Bajaj. Motorized 3-wheeler, usually bright orange. Bargain the fare before you get in: 50¢ for short hops in town. Faster through the traffic than buses, but avoid rush hour. Not for long distances; if the noise doesn't kill you, the carbon monoxide will.
Bemo. A 7–10 seat minibus. Get on and off where you want. Fares from 10¢ according to distance. Operate mostly off main roads, in the suburbs.
Bus. Very cheap but hot, crowded and dilapidated. Not good for tall people. Standard fare is about 15¢. Smaller *Patas* buses are slightly more expensive at 30¢, but less crowded and stop anywhere. Beware of pickpockets. City bus route maps are (sometimes) available at the Visitor Information Center in Djakarta Theatre building on Jl Thamrin.
Taxis. Taxis are plentiful and can be flagged down anywhere. Fares are cheap by international standards. $4 will get you almost anywhere in the city. You can also phone for a cab. AC flagfall is 50¢, 25¢ per km thereafter. Make sure the meter is on. Bluebird and most other phone taxis are reliable- and drivers often speak some English. Negotiate for hourly or longer rates. Gamya taxis accept credit cards. For **24-hour taxis** ☎ Bluebird 325607; Express 5706705; Gamya 3101215; Metropolitan 672827; Steadysafe 333333; Kosti Jaya 7801333.
Car rental. Many companies now offer both "chauffeur-driven" (CD) cars with driver and gas included, as well as "self drive" (SD) cars. Special one-way drop-off rates to Bali, Yogya, Surabaya and Medan are also available. CD daily rates (12 hrs) range from $79 (Toyota Kijang/Ford Laser) to $192 (Mercedes 280/230 E). SD daily rates, including insurance, range from $55 (Kijang/Laser) to $92 (Toyota Corona/Mitsubishi Gallant). Deposit required.
Avis Jl Diponegoro 25 ☎ 334495, 332900.
Budget Jl Gelong Baru 35 ☎ 5602954.
Hertz Head Office ☎ 518089.
National Kartika Plaza Hotel ☎ 333423, 337792.
Toyota Rent-A-Car Jl K H Hasyim Ashari ☎ 361861.
Bluebird Counters at the entrances to the Hilton and Hotel Indonesia, or call 325607. CD Volvo 740 GLEs, Cressidas and Mercedes by the hr (2 hours minimum) or by the day (2 days minimum). A non-AC Isuzu minibus can be hired for $20 an hour (minimum 6 hrs). Prices apply to city use only.

City Tours

Many travel agents offer coach tours of major city sights as well as Bogor Botanical Gardens, Puncak and nearby islands. Coaches pick up at the major hotels. Price is about $20–25/half day. Contact an agent in your hotel or call **Panorama Tours** ☎ 376782 or **Boca Pirento** ☎ 5664481.

ACCOMMODATION

Hotels in Jakarta range from budget roof-over-your-head *losmens* to penthouse luxury suites with a private helipad outside your door. For booking information see above for Indotel Booking Counter at Sukarno-Hatta Airport. Booking hotels through a travel agent is usually much cheaper than walking in off the street.

Budget ($4–$25)

Jakarta's cheapest rooms are found in *losmen* on Jl Jaksa and Jl Kebon Sirih, right downtown. The most popular ones are **Wisma Delima** Jl Jaksa 5 ☎ 337026 and **Borneo** Jl Kebon Sirih Barat Dalam ☎ 320095. Both provide rooms with fan and shared or private bath plus cheap breakfast. Prices range from $7–10 a night. If you want AC, double the price and check out either **Djody** Jl Jaksa 27/35 ☎ 3846600, or **Karya** Jl Jaksa 32 ☎ 320484.

A more refined alternative to the *losmen* are private guest houses which tend to attract longer staying guests. **Jl Teuku Umar 66** ☎ 3100599 is probably the best budget place in town—a rambling three-story house with a central courtyard. Rooms range from monastic single cells to balcony rooms with AC and en suite bath. Prices from $12 up to $25 for AC rooms, breakfast included. **PGI Guest House** (Christian Guest House) at Jl Teuku Umar 17 ☎ 3909427, has a variety of rooms (fan and AC), well-maintained, simple and spacious. Location is residential and central. Friendly staff. $12–22, breakfast included.

Intermediate ($50–$100)

Atlet Century Park (633 rooms) Jl Pintu Satu Senayan ☎ 5712041; fax: 5712191. Newly opened hotel strategically located next to Senayan Sports Complex, golf course and driving range. Excellent value at $95 and up. Former athlete's village.
Betawi Sofyan (69 rooms) Jl Cut Mutiah ☎ 3905011; fax: 3902747. $55 and up.
Cikini Sofyan (115 rooms) Jl Cikini Raya 79 ☎ 33-5928; fax: 3100432. Good value. $54.
Cipta (48 rooms) Jl KH Wahid Hasyim 53, Menteng ☎ 3904701; fax: 326531. Opened in 1991. Centrally located near shopping and business center,

Jl Jaksa and nightlife. $63.
Garden (117 rooms) Jl Kemang Raya, Kebayoran ☎ 7980760; fax: 7980763. In the south of the city in a quiet residential area near shops and supermarkets. $65 and up.
Kartika Plaza (270 rooms) Jl MH Thamrin ☎ 321-008; fax: 322547. Recently upgraded, very central and popular with businessmen. $105 and up.
Kemang (100 rooms) Jl Kemang Raya ☎ 7993208; fax: 7993620. In the south of the city, access to town difficult during rush hours. $67 and up.
Marco Polo Jl Cik Ditiro, Menteng ☎ 326679; fax: 3107138, 327617. Swimming pool. $63.
Menteng I/II (80 rooms) At Jl Suroso 28 ☎ 325-208 and Jl Cikini Raya 105 ☎ 325543. $47.
Sabang Metropolitan (130 rooms) Jl HA Salim 11 ☎ 372450; fax: 372642. $45 and up.

First Class ($100–$150)

Hotel Indonesia (579 rooms) Jl MH Thamrin ☎ 320008; fax: 321508. Built in the 1960s by the Japanese as a war reparation, "HI" (pronounced Ha-ee) was the first "modern" hotel in Jakarta and is still a major landmark. The "old lady" has been given a facelift, though still only rates 4 stars. The bizarre, art deco Ramayana Terrace has a stained glass ceiling, murals and aviary. The small and dim lobby bar, gathering place of foreign journalists in C.J. Koch's novel *The Year of Living Dangerously*, has now regrettably disappeared. $150 and up.
Horison (440 rooms) Jl Pantai Indah, Ancol ☎ 68-9333; fax: 689322. Large hotel near the coast in the north of the city. $135 and up.
Jayakarta Tower (426 rooms) Jl Hayam Wuruk ☎ 6294408; fax: 6295000. $95 D; $85 S.
Kartika Chandra (143 rooms) Jl Gatot Subroto ☎ 5205000; fax: 5204238. Plain but economical. Favored by long-staying guests. Pool area is seedy; bowling alley and cinema next door. $110 and up.
President (311 rooms) Jl MH Thamrin ☎ 3901122; fax: 333631. Recently renovated Japanese hotel across from Plaza Indonesia. $127 and up.
Wisata International (181 rooms) Jl MH Thamrin ☎ 320308; fax: 324597. Centrally located, walking distance to Plaza Indonesia. $105 and up.

Luxury ($150 and up)

A growing number of 5-star hotels offer quality service and facilities. Room rates are for single standard rooms, *before* 21% tax and service. For spacious luxury the Jakarta Hilton and Borobudur Intercontinental are recommended. The new Grand Hyatt has the best location and restaurants.
Borobudur Intercontinental (860 rooms) Jl Lapangan Banteng Selatan ☎ 3805555; fax: 3809595. Palatial marble lobby with a lovely lounge overlooking a large garden. Biggest pool in town, and a very popular disco (The Music Room). Garuda and Cathay airline offices. $190 and up.
Grand Hyatt Jakarta (450 rooms) Jl MH Thamrin ☎ 3107400; fax: 335502. Jakarta's top hotel. For total indulgence, this is *the* place. Excellent specialty restaurants and pub. $260 and up.
Hyatt Aryaduta (331 rooms) Jl Prapatan ☎ 3861234; fax: 3809900. Recently renovated; very comfortable with lots of extra touches in the rooms. Jazz pub, and great Italian food. $180 and up.
Jakarta Hilton International (664 rooms) Jl Gatot Subroto ☎ 5703600; fax: 5733089, 5733091. A hub of Jakarta's business and social life. Sprawling grounds with an enormous pool, tennis courts, jogging track and a plush disco. Garden Tower rooms are more expensive but are tastefully decorated in pastel tones and *ikat*. $180 and up.
Le Meridien Jakarta (265 rooms) Jl Jend. Sudirman ☎ 5711414; fax: 5711639. With all the amenities of the larger hotels, the small Meridien is wonderfully inviting. Great attention is paid to guest comfort. Beautiful rooms. Buffet lunch is excellent value. $180 and up.
Mandarin Oriental (467 rooms) Jl MH Thamrin ☎ 3141307; fax: 3141407, 3148680. Small site with no grounds, but a classy "city" hotel with fine food and service. Biggest rooms in town and huge, soft beds. Great coffee shop and bar. $180 and up.
Sahid Jaya (750 rooms) Jl Jend. Sudirman ☎ 57-04444; fax: 5733168. Newly renovated. A big hotel popular with tour groups. The Sahid Grill on the top floor is very good. $170 and up.
Sari Pan Pacific (501 rooms) Jl MH Thamrin ☎ 32-3707; fax: 323650. Excellent food, with the city's best bakery. Popular coffee shop, jazz lounge and disco. Conveniently located near Sarinah department store and cinemas. $155 and up.

FOOD

Whatever your preference, Jakarta has it, from roadside stalls serving delicious steamed crabs to elegant European restaurants serving *coq au vin*. You can sample regional dishes from all 27 of Indonesia's provinces or dine on a Big Mac.

Indonesian

Tan Goei opposite Hero Supermarket on Jl Cokroaminoto has indoor and outdoor seating, fountains and great *sate*. The fresh yoghurt drinks are tasty. Good for late-night beer and *sate* when a cool breeze is blowing. **Senayan Sate House** is a chain of restaurants serving delicious *sate* and other local dishes. Branches on Jl Cokroaminoto, Jl Kebon Sirih in Menteng and Jl Pakubuwono in Kebayoran.

Sundanese (West Javanese) cuisine is served in restaurants which usually have indoor gardens and pools where you can choose live carp or *gurame* for frying or grilling. Try **Ikan Bakar Kebon Sirih** on Jl Kebon Sirih or **Raden Kuring** on Jl Raden Saleh. For hot Padang food, **Natrabu** at Jl HA Salim 29 has won prizes for its food and its waiters' ability to carry 20 or more plates at once. Inexpensive too.

Food Stalls

The cheapest Indonesian food is served at *warung* street stalls or from mobile carts known as *kaki lima*. The drawback of these places is that they have no water supply, and hygiene standards are often dubious. Not for weak stomachs.

Jl Kendal has roadside stalls serving *sate* and soups made from all parts of goat. Open from midday until the wee hours.
Jl Pecenongan (off Jl Juanda) Stalls are open only at night and are famous for their fresh seafood (crabs and prawns) and Chinese dishes.
Jl Sabang stalls, open after dark, serve some of Jakarta's best *sate*, delivered to your car window.
Pasaraya Shopping Center in Blok M has a number of foodstalls in the basement, a safer place to test your tolerance for street food.

Dutch/Indonesian

Arts & Curios Jl Kebun Binatang IV off Jl Cikini, serves Dutch and Indonesian dishes in a quaint old curiosity shop atmosphere at moderate prices. A favorite of literary and arty types. **Memories** in the Indocement Building on Jl Sudirman is full of colonial memorabilia and rich and quite pricey Dutch food. Dutch food and atmosphere also at **Club Noordwijk** Jl Juanda. **Oasis** on Jl Raden Saleh Raya, is a fine Dutch villa, in a class of its own for old-world charm and *rijsttafel* served by a long line of young girls, each carrying a different dish. Average food, but a must for the atmosphere and style.

Seafood

On Jl Melawai VIII in Blok M, Kebayoran, and on Kemang Raya 37, **Ratu Bahari** serves good Chinese seafood at moderate prices. Even better but crowded at lunch time is **Nelayan** in Manggala Wanabakti building on Jl Gatot Subroto. **Nelayan** (no relation) in the Borobudur hotel is the best up-market seafood restaurant. The seafood basket, served with pliers and other tools, is messy and mouth-watering.

Chinese

For medium-priced Szechuan and Cantonese food, try **Summer Palace**, Jl Menteng Raya 29 and **Hong Kong** on Jl Blora 27. The **Spice Garden** in the Mandarin is up-market Szechuan, all red and gold and often full of ostentatiously wealthy patrons. The food and service is superb. For excellent Cantonese food, try **Han Restaurant** in the Grand Hyatt. **Bakmi Gajah Mada** on Jl Melawai IV in Blok M, and near Sarinah Thamrin does a roaring trade in Chinese noodles. Cafeteria style, fast service.

Japanese

On Jl Cikini IV, **Kikugawa** offers reasonably priced Japanese food and a "country inn" atmosphere. For *shabu shabu* with panoramic views, try **Sky Garden** on the 28th floor of Wisma Nusantara. **Nippon-Kan** in the Hilton is the most pleasant top-of-the-line Japanese restaurant, overlooking a lake with swans and lotus blooms. **Sumire** in the Grand Hyatt and **Shima** in the Aryaduta are excellent. **Tokyo Garden** in the Lippo Building on Jl Rasuna Said is also good, but expensive. **Sumimbian** Chase Plaza, Jl Sudirman, specializes in charcoal-grilled *yakiniku*, with a view. Yuppie haunt.

Korean/Vietnamese

Koreana on Jl Melawai in Blok M has reasonable prices. Also good is **Korea Garden** on Jl Teluk Betung. **Korea Tower** atop the Bank Bumi Daya building has spectacular views. In the medium price range are the two **Arirang** restaurants, one on Jl Gereja Theresia I in Menteng and the other on Jl Mahakam I in Kebayoran Baru.
Paregu I on Jl Sunan Kali Jaya in Kebayoran has excellent Vietnamese fare, refined service and piano music.

French

Jakarta's best is the **Club Room**, in the Mandarin hotel. The food is excellent, the ambiance refined and the service first class. Running a close second are **Taman Sari** in the Hilton, **Jayakarta Grill** in the Sari Pan Pacific and **Toba Grill** in the Borobudur. The newly opened **Le Maritime** in Le Meridien specializes in French-style seafood. Finish the meal with a pastry, truffle or cake from **La Boutique Gourmande** on the hotel's ground floor. **Le Bistro** on Jl Wahid Hasyim is cozy and moderately priced. An intimate, expensive but elegant French restaurant for romantic trysts is **La Rose** on the ground floor of Landmark Centre on Jl Sudirman.

Indian

Akbar Palace in Wijaya Grand Center, Kebayoran, serves excellent North Indian food, specializing in tandoori dishes. Nearby **Eastern Promise**, Jl Kemang Raya, serves a range of Indian meals and European dishes. The **New George and Dragon Curry House** at Jl Talang Betutu 7, and **Copper Chimney** on Jl Antara, Pasar Baru, are also recommended.

Italian

Jakarta's only up-market Italian restaurant is **Ambiente** in the Hyatt. A potential rival is the newly opened **Il Punto** in the World Trade Center. **Maxi's** in Plaza Indonesia has very good food and a pleasant atmosphere. Less fancy are **Pinnochio** in Wisma Metropolitan I on Jl Sudirman (caged apes and an excellent value buffet lunch). Despite the balmy tropical nights, there are few places where you can eat outdoors in Jakarta. The Hilton's **Pizzaria**, in the garden behind the hotel, is one. Built on a lake, it has a live band every night except Tuesday. Popular on Friday and Saturday nights. The **Pizza Boat** in Pondok Indah (nautical decor) also has good pizza.

American/Mexican

The **Hard Rock Cafe** in Sarinah Jl Thamrin draws the crowds it does the world over. The **Ponderosa** chain (Widjojo Centre, Wisma Antara, Centrepoint, Arthaloka Bldg) specializes in steaks and Mexican food. **Green Pub** in the Jakarta Theatre building on Jl Thamrin has Tex-Mex food, country-western music and huge margaritas which come in a glass you can take home. Green Pub's brother, **Amigos**, in Kemang Club Villas (follow the signs off Jl Kemang Raya) offers the same combination.

Fast Food

You can't miss the golden arches and Buddha-like Ronald McDonald sitting on top of Jakarta's 24-hour **McDonald's** on Jl Thamrin. A second McDonald's has opened in the new Blok M Mall. **Wendy's** (Pondok Indah Mall, Plaza Indonesia) now has a fax for incoming orders. **Burger King** is in Plaza Indonesia. **Pizza Hut**, **Dairy Queen**, **Kentucky Fried Chicken**, **A&W** and **Swenson's**, all have numerous outlets throughout the city.

SHOPPING

Caveat Emptor—the buyer beware! Jakarta is a great place to shop for souvenirs, artifacts and handicrafts from around the archipelago, and real bargains can be found. But for the uninitiated there are perils in doing business with the city's sly traders. In practical terms, consumer's rights can be considered non-existent, so check and double-check your purchases before you pay.

One-Stop Gift Shopping

Sarinah department stores (Jl MH Thamrin across from Jakarta Theatre) and **Pasaraya** (in Blok M, Kebayoran) carry a range of handicrafts representing almost everything you can buy in Indonesia, except antiques; **Blok M**'s new "underground" mall is another first-time shopper's wonder. Prices are reasonable and quality consistent.

NOTE: For each purchase you get a *bon* (bill) which must be paid and stamped at the cashier then taken to a desk where the goods are collected. Rather than lining up to pay several times, collect several bills and make one trip to the cashier.

Antiques

There is a thriving cottage industry of "instant antiques"—reproductions which look like the real thing. Never pay an exorbitant price for something unless you are certain you know its value. Even so-called reputable dealers are not always reliable. While some up-market shops have excellent pieces, they also have New York prices. Inexpensive but well-made reproductions can be a good alternative.

Jl Palatehan in Kebayoran has several fancy antique shops that are good but pricey.

Jl Surabaya has an "art market" with many stalls selling curios, junk, souvenirs, antiques, old beads, cloth, china, bric-a-brac and furniture. Bargaining is expected. If you pay more than half the asking price you have definitely made a bad deal.

Jl Kebon Sirih Timur Dalam is a crowded sidestreet choked with traffic and lined with antique and furniture shops. Some great finds here. Bargain hard.

Jl Ciputat Raya is 45 minutes south of town, but its shops have a great selection at cheap prices.

Furniture

Genuine antiques are rare. Good reproductions are cheaper, sturdier and last longer. Many shops will arrange packing and shipping and are reliable, especially if you let them know you have a Jakarta contact who will chase them if there is a delay. Shop for antique spice chests (from $45), old puppets (from $3) chairs (from $30) and bigger pieces including ornately carved Chinese four-poster beds ($750 or more) along **Jl Palatehan**, **Jl Surabaya**, **Jl Kebon Sirih Timur Dalam** and **Jl Ciputat Raya**. Modern rattan furniture is now produced for export in Jakarta. Look in the shops along **Jl Kemang Raya**; bargain for at least 15% off the asking price.

Brass

Inexpensive modern brass is available in Sarinah and Pasaraya (Blok M). Jl Surabaya has mostly new copies but some originals, especially **Dutch lamps** and **ship chandlery**. Old brass has a slightly reddish tint even when polished. Have wiring checked by an electrician at home before using converted antique lamps, priced around $18 and up.

Porcelain

Again, few genuine antiques are left. Some **Ming** pieces can be found but price is no guarantee of authenticity. **Jl Pelatehan**, **Jl Surabaya**, **Jl Kebon Sirih Timur Dalam** and **Jl Ciputat Raya**.

Textiles

Indonesia produces some of the world's most sophisticated ethnic textiles. Most famous is Javanese batik—produced by a wax-resist process. *Batik tulis* (hand-painted batik) is the most refined and expensive, followed by *batik cap* (block-printed). Avoid cheap prints on poor material, which have a design on one side only.

Ikat weavings are also highly developed. Traditional cloths use vegetable dyes and natural fibers. Commercial dyes are brighter and artificial fibres melt when held over a match. Fine fabric and complex designs indicate quality.

For reasonably priced textiles such as batik, East Indonesian *ikat*, Kalimantan weavings and other regional examples, shop at Sarinah and Pasaraya. Look for antique *ikat* ($70 plus) or antique and gold-leafed batik ($30) on **Jl Kebun Sirih Timur Dalam**, **Jl Surabaya** and **Jl Ciputat Raya**. Other reasonably priced batik shops are **Batik Keris** (numerous locations) and **Danar Hadi**, Jl Raden Saleh 1A. **Iwan Tirta**, Jl Panarukan 25, designs expensive high fashion batik garments, often on silk (has another shop in Hotel Borobudur). **Batik Hajadi** at Jl Palmerah Utara 46 has a huge range of cotton upholstery and curtain fabrics by the meter for reasonable prices.

Paintings

Apart from Balinese painting, Indonesian art has little commercial value overseas. Works by well-known, traditional Balinese painters are expensive. See works in progress at **Pasar Seni** in the

Ancol complex where paintings and commissioned portraits are sold. Several galleries in Jakarta have collections of modern Indonesian painting; quality and prices vary. Most old maps and prints of Indonesia found in Jakarta come from Europe and are priced accordingly.
Duta Fine Arts is a renowned gallery in a Mediterranean style villa at Jl Kemang Utara 1/55A.
Edwin's Gallery Jl Kemang Raya 21. Good selection.
Santi Fine Arts Gallery Jl Benda 4, Cilandak Timur, has a number of regular exhibitions.
Toraya Framers on Jl Kapten Tendean (turn down the side road just after the post office) do professional framing at very reasonable prices.

Wooden Artifacts

"Old" pieces are artificially aged by burying or staining. Check for sharp, newly carved edges. Genuine pieces will be smooth in areas frequently handled. Most carvings have been produced for tourists; buy according to aesthetic value and quality of workmanship. **Jl Ciputat Raya** and **Jl Kebon Sirih Timur Dalam**.

Gold and Silver

Contemporary gold jewelry is relatively cheap and workmanship is good. Price is based on the daily gold rate plus around 10% for workmanship. Old gold and ethnic jewelry is usually real but prices may be higher than in Europe or the US.

The silver plating used for modern tea sets, etc is usually thin and soon tarnishes. Sterling silver from reputable shops is a better buy.
Spiro Jewellers (Mandarin, Sari Pacific & Hilton hotels) produces quality gold and silver reproductions of traditional ethnic designs. Prices start at around $100 but the quality makes it worth it.
Pasar Ikan and **Blok M** Gold dealers can also be found here. Request a certificate of karat and weight.

Fashion

Indonesia has a young but thriving fashion industry and talented designers are beginning to make an impact on the international scene. Indonesian designer fashions can be bought at reasonable prices. Workmanship varies (watch out for poor fabric) but a careful eye can find excellent bargains. Leading the local fashion revolution are Iwan Tirta (high fashion batik), Poppy Dharsono and Arthur Harland (chic office & day wear), Ghea Sukasah (inspired ethnic revivals), Ramli (embroidery), Hanum Gularso (batik and traditional fabrics). **Sarinah Jaya and Keris Gallery** Jl Cokroaminoto, carry complete designer ranges.
Esterliana Designs Jl Taman Kebun Sirih 1/123, specializes in hand painted silk and linen dresses.

MARKETS

Every neighborhood has a *pasar* (from the same Arabic root as the English "bazaar"), which is a hub of social as well as commercial life. The typical *pasar* is hot, crowded and noisy. When you go, carry only as much money as you plan to spend. Prices may be either higher or lower than in the stores—bargaining is expected. Shopkeepers rarely have change for large bills.
Pasar Baru is the place to shop for fabrics by the meter, clothes and shoes. **Pasar Tanah Abang** has fabric, haberdashery, upholstery etc. **Blok M**, **Glodok**, and **Pasar Benhil** for electronic goods. **Blok A** for household wares. **Pasar Barito**: bird market, rabbits, squirrels, monkeys and fish for sale. **Pasar Ikan** for fresh fish, ship's chandlery, kitchen utensils. **Pasar Seni** for paintings and handicrafts.

Supermarkets

Kemchicks on Jl Kemang Raya is a favorite with westerners, almost everything is available, including fresh bread. **Golden Truly** in the Jakarta Theater Building is the most central supermarket. Also good are the **Hero** supermarkets on Jl Cokroaminoto in Menteng and in the basements of Ratu Plaza and Pasaraya, Blok M.

PHOTOGRAPHY

There are numerous one-hour photo processing stores throughout the city. **Jakarta Photo** on Jl H Agus Salim 35A, Menteng and Jl Panglima Polim Raya No. 127 A, is the best all-round photographic store, has a one-day service for slides and does camera repairs. Professional slide processing available at **Ekta** Jl Cideng Barat 80.

MUSIC & ELECTRONICS

Copyright laws have wiped out cheap, pirated cassettes and computer software.
Duta Suara Jl H Agus Salim 26, is the best store for music tapes and CDs.
Trio Tara Jl Hayam Wuruk 96. Wide range of CDs.
Video shops worth checking out are in Wisma Kosgoro, Jl Thamrin and in Kemchicks, Kemang Raya.
Istidata Jl H Agus Salim 100, is good for computers.

BOOKS

Times in the new Plaza Indonesia complex is the best-stocked bookshop in town. Also check out the **Kinokuniya** shop inside Sogo department store above Times. **Ken Chick's** supermarket in Kemang has a full range of paperbacks and books on Indonesia. **Pondok Indah Mall** has three bookstores, **Times**, **Gramedia** and **Gunung Agung**.

NIGHTLIFE

Jakarta is a 24-hour city. Almost as much goes on at night as in the day, minus the traffic and heat. Restaurants, however, close early so eat before 9 pm. **Nightclubs** and **bars** get going around 10 pm and some go on until dawn. Late-night supper makes a good nightcap, and you can always grab a snack on the street.

Awareness of social codes will help; Indonesian women rarely go out alone at night and although it is usually safe for Western women to do so, it is unwise unless you want to attract enough males to start your own football team. western males are attractive to bar girls, usually for financial reasons.

Bars

Good places for apéritifs are the **Kudus** Bar of the Hilton, the **Pendopo Bar** of the Borobudur and the lobby lounge of the Hyatt Aryaduta. Favorite after dinner watering holes are the **Captain's Bar** in the Mandarin Hotel, particularly on Beatles' night and the **Melati Lounge** in the Sari Pacific which features a pianist and Filipino bands. **O'Reiley's** in the Grand Hyatt is the most popular bar in Jakarta for pub lunches, live CNN and BBC broadcasts on big video screen, and live entertainment.

Jakarta would not be Jakarta without the hotel lobby. Batak entertainers can be seen in the early evening in the mezzanine coffee lounge at the Mandarin, outdoors at **Tan Goei** on Friday and Saturday nights and at Hilton's **Pizzaria** on Tuesday nights. Enthusiastic Bataks perform at **Oasis** restaurant nightly. Bataks dressed as Mexicans visit the Borobudur's Pendopo Bar.

Supper Clubs

Pizzaria in the Hilton garden is a good spot for music with dinner, with lights reflecting in the lake, and energetic Filipino bands. Gets very lively on Fri & Sat nights.
Temptation on Jl Kemang Raya and **New Parrots Videotheque** on Jl Wahid Hasyim are music lounges which serve meals and later turn into discos.
The Tavern, downstairs in the Hyatt Aryaduta, is a popular bistro-style bar with live music, famous for their "hot-stone" steaks you cook yourself.
Green Pub in the Jakarta Theatre and **Amigos** in the Kemang Club Villas complex draw expat crowds with lethal margaritas, rock and country music.
The News Cafe in the Setiabudi building has a very European feel. The decor is excellent, the menu original, and the staff friendly. Live music every night.
Jazz N' Rock Cafe ATD Plaza, Jl Thamrin has a spacious layout to pack in the crowds. International food and live bands every night.
Hardrock Cafe, Sarinah complex, Jl Thamrin, gourmet burgers to the beat of the band.
Blue Ocean on Jl Hayam Wuruk is a Chinese fantasy of bad taste with an unmissable floorshow.

Pubs

English teachers frequent the **Chicago Entertainment Club** and **Top Gun** in Blok M. Oil men like **King's Head** in Kebayoran. The **Jaya Pub** in the Jaya Building on Jl Thamrin is an institution; noisy, crowded and always raging. It is owned by veteran Indonesian film stars Rima Melati and Frans Tumbuan, who also own **The Tavern** ands **Le Bistro**. **JJ "Do It"** at Jl Tanah Abang Timur, is an up and coming club. DJ specialists showcase theme music rotating everyday of the week.

Discos

The cover charge at discos and clubs usually includes the first drink. The legendary **Tanamur** on Jl Tanah Abang Timur, is said to be the most densely packed building on the world's most densely populated island. Wall-to-wall cigarette smoke, bar girls: seedy and loved by all. This seems to be one of the few discos with no dress code. Also popular are the **Music Room** in the Borobudur, and the **Oriental** in the Hilton. **Fire** in the Plaza Indonesia is trendy and always crowded. **Ebony** on Jl Rasuna Said in Kuningan is a flashy version of Ancient Egypt with waitresses in Nubian costumes and some good Indonesian bands. The **Pitstop** in the Sari Pan Pacific features a Filipino band. **Stardust** in Kota is a huge converted cinema favored by Chinese teens. If karaoke is your bag, **Dynasty** in Glodok Plaza has a huge venue for performers. For a more up-market spot with similar entertainment try the **Hailai Executive Club** in Ancol.

Late Night

As the night turns into morning, action shifts to the Blok M bars—seedy dives well populated with bar girls and drunken expatriates. **The Club** and **Sundowners** are usually crowded. **Tambora** and **The K Bar** which are sleazier and stay open later, are traditional places to wind up when you can no longer stand up. More refined night owls gather in the **Peacock coffee shop** in the **Hilton** for *bubur ayam* (chicken porridge) and *mie kangkung* (noodles with quail eggs and swamp greens), both excellent pick-me-ups after a night on the town. The **Ramayana Terrace** in the Hotel Indonesia and the **Bogor Brasserie** in the Borobudur are also late-night supper stops for wealthy all-nighters. Cheap late-night/early-morning food can be found nearby on **Jl Kendal**; there is a rehabilitating soup made from sheep parts. Sate stalls are also open late along **Jl Sabang**.

CULTURAL EVENTS

For a more genteel sampling of Jakarta's cultural offerings, start in the early evening with *gamelan* music in the Hilton lobby then visit **Bharata Theater** at Jl Pasar Senen 15 for traditional Javanese *wayang orang* and *ketoprak* performances (8 pm nightly). Free traditional shadow puppet performances, *wayang kulit*, at the Wayang Museum every Sunday at 10 am.

Check the *Jakarta Post* newspaper for listings at the following cultural centers:
Taman Ismail Marzuki Jl Cikini Raya 73 ☎ 322606,

Jakarta's cultural and performing arts center; dance, theater, music, art exhibitions, poetry readings, etc. Has several halls, theaters, cinemas and a planetarium. Get a monthly calendar of events from the center.

Gedung Kesenian, on the corner of Jl Pos and Jl Kesenian ☎ 371892. For a touch of nostalgia take in a show (usually dance or music) at the recently restored Dutch colonial Schouwburg playhouse, it's worth a visit just for the atmosphere.

Art Market Pasar Seni in the Jaya Ancol Dreamland complex, features many traditional performing arts as well as shops selling a wide range of handicrafts and paintings. Open air restaurants, paved boulevards and a sea breeze make it a pleasant place to while away an evening.

Taman Mini Jl Pondok Gede Raya ☎ 8401719. Beautiful Indonesia-in-miniature park in a 160-hectare cultural park with models of the country's 27 regional provinces. Also has an aviary with 112 native bird species, an orchid garden, museums, cinemas and theater performances.

Many foreign embassies have cultural centers with libraries, films and other cultural programs. The **Ganesha Society** run by volunteers, has a weekly program of films and lectures on Indonesian culture and National Museum tours.

American Cultural Center (excellent library) Wisma Metropolitan II, Jl Sudirman ☎ 5711503. **Australian Cultural Center** Jl H Rasuna Said Kav C 15-16 ☎ 5227111. **British Council** (good library), Jl Jend. Sudirman 71 ☎ 5223311. **Centre Culturel Francaise** (French) Jl Salemba Raya 25 ☎ 4218585. **Erasmus Huis** (Dutch) Jl H Rasuna Said, Kav. 5–3 ☎ 5252321. **Goethe Institute** (German) Jl Matraman Raya 23 ☎ 8509719. **Indonesia-America Friendship Soc.** Jl Pramuka 30 ☎ 8583241. **Italian Cultural Center** Jl Diponegoro 45 ☎ 337445. **Japan Cultural Center** Summitmas Bldg, Jl Sudirman ☎ 5255201.

OTHER PLACES OF INTEREST

Istiqlal Mosque, near Banteng square, is the largest mosque in S. E. Asia. Take off shoes before entering.

Ragunan Zoo Jl Harsono RM No. 1, has over 3,600 animals and birds. The official name of the zoo is Ragunan Wildlife Reserve. English-language day tours are available through Sahabat Satwa ("Friends of the Zoo") call the office (Mon–Fri, 9 am–noon) at ☎ 7806164 for details. Open 7 am–5 pm.

Museums

Most Museums are closed Mondays and open Tue–Sun from 9 am–4 pm, closing earlier Fri and Sat. Admission fees are minimal.

Adam Malik Museum (Museum Adam Malik) JlDiponegoro 29 ☎ 337403. Open: 9:30 am–2 pm. Admission: Rp1,000. Former Vice President and Foreign Minister Adam Malik's home with his eclectic collection of ceramics, wooden artifacts, antiques, paintings and icons. Near Jl Surabaya antique stalls.

Armed Forces Museum (Museum Satria Mandala) Jl Gatot Subroto 147 ☎ 5745537. Open: 9 am–3 pm (Closed Mon). Admission: Rp200. Celebrates the armed forces' role in the revolution. Also the former residence of Dewi Soekarno, one of the first president's many wives.

Ethnographic Museum (Museum Bentara Budaya) Jl Palmerah Selatan 17 ☎ 54883008 ext. 7233. Open: 10 am–2 pm. Admission free. Changing exhibitions as well as a permanent collection of Indonesian paintings and ceramics in a beautiful old carved teak-wood house.

Fine Arts Museum (Balai Seni Rupa) Jl Pos Kota 2 ☎ 6907062. Open: 9 am–3 pm, Fri 9 am–2:30 pm, Sat 9 am–12:30 pm, closed Mondays. Admission Rp150. Modern Indonesian art, old ceramics and statues in Batavia's former Hall of Justice.

Jakarta History Museum (Museum Fatahillah) Taman Fatahillah square. Former city hall (*Stadhuis*) of Batavia. Houses large collection of antiques and artifacts from the Dutch colonial period.

Maritime Museum (Museum Bahari) Jl Pasar Ikan 1 ☎ 6693406. Open: 9 am–4pm (Closed Mon). Admission: Rp150. Traditional boat models, fishing gear, photographs, charts, paintings. Fusty but fun.

Museum Indonesia (in Taman Mini Indonesia Indah) Jl Pondok Gede ☎ 8401719. Open: 9 am–5 pm. Admission: Rp200. Traditional costumes and agricultural tools housed in a large "Balinese" pavilion.

National Monument (Monumen Nasional, "MONAS") Jl Silang Monas ☎ 340452. Admission Rp100–200. Dioramas of Indonesian history from prehistoric times until the New Order. Elevator to see the view from the top costs Rp5,000.

National Museum (Museum Nasional) Jl Medan Merdeka Barat 12 ☎ 360976. Open: 8:30 am–2:30 pm Tue–Thur, Sun, Fri to 11 am and Sat to 1 pm. Closed Mondays. Admission: Rp100–200. Indonesia's largest museum. Fine antiquities, jewelry and ceramics. Free tours in English, French and Japanese beginning at 9:30 am on specified days.

Taman Prasasti (Inscription Park) Jl Tanah Abang 1 ☎ 377907. Open: 9 am–3 pm. Admission is free. Historic graves, some from other city cemeteries. Stamford Raffles' wife Olivia is buried here.

Textile Museum (Museum Tekstil) Jl KS Tubun 4 ☎ 365367. Open: 9 am–2 pm; Fri 9 am–11 am. Closed Mon. Extensive collection in a period house.

Wayang Museum Jl Pintu Besar Utara 27 ☎ 679-560. Open: 9 am–3 pm, closing early on Fri (2:30 pm) and Sat (12:30 pm). Closed Mondays. Admission Rp150. Puppets from all over Indonesia and abroad. Free shows every Sunday at 10 am.

MEDICAL SERVICES

There are a number of clean and reliable Western-style clinics. Among the best are the following:

British Medical Scheme in the Setiabudi Building on Jl Rasuna Said ☎ 5201034, ($35 surcharge for non-members).

SOS on Jl Puri Sakti 10/10, Cipete, South Jakarta ☎ 7505980. No appointment required.

Metropolitan Medical Center is (MMC) Jl Rasuna Said, Kav. C21, Kuningan ☎ 5203435. Reliable non-member clinic. No appointment required and usually minimal wait.

Bunda Hospital on the corner of Jl Sutan Syahrir

and Jl Cik Ditiro ☎ 322005, has family planning and gynecological clinics.
Pertamina Hospitals Jl Kyai Maja, Kebayoran Baru and Pondok Indah ☎ 7200289, are well equipped and professionally-run.
Jakarta Central Emergency Service ☎ 118 or 334030, is a 24-hour ambulance service which covers all of Jakarta and will transport to any hospital. Probably the quickest way to get to a hospital. If you don't need emergency treatment on the way, however, call a Bluebird taxi ☎ 325607.

24-Hour Dispensaries

Apotik Raden Saleh Jl Raden Saleh 2 ☎ 323550.
Apotik Jaya Jl Panglima Polim IV/18 ☎ 770137.
Apotik Titi Murni Jl Kramat Raya 128 ☎ 3909682.

Pharmacies

Commonly prescribed drugs can often be purchased without a prescription. Avoid medicines from roadside stalls or a *pasar,* some are fake.
Apotik Senopati Jl Senopati 15, Menteng, **Apotik Menteng** Jl Dr Sam Ratulangi 6 and **Apotik Melawai** Jl Melawai Raya No. 191, Kebayoran, are all large dispensing pharmacists.
Optik Melawai Jl Cokroaminoto 78, Jl Melawai Raya No. 191, and in Ratu Plaza and **Optic Seis** Jl Melawai IX/28, and Ratu Plaza, are reliable for eye tests, spectacles and contact lenses. Glasses can be made in 24 hours if required.

POSTAL SERVICES

The new main **Post Office** is on Jl Lapangan Banteng Utara and is spacious and efficient. Open: 8 am–4 pm Mon to Sat, but some counters close at 1 pm. Branch offices handling most services are found in Sarinah Thamrin (ground floor) and on Jl Kapten Tendean in Kebayoran. These close at 11 am on Fri and 12:30 pm on Sat.

TELEPHONE

Public telephones in Jakarta take either Rp50 or Rp100 coins but rarely work. A more convenient and reliable option is to purchase a phone card in *wartel* offices found throughout the city (try the lower level of Plaza Indonesia) or at hotel counters. These sell by units which translate into talking hours. A 60 unit card costs $2.50 and allows for three hours of intercity gabbing.

Many locations now offer IDD **Home Country Direct**: Hotel Indonesia, Sukarno-Hatta Airport, President Hotel, Jakarta Hilton, Taman Mini, and *Wartel* offices. The telecom center in the Djakarta Theater building is efficient and open 24 hours.

IMMIGRATION

The main immigration office is on Jl Teuku Umar 7, Menteng. Open 8 am–3 pm Monday–Thursday; 8–12 am Friday; 8 am–2 pm Saturday.

NATURE RESERVE PERMITS

The **PHPA** office for permits and information on Indonesia's parks and nature reserves is located at Jl Merdeka Selatan 8–9, Blok G, 21st Floor.

CONSULATES

Australia Jl Thamrin 15 ☎ 323109. **Belgium** Jl Cicurug 4 ☎ 348719. **Britain** Jl Thamrin 75 ☎ 330904. **Canada** Wisma Metropolitan I Fl 5, Jl Sudirman ☎ 510709. **Denmark** Jl Rasuna Said kav 10 ☎ 5204350. **France** Jl. Thamrin 20 ☎ 332807. **Germany** Jl Thamrin 1 ☎ 323908. **Italy** Jl Diponegoro 45 ☎ 337422. **Japan** Jl Thamrin 24 ☎ 324308. **Korea** Jl Teuku Umar 72–74 ☎ 332846. **Malaysia** Jl Imam Bonjol 17 ☎ 332664. **Netherlands** Jl Rasuna Said kav S 3 ☎ 5251515. **New Zealand** Jl Diponegoro 41 ☎ 330680. **Norway** Jl Rasuna Said kav. 10 ☎ 510638. **Singapore** Jl Rasuna Said B1 X/4 Kav 4 ☎ 5201469. **Spain** Jl Thamrin 53 ☎ 325996. **Switzerland** Jl Rasuna Said B1/X3 Persil 2 ☎ 516061. **Thailand** Jl Imam Bonjol 34 ☎ 343762. **United States** Jl Medan Merdeka Selatan 4–5 ☎ 360360.

AIRLINE OFFICES

Cathay Pacific Hotel Borobudur, Jl Lapangan Banteng ☎ 3806664. **China** Duta Merlin, Jl Gajah Mada ☎ 354448. **JAL** Wisma Nusantara, Jl Thamrin ☎ 322207. **KLM** Plaza Indonesia, Jl Thamrin ☎ 3140708/3107657. **Korean** Wisma Metropolitan II, Jl Sudirman ☎ 5780236. **Lufthansa** Panin Centre, Jl Sudirman ☎ 710247. **MAS** Hotel Indonesia, Jl Thamrin ☎ 320909. **Saudia** Wisma Bumiputera, Jl Sudirman ☎ 57-80615. **Singapore** Chase Plaza, Jl Sudirman ☎ 5206899. **Swissair** Hotel Borobudur, Jl Lapangan Banteng ☎ 373608. **Thai** BDN Bldg, Jl Thamrin ☎ 320607. **United** Hotel Borobudur, Jl Lapangan Banteng ☎ 362707. **UTA** Jaya Bldg, Jl Thamrin ☎ 323609. **Philippine** Hotel Borobudur, Jl Lapangan Banteng ☎ 370108. **Qantas** BDN Bldg, Jl Thamrin ☎ 327707. **Royal Brunei** Hotel Sabang Metropolitan, Jl HA Salim ☎ 327214.

FOREIGN BANKS

ABN Jl Juanda 23–24 ☎ 362309. **AMEX** Arthaloka Building, Jl Sudirman 2 ☎ 5702398. **Bank of America** Wisma Antara, Jl Merdeka Selatan 17 ☎ 348031. **Bank of Tokyo** Jl Sudirman kav 10–11 ☎ 5780709. **Chase Manhattan** Jl Sudirman kav 21 ☎ 5782213. **Citibank** Jl Sudirman kav 70A ☎ 5782007. **Hong Kong & Shanghai** Wisma Metropolitan II, Jl Sudirman ☎ 5780075.

Jakarta's Best Bets

Every great city has its secrets—from the restaurant discovered by accident or recommended by a friend, to the curiosity shop tucked down an alley. A few tried and true suggestions in Jakarta are:

Irish Coffee In the bar at the Jayakarta Grill, Sari Pacific Hotel. An elaborate performance: a *sarong*-clad waitress wheels a trolley of gleaming copper utensils to your table and prepares it as you watch, letting rivulets of caramel dribble down the glass.

Cultural Enclave From rock concerts to Irian Jaya art exhibitions and Russian ballet, Taman Ismail Marzuki, or TIM, has it all. At Jl Cikini Raya 73. A monthly program of events is available at the box office and other outlets in the city.

Late Night Sate On Jl Agus Halim (Jl Sabang), pull up to any stand and eat tasty midnight snacks delivered to your car. Saturday-night teenagers' hangout.

Shop Till You Drop To avoid this, shop at Sarinah. The handicraft and batik floors are excellent. A wide range of arts and crafts from every corner of Indonesia; reasonable prices.

Big Value Breakfast From 7 till 10 am, the coffee shop in the Marco Polo Hotel (Jl Cikditiro in Menteng) serves a giant all-you-can-eat smorgasbord and endless cups of coffee.

Goats' Head Soup The *warung* on Jl Kendal behind the Duku Atas railway station in Menteng serve delicious dishes made from all parts of sheep and goat. Choose from large bowls of feet, eyes, ears, meat, testicles (men only).

Eat Your Way Through the Archipelago Street food without the peril. The basement of Pasaraya department store in Blok M has stalls selling Indonesian dishes, Western pizza, spaghetti and steaks. Great food, cheap, clean and efficient.

Salad Days When you crave vegetables, try the salad bars in the Ponderosa or Pizza Hut. One charge for all you can pile on your plate. Skilled structural engineers can get as much on a side-order plate as novices on a main.

Sweet Death Made-to-order *martabak manis,* a thick circular pastry filled with melted chocolate, peanuts and cheese. Delicious, rich and so filling you may need to lie down. Look for *kaki lima* carts after dark.

Post Office To avoid erratic opening hours and long post-office queues, use Hilton or Mandarin hotel postal counters. Open all hours.

Cheap Thrills The roller coaster in the Dunia Fantasi amusement park does a loop-the-loop and double corkscrew. In Taman Impian Jaya Ancol, Dreamland for short, a 200-hectare (500-acre) recreation complex next to Sunda Kelapa. Has golf course, drive-in, marina, swimming pools and Pasar Seni, an art market with tiled walks and piazzas.

City Cruising Now a dying breed, the *becak* pedicab comes into its own at night. Hire one for an hour (50¢) and ride with the night breeze in your hair. Cruise the streets and explore Jakarta after dark.

Delicious Discount The Mandarin Hotel's cakeshop sells goodies half-price after 7 pm. Take away or eat in the Clipper Lounge with satanically strong coffee.

Massage After a tiring day, drop in at Bon Vita, Jl Cisanggiri 10, behind Pasar Santa, Kebayoran Baru, for a revitalising massage and hot towel rubdown. For both sexes, clean and at $3.50 per hour, far cheaper than the hotel fitness centers.

For Ladies House of Beauty, Jl Jambu, Menteng gives the best "cream bath"—hair conditioning with a head, neck and back massage. Relaxing and reasonably priced. Also try a manicure and pedicure.

Hill Therapy A refreshing break from Jakarta's heat can be found in the hill resorts near Puncak Pass. Breathtaking scenery, tea plantations, roadside flower and fruit stalls, and lovely bungalows. Return early afternoon or late night to avoid traffic.

Pizza To Go Pizza Hut delivers deep-pan pizzas. Staff told to "order, cook, go, so no wait." Call 352064 10 am–10 pm, no delivery charge.

Pulau Seribu

See map, page 101.

Just 2.5 hours north of Jakarta, Pulau Seribu (Thousand Islands) is a paradise for **watersports** enthusiasts. Beautiful beaches and diving among the coral reefs surrounding each island make the metropolitan mania of Jakarta seem miles away.

Ferries depart daily around 7 am from the Ancol Marina, usually without prior booking. The return ferry leaves the islands around 2:30 pm. Speedboats and hydrofoils take about one hour. Enquire at Putri Pulau Seribu Paradise office in Djakarta Theatre building. Charter flights at Kemayoran airport, or enquire at the resorts.

Take sunscreen, insect repellent, shoes for walking on the reef. Look for fruit bats, lizards, birds, turtles, pearly dawns and shooting stars.

RESORT BOOKINGS

Pulau Ayer PT Sarotama Bumi Perkasa, Jl Ir H Juanda III/6 ☎ 342031. **Pulau Bidadari** PT Seabreeze, Marina Ancol ☎ 680048. **Pulau Kotok** Duta Merlin Shopping Arcade ☎ 362948. **Pulau Pantara Timur** and **Barat** PT Pantara Wisata Jaya, Hotel Borobudur ☎ 3805017. **Pulau Putri**, Pelanggi, Panjang and Papa Theo are booked through PT Pulau Seribu Paradise, Setiabudi Bldg I, Ground Floor ☎ 515884. **Pulau Sepa** PT Thousand Island Resort Diving Centre, 29 Jl Kalibesar Barat ☎ 678828.

To visit the **bird sanctuaries** on **Pulau Rambut** or **Pulau Bokor**, contact PHPA, Dinas Kehutanan, DKI Jakarta, Jl Rasuna Said Kuningan ☎ 520142.

TOURS

All dive shops in Jakarta organize **diving** trips to Pulau Seribu. Prices are similar. Dive gear can be hired and is usually well-maintained.

Jakarta Dive School ☎ 5703600 ext. 9008; fax: 3803567. **Dive Indonesia** ☎ 370333 ext. 76024; fax: 370447. **Divemasters Pro Shop** ☎ 583051 ext. 9037. **Stingray Dive Centre** ☎ 5700272.

— Janet Boileau/Christie Blom

2 West Java PRACTICALITIES

INCLUDES WEST COAST, BOGOR, BANDUNG & EAST OF BANDUNG

Prices in US dollars, excluding tax & service (10–30%).
S = Single; D = Double; AC = Air-conditioning.

West Coast Beaches

(ANYER AND CARITA)

Beyond Merak and Cilegon, the acrid exhaust fumes of the Jakarta-Tangerang toll road are replaced by a fresh salty breeze and traffic is left in the distance as the highway fades into a two lane shoreline road. There are miles of white sand beaches along the coast between Anyer and Labuan, offering the perfect serene antidote to Jakarta's endless noise and heat.

GETTING THERE

Though not cheap, the easiest way to reach the west coast is **by car**—rent one in Jakarta through any of the agencies (see Jakarta Practicalities). Don't worry about facing the hustle of highway traffic as most agencies provide a driver.

You'll have no trouble reaching the western beaches via **public transportation**, however, as buses run the coastal road between Cilegon and Labuan every ten minutes or so. Starting from Jakarta's Kalideres station, it takes the Merak bus about two hours to reach Cilegon, where you can hop off and catch a minibus south to reach Anyer in about another half hour.

If you're headed for Carita, the direct bus to Labuan is a bit faster; four hours to the main bus terminal, then a 100-meter walk to the gravel parking lot where you transfer to a minibus for the 10-minute ride to Carita.

From Sumatra, the **ferry** across the Sunda Straits to Merak takes about two hours and runs all night, with frequent buses from the terminal all the way to Sumur.

ACCOMMODATION

Unless you're taking a break from a long trans-Javan or Sumatran journey, pass up the rather ordinary Merak and Labuan hotels and head for the more attractive coastal offerings of Anyer and Carita. There is something for travelers of every budget; basic *losmen*, simple beach-front rooms, business-style hotel suites and deluxe bungalows—all within walking distance of the beach if not directly on it.

During weekends and holidays this area becomes crowded with city-dwellers and surcharges of 20–50% are common. Reserve beforehand if you know you'll be competing with the regular crowds, otherwise stick to weekdays.

Budget (under $20)

These hotels offer low-cost accommodation that is clean, central to activities and close to beaches on the Carita-Anyer road.

Carita Krakatau Beach Resort Jl Raya Anyer. Simple bungalows offer both dormitory and private rooms for $4–6, or beachfront rooms for $9–30 a night. Though a bit run-down this is still a good place to meet other travelers and useful for information on boats to Krakatau and trips to Ujung Kulon. Has a small library and info center, and the Krakatau Museum nearby. Bring the *Krakatau Newsletter* (get from tourism offices in Jakarta) for 25% discount on weekdays, 10% on weekends and holidays.

Drever Room Jl Raya Karang Bolong, Anyer (opposite Anyer Beach Hotel). Three simple, clean rooms with shared *mandi;* family-run, with a good *warung* in front. Fruit and tea included in the $5–10 price.

Hotel Caringan Jl Perintis Kemerdekaan, Labuan (100 m before the PHPA office). Clean, quiet rooms with private *mandi.* $5 and up.

Narida Beach Inn Jl Raya Anyer. For $20, you'll get a comfortable room with breakfast included.

Sunset View Jl Raya Anyer, Carita. A small resort with quiet bungalows. $5–7.50.

Yusi Inn Jl Raya Anyer, Carita. Hidden between the bungalows across from the beach along the main coastal road, this colorful inn is basic but has a definite local flavor. Rates $5–7.50.

Intermediate ($20–$60)

Anyer Beach Hometel and Resort (103 rooms) Jl Raya Karang Bolong Km 17, Anyer Serang 42166. ☎ (0254) 601376. Huge resort with a Western 'community' feel and a lively, businesslike atmosphere. Superior recreation/business facilities. Bungalows are $40–50 for one room and $75–125 for two- to four-bedrooms including AC, hot water, kitchenette, minibars. Double on weekends and holidays.

Desiana Cottage Jl Raya Anyer ☎ (0254) 201010. A small, charming resort on the Carita beach strip with a real Indonesian feel. Excellent restaurant. Cottages run $40–80, with economy rooms for

around $15; add 30% on holidays and weekends.
Griya Indira Jl Raya Anyer. Large beach-side bungalows $41; $25 for 2-bedroom cottages.
Guna Sangiang Jl Raya Anyer. Near the beach. Comfortable, basic cottages for $25–50 a night. Good restaurant. Also has karaoke and a pool table.
Hideaway Cottage Jl Raya Anyer; for reservations ☎ (0254) 3106369. Seven comfortable cottages on a quiet beach; no restaurant but a nice pool. $30 for one-bedroom cottages, $75 for a three-bedroom dwelling suitable for up to 10 persons.
Lucia Cottage Jl Raya Anyer, Carita. Quaint rooms across from the beach. $20–30.
Matahari Beach Resort Jl Raya Anyer. Nine bungalows with AC and breakfast. $44–85.
Merak Beach Resort Jl Raya Merak ☎ (0254) 71015. Basic but efficient, rooms face a rocky beach. Try Wing B for a deck over the water; $26S, $29D.
Sanghyang Indah Resort Hotel Jl Raya Anyer ☎ (0254) 601292. Attractive setting in a small teak forest. Swimming pool and tennis court. $40–70.
Selat Sunda Jl Raya Anyer. Unique circular cottages close to the beach. Restaurant open only on Saturday nights. $25–40.
Wira Carita Jl Raya Anyer, Carita ☎ (0254) 200016. Between the Krakatau Museum and the Carita Tourist Office, this Western motel-style resort caters to many group tours. Across the road from the public beach, amenities include tennis courts, a playground and large restaurant. Room rates are $20–30, with cottages at $25–35 a night; group discounts may be available.

First Class ($60 and up)

Anyer Beach Motel (62 rooms) Jl Raya Bandulu; or PO Box 01/ANL, Anyer-Serang 42166 ☎ (021) 510503. This sprawling complex is a quiet western-style resort with roomy bungalows, a strip of beach, tennis courts and a good restaurant with a fun Saturday night barbecue. Deluxe rooms $80, Super Deluxe $90, Suites $225. Family deals and net meal rates available. Popular with business travelers.
Mambruk Quality Resort Jl Raya Karang Bolong; or PO Box 10, Anyer 42166. ☎ (0254) 601602; fax: (0254) 601723. Luxury resort with excellent recreation and business facilities, bright flower gardens and a seaside setting. Two restaurants, a disco, a kid's playground and a lovely pool with a swim-up bar. Shopping arcade, medical, massage and travel services also available. Rooms $70–160; $180–210 for four-person bungalows.
Marina Village (24 rooms, 6 bungalows, 1 suite) Jl Raya Anyer ☎ (0254) 601585. Attached to a small, picturesque marina, this large resort offers first-class ocean sporting facilities, including charters to Krakatau and Ujung Kulon. Accommodation is pleasant, facing the marina or beach; rooms run $55 with AC, $155–210 for two-bedroom bungalows with kitchen;$260 for four-bedroom suite.
Pondok Tu Bagus Jl Raya Anyer; for reservations write to Jl Permata Hijau, Blok G No. 26, Simpruk, Jakarta Selatan ☎ (021) 5484490. A smaller seaside resort set in quiet gardens and breezy palms, bungalows cost around $100 and are often full so be sure to book early.
Puri Retno I and II Jl Raya Anyer ☎ (0254) 201228. This full-facility resort is a first-class escape to Balinese-style serenity with charming bungalows and private beach-side location. Rates are $100 and $200, respectively, for Standard two-room and Deluxe 3-room dwellings, with breakfast.
Siyoni Anyer Seaside Cottage Jl Raya Karang Bolong Km 35; for reservations write Jl Kapten Muslihat No. 21, Bogor ☎ (0251) 327819. Set a half-kilometer off the main road, this quiet resort is often used by business travelers. Comfortable cottages run $66–76, with breakfast.

FOOD

The West Coast offers a broad range of local and international cuisine. Heading south from Cilegon along the main coastal road, a few tasty places to try include:
Cafe de Paris (in Sambolo) is a bit pricey but has excellent cordon bleu and a craft shop next door.
Carita Tourism Office has a basic, inexpensive menu of tasty *nasi goreng*, toast and fruit.
Desiana, just down the road, also has good seafood. Eat shrimp in oyster sauce and fresh grilled fish outside on the patio for a terrific sunset meal.
Guna Sangiang restaurant has a good selection of tasty seafood—try the enormous *udang bakar* (grilled shrimp) and sweet-and-sour fish.
Krakatau Beach Hotel has a fruit salad favorite, served in a coconut shell and topped with ice cream—a delicious snack for a hot day.
Mambruk has a Sunday buffet breakfast and brunch for $10 that includes free use of the huge hotel pool.
Marina Village has a unique bar built from an old wooden fishing boat; facing the western horizon. A relaxing setting for an afternoon seaside cocktail.
Nyenil, next to the Krakatau Museum, is the traditional backpackers' hangout, where you'll find good Indonesian food at budget prices, as well as video games and nightly television gatherings.
Ponderosa at the Mambruk Quality Resort is the place for a quiet afternoon game of chess and a cup of tea. Good hamburgers and a two-for-one happy hour.
The Red Burn (about 10 km past Cilegon across from Krakatau Steel), a lively expat hangout with juicy steaks grilled right at your table, french fries, and good mixed drinks; prices are moderate and a band often plays on the weekends.

DAY TRIPS

In the western beaches area there are a number of short and convenient tour options. The deserted island of **Sangiang**, a small paradise filled with mangroves, monkeys and the remains of a Japanese fort, can be reached in about 2 hours by boat from one of the hotel marinas in Anyer. Also, about 3 km past the Anyer Beach Hotel going south is the turnoff to the natural hot springs just 25 km to the east. **Karang Bolong**, 6 km south of Labuan, is a pleasant stretch of public beach with a large rock arch;

a nice place for a picnic. For a short hike, ask the Carita Tourist Office about the walk to the **Curug Gendang Waterfall**, a leisurely half-day trip that winds through the west coast forests.

Krakatau

See map, page 111.

Visiting Krakatau, one of the most fascinating stops on any traveler's itinerary, requires three things: a reliable boat, a group of friends and patience. No matter where you plan to begin your Krakatau adventure, boats will be easy to find—the key is to get one that is safe. The easiest method is to join one of the many tour packages available from the larger hotels in Jakarta or through major travel agencies. Most hotels along the Anyer-Carita-Labuan strip will also provide information on the various options.

If you're thinking of planning your own trip, try the docks at Tanjung Priok in Jakarta for renting a boat, or simply head to Carita, Labuan or Sumur and ask around. Keep in mind the size of your group, what the price includes (food, petrol, crew, etc) and the amount of time you plan to rent the boat. You'll probably have to bargain hard; a trip for a party of four can run $50–250, depending on the captain and the condition of his boat.

Be careful, as many of these ships are in less than reliable condition. A few years ago, two women drifted off-course all the way to Benkulu, Sumatra, surviving for several weeks on only toothpaste and hope. Consider it safer to arrange something through the Tourist Office in Jakarta, Labuan or Carita, or through your hotel if you're not keen on a package tour. One of the better deals is through PT Wanawisata Alamhayati, at the Tourism Management Board for Ujung Kulon National Park. They have a charter boat that sails between Labuan and Peucang Island via Krakatau for $200 for up to 20 people.

It takes about 4 hours to sail to Krakatau, two or three to climb up and walk around, and then four more hours back to the docks at Labuan, Sumur or the Carita hotels. You'll start early and the weather is often windy and unpredictable, so bring a light jacket, plus a hat and sun block. Wear sturdy, comfortable shoes—high tops or hiking boots are ideal—and don't forget snacks and water for the trek and the boat ride back. A few other things to bring: a canteen which leaves both your hands free for climbing, an extra pair of socks, a handkerchief or small towel, sunglasses and a plastic bag in which to dispose of any trash. The journey becomes very exciting as you sail towards the awesome remains of the legendary 1883 explosion, and a good camera will capture the stunning scenery as well.

Ujung Kulon National Park

See map, page 117.

Ujung Kulon is a subtle paradise of endless jungle trails and bright coral coves that tease the imagination with the promise of adventure and wildlife—and usually deliver. As tourism encroaches, the park is going through many changes. In the last decade, programs in environmental education, conservation and training local Sundanese to run and maintain the area are just a few advances that have enhanced the attraction of the park to visitors worldwide.

GETTING THERE

Besides the package tours from Jakarta, Carita and Labuan, you can start your journey from the PHPA office in Labuan after obtaining a permit ($2.50) and insurance (75¢) and maps and other materials. Stop in the Wanawisata office for additional ideas and information; they also have a booklet on accommodation costs and boat schedules for the islands and peninsular park.

By bus, once you're in Labuan, head south for Sumur ($1), then either hitch or hire a motorcycle ($2.50) for the final 20-km stretch of rugged coastal road to Taman Jaya.

The easiest means of arrival is by car, but past Labuan, the road turns ugly so be sure you either have a good jeep or similar tough vehicle.

GENERAL INFORMATION

Ujung Kulon is great for trekking, wildlife and culture at any time of the year, although from November to June, the rains may limit hiking and camping opportunities. For the best weather and wildlife sightings, plan to stay at least a week between May and October; the dry climate makes trekking easier and animals are more likely to gather near watering holes.

Although most trails are level and easy to follow, guides are required for any trek through the park—plan on paying around $5 a day plus food. Many of these guides are from the nearby Sundanese villages, and their forest experience makes them an invaluable source of stories and information about the park. Treat your guide as a friend rather than a porter and you will be richly rewarded.

If you plan to trek, things to bring include a good pair of walking shoes, insect repellent and anti-malarial pills—the disease is prevalent in the park. Wear a hat for protection from the wickedly hot sun along the coastal routes. Nights are cool and comfortable; a sleeping bag isn't necessary as a *sarong* will provide enough warmth and cover. There are plenty of clean beaches and river pools along the way, so bring your swimsuit. Take thongs or sandals to wear after a long day's trek. Plastic bags are useful both for trash and to protect your camera and clothes during rain and river crossings.

Further Details

For general information on the Krakatau and Ujung Kulon adventures, try the Tourist Offices in Jakarta. The friendly staff can at least start you off in the right direction.

You can get details on reservations and permits from the **PHPA** (Forestry and Nature Protectorate) office at Wisma Manggala Wanabakti, Blok I L&B, Jl Garat Soebroto in Jakarta or at Jl Juanda 9 in Bogor (next to the Botanical Gardens). The office for **PT Wanawisata Alamhayati**, which handles most of the travel options to Ujung Kulon, can also provide pamphlets on trails, accommodation and boat schedules. Write to: Gedung Manggala Wanabhakti Blok IV, Lantai II, Wing-A, Jl Jenderal Gatot Subroto, Senayan, Jakarta 10270 (☎ 5710392 from Jakarta). If you'd like to learn more about the history and species of Ujung Kulon or current projects in the park, try the **World Wide Fund for Nature** located at Jl Pela Raya No. 3, Gandiara Utara, PO Box 7928 JKISKM Jakarta 12079.

The best option to get your **permit** is at the PHPA office in Labuan (Jl Perintis Kemerdekaan No. 43) on your way to the park. The Wanawisata office is just 100 m down the street, and both organizations will be able to provide you with maps, advice and ideas. Just 7 km north along the same road, the Krakatau Beach Hotel is another useful source of information, with brochures, maps and newspaper clippings about the area.

In Carita, one km north of the Krakatau Beach Hotel, the eager staff at the **Tourism Office** can help you plan a more individualized journey, and give ideas for things to do in the west coast area. The **Krakatau Museum** (open 10 am–1 pm daily), across from the Krakatau Beach Hotel, is an excellent source of information and historical background for West Java, with artifacts and displays ranging from skulls recovered from Banten and the studies of volcanoes to current research on the flora and fauna in Ujung Kulon.

ACCOMMODATION

Where you stay in the park will depend much on what you want to do: there are endless activities and several accommodation options. The best deal anywhere are the shelters along the trails, simple wooden structures which provide a protective roof, a cool breeze and a clean ocean or river in which to play—all for free!

For those who enjoy more amenities, the deluxe guesthouses are on **Peucang Island**; overlooking a lush field filled with wildlife including deer, monitor lizards and macaques. These huge ranch-style cottages are complete with wide verandas, private baths, running water, electricity at $25–80 per night. Most package tours stay here, as there is a good restaurant, an information center, and a picture-perfect beach. The island is also central to most of the mainland trails, which are easily reached by boat from the Peucang dock. With boating, snorkeling and swimming options as well as a variety of wildlife including primates, pigs, birds, deer and several Javan rhino, many visitors simply relax here and never step onto the peninsular park.

Handeuleum Island is also a popular package stopover, although there is no restaurant and facilities are limited. With four rooms, ten visitors maximum, it is conveniently located across from the Cigenter Grazing Ground—one of the prime rhino-spotting locations. Rooms are reasonably priced, with doubles at $15, though many travelers choose to camp at the watchtower beside the grazing ground instead; for late-night and early-morning glimpses of wildlife.

Panaitan Island has no formal accommodation; but beach camping with the surfers is fun. As the island is as yet undeveloped, the wilderness is dense and beautiful, with several trails to explore and mountains to climb and plenty of ideal camping spots along the way.

Just beyond the rocky western bay and a shady coconut grove, **Taman Jaya** offers a room and breakfast in one of several comfortable guesthouses for $10 S and $20 D a night, with shared living areas and *mandis*. Across the street are the PHPA, Wanawisata and World Wildlife Fund offices.

WALKS AND WILDLIFE

Trekking and wildlife-watching are the most common reasons for coming to Ujung Kulon; your options are limited only by time and imagination. Trails run all around the peninsula, as well as through Peucang and Panaitan Island, ranging from easy one hour walks to challenging jungle and mountain treks for outdoor enthusiasts of every age and physical condition.

Wildlife is everywhere, but your best chances for seeing primates, birds, wild deer, pigs and *banteng* are in the mornings and evenings; for sightings of larger animals, try the Cigenter and Cidaon grazing grounds. A day's walk through the cooler forest areas can provide glimpses of everything from macaques to butterflies, snakes and perhaps, the slow movement of spots as a leopard slinks through the shadows, or the deep tracks of the rare Javan rhino.

SWIMMING AND SNORKELING

Watersports are another reason for a visit to

Ujung Kulon. A variety of diving and snorkeling tours that depart from the docks at Tanjung Priok are available from larger hotels and travel agencies in Jakarta. Hotels in the Carita-Anyer area have similar deals. Try Marina Village, Anyer Mambruk Quality Resort and Beach Hometel, or Wanawisata and the Carita Tourist Office. You'll also find many options for boating and fishing tours at these places. An alternative is to bargain for daily small boat rental at the docks of Labuan, Peucang, Sumur and Taman Jaya.

Peucang is quiet, secluded and clean: ideal for swimming and sunning. Panaitan Island attracts a lively surfing crowd drawn by challenging waves and beach camping. Trekkers along the coastal peninsula will find plenty of sandy beaches and sunlit jungle rivers for that revitalizing swim after a tough day in the jungle.

SUNDANESE CULTURE

For culture, a stay in Taman Jaya offers a chance to learn the Sundanese ways. Many villagers enjoy talking with visitors and, if you're lucky, you may be allowed to observe traditional craft-making, methods of cooking or even a wedding.

Staff at Wanawisata or the PHPA in Labuan might be able to arrange such a trip. Also try the Wanawisata or WWF offices next to the guest-houses in Taman Jaya. Very little English is spoken in the villages, so it helps to have a good knowledge of Bahasa Indonesia or Sundanese—or at least travel with someone who does.

—Holly S. Smith

Bogor

See map, page 118. Telephone code is 0251.

GETTING THERE

Bogor (population 300,000) lies on the Jakarta-Bandung route, though the Jagorawi toll road bypasses Bogor. Express trains leave from Gambir Station in Jakarta twice a day (75¢); otherwise slow trains depart almost every hour during the day. No trains leave for Bandung from here, but there is a train to Sukabumi twice a day. The Bogor train station is in the center of town on Jl Raya Permag.

The bus from the Kampung Rambutan bus terminal in east Jakarta costs about 50¢ or 75¢ with AC. Further connections can be made from from Bogor's Baranangsiang bus terminal to Sukabumi, Bandung, Cirebon and Pelabuhan Ratu. Another bus station (Merdeka) is near the train station. Numerous *becak* ply the streets of Bogor; *bemo* cost Rp250 for short distances and Rp500 for longer ones. There's a taxi terminal across the road from the Zoological Museum on Jl Juanda.

ACCOMMODATION

Many of these rates are due to rise in the next two years; for exact rates, contact the Tourism Office or your travel agency.

Abu Pensione (18 rooms and dormitory) Jl Mayor Oking 15 ☎ 322893. A very informal and friendly hostel, popular with foreign tourists. Dorms and private rooms. The elevated terrace restaurant is a nice place to have a cool drink and write post-cards. Offers various tourist services, including airport pickup for $25. Dorms $2.50, rooms $6–23.

Bogor Inn (20 rooms) Jl Kumbang 12 ☎ 328134. An intimate little guest house on a quiet side street. A little overly decorated in pinks and whites, the rooms are very nice. $12 per person, regardless of room. A small restaurant is attached.

Dewi Sartika (34 rooms) Jl Dewi Sartika 6A ☎ 312343. Brand new and modern. Restaurant. $20–32.

Firman Pensione (14 rooms) Jl Paledang 48 ☎ 323246. A clean, reasonably priced *losmen* 100 meters from the Botanical Gardens. With breakfast, $6. $9 with bath; $11 for a 3-person room.

Pangrango (73 rooms) Jl Pangrango 23 ☎ 328670; fax: 314060. New and the best in town, on a quiet side street off Jl Pajajaran. Restaurant, pool, TV, mini-bar. $16 standard, $43 Suite.

Puri Bali (15 rooms) Jl Paledang 30 ☎ 317498. Shady, clean rooms near the Botanical Gardens. Rooms including breakfast $10.

Ririn (30 rooms) Jl Ciburial Indah I & II, Baranangsiang ☎ 314070. This new modern hotel is just a couple of kilometers past the hustle and bustle of Bogor. Located south of the bus terminal and off the road in a rural setting. $15–38.

Salak (54 rooms) Jl Juanda 8 ☎ 312090. Previously a charming but run-down old colonial place, it is currently being renovated and promises to become one of the best places to stay in town. Just opposite the Presidential Palace. Due to open early '95.

Wisma Ramayana (21 rooms) Jl Juanda 54 ☎ 32-0364. Near the entrance of the Botanical Gardens. Pleasant inner courtyard. Ask about the tour to Gunung Salak waterfalls and hot springs. Reasonable rooms, breakfast included. $8–19.

FOOD

Bunga Seruni Jl Perintis Kemerdekaan 7. Good Sundanese cuisine.

Bogor Permai Jl Sudirman 23A. The best Chinese food in town. Popular with tour groups.

Jumbo Bakery Jl Sudirman 3F.

Kentucky Fried Chicken Jl Raya Pajajaran 8.

Lautan Jl Sudirman 15. Chinese & Western.

Multia Steakhouse Jl Pajajaran. Near Wisma Permata.

Trio Permai Jl Juanda 38. Indonesian food.

Plaza Kapten Muslihat (also called Taman Topi). By the train station. Indonesian food and recreation park. Kid's rides.

NOTE: Many places along Jl Suryakencana serve the Bogor specialty *asinan* : vegetables pickled in brine.

MISCELLANEOUS

Bogor Tourist Information Center Jl Juanda 10, between the City Hall and Hotel Salak. Ask for the informative *Guide to Bogor Town* booklet.
Hospitals RS Karya Bakti, Jl Dr Semeru; Red Cross, Jl Pajajaran Raya (east side of Botanical Gardens).
Main Post Office Jl Juanda 5.
Main Telecoms Office Jl Pengadilan 8.
Bank Bumi Daya Jl Juanda 12.
Bogor Botanical Garden Entrance on Jl Juanda.
Sukarna's Gong Workshop Jl Pancasan 17.

SHOPPING

Bogor Internusa Shopping Centre Jl Raya Pajajaran.
Dewi Sartika Plaza Jl Dewi Sartika 1. Big shopping center just north of the bus terminal.
Matahari Jl Paledang 15. Various handicrafts.
Shangri-La Department Store Jl Merdeka 6.
Art Shop Delima Jl Suryakencana 54. *Wayang golek*, paintings and wall hangings.

Puncak Area

See map, page 120.
This cool, misty resort area really fills up on the weekends with the exodus from Jakarta. No air or rail connections, but many buses run between Jakarta and Bandung, and by *bemo* hopping you can even get here from Bogor.

This area encompasses a number of distinct areas on both sides of Puncak Pass. Many villas, guest houses, hotels and restaurants are on both sides of the summit. Room rates tend to go up on the weekends and holidays. It's possible to find bungalows by asking in small restaurants off the main road.

Ikan mas (goldfish) and *gurame* (another kind of fish) are a culinary specialty of the area. Above Cipanas it is less populated and cooler. Just below the summit on the western side are a number of stalls selling fruits and vegetables, as well as souvenirs such as strange man-high tea roots.

Summit Panghegar (112 rooms) ☎ (0255) 511335, 512785. The best hotel in the area: thoughtfully designed and well-suited for private gatherings or conferences. Located in Pacet, close to the Cibodas Botanical Gardens. $54–75.

Puncak

Telephone code is 0255.
Puncak Pass (41 rooms) Jl Raya Puncak ☎ 512503; fax: 512180. Nearest the summit and with colonial charm. Bungalows and rooms with a wide, lovely view. The grounds are spacious and well kept. Very cozy bungalows, most with a fireplace. Good restaurant, pool and playground. $50–108 (5% discount weekdays).
Bukit Indah (120 rooms) Jl Puncak Raya ☎ 512903; fax: 513167. Another of the older, established hotels (3-star) in the area just below Puncak Pass Hotel. The standard rooms are nice but small. With 6 conference rooms, this is a favorite place for Jakarta groups to hold conferences and seminars. A new wing has just been built. Swimming, tennis, and restaurant. $38–110.
Ciloto Indah Permai (126 rooms) Jl Raya Ciloto ☎ (0255) 512645; fax: 512644. Below the road 25 m and very quiet. Good facilities: a pool, playground, fitness center, billiard room, restaurant and disco. The single and double rooms are unexciting, but the bungalows are spacious and comfortable. $32 double room; $132 4-room bungalow.

Cisarua & Cibeureum

Telephone code is 0251.
Cisarua lies 10 km east of Bogor on the road to Puncak Pass, near the sprawling Gunung Mas tea plantation. It's a good base for scenic rural walks.
Kopo International Youth Hostel (49-person capacity) Jl Raya Puncak 557, Cisarua ☎ 4296. Clean budget rooms. Breakfast included and some rooms with TV. Private rooms available. Dormitory-style bed $2.50.
Perama (28 rooms) Jl Raya Puncak Km 22, Cisarua ☎ 4735. Huge, artificial rocks everywhere. Quiet grounds. $22 S; $24 D.
Permai International (10 rooms) Jl Raya Puncak km 82 ☎ 4864. Near the turnoff to Taman Safari. The standard rooms are small but comfortable and quiet, with a nice view over the valley. Deluxe rooms are next to the busy road. $20–30.
Safari Garden (300 rooms) Jl Raya Puncak 601 ☎ 4148; fax: 4111. Large complex of rooms, bungalows and facilities amid 7-hectare site. A wide range of accommodation from $15–56.

Taman Safari

This safari park comprising 168 hectares is near Cisarua: look for the well-marked intersection with the sign pointing to Taman Safari. A *bemo* costs Rp500 for the 2.5 km ride to the park. Entrance fee is $2.50 for adults; $2 for children under 6. A van with a guide will take you around, or you may drive your own car. ☎ (0251) 4422.

Selabintana

Telephone code is 0266.
Selabintana lies south of the Puncak area, on the slopes of Gunung Gede. Access is via Sukabumi. There are rail connections to Sukabumi from Bogor and Bandung. Buses to Sukabumi run from Jakarta and Bogor via Cibadak and from Bandung via Cianjur. From the *alun-alun* in Sukabumi *bemo* run the length of Jl Selabintana.

Bukit Idaman (28 rooms) Jl Selabintana 137 ☎ 22-2853. Traditional Sundanese bungalows with lots of character. Restaurant attached. $22–32.
Hotel Selabintana (163 rooms) Jl Selabintana Km 7 ☎ 223204; fax: 221501. Located at the end of the road. The best place to stay in the area. A huge 2-star hotel complex in the colonial tradition. Lovely manicured grounds. Sundanese restaurant, swimming, tennis, golf and hiking (ask where to get permission to hike up G. Gede and G. Pangrango).
Pondok Asri is a new addition to the Hotel Selabintana which has very nice three-bedroom split-level bungalows. $17–$22 (excludes 20% tax and service).
Pangrango (20 bungalows) Jl Selabintana Km 7 ☎ 221520. Large recreation area, but rooms are rather run-down and dull. $9–20 (add 21%).
Sukabumi Indah (28 rooms) Jl Selabintana Km 6.3 ☎ 224818. Brand new. Swimming pool, tennis and restaurant. $25–100.

Many restaurants and *warung* line Jl Selabintana. Try rabbit *sate* at Sate Kelinci, Km 7.

Pelabuhan Ratu

Telephone code is 0268.
This picturesque fishing village some 50 km south of Bogor fills up at weekends with local tourists. There is no rail or air service to Pelabuhan Ratu. Buses and minibuses run frequently between Pelabuhan Ratu and Cibadak or Sukabumi, or Bogor directly. The bus station is in the center of town near the fish market.

ACCOMMODATION

After turning left at the intersection onto Jl Siliwangi to go into town, there are some inexpensive *losmen* on the right-hand side, such as Laut Kidul and Karang Naya. Most hotels in Pelabuhan Ratu charge more on the weekends and holidays.
Bayu Amrta (17 rooms) ☎ (02669) 41031 for reservations. Past Buana Ayu and situated above the ocean cliffs off the road. Most rooms have been newly re-decorated. Very clean and comfortable. Good value for the price. Open air terrace restaurant. No direct access to the beach. $9–23.
Buana Ayu (8 rooms) ☎ (022) 440882 in Bandung for reservations. Also known as Hoffman's. Just around the bend from Wantilan Restaurant. Bungalows overlooking the ocean. No grounds to move around on, but it has a well-known restaurant. All rooms with AC, fridge and terrace. $13–43.
Cleopatra (38 rooms) Jl Raya Citepus 114 ☎ 41-185. Plain, clean rooms in a new hotel complex about 5 km west of town. Rooms and cottages. Pool for children and a restaurant. $20 double with fan; $38 for a 3-person room with AC and TV.
Karang Sari (31 rooms, 6 bungalows) Jl Raya Cisolok ☎ 41078. Landscaped complex across the road from the beach. Small restaurant. Adequate rooms for $9; comfortable AC bungalows $38.
Pondok Dewata (41 rooms) ☎ 41022. Not far from the fish market. Bungalows spread out in a Bali-style complex. Right on the beach. Disco on the grounds. The new, large bungalows are a great deal for $43, with AC and TV. Non-AC $30.
Samudra Beach (100 rooms) Jl Raya Citepus ☎ 41-200, or (021) 3840601 for reservations in Jakarta. About 6 km west of town. The area's only "luxury" hotel. A little expensive but it's got everything. The rooms are in need of renovation but comfortable. Seaside pool, tennis, restaurants, lounge and disco. Room 308 is a "meditation" room for *Nyai Loro Kidul*, goddess of the southern coast, so bring an offering. All AC. $60–225.
Wisma Handayani (14 rooms) Not far from Karang Sari towards town, up a small road in a *kampung*. The rooms are very basic. $10–20.

FOOD

Wantilan Restaurant Part of the Pondok Dewata Hotel complex. Cozy place to enjoy good seafood, Chinese and western dishes. **Bayu Amrta** serves seafood and western food. **Buana Ayu** is said to have the best food in town. About 4 km west from town are some small beachside *warung* under the palm trees: **Ratu Sari** (Chinese, seafood), **Restoran Sanggar Sari** (Chinese, seafood, chicken) and **Restoran Gemini** (seafood, fried chicken).

MISCELLANEOUS

Bank BCA Jl Siliwangi 141. **Hospital** Set back from the road on the right coming into town. **Goa Lalay Bat Cave:** the road is near the BCA bank. Sign only visible when coming into town. 4.2 km to the cave—the bats swarm out just before sunset.

— *Gary Crabb*

Bandung

Telephone code is 022.
Bandung is known for its colonial past and its cool climate. Spend a day or two exploring the city's sights and attend a performance of Sundanese *wayang golek*, music or dance in the evenings. Then head for the hills. Weeks could be spent exploring the highlands around the city.

ARRIVAL/DEPARTURE

You can get to Bandung by air, road or rail. Better to go by train or bus to catch glimpses of the area's magnificent scenery. Flights from Jakarta to Bandung fly from Halim airport, south of the capital.

By Air

Merpati, Bouraq and Sempati serve Bandung regularly from Jakarta, Surabaya and Yogyakarta.

Merpati's shuttle flights leave Jakarta's Halim airport about eight times daily between 8 am 4 pm, while Bouraq (daily at 4 pm) and Sempati (twice daily at 8 am and 4:15 pm) fly to Bandung from Jakarta's Sukarno-Hatta International airport. From Surabaya there are daily Merpati flights scheduled at 8:50 am and 1:50 pm, and from Yogyakarta, Bouraq flies daily at 2 pm.

Departure. Merpati, Bouraq and Sempati fly regularly from Bandung to Jakarta, Surabaya, and Yogyakarta. Merpati's shuttle flights leave for Jakarta's Halim airport about eight times daily between 7 am–4 pm whilst Bouraq (daily at 3:50 pm) and Sempati (twice daily at 9:05 am and 5:20 pm) fly to Jakarta. There are daily Merpati flights to Surabaya at 7 am and 11 am, and Bouraq fli\es to Yogyakarta every day at 7 am.

By Road

Bus services to Bandung run from nearly every location in Java. Innumerable vehicles regularly ply the scenic road between Jakarta and Bandung, leaving the capital from the new Kampung Rambutan bus terminal in the east.

You should not have a problem finding a bus to Bandung from Central Java or even East Java, but you might have to change in Purwokerto (Central Java) or Banjar (West Java). Bandung can also be easily reached from Cirebon, Pangandaran, Bogor, and Sukabumi.

The 4848 Company (Jakarta office: Jl Prapatan, near Aryaduta Hotel ☎ 364448) runs **long-distance taxis** to Bandung which take you right to your door. $6 per person from Jakarta or $30 if you charter the whole vehicle.The latter may be more comfortable if you want to stop in Bogor or the Puncak area ($3 extra is charged for every hour of stopover time). **Media Taxi** ☎ 33-0868, also run Intercity taxis to Jakarta. Round-trip including driver, gas, AC costs about $70.

If you hire a **self-drive car** from Jakarta you have the choice between two approach routes: the toll road east of Jakarta via Purwakarta or Subang, or the southern route via Puncak or Sukabumi. The Puncak road is the most scenic but it is often crowded.

GETTING AWAY. All types of buses leave Bandung regularly to just about anywhere in West Java, as well as other destinations: Yogya via Tasikmalaya; Jakarta via Bogor, the north coast via Cirebon; and even Malang in East Java.

Most buses leave from one of the two main terminals: Kebun Kelapa, a.k.a. Abdul Muis, on Jl Pungkur (westbound buses) or Cicaheum, on Jl Suniaraja (eastbound buses), the various levels of comfort are usually indicated by prices. **Long-haul buses** to Yogyakarta and Malang tend to depart from outside the company offices, so be sure to check the location long before your departure time.

The **4848 Taxi Company** can pick you up from wherever you are to take you on to Jakarta or Bogor for $6 ($30 for a chartered limousine), or to an eastern destination such as Pangandaran. To book, contact their office in Bandung located on Jl Suniaraja 14 ☎ 434848.

By Rail

The rail journey either from Jakarta or from Yogyakarta is a particularly scenic way of getting to Bandung.

From Jakarta. Parahyangan express trains reach Bandung in three hours, leaving Jakarta's Gambir station daily at 5:40, 9:30, 11:30 in the mornings and 1:30, 3:30, 5:30, 6:50, 8:40 and 9:30 in the evenings, with an additional train at 4:50 pm on Sundays and public holidays. Fares are $5–10, depending on class.

From Yogyakarta the train takes 8 hours, leaving daily at 8 am, 11 am and 11:20 pm. Take the early morning train so as not to miss the scenery. On Sundays and public holidays there is an additional train from Banjar, (Pangandaran) leaving at 6:20 am.

On all these journeys, the last hour and a half before you reach Bandung takes you through spectacular scenery, so make sure you are awake: especially on the night train from Surabaya and Yogyakarta.

GETTING AWAY. Jakarta-bound Parahyangan express trains leave Bandung daily at 5 am, 6 am, 9 am, 11 am and at 1 pm, 3 pm and 6:20 pm; with extra trains on Sundays and public holidays at 5 pm and 7:30 pm. Fares are $5–10, depending on class.

Eastbound trains leave the station at 5:25 am, 7:40 am and 5:40 pm, and arrive in Tasikmalaya about three hours later; in Banjar after four hours; in Yogyakarta after 6.5 hours; and in Surabaya after some 14 hours. On Sundays and public holidays an extra train leaves Bandung for Banjar at 1 pm. The sections just west of Bandung and between Cicalengka (half an hour east of Bandung) and Cibatu (1.5 hours away) offer the most beautiful views.

LOCAL TRANSPORT

A number of companies operate **metered taxis** in the city. The tariffs have been fixed by the Transportation Ministry and are very moderate at about 50¢ per kilometer. **Car hire** per hour or per day can be arranged by the better hotels or by the 4848 taxi service (see above).

The countless small minibuses have colored stripes referring to their respective destinations. Most of these vehicles are called *angkot* (an abbreviation of *angkutan kota*: urban transport) and ply routes from the four big terminals of Station Hall, Cicaheum, Ciroyom, or Abdul Muis (alias *Kebun Kelapa*). The destinations are displayed fairly clearly on the windscreens. Tariffs vary between 5¢ and 20¢.

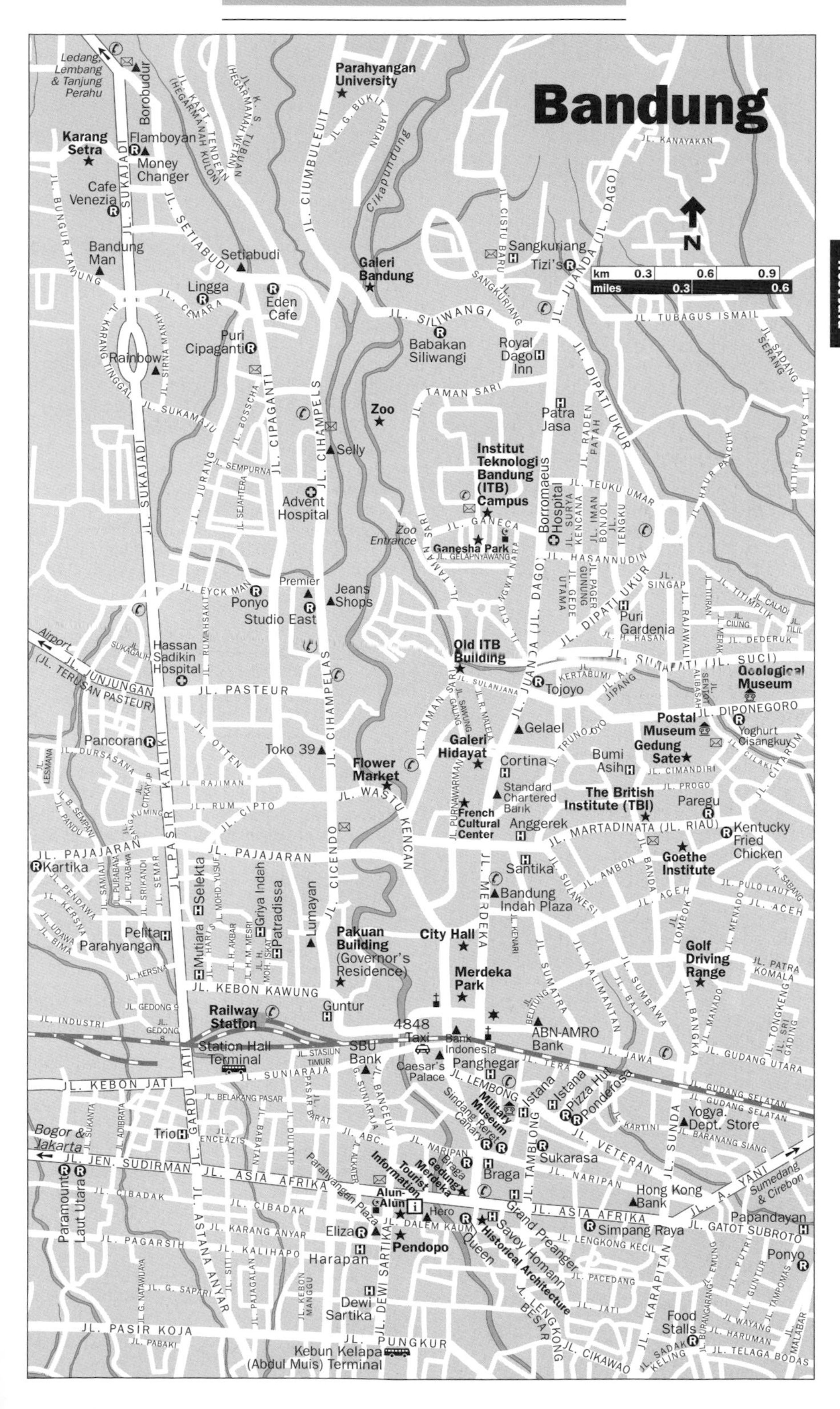
Bandung
km 0.3 0.6 0.9
miles 0.3 0.6
N
Parahyangan University
Galeri Bandung
Zoo
Institut Teknologi Bandung (ITB) Campus
Ganesha Park
Old ITB Building
Geological Museum
Postal Museum
Gedung Sate
The British Institute (TBI)
Goethe Institute
Golf Driving Range
Galeri Hidayat
French Cultural Center
Flower Market
City Hall
Merdeka Park
Pakuan Building (Governor's Residence)
Railway Station
Station Hall Terminal
Kebun Kelapa (Abdul Muis) Terminal
Pendopo
Historical Architecture
Military Museum
Gedung Merdeka
Tourist Information
Karang Setra
Money Changer
Advent Hospital
Hassan Sadikin Hospital
Borromaeus Hospital
Airport
Bogor & Jakarta
Sumedang & Cirebon
Ledang, Lembang & Tanjung Perahu
JL. SUKAJADI
JL. SETIABUDI
JL. CIPAGANTI
JL. CIHAMPELAS
JL. SILIWANGI
JL. JUANDA (JL. DAGO)
JL. DIPATI UKUR
JL. PASTEUR
JL. PAJAJARAN
JL. MERDEKA
JL. ASIA AFRIKA
JL. JEN. SUDIRMAN
JL. KEBON JATI
JL. A. YANI
JL. GATOT SUBROTO
JL. MARTADINATA (JL. RIAU)
JL. DIPONEGORO
JL. SUMATRA
JL. JAWA
JL. WASTU KENCAN
JL. CICENDO
JL. TAMAN SARI
JL. GANECA
JL. TUBAGUS ISMAIL
JL. KARAPITAN
JL. PUNGKUR
JL. DEWI SARTIKA
JL. ASTANA ANYAR
JL. PASIR KOJA
JL. VETERAN
JL. SUNDA
JL. BANGKA
JL. LEMBONG
JL. NARIPAN
Braga
Savoy Homann
Grand Preanger
Sukarasa
Simpang Raya
Papandayan
Ponyo
Yogya. Dept. Store
Hong Kong Bank
ABN-AMRO Bank
Bank Indonesia
SBU Bank
4848 Taxi
Caesar's Palace
Panghegar
Istana
Pizza Hut
Ponderosa
Alun-Alun
Hero
Eliza
Harapan
Dewi Sartika
Food Stalls
Trio
Paramount
Laut Utara
Kartika
Pelita
Parahyangan
Mutiara
Selekta
Griya Indah
Patradissa
Lumayan
Guntur
Santika
Bandung Indah Plaza
Anggerek
Standard Chartered Bank
Cortina
Gelael
Tojoyo
Bumi Asih
Paregu
Kentucky Fried Chicken
Yoghurt Cisangkuy
Puri Gardenia
Patra Jasa
Royal Dago Inn
Babakan Siliwangi
Sangkuriang
Tizi's
Setiabudi
Lingga
Eden Cafe
Puri Cipaganti
Rainbow
Flamboyan
Borobudur
Cafe Venezia
Bandung Man
Selly
Premier
Jeans Shops
Ponyo
Studio East
Toko 39
Pancoran
Zoo Entrance

West Java 2

ACCOMMODATION

Budget (under $20)

Most of the less expensive hotels are near the railway station. They are simple and efficient, but do not accept credit cards.

Cianjur (15 rooms) Jl Abdul Muis 169 ☎ 56834. Very nice *losmen*. Walk from bus depot. $4.

Harapan Eka Graha (29 rooms) Jl Kepatihan 14–16, ☎ 4204212, 4200204. Simple Dutch-style hotel close to the city centre, just behind the *alun-alun* (town square). No AC. $11–22.

Mawar (10 rooms) Jl Pangerang 14 ☎ 51934. Near the *alun-alun*. Clean. $4–6.

Nugraha (17 rooms) Jl Haji Mesri 11 ☎ 436146. Tasteful bamboo decor. No AC. $7–20.

Pasifik (8 rooms) Jl Abdul Muis 79 ☎ 56027. Dutch-style hotel near bus station; no AC. $10–15.

Patradissa Jl M Iskat 8 ☎ 4206680. Within walking distance of the railway station's northern exit.

Sakadarna (15 rooms) Jl Kebonjati 34 ☎ 439897. Cramped but clean, near train station. $3–5.

Intermediate ($20–$60)

Major credit cards are generally accepted.

Abadi Garden Jl Setiabudi 287, Bandung 40154, ☎ 210987. Rooms at $37 and suites at $85.

Anggrek Jl Martadinata 15 ☎ 4205537. Convenient location, but somewhat run down. $33.

Arjuna Plaza Jl Ciumbuleuit 114 ☎ 231328. High up on the slopes above the city in the Ciumbuleuit residential area. Cool evening breezes. $13–37.

Cipaku Indah Jl Cipaku Indah II 2, Bandung 40143 ☎ 210221/2/4; fax: 210223. At the edge of the city this hotel is designed like a motel, with individual bungalows for $22–50. Situated near recreation facilities (heated and unheated pools, tennis courts, fishing pond). Arrive by taxi, as public transport may be difficult to find to this area.

Cortina (27 rooms) Jl Juanda 32, next to Gelael supermarket, ☎ 4206778. $30 and up.

Griya Indah near the railway station's northern exit on Jl M Iskat 21 (off Jl Kebon Kawung). Very new: good value for money. ☎ 4204263. $20–30.

Guntur near the railway station at Jl Oto Iskandardinata 20 ☎ 4203763. Popular with Indonesian business travelers. $18 and up. Good value.

Istana Jl Lembong 21 and 44 (one building on either side of the street) ☎ 436079. Rooms between $38–52, suites from $95.

New Naripan Jl Naripan 31 ☎ 439473. Convenient: in city center near Jl Braga. Regular *wayang golek* show. $36 and up.

Patrajasa (26 rooms) Jl Juanda 132 ☎ 2502664. North of town. Not bad; rooms from $37.

Puri Gardenia (50 rooms) Jl Dipati Ukar 30 ☎ 21-0001, 82345. Tucked away in the tree-lined streets of the old colonial residential quarter. Rooms are good value, at $13–45, but there's no restaurant.

Sangkuriang Guest House Jl Cisitu 45B (off Jl Siliwangi) ☎ 2504707; fax: 82420. Popular despite out-of-the-way location. Pleasant rooms. $25 and up.

Talaga Sari Jl Setiabudi 269–275 ☎ 212632, 210916, 214107. Conveniently near a swimming pool and the Glosis restaurant, as well as the Chinese restaurant next door. $25–110.

First Class ($60 and up)

All of the following feature swimming pools, 24-hour restaurants and accept major credit cards.

Grand Hotel Preanger (176 rooms) facing Jl Asia-Afrika at 81, PO Box 1220, Bandung 40111 ☎ 431631, 430682/3; fax: 430034. The best hotel in town, one of Bandung's holdovers from the colonial era. Right in the city center. Highest standards of luxury, including bullet-proof presidential suite. Rooms from $120, suites from $600.

Horison (253 rooms) Jl Maskumambang 8, Bandung 40264. ☎ 305000; fax: 445993. One of Bandung's newest hotels. Southeast of the center. Large compound with olympic-sized pool. Rooms from $75.

Kumala (63 rooms) Jl Asia-Afrika 140, ☎ 4205141. A good hotel for this price range. Rooms around $60.

Panghegar Jl Merdeka 2, ☎ 432286/7, 432296/8. A hotel from the Sixties, with a Sundanese touch. The revolving rooftop restaurant stages Sunda dance shows on Wed and Sat nights. $65 and up.

Papandayan Jl Gatot Subroto 83, Bandung 40263. ☎ 3100799; fax: 4205993. A new hotel out of the city center to the east. Has a lovely open restaurant. Rooms from $88.

Santika Jl Sumatera 52–54. PO Box 1314, Bandung 40115. ☎ 4201038; fax: 439601. Modern hotel with an appealing design. Conveniently near to the shopping area on Jl Merdeka. Cozy bar. Rooms from $80, suites from $115.

Savoy Homann (153 rooms) opposite the Preanger in Jl Asia-Afrika 112 ☎ 432244, 430083; fax: 436187. An art deco architectural monument. This place has a nostalgic air, with a cozy coffee shop and lovely tropical garden. Rooms $75–80; deluxe suites around $110.

Sheraton Inn Bandung Jl Ir H Juanda (popularly known as Jl Dago) 390, Bandung 40135. ☎ 2500-303; fax: 2500301. Some way out of town, at the foot of the hills. Restaurant closes at 11 pm. Rooms from $80, suites from $180.

FOOD

Sundanese

All of the following restaurants are popular with locals, with bustling atmosphere, delicious smells and soothing Sundanese music.

Babakan Siliwangi Jl Siliwangi. Bandung's most famous Sundanese restaurant. Overlooking a green area, you dine in casually designed gazebos.

Sindang Reret Jl Naripan 7–9. Also well-known and very conveniently located in the city center. Housed in the same building as the Cultural Center Foundation. Very elegant. Renowned for its Sundanese cuisine but also serves a variety of other Indonesian dishes. *Wayang golek* performances are held every Saturday night on the stage in the back of the restaurant.

Ranggon Selera Jl Surapati 229. Modern and clean. You select your meal from a variety of Sundanese dishes brought to your table. It operates in much the same way as a Nasi Padang restaurant: you only pay for what you eat.

The same also goes for the **Ponyo** chain of restaurants, the two most conveniently located for tourists are at Jl Malabar 60 and in Jl Eyckman 11.

Other Indonesian

Bandung has countless Indonesian restaurants, but these are recommended:

Mie Naripan on Jl Naripan is an old noodle shop in the center of town, popular with locals and Japanese. **Tojoyo** on the corner of Jl Juanda and Jl Prabudimuntur is famous for its crunchy chicken legs. Other restaurants specializing in chicken are **Nyonya Suharti** and **Ayam Goreng Cianjur** on Jl Sunda. For Nasi Padang, try **Simpang Raya** on Jl Asia Afrika, or the **Sari Bundo** on Jl Dalem Kaum.

Nirwana Jl Sukajadi 143. Newly opened. Good cheap Indonesian and Chinese food. Cheerful, clean surroundings. Bakery attached.

Chinese and Seafood

There are a considerable number of Chinese restaurants in Bandung, which are often the best bets for good seafood.

Queen Jl Dalem Kaum 79 is reputedly the best in town. Extensive menu but not especially cheap.

Talaga Sari Jl Setiabudi 269. Great food, popular and has both indoor and outdoor tables.

Flamboyan Jl Sukajadi 234. Also very popular, offering Chinese, Thai and other international dishes.

Pancoran on Jl Sukajadi and the **Kartika** on Jl Pajajaran (near the airport) are among the restaurants specializing in seafood worth trying.

Japanese, Korean, Indian

Bandung has a number of Japanese restaurants, with **Daishogun** in Jl Cihampelas 125 considered to be the best. Others include the **Eden Cafe** (which also has a Korean menu) on Jl Setiabudi 29A, and **Paregu** on Jl Martadinata.

Hoka-Hoka Bento a Japanese fast food restaurant on Jl Merdeka and Jl Setiabudi, is surprisingly good yet cheap. **Hanamasa** is on the same street. Korean restaurants are fewer; the most popular being the **Korean House** on Jl Sukajadi 175.

For Indian food, most people head for the **Braga Pub** Jl Braga 17–19. Has a wide variety of dishes, with set menus at $5: highly recommended.

International/Western

Most of the larger hotels have restaurants catering to international tastes; try the **Papandayan**, the **Sheraton**, the **Preanger**, the **Panghegar**, or the **Savoy Homann** if you want western fare.

Braga Permai on Jl Braga 58 sidewalk cafe on colonial street offering European, Chinese and Indonesian food.

Western fast food outlets include **Pizza Hut**, **Ponderosa** (both in the same building on the corner of Jl Naripan and Jl Sunda). Steak houses include **Sukarasa** (Jl Tamblong 52) and **Canary** Jl Juanda 16 and **Angus**, high above the city in Jl Setiabudi. **Kintamani** is a new and fashionable restaurant in Jl Lombok 45, boasting 24-hour service and a wide variety of cuisines.

For atmosphere, however, all these are no match for **Glosis**, with its main restaurant set in a lovely, large compound in the posh Ciumbuleuit residential area at Jl Gunung Agung 8. There is now a second Glosis in the top floor of the Talaga Sari Chinese restaurant with a roof terrace with a lovely view over Bandung, especially in the evenings.

Café Venezia Jl Sukajadi 205 has an appealing range of western, Japanese and Korean dishes. Very popular place with tables set in a lovely garden, the atmosphere enhanced by soft live music.

Yoghurt Cisangkuy is a "milk bar" situated on Jl Cisanguy between the Geological and the Postal museums. It's the ideal place for resting tired feet while sitting and sipping a Strawberry Special. Students and secretaries meet here in the afternoons and it's a good place for a chat.

SPORTS FACILITIES

The Bumi Sangkuriang sports center, on Jl Kiputih in the Ciumbuleuit colonial residential area has the most nostalgic air and is Bandung's largest sports complex, with tall trees and tennis courts.

Golf lovers can find courses in Arcamanik (east of the city center), Sulaiman (south of the city in the Sulaiman airbase), Dago (north of the city, with beautiful views but high prices), in Lembang (a moderately priced nine-hole course), and perhaps the best of them all is Jatinangor, about 20 km east of Bandung. There is also a driving range on Jl Lombok, in the city center.

NIGHTLIFE

Laga Pub Jl Junjungan 164 is an institution, with live music and a small dance floor. The place is popular among resident expatriates and young Indonesians; admission: $1.50.

Prince on Jl Eyckman calls itself a pub but is more of a small restaurant.

The Enhaii Jl Setiabudi. Live music and a few tables in a casual setting. Popular.

Mientje Pub Hotel Papandayan. Popular with expats.

Studio East Jl Cihampelas 129 is Bandung's biggest disco and among the most sophisticated in the country; expect crowds on Saturday nights.

Lingga Jl Cemera. Another pub popular with westerners; country style. Live music, no cover charge.

Shangri-La is a disco in the northern part of town on Jl Setiabudi 29A, right next to the Eden Cafe. It is fairly popular with foreigners and smaller than the two above; admission is $4 and it's always full on Friday and Saturday nights.

Caesar's Palace Jl Braga 129, directly south of the railway crossing is in the impressive old Landmark building, part of Bandung's architectural heritage. Hefty admission charge of $12 per person.

Dankhdut Disco Jl Braga, just south of Caesar's Palace. *Dangdut,* as it is mostly spelled, is a popular Indonesian dance music style influenced by Indian elements. This place doubles as a pick-up joint, and Asian women may find it unpleasant.

Marabu. This dance shop and pick-up bar on Jl Suniaraja Timur 7, just around the corner from Jl Braga, is definitely sleazy. The music is not bad, and many expatriates seem to like it.

Lipstick in the shopping complex on the east side of the *alun-alun* is a roller skate disco. Monopolized by the young generation: admission $1.50.

MUSEUMS

Geological Museum Jl Diponegoro 57, next to Gedung Sate. The city's most well-known museum. It features some interesting dioramas of volcanoes, skeletons of fossil animals and a replica of the Java Man skull found in East Java in 1896.

Nearby is the **Postal Museum**, housed in a side wing of Gedung Sate, which has a fascinating collection of stamps and other postal items from the colonial era until today. Open Mon–Thur 8 am–2 pm, Fri 8 am–11 pm, Sat 8 am–1 pm. Closed Sun.

The **West Java Provincial Museum** "Sri Baduga" has Jl Oto Iskandardinata 638 as its official address but it is in fact located on the southern side of Jl Lingkar Selatan, just south of the large Tegal Lega field. It mainly displays items relating to the cultural history of the province. Replicas of the famous "Batu Tulis" (Inscribed Stone) from the Bogor area as well as other stone statues found in West Java can be found near a Baduy house, a gamelan set, and other artifacts. The building is cool and the displays well designed, but unfortunately the explanatory descriptions are only very sketchy. Open Tue–Sun, 8 am–4 pm and closed on Mon and public holidays.

Wangsit Siliwangi (military museum) Jl Lembong 38 displays WWII weapons also used in the war of independence. Other items include photographs, captured flags and uniforms from various regional rebels and separatist movements that troubled Indonesia's central government during the 1950s and 1960s. Open daily in the morning.

Museum Asia Afrika in the east wing of Gedung Merdeka in Jl Asia-Afrika 65 (corner with Jl Braga) commemorates exclusively the famous Asia Africa Conference which took place in Bandung in 1955. Open Mon–Sat in the morning.

PERFORMING ARTS

Bandung is rich in performing arts traditions and has numerous venues where shows take place.

Sindang Reret restaurant in Jl Naripan 7–9 presents *wayang golek* performances every Saturday evening from about 8 pm till midnight.

Performing Arts Academi (STSI) Jl Buah Batu 212 is the city's academy of traditional music and dance. Conveniently located on Abdul Muis/Buah Batu *bemo* route. Classes are held until noon Mon–Sat. Visitors may politely walk around and watch.

Kencana Wungu. Small nightclub featuring two traditional Sundanese social dance forms called *ketuk tilu* and *jaipongan.* A gamelan orchestra plays Sundanese pop songs, and dance hostesses take the floor in traditional *sarung-kebaya* dress. There is a modest cover charge and drinks are served. The club is open 9 pm–midnight everyday, and until 2 am on Sat. Patrons (male and female) can dance with the hostesses for a small fee: this is enormous fun, so don't be shy: just imitate the hostesses and follow the beat of the drums.

Rumentang Siang Jl Baranang Siang 1. This government-sponsored auditorium stages both traditional and contemporary performing arts. Check with the Tourist Information Service on the *alun-alun* for current programs. On Thursdays at 4 pm there is a dance program for tourists. Wednesday evenings on alternate weeks there is a 3-hour *wayang golek* or other traditional performance. On the first and third Sat evening of every month there is an all-night *wayang golek* performance that is broadcast on the radio. Sundanese *sandiwara* (classical performances similar to Javanese *wayang wong*) are offered on three weekends each month.

Padepokan Seni Jl Lingkar Selatan 17. Local government sponsored shows of various performing arts on Wed and Sat, 8 pm–11 pm.

Debus performances. Every Saturday night, a *debus* at the **Sakadarna Homestay**, Jl Kebonjati 34, provides a demonstration of "white magic": eating glass and razor blades, sticking long spikes through his cheek without drawing blood, cracking a coconut with his head, and other strange feats.

Kebon Binatang (Zoo) Jl Taman Sari. Performances of *wayang golek*, dance, *penca silat,* etc. are held every Sunday from 9 am onwards.

West Java Provincial Museum on Jawa Barat Jl Oto Iskandardinata 638 puts on various performances, including *jaipongan* dances every Wed at 2 pm ($1.50).

Panghegar Hotel on Jl Merdeka 2, sponsors a number of events, including a buffet dinner in the Pasundan Restaurant on Wed and Sat at 7:30 pm accompanied by dancing and other traditional arts. Cover charge is $7 a head. *Tembang Sunda* (classical sung poetry) and *kacapi suling* (traditional zither and flute) can also be heard in the lobby free of charge from 5 pm on Wed and Sat.

Ram fights (*adu domba*) take place every second Sunday of the month. These traditional spectacles are held near the Ledeng minibus terminal, down Jl Sersan Bajuris in a bamboo thicket behind the power station.

TOURIST INFORMATION

Tourist Information have a kiosk on the eastern side of the city square (*alun-alun*). They have up-to-date information about upcoming events and can arrange trips out of town. Open Mon–Sat am.

The **Immigration office** is at Jl Surapati 80, opens daily at 8 am, closing Mon–Thur at 2 pm, Fri at 11 am and Sat at 1 pm.

The main **police station** is on Jl Jawa, off Jl Merdeka, near the City Hall.

BANKS & MONEYCHANGERS

The number of banks in Bandung has increased dramatically since a major deregulation of the banking system took effect in 1988. Although **traveler's cheques** should in principle be exchangeable in any bank, there is often an annoying reluctance to provide this service.

Sejahtera Bank Umum at Jl Suniaraja 53–55 and **Standard Chartered Bank** at Jl Juanda 16 seem to give the best rates and are the most efficient. Two reputable money changers offer their services at Jl Lembong opposite the Panghegar Hotel and at Jl Sukajadi 232 next to the Flamboyan restaurant (Mon–Sat 8:30 am–12 noon and 2 pm–4 pm).

POST & TELECOMMUNICATIONS

There are a large number of post and telecoms agents dotted around the city. An impressive range of telecoms facilities is provided by the many privately run agents (*Wartel, Warpostel,* or *Warparpostel)* including long-distance and international calls as well as faxes. They are generally efficient and some accept credit cards. Some stay open 24 hours daily. Ask at your hotel for the nearest location.

SHOPPING

Bandung's major shopping districts include Jl Merdeka (around the Bandung Indah Plaza), the area around the *alun-alun* and Jl Dalem Kaum (Parahyangan Plaza), Jl Sunda (near the Yogyakarta Department Store), and the Kosambi area along Jl A Yani, the latter being a low-price shopping area for locals. The **Bandung Indah Plaza** is the city's flashiest shopping center, but the big department stores in the other areas are also convenient. **Sarinah Department Store** in the southern part of Jl Braga, is another convenient one-stop shopping place, for batik, souvenirs and handicrafts.

Two streets in Bandung have a reputation as specialized shopping areas: Jl Cihampelas for jeans, T-shirts and casual wear and Jl Cibaduyut for shoes. Souvenir, antique and gift shops worth trying include: **Rainbow** Jl Sukajadi 168 (near the petrol station) which has a wide choice of antiques and other gifts. **Syiwa** Jl Gegerkalong 36; **Selly** on Jl Cihampelas 232; **Lumayan** in Jl Cicendo 5 and **Toko 39** in Jl Cihampelas 39, which sometimes has less-than-friendly service. There are two shops specializing in batik on Jl Tamblong.

TRAVEL AGENTS

Big travel agencies include **Interlink**, Jl Wastu Kencana 5 ☎ 435529; **Vayatour** in Hotel Panghegar Jl Merdeka 2 ☎ 430331; and **Pacto** in Hotel Savoy Homann ☎ 445739.

— *Roggie Cale/Gottfried Roelcke*

East of Bandung

See map, page 132.

This section covers all noteworthy destinations along the route east of Bandung to Yogyakarta.

Sumedang

Telephone code is 0261.

Sumedang is on the main Bandung-Cirebon highway, with frequent bus connections from either direction. No rail or air connections. Many *becak* in town, no taxis. The bus terminal is in the center of town, and all local *bemo* stop here.

ACCOMMODATION

Penginapan Kencana (10 rooms) Jl P Kornel 198. ☎ 81642. Modernized Dutch-era guest house; best in town. $10 a night.

Penginapan Abadi (14 rooms) Jl P Geusan Ulun 102. Clean and friendly. Close to the museum. $4.

FOOD

The local specialty is *tahu Sumedang,* produced by over 200 cottage industries in Sumedang and served all over town. Small cubes of fresh bean-curd are deep-fried until crisp, then served with sweet soya sauce and chili *sambal*—absolutely delicious! Passing motorists buy huge baskets of the stuff to take back home with them.

Rumah Makan Bandung Jl P Geusan Ulun 97.

Ojo Lali Jl Mayor Abdurachman 146. Simple Sundanese and Indonesian dishes.

SUMEDANG MUSEUM

To request access to their special collection in advance, write to: Museum Prabu Geusan Ulun, Jl Prabu Geusan Ulun 28, Sumedang, attention: RM Abdullah Kartadibrata. Send the letter to arrive at least a week in advance of arrival and hope that someone meets you on the appointed day. Be sure to arrive at the museum before noon.

Garut

Telephone code is 0262.

There is no air or rail connection to Garut. For those who have been to Garut before, note a change of street names for the northern entry into the city: Jl Raya Tarogong has become Jl Oto Iskandardinata. Guntur bus terminal is on the north side of town, with easy connections to Bandung, Jakarta, Banjar and Pameungpeuk.

Bemo and horse-drawn carriages travel throughout the town. There's a small *bemo* terminal near the post office on Jl Achmad Yani. Take the No. 4 bemo 6 km to Cipanas. The main shopping district is on Jl Achmad Yani. For batik, ask for Ibu Uba on Jl Papandayan. There are no museums in Garut, but there is ram fighting. Rather than staying in Garut itself, your best bet is to stay in nearby Cipanas.

ACCOMMODATION

Ngamplang (20 rooms) Jl Raya Tasikmalaya Km 3. ☎ 81800. New resort hotel on old Dutch foundations, 4 km south of Garut and 200 m off the Garut-Tasikmalaya road. Lovely rural hilltop location overlooking 4 volcanoes. Very quiet. Golf, tennis, a pool and hikes up Gunung Cikurai's volcano. Modern rooms. 10% discount weekdays. $25–40.
Paseban (37 rooms) Jl Oto Iskandardinata 260A, Tarogong ☎ 22307. About 1 km south of the road to Cipanas. A sleepy, shady place with modest rooms. Small restaurant. The economy rooms are a good deal. $4.50–15.
Sarimbit Guest House (9 rooms) Jl Oto Iskandardinata 236, Tarogong ☎ 21033. Small and friendly. Near road to Cipanas. Will arrange tours. No AC or TV. Breakfast. Some rooms with hot water. $5–15.
Wisma PKPN (51 rooms) Jl Ciledug 79 ☎ 21508. Unexciting location and decor, but the rooms are clean and a good value. With breakfast. $7.50–15.
Wisma Rana (5 rooms) Jl Achmad Yani 27 ☎ 81-853. Very nice, super-clean rooms in an old Dutch colonial house. Beautiful wood furniture. Central location near post office and shopping district. $25–40.

2 West Java

FOOD

Wan Sa Min Jl A Yani 69–71. Superb Sundanese food. The owner, Haj Jumhana, is friendly and knows a lot about where to go and what to do.
Rumah Makan Garut Jl Achmad Yani 113. Established in 1930. The best Chinese food in town.
Rumah Makan Padang Sago Jl Achmad Yani 45. Typical Padang food.

MISCELLANEOUS

Tourist Information Center Jl Merdeka 117, near the bus station. **Public Hospital** (Rumah Sakit Umum) Jl Rumah Sakit 113. **Post Office** Jl Achmad Yani 40, near main shopping area. **Asia Dept Store** Jl Achmad Yani 142–144.

Cipanas

Cipanas is a hot springs resort area just 6 kilometers north of Garut (No. 4 *bemo*). From the main road it's 1 km. Most guesthouses and hotels are in one area called Complex Pariwisata Cipanas. Rates given are for weekdays; weekends see an increase of 10–30%, and more on public holidays. All hotels have a hot pool on the grounds, and most have one in each room.

ACCOMMODATION

Sumber Alam (14 rooms and bungalows) Cipanas ☎ 21027. Very tastefully done. Restaurant with modest menu. Largest pool in Cipanas. Small tidy rooms for $14. Bungalows built out over ponds: $16–40.
Tirta Ganga Cipanas Undergoing total renovation. The first multi-story luxury hotel in Cipanas. $25–65.
Tirta Merta (22 rooms) Cipanas ☎ 21085. Located just before main entrance to Complex. Modest, clean rooms and bungalows with a small restaurant. Hot springs pool in room. Motel layout. $7.50–20.

— *Roggie Cale/Gary Crabb*

Climbing Gunung Papandayan

Papandayan, some 30 km southwest of Garut, is classified as an "A-type," or highly unstable, volcano. Understandably, it is constantly monitored. Papandayan's first recorded explosion was in August 1772, when it blew one cubic kilometer of its cone into the sky, killing 3,000 people and burying 40 *kampungs*.

Exploring Papandayan's active crater today is like visiting another planet. A desert of rough lava and black ash is punctuated by bright yellow pockets of sulphur, while hissing acid rivulets and hot mud pools making outlandish belching noises compound the alien effect.

Kawah Mas (Golden Crater) is Papandayan's 150-meter-wide central dome. Here roaring fumaroles sounding like jet engines exude scorching vapor, and the residual heat from previous eruptions glows ominously in the volcano's interior.

From the top you get a good view into Papandayan's acid-spewing throat. Watch your step in this area; the ground is uneven and dotted with percolating mud pools. If the wind unexpectedly changes direction, cover your face with a cloth for protection against the fumes.

After visiting this nether world, you may feel like having a picnic in the fresh breeze. Climb up the left side of Kawah Mas, if facing the road, where a 15-minute walk leads up to a small plateau with a lovely view over the Garut plateau.

GETTING TO PAPANDAYAN

If this is to be your first encounter with a volcano we strongly recommend you hire a guide from Cisurupan or Cileet.

The gateway to Gunung Papandayan is Cisurupan, a *kampung* 20 km southwest of Garut on the highway to Java's south coast. Take a *colt* from the bus terminal in Garut to Cisurupan: 50¢. In the center of town, where the highway forks to the left, the paved road to Papandayan bears right. Look out for the white signpost. Tell the driver in advance "Ke Gunung Papandayan" and he will drop you off at this junction.

During most of the day there's no public transport uphill to the farming villages of Cileet (3 km) or Janggol, one km further up. If you aren't a passionate trekker looking forward to hiking up 10 km (1,500 meter altitude gain) from Cisurupan to Papandayan, hire a motorbike and rider, $1 is the standard one-way fare. Usually a group of bike taxis waits around the signpost.

ACCOMMODATION/GUIDES

There are no *losmen* near Papandayan, except for a few private houses. For a half-day trip stay in Garut and bring all the food you need from there. Public transport to the volcano and back takes about 4 hours, so it's better to charter a *bemo*. Early risers should start at daybreak. Between 10 am and noon Papandayan's cauldron gets very hot: pack a hat and sun-block.

Ask one of the bikers in Cisurupan (most of whom also act as guides) about private accommodation. A friendly and charming guide/rider is Mr Yan. If you don't meet him at the junction, take another bike for 3 km to Kampung Cileet and ask for him.

He offers stays in a bamboo house with bedroom and kitchen, but outdoor *mandi*. Toilet facilities consist of the coffee trees at the back. If that doesn't bother you, this is a great place to prolong your stay. There's a tiny shop In Janggol where you can get rudimentary supplies and simple food.

—*Tom Otte*

Tasikmalaya

Telephone code is 0265.

Tasikmalaya is a transit town on the Bandung-Yogya route. Businessmen and stopover tourists are the primary guests in the over 30 hotels.

Trains serve Tasik daily from Bandung and Yogya; the train station is at the northern end of Jl Tarumanegara, not far from the center of town *losmen*. Cilembang is the main bus terminal (4 km south of town), there's also another terminal just off Jl Martadinata in the north (at the junction near Hotel Ramayana).

ACCOMMODATION

Borobudur (50 rooms) Jl Raya Singaparna 25 ☎ 33176. The best place in town. AC $15–25.

Crown (61 rooms) Jl Martadinata 45 ☎ 30269; fax: 33967. The best on the town's main thoroughfare with clean and modern rooms. All rooms with TV and breakfast. Restaurant with Japanese, Chinese, European and Sundanese food. $15 standard; from $30 with AC, hot water and mini-bar.

Indah (18 rooms) Jl Martadinata 242 ☎ 31344. Spacious but rather dismal rooms. Prices include breakfast $7; $13 with fan & TV.

Kencana (36 rooms) Jl Yudanegara 17 ☎ 32464. Cheap rooms near mosque. Breakfast. $3–11.

Mandalawangi (21 rooms) Jl Martadinata 177 ☎ 31347. Nice garden entrance and set back off the main street. Room service from Alum Sari Restaurant next door. $16 economy; from $24 AC.

Penginapan Sunda (9 rooms) Jl Tarumanegara 21. Built in the 1920's, this *losmen* has very basic rooms in a quiet courtyard. Natural garden lends a country feel to the place. $11 for 1–3 persons.

Ramayana (10 rooms) Jl Martadinata 333 ☎ 31340. Near the bus terminal in the north part of town. Clean rooms but a little too near the main road. Restaurant. $20 fan and TV; $23 AC and TV.

Widui (30 rooms) Jl Martadinata 51 ☎ 34342. Faded Art Deco charm and somewhat musty. The economy rooms in the back are quiet. All rooms with breakfast, some with AC. From $6–28.

FOOD

Alum Sari Jl Martadinata (next to Hotel Mandalawangi). Typical Sundanese dishes.

Fast Food Jl Yudanegara (across from Kencana Hotel). Not very fast, but lots of Chinese dishes.

Mie Baso Lekker Jl Tarumanegara 12. Nice surroundings. Sundanese specialties and noodles.

Restaurant Ramayana Jl Martadinata 333. At the Hotel Ramayana. A favorite for visitors passing through. Cool and friendly. Try the *filet d' ikan mas* (goldfish) from the in-house pond.

SHOPPING

Embroidery and **handicrafts** are the main industries. Just north of town on the main road is an area with many handicraft shops specializing in baskets and rattan. Tasik is also well known for making 3-tiered ceremonial **umbrellas**.

Department stores are on Jl Mustofa 8: Jogja, Asia and Gunung Agung.

Pusat Kerajanin Kusumah (Jl Martadinata, near Hotel Ramayana) is a major handicraft emporium.

Kandaga Art Shop Jl Dr Sukarjo 7 off Jl Mustofa.

Batik Bordir Kota Resik Jl Seladarma 96.

MISCELLANEOUS

Tourist Information is at Jl Oto Iskandardinata 2 ☎ 30165.

Post Office Jl Oto Iskandardinata 6.

There are several **banks** on Jl Mustofa and nearby.

Public Hospital is located at Jl Rumah Sakit 33.

— *Roggie Cale/Gary Crabb*

Climbing Gunung Galunggung

In 1982 Gunung Galunggung hit the international headlines. On April 5, artillery-like rumblings and rattling windows alarmed thousands of people in the Tasik area. Within a few hours, a serene landscape of rice paddies and clove plantations was transformed into a smoldering black desert. After lying dormant for 64 years, Galunggung's lava dome, Gunung Jadi, had erupted.

The crater spewed 35-meter-thick pyroclastic flows of lava and spat flaming rocks as far as 5 kilometers away. It emitted lava and hot ash continuously for ten months, causing several emergency aircraft landings in Jakarta that year.

The omnipresent ash caused a fresh water

shortage in the region and 35,000 people were evacuated. Many Cipanas residents had to stay in a school in the nearby town of Tasik for nearly two years. But by January 1983, Galunggung had become dormant again and life for the locals returned to relative normalcy.

PREPARATIONS

As this is a day trip no special preparations are necessary, with the exception of good hiking footwear. There are several *warung* at Cipanas hot springs selling meals, snacks and drinks.

Don't forget to pack your swimming costume for a swim after the climb. There's no shade on top of this black cone, so bring a hat to prevent sunburn: it gets mercilessly hot around noon. If you wish to stay inside the crater overnight bring a sleeping bag or a rented tent. There are some great camping spots on the lake shore.

GUIDES

You don't really need one, but if you arrive alone and would like some company go to the parking lot near Cipanas springs. Try Dandy, who enjoys climbing barefoot on razorsharp lava. He charges around $2 depending on your bargaining ability and the duration of your trek.

GETTING TO CIPANAS

The 24-km trip from Tasikmalaya to Cipanas takes 1.5–2 hours. To avoid an ascent under the hot sun and to have morning light for taking pictures, start very early. In the center of Tasikmalaya catch *bis kota* number 05, which tours around the city.

You reach Indihiang village (c. 7 km) 20 to 30 minutes later. Ask the driver to drop you at the Bank Rakyat Indonesia on the left-hand side of the road. Just next to the bank there's a turnoff to the left leading to Cipanas and Galunggung.

A mob of motorcycle taxis hangs around here eager to take a fare. Just face in the direction of Galunggung and you'll soon be surrounded. Don't feel hassled, take your time, bargain, and get the fare down to about $2 one way.

The rough 17-km journey takes around 45 minutes. The road is still covered with ash from the 1982 eruptions, making for a slippery motorcross ride, but the surrounding countryside is breathtakingly beautiful.

At Cipanas village (*ci* means water and *panas* hot) below the springs, you pay the 30¢ admission fee. If you intend to climb up to the craters, which might take 5 to 6 hours, fix a time in the late afternoon for your motorcycle to pick you up for the return trip. There's a regular *bemo* service from Indihiang to Tasik, even at night.

THE ASCENT

Beyond Cipanas' hot spring pools and through a small gate is the beginning of the trail up Gunung Galunggung. Immediately after crossing the yellow bridge, turn right. From here there are no more turn-offs, just follow the trail up to Galunggung. Orientation is very easy, you face the Jadi crater for most of the hike.

The well-trodden ash trail leads over hilly areas covered with older vegetation that survived the 1982 eruption. After about half an hour you enter the devastated belt. It still looks like a desert here. Note the young casuarina trees which have grown to an average height of 1 meter from the bed of ash in the past 11 years.

The trail then leads to the base of Gunung Jadi. Beyond the shelters to the left the path gets steep and the final 300 meters is very slippery: it often feels like one step forward, two steps back, but perseverance is rewarded. You should reach Jadi's crater-rim after 1 to 2 hours in all.

EXPLORING THE CRATER

Standing beneath Gunung Galunggung's 2,500-meter-wide, sheer caldera wall is an impressive experience. Note the huge blown-off part on the east side of the volcano. Galunggung's beautiful, black-green crater lake lies 80 meters below and from its northern shore the caldera wall rises up a sheer 800 meters.

Thousands of kaliandra trees have been planted into the fine ash on the eastern and southern sides of Gunung Jadi, to prevent erosion of the cone and thus preserve the lake. From the rim there are stunning views over the lowlands, to Tasik and Gunung Panjalu in the east.

Walk along the rim to the left and relax under the shady bamboo hut. From there slide down the narrow path to the lake for a refreshing swim.

Nature-lovers should explore the area between Gunung Jadi and Galunggung's caldera wall. There are canyons with exotic vegetation, riverbeds, caves and precipitous waterfalls awaiting discovery.

The return journey involves sliding from the rim down the volcano and then hiking back to Cipanas. It should take about an hour. On the way back to Indihiang stop in the upper villages to see the ruined houses and crumbling mosques. Finish off the trek with a soothing bath in either Curug Panoongan waterfall or Cipanas hot springs.

—Tom Otte

Ciamis

Telephone code is 0265.

This small town, 17 km from Tasikmalaya, lies on the main route between Bandung and Yogya.

The train station is a five minute walk from the bus station which is on the main road, near the area where most hotels are located.

ACCOMMODATION

Budi Famili (35 rooms) Jl Jend. Achmad Yani 72–74 ☎ 71169. Still the best in Ciamis at all levels. Garden courtyards. All rooms with breakfast. $3–10 no AC; $17 AC.
Saung Puja Seda (8 rooms) Jl Jend. Achmad Yani 44 ☎ 72475. Cozy rooms with view of a small river. All rooms with TV, private bath, fridge and breakfast. Sundanese restaurant. $15–23 with AC.

FOOD

Ponyo Jl Jend. Sudirman 26. Sundanese food.
Saung Puja Seda Jl Jend. Achmad Yani 44. Cheap Sundanese food. Choose the live fish yourself.
Nikmat Jl Jend. Achmad Yani 37. Sundanese food.

MISCELLANEOUS

Post Office Jl Jend. Achmad Yani 2.
Telephone Office Jl Jend. Sudirman 88A.
Bank BCA Moneychanger, Jl Jend. Achmad Yani 33.

Pangandaran

Telephone code is 0265.
There are no air or direct rail connections to this area. From Jl Jaksa in Jakarta *(losmen* area), there is a direct connection to Pangandaran daily by AC minibus; tickets are $14 and are available at RTQ Wartel, Jl Jaksa 15C, or call Jakarta (021) 39294.

From Banjar on the Bandung-Yogya route, you can get a bus to Cijulang (just west of Pangandaran) for $1. From the bus terminal in Cijulang, a *becak* to the beach areas costs 25–50¢ (1.5 km). Coming from Yogya or Wonosobo, take the ferry in Cilacap to Kalipucang (nice backwater trip), walk to the main road (5 min) and catch a local bus to Pangandaran for 25¢.

To enter the beach area, you pay a tourist tax of 50¢ per person, which includes a kind of insurance during your stay in Pangandaran. To drive vehicles into Pangandaran costs $3–6. *Becak* are everywhere. Bicycles can be rented from several places, and motorbikes at Luta Travel Agency (Jl Kidang Pananjung 107, next to the post office). Luta also organizes minibus rental, tours, taxis and boat trips to Yogya. Hire snorkeling equipment from Jl Kidang Pananjung 203.

Boutique La Bougainville, at the same address as Luta Travel Agency, has a selection of souvenir items including batik and wayang puppets.

ACCOMMODATION

All room rates are for the regular season. On major holidays, rates double and all hotels are completely full. Most include breakfast.

Under $10

Losmen Mini Dua (10 rooms) Jl Kalenbuhaya. Central, simple and clean. $2–4 a night.
PW Argaloka (13 rooms) Jl Pamugaran, west beach. Good value for money. $5.
PW Sandaan (11 rooms/cottages) Jl Pamugaran, west beach. Nice. $3–6 a night.

$10–$15

Adam's Homestay (5 rooms) Jl Pamugaran, west beach. Uniquely designed Mediterranean-style compound with bookshop attached. $15.
Losmen Panorama (13 rooms) Jl Kidang Pananjung 187, east beach. European-tropical decor. $6–12.
Penginapan Lugina (18 rooms/bungalows) Jl Kidang Pananjung 193, east beach. Tasteful. $10–20.
PW Bulak Laut (10 rooms) Jl Bulak Laut, west beach. $6–10.

$15 and up

Bumi Nusantara (25 rooms/bungalows) Jl Pantai Barat, west beach. Traditional architecture. Recent renovations. With AC $25–35.
Nyiur Indah (14 rooms) Jl Pantai Barat 79, west beach. Very nice! Chinese restaurant attached. $12; $17 AC.
Pantai Indah Barat, Jl Talanca 153 ☎ 39004, fax: 39327. Best hotel in town. Modern low rise located on the main road, near the beach. AC, TV, fridges, baths, hot water. De luxe $35–90. Suites $70–145.
Putri Duyung, Jl Pamugaran ☎ 39210. Hotel and bungalows. Very clean, pleasant. AC double: $22.
Sunrise Homestay (10 rooms) Jl Kidang Pananjung 175, east beach. Traditional decor. $15–45.
Wisma Pelangi (13 rooms/bungalows) Jl Pasanggrahan 7. Central, attractive and simple. $8–25.

FOOD

Gatul's (east beach by the fish market) has the best seafood around, according to locals. Choose your entree right off the chopping block out back. Lobster, shark, shrimp and fish. Open in the evenings.
Inti Laut, Jl Pamugaran 28 ☎ 39224. Hotel/restaurant which serves excellent seafood.
Rumah Makan Cilacap Jl Kidang Pananjung 187, is a popular hangout. Western breakfasts and a little of everything else. Food and service is so-so.
Rumah Makan Sari Harum Jl Pasanggrahan 2, is a nice Sundanese restaurant. They have *ikan jambal* (salted fish) right off the local drying racks.
Rumah Makan Nanjung Jl Nurbaen Pantai Barat, is a seafood extravaganza. Big tourist business.
Putra Galunggung Jl Kidang Pananjung 164. *Sate kambing* only: for when you're tired of eating fish.

— Roggie Cale/Gary Crabb

3 Yogyakarta PRACTICALITIES

Yogya's rich and ancient cultural heritage has made it Indonesia's second most popular tourist destination, after Bali. Visitors are attracted by the traditional way of life and the numerous sights in and around the city. Hotels, restaurants and other services have improved greatly in recent years. Parks now surround Borobudur and Prambanan, and nearby beaches and caves are rapidly being developed as tourist *"obyek."* Yogya's true charm, however, lies in her quiet, unhurried pace. To rush Yogya is to miss her essence, so take her gently.

Prices in US dollars excluding tax and service (10–30%). AC = Air-conditioning. Telephone code is 0274. *See Kraton Yogyakarta and Yogyakarta Sidetrips maps, pages 157 & 172.*

GETTING THERE

By Air

Most visitors arrive and leave via Adisucipto airport, 9 km (5.6 mi) east of the city, on direct flights to and from Jakarta or Bali. **Garuda** has 7 daily flights to/from Jakarta ($62 economy, $82 executive) and 6 to/from Denpasar ($58). International connections can be made through both cities. **Sempati** also has flights to Jakarta and Denpasar for similar prices. **Merpati** and **Bouraq** have daily flights to other cities, including Surabaya, Banjarmasin, Balikpapan, Palu, Kupang and Maumere. All travel agencies can make domestic ticket reservations. Only two, Vayatour and Pacto, can make international bookings (see "Travel Agencies" below).

Garuda: Jl P Mangkubumi 56 ☎ 5184, 86440. Open Mon–Thur 7:30 am–4:30 pm; Fri 7:30 am–11.30 am, 2 pm–4:30 pm; Sat–Sun 9 am–1 pm.
Merpati: Jl Jend. Sudirman 63 ☎ 4272. Open Mon–Fri 8 am–4 pm; Sat–Sun 9 am–2 pm.
Bouraq: Jl Mataram 60 ☎ 62664. Open Mon–Fri 8 am–4 pm; Sat–Sun 9 am–2 pm.

Major hotels and many guest houses offer free transport to and from the airport. Taxi fare to the city is $3.50. Otherwise, walk to the main highway and catch a public minibus traveling to the left (west) into the city. They stop at the Terban terminal; from here take a *becak* or city bus to the Malioboro or Prawirotaman hotel areas.

By Train

The **Bima Express** is a first-class train that runs the Jakarta-Yogya-Surabaya route every night. Reclining seats and AC, but no sleepers. Leaving Jakarta Kota Station at 4 pm, it pulls into Yogya just after midnight. Be sure to wake up, or you'll end up in Surabaya! $22–30 each way.

The **Senja Utama Yogya** leaves Jakarta's Gambir Station at 7:45 pm and has one AC car. It arrives in Yogya at around 4:30 am ($22). The **Senja Utama Solo** (2nd class) and **Senja Ekonomi** have similar timetables. For a pleasant, 8-hour daytime ride, the **Fajar Utama** (one AC car), arrives in Yogya at mid-afternoon ($20). There is also the **Mutiara Selatan** from Bandung ($18). All these trains can be taken in the other direction when leaving. Check your hotel for schedules.

Upon alighting at Tugu Station, walk out by the back exit (across the tracks) and not through the front: it's closer to the Pasar Kembang area and the *becak* drivers are not as aggressive.

By Bus

Inter-city express buses from Jakarta, Bandung, Surabaya and Bali travel all night and deposit weary riders in the early morning at a bus terminal on the southeastern corner of the city. Some companies take you right to your final destinations. From the terminal, take a city bus or taxi into town. Jakarta to Yogya takes about 10 hours and costs around $10.

Buses depart for all destinations on Java, Bali and Sumatra throughout the day and night from the main terminal at Umbulharjo (☎ 87834). Day buses are crowded, hot and slow, but cheap. Night AC express buses depart from their offices (many along Jl P Mangkubumi) between 3–7:30 pm before stopping at the bus terminal to pick up additional passengers. Ticket agencies along Jl P Mangkubumi, Jl Sosrowijayan, and Jl Prawirotaman, have information on current fares, seating and routes as well as photos of the buses. City buses No. 1 and No. 14 take you from the Malioboro and Prawirotaman areas to Umbulharjo (during daylight hours).

By Minibus

Privately-run minibuses (called "travel" or "colt") to and from nearby cities such as Solo and Semarang run throughout the day. Seats are reserved, they are safe and reliable, and they deliver you right to the door. Pick-ups can be arranged. Offices cluster just west of the Tugu monument (SAA is the most reliable) and on Jl Dr Wahidin (Trisula), just east of Bethesda Hospital. Cost is only $1.75 to/from Solo and $3 to/from Semarang.

TOURIST INFORMATION

The **Tourist Information Center** (Jl Malioboro 16, just south of the Mutiara Hotel ☎ 3543, 2811 ext. 11) is run by the Regional Tourism department. Open Mon–Sat 8 am–9 pm. Closed on Sun and holidays. The friendly and helpful staff can provide a calendar of events, city and regional maps, train and bus schedules, city bus routes (which tend to change), performance and tour details, travel books, maps and postcards.

GETTING AROUND

Yogya's main street, Jl Mangkubumi-Malioboro-Ahmad Yani, runs north-south from the *keraton* up to the Tugu monument at the top of Jl Mangkubumi. Running east from the monument, Jl Urip Sumoharjo (known popularly as Jl Solo) is another major shopping street. First class hotels are located either on Jl Malioboro or the road leading out to the airport. Jl Prawirotaman in the south of the city is packed with great value-for-money guest houses ($10–25 a night including breakfast). Souvenir and art shops are scattered around Prawirotaman and its extension, Tirtodipuran, as well as around the *keraton*, the Taman Sari complex and on Jl Malioboro.

Local Transportation

The best way to get to know Yogya is by walking.
Becaks. The next best way is by *becak*: the ubiquitous three-wheeled pedicabs with seats for passengers in the front and a bicycle seat for the driver in the back. Trips within the city cost around Rp500 (25¢) per km, but rates vary according to the number and size of passengers, time of day (night costs more than day), weather (fares are higher in the rain) and difficulty of the trip (the city inclines slightly south to north, so heading north is slightly more expensive).

Fix a price before getting in and don't be shy about walking away after stating your final offer. Chances are the driver will call you back and tip the *becak* forward, which means he accepts your offer. Some drivers will wait while you visit museums or shops: figure on Rp1,000 (50¢) an hour. Those who offer very cheap rates actually want to take you shopping in the hope of getting a fat commission from shops. The *becak* is a very pleasant way to travel.
Bicycles cost $1.50 a day to rent, with the better bikes going out earlier in the morning. Parking fee is Rp25. Many hotels and *losmen* in the Pasar Kembang/Sosrowijayan and Prawirotaman areas have bicycles for rent. Ask around.
Motorcycles for rent at $5 a day are available along Jl Pasar Kembang at Java Motorbike Rental, Fortuna, other outlets and through numerous tourist services in the Prawirotaman area.
Rental cars. Self-drive cars now available at the Bali Car Rental Service in front of Adisucipto airport ☎ 62548. Open every day, they have cars and jeeps for $20 to $50 per day (with and without insurance). Valid international license is required. Drivers can be hired for $10 for a 12-hour day. In town, Fortuna, Jl Jlagran 20 (☎ 64690) also rents cars at $25 to $40 a day.
Taxis. Hotels, travel agencies and tourist information offices can arrange for taxis (max. 4 people) and minibuses (5 to 8 people) with drivers. For trips outside the city, rates depend on the demand and the distance. For one day, out-of-town round-trips, the following are rough estimates:
Ambarawa/Bandungan $36
Baron Beach $40 Borobudur $17
Dieng Plateau $55 Imogiri $13
Kaliurang $15 Kasongan $13
Parangtritis $20 Prambanan $14
Samas $20 Sendangsono $20
Surakarta (Solo) $28
Metered taxis roam Yogya's streets. Hail one or call Centris ☎ 2548/4877. Indra Kelana ☎ 5819, 63910. ASA ☎ 2027, 88018. JAS ☎ 73737. Vetri ☎ 63551/63555. Rajawali ☎ 2976. Pandawa ☎ 6311/88353. Pataga ☎ 71725. Open door is Rp800 + Rp400/km. Only JAS sticks to the meter for out-of-town rides (within DI Yogya province).
City buses. A fleet of city buses runs throughout the city, with end points at the Umbulharjo terminal (in the southeast) and the Gajah Mada University campus (in the north). Red-orange Kopata buses (routes No. 1–9) and blue Aspada buses (routes No. 10–15) operate from 6 am to 6 pm. White Damri buses (routes No. 14 and No. 15) run until 8:30 pm. Yellow Kobutri vans have two routes running clockwise and counter-clockwise from the shopping center east of the post office and Gajah Mada. Fare is Rp250.

Tour and Travel Agencies

An easy way to see the sights is to join a package tour. All agencies offer day and half-day tours of the city (including the *keraton*, Taman Sari, batik and silver workshops), Borobudur, Dieng, Prambanan, craft villages, Parangtritis, etc. Day tours cost $10–15 (city tour) and $35 for a tour of Borobudur and Dieng. Hire cars with guides for personalized tours. Most agencies handle domestic airline and hotel bookings; Vayatour and Pacto can arrange international ticketing.

Hotels also offer tours. Budget tours are available in the Sosrowijayan-Pasar Kembang and Prawirotaman areas. Most agencies are open Mon–Fri 8:30 am–4 pm, Sat until 1 pm. Check at your hotel reception for details.

For the adventurous, there are mountain treks and camping trips to Dieng, Gedong Songo, Merapi, Borobudur, caves and secluded beaches. Equipment, transport and guides are provided. Contact: **Gypsy Adventure Tours** Jl Tirtodipuran 21 ☎ 4984 and **Kartika Trekking Service** Jl

Borobudur, Magelang, Semarang
Gajah Mada University
JETIS
JL. W. MONGINSIDI
JL. TRI MARGO
JL. DR. SARJITO
JL. A.M. SANGAJI
JL. SIMANJUTAK
JL. TERBAN
JL. CIK DITIRO
Panti Rapih Hospital
Indraloka Homestay Service
JL. KARTINI
JL. DEWI SARTIKA
JL. CANDRAKIRANA
JL. SAGAN
JL. RAHAYU SAMIRONO
Valentino's Rest.
JL. PAKUNINGRATAN
JL. KRANGGAN
JL. ASEM GEDE
JL. PONCOWINATAN
Bus-stop (to Borobudur)
Santika Hotel
Army Museum
JL. KYAI MOJO
JL. DIPONEGORO
JL. JEND. SUDIRMAN
JL. UR
Tugu Monument
Garuda Airlines
Bethesda Hospital
TEGAL REJO
JL. TENTARA RAKYAT MATARAM
JL. PINGIT KIDUL
Pesta Perak Rest.
JL. TENTARA PELAJAR
JL. BUMIJO LOR
JL. BUMIJO
JL. GOWONGAN LOR
Arjuna Plaza
JL. SABIRIN
JL. SUHARTOYO
JL. SUPADI
JL. HADJUAR SONO
JL. JUADI
JL. SAJIONO
JL. SUNARYO
JL. PATIMURA
JL. UNGARAN
JL. SUROTO
JL. YOS. SUDARSO
JL. DR. WAHIDIN SUDIROHUSODO
JL. KOESBINI
JL. DANI
JL. TRIMO
KOTA BARU
Kridosono Sports Stadium
JL. BUMIJO TENGAH
JL. GOWONGAN KIDUL
JL. SURYONEGARAN
JL. WONSODIRJAN
New Batik Palace
JL. P. MANGKUBUMI
Syuhada Mosque
RRI Kota Baru
JL. A. JAZULI
JL. ABU BAKAR ALI
JL. KRASAK
JL. SIKARTO
Diponegoro Monument
Tugu Station
JL. PEMBELAH TANAH AIR
JL. JLAGRAN
JL. PASAR KEMBANG
Kota
Asia-Afrika
Batik Palace
Mendut
Superman I Rest.
Superman II Rest.
Ana's Rest.
Aziatic
Gandhi Losmen
Natour Garuda
JL. LEMPUYANGAN
LEMPUYANGAN
JL. PRINGGOKUSUMAN
JL. KEMETIRAN
JL. SOSROWIJAYAN
Legian Rest.
DANUREJAN
JL. PENGOK
Batik Palace Cottages
Zamrud
JL. MATARAM
JL. SOSROKUSUMAN
JL. MAS. SUHARTO
JL. MACANAN
JL. DR. SUTOMO
JL. CIK DI TIRO
JL. KEMETIRAN KIDUL
JL. DAGEN
JL. JOYONEGARAN
JL. MALIOBORO
GEDONG TENGEN
Peti Mas
Sri Wibowo
Mutiara
Tourist Information Center
JL. TEGAL PANGGUNG
JL. HAYAM WURUK
Kali Winongo
JL. COKROAMINOTO
JL. LET. JEN. SUPRAPTO
JL. PAJEKSAN
JL. SURYATMAJAN
JL. JEMINAHAN
JL. BAUSASRAN
PATOK
JL. BESKALAN
JL. KETANDAN
PAKUALAMAN
JL. PURWANGGAN
JL. AIP II KS TUBUN
JL. GADEAN
NGAMPILAN
Margomulyo Church
JL. REMUJUNG
Beringharjo Market
JL. REKSOBAYAN
JL. PABRINGAN
JL. BHAYANGKARA
JL. A. YANI
JL. MAYOR SURYOTOMO
JL. JAGALAN
JL. GAJAH MADA
JL. JAYENG PRAWIRO
JL. HARJO WINATAN
JL. SURYOPRANOTO
JL. KI MANGUNSARKORO
State Guest House
Fort Vredeburg (Benteng Budaya)
Gedong Senisono
Pakualaman Palace
JL. BEJI
JL. MESJID
ISI Graphic Arts Faculty
JL. WIROBRAJAN
JL. K.H. AHMAD DAHLAN
JL. SENOPATI
JL. SULTAN AGUNG
JL. TRIKORA
Nitour Office
Sono Budoyo Museum
Cetiya Budda Prabha
St. Francis Xavier
Biology Museum
JL. BINTARAN
Sasmita Loka Pang. Jend. Sudirman
GONDOMANAN
JL. BINTARAN KIDUL
Dalem Notoprajan
Grand Mosque
Alun-alun Utara
JL. IBU RUSWO
JL. KENEKAN
JL. SUROKARSAN
JL. NOTOPRAJAN
JL. KAUMAN
JL. KADIPATEN LOR
KERATON
Pagelaran
JL. WIJILAN
JL. MANGUNNEGARAN KULON
JL. MANGUNNEGARAN WETAN
JL. GONDOMANAN
JL. LEDOK GONDOMANAN
JL. ROTOWIJAYAN
JL. KEMITBUMEN
JL. NGASEM
JL. KADIPATEN KULON
JL. WAHID HASYIM
Sultan's Palace (Keraton)
JL. P. MANGKURAT
JL. PAKARYAN
JL. PANEMBAHAN
JL. SURYOMENTARAMA
JL. BRIGJEN KATAMSO
MERGANGSA
Kali Code
JL. TAMAN SISWA
JL. POLOWIJAN
JL. IREDA
JL. LET. JEN. S. PARMAN (Taman Sari)
Ngasem Bird Market
JL. MAGANGAN LOR
Purawisata
JL. MAKAN
JL. MANTRIGAWEN LOR
JL. MANTRIGAWEN KIDUL
Water Castle (Taman Sari)
JL. NOGOSARI KIDUL
JL. NOGOSARI KULON
JL. TAMAN
Sasono Hinggil
JL. SURYOPUTRAN
JL. PASINDENAN
JL. GAMELAN LOR
JL. LANGENSURYO
JL. GAMELAN KIDUL
TAMAN
Mesjid Soko Tunggal
JL. NGADISURYAN
Alun-alun Selatan
JL. LANGENASTRAN LOR
JL. NAMBURAN LOR
JL. NAGAN LOR
JL. PATEHAN
JL. LANGENASTRAN KIDUL
JL. NAMBURAN KIDUL
JL. NAGAN TENGAH
JL. PATEHAN TENGAH
JL. NAGAN KIDUL
JL. PATEHAN KIDUL
JL. GADING
JL. LANGENARJAN LOR
JL. LANGENARJAN KIDUL
JL. SILIRAN LOR
JL. SILIRAN KIDUL
Dalem Pujokusuman Dance School
JL. SUGENG JERONI
JL. GEDONGKIWO
JL. LET. JEN. M. T. HARYONO
JL. MAY. JEND. SUTOYO
JL. KOL. SUGIYONO
JL. MEN
GEDONG KIWO
JL. BANTUL
PUGERAN
JL. PANJAITAN
JL. PARANGTRITIS
Perjuangan Museum
Agastya Art Foundation
ISI Music Faculty
JL. SISINGAMANGARAJA
JL. MBARAKAN
JL. PRAPANCA
JL. SURYODININGRATAN
JL. TIRTODIPURAN
Borobudur
Sriwijaya
Hanoman's Rest.
Vagabond
Sartika
JL. PRAWIROTAMAN
Batik Factories
Airlangga
Delta Homestay
Palm House
Duta
Rose
Metro
Galunggung
MANTRIJERON
JL. KARANGKAJEN
JL. SOROSUTAN
JL. MANGKUYUDAN
Matahari
Samas, Glagah, Bantul & Kasongan
Parangtritis

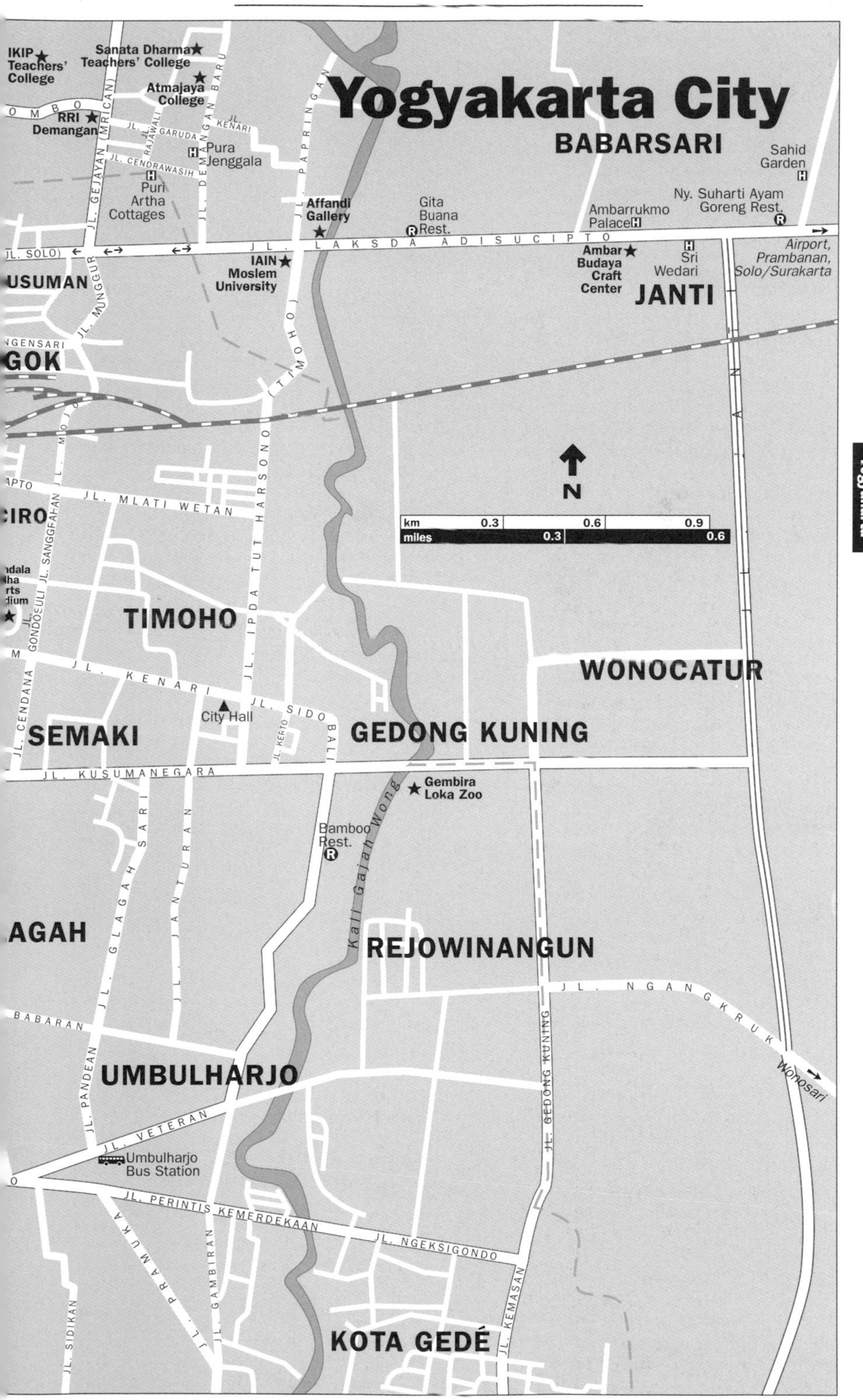
Yogyakarta City
BABARSARI
JANTI
USUMAN
GOK
CIRO
TIMOHO
WONOCATUR
SEMAKI
GEDONG KUNING
AGAH
REJOWINANGUN
UMBULHARJO
KOTA GEDÉ
IKIP Teachers' College
Sanata Dharma Teachers' College
Atmajaya College
RRI Demangan
Pura Jenggala
Puri Artha Cottages
Affandi Gallery
Gita Buana Rest.
Ambarrukmo Palace
Ny. Suharti Ayam Goreng Rest.
Sahid Garden
IAIN Moslem University
Ambar Budaya Craft Center
Sri Wedari
Airport, Prambanan, Solo/Surakarta
City Hall
Gembira Loka Zoo
Bamboo Rest.
Kali Gajah Wong
Umbulharjo Bus Station
Wonosari
JL. LAKSDA ADISUCIPTO
JL. SOLO)
JL. GEJAYAN (MRICAN)
JL. DEMANGAN BARU
JL. PAPRINGAN
JL. KENARI
JL. GARUDA
JL. RAJAWALI
JL. CENDRAWASIH
JL. MUNGGUR
(TIMOHO)
JL. MLATI WETAN
JL. IPDA TUT HARSONO
JL. SANGGRAHAN
JL. GONDOSULI
JL. CENDANA
JL. SIDOBALI
JL. KERTO
JL. KUSUMANEGARA
JL. GLAGAH SARI
JL. JANTURAN
JL. NGANGKRUK
JL. GEDONG KUNING
JL. PANDEAN
BABARAN
JL. VETERAN
JL. PERINTIS KEMERDEKAAN
JL. NGEKSIGONDO
JL. PRAMUKA
JL. GAMBIRAN
JL. SIDIKAN
JL. KEMASAN
km 0.3 0.6 0.9
miles 0.3 0.6
N

Sosrowijayan 10 ☎ 87016.

ACCOMMODATION

Yogya offers an enormous range of accommodation, with excellent value for money in every category. The greatest choice is in the middle and lower ranges, as Yogya has always been popular with budget travelers, but a number of major luxury hotel projects are now underway.

Budget (under $15)

Budget travelers congregate in the Pasar Kembang district around the train station. Dozens of small hotels and *losmen* are crammed into this densely populated area between Jl Pasar Kembang and Jl Sosrowijayan, especially along the alleys (*gang*) running between them. Accommodations are basic, for as little as $1 a night.
Aziatic (12 rooms) Jl Sosrowijayan 6. Friendly.
Delta Homestay MG III/587A. Behind Jl Prawirotaman. Nice garden, small pool. $8 S, with breakfast.
Gandhi Losmen on Jl Sosrowijayan (Gang II) at $1.50–2 a night, with garden and helpful staff. The small gallery features batik portraits.
Hotel Wisnugraha, Jl Kusumanegara 114 ☎ 71413. Very clean and friendly. $12. $18 AC.
Kota on the western end of Jl Pasar Kembang, at Jl Gandekan Lor 79, offers clean and spacious rooms, pleasant garden and good security.
Losmen Prastha Jaya (11 rooms) Sosrowijayan Wetan GT I/118 ☎ 63522. $4–5.
Sartika Homestay Jl Prawirotaman 44A ☎ 72669. At the very end of the street; quiet and friendly. $6.50–12.50.
Sri Wibowo (40 rooms) Jl Dagen 23 ☎ 63084; $10.
Vagabond Youth Hostel Jl Sisingamangaraja 28B (off the east end of Jl Prawirotaman) ☎ 71207. An associate member of the International Youth Hostel Federation. Dorm beds for only $2.50 or $6 D. Discounts during low season.
Zamrud Jl Sosrokusuman 180 ☎ 2446. On a small street off the east side of Malioboro. Quiet and safe. $8 a night.

Guesthouses ($15–$25)

Guesthouses are converted Javanese homes run by the owners, most of whom still live on the premises. Almost every house on Jl Prawirotaman appears to have been converted into a guesthouse; a few are also found just off Jl Malioboro on Jl Dagen. Walk these streets until you find something you like.

Away from the bustle of Malioboro, the Prawirotaman guesthouses have pleasant gardens and many have pools, minibus tours and other services. The **Airlangga** has luxury-class rooms in its new wing, and the **Metro**, on the street behind Prawirotaman, provides very peaceful surroundings. **Galunggung** has the biggest pool. Prices for these are a great bargain at around $15–25 for a room with AC ($10 with fan), including breakfast, tax and service. Rates depend on the season. Discounts available during slow periods, especially for longer stays.

Rates in Prawirotaman are even cheaper than these: as little as $3.50 to $9 (regular rates).
Airlangga (30 rooms) Jl Prawirotaman 6–8 ☎ 63-344, 71427. $17 fan, $20 AC. **Borobudur** (10 rooms) Jl Prawirotaman 5 ☎ 63977. $7.50–10. **Duta** (27 rooms) Jl Prawirotaman 20 (26) ☎ 72064. $18.50 fan, $24 AC. **Gajah** (36 rooms) Jl Prawirotaman 4 ☎ 5659, 5037. **Galunggung** (20 rooms) Jl Prawirotaman 28/36 ☎ 2715. $9–17.50. **Metro** (30 rooms) Jl Prawirotaman 71, ☎ 72004. $14 fan; $20 AC. **Rose** (25 rooms) Jl Prawirotaman 22 ☎ 87991. $7.50–17.50. **Sriwijaya** (25 rooms) Jl Prawirotaman 7 ☎ 71870.

Homestay Service

A bed-and-breakfast room with a Javanese family can be arranged through the **Indraloka Homestay Service** 18 Cik di Tiro ☎ 64341. Run by Mrs Moerdiyono, the service provides rooms with English or Dutch-speaking families for $20–25 a night (incl. breakfast). Home-cooked lunch and dinner extra. All rooms have western amenities and fan. Homestays in other cities can be arranged.

Intermediate ($20–$40)

All of the following are newer hotels in the center of town, with AC rooms. Breakfast and service charges additional.
Batik Palace Hotel (26 rooms) Jl Pasar Kembang 29 ☎ 2149, 63824. Very convenient, right near the train station and Jalan Malioboro. $19–33.
Batik Palace Cottages (35 rooms) Taman Yuwono Dagen Sosromenduran ☎ 61828; fax: 63824. Convenient location and peaceful environment. AC room $22 S; cottages $27–44.
Matahari (50 rooms) Jl Parangtritis 23 ☎ 72020; fax: 72737. Southern end of town. $22–50 S.
Mendut (52 rooms) Jl Pasar Kembang 49 ☎ 63435, 66244. Just opposite south exit of train station so convenient for late night train arrivals. $20–63.
Peti Mas (34 rooms) Jl Dagen 39 ☎ 2896. With a pleasant garden.

First Class ($40 and up)

Aggressive competition among these hotels means that discounts of up to 50% are available during low season. Buy a voucher through a travel agent in town or at the airport counter.
Ambarrukmo Palace (265 rooms) Jl Laksda Adisucipto, Yogyakarta 55281 ☎ 66488; fax: 63283. Yogya's top hotel was built as a war reparation by the Japanese in the 1960s, on the site of a royal rest house. Several of the original structures remain: a graceful *pendopo,* a royal *dalem* residence hall and a *bale kambang* (a two-story circular pavilion set in a lake, now a floating restaurant). Pool and tennis courts. $85 to $800 for the presidential suite.
Aquila Prambanan (220 rooms) Jl Laksda Adisucipto, No. 48, PO Box 82, Babarsari. ☎ 65005, 65100; fax: 65009. Yogya's newest fancy hotel,

only 3 km from the airport (5 km from the city). $80 S, $110 for a cottage. Great food.

Century Yogyakarta International (220 rooms), Jl Laksda Adisucipto 38. ☎ 64750, 64727; fax: 64-171. Newly renovated. $90 S, $350 for a suite.

Melia Purosani (300 rooms), on the corner of Jl Suryotomo and Jl Suryatmajan. For reservations ☎(21) 5221855; fax: (21) 5221853. Brand new luxury hotel. All rooms have bathroom and shower, IDD phones, AC, TV, mini bar and fridge. Also shops, a pool, fitness centre and conference facilities. Standard $115 S, $125 D. Superior $125 S, $135 D. Rates excluding 17.5 percent tax.

Mutiara (125 rooms) Jl Malioboro 18 ☎ 4531, 63-814, 5173; fax: 61201. Right in the heart of Malioboro, close to shops and the *keraton*. The north wing is older and cheaper ($25 S, $35 D) than the south wing ($52 S, $58 D).

Natour Garuda (102 rooms) Jl Malioboro 60 ☎ 66-353; fax: 63074. Recently renovated; centrally located on Jl Malioboro. Has a number of lovely old colonial suites with terraces. Luxury rooms, $106 S, $136 D. Suites $204–600.

Puri Artha (60 rooms) Jl Cendrawasih 36 ☎ 5934, 63288; fax: 62765. Cozy up-scale guesthouse in a quiet neighborhood. Very friendly atmosphere. Small pool and shops. $40 standard, $75 suite.

Queen of the South Beach Resort (38 rooms) Girijati, Kec. Panggang, Parangtritis ☎ 67196; fax: 67197. Perched on the cliffs overlooking Parangtritis, this is the ideal spot for beach activities. Open-air, idyllic. $60 standard, $120 suite.

Sahid Garden (140 rooms) Jl Babarsari ☎ 87078. Offers both high-rise rooms and pleasant garden cottages. Free transport to and from town. $40 S, $55–120 for cottages.

Santika (148 rooms) Jl Jend. Sudirman 19 ☎ 63036, 61910; fax: 62047. Part of the Santika chain, this is luxurious elegance. $80 S, $175–600 suite.

FOOD

Although out of the way, several Indonesian restaurants are well worth the extra effort to find.

Pesta Perak Jl Tentara Rakyat Mataram 8 ☎ 632-55. Open 11 am to 9:30 pm. Great lunch and dinner buffets. Has a small garden and a wide selection of curries, fried chicken, fish and fruits.

Selera Kuring Jl HOS Cokroaminoto 174, specializes in fresh Sundanese-style fish, fried or curried. Fish (*gurame*) come from their own ponds on site. Open 10 am–3 pm, 5–10 pm.

Pring Sewu Jl Magelang Km 6 ☎ 64993. Specializes in grilled *gurame* served plain, with a curry sauce or with a brown bean sauce. The fried rice and satay are good too.

Yogya's answer to Colonel Sanders is the delicious Javanese *ayam goreng*—chicken simmered in coconut cream (*santen*), pepper, onions and coriander, then flash-fried. A visit to Yogya is not complete without trying this at the famous **Suharti** restaurant just past the Ambarrukmo (Jl Laksda Adisucipto km 7 ☎ 5522). A whole chicken costs $5. To be eaten with sweet chili sauce, fried *pete* beans, *lalap* salad and *sayur asem*, a sweet-sour vegetable soup.

Padang restaurants, recognizable by the rows of dishes in the front window, are all over the city. Very hot and spicy, there is beef *rendang*, chicken curry, fried beef lungs, fish and vegetable curries, potato cutlets and lots of rice. Order as you go in or have the waiter bring a whole selection of dishes to the table (you pay only for what you eat). **Sinar Budi** (Jl Mangkubumi 41), and **Minang Mini** (Jl Mataram in back of Kepatihan, at the end of the alley which runs off Malioboro just north of the Mutiara Hotel) are conveniently located and justly popular.

Specialties of a Yogyanese palace banquet are prepared everyday at a buffet luncheon at the home of **Prince Joyokusuma**, Jl Rotowijayan 5 ☎ 73520, just outside the entrance to the *kraton*. $5. Lunch and dinner are served with a fantastic beach panorama at the **Queen of the South Beach Resort**, Parangtritis. ☎ 67196. **Baleanda Gallery and Restaurant** (Jl Tirtodipuran 3 ☎ 76114) is cool and cozy. Browse through the gallery of modern Indonesian paintings while savoring *pepes jamur* (mushrooms steamed in banana leaves) or spaghetti verde.

For western food, **Gita Buana**, Jl Laksda Adisucipto 169, offers AC respite with steaks, salads and white tablecloths. **Legian Restaurant** (Jl Perwakilan 9 ☎ 87985) is a delightful, roof-top terrace overlooking Jl Malioboro serving steaks, chops, grilled fish and fruit-salad yogurt at reasonable prices. Tiny **Lima Restaurant** on Sosrowijayan Gang I in the Pasar Kembang area has juicy, spiced grilled lamb chops for under $2. Homesick expats' favorite.

Also near Pasar Kembang-Sosrowijayan are **Superman I** and **II** (Sosrowijayan Gang I/99 and I/71) and **Ana's Restaurant** (Sosrowijayan Gang II/127). Popular with the budget crowd, these places serve great pancakes, yoghurt and fresh fruit juices as well as western snacks.

Restaurants serving Indonesian, Chinese and western dishes are also found in the Prawirotaman area. **Tante Lies** at the corner of Jl Parangtritis and Jl Prawirotaman is a popular nighttime hangout. The *nasi rames* and *laksa* soup at **Palm House** on Jl Prawirotaman are tasty and tastefully served. Down the street, **Hanoman's Forest** (which stages nightly performances of dance and puppetry) and **Gorontalo Indian** (nearby on Jl Parangtritis), are very pleasant.

Billed as Yogya's specialty, *gudeg* is a stew of young jackfruit simmered for hours in coconut milk and spices and served with chicken, egg or *tofu*. Available in restaurants such as **Juminten** (Kranggan 69) and **Bu Citro** (opposite the airport), *gudeg* actually tastes best eaten at sidewalk stalls in the evening. Dozens of vendors along Malioboro serve *gudeg* at night, but the tastiest is doled out by huge, friendly women at stalls south of the entrance to the Chinese temple on Jl Brigjen Katamso, and behind the Permata cinema on Jl Gajah Mada.

Restaurants all along Malioboro serve refreshing shaved ice drinks with every imaginable tropical fruit (in season), as well as a variety of western, Indonesian and Chinese dishes.

For fast food freaks, there's **Pizza Hut**, Jl Jend. Sudirman 3; **Kentucky Fried Chicken**, Jl Malioboro 137 and Jl Laksda Adisucipto (Gelael); and **California Fried Chicken**, Jl Malioboro 85 and Jl Laksda Adisucipto (Hero's) and MacDonald's at Malioboro Mall.

PERFORMING ARTS

In this age of electronic entertainment, the traditional arts must adapt to survive. Classical dances are shortened for television audiences, eight-hour *wayang kulit* performances are broadcast over the radio, gamelan recordings are played at wedding receptions, and *ketoprak* troupes have TV and radio devotees.

Live performances have become more expensive and are less common at ceremonies. A case can be made for the positive impact of tourism on the traditional arts. Many tourist shows maintain high artistic standards and serve to support the artistes.

Gamelan Music

The **Kridha Mardowo** musicians rehearse in the Yogya *keraton* every Mon and Wed, 10:30 am–12 noon (except during the fasting month). On Sunday Pon (every five weeks) there is a live radio gamelan broadcast from the **Pakualaman Palace**, 10:30 am–1 pm, except during the fasting month of Puasa. No admission charge.

Two hotels have ensembles in their lobbies played every day: **Ambarrukmo Palace Hotel** (10:30 am–12:30 noon, 4–6 pm) and the **Natour Garuda Hotel** (12 noon–2 pm, 6:30–8:30 pm). Sunday lunches at **Ny. Suharti's Restaurant** can be savored while enjoying a noon concert (11 am–3 pm). The best selection of Javanese gamelan recordings is available at **Podo Moro** on Jl Malioboro, north of the Mutiara Hotel.

Dance Performances

Dance rehearsals held in the *keraton's* Bangsal Kasatriyan every Sun, 10:30 am–12 noon. Warm-up movements are followed by run-throughs of several classical dances in which young dancers are almost imperceptibly prodded into position by the teachers.

Dance performances are presented in the **Sri Manganti pavilion** in the *keraton* on Sundays (except during the fasting month), 11 am–12:30 pm. Performing groups alternate between private dance schools and formal dance academies.

Excellent presentations of classical Javanese dance are staged three nights a week at **Dalem Pujokusuman**, Jl Brigjen Katamso 45. Performed by students of two renowned schools, these concerts feature solo and duet dances as well as a *Ramayana* dance-drama (*sendratari*) fragment (Mon, Wed, Fri 8–10 pm). Admission: $4.

Dinner shows feature a variety of dances, mostly of the Solonese tradition, at the Borobudur restaurant of the **Ambarrukmo Palace Hotel** (Tue, Fri, Sun 8 pm), the French Grill restaurant of the **Arjuna Plaza** (Mon, Wed, Fri 8 pm–10 pm) and **Hanoman's Forest Garden Restaurant** at Jl Prawirotaman 9B (Tue, Sat 7:30 pm–9 pm).

Schools and Rehearsals

If you are interested in seeing how traditional dance is studied, drop by on on one of the schools while classes are in progress and observe. The **Siswo Among Bekso** school holds classes for beginning groups on Tue and Thur, and for advanced students on Wed and Fri, starting at 4 pm at Dalem Purwodiningratan, Jl Kadipaten Kidul 46. The **Pamulangan Bekso Ngayogyokarto** school holds classes at Dalem Pujokusuman (Jl Brigjen Katamso 45) on Mon, Tue and Thur, between 4–6 pm. **Mardowo Budoyo** holds its classes here Sun and Fri, 5 pm.

The performing arts high school, **Sekolah Menengah Karawitan Indonesia**, in Kasihan, Bantul, has classes every day (except Sunday), 7 am—2 pm. At the Performing Arts campus of the **Indonesian Institute of Arts** (ISI, formerly ASTI) at Bulaksumur, classes run all day, Mon–Sat; rehearsals often go into the night. Dance classes for children are organized by ISI and held on campus on Sunday mornings.

The **Dance Center** (Pusat Latihan Tari) of Bagong Kussudiharjo holds rehearsals of modern choreographies based on traditional dance movements at Singosaren, Jl Martadinata 9 (Wed, Thur, Sat, Sun 4–6 pm ☎ 2982). Bagong's Art Colony, Padepokan Seni Bagong Kussudiharjo, Desa kembaran, Kal. Tamantirto, is hidden away in a small village in Kasihan in the Bantul district. Only 15 mins from town by car, the colony brings together students, teachers and afficionados from all over Indonesia. Workshops are held everyday, 8 am–1 pm and 4 pm–6 pm.

Classical Solonese dances are rehearsed every Thursday evening 7–9 pm at the **Pakualaman Palace**, Jl Sultan Agung.

Wayang Wong and Sendratari

The most spectacular *sendratari* is the outdoor **Ramayana Ballet** performance at Prambanan. Four episodes (*The Abduction of Sinta*, *Hanoman's Mission*, *The Death of Kumbakarna* and *Sinta's Trial of Purity*) are spread over four nights (Fri to Mon) of the two weekends closest to every full moon between May and October. A cast of hundreds fills the open-air stage, with the ancient Siva, Visnu and Brahma temples forming an illuminated backdrop, 7–9 pm. Tickets: $2–12.50 VIP. Minibus taxi service back to your hotel in Yogya is available.

A different dance company also performs each month in the new indoor **Trimurti Theater** at Prambanan, shows every Tue, Wed and Thur night, 7:30–9:30 pm all year round. $3.50–7.50.

Nightly performances of the Ramayana (Solonese style) are held at **Purawisata**, on Jl Brigjen Katamso, 8–9:30 pm. Dinner shows at **Ambarrukmo Palace Hotel** (Mon, Wed, Sat 8–9 pm) and **Arjuna Plaza** (Thurs 7–9 pm) present fragments of the Ramayana in *sendratari* form.

The annual **Sendratari Festival** sponsored by the Education and Culture Ministry is usually held in October at the Kepatihan pavilion.

Wayang Kulit

Complete 8-hour performances of shadow puppet plays are staged on the second Saturday of every month at **Sasono Hinggil Dwi Abad** in the south square. Sponsored by the national radio station (RRI), the television station (TVRI) and the local newspaper (Kedaulatan Rakyat), these usually feature Yogyanese *dalangs* (puppeteers), but occasionally have Solonese or Banyumas performers. 9 pm–5 am. VIP tickets cost $2.

On the fourth Sunday of the month, a complete performance is broadcast live from **RRI**, alternating between Sasono Hinggil in the south square and RRI's new studio-auditorium on Jl Gejayan. 9 pm–5 am, admission free.

Bedol *songsong wayang* performances are held at the *keraton's* south Kemagangan courtyard on the nights after Grebeg Mulud and Grebeg Puasa. Set in a small pavilion, the ambience here is more appropriate than large auditoriums.

The **Agastya Art Foundation**, Gedong Kiwo MJ 3/237, presents two-hour *wayang kulit* fragments every day except Saturday, from 3–5 pm. **Ambar Budaya** presents a short fragment at the Yogyakarta Craft Center on Jl Laksda Adisucipto, across from the Ambarrukmo Hotel, on Mon, Wed and Sat, from 9:30 pm–10:30 pm.

Two hour fragments are presented nightly at the pavilion next to **Sono Budoyo Museum** between 8 pm to 10 pm.

Dinner shows at three restaurants also feature short fragments: **Bale Kambang Floating Restaurant** at the Ambarrukmo on Thurs (8 pm), **Arjuna Plaza Hotel** on Tue 7–9 pm and **Hanoman's Forest Garden Restaurant**, Jl Prawirotaman 9B, on Wed and Fri, 7:30–9:30 pm.

Classes for *dalang* training in the classical Yogya *keraton* style are held every evening except Thur and Sun, 7–10 pm at the **Habiranda Dalang School** in Pracimasono, on the southwest corner of the north square.

Wayang Golek

Yogyanese *wayang golek* is presented at the **Nitour** office tucked away in a corner of the yard at Jl KHA Dahlan 71, everyday except Sun 11 am–1 pm. If you last through the initial court scene, which by definition contains much formal dialogue, then you will see battles on horseback, lively monkeys and giants who get beheaded. A similar performance in pleasanter surroundings is offered by the **Agastya Art Foundation** (see above) on Saturday, 3–5 pm.

Dinner shows featuring *wayang golek* include the **Ambarrukmo Palace Hotel** on Mon 8–10 pm, **Arjuna Plaza Hotel** on Sat 7–9 pm and **Hanoman's Forest Garden Restaurant** on Mon and Thur 7:30–9:30 pm.

Ketoprak

The extremely popular *ketoprak* folk drama remains inaccessible to most westerners, as the improvised dialogue is in rapid-fire Javanese. It may be fun, however, to see the outlandish costumes and melodramatic acting. **RRI** stages live performances at their Demangan studios at Jl Gejayan on the first Friday and Saturday of the month. Amateur performances can be seen on temporary stages along the streets around Independence Day (August 17) and in the night fair preceding the week of Sekaten.

Modern Drama and Poetry

A variety of modern drama, poetry readings, pantomime, and pop concerts is presented periodically at three separate arts centers. **Gedung Senisono**, kitty-corner to the main post office, has an open-air stage which features live entertainment on Saturday nights. **Taman Budaya** on the Gajah Mada campus, and **Bentara Budaya** on Jl Suroto (in Kota Baru), also feature various forms of modern entertainment. Ask at tourist information for current listings.

SHOPPING

Yogya is a shopper's paradise, a production center of both traditional and modern handicrafts. Top of the list are the famous Javanese batiks.

Textiles

Numerous small factories and cottage industries in Yogya make traditional hand-drawn *batik tulis*, as well as the stamped *batik cap*, in ready-to-sew lengths. Many are found along Jl Tirtodipuran in the south of Yogya. Visitors are welcome to view the batik process in back of the showrooms. A few of the best-known showroom/factories are:

Ardiyanto's Jl Magelang km 5.8 ☎ 87777.
Plentong Jl Tirtodipuran 28 ☎ 2777.
Rara Djonggrang Jl Tirtodipuran 6A/18 ☎ 88653.
Suryakencana Jl Ngadinegaran MD VII/98 ☎ 3798.
Tjokrosuharto Jl P Mangkurat 58 ☎ 3208.
Winotosastro Jl Tirtodipuran 54 ☎ 62218.

Batik stores offer similar merchandise, but do

not produce their own cloth. The widest selection of material, both hand-drawn and stamped, as well as printed, is available at **Terang Bulan** on Jl Malioboro. Prices are fixed and reasonable. Traditional Yogyanese patterns are getting harder to find, as the trend is towards material for modern clothing. Medium-quality *tulis* pieces can still be found at Terang Bulan, Juwita and Tjokrosuharto. Batik Keris, Batik Semar and Danar Hadi are branches of Solonese factories.

Batik Keris Jl Ahmad Yani 104 ☎ 2492.
Batik Semar Jl Urip Sumoharjo 107.
Danar Hadi Jl Laksda Adisucipto 3 ☎ 88083.
Griya Batik Timur Jl Ahmad Yani 25 ☎ 2844.
Juwita Jl Ahmad Yani 36 ☎ 3981.
Makmur Jl Ahmad Yani 63 ☎ 2798.
Margaria Jl Ahmad Yani 69 ☎ 2669.
Mirota Jl Ahmad Yani 9 ☎ 61990, 88524.
Suryo Puri Jl Kadipaten 3/5.
Terang Bulan Jl Ahmad Yani 76 ☎ 2488.

The highest quality batik is not found in stores, but in dealers' homes. **Bapak Hadiwasito** (Taman Kp III/116, on the alley just north of the entrance to Taman Sari) still maintains high standards in his traditional batik (about $20–50 for a 2-m length). **Ibu Mangunwinoto** (Jl P Mangkurat 158, just south of Tjokrosuharto's) has excellent examples of traditional Yogyanese batik from the Imogiri area villages ($25–100 range).

Lurik is the coarse, woven material traditionally used for men's jackets and *sarong*. Weaves have been refined and bright colors added so the cloth can be used for clothes. Most batik stores offer a selection of *lurik*. **Logro** (Jl Wirobrajan 44) has pieces of *lurik* woven on the traditional back-strap loom, which can be sewn into handsome jackets, shirts, blouses, and simple dresses. **Rumah Tenun "Charindra"** (Jl Modang 70B, off Jl Mangkuyudan ☎ 2480) produces export quality *lurik* on large looms.

Batik Paintings

Batik paintings are as varied as the artists who paint them. The range of styles and themes expressed in this medium is impressive. Check out several painters before buying. Amri Yahya, Bagong Kussudihardjo, Kuswaji and Sapto Hudoyo are the pioneers. Bargain, but remember that these are originals, not overpriced copies.

Many artists at newer galleries (notably Tulus Warsito and Slamet Riyanto) run batik courses. The **Batik Research Center** also offers intensive personalized courses tailored to the needs of the individual or group.

Pak Hadi Pranoto, Ngadinegaran MJ 3/65 offers full-day and half-day courses, and Pak Hadjir (just to the left of the entrance to Taman Sari) has years of experience teaching western tourists in 3 or 5 day courses. The best-known artists/galleries are:

Amri Yahya Gallery Jl Gampingan 67 ☎ 5135.
Galar Gallery Jl Parangtritis 11.
Kuswaji southwest corner of the north square.
Saptohudoyo Jl Laksda Adisucipto Km 9 ☎ 87443.
Slamet Riyanto Jl Tirtodipuran 61A.
Tulus Warsito Jl Tirtodipuran 19A.

Silver and Gold

Silver factories line the streets of Kota Gede. The merchandise is similar in most of these places—jewelry, plates, vases, souvenir items (silver *becaks, andong* and even replicas of the sultan's carriage). Some of the better ones are: **HS** Mondorakan Barat RT 01 ☎ 88872. **MD Silver** Jl Keboan, Kota Gede ☎ 2063. Takes special orders. **Tom's Silver** Jl Ngeksiganda 60, Kota Gede ☎ 3070, 2818. Top quality work, but expensive. In the city, **Tam Yam An** Jl AM Sangaji 10 ☎ 62164, takes special orders.

Puppets

For excellent *wayang kulit* puppets, go to the **Ghriya Ukir Kulit** run by Sagio in the village of Gendeng, 4 km west of Kasongan, just west of a broad intersection shaded by a big banyan tree. Open 9 am–4 pm. Puppets $25–35, or with real gold-leaf $75 to $130, depending on size.

In the city, **Moelyosoehardjo** (Jl S Parman 37B ☎ 2873) has good *wayang kulit*. **Pak Ledjar** (Jl Mataram DN I/370) makes Solonese-style puppets. Order the characters you want; he can make much better ones than those on display. **Bapak Sukasman** (Mergangsan MG III/173, turn east from Jl Taman Siswo opposite the Islamic University) has experimented with new forms of *wayang kulit*. He has some puppets on sale and is always willing to explain his ideas.

Yogyanese *wayang golek* rod puppets are rarer than the Sundanese ones, and cost at least twice as much ($30 and up). The **Nitour office** and **Agastya Foundation** (see above) both have quality puppets for sale.

Masks

Traditional masks of characters from the indigenous Panji tales are still made. True collectors' items can be found in the village of Krantil, Pendowoharjo district, at the home and workshop of **Pak Warno Waskito.** Take Jl Bantul, turn right at the 7.6 km marker, continue about 300 meters and turn left. Signs indicate the first house on the right.

Leather Goods

Leatherwork has been refined over recent years and bags, belts, wallets, and shoes produced in Yogya are much more durable and sophisticated than before.

Some of the finer quality workshops can handle special orders for coats, briefcases, boots, etc. The best shops are:

Fancy Art Shop Jl Malioboro 189A. **Kerajinan Indonesia,** Jl Malioboro 193 ☎ 61995. **Budaya** Jl

Prawirotaman 15B ☎ 5071. **Kusuma** Jl Kauman 50.

Buy beautiful export-quality leather bags and wallets, soft toys, and wooden craftwork at **Pusat Rehabilitasi YAKKUM** (Rehabilitation Center for the Physically Handicapped), Jl Kaliurang 13.5, ☎ 95386. Mon–Fri 8 am–4 pm, Sat till 12 noon. Stop by on your way to Kaliurang. It's worth it.

Antiques

Antique and curio stores are great fun. Finds can include Chinese porcelains, old batik and textiles, lamps, *keris* daggers, lance points, shadow puppets, *wayang golek* , masks, silver jewelry, coins, glass paintings, batik stamps, *loro blonyo* bridal figures and musical instruments. Many are not genuine antiques but replicas. Some of the better shops are:

Ancient Arts Jl Tirtodipuran 50.
Ardiyanto's Jl Magelang km 5.8 ☎ 87777.
Delly Art Shop and Antiques Jl Tirtodipuran 22B.
Dieng Art Shop and Antiques Jl Tirtodipuran 30.
Kerajinan Indonesia Jl Malioboro 193–195 ☎ 61995.
Alia Jewelry on Jl Tirtodipuran 46 has beautiful Javanese black opal jewelry.

Miscellaneous

A wide variety of rattan baskets and furniture can be found in stores on the east bank of the Code River in Kota Baru or go straight to the **Tunggak Semi workshop** on Jl Godean in Malangan, Sumberagung, Moyudan, Sleman.

Tea (check the expiration date), coffee and an array of local snacks can be picked up at either the market sections of the Ramai, Matahari department stores along Malioboro or food stores along Jl Pajeksan (west of Malioboro).

The **Cemeti Modern Art Gallery** Jl Ngadisuryan 7A, has a monthly exhibit of paintings by Indonesian and Western artists who have lived in Indonesia. Open Tue–Sat, 9 am–1.30 pm. ☎ 71015.
Gamelan instruments Pak Suhirdjan, Gedong Kino MJ I/951, individual instruments and whole ensembles made to order.

MAIL

The main post office is near the main junction at the bottom of Malioboro. Open Mon–Thur 8 am–8 pm, Fri 8–11 am and 2–8 pm, Sat 8 am–5 pm.

CHANGING MONEY

Banks give better rates than money changers. **Bank Negara Indonesia 1946** (Jl Trikora 1 ☎ 48-64) Opposite the post office. Mastercard and Visa cash withdrawals can be made at **Bank Central Asia** (Jl Urip Sumoharjo 49 ☎ 86455) and **Bank International Indonesia** (Jl Jend. Sudirman 46 ☎ 62269). Open Mon–Fri 7:30 am–2:30 pm, Sat until 10:30 am. **Pacto Travel Agency** at the Ambarrukmo is an AmEx agent and handles checks, replacements, mail and cash advances up to $1,000.

PHONE AND FAX

The **Telecommunications Office** Jl Yos Sudarso 9 ☎ 86996, is open 7 am–12 midnight for domestic and overseas operator-assisted calls.

Telecoms agents (*WarPosTel*) are scattered in convenient locations all over the city. Open 24-hours, they can place direct domestic and international calls, send telegrams, telexes and faxes. Ask at your hotel for the nearest location.

MEDICAL FACILITIES

The best hospital is the Catholic-run **Panti Rapih** (Jl Cik di Tiro 30 ☎ 63333), but the most efficient emergency services are at **Bethesda Hospital** (Jl Jend. Sudirman 70 ☎ 85000, 87776). Although the equipment and specialist staff at Gajah Mada's **Dr Sarjito Hospital** (Jl Bhineka Tunggal Ika ☎ 87333, 5209) is modern, the nursing service is lethargic and unsanitary. *Apotik* (pharmacies) are everywhere, but only **Kimia Farma** Jl Malioboro 123, is open 24 hrs.

IMMIGRATION

Immigration Office Jl Laksda Adisucipto Km 9.4 ☎ 4948. Near airport. Open Mon–Thur 8 am–2 pm, Fri till 11 am, Sat. till 1 pm. Main counter shuts an hour before closing time.

— *Joan Suyenaga*

4 Temple PRACTICALITIES

INCLUDES BOROBUDUR, KEDU, DIENG AND PRAMBANAN

There are large parks around Borobudur and Loro Jonggrang (Prambanan). These charge an entrance fee (Rp4,000), plus Rp500 for cameras. At most other sites, visitors are asked to sign a guest book and make a small donation (Rp500 per person) to the otherwise unpaid caretaker (*juru kunci*). Guides can be hired at the information counter at both Borobudur and Prambanan.

Prices in US dollars excluding tax & service (10–30%).

Borobudur

Borobudur can be reached by car in an hour from Yogya. The road is good, and the drive leads through small towns and rice fields. Borobudur lies at the edge of a tiny village by the same name. The inhabitants are mainly farmers and souvenir vendors; most are Muslims.

Early morning is the best time to visit Javanese temples, Borobudur included. The gate opens at 6 am, around sunrise. The view of the surrounding volcanoes and the Bukit Menoreh range to the south is clearest at dawn, although mist sometimes obscures the view until 8 am.

To get to the temple you have to walk 500 meters to the base of the hill then climb a series of steps to reach the temple foot. Seeing all the reliefs entails a walk of more than 2 km, including several flights of steps.

The minimum time needed at the site is 1.5 hours. To view all the reliefs takes at least 3 hours. No large bags are allowed on the monument; these can be safely left at the entrance. There's a drinks kiosk just outside the entrance. Take water if you're staying for a while.

GETTING THERE

There are many ways to get to Borobudur. You can hire a car with driver in Yogya; a half-day trip costs about $20. Hotels and tour operators arrange group bus tours (see Yogya Practicalities). Alternatively, take a public bus or minibus from Yogya to Muntilan, change at the terminal here to another bus for the temple. Pickpockets sometimes operate on these buses, so beware.

ACCOMMODATION

Saraswati Inn and **Pondok Indah** are pleasant and inexpensive places to stay. Both are on the Yogya road, 100 meters from the Borobudur parking lot. They have simple but good restaurants.

Borobudur Guest House is at the edge of the temple site. ☎ (0293) 8131. Luxurious, modern Javanese style. 20 AC rooms, private baths, hot water. Double $31; Twin $33. Includes breakfast.

Kedu Plain

See map, page 192.

A full-day excursion can be made with Borobudur as its focal point. The temples of Mendut and Pawon are nearby. **Pawon** is just 2 km east of Borobodur and 100 meters south of the main road in a small village. **Mendut** is 3 km east of Borobudur, on the right side of the main road coming from Yogya. In the late afternoon (on a clear day) the sun illuminates the sanctuary and the three marvelous statues within.

After Mendut you have a choice of two routes. One includes returning to Yogya via the main road and stopping in **Mungkid** village. Craftsmen here learned stonecarving during the Borobudur restoration, and now sell sculptures from the same volcanic rock from which Borobudur is built.

From Mungkid, continue along the main highway, making detours to **Candi Ngawen** and **Candi Canggal**. Both are a few km west of the highway along unpaved but serviceable roads.

The alternative is to go east along the road between the twin peaks of Merapi and Merbabu, via Selo and Boyolali and back to Yogya. Points of interest include three small Hindu temples collectively called **Candi Kuning**. To reach them, take the small road leading south before Selo. These partially restored temples set amid rice fields (Asu, Pendem and Lumbung) date from the 9th century. Lumbung is on the edge of a sheer ravine, 10 m above a beautiful stream. The road up to Selo has spectacular views across the Kedu Plain. Get an early start, this is a long trip.

Dieng Plateau

See map, page 194.

The Dieng Plateau can be reached from Yogya in about 3 hours by car. It is advisable to start early and get there before noon. Because of its altitude, the plateau is often shrouded in mist by early afternoon. Hire a car and driver from Yogya for about $50 a day. Bus tours can be arranged by many companies for about $10 per person. By public transport, go first to Magelang and change for Wonosobo or take a minibus to Wonosobo directly from Yogya (Rp3,000). You can get a minibus from the terminal here to Dieng.

The sites on the plateau can be reached on foot from Dieng village minibus terminal; the furthest temple, **Candi Bima**, is only 1.5 km away. The furthest point of interest, the Sikidang mud crater, is 500 m beyond this. A road leads around the valley, with parking areas near the main sites. Visitors who get out at Dieng will be approached by local guides. Negotiate the fee in advance. A reasonable fee for a 3-hour tour is about $3.

During weekdays the small museum near **Candi Gatotkaca** may be open, and is worth visiting. There are several small *losmen* in Dieng village. Bring a sweater and extra pair of socks.

Wonosobo

Although there are small *losmen* on the Dieng Plateau itself, more comfortable lodgings are found in this town just below Dieng. This is also the best place to hire guides for Dieng. Wanosobo has a picturesque *alun-alun* (square) surrounded by columned pavilions and banyan trees.

The **Tourist Office**, Jl Pemuda 2 ☎ (0286) 21194, is open 7 am–2 pm. Guides can be hired here.

Sri Kencana Jl A Yani 81 ☎ (0286) 21522. Rooms for $15, family rooms for $30; including breakfast.

Nirwana Jl Resimen 18/36 ☎ (0286) 21066 charges $22.50 for first class rooms.

Bima Jl Achmad Yani No. 4 ☎ (0286) 21233. West of the *alun-alun* charges $16 per room per night.

Asia Jl Angkatan 45, no 35. (200 m southwest of the *alun-alun*) is an excellent Chinese restaurant.

Prambanan Plain

See map, page 196.

A tour of all the main temples takes a full day. To view the lesser-known sites takes another day. If time is short, go straight to **Loro Jonggrang temple**, 19 km (12 mi) from Yogya, which opens at 6 am. The trip takes about 30 mins. A round-trip with car and driver costs about $15 for 4 hours. Public transport will cost much less.

The main points of interest at Loro Jonggrang can be seen in an hour or two. Amateur guides at the entrance can explain the principal narrative relief panels. $1–2 for a 45-min tour.

OTHER PRAMBANAN TEMPLES

From Loro Jonggrang, proceed by trolley to Sewu, within the park, passing two smaller ruins, **Candi Lumbung** and **Candi Bubrah**. An ideal way to get around is to hire a horsecart (either a two-wheeled *dokar* or a 4-wheeled *andong*) at the market in Prambanan. This is a sedate way to visit **Plaosan** and **Sojiwan**. Total distance is about 6 km, requires 3–4 hours, and will cost about $6.

The **Ratu Boko** "palace" on the Siva Plateau is reached by car or minibus via a small road leading south from Prambanan to Piyungan. After crossing a river, turn off to the left at a microwave station, then left again, following the pavement until the end. An alternative is to take a horsecart or minibus to the foot of an ancient stairway, about 200 m on the left after crossing the river. From here, climb about 100 m up a steep and slippery path cut into the stone.

On reaching the plateau, the gateway and viewpoint over the Prambanan plain are only a short walk. To the right of the gate is a small guardpost. Sign and give a small donation. A visit to the other two parts of the site, the palace and cave areas, is about a 2 km round-trip walk.

At midday the climb and walk can be tiring. You can get drinks at a small stall just south of the gateway. The best time to visit the plateau is late afternoon. Allow 1.5–2 hrs for a visit.

Another half a day can easily be spent visiting Sambisari, Kalasan and Sari near the road out to Prambanan. To see Watu Gudik, Banyunibo, Dawungsari, Barong, Ijo, Gopolo, Abang and Payak on the Prambanan to Piyungan road, south of Ratu Boko takes a further half-day at least.

GLOSSARY

Some basic vocabulary connected with ancient Indonesian sites and history may be useful to visitors who wish to learn more about them.

bodhisattva A being who has reached the stage of entering Nirvana, but who voluntarily holds back to assist other beings to reach that stage.

candi Temples, gateways, bathing places and other stone remains dating from the pre-Islamic period in Indonesia.

cattra A parasol, often consisting of several tiers, symbolizing royal status.

kala A monster head, probably deriving from Indian depictions of lions. Used to decorate temple niches and portals, probably to frighten away evil influences. Often combined with a *makara*.

kalpataru A "money tree" festooned with jewels, surrounded by pots of treasure; a symbol of heaven.

kinnara Celestial being with a bird's body and a human head.

lingga A three-dimensional phallic symbol carved of stone, symbolizing Siva.

makara A monster head composed of an elephant trunk and tusks, a crocodile's jaw; sometimes with fore-paws. Often found at the ends of stairway walls and the bottom corners of temple niches.

mudra Symbolic hand positions.

pradaksina A ritual circumambulation of a shrine.

stupa Buddhist symbol resembling a bell. It was customary to build stone or brick structures in this shape to shelter relics of Buddha or monks.

yoni A stone base for a *lingga*, usually with a square upper surface and a spout symbolizing the vagina. In rituals the *lingga* was washed with water which then poured out of the *yoni* to be collected. This water was thought to confer fertility.

— *John Miksic*

5 Surakarta (Solo) PRACTICALITIES

INCLUDES SOLO SIDETRIPS

Prices in US dollars. S = Single; D = Double; T = Triple; AC = Air-conditioning. Telephone code is 0271.

GETTING THERE

From Yogya and East Java. Taxis between Yogya and Solo cost $17.50. No matter what vehicle you choose, be forewarned that the 2-hour ride from Yogya to Solo is one of Java's more nerve-jangling routes. From nearby cities it may be more convenient to take an 8-passenger "travel" minibus, which will drop you off at any address in Solo. They are more expensive than public buses but will save you a *becak* fare at the other end.

"Travels" leave from **Surabaya** and **Malang** every 2 hours ($6 AC); and from **Semarang** ($1.75, $3 AC) and Yogya ($1.25, $2 AC) every half hour. Buy tickets at "travel" agents in each city.

Intercity public buses depart every 10 mins from Surabaya, Malang, Yogya and Semarang to Solo: 50¢–$1. On some longer routes, AC *patas* buses offer comfortable limited-stop "travel" which costs slightly more. Regular buses can be flagged down anywhere along their routes, but you are less likely to get a seat this way. Guard your bag.

There are five AC express night trains a day leaving from Yogya costing $1–2.25, depending on class. Trains from Probolinggo (Bromo) take 9 hours and trains depart every evening at 8:30 pm, tickets cost $2 to $4.50.

From Jakarta. Garuda/Merpati and Sempati both have daily flights ($62 one way) as well as Denpasar/Surabaya ($68) to Solo.

Arrange *departing* tickets through either Nusantara Tour & Travel Jl Urip Sumoharjo 65 ☎ 47551; Garuda office at the Kusuma Sahid Prince Hotel; or Sempati Air's office at the Lippobank on Jl Slamet Riyadi (west of Pasar Pon).

AC express **night trains** run between Solo and Jakarta every evening.

"Travel" minibuses run from Jakarta to Solo, leaving at noon and arriving at 4 am, ($15).

You can catch AC express **night buses** between Solo and Jakarta at 3–5 pm ($13) and

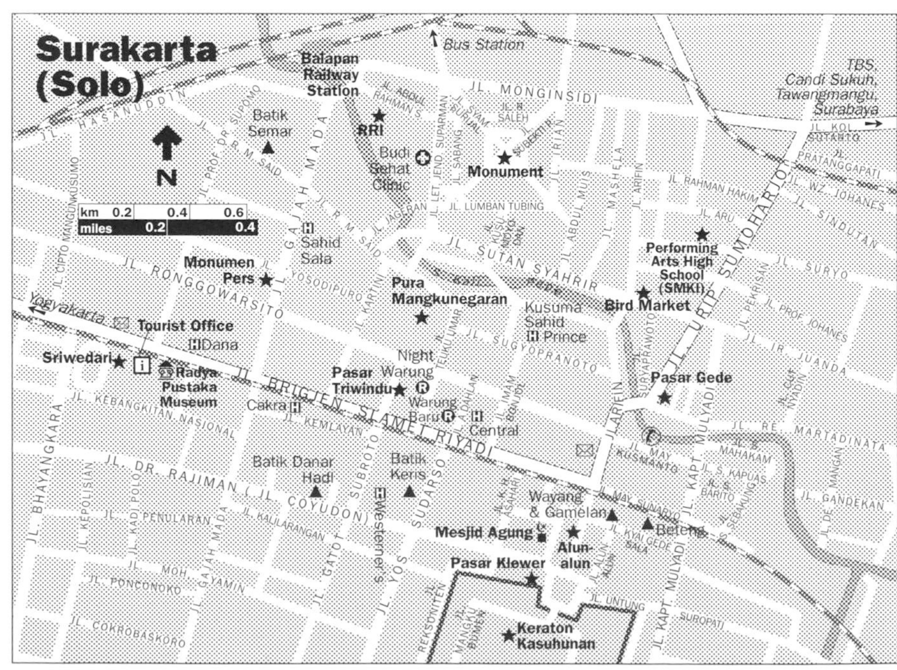

from Probolinggo before 10 pm ($10). Tickets can be arranged at the bus stations, through "travel" agents or directly from the bus company offices in every city. For the ultimate in wheeled luxury between Jakarta and Solo, take the **Big-top Class buses** offered by Muncul and Mulya Indah ($16).

From Bali. Daily flights cost $77 o/w. Night buses leave Denpasar before 4:30 pm, $18 o/w.

Leaving Solo. Catch **intercity public buses** at the Gilingan Bus Terminal. **Buses.** SAA runs **"travel" minibuses** to Semarang and Yogya from Hayuningrat at the Keraton Kasunanan ticket office. Other agents are located on Jl Honggowongso on the left south of Jl Slamet Riyadi. The biggest selection of travels is at the minibus terminal at Gilingan. Book **AC Express night buses** through **Rosalia Indah** Jl Slamet Riyadi 102 ☎ 32437; or **Warung Baru** (see "restaurants").

GETTING AROUND

Taxis from Solo airport charge $5. A taxi to the airport from anywhere in Solo costs $4.50. Solo's taxi service is Solo Central Taxi. ☎ 45678, or go to Matahari Department Store, Pasar Gede and on Jl Slamet Riyadi. Drivers have a list of fixed prices for destinations outside Solo.

Car rental with driver is around $50 a day to destinations such as Tawangmangu. Try the cooperative that operates from just east of the Gading gateway on Jl Veteran.

There is not yet an official place to **rent motorbikes** but ask around at the homestays, or try one of the dealers along Jl Slamet Riyadi.

Bicycle rentals cost from 50¢ to $1.25 a day depending on whether it is a classic one-speed from Rosalia Indah (see above) or mountain bikes from one of the homestays or Warung Baru (see "restaurants"). Nobody's bikes are in very good repair. A stop at the one dependable bike shop, Bridgestone (next to the Holland Bakery on Jl Slamet Riyadi) couldn't hurt.

Becak are everywhere in Solo and still the best way to get around. From Gilingan Bus Station to Kemlayan where most of the homestays are, $1.50 is a reasonable fare. Decide where you want to stay and stick to it as *becak* drivers get commissions for delivering guests to certain homestays. Work out a price before getting in a *becak* or be prepared to pay whatever they ask at the end of the ride. 75¢ from the *Alun-alun Lor* to Sriwedari is reasonable.

ACCOMMODATION

The **Kusuma Sahid Prince** is still the best. The **Ramayana** Guest House is the winner in the intermediate category and recent stiff competition for the budget traveler provides many choices in the *gangs* of Kemlayan with **Relax Home Stay** leading the pack at the time of writing.

Budget (under $10)

Bamboo Homestay (16 rooms) Jl Setyaki 1 behind Sriwedari ☎ 35856. Looks like a scene from a Kafka novel. They've turned bare wood floors and bamboo walls into an industrial loft æsthetic. If it remains clean, it works. $2.50 S to $4 D.

Central (25 rooms) Jl Achmad Dahlan 32 ☎ 42814. An Art Deco classic and truly central. Choose rooms on the front to overlook the street from the second floor terrace or the back to avoid the noise. Could be cleaner. $3 D shared bath.

Happy Homestay (8 rooms) Gang Karangan 12 off Jl Honggowongso. Friendly and clean. Take one of the three rooms upstairs which have a terrace, are bigger and offer greater privacy. $2.50 S, $4 D.

Joyokusuman (15 rooms) Jl Gajahan. Long time favorite of dancers and meditators. What the short term rooms lack in comfort and hygiene is redeemed by the large garden and traditional feel. Upkeep has slackened of late. There are plans to move and change the name to Hendra's Guest House. $3 D.

Mama's Homestay (10 rooms) Gang Kauman III/49 off Jl Yos Sudarso to the east ☎ 52248. A small space dominated by the funky and forceful Mama who runs a batik course and serves huge breakfasts. The two nearby mosques may disturb your sleep in the early hours. $3 S; $4 D.

Relax Homestay (16 rooms) Gang Empu Sedah 28, off Jl Yos Sudarso. Rooms are simple with Pak Julian's arty touch. Two hammocks in the spacious yard justify the name. Diligently scrubbed *mandi*. $3 S and $4 D.

Solo Homestay (11 rooms) Jl Achmad Dahlan, Gang Banda 2. Near Warung Baru and the Central Hotel. Simple rooms and a pleasant and comfortable place to relax. $2.50 S, $3 D all with fans and shared bath.

The Westerners (12 rooms) Gang Kemlayan Kidul 11 off Jl Yos Sudarso to the west ☎ 33106. The travelers' standby but currently resting on the laurels of its former near monopoly of the budget market. $2.75 dorm, $3 S, $3.75 to $4.50 D.

Moderate ($10–$40)

Arini (22 rooms) Jl Slamet Riyadi 361 ☎ 46525. Quiet, clean and comfortable. $12 fan, $19–24 AC.

Dana (47 rooms) Jl Slamet Riyadi 286 ☎ 41976; fax: 43380. Rooms are either newly renovated ($50 AC to $75) or of an older vintage with dark wood paneling ($12 fan to $20 AC). Superior Suite $81.

Putri Ayu (29 rooms) Jl Slamet Riyadi 331 ☎ 46-155. Very comfortable and clean rooms around a two story courtyard. One of the best deals in this price range. 2 km from the center of things but still close to good food. $12 fan, $18 AC.

Ramayana Guest House (8 rooms) Jl Dr Wahidin 22 ☎ 32814. The homely feel and garden courtyard here are popular with westerners. The birds will prevent you sleeping in. $15 with fan, $19 AC.

Wisata Indah (26 rooms) Jl Slamet Riyadi 173 ☎ 43753, 46770. A good bet in the heart of town. Clean, but nothing spectacular. Standard $25, Deluxe $30 and Superior $35.

First Class ($40 and up)

Cakra (79 rooms) Jl Slamet Riyadi 201 ☎ 45847; fax: 48334. Close to the center of things and has a few good rooms. The upper floor west side standard rooms are the best bet and offer a view. The old Junior Deluxe rooms open out to the garden in the rear. Stark swimming pool, live gamelan and a mediocre restaurant. $45 Standard, $60 Junior Deluxe, $71 Deluxe. Cottages $80 to $195.
Kusuma Sahid Prince (88 rooms) Jl Sugyopranata 20 ☎ 46356; fax: 44788. Once a palace, this is now Solo's best hotel. Elements of the original palace are still visible. Decent restaurant and bar, Solo's best pool, gamelan music, shops and a moneychanger are all here. Cabanas are $85 S, $95 D. The best rooms are the newly renovated Superior rooms for $150. Suites range from $115 to $760 for the Royal Suites with a secret passage for hiding your illicit lover.
Riyadi Palace (48 rooms) Jl Slamet Riyadi 335 ☎ 47181; fax: 51552. Solo's newest hotel. $44 Standard, $60 to $80 Deluxe and Suites for $107.
Sahid Sala (39 rooms) Jl Gajah Mada 82 ☎ 35889; fax: 44133. Gamelan in the afternoon and karaoke in the restaurant. The cottages in the garden are especially comfortable. $77 S and $88 D Standard, Suites $110. Cottages $117–285.
Solo Inn (32 rooms) Jl Slamet Riyadi 366 ☎ 46077; fax: 46076. Very comfortable. Good service. $36 S to $46 D Standard and $75 for a Suite.

FOOD

There are some wonderful night *warung* in Solo where you can sample such local specialties as *nasi liwet* (coconut milk and chicken over rice in a banana leaf) and *nasi gudeg* (young jackfruit with papaya leaves and coconut milk).
Jalan Teuku Umar is the street of milk and honey, offering fresh milk mixed with ginger, honey or egg either iced or hot. It is also the heart of Solo's *warung* society, offering rice meals, a dizzying variety of fried, jellied or baked *jajan* snacks.

At night in Solo, where there's smoke there's *saté* and there's always plenty of it coming from the corner of Jl Yos Sudarso and Jl Slamet Riyadi where grills are furiously fanned to render chicken and goat in various shades of char.

Daytime Warungs

Bu Hadi is reputedly the best cook in Solo. The menu at her little kitchen (behind the Kantor Lurah at the corner of Jl RM Said and Jl Gajah Mada) changes daily and is consistently good, mainly vegetable and chicken dishes. Open early morning until 2 pm. Go before noon if you want a good choice.
Monggo Mampir is in Gajahan, east of Jl Yos Sudarso on Jl SM Sangaji 49. A relaxing place to sit out the hot afternoon and munch on fresh vegetables.

Night Warungs

Bu Mitro, the sour lady, serves great *gudangan* (vegetable greens over rice) or *sayur lodeh* (vegetables in coconut milk) with a sneer and, if she really likes you, some verbal abuse. At night in front of Losmen Aida, Jl RM Said, just east of Jl Gajah Mada.
Bu Yati is the *nasi gudeg* queen of Jl Teuku Umar (and thus Solo) at the corner with Jl Ronggowarsito.
Bu Wongso Lemu mid-block on Jl Teuku Umar at night. Best spot for the Solonese specialty *nasi liwet.*
Warung Kobra on Jl Veteran near the Gading gate at night. You choose the snake; they kill it, skin it, cook it and serve it. High entertainment value for the non-squeamish, and tasty too.

Restaurants

Warung Baru at Jl Keprabon Tengah 23 (Jl Achmad Dahlan) across from the Hotel Central, is *the* coolest place to hang out and soak up Solo vibes. Low prices for everything from *pisang goreng* to Probolinggo bus tickets. Lots of good advice and extra services. Some of the best western food in town.
Kantin Bahagia at Jl Gatot Subroto across the street from Matahari Department Store. Good Chinese-Indonesian-European menu aimed at travelers.
Malioboro Jl Gatot Subroto 14. The best fried chicken in Solo.
Lesehan Lezat is the best of the wide selection of food stalls at Sriwedari Park with excellent baked fish. The *teh poci gula batu* is tea poured over a huge sugar crystal. Interesting. Open 24 hours a day.
Andalas Jl Ronggowarsito 111 opposite the Mangkunegaran Palace. The best Padang food in town.
Kusuma Sari at the southwest corner of Jl Yos Sudarso and Jl Slamet Riyadi. A comfortable centrally located eatery popular with locals and foreigners alike. The food is only so-so but this is the place for ice cream between dinner and the *wayang.*
Tio Cio 99 Jl Slamet Riyadi 248. Good seafood.
Bakso Kalilarangan Jl Yos Sudarso 129. Serves *bakso* meat balls made from various things: *babat* is stomach and *otot* is veins. Closed Wednesdays.
Swikee Asli Purwodadi Jl Yos Sudarso 168. Solo branch of Purwodadi chain. Specialty? *Kodok* (frog).
Pringgondani Jl Widuran 79, is a *lesehan* restaurant where the *ayam goreng* (fried chicken) is made from free range chickens: skinnier but tastier. Let the kids loose to romp in the pool of plastic balls.
Purimas 3 is across the street from Pringgondani and sells 5 snack size cakes for 50¢ in its bakery section. Next to the bakery is a pavilion where you can sample the foods that are typical of the ubiquitous *kaki lima* (five-legged) mobile stalls.
Serabi Kalilarangan at Jl Yos Sudarso 51 has for over 70 years been serving excellent egg and coconut filled crepes. Great for breakfast.
Rasa Mirasa Jl Raya Solo, a $2.50 taxi ride away in Kartasura. A *lesehan* restaurant (you sit cross-legged at low tables) out of town with perhaps the best food in the area, the baked fish can't be beaten. A relaxed atmosphere (if you can get them to disconnect the speaker at your table).
Orient Jl Slamet Riyadi 397, Purwosari is the best Chinese food in Solo at reasonable prices. Live music three nights a week.
Sari is a little further down the same street and serves the tastiest sit down menu of Javanese food.

Nikoo is a new Japanese restaurant with surprising authenticity for Solo. on Jl Slamet Riyadi next to the Gelael Supermarket & Kentucky Fried Chicken. **Rindu** is a chain of clean and reliable Padang style places, expanding quickly all over Solo. If you stumble on one when hungry, drop in.

Tours & Meditation

The **Keraton Kasunanan** is open for tours every day but Friday from 8:30 am until 1 pm. Admission is 30¢ plus a 50¢ camera or $2.50 video fee. The **Mangkunegaran Palace** is open daily, 9 am to 2 pm; 9 am to 12:30 pm on Saturdays.

What Solo lacks in big time attractions it makes up for in soul and the simple fascinations offered by the popular bicycle tour of the area making stops to look in on some of the local industries of batik production, *tofu* making and an *arak* (rice wine) distillery among others.

These tours are offered by many of the homestays and Warung Baru, which was the original, has the best guides. The going rate is $4 per person (2 minimum) including the bicycle, or $10 per person by horse and cart (4 minimum).

Solo also offers a great opportunity to try your hand at the batik process with many places offering **batik** courses. Among them are Mama's Homestay (see "accommodation" above) and **Batik Keris** (see "batik" below).

Solo is a major center of **meditation** with four guides commonly accommodating foreigners. The most accessible of these is Pak Suyono at Shanti Loka, Jl Ronggowarsito 60, a fluent English speaker offering morning and evening **new age relaxation meditation** five days a week. Pak Wondo practises Sumarah traditional **Javanese meditation** in Keratonan on Gang I and holds Wednesday evening sessions with a translator. Pak Hardjanto at Jl Sidikoro 10A in Baluwarti to the east of the Keraton, teaches **yoga**. A commitment of 40 days (and 40 nights) is advised as an introduction to this demanding practice involving the Javanese tradition of daytime sun and nighttime water tank meditation. Pak Prapto Suryodarmo, located on the north edge of Solo in Mojosongo, instructs Buddhist-related **dance and movement meditation**. He is popular among Europeans.

PERFORMING ARTS

Aside from the regularly scheduled happenings listed below, word-of-mouth is the way to find out about the performing arts when you're in town. Also check at the **Tourist Information Center** at Sriwedari. Especially popular are the Wednesday morning dance rehearsals at the Mangkunegaran Palace.

Music & Dance

You can hear some of the musicians who helped make Solo famous for its special style of gamelan play in the lobbies of the **Kusuma Sahid Prince** and **Sahid Sala** hotels every afternoon. The **Mangkunegaran Palace** holds dance rehearsals with live gamelan in their huge reverberant *pendopo* that are open to the public every Wednesday morning from 10 to around noon, preceded and followed by gamelan *klenengan* jam sessions. On Monday and Thursday evenings, at around 8 pm, dance performances are staged for package tourists and the occasional discrete ad hoc guest.

Every 35 days on the eve of *Sabtu Pon* of the Javanese calender (always a Friday night) the Mangkunegaran gamelan troupe broadcasts their sound from this hall over **Radio Republik Indonesia (RRI)**. RRI has an auditorium, just south of Balapan Train Station, from which it broadcasts live performances of gamelan every second and fourth Thursday of the month from 9:30 pm until midnight. Although not the ideal venue to view traditional performances, it is open and free to the public.

At the **Keraton Kasunanan Surakarta** every fifth Monday night on Malam Selasa Legi gamelan is performed and broadcast by RRI. The best time to see performances at the **STSI Performing Arts Academy** in Kentingan just north-east of town is during the final exam periods in December and June and at the **SMKI High School for the Performing Arts** in April and May. The **TBS Performing Arts Center** is also in Kentingan and has a monthly calendar of events.

Wayang

Wayang kulit shadow puppet plays are an important part of many common rituals in Java. Performances are frequent and usually advertised by word-of-mouth. If you can find someone to translate for you all the better but this is by no means essential. Saturday nights are *wayang kulit* night at **RRI,** broadcasting live from rotating locales. The first Saturday of every month it is at **STSI,** on the third it is at RRI, on the fourth at the Pagelaran (of the **Keraton Kasunanan**) on the south side of the *Alun-alun Lor,* and the fifth Saturday, when it occurs, it is at **TBS.**

Central Java's most celebrated puppeteer, **Ki Anom Suroto**, sponsors *wayang* performances on his Javanese birthday occurring on the eve of *Rebo Legi* (a Tuesday night every 5 weeks) at his home behind Hotel Wisata Indah.

At the **Sriwedari Park** there is *wayang orang* performed every evening at 8 pm except for Sunday when there is a matinée at 9 am. In addition, RRI broadcasts live performances of *wayang orang* every first and third Tuesday of the month from 9:30 pm until midnight.

SHOPPING

Solo has long been famous as a place to buy

its characteristically rich orange and yellow batik, this can be found at **Pasar Klewer** and the big batik stores (see below).

Other shopping opportunities are found in **Pasar Triwindu** or the historic **Pasar Gede**. Solo has two shopping malls: one on Jl Gatot Subroto and the new mega mall **Beteng** on the extension of Jl Slamet Riyadi just east of the entrance to the *Alun-alun Lor*. Both have branches of **Matahari Department Store**.

Galael is a western-style supermarket on Jl Slamet Riyadi, west of Sriwedari, where there is also a **Swensons** ice cream parlor and a **Kentucky Fried Chicken**.

Batik

The three biggest batik producers in Java have major stores in Solo. These are **Batik Keris** at Jl Yos Sudarso 62, **Danar Hadi** at Jl Slamet Riyadi 217, and **Batik Semar** at Jl RM Said 148. They have helpful staff, fixed prices and a wide selection of batik cottons, silks and finished clothing as well as some other handicrafts.

Once you have a feel for what you're looking for, such as the difference between *cap* (wax is applied using a metal stamp) and *tulis* (more painstaking and refined hand drawing process), you may want to try your bargaining skills out at **Pasar Klewer** at the southwest corner of the *Alun-alun Lor* in front of the Keraton Kasunanan. This is more of a classic Southeast Asian market experience with all of the bustle and shove. It is most pleasant early in the day when you can get "morning prices" (lower).

Prices depend on the process employed, the detail of design, the quality of the cloth, the number and quality of dyes and the presence or absence of defects. Inspect each cloth carefully for consistency, as patterns can change within a single piece. Machine-printed batik can cost as little as $2 a meter. The best *cap* is $5 for a sarong length of 2.25 meters. The finest quality *batik tulis* starts around $40 and goes as high as $300 for the best pieces which have taken from one to two months of patient work.

A good shop to see batik is **Siti Sendani** Jl Slamet Riyadi 208 across from Hotel Cakra with mixed *batik cap* and *tulis* for $20 and good *tulis* for $50 to $75.

For the highest quality work, go to the designers' home factories. These are the aristocrats of Solo so the rules are different here than in Pasar Klewer. The most well-known are: **KRT Hardjonegoro**, Jl Yos Sudarso 101; **Bu Praptini**, in the Tumenggungan district; **Bu Barjo**, Jl Pangeran Mijil 5, Pringgolayan; **Bu Hartini**, Jl Kalilarangan 5. Also try **Nora Art Gallery** Jl Slamet Riyadi 280: paintings and antiques for the serious collector.

The place to buy a dance costume is **Bedoyo Srimpi** on Jl Dr Supomo. Other traditional outfits can be found at **Busana Jawi** on Jl Teuku Umar 14 or at **Sadinoe** Jl Siswo 60.

Wayang Puppets

The best place to buy leather *wayang kulit* shadow puppets is the south-east corner of the *Alun-alun Lor*. These full-sized new puppets come in two price ranges, depending on whether real gold leaf is used or not. For non-gold, a figure of Arjuna may be had for as little as $25 (with a little bargaining). Larger characters are more expensive. Smaller sized so-called "children's" shadow puppets can be found at the **Balai Agung** on the north side of this same square.

Avoid the overpriced shops at Sriwedari. At the **Mangkunegaran Palace** gift shop you can find good shadow puppets for just a little more than you might pay elsewhere ($30 for a small character, to $100 for a *gunungan* tree of life). The highest quality puppets are available only through craftsmen in the surrounding villages and usually must be ordered in advance.

A wonderful example of Javanese traditional arts continuing to evolve and develop is the output of **Pak Hajar Satoto** producing *wayang kulit* puppets, colorful carved furniture and *topeng* masks as well as sculptures and paintings. He has galleries at Joyontakan 01/01 (go south on Jl Yos Sudarso past the second bridge after Jl Veteran and take the first little street to your left) and at Gembongan in Kartosura.

Central Javanese *wayang golek* wooden puppet figures can be bought from Pak Sunarso at STSI, the performing arts academy in Kentingan.

Kris

Dance kris daggers that are for show only (they do not have the mystical power of a real *kris*) and can be found at **Busana Jawi** on Jl Teuku Umar or inside **Pasar Triwindu** for between $5 and $30. Another place to find *kris* is the eastern side of the *Alun-alun Lor*. One dealer here, **Pak Abdul Chanan** has an impressive collection on sale with prices ranging from $200 to $30,000. **Pak Triyono Widodo** makes high quality *kris* and sheaths and can talk informatively on the topic in English. Ask for him at TBS, the Performing Arts Center just northeast of town in Kentingan. Also try **Pak Fauzan** at Yosoroto Rt 28/Rw 82, Badran (in the west of town) for high quality *kris*.

Antiques

Smaller items and furniture can be found at **Pasar Triwindu**. Check out the wooden sculptures of the seated couple Loro Blonyo that traditionally adorn the central, most sacred, room of a Javanese house. Also available at Bali Art Shop at Kauman gang II (some call it Jl Tri Sula).

Pak Nindyo at Hanindyosaputro, Jl Bremoro 10A, Danukusuman, is a major dealer in antiques and reproductions, shipping items all over Java and the world. He has a large workshop and produces beautiful reproductions as well as having a large selection of originals. Of the smaller hole-in-the-wall shops, the two next-door neighbors on Jl Reksoniten (also called Jl Baluwarti), **Pak Gasim** and **Pak Sauman** between them have a good collection including old *lemari* (armoire if you're French) running from $75 to $800. Another spot is **Pak Willy Moertoyo Widodo** at Jl Urip Sumoharjo 113.

Gamelan Instruments

Suling flutes are the least expensive and most transportable traditional instrument of Solo. You can buy these as well as a two string fiddle *rebab* or a *siter* (zither) near the south-east corner of **Pasar Triwindu**. You can visit the Balai Agung workshop at the north side of the *Alun-alun Lor* and watch them make iron instruments (the least expensive material) and carve wooden drums. **Pak Mulyadi's** at Loji Wetan Rt 04/VII past the Beteng shopping mall, has good iron and brass instruments—$50 to $100 for a *gender* metalaphone with tube resonators.

For the best quality, bronze is the metal and **Pak Tentrum** (Ngepung Rt 02/Rw II Semanggi) is the maker. A *gender* from here will cost around $150 to $200.

Cassettes

For **traditional music** go to Radio Garuda on Jl Slamet Riyadi 122 where the sales people are the most helpful. A wider selection can be found at Istana Cassette at the corner of Jl Diponegoro and Jl Slamet Riyadi (no sign). Single tapes run $1.50 or $10 for a whole 8-tape *wayang* story.

SERVICES

The tourist information office is on Jl Slamet Riyadi at Sriwedari. The main **telephone office** at Jl Mayor Kusmanto 3 is open round the clock. They can receive **faxes** and deliver them anywhere in Solo for 30¢ a page. Special pay phones for billing international calls to your calling card company are found at both palaces in town. Ask for the **Home Country Direct Indosat** telephone. There is a centrally located *Wartel* on Jl Slamet Riyadi at Pasar Pon. The **post office** is open from 8 am to 7 pm at Jl Jenderal Sudirman 7. Elteha is a packing and shipping service located across from the Sala Sahid Hotel on Jl Gajah Mada. For major **shipments** to send home your furniture or gamelan purchases, use PT Sunaryo Jl Yos Sudarso 1 in Yogya ☎ 5072. **Change money** at Bank Bumi Daya which is also the American Express agent. When the banks are closed you can change money at Sahid Artha Sari at the Kusuma Sahid Prince Hotel 8 am to 7 pm Mon to Sat and 11 am to 3 pm on Sun, or at some of the gold stores on Jl Coyudan near Pasar Klewer. **Photography** needs are best handled at Sudio Hari Jl Honggowongso 26. The best **swimming pool** is at the Kusuma Sahid Prince Hotel for $1.25 (50¢ extra to use one of their towels) unless you want to swim laps in which case the 50 m pool at Bengawan Sport out in Kentingan is the preferred spot (40¢, bring your own towel). The best **disco** is Freedom, 4 km away from Pasar Pon in Manahan. Legend is a new dance hall at Jl Honggowongso 81A near Pasar Kembang. There are also two popular **nightclubs** in town: the Holland Pub above the Holland Bakery on Jl Slamet Riyadi and Central Restaurant at the Central Hotel.

For **movies** go to the three theaters at Matahari Department Store, Jl Gatot Subroto or take a taxi out to Solo Baru to see one of the eight movies at Atrium: for a brief moment this was the biggest cinema in Indonesia. Check the banners at the corner of Jl Yos Sudarso and Jl Slamet Riyadi to find out what's on. For **minor medical problems** that call for more than a stop at the *apotik,* go to clinic Budi Sehat at Pasar Legi open until 7 pm. The recommended dentist is Dr Shirley behind Pasar Gede and the best hospital in town is Rumah Sakit Dr Oen.

— *Bob Cowherd*

Solo Sidetrips

See map, page 218.

Tawangmangu

Buses to Tawangmangu from Solo cost 35¢ and take a grueling 2 hours to travel 40 km. If you don't want to stand up the whole way, be sure to catch it from Solo bus terminal. Note: the last return bus leaves Tawangmangu at 4 pm.

Taxis costs $12.50 one way and a bit less than twice that for a return trip with a bit of cruising around Tawangmangu.

Alternatively, **hire a "colt"** for a whole or half day trip ($15–30) from various restaurants and hotels in Solo (try Westerners', Happy Homestay, or Warung Baru). Drivers from these places often speak some English and make good guides. They are usually more prepared to visit sights and wait, as opposed to taxis which often charge for waiting and for each extra destination.

A recommended trip is to go to Candi Sukuh and take the beautiful 2 to 3 hour hike from there to Tawangmangu while your driver goes the long way round and meets you at the top of the stairs to the waterfall. It is best to book a "colt" at least a day in advance.

Once in Tawangmangu, you can hire horses for about $1.50 an hour, although it is probably easier and more comfortable to walk.

ACCOMMODATION

Tawangmangu is Solo's weekend getaway resort, and places to stay tend to be crowded or full in holiday periods, and almost deserted at other times. Note: prices can go up as much as 300% at peak times.

A wide range of accommodation is available, mostly centered on the main road up the hill from the bus station, and around Bale Kambang near the entrance to the waterfall, Grojogan Sewa.

Pondok Lawu Jl Lawu 20 ☎ (0271) 97020. Probably the best value for money. Double or twin rooms $12.50 and $17.50. Hot showers, in-house videos and wall-to-wall carpeting. Spotlessly clean.

Komajaya Komaratih Hotel Jl Lawu 150–151 ☎ (0271) 97125. Tawangmangu's largest and fanciest hotel. Good restaurant, karaoke bar, a pool and tennis courts. Standard rooms $29 D, $25S. Also suites for 4 to 16 people ($52–116) with their own dining and sitting rooms, and western-style bathrooms.

Losmen Muncul Sari Jl Raya Kaliosoro 87 is cheap and pleasant, with twin and double beds ranging from $5 to $10. The more expensive rooms have their own bathrooms with hot water.

Pak Amat's, next to the bus station, must be the cheapest place in town. Adequate, maybe. $3.75.

FOOD

Food in Tawangmangu tends to be more expensive than in Solo, with less variety. However, try the local specialty, *saté kelinci* (rabbit saté). Vegetables and fruit here are good, cheap and fresh so salads, vegetable soup, *gado-gado* and similar dishes are likely to be good as well.

Puas Siti Sari, near the waterfall, has an extensive Chinese and Indonesian menu, offering dishes such as oxtail soup and fried chicken.

Sapto Argo, on the left side of Jl Raya Lawu, up the road from the bus station is also popular. There are several *warung* near the bus station and at the entrance to the waterfall.

Out of town, on the road to Solo, are several places set amid rice fields, offering fresh goldfish and catfish. You usually eat sitting on mats at bamboo tables and at some, you can fish your meal out of a pond! Easily seen from the main road, they often use the word *lesehan* in their name.

Sarangan

Sarangan is 14 very steep and windy km from Tawangmangu. You can catch a **public "colt"** from Tawangmangu for 35¢, slightly more on Sundays. Mainly used by village women carrying produce to market, these are great for local color, but are very crowded and stop a lot. Also, they tend to stop running by mid-afternoon. You can **hire a colt** from Tawangmangu for about $12.50 return or a **taxi** from Solo for about $25 one way.

ACCOMMODATION

Accommodation in Sarangan is a bit more expensive than in Tawangmangu with little low budget accommodation available. Prices are very high during holidays, cheaper on weekdays.

Hotel Sarangan ☎ (0351) 98022. Has a great lake view and a dusty old-fashioned charm, with a huge lobby with pool tables, table tennis, and a fireplace. Rooms are large and comfortable, and have bathrooms with hot water. $23 S; $28 D and up.

Grand View Cottages is good for groups, with cottages for 7 next to the lake. Cottages are spacious and clean, and have dining rooms, sitting rooms, color TV, and telephone. Tennis courts and a karaoke lounge are available. Cottages $75 and up.

There are a lot of simpler places in the $10 to $15 category on the main road to the lake. **Sari Rasa**, is recommended: very clean, with a pleasant lounge, and blankets and hot water in rooms for $10 D.

FOOD

Food in Sarangan is a bit limited, with a choice between the simple *warung* next to the lake, and the hotel restaurants. **Pondok Bamboo Restaurant** at Grand View Cottages is quite good, with a range of Chinese dishes, but a little expensive. **Sari Rasa** has very good fish and oxtail soups.

Sangiran

To get to Sangiran using public transport, catch the Purwodadi bus from Solo, and get off at Kalijambe (20¢). From there, you can either walk 3.5 km through rice fields to the museum or ask someone to take you on their motorbike for about $1 round trip. Lots of motorbikes wait for passengers at the T-intersection here. Alternatively, a taxi from Solo costs about $6 one way. The museum is open 7 am to 5 pm, 7 days a week, and entrance is 8¢. Simple Indonesian food is available at the *warung* outside the museum.

Pacitan

A $1, 4-hour bus ride from Solo passes through Wonogiri before arriving in Pacitan (5 km past the beach). Pacitan is a fairly large town with a military base and several places to stay and eat. **Gua Tabuhan** is nearby with stalagtites upon which gamelan music can be played. There are a lot of jewelry and agate sellers at the entrance.

Tell the bus driver if you want to go to the beach and get off before you get to town. From here it's less than 1 km. Sometimes you can catch a *dokar* horse carriage ($1) back to the beach. Beautiful and uncrowded sands with good swimming. Watch out for riptide in some spots.

ACCOMMODATION

Happy Bay Beach Bungalows at the beach, Pacitan ☎ (0357) 81474. Run by "Eric, the half crazy Australian." Polite staff and pleasant grounds. Clean rooms and beautiful bathrooms. $5 S and $6.25 D to $9 for a room for four. No fans or AC but all rooms have private baths. Surf and boogie boards for hire, also bicycles ($2 a day) and motorbikes ($10). The good surf is 3 km away. If Happy Bay is full try the **Bali Beach Queen Hotel** in town.

— *Tim Kortschak*

6 North Coast PRACTICALITIES

INCLUDES CIREBON, PEKALONGAN & SEMARANG

Prices in US dollars, excluding tax & service (10–30%). S = Single, D = Double, T = Triple.

Cirebon

See map, page 230. *Telephone code is 0231.*

GETTING THERE

Cirebon can be reached from Jakarta via the flat and boring north coast highway in 4 hours. The traffic is very heavy, with many buses and trucks. From Bandung, Cirebon is 125 km and just over 2 hours via Sumedang along a very scenic road. **By bus** from Jakarta or Bandung costs $3. The Cirebon bus terminal is at the southern end of the city. Frequent **trains** from Jakarta cost about the same and arrive at the station on Jl Siliwangi, just north of the center of town, where most hotels are located.

On arrival, you may find a visit to the **Tourism Office** on Jl Brigin Darsono 5 ☎ 208856 useful to get a schedule of events.

ACCOMMODATION

Budget (under $15)

Asia (31 rooms) Jl Kalibaru Selatan 15 ☎ 202183. Well-maintained old house with atmosphere and friendly people. Excellent information about Cirebon. Will arrange tours. All rooms include breakfast. $6 no bath; $7–13 with bath.
Cordova (44 rooms) Jl Siliwangi 87 ☎ 204677. Cheap but not too clean. Drivers whose employers stay at the nearby up-market hotels often stay here. $6 double, bath & fan; $14 double, AC & TV.
Nusantara (43 rooms) Jl Tentara Pelajar 39/41 ☎ 203941. Super budget *losmen*. Lively and friendly. No AC. All rooms with breakfast. One room, one person, $3; two people, bath in room, $6.
Slamet (38 rooms) Jl Siliwangi 95 ☎ 203296. Sparkling clean but lacking character. Cleanest and most reasonable in this price range. Bath in all rooms. $10 for 2 beds & fan; $14 AC & TV.

Intermediate ($15 and up)

Grand (28 rooms) Jl Siliwangi 98 ☎ 208867; fax: 208632. Centrally located faded-glory hotel near the town square, built in 1923. Rooms are comfortable, spacious but water stained. AC & TV. Prices include breakfast. $15–25. Good value.
Kharisma (101 rooms) Jl Kartini 60 ☎ 207668; fax: 202295. A new building has been recently built where upper range rooms are housed. Swimming pool, fitness center, disco. The older rooms are a bit pricey. $25–90.
Niaga (18 rooms) Jl Kalibaru Selatan 49 ☎ 206-718. Simple and clean. Breakfast included. $18–25.
Omega (55 rooms) Jl Tuparev 20 ☎ 204291. A little run-down for the price, but rooms are adequate. Restaurant attached. $20 standard room.
Priangan Jl Siliwangi 108 ☎ 202929. Centrally located near a shopping district. Very clean. $12 non-AC double; $15 with AC; $27 with AC & TV.
Sidodadi (44 rooms) Jl Siliwangi 74 ☎ 202305; fax: 204821. Comfortable. Restaurant, bar, pool table. $15 standard single; $34 deluxe.

First Class ($40 and up)

Bentani (83 rooms) Jl Siliwangi 69 ☎ 203246; fax: 207527. Three-star hotel with full facilities. The rumbling of the disco reaches most rooms until late. $49 standard single; $54 double.
Park (99 rooms) Jl Siliwangi 107 ☎ 205411; fax: 205407. New and plush three-star hotel in four stories. The best place in town. $50 for a standard single; $60 double.
Patra Jasa (53 rooms in 28 bungalows) Jl Tujuh Palawan Revolusi (Tuparev) 11 ☎ 29400; fax: 27696. Northwest of town on the way to Bandung. Not much on style but the rooms are quite spacious. Swimming pool and restaurant. $42 to $96.

FOOD

The seafood in Cirebon ("Shrimp City") is wonderful, and most eateries have tanks of live creatures in house. Another of Cirebon's specialties is frogslegs or *swike* ("water chicken").
Jumbo Restaurant & Seafood Jl Siliwangi 191 ☎ 23606. Try this place if you like to cook your seafood yourself. There's a gas cooker in each table (*meja panas*), Japanese style.
Maxim's Jl Bahagia 3. A huge Chinese restaurant in plain surroundings with amazing seafood. Try the *udang mabak* (drunken shrimp), prepared with *arak* (Indonesian schnapps). Also big steamed crab. The extensive menu is also in English.
Kopyor Jl Karanggetas. Chinese food and *es kopyor* (coconut milk with syrup).
Jogja Department Store Jl Siliwangi in the main shopping area. Try *nasi jamblang* or *soto kudus*.

SHOPPING FOR BATIK

There are several batik makers in Trusmi (Plered) village 12 km from Cirebon. Take the main road west towards Bandung, turn west in Plered at the intersection (many *becak* here). Atmospheric Trusmi is about 500 m down the road. This is a great place to walk around in the cool morning hours. The small and friendly batik shops usually have a *pabrik* (workshop) attached which you can visit. You will find batik *megamendung, pedalaman, pesisiran, keratonan* and others.

H Masina is located on the right as you enter Trusmi. Some batiking goes on right in the courtyard. The well-stocked shop is a place to sit on the floor, relax, drink tea and view the wares. ☎ 31030.

Batik Adi Putro is down the first street to the right about 20 m. It doesn't have much of a display room, but out back the workshop, where 20 workers sit around pots of hot wax, makes a strong impression.

Batik Genung Jati is a little further down from Batik Adi Putro on a side street. This big new stylish shop has a wide selection and a workshop next door.

MISCELLANEOUS

Tourist information Jl Brigin Darsono 5 ☎ 208856.

Pekalongan

Telephone code is 0285.

Pekalongan lies on the main north coast bus and rail routes. No air connections. Rail connections from Jakarta ($3 economy; $16 with AC) and Surabaya (prices similar); railway station is on Jl Gajah Mada. Buses east and west leave from the terminal east of town on Jl Raya Batang.

ACCOMMODATION

Budget (under $15)

Agus Salim (5 rooms) Jl Agus Salim 44. Cheap rooms. $2 single.

Gajah Mada (20 rooms) Jl Gajah Mada 11A ☎ 41185. Its biggest asset is that it's across from the train station. An old house, rooms a bit shabby. $4 double, no bath or fan; $5 with bath.

Indah (15 rooms) Jl Gajah Mada 33 ☎ 81344. Dusty *losmen*. $5 to $6.

Melati (34 rooms) Jl Gajah Mada 2 ☎ 4132. Basic rooms. $6; $9 AC.

Sari Dewi (32 rooms) Jl Hayam Wuruk 1 ☎ 21248. Friendly and central. Reasonable rooms for the price. Ask for Ibu Itok to guide you around town. $5 double, no bath; $15 AC & TV.

Sendang Sari (20 rooms) Jl Sudirman 29, Batang ☎ 91016; fax: (0285) 81398. Located about 5 km east of town in Batang. Reasonable rooms. $3 economy; $10 AC, TV and bath.

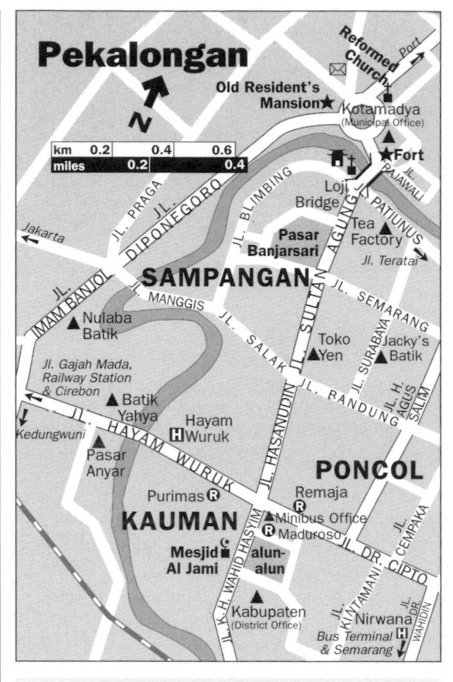

Intermediate ($15 and up)

Hayam Wuruk (51 rooms) Jl Hayam Wuruk 152 ☎ 81322. One-star and good value. Conveniently near to seven batik shops. $22 to $40.

Istana (48 rooms) Jl Gajah Mada 23–25. Two-star hotel. Clean, nicely decorated rooms. Restaurant and billiards. $12 fan; $20 AC.

Jayadipa (46 rooms) Jl Raya Baros 29 ☎ 81938. A brand new hotel with comfortable rooms. The drive-in rooms are right for those who don't want anyone touching their car: $28. $11 for standard with fan. The $18 rooms have AC, TV & fridge.

Nirwana (63 rooms) Jl Dr Wahidin 11 ☎ 41691. Two-star hotel with very cushy rooms. Probably the best place in town. Huge swimming pool with slides. Restaurant, billiards, and gift shop. $10 single standard. $22 single standard AC.

FOOD

Rumah Makan Puas Jl Surabaya 32. Near Jacky Batik and the hospital. Very good and cheap food. Try Pekalongan specialities such as *nasi kebuli* (beef), *nasi mekoro* (with shredded *nangka*) or *soto kerbau* (water-buffalo soup).

A Karim Jl Gaja Mada 1. Great *sate* and *gulai kambing* (mutton stew).

Bu Nani Jl Raya TIrto. About 2 km west of town. Best seafood around. Try the frogs' legs too.

Purimas Bakery Jl Hayam Wuruk 191 ☎ 21219. Fresh breads, ice-cream and snacks.

Remaja Jl Dr Cipto 20 ☎ 21019. Good Chinese food, centrally located near the *alun-alun*.

Tirto Permai Jl Tirto. Javanese food and seafood, *lesehan* style (mats on the floor).

BATIK

Oey Soe Tjoen Jl Raya Kedungwuni 104 ☎ Kedungwuni 68. 9 km south of Pekalongan. This shop is famous. The only batik maker in town that doesn't use *cap* (stamp): all hand-painted. *Kain* and *sarung* cost about $250 and wall hangings about $63. Not much in stock, but you can order, pay now, and it will be sent within Indonesia (but not abroad). Over 100 designs. Expect a 9-month wait. Pak Mujadi Widjaja runs the shop and is eager to explain the process and show work in progress.
Ridaka Jl HA Salim, Gang VI/4 ☎ 21794. Specialists in handwoven textiles made from banana leaf and stalk, and water hyacinth. Shirts, jackets, vests as well as baskets, bags, lamps, etc. Ask to see the rewoven batik. Also tapestry, rugs and wall hangings.
Jacky Batik Jl Surabaya VA/1 ☎ 61649. Exclusive boutique. Batiks made in the workshop in back. Silk set for $125. At Jacky's other shop, Jl Gajah Mada 36, various garments and textiles from other parts of Java are available.
Achmad Yahya Jl Pesindon 221 ☎ 41413. Medium quality export fabrics. His specialty is decorative floral upholstery patterns. Prices are reasonable.
H Abdullah Jl Jlamprang Gang I/27 and H Zahro, Jl Jlamprang 274B. These are workshops in the Krapyak district, usually with some stock for sale.

MISCELLANEOUS

Tourist information Jl Jetayu 3 (City Hall) ☎ 61223.
Anatama Tour Jl Mansyur 25 ☎ 81121.

— *Gary Crabb*

Semarang

See maps, pages 238 & 241. Tel. code is 024.

GETTING THERE

By air. A convenient Garuda/Merpati air shuttle operates almost hourly to/from Jakarta's Sukarno-Hatta airport ($55). No advance bookings; go early and buy a ticket at the counter in Terminal C. Twice-daily flights to/from Surabaya ($35). Bouraq and Mandala operate less frequent flights to Jakarta and Banjarmasin. Semarang's A Yani airport is 5 km west of town. A taxi costs $3 but you can walk to the highway (a bit of a hike with luggage) and hail a bus or *colt* going east (to your left) into town; only Rp200.
Garuda office Jl Gajah Mada 11 ☎ 20178.
Bouraq office Jl Pemuda 40A ☎ 23779.
Mandala office Jl Pemuda 40 ☎ 285319.
Merpati office Jl Gajah Mada 58B ☎ 23027.
Sempati office Hotel Graha Santika ☎ 414086.
By train. From Jakarta or Surabaya via the AC Mutiara Utara night express costs $18 and takes 8–10 hours. The second-class Senja Utama also travels at night and costs $6.50 (non-AC). Both are often delayed. You arrive in the dead of night in Tawang Station. Hire a *becak* or cab, but bargain hard. Onward tickets can be bought at Tawang before departure, or in advance from PT Pusaka Nusantara at Jl Thamrin 84 (☎ 20720).
By minibus. The best way to get here from Yogya, Solo or Cirebon. Semarang's minibus terminal is at the corner of Jl MT Haryono and Jl HA Salim. Departures for Solo, Yogya, Pekalongan, Cirebon, Bandung, Jakarta every hour during the day. Most with AC. From $3 to $11 depending on distance.

GETTING AROUND

By taxi. Taxis are metered; rent by the hour or day. Ask your hotel or call Atlas: 315833; Indra Kelana: 22590; Puri Kencana: 288291; Surabaya: 313299.
By *becak*. Can be a good way to see the harbor and old city. Hire one on an hourly basis, around $1 per hour, and tell him you want to *putar-putar,* to go around: forbidden on major streets, however.

ACCOMMODATION

Choose between busy downtown or the hills behind (Candi Baru or Gombel). The latter are cooler, quieter and generally nicer, but pose transport problems unless you have a car.

Budget (under $20)

Budget places are mostly downtown. For convenience try the Blambangan. For bottom-end rates Arjuna or Oewa Asia. The Continental in Candi is a really good deal—almost first-class rooms at budget prices!
Arjuna Jl Imam Bonjol 51 ☎ 24186. Well maintained old house. $5 double; $6.50 triple.
Blambangan Jl Pemuda 23 ☎ 21649 and 27645. Simple but clean. Enjoy the aroma from a *jamu* factory in back. Small dorm $15; $7.50 double.
Continental (10 rooms) Jl Dr Wahidin 195, Candi ☎ 311969. Small, friendly and good service, the best deal around. Clean, modest rooms $12. Suite $20.
Djelita (34 rooms) Jl MT Haryono 85–87 ☎ 23891. Well-maintained. $11 AC; fan $8.
Grand Rama Jl Pelampitan 37–39 ☎ 21739. Old hotel, big rooms, some sleeping six ($15), $14 AC.
Green Guest House Jl Kesambi 7 ☎ 312528. Small place with view of the city. Clean and good value. $10–12 with fan, $13–24 with AC.
Johar Jl Mpu Tantular 1 ☎ 288585. Opposite the market. $7 D with bath and fan. $12 with AC.
Nendra Yakti (27 rooms) Gang Pinggir 68 ☎ 22538. Newly-renovated, clean and in the center of Chinatown, with a temple next door. $8 double; $15 VIP.
Oewa Asia (30 rooms) Jl Kol Sugiono 12 ☎ 22578. Cheapest AC room in town, $10. Non-AC $6.50 double. Ask for the renovated rooms.

Intermediate ($20–$70)

Many of these are older hotels, some renovated. Great value for money; some with first-class rooms at bargain rates. Most rates include breakfast. Recommended are Telomoyo for convenience, Bukit Asri for value, and Candi Baru for colonial ambience.

Bukit Asri (35 rooms) Jl Setiabudi 5A, Candi ☎ 315743. Quite new, with clean and private rooms. All AC, with TV and 24-hour video. $25.

Candi Baru (32 rooms) Jl Rinjani 21, Candi ☎ 31-5272. Charming old hotel with spacious rooms and high ceilings. Even if you aren't staying here, have a look at their big suite, with antique tiles and stained glass. $20 for standard AC room.

Dibya Puri (78 rooms) Jl Pemuda 11 ☎ 27821. Rather decrepit. Big rooms. $27 incl. breakfast.

Metro Grand Park (103 rooms) Jl H Agus Salim 24 ☎ 27371. Central but noisy. Ask for a renovated room. $48 single and $55 double. Suites $125.

Plaza (55 rooms) Jl Setia Budi 101–103, Candi. ☎ 473188, 473215. Fancy rooms from $27 S.

Queen (29 rooms) Jl Gajah Mada 44–52 ☎ 27063. In town. Large room sleeping four costs only $43. Some have private sitting areas. $25.

Siranda (60 rooms) Jl Diponegoro 1 ☎ 313271. On way to Candi. Nice view of Simpang Lima square. Good service and value. $35 1st floor; $20 3rd floor.

Srondol Indah Jl Setiabudi 221, Candi ☎ 318180, fax: 310303. Good value. Check out their karaoke bar. $19 single, $21 double.

Telomoyo (72 rooms) Jl Gajah Mada 138 ☎ 28926 and 25436. Popular place for foreigners, right downtown; quiet rooms with verandahs. Standard rooms $26 single and $33 double.

First Class ($70 and up)

Graha Santika (125 rooms) Jl Pandanaran 116–120 ☎ 413115, 413121. The newest and best in town. Pastel colors, photos of old Semarang. Pool, fitness center. $70 single and $76 double for standard rooms; up to $190 for suites.

Patra Jasa (147 rooms) Jl Sisingamangaraja, Candi Baru ☎ 31441, fax: 31448. 1970s-style hotel with motel bungalows. View of the town. Pool, bowling alleys, karaoke bar. Golf course nearby. Whirlpool in the suites, $102. Spacious verandahs in the Argasoka wing. $70 S, $80 D.

FOOD

Semarang is a great place to eat, with some of the best Chinese food in Java. Many eccentric places, like a shop that started in the train station selling *wingko babat* (coconut cakes) and now ships them all over the island (Wingko Babat Cap Kereta Api, Jl Cendrawasih 14 ☎ 22064). And Toko Oen, popular for over half a century.

Indonesian

Bandeng Presto Jl Pandanaran 67 ☎ 319530. The owners of this small place specializing in smoked *bandeng* fish, a Semarang specialty, had the idea of vacuum-packing their product and calling it Bandeng Presto. Today, many of their neighbors have imitated them, but the original (first on your left as you come from Simpang Lima) is still the best.

Mbok Berek Jl A Yani 170 ☎ 316346. Great Yogya-style fried chicken, with rice and sweet *sambal*.

Sari Medan Jl Pemuda. Best Padang food in town.

Timlo Solo Jl A Yani 182 ☎ 316491. Branch of the famous Solo eatery; cheap Javanese food.

Chinese

The best restaurants are on Jl Gajah Mada, and in Chinatown, around the Tay Kak Sie temple.

Istana Jl MT Haryono 836 ☎ 21754. Specializing in *sukiyaki* and Chinese fire pot. Expensive.

Kit Wan Kie Gang Pinggir 23–25 ☎ 20973, 20543. Right in Chinatown. Great food.

Loempia Semarang Gang Lombok 11 (just before Tay Kak Sie temple). *Lumpia* spring rolls filled with shredded carrots, bamboo shoots and meat are a Semarang delicacy. Vendors line Jl Pemuda and Jl Gajah Mada. Open 9 am until 7 pm.

Pringgading Jl Pringgading 54 ☎ 288973. Best Chinese seafood in town; reasonable prices.

Tan Goei Jl Tanjung 23 ☎ 22521. An old standby, serving Indonesian and Chinese favorites, including all-you-can-eat specials for $2.

Western

Boundy Jl JH Thamrin. Steaks and hamburgers.

Danish Bakery Jl Pandanaran. Serves passable pizza and western dishes. Reasonable prices.

Ritzeky Pub Jl Sinabung Buntu. An expat hang-out, with darts, pool tables and a squash court. Serves pizza, veal cordon bleu and other dishes.

Sukarasa Jl Ungaran, near the Patra Jasa. An attempt at French cuisine. Reasonably priced food and wine.

Toko Oen Jl Pemuda 52 ☎ 21683. A favorite with Indonesians and westerners since the colonial period, Toko Oen has kept up their spare ribs, tournedos grillée, *uitsmijters,* rissoles and a wide selection of ice creams, cakes and sweets.

PERFORMANCES

Semarang is rapidly fading as a center for Javanese folk arts. Its residents, once enthusiastic theater-goers, seem to enjoy TV more than *ketoprak* and *wayang kulit* these days.

Ngesti Pandowo Jl Pemuda 116. Performances of *ketoprak* on Mon and Thur, and *wayang orang* the rest of the week. Shows at 8:15 pm.

Sobokarti Folk Theater Jl Cipto 31–33, north of the Dargo market. Holds lessons for children on Saturday mornings. Visitors are welcome. *Wayang kulit* performances held every Saturday night, 8–11 pm.

RRI (Radio Rebublik Indonesia) Jl A Yani, also holds *wayang kulit* performances on the first Saturday of every month.

Bandungan

Telephone code is 0298.

This mountain resort town is some 38 km south of Semarang. By public transport, go first to Ambarawa by bus or minibus (40¢) from Semarang. Then catch a local minibus heading to Bandungan (15¢). By private car, take the scenic back road by turning off to the right about 10

km (6 mi) past Ungaran. Lots of good hotels here.
Amanda (48 rooms) ☎ 91145. Luxurious new rooms with large verandahs. Great views. $20–59.
Kusuma Madya (45 rooms) ☎ 91136. Variety of rooms; $7–12. Some cottages too.
Rawa Pening Eltricia (43 rooms). Across the street from the RP Pratama. Bungalows for three at $18, up to $53 for six persons, breakfast included.
Rawa Pening Pratama (39 rooms) ☎ 91134. About 1 km from Bandungan; turn left at the main junction; it's on the right. Colonial mansion with high ceilings and several adjacent bungalows. Gorgeous views. Breakfast is free on Sundays. $12–33.
Wina Wisata Inn (43 rooms) ☎ 91120. Clean double rooms for $6.50. Bigger ones (up to 10 persons) with color TV, are also available for $30.

Kopeng

This is another cool hill station southwest of Salatiga, 60 km (38 mi) south of Semarang.
Hotel & Pemandian Kopeng ☎ (0298) 81344. An old lodge with a big pool and park, a paneled lounge and dining room with fireplace. Popular local Sunday picnic spot. Tennis courts and vegetable market nearby. Rooms are not in good shape, but are very cheap: $3 double. $18 for one that sleeps six.
Kenanga Indah (8 rooms) is small but pleasant. $5. To get there, take a bus to Salatiga (50¢) and change to a minibus up to Kopeng (30¢). A very scenic road continues from here over the mountain to Magelang, near Yogya.

East of Semarang

See map, page 244.
You can visit Demak, Kudus and Jepara as a day trip from Semarang. To see Rembang and Lasem you will need to spend the night. Tuban is farther—just a couple of hours shy of Surabaya. Kudus has the best facilities, but Pati is better value. The only other place to stay here is Rembang. Allow two full days to cover Demak, Kudus, Jepara, Rembang and Lasem.

All towns except Jepara lie on the main rail line running east from Semarang. Jepara can only be reached by road. Inter-city minibuses are available from Semarang to any of these cities, Rp350, until 8 pm. Once there, *becak* is the best way to get around: 50¢ to $1 per hour. People here are devout Muslims, particularly in Kudus and Demak, so dress modestly and remove shoes when entering a mosque.

Kudus

See map, page 246. Telephone code is 0291.
The most developed town on the northeast coast, Kudus is the center of Indonesia's clove cigarette industry. Visit the *kretek* museum, a joint effort of cigarette companies in Kudus. A traditional Kudus house is also in the same complex.
Air Mancur (46 rooms) Jl Pemuda 70 ☎ 22514. Packed with salesmen; okay also for budget travelers. $15 double, $20 triple.
Kudus Asri Jaya (33 rooms) Jl AKBP R Agil Kusumadya ☎ 22449. Out of town, on the road leading to Semarang. The best in Kudus. Facilities include color TV with satellite dish, pool and exercise room. $10 economy, $30 standard.
Notosari Permai (27 rooms) Jl Kepodang 12 ☎ 21-245, 21227. Relatively pricey, but with excellent service. Rooms vary, so have a look at them first. $11 up to $25 for the suite.
There are a number of good restaurants along Jl Agil Kusumadya: **Pondok Gizi** ☎ 22380. **Sari Lembur Kuring** ☎ 22555. A must is the famous *soto Kudus*, available at **Soto Ayam Pak Denuh**. Run by the son of the founder; it started in the bus terminal and now has branches in Simpang Tujuh Department Store, Ramayana Theatre and on Jl Agil Kusumadya.

Pati

Telephone code is 0295.
Kurnia (45 rooms) Jl Tondonegoro 12 ☎ 81133. Wide options of rooms. $22 D for a VIP room; $5 for economy.
Merdeka (44 rooms) Jl Dipenogoro 69 ☎ 81106. Very reasonably priced. $13 for AC room that sleeps three. Cheaper one is $4, with good ventilation. Rather noisy.
Pati (60 rooms) Jl PB Sudirman 60 ☎ 81313. Comfortable rooms. Pool. Their bottom-end rates are $5; the best rooms cost only $13.
Rama Jl Supriyadi 100 ☎ 81243. *The* place to stay. Clean, a great bargain. $12 for VIP room; $3.50 for economy. Filling breakfast, afternoon drinks and snacks. Friendly, helpful staff.

Tasty, spicy fried chicken is available in **Kembang Joyo restaurant** Jl Pemuda 278 ☎ 81783. Reasonably priced, quick service. For good seafood try **Mlroso** Jl P Sudirman 150 ☎ 81381.

Rembang

Rembang's main street, Jl Sudirman, runs east-west along the coast. The big Chinese temple is at the western end of town, on the coast facing the sea. From the main intersection, a road leads south across limestone hills to Blora.
Losmen Restu (25 rooms) Jl PB Sudirman 38 ☎ 91408. Fairly priced; the front rooms are best. $4 D; $11 for AC with private bath.
Perdana (11 rooms) Jl PB Sudirman 76 ☎ 91381. $2.50 S, $3.50–5 D.

You can never go wrong in **Andri,** Jl Perikanan 6B, a little Chinese restaurant on a lane off Jl Sudirman, specializing in seafood. Try their fresh steamed prawns (*udang rebus*).

Rembang is also one of few places where you can try the fruit known as *kawis*. Juice made from its sweetened syrup is served in any restaurant.

— Sandra M. Hamid and Amir Sidharta

7 East Java PRACTICALITIES

INCLUDES SURABAYA, MADURA, MALANG, BROMO & THE EASTERN TIP

Prices in US dollars, excluding tax & service (10–30%). S = Single; D = Double; T = Triple.

Surabaya

Telephone code is 031.

GETTING THERE

Garuda runs shuttle flights departing almost hourly from Jakarta, 4 flights a day from Singapore, 5 from Lombok, 4 from Bali and daily from Sydney, Sulawesi, Sumatra, Yogyakarta and Solo. Reach Garuda at Jl Tunjungan 29 ☎ 515590–1 and Jl Pemuda 12 ☎ 41508, 46690 or at Juanda Airport ☎ 817161.

Merpati is at Jl Pemuda 31–37 ☎ 516040, 516044, 516096–7. **Sempati** is at the Hyatt Regency ☎ 525804–7 and flies from Taipei, Kuala Lumpur, Perth and Singapore as well as the same domestic destinations as Garuda. Other airlines have offices at the Hyatt Regency ☎ 51-1234. Take a $4 taxi ride from **Juanda Airport** 15 kilometers into the city.

See "Travel Advisory" for information on the two AC express trains with nightly departures between Jakarta and Surabaya via Yogyakarta and Solo or Semarang which arrive early in the morning: **Bima Express** (Gubeng Station) and **Mutiara Utara** (Pasar Turi Station).

Night buses and **public intercity buses** arrive at Purabaya (also called Bungurasih). The terminal is about 15 km south of downtown. To book a ticket, go straight there or to the company offices along Jalan Arjuna. From here you can take **city buses** that crisscross the city for 15¢ (more for the AC buses). You may prefer to take a **taxi**: Zebra: 515555, 512233; Merpati: 513831, 513835; Supra: 814460, 810748.

For longer rides **private cars** (*plat hitam/taksi gelap*) can be hired from the parking lots of the larger hotels for $2.50 an hour (two hour minimum), $50 for a night trip to Bromo and $40 for a day trip to Tretes.

City buses and *bemo* are Rp300 a ride and reaching your destination will require luck and/or a map (available from the malls or from **Gramedia** Jl Basuki Rakhmat 95). *Becaks* are limited to short trips within areas bounded by the larger streets from which they are banned. **Rent bikes** for 50¢ to $1.50 a day or a motorbike for $5, if you dare, from the Bamboe Denn (see below).

ACCOMMODATION

As Indonesia's second largest city, hotels tend to be more expensive and/or less well looked after than those in the rest of Java. It is also one of the hottest places in Java and air-conditioning becomes an appreciated comfort. There are some inexpensive places as well as the likes of the **Hyatt Regency**. **Hotel Remaja** is the best value and the budget favorite is **Bamboe Denn.**

Budget (under $20)

Asia (40 rooms) Jl Tembaan 55 ☎ 40194, 526579. Similar to Hotel Centrum in quality but with toilet seats. $15 fan, $20–30 AC.

Bamboe Denn (20 bed dorm and 7 rooms) Jl Ketabang Kali 6A ☎ 40333. The travelers' favorite. Cramped but friendly. You will be asked to converse with students of the affiliated English school to supplement the low rates. The manager, Bruno is a walking tourist information service. Free passes to Atom Disco Thursday and Saturday nights. $1.75 for a bed in the dormitory; rooms are $2.50 D to $5.75 for 4 people.

Centrum (41 rooms) Jl Bubutan 16–22 ☎ 40219; fax: 520185. Somewhat neglected. $8.75 shared bath, $18 to $24 fan; $25 AC & TV.

Ganefo (55 rooms) Jl Kapasan 169–171 ☎ 311169; fax: 361390. Beautiful wooden doors in the front. Simple rooms. $8.25 shared bath, $13 with bath but no fans. $16.25 AC.

Irian (26 rooms) Jl Samudra 16 ☎ 20953, 334937. Inexpensive rooms grouped around the courtyard of an old colonial building with 4-meter-high ceilings. Often full. $9 S and $11.50 D shared bath and fan. AC & private bath $16 S to $19 D.

Paviljoen (18 rooms) Jl Genteng Besar 94–98 ☎ 43449. Traditional feel despite recent renovations. $12.50 fan or $17.50 AC.

Rejeki (16 rooms) Jl Samudra 54 ☎ 21746. The best of the 7 similar old Dutch hotel buildings in this area. Open your door and close the louvered half doors for ventilation and privacy. Four poster beds with mosquito netting. $3.75 S and $4.25 D.

Remaja (19 rooms) Jl Embong Kenongo 12 ☎ 41-359, 510045; fax: 510009. Almost always full. Call ahead. The best bet in Surabaya with AC rooms from $19 S to $25 D.

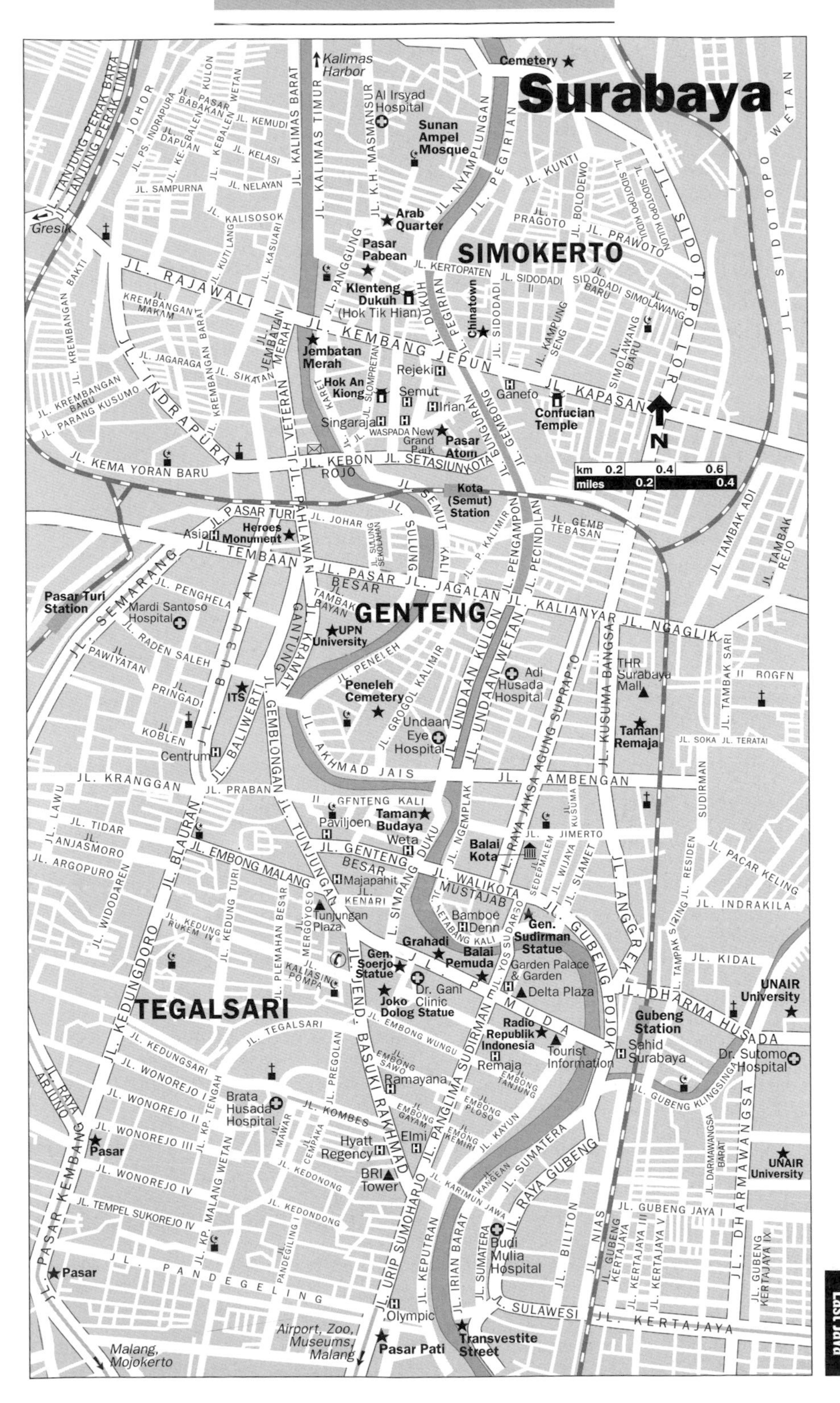
Surabaya
Kalimas Harbor
Cemetery
Al Irsyad Hospital
Sunan Ampel Mosque
Arab Quarter
Pasar Pabean
SIMOKERTO
Klenteng Dukuh (Hok Tik Hian)
Chinatown
Jembatan Merah
Rejeki
Hok An Kiong
Semut
Irian
Ganefo
Confucian Temple
Singaraja
WASPADA
New Grand Park
Pasar Atom
Kota (Semut) Station
km 0.2 0.4 0.6
miles 0.2 0.4
N
Gresik
Asia
Heroes Monument
Pasar Turi Station
Mardi Santoso Hospital
GENTENG
UPN University
ITS
Peneleh Cemetery
Adi Husada Hospital
THR Surabaya Mall
Taman Remaja
Undaan Eye Hospital
Centrum
Paviljoen
Taman Budaya
Weta
Balai Kota
Majapahit
Tunjungan Plaza
Bamboe Denn
Gen. Sudirman Statue
Grahadi
Balai Pemuda
Gen. Soerjo Statue
Dr. Gani Clinic
Garden Palace & Garden
Delta Plaza
Joko Dolog Statue
TEGALSARI
Radio Republik Indonesia
Tourist Information
Gubeng Station
Sahid Surabaya
UNAIR University
Dr. Sutomo Hospital
Remaja
Ramayana
Brata Husada Hospital
Hyatt Regency
Elmi
BRI Tower
Pasar
Budi Mulia Hospital
Olympic
Airport, Zoo, Museums, Malang
Pasar Pati
Transvestite Street
Malang, Mojokerto
JL. RAJAWALI
JL. KEMBANG JEPUN
JL. KAPASAN
JL. KEMA YORAN BARU
JL. KEBON ROJO
JL. SETASIUN KOTA
JL. PASAR TURI
JL. TEMBAAN
JL. SEMARANG
JL. PASAR BESAR
JL. JAGALAN
JL. KALIANYAR
JL. NGAGLIK
JL. INDRAPURA
JL. BUBUTAN
JL. KRAMAT GANTUNG
JL. PAHLAWAN
JL. AKHMAD JAIS
JL. AMBENGAN
JL. KRANGGAN
JL. PRABAN
JL. GENTENG BESAR
JL. EMBONG MALANG
JL. BLAURAN
JL. TUNJUNGAN
JL. WALIKOTA MUSTAJAB
JL. GUBENG POJOK
JL. PANGLIMA SUDIRMAN
JL. BASUKI RAKHMAD
JL. URIP SUMOHARJO
JL. RAYA GUBENG
JL. DHARMA HUSADA
JL. KEDUNGDORO
JL. PASAR KEMBANG
JL. RAYA ARJUNO
JL. PANDEGELING
JL. SULAWESI
JL. KERTAJAYA
JL. KUSUMA BANGSA
JL. UNDAAN KULON
JL. UNDAAN WETAN
JL. SIDOTOPO LOR
JL. TAMBAK ADI
JL. SIDOTOPO WETAN

Intermediate ($20–$80)

Cendana (23 rooms) Jl Kombes Doeryat ☎ 42251; fax: 514367. One of the better hotels in this price range. Run by the Surabaya Inn Group. If full they can put you in touch with the others in the chain. AC and hot water. $32 S and $37 D standard, $41 S and $46 D suite.

Jane's House (38 rooms) Jl Dinoyo 100 ☎ 577722. Another Surabaya Inn Group hotel but this time with great carved traditional furniture, although you have to pay for a deluxe before you get some of the furniture into your room. AC and hot water. Standard $27 S and $31 D, deluxe $38 S and $43 D.

Majapahit (105 rooms) Jl Tunjungan 65 ☎ 43351; fax: 43599. A tourist destination itself, this hotel is a beauty from the colonial past. Standard rooms (1970's) are $49, while the untouched original, though mothbally, atmosphere can be found in the Economy wing for $40.

New Grand Park (101 rooms) Jl Samudra 3–5 ☎ 331515; fax: 333194. Upmarket establishment near Pasar Atom and the Kota/Semut Train Station. Standard $62, deluxe $89, suites $172.

Pondok Asri Family Homestay Jl Kalibokor Selatan 108 ☎ 582377, 578433; fax: 578433. A cozy place near the central business district. Clean and quiet. Popular with Dutch groups. Reasonably priced with hot water, AC, TV. $20–25.

Semut (51 rooms) Jl Samudra 9–15 ☎ 24578, 332601. A pleasant place to stay in the busy old part of town. Standard $20, superior $27.

Wisma Mawarani Jl Embong Kenongo 73 ☎ 44839, 45435; fax: 45435. Almost always full. $30 to $40.

First Class ($80–$150)

Altea Mirama (105 rooms) Jl Raya Darmo 68–76 ☎ 69501–4; fax: 571943. In a quieter part of town. Great ambience. Wonderful use of plants and color throughout. Standard $103 S and $115 D, club room $145 and $212 for a suite.

Elmi (140 rooms) Jl Panglima Sudirman 42–44 ☎ 522571–9; fax: 515615. Centrally located and cheaper than the Hyatt. Standard $80 S and $93 D, deluxe $106, suites from $222 to $271.

Garden Palace (203 rooms) and **Garden** (100 rooms) Jl Pemuda 21 ☎ 520951; fax: 516111. Some good food here as well as being close to the malls. Garden palace: from $124; Garden: from $81 S and $88 D.

Sahid Surabaya (216 rooms) Jl Sumatra 1 ☎ 526-632; fax: 516292. The public areas are a bit stuffy but the rooms themselves are great. Standard $88 S, $101 D, suites are $132–484.

Weta International (100 rooms) Jl Genteng Kali 3–11 ☎ 519494, 523424; fax: 45512. $85. Almost always empty so ask for a discount.

Luxury ($150 and up)

Hilton International (120 rooms) Jl Gunungsari ☎ 582703; fax: 574504. A bit out of town next to the 18-hole golf course. $157 for twin beds, $182 for a queen, suites for $266 and $472 for a villa.

Hyatt Regency (268 rooms) Jl Basuki Rakhmat 124–128 ☎ 511234; fax: 521508. In the heart of the business and entertainment district. Club rooms include extra special treatment and services. This is where many of the best restaurants and a number of airline offices can be found. Rooms from $220.

FOOD

Western

Hugo's Restaurant at the Hyatt Regency has the best steak in town and the **Arumis Terrace Cafe** downstairs is excellent value for money with especially popular breakfast and lunch buffets. **Bon Cafe Steak House** is also good.

Cafe Venezia at Jl Ambongan 16 has some decent meat dishes although their forte is Japanese food. They also have Korean and Chinese food and a big ice cream menu. **Turin Ice Cream** is at Jl Embong Kenongo, around the corner from Jl Pemuda. **Pizza Hut**, **McDonald's**, **Dairy Queen** and **KFC** have all been spotted at various locations in Surabaya (at the shopping malls).

Seafood and Chinese

Ceshiang Garden is the best, again at the Hyatt Regency. **Mahkota Restaurant** offers an out-of-the-ordinary floor show with dinner at Jl TAIS Nasution 23–25. **Mina Seafood** is at the Sahid Surabaya Hotel. **Balai Shabat Surabaya** Jl Gentengkali, has an extensive vegetarian menu.

Japanese

Surabaya has many good Japanese restaurants reflecting the business community that it increasingly serves. **Nishika Japanese Restaurant** at the Garden Palace Hotel is perhaps the best while **Shima Japanese Restaurant** at the Hyatt Regency is also excellent although pricey.

Indonesian

Handayani has good Javanese dishes at Jl Kertajaya 42 and other locations around Surabaya. **Puri Garden** is on the 1st floor of Surabaya Plaza and offers a tamer version of Indonesian specialties. **Kayoon Park** has many food stalls overlooking the muddy waters of the Kalimas River. **Pasar Malam Genteng** at Jl Walikota Mustajab is an inexpensive eatery with variety and color open from 6 pm to midnight.

SHOPPING

Shopping is one of the best things that Surabaya has to offer and the thing that Surabayans are best at, accounting for a lot of the traffic. The malls offer a cool oasis away from the traffic and midday heat as well as bountiful food courts, especially **Tunjungan Plaza**.

Malls

The following are the best malls in town offering a sophisticated selection of shops, rare outside Jakarta, with lower prices than the capital:
Tunjungan Plaza I & **II** at Jl Basuki Rakhmat 8.
Plaza Surabaya at Jl Pemuda 31–37.
Andhika Plaza at Jl Simpang Dukuh 38–40.
Surabaya Mall Jl Kusuma Bangsa 116–119.
Indo Plaza at Jl Semut Kali 9.

Antiques

Reproductions are common so beware you're not paying top antique prices for these. There are several homes with collections in the Gubeng Jaya alleys off Jl Dharmawangsa.
Pinguin Antiques in the mornings at Jl TAIS Nasution 45 ☎ 40650. Rather expensive.
Mandala Arts & Antique, HA Tawwab Hadlory, Jl Nyamplungan XI/7, first destination of traders from rural area to sell their finds. Very good prices.
Soerabaia Oriental Art, Kitty Naéyé Frans & Cece, Jl Kris Kencana Blok J 45–46. ☎/fax: 571971. Wide collection of wood carvings. Good prices. Has warehouse at Mojosari, 50 km out of town.

Batik and Handicrafts

Two of Java's major batik producers have stores in Surabaya: **Batik Keris** Tunjungan Plaza and Surabaya Plaza; and **Danar Hadi** Jl Raya Diponegoro 184, and Jl Pemuda 1J. **Sarinah Department Store** at Jl Tunjungan 7, has batik from various producers as well as handmade items from all over Indonesia. Also try **Kampar Batik & Handicraft** Jl Indragiri 43, and **Mirota Art & Craft** Jl Sulawesi 24.

ATTRACTIONS

Surabaya's **Zoo** is at the intersection of Jl Raya Diponegoro and Jl Raya Darmo opposite **MPU Tantular Museum**. The Komodo dragons are fed on the 5th and 20th of each month at 12:30 pm. Avoid Sundays. Open daily from 7 am to 5:30 pm.

The three best of Surabaya's many **discos** are **Studio East** at Andhika Plaza fourth floor, **Fire** at Tunjungan Plaza and **Atom** at Pasar Atom 5th floor, Jl Waspada.

The most comfortable **movie houses** are: **Studio** at Tunjungan Plaza and **Mitra** on Jl Pemuda and at Surabaya Plaza.

SERVICES

Change money at Bank Bali Jl Tunjungan 52 ☎ 43245 and seven other branches; Bank Negara Indonesia (BNI) Jl Pemuda 36 ☎ 41351; Jl Urip Sumoharjo 55 ☎ 46712; Bank Niaga Jl Tunjungan 47–51 ☎ 43537, 41552 and five other branches; Pasopati Jl Raya Darmo 1A ☎ 574000, 575000; Jl Kusuma Bangsa 116 ☎ 44000; major hotels and travel agents. **Get cash advances** with your Access, Visa or MasterCard at Bank Duta Jl Pemuda 12 ☎ 470975.

Tourism information is available at Juanda Airport ☎ 817161 or 811542 ext. 603. Jl Pemuda 118 and Jl Darmo Kali 35 ☎ 575448–9. The main **post office** is at Jl Kebonrojo 10 ☎ 22096–9 with branches at 30 other locations. There are *Wartel* **telephone** offices all over Surabaya, 48 at last count. The preferred **hospital** is Rumah Sakit Dr Sutomo, Jl Prof Dr Mustopo 6–8 ☎ 40061, 40065.

TRAVEL AGENTS

Recommended agents:
Pacto Ltd. Taman Hiburan Rakyat (THR) Surabaya Mall, Jl Kusuma Bangsa ☎ 45776.
Pasopati (see "services" above for address).
Orient Express Jl Basuki Rakhmat 78 ☎ 515253–7.

Madura

GETTING THERE

There are two ways of getting to Madura, by bus or ferry. By **public bus**, leave from Surabaya's Bungurasih terminal (also called Purabaya) on buses bound for Sumenep, east Madura. *Patas* buses cost $2.50 and run three times a day; non-AC buses leave every 10 minutes and cost $2.

To catch the ferry, take a city bus from the center of Surabaya to the port of Tanjung Perak. From here cross the Madura Strait on the ferries which run every half hour and cost 15¢.

Towns on Madura are best reached by "colt". The journey to Pamekasan takes 2 hrs and costs $1. Trips to Sumenep via Bangkalan, Sampang and Pamekasan take 3.5 hrs and cost $1.75.

To see the north coast, the batik of Tanjung Bumi and the beach at Siring Kemuning charter a "colt" from the ferry terminal in Kamal for around $25 for a day trip to Sumenep or take local "colt" between villages. 25¢ to $1 per ride.

If you're heading to points east from Madura you can avoid the backtrack through Surabaya by taking the **boat** from Kalianget near Sumenep to Jangkar on Java.

Boats leave at 7:30 am daily and take about 5 hours for $2 including the bus ride on to Situbondo. In the other direction, the boat from Jangkar to Kalianget is at 1:30 pm. From Sumenep's Giling Terminal you can get "colts" to **Selopeng Beach** (25¢, 45 minutes) or **Lombang Beach** (35¢, 45 mins ride to Pulau Hijau terminal and a 35¢, 3 km *becak* ride to the beach).

BATIK

Madura batik is extremely varied and often

startlingly beautiful, also the finest woodcarvers of the royal courts of Central Java all hailed from here (see "Sumenep" below). The most *halus* (refined) batik designs are made in the village of Tanjungbumi on the north coast but a small selection of its products can be found in Sumenep's Pasar Anom in Bu Paula's **Toko Mulia** or her husband's shop **Koleksi Batik Madura Citra** (open evenings) at very competitive fixed prices. The product of up to three months of drawing in wax can be purchased for between $50 and $150.

The most complete selection can be found in Pamekasan at **Pasar 17 Agustus** (Thurs and Sun mornings only). At other times try **kampung Arab** (the Arab quarter) in Pamekasan for shops selling *sarong* from $3 to $50.

Bangkalan

Telephone code is 0323.

Melati (20 rooms) Jl Mayjen Sungkono 48. Tucked away down a narrow alley are these fairly new, nice rooms although the new management leaves room for doubts about the future. $8 with fan, $5 no fan, $4 shared bath.

Ningrat (28 rooms) Jl KHM Kholil 113 ☎ 398388. Has the most pleasant rooms on Madura with colorful carved furniture. A reasonable alternative to staying in the much more expensive hotels in Surabaya a little more than an hour away. VIP $25 S, $36 D; standard $11 S, $17 D; economy rooms are tiny with shared bath $6.

There is a row of shops including restaurants along Jalan Mayjen Sungkono the best of which is **Rumah Makan Cipta Rasa** serving Javanese food at number 29A.

Sampang

Telephone code is 031.

Camplong Cottages (14 rooms) 9 km east of Sampang ☎ 513051. Camplong beach is wide and sandy with a coral reef close to shore and gentle waves. Oil tanks temper the beauty a bit. Standard $13 or $18. Deluxe $23 (closer to the waves). To get even closer, the 13¢ ticket to use the nearby park and facilities entitles you to camp on the beach.

PKPN (24 rooms) Jl Rajawali 9 ☎ 21166. $4 for older rooms with 5 beds and shared bath. Newer rooms are $5 for 2 beds with fan and private bath. $10 AC.

Setia (10 rooms) Jl Imam Bonjol 8–10 ☎ 21063. A clean, comfortable and friendly place. $3.25 to $4.50 with fan and shared bath.

Pamekasan

Telephone code is 0324.

Madura Indah (15 rooms) Jl Jokotole 4C ☎ 81773. The Governor made them to drop their former name, the Green Peace Hotel, and changed their peace sign into a Mercedes Benz logo. $2.25 S, $2.50 D, $3.75 with fan and $5 with private bath.

Ramayana (30 rooms) Jl Niaga 55–7 ☎ 81406. Best rooms in town. $8 with fan, $6.50 without. $11 to $17 AC. Older economy rooms $2.50.

Trunojoyo (23 rooms) Jl P Trunojoyo 48 ☎ 81181. Clean and quiet. $2.75 shared bath, $6.25 with fan and $9 to $17 AC.

Pamekasan's restaurants feature Chinese and Indonesian menus. **Rumah Makan Telomoyo** Jl Trunojoyo 47 is the best and **Lezat** has the best location on the *alun-alun*. **Rumah Makan GTR** Jl Agos Salim 18 is clean and has great fried chicken.

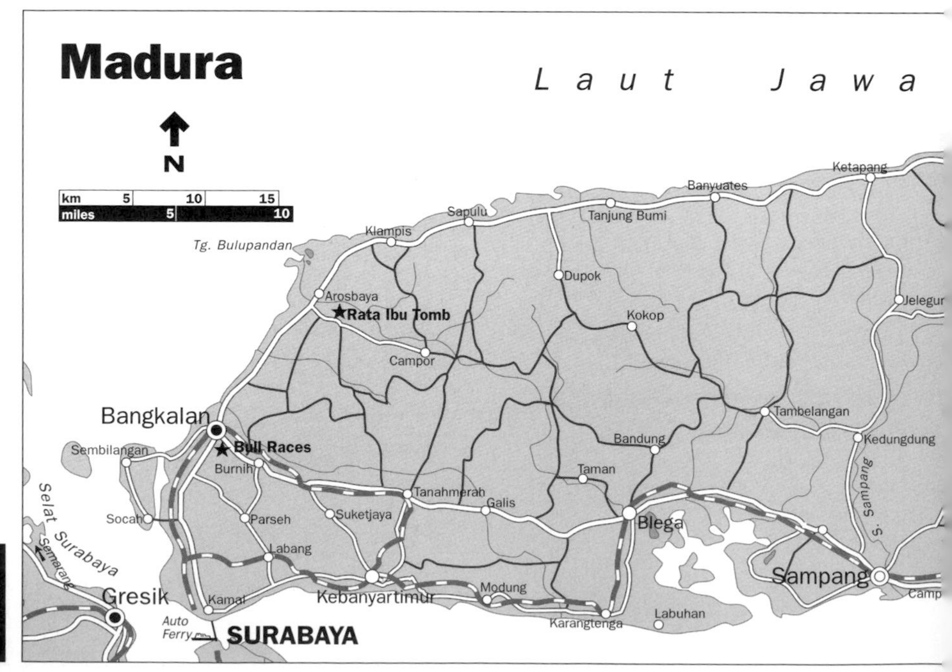

Sumenep

Telephone code is 0328.

Losmen Syafari Jaya (57 rooms) Jl Trunojoyo 90, ☎ 21989. Just south of town. More private than most, with a wide second floor terrace. Could be cleaner. $2.25 shared bath, $3.30 to $4.40 with bath. Rooms with AC & TV are $8.50.

Wijaya I (62 rooms) Jl Trunojoyo 45–47 ☎ 21433. This is *the* place to stay in Sumenep. It is a short walk from the bus terminal and the center of town, well run and clean. $3 D shared bath, $4.25 D with bath, $10 to $17.50 AC.

Wijaya II (39 rooms) Jl KH Wahid Hasyim 3 ☎ 215-32. The same quality as Wijaya I but quieter and closer to town. $2.50 S and $3.50 D shared bath, $4.25 to $4.75 with bath and $12.50 AC.

FOOD

In addition to the usual Indo/Chinese fare, some Madurese specialties are available like *ayam goreng Sumekar* at **Rumah Makan Anugrah** and *nasi soto babat* next door at **Rumah Makan 17 Agustus**. **Rumah Makan Padang Bimba** offers tasty Sumatran food. Also try the night market north of the town square. *Bubur kacang hijau* is a popular green pea porridge from the day market south of the mosque for 8¢.

WOODCARVING

Wedy S at Jl B Abdullah 447 just east of the Kraton in Sumenep has models of wooden boats and chests used in Madurese engagement rituals as well as other antiques.

Edhisetiawan Jl Sudirman 34, Sumenep has some competitively priced small items as well as the biggest wooden bells you are ever likely to see.

Toko Prima Art Shop, Jl A Yani 88, Sumenep. Has a well displayed collection of antiques.

MISCELLANEOUS

The **Kraton Sumenep** is now the home of the Bupati (regency officer) and is in fairly good shape, check out the wild swimming pool design. Museum and palace are open 7am to 2 pm and close at noon on Sunday.

The big **bull races** are in September but you can still catch practice-runs in Ambunten or at Sumenep's Lapangan Serba Guna Giling every Saturday afternoon or in Bluto every Monday afternoon. **Change money** at Bank Panin at Jl Trunojoyo 176, Sumenep 8 am to noon Monday through Friday and until 11 pm on Saturday.

Malang

See map, page 270. Telephone code is 0341.

GETTING THERE

Malang's airport, Abdulrahman Saleh, opened on April 1st 1994. Some 15 km to the east of the city, traveling there takes 20 minutes. There are daily Jakarta to Malang flights at 8am; and

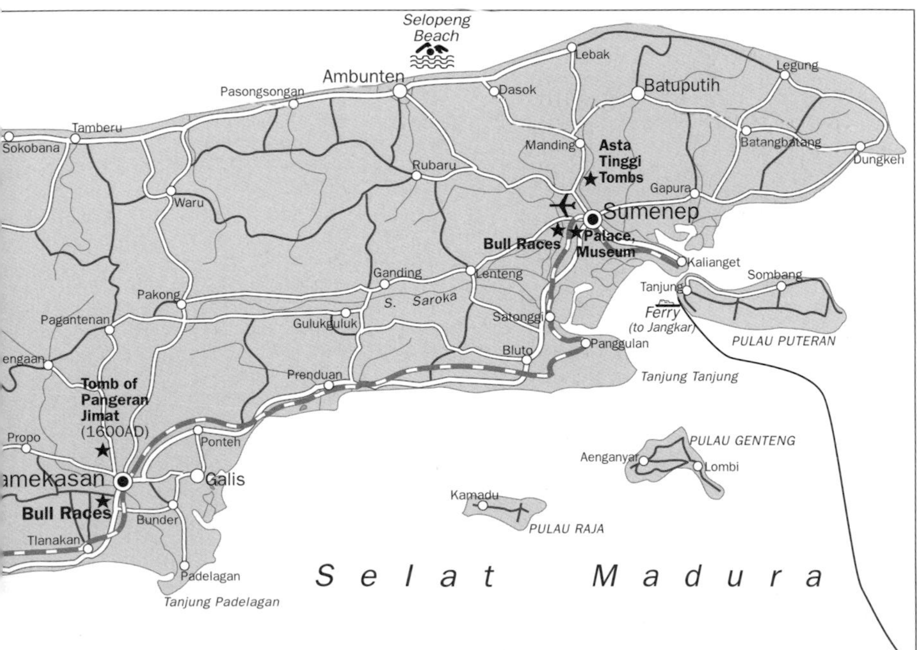

from Malang to Jakarta flights leave at 10.15 am both services are on Merpati Airlines.

Second class **trains** from Surabaya arrive every afternoon from Solo and Yogya ($6). Sit on the south (downhill) side for a great view. **Night buses** to and from Denpasar are $11 from Bali Cepat, Jl Dr Cipto 30 ☎ 67977. **Intercity public buses** go to Probolinggo (the main route to Bromo) from Ardjosari Terminal (80¢).

Travel (minibuses) run the Malang-Surabaya route nine times a day ($4 from Mandala Travel, Jl Adisucipto ☎ 42426/42429) and Solo/Yogya eight times a day ($9 from Rosalia Indah, Jl KHA Dahlan ☎ 24804/64841).

AC **taxis** run the route from Juanda airport to Malang for $21 one way. Taxis to the airport can be ordered via travel agents. Frequent **Angkota** (Mikrolet vans) crisscross Malang for 15¢ a ride.

GETTING AROUND

Malang's **taxi** services are Citra Kendedes ☎ 45101, 43736 and the recently set up Argo Perdana Taxi ☎ 40444, which provide passengers with printed fare receipts. **Car rental** with driver is $40 a day to destinations such as Balekambang, Bromo and Batu from Mujur Surya at Jl Bromo 33 ☎ 27955. **Motorbikes** can be rented from Saudara Lely, Jl Menari 10 ☎ 66839. ***Becaks*** are still ubiquitous: 50¢ between the *alun-alun* (town square) and Tugu Park.

Malang is compact and the mature trees which account for so much of its charm shade the streets, making it a pleasant place to walk.

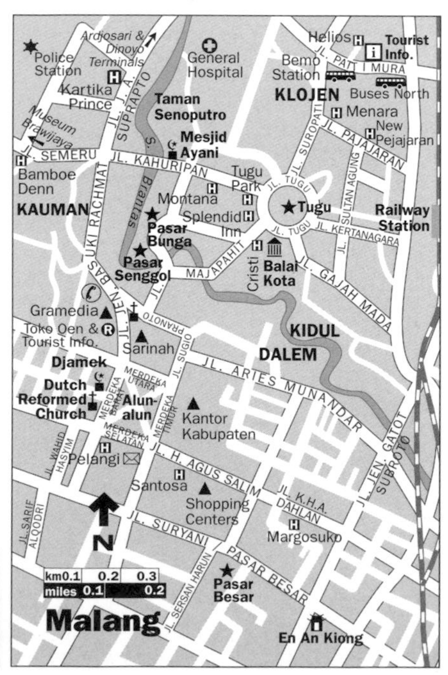

ACCOMMODATION

If you're looking for a chance to stay in style in this part of the world you could do no better than the wonderful Tugu Park Hotel.

At the other end of the scale, Bamboe Denn is a budget travelers' favorite. For a little more money the Menara is also good value.

You can often get substantial discounts by buying hotel vouchers from travel agents rather than dealing with the hotels direct.

Guesthouses($10–$25)

Cristi Guest House (7 rooms) Jl Majapahit 3A ☎ 61596. On the road between the town square and Tugu Park. Smallish rooms. $10 D to $15 D.

Enny's Guest House (15 rooms) Taman Wilis 1A. ☎ 51369. A long-time favorite of Dutch travelers with a comfortable living room and a scale model of Mt Bromo in the garden. $28 D for the funky bamboo bungalows in the roof garden. $23 D for regular rooms with baths and hot water.

Guest House Kawi 40 (Bu Darwis) (20 rooms) Jl Kawi 40 ☎ 51351. Family style meals for $1.25 breakfast; $2.50 for lunch or dinner. $13 D to $25 D.

Budget (under $20)

Aloha (29 rooms) Jl Gajah Mada 7. ☎ 26950. A converted old house in a quiet neighbourhood just behind the Balai Kota. Rather gloomy lobby, but the rooms are clean. Private bath in all rooms. Standard $12; with TV $16.

Bamboe Denn (11 beds) Jl Arjuna 1 ☎ 66256. Attached to an English school where you will be asked to talk to the class. A good chance to get to know the Javanese. $2 in the dorm. The one private room is $4 D to $7 for four people.

Emma Mustika Sari (7 rooms) Jl Laksamana Martadinata 18–24 ☎ 64939. A renovated 1898 building surrounded by a wall and away from the street. $7.50–15 with bath; $6.25 shared bath.

Helios (24 rooms) Jl Pattimura 37 ☎ 62741. Friendly and well-run. $4 S to $7 T with shared bath. $9 D with bath.

Megawati (29 rooms) Jl Pang Sudirman 99 ☎ 64724. Very homely although the rooms, decorated in traditional colonial style, are rather dark. Rooms in front have large genuine antique beds. The owner is Mrs Warokka, a pleasant Dutch-speaking Manadonese lady. Popular with Dutch travelers. Standard $14; with fan $17. TV $1 extra.

Menara (15 rooms) Jl Pajajaran 5 ☎ 62871. Rooms are clean and all have private bath with hot water and AC. $12 D to $20.

Riche (56 rooms) Jl Basuki Rahmat 1 ☎ 25460, 63770. Excellent central location right at the corner of the *alun alun* plaza. Needs renovation. Standard $14; Standard with 6 beds $26.

Santosa (60 rooms) Jl H Agus Salim ☎ 66889; fax: 67098. Sandwiched between two shopping centers. $8 D to $12 shared bath. $11 D to $22 (4 beds) with bath. $28 T for rooms with hot water and TV.

Moderate ($20–$40)

Margosuko (43 rooms) Jl KHA Dahlan 40–42 ☎ 25270, 66169; fax: 65750. Downtown location. All rooms have a private bath and hot water. Standard: $15; VIP with AC $24.

Montana (38 rooms) Jl Kahuripan 9 ☎ 62751, 28370; fax: 61633. Rooms are small but clean. One of the most popular hotels in town, due to its location. $29 Standard with fan. $37 Standard AC. $47 Deluxe AC.

Pajajaran Park Hotel (18 rooms) Jl Letjen Sutoyo 178 ☎ 41347. Newest hotel in town. Clean and efficient. On the main road to Surabaya. Good value for money. Standard $15; deluxe $34; jumbo $40; suite $50.

Pelangi (84 rooms) Jl Merdeka Selatan 3 ☎ 65156, 65157. One of the oldest, and most centrally located hotels in Malang, on the corner of the *alun alun*. The upper floors are more private, airier and cheaper. Some rooms have spacious private verandahs. The buffet breakfast is grim. $28 D with fan. $35–43 D with AC. A few economy rooms for $12 D.

First Class ($40 and up)

Kartika Prince (79 rooms) Jl Jaksa Agung Suprapto 17 ☎ 61900; fax: 61911. Has the biggest pool in this price range. The Peacock Ballroom (capacity 1,500) is the most prestigious hall in the city and holds major performances and banquets. There's also a disco and karaoke bar. $55 Standard. $75 Superior. $220 for the two story Ambassador Suite complete with piano.

Regent's Park (99 rooms) Jl Jaksa Agung Suprapto 12–16. ☎ 63388, 62966; fax: 61408. $61 Standard. $75 Superior. $252 for the special Japanese style suite. If you don't mind the slightly gloomy atmosphere, the Chinese food at the Wan Sho restaurant is among the best in town.

Tugu Park (36 rooms) Jl Tugu 3 ☎ 63891; fax: 62-747. Winner of the best commercial public building in Indonesia award. Built around the remarkable collection of historic artifacts of Pak Anhar and lushly filled with tropical plants and giant trees he rescued from Malang's botanical garden (now a housing development) in a midnight helicopter raid. Call a few weeks ahead of time. Superior Deluxe $70. Suites $90. The antique-strewn Dutch colonial Honeymoon Suites are $125.

FOOD

Toko Oen was once a chain of Dutch restaurants strung across Java; one of the last survivors this era is this Malang institution northwest of the *alun-alun*. To get a flavor for what this landmark once was, sit in the low slung chairs and take in the blues and greens of this classic space: but don't venture beyond the drinks on the menu. Then rush over to **Und Corner** at Tugu Park where the Toko Oen baking team still turns out the best pastries around. The core of the staff is fortunately intact and turning out wonderful Indo-Dutch food at the adjoining beautiful **Melati Pavilion Restaurant**. Live jazz piano every night.

Amsterdam Restaurant (Jl Terusan Kawi 2) has good Chinese, Indonesian and European food. Live music every night and a convivial atmosphere. Another favourite with a similar range of cuisines is **Santapuri Restaurant** (Jl JA Suprapto 56, on the main road from Surabaya) where they also serve Japanese dishes.

There are some great places outside of town. About 3km south of the Sukun Cemetery, on the left hand side of the road, you will find **Warung Ikan Segar**. This is a very pleasant floating restaurant where they serve deep fried fish, Indonesian dishes and other seafood: you can also order the fish of your choice. They have *lesehan* seating style on cushions around low tables. Try their excellent *pecek telor*: a boiled egg crushed in a salty but sweet sauce.

Some 15 km north of town, 500 m before Singosari on the left side of the road is **Pondok Alam** (Jl Raya Singosari 123B). They serve delicious seafood here. Further north, at no. 169, is the **Kantri Club**, which has separate pavilions set among fish ponds. A popular place for evening meals.

Fried chicken lovers should try the local *ayam kampung* (village chicken). **Ayam Goreng Pemuda** at Jl Semeru 38A; **Remaja** on Letjen Sutoyo and nearby **Ayam Goreng Kertasari** at Jl Letjen Sutoyo 80 are all favourites, the latter being a nice place for a variety of dishes. Their Javanese dessert *es puter* (coconut ice in a number of different flavours) is a favorite.

Noodle fans should head for the specialists: **Bakmi Gajahmada** at Jl Pasar Besar 21, **Bakmi Gang Jangkrik** at Jl Kawi Atas kios 26 are two recommended spots. All along Jl Kawi Atas there are numerous small *depot makan* restaurants for those on a budget.

The best Chinese food can be had at **KDS**, Jalan Gatot Subroto 9C, especially the peanut or pork filled dumplings (*swee kow*). **Nikmat Lezat** on the same street at no. 94 and **Dirga Surya** at no. 77 are also well known. **Dragon Phoenix** at Jl KHA Dahlan 27-29 is the biggest Chinese restaurant in town. Budget conscious travelers who don't mind a simple atmosphere but want good quality food, should head for **Santai** or **Depot 21** at Jl Slamet Riyadi 108 and 94A.

Sumatran Padang food is available at **Rindu**, Jalan Agus Salim 29 near Mitra I shopping center. Good *nasi rawon* (rice, beef and a flavorful broth) is also available in the nearby **R M Nguling**, Jalan Zainul Arifin 62 and the renowned **Warung Brintik** at Jl KHA Dakhlan 39.

For East Javan cuisine check out the perpetually packed **Soto Rampal** at Jl Pang Sudirman 71A. For a uniquely Malang-style chicken soup (*soto ayam*) try **Soto Lombok** which adds the special ingredient of brown coconut powder (*koya*) to achieve a unique flavor. Also try the delicious *soto Madura* style which can be sampled at **Soto Ambengan** at Jl Pattimura 11, or

Soto Lamongan at Jl Slamet Riyadi 147C. Don't miss the old favourite **Warung Pojok** at Jl Pejajaran 25B, which is well-known for its *rujak* (crunchy salad smothered in sweet peanut sauce) and *rawon*(beef stew) and traditional dessert *es dawet* (green rice pudding in coconut sauce).

Stir-fried vegetables with cow's snout is called *rujak cingur* and can be found at the *warung* owned and run by Pak Ban half way along Jl Tenes, just north of Jl Kawi.

Some of the cheapest places to sample Malang's specialties, *nasi rawon* and *bakso Malang* (meatballs in a noodle soup topped with *tofu* and a tomato, chili or sweet soy sauce) are the *warung* (food stalls) that set up at night at various spots in town. **Pasar Senggol** on Jalan Tumapel between the *alun-alun* and Tugu Park is the most central night *warung* area.

Also try grilled corn-on-the-cob, seafood and various cooked birds at **Jalan Pulosari** at night just north of the many small *depot makan* restaurants of **Jalan Kawi Atas**. As always, keep a critical eye on the purveyors' attitude towards cleanliness when choosing a place to eat.

The desperately homesick should head for **Kentucky Fried Chicken** at Malang Plaza, or to the **California Fried Chicken** on the third floor of Malang Plaza, or at Mitra II (Jl Letjen Sutoyo). **McDonald's** is at Sarinah Plaza, but try the food court first. There's another food court at Mitra I, and most of the stalls at the **Food Bazaar** at the Matahari Dept. Store on the second floor of Pasar Besar (Jl Pasar Besar) are good.

SHOPPING

The Mayor of Malang has done his best to ensure that visitors to his city will not lack for convenient shopping opportunities: there are 5 shiny new malls: **Malang Plaza**, **Gajahmada Plaza**, **Mitra I**, **Mitra II** and **Sarinah Plaza**, and a sixth, **Mataram Plaza**, will be opening soon.

There are some good antiques to be had at **Kendedes Art & Furniture** Komplek PTP 23 Nos. 1, 2, 4 Jl Raya Karanglo (Banjararum-Singosari) ☎ 42756–7. Mr Hadi, the owner, stocks rocking horses, other antiques and reproductions. He regularly receives orders from abroad. Also try **Wisma Antik** Jl Ciliwung 1–1A ☎ 41420.

For copies of traditional Chinese ceramics, head towards Batu. A number of workshops can be found in the Dinoyo area, near Brawijaya University.

Sarinah Plaza on the north side of the *alun alun* houses the Sarinah department store specializing in handicrafts from across the archipelago. **Barang Lama** in Purwosari (half-way between Surabaya and Malang) has a wide selection of old furniture at very reasonable prices, as well as ceramics, china, brass and cast-iron Dutch lamps.

For English and foreign newspapers, magazines and books about Indonesia go to **Wise Owl**, Jl Kawi 26 ☎ 62700. Another option is **Gramedia** at Jl Jend. Basuki Rahmat 3: it's easy to find, next door to Toko Oen.

SERVICES

Tourist information is best gotten from Toko Oen at Jl Basuki Rahmat 5 ☎ 64052, 25221; open 8 am to 9 pm. The main **telephone office** at Jl Basuki Rakhmat 7–9 is open 24 hrs (fax: 69111). There are also 17 *wartel* around town. The **post office** is on the south side of the square (*alun alun*).

Change money at Bank Bumi Daya on the west side of the square or BCA Bank, Bank BNI or Bank Niaga all of which are found along the central Jl Jend. Basuki Rahmat. The Kartika Prince Hotel (Jl Jaksa Agung Sprapto 12–16) operates a 24 hr money changing service.

Some recommended **travel agencies** are: **Mujur Surya** (next to **Putra Jaya** car rental) Jl Bromo 33A ☎ 27955–57; fax: 61633. **Pasopati**, Jl Jend Basuki Rahmat 11E ☎ 20270; fax: 64750. **Tanjung Permai** Jl Jend Basuki Rahmat 41 ☎ 27141; fax: 24348. **Angkasa Express** Jl S. Wiryopranoto 3 c ☎ 662385. The **Sempati Air** office is in the of Malang Regent's Park Hotel ☎ 63388.

NIGHTLIFE

There are two lively discos: **My Place** at the Kartika Prince Hotel and and **Basement** at Gajahmada Plaza. If you don't feel like dancing till dawn, try the movies. **Mandala Theatre** at Malang Plaza has 4 screens and **Sarinah Theatre** at Sarinah Plaza has 3.

Lawang

Telephone code is 0341.

A minibus from Malang's Arjosari Terminal costs 15¢. Take a break from the temples to see a relic of the more recent past at the brooding **Hotel Niagara** (13 rooms) Jl Dr Sutomo 63 ☎ 96612. Five stories of balconies, stained glass, marble, glazed tiles and 20 foot ceilings in a state of slow decay. It looks haunted and, apparently, it is. Even if you don't stay, ask to go on top of the building to see the view. $6 economy, $8 standard and $13 first class. **Arjuna View Hotel** (23 rooms) Jl Dr Wahidin 33 ☎ 96392. $17–28 D. **Hotel Sumber Waras Jaya** (10 rooms) Jl Sumber Waras 36 ☎ 96190. $8 D.

Eat excellent Javanese food at either **Kertosono** or **Depot 29;** or try cobra, turtle or aardvark at **Depot Surabaya**.

Batu and Selekta

Telephone code is 0341.

More laid-back than Tretes, this is the place for apples, great views and an opportunity to use the sweater you packed. Don't even think about it on Sundays, holidays and school vacations: the crowds are unbearable and some room rates double. Take a 15¢ Mikrolet to Dinoyo

Terminal and catch a violet minibus for 25¢ to Batu's bus terminal. From here it's another 15¢ to the area north of the town square where the hotels are. Songgoriti is just 2 km further up tucked into the hills and more surrounded by the forest. Selekta is 4 km to the north.

ACCOMMODATION

Budget (under $15)

Apple Green Home Stay (19 rooms) Jl Panglima Sudirman 104, Batu ☎ 91747. A 1938 Dutch Moderne house with cramped rooms at $13 D and more comfortable new rooms at $15 D.
Arumdalu (43 rooms) Jl Arumdalu, Songgoriti ☎ 91266. Economy $6 D. Standard $10–13 D.
Perdana (65 rooms) Jl Panglima Sudirman 101, Batu ☎ 91104. Decent but soulless. $10–18 D.

Intermediate ($15–$35)

Batu Permai (29 rooms) Jl Hasanudin 4, Batu ☎ 91077/91934; fax: 92512. Quiet side street location. Clean. $14 to $24 D.
Metropole (49 rooms) Jl Panglima Sudirman 93, Batu ☎ 91758, 91759; fax: 91760. The newest rooms are the nicest and cheapest at $26 D. Others are $35 to $55 D.
Nirwana (46 rooms) Jl Arumdalu 5, Songgoriti. ☎ 92990/92991. Small and clean. $23 D to $27.
Selekta (46 rooms) Selekta ☎ 91025, 92369. Part of a hotel/garden/pool complex. Boasts a pool slide that's big enough to be an Olympic ski jump. The rooms with the best views are numbers 6–8 ($30 D) in the classic Moderne Selekta 2 building.
Wijaya Inn, Jl Raya Selekta 56 ☎ 92694; fax: 92223. An efficient, good value hotel with good food. Standard (3 persons) $17; standard deluxe $16 (2 persons) $21 (3 persons); VIP $27 (2 persons) $35 (3 persons).

First Class ($35 and up)

Bukit Cemara Emas Bungalows Jl Flamboyan 9, Batu ☎ 92987. Agricultural tourism: improved by the genuine bucolic atmosphere. $50.
Kartika Wijaya (66 rooms) Jl Panglima Sudirman 127, Batu ☎ 92600/92601; fax: 92604. The stained glass and wood in the lobby retains a Dutch elegance. Standard $64 and Superior $73. Regional theme bungalows are $83.
Kusuma Agro Wisata Jl Abdul Gani Atas (1 km up Kawi mountain) ☎ 93333–36; fax: 93196. Unbeatable views of the mountainous Batu area. Boasts an apple and orange orchard where you can pick and buy fruit. Horse riding, a pool and sports facilities. A very nice place. Standard $34; superior cottage $54; deluxe cottage $90.
New Victory (60 rooms) Jl Raya Junggo 107, Selekta ☎ 93011, 93012. Brand new, with a tiny exposed pool. $37 to $45 D.
Purnama (144 rooms) Jl Raya Selekta 1–15, Selekta ☎ 92700; fax: 92710. Fresh mountain water pool. Standard $36 D but only some of the Superior rooms ($84 D) have a view.
Royal Orchids Garden (19 condominiums) Jl Indragiri 4, Batu ☎ 93083; fax: 91064. A gingerbready new condo village for the family car vacationers of Surabaya. $110 to $400.

FOOD IN BATU

Warung Bethania is a real must for lovers of local food in an extraordinary ambience. Serving excellent Javanese food in a forest setting straight out of *The Wizard of Oz,* this place is patronized regularly by celebrities and ministers. Their deep fried *gurame* eel is exceptional accompanied by *tempe* and *tahu* (soy cakes and *tofu*), *sayur lodeh* (vegetable soup). Highly recommended.

Further east are the warm and woody open terraces of **Amsterdam Restaurant**. European, Chinese and Indonesian menu, with a big ice cream section. Great deep-fried fish. **Prameswari Restaurant** is closer to the center. Roasted corn-on-the cob is sold on the roadside. **Sate Hot Plate** at the east end of town has goat *sate.* **Batu Plaza** at the town square has a food court, department store and movie theater.

Tretes

Telephone code is 0343.

The cool mountain air and panoramic views made this town on the slopes of Mt. Arjuna a favorite weekend family destination in the past, but more recently it has become the site of a huge prostitution business catering to Surabayan businessmen. Nevertheless it is still a good spot from which to base yourself: swim, cool off, do some hiking or even a dawn to dusk horseback ride to the peak of Mt. Welirang ($25, dry season only). Many ultra-luxury resorts are under construction in these hills but modest accommodation is still to be found primarily in the form of rooms rented in private homes *(pila)* for $10 a night. Nicer ones with hot water run from $25 to $50 a night. Nearby Trawas and Pacet offer more serenity and seclusion.

ACCOMMODATION

Mirama Indah (21 rooms) Jl Wijayakusuma 60 ☎ 81-217. The best of the bottom end—in the old red light district. $7.50 with hot water, $5 without.
Natour Bath Tretes (70 rooms) Jl Pesanggrahan 2 ☎ 81776, 81777; fax 81161. The former best place to stay in Tretes with an ice-cold spring fed swimming pool. Standard $60, superior $70.
PPLH (Center for Environmental Education) Seloliman, Trawas. Reserve through the Surabaya office: Jl Adityawarman 54 ☎ (031) 575884. Beautifully set up in a tropical rainforest by an Indonesian environmentalist and a German architect. Caters mainly to groups from Surabaya and Europe. Individual deals can be arranged by calling ahead of time. Vegetarian food, quiet atmosphere. A unique way to see natural Java even if expensive. Day hike $30,

2-day program $70, 3-day program $120 (prices are per person including food and bungalow).

Surya Hotel and Cottages (151 rooms) Jl Taman Wisata ☎ 81911; fax: 81708. Even if you don't stay here you can take advantage of the facilities: pricey restaurant, disco, tennis and squash courts, fitness center with sauna, hot tub and massage, and a wacky shaped heated swimming pool ($1.75 during the week). Standard $115, superior $140 and suites for $157 to $726.

Swiss Ind (22 rooms) Pacet ☎ (0321) 23420. A group of cottages situated on a high mountain slope crossed by cold streams. Better views and seclusion than you'll find in Tretes. $30 with breakfast. Add $5 for lunch and dinner.

Tretes View (64 rooms) Jl Gadjah Mada 6–7 ☎ 81-700; fax: 81758. Until the prices go up, this is the best luxury deal. Standard $47, superior $67.

Wisma Sri Katon (16 rooms) Jl Raya 53 ☎ 81122. Clean and simple. No hot water. $10 with bath.

MISCELLANEOUS

Depot Abadi has three branches serving free range chicken *(ayam kampung)* which is scrawny but very tasty. For your excursions into the mountains Viking Restaurant offers a lunch box with fried chicken "à la Kentucky" for $4.50.

Candra Wilwatikta is a performing arts center in Pandaan 45 mins south of Surabaya on the road to Tretes presenting Javanese dance spectacles twice a month at the new and full moons. ☎ (0343) 31841. Eat at Depot Sri opposite before the show.

— *Bob Cowherd/Paul Zacharia*

Climbing Arjuno-Welirang

Arjuno-Welirang is an active volcanic massif, 50 km south of Surabaya. Gunung Arjuno (3,339 m) is dormant, and forms part of the Arjuno Lalijiwo Reserve, a 5,000 hectare montane wildlife park. A 2,700-m-high saddle connects Arjuno with its active neighbor, Gunung Welirang (3,156 m). Seismologists classify Arjuno-Welirang as "A–type": the most dangerous.

Some of Java's most picturesque mountain resorts: Tretes, Batu, Pandaan and Selekta, lie on the slopes of the massif. This area is an ideal base for mountain-lovers.

Although only recommended for experienced trekkers, the Arjuno-Welirang route offers one of Java's most spectacular treks: from Selekta to Tretes via both peaks and the Lalijiwo Reserve.

If you want to climb the peaks individually, start the Arjuno climb from Selekta (a shorter route) and approach Welirang from Tretes. The trail to Arjuno leads you through magnificent Alpine forests to one of Java's highest summits.

GUIDES

Unpredictable weather conditions, and the fact that many paths are hidden, make hiring a guide essential for climbing Arjuno. Guides here speak very little English, so you should either speak some Indonesian or hire an interpreter. Mr Asir, who lives in Kampung Junggo, 2 km north of Selekta, is recommended. His house is 50 m to the left of Pos Tulungrejo. He charges about $5 per day. To reach him, rent a motorbike in Selekta at *losmen* Mona Lisa, Jl Raya Selekta 83.

PREPARATIONS

The route described below follows the trail from Selekta to Tretes. The total walking distance of 35 km includes both peaks, the Lalijiwo Reserve and sulphur-collectors' camp. Allow 2 to 3 days, bring energy-rich foods, a water-resistant jacket and a sleeping bag. One bottle of water is sufficient—more is available up the mountain.

SELEKTA TO GUNUNG ARJUNO

From Selekta either walk, or ride a motorbike, to Kampung Junggo. The trek begins among asparagus plantations. After 1.5 hours walking you enter montane forest, where a narrow footpath winds up Arjuno's western slope. This path is often hidden under thick ferns, particularly after the rainy season.

After 3 hours you should reach the top of a 100 m gorge. This is an excellent picnic spot. Keep quiet and you might see black and red monkeys on the opposite side of the canyon.

The path continues precipitously to Arjuno's peak region where some sections are as steep as 45 degrees. After another 2 hours of crawling between tall conifers you reach the tree line and an open plateau. Keep left at the turnoff: the path on the right descends to Singosari and Malang.

It's another 30 minutes from the plateau to the peaks (6 to 7 hours in all from Kampung Junggo). A few hundred meters below Arjuno's summit look for a big cave on your left, this is a useful spot to bivouac in bad weather. If the weather's clear when you arrive at Arjuno's summit, which lies at 3,339 m above sea level, you get stunning views of East Java's volcanoes stretching into the distance.

A steep and arduous path leads from the summit to Lalijiwo Plateau. After 12 noon it often gets very misty along this section: sometimes you can't even see your guide walking directly in front of you. If the mist descends, *do not* stray from the footpath: in certain places it winds alongside a deep, invisible nothing.

Take it easy and allow two hours to reach the fairytale-like Lalijiwo Plateau. High meadows of *alang-alang* grass with muddy swamps, pools of clear mountain water, surrounded by stands of tree fern, groups of rustling casuarinas and pretty alpine flowers await you at this idyllic resting place.

If you don't want to bivouac on Arjuno's icy summit or foggy Lalijiwo Plateau, make sure you leave the summit by 2 pm to ensure that you can reach Pondok Welirang, the sulphur collectors' camp, which lies at 2,400 m.

Continue northwest after the pools at Lalijiwo and find the path with a plastic tube snaking along it. The tube provides the sulphur men with fresh drinking water, and climbers with freezing showers. Just follow it and 30 minutes later you enter a clearing in which lies Pondok Welirang, looking like a Tibetan mountain village.

TO WELIRANG & BACK TO BASE

Leave the camp before daybreak (4:30–5 am) to give you enough time to explore Gunung Welirang's craters and descend to Tretes without undue haste. From the camp start on the trail which climbs straight up. The turnoff to the left behind the watertank leads back to Gunung Arjuno, Lalijiwo and back down to Selekta.

After ascending at a gentle 15 degrees, the rocky trail suddenly becomes steep. It climbs up onto the small Bluntu plateau, winds around some smaller peaks on the saddle between both volcanoes, and finally zigzags up Welirang's steep flank from the southeast.

Around 3 hours later you reach Welirang's flat crater complex. The first one you pass is extinct but a bit higher up is a bigger, active crater. WARNING: Do not stand on the edge of the crater rim, especially if it is still dark. Crater walls consist of porous ash and loose debris and are often overhanging. Just a small step too far and that's it...

From the highest point (3,156 m) you can enjoy marvelous views over the region. Try to get here before 9 am, when clouds begin to travel from the humid lowlands and engulf the surrounding area, including you, by noon.

To witness the sulphur collectors doing their hellish work, trek back to the extinct crater. Off the main trail to the west lies a track that descends 100 m to a parasitic crater which faces the Selekta valley. This is called "the kitchen" and it is Welirang's acidic heart. Here sulphurous vapor condenses to form a yellow mass which workers gather in blocks. After carefully loading their baskets they carry the sulphur down the rocky serpentine paths—some only wearing slippers and smoking *kretek* cigarettes at the same time.

Count on another 4.5 hours from Welirang's peaks to Tretes. The trail ends at the gate which forms the entrance to Taman Rekreasi park. There's a campsite and waterfalls here, if you can't face returning to Selekta on day two.

To get to Tretes by public *bemo*, continue for 200 m beyond the gate, turn right and continue for another 200 m until you reach the Tanjung Plaza Hotel. Wait opposite it for minibuses heading for Pandaan.

If you want to continue back to Selekta, go to Pandaan and change onto another minibus to Malang (Pattimura station). From there take a minibus to Batu and another one to Selekta (around 2.5 hours and Rp2,000 in total). You'll reach your *losmen* much more exhausted than the sulphur-men arrive in Tretes, and you will be two kilograms lighter than when you began.

— Tom Otte

Balekambang, Ngliyep & Sempu

The currents can be dangerous in this area south of Malang along East Java's rugged coast, so seek local advice before going swimming.

To reach **Balekambang** take the "colt" to Bantur from Gadang Station for 75¢ then another on to Balekambang for 25¢. Visitors stay in villagers' homes for $5 a night, $7.50 when crowded.

Ngliyep is a bit harder to reach by public transportation. From Gadang Station south of town take a "colt" to Karangkates, then to Donomulyo. On Sundays, "colts" run to Ngliyep for 25¢. On other days you have to hire an *ojek* (a guy on a motorbike) or a "colt" for $2.50 to the beach about an hour away. There's a *losmen* with 10 rooms for $5 a night (shared bath). A beautiful wide beach with large dangerous waves.

Pulau Sempu (300 m off the coast of Sendang Biru) is a pristine uninhabited island with some magical places. There are government owned bungalows for $5 a night (always full on Saturday nights). From Gadang Station, take a 40¢, 1–1.5 hours "colt" ride to Sumber Manjing Wetan and a ±$1 *ojek* on to the Sendang Biru. A boat to the island is $5 round trip.

— Bob Cowherd/Paul Zacharia

Bromo

See map, page 284.

Most visitors to the high altitude villages on the slopes of the Semeru massif arrive in buses in the dark and leave before the sun gets hot, but this is actually a great place to explore for a few days of great walks and mountain air.

There are four approaches to Bromo. From Probolinggo in the northeast, to Sukapura and then up (the most popular route). From Pasuruan in the northwest, via Tosari and then to the caldera by jeep. Or along the backroad from Malang in the west, to Ngadas, on the southern side of the caldera rim (the trekkers' route). The final approach, from Malang via Lawang, Purwodadi, Nongkojajar and Wonokitri is highly recommended. The road is smooth and the views are spectacular all the way to Wonokitri. The whole trip takes 1 hour 45 minutes by car.

The sunrise is touted as Bromo's big event.

Get up early anyway to see the landscape at its best, although you don't have to be hustled by guides Into going down to Bromo at unearthly hours of the morning: the best view of the sunrise is from the rim of the caldera, not from the edge of Bromo itself. In the villages around the rim one can generally find homestays for $2.50 to $5 if you don't mind roughing it out. It helps to have your own bedding, a few words of Indonesian, and a sense of adventure.

Pasuruan

Telephone code is 0343.
This is the town described in L. Couperus's book *The Hidden Force* (De Stille Kracht) which makes for good travel reading. It has some interesting colonial architecture on its side streets. Pasuruan is a 1-hour, 50¢ bus ride from Surabaya.
Pasuruan Hotel (36 rooms) Jl Nusantara 46 ☎ 41-494. The best in town but nothing special. $8.25 shared bath, $11 private bath, $12 with AC.
Wisma Karya (46 rooms) Jl Raya 160 ☎ 61655. Popular with Indonesian salesmen. $4 shared bath, $7 private bath, $12 to $14 AC.
Depot Hayam Waruk, Jl Hayam Waruk 19A, has good Chinese and Indonesian food. There are *warung* at the *alun-alun* (town square) at night; especially crowded on Tuesdays when villagers flock here in traditional dress.

Tosari & Wonokitri

Telephone code is 031.
From the bus terminal in Pasuruan, catch a "colt" to Pasrepan, another to Tosari and a third to Wonokitri. A chartered van costs $25 to Wonokitri and $12.50 more to get to the peak of Mt Penanjakan (2,775 m)—a 13-km climb. Unless you want to do it on foot, arrange for transportation the night before at your hotel. Departures are at 3:30 am to catch the sunrise. Buy food and drink the night before to help keep you warm. Pay Rp1,500 entrance fee at the checkpoint at the top of Wonokitri.

Mt Penanjakan provides the best views of the area and is only readily accessible from the Tosari-Wonokitri approach. A new road has been started from Cemara Lawang to this vantage point but is still a long way from completion. You can walk, ride a horse or get a van driver to take you to the top of this road and walk one hour up the steep, poorly marked footpath. On this and other pre-dawn excursions take a flashlight, spare batteries, warm clothes, water and some food.

From the peak, there's a steep trail to where the unfinished road finishes, leading the rest of the two hour trip along the rim to Cemara Lawang. There is a good road leading down to the edge of the sand sea from where cars have not yet been banned, but it's better to make the 8 km walk from this edge across the sand to Mt Bromo.

Bromo Surya (21 rooms) Wonokitri. Just before the checkpoint. Over-priced but the only hot water in Wonokitri. $25 and $20 rooms.
Pondok Wisata Surya Nata (9 rooms) Wonokitri. Run by Pak Budi the village head. Very simple rooms and water that is really cold. $12.50.
Grand Bromo Cottages (80 rooms) Tosari ☎ 336-888, fax: 336833. The only 3-star accommodation in the area. A mountain lodge feel in the restaurant. In clear weather, the views out over the lowlands to Mt Arjuno and the Java Sea are great. $48 for a decidedly sub-standard Standard; Superior $61 S and $67 D; $121 to $218 for Suites.

Probolinggo

Telephone code is 0335.
Some people prefer to stay here and go up to Bromo just for the day.

From the Bali ferry terminal at Banyuwangi to Probolinggo, it's $1.60 for regular buses (5 hours) or $2.50 for *patas* (4 hours). From Surabaya or Malang, Probolinggo is an 85¢, 2-hour public bus ride away. It's $1.25 and an hour-and-a-half by *patas* AC public minibus.
WARNING. Beware of transportation scams to Bromo via Probolinggo. Hustlers are rife and people will deceive you if you permit them. Don't get locked into an all-inclusive package deal unless you really want to: maintaining your independence can be more rewarding—and cheaper.
- Make it clear well ahead of your arrival that you will not get off the bus anywhere but Probolinggo bus terminal. It's easy to see, even at night: there's a clear sign as you enter, and the place houses dozens of buses.
- Don't get pressured into purchasing return trip tickets ahead of time. You can take a scheduled regular or AC *patas* public bus during the day. Alternatively, you can get a seat on a bus via an informal arrangement with the conductor of whatever bus is passing through on its way to Yogya/Solo or Bali. This does not involve a ticket but a price you arrange directly with the conductor or which an agent in Probolinggo arranges for you. Ask at the *loket* in the terminal what the fare for public *patas* AC bus is to your destination. The prices offered you by private companies should not be too much more.
- The price of public transport up to Ngadisari and Cemara Lawang is fixed by the government at Rp1,500 and Rp2,500 respectively. If you arrive at a reasonable hour (6 am to 6 pm) there will be "colts" and special gray tourist jeeps running regularly from Probolinggo Terminal to Ngadisari Terminal. Or charter a *bemo* for Rp15,000 or Rp12,500 if you are a good bargainer. At Ngadisari pay Rp1,550 entrance fee.
- Decide where you want to stay and insist on being taken there. Drivers get paid commissions for delivering you to specific hotels.

Train fares (2nd class) from Probolinggo to anywhere within 210 km, including Surabaya,

Malang and Banyuwangi, cost $2.50.

The Government approved **Tourist Information Center** at Jalan Lawayan is the best bet for good information and fair ticket prices. **Change money** at Bank Bumi Daya. The **phone office** is at the northeast corner of the *alun-alun.*

ACCOMMODATION

Losmen Bromo Permai (41 rooms) Jl Panglima Sudirman 237 ☎ 41256. Popular with travelers and the best bet in Probolinggo. The older building has a more comfortable atmosphere, with rooms set around a two story courtyard and a nice place to eat. A variety of rooms from $2.25 S shared bath to $4.25 D private bath and a few rooms with AC $7.50 to $11.

Ratna (48 rooms) Jl Panglima Sudirman 16 ☎ 21-597. Well run and comfortable. $3 shared bath, $7.50 to $10 D private bath, $15 D AC.

Tampiarto Plaza (64 rooms) Jl Suroyo 15 ☎ 21288/41436; fax: 41103. Restaurant, a decent pool, disco. Recently renovated. $5.50 S to $8 D with fan and bath, $15 S to $21 D with AC and hot water.

Cemara Lawang & Ngadisari

No telephones yet. Numbers given are to make reservations only.

From Ngadisari pay a Rp1,550 entrance fee to the national park and Rp1,000 for a ride in a tourist jeep up to Cemara Lawang perched on the rim of the caldera.

In Cemara Lawang, horses can be rented at the official rate of Rp10,000 round trip or from the bottom of the stairs at Mt Bromo for Rp5,000 for just the return trip across the sand and up the caldera wall. The horses are small and are limited to a brisk walk with their owner walking alongside. Prices go up for the Kasodo Ceremony in December, Lebaran in January or February and the New Year.

It gets very cold here and sometimes stays that way all day. Better rooms have hot water and many cheaper rooms include access to hot showers for a small fee. There are some camp sites on the rim of the caldera 500 m from the PHPA (Forestry) Office. Wisma Ucik adjacent to the Ngadisari terminal is a government guesthouse with only 6 rooms and problems getting water but may have some empty rooms or be able to arrange a homestay for you. Yoschi's Guest House can't be beat for the best food, most comfortable rooms, relaxing atmosphere and good value. In ascending geographical order:

Sukapura Permai (14 rooms) Sukapura ☎ (0335) 21379. Rooms with views available. $15 with hot water, $12.50 without.

Grand Bromo (65 rooms) Sukapura ☎ (031) 711802; fax: (031) 715798. The up-market alternative. Also the fanciest restaurant. The "tourist" rooms are in poor repair for $42. $61 standard, $73 superior.

Bromo Home Stay (27 rooms) Wonokerto. Mainly for package tour guests. If Yoschi's is full but you want to stay close to her cooking. Prices include the pre-dawn jeep ride to Cemara Lawang. Unpleasant staff. $5 shared bath, $8 with cold water bath, $12.50 with hot bath.

Yoschi's Guest House (20 rooms) Wonokerto (2 kilometers downhill from Ngadisari). *The* place to stay near Bromo. Run with German flair by Uschi. Comfortable and clean. 50¢ for a half hour hot shower. $2.75 to $5 with shared bath, $7.50 for private bath with hot water. $9 to $12 for cottages.

Losmen Cafe Lava (25 rooms) Cemara Lawang. The last resort. Inedible food. Rates seem to change according to how much they think they can get. Sometimes they are $2.50 S, $5 D.

Cemara Indah (34 rooms) Cemara Lawang. Strategically perched on the rim; great view from the restaurant. $3 S to $7.50 T with shared bath, $17.50 without hot water, $22.50 with hot water.

Bromo Permai I (63 rooms) Cemara Lawang ☎ (03-35) 21626. Great location. A variety of rooms; $1.75 dorm, $5 D, $7.50 T shared cold water bath, $17–22 with hot water, $34 with charcoal stove.

FOOD

By far the best food is at **Yoschi's**. Try the Bromo soup and the potato pancakes with hot sauce. There are some good *warung* near the "colt" terminal at Ngadisari as well as **Wisma Ucik Restaurant. Bromo Permai** is a nice place for breakfast after the morning hike.

Climbing Java's Highest Peak

Gunung Semeru in the south of the Bromo-Tengger-Semeru National Park is Java's highest peak at 3,676 m, it is also one of the world's most beautiful volcanoes. But the beauty of Indonesia's Fujiyama masks treachery.

In 1909 an explosive eruption killed 220 people and destroyed more than 1,400 houses, and since 1967 Semeru (also known as Gunung Mahameru) has been constantly active. In 1987 alone, volcanologists noted 22,073 seismic events. Understandably, scientists classify it as a highly dangerous "type A" volcano.

There are four possible approaches to Semeru, each being long and strenuous due to the remote location of this volcano. Even from Ranupani (the nearest Tengger village and start off point) which you can reach by *bemo*, it is still a 28 km trek to the base.

Cooking-gear, bivouac equipment and enough food and water are necessary for this trip and even the fittest must count on three days. Once at the base of Gunung Semeru, the final 700 m is extremely strenuous, but technically the climb is easier than Gunung Merapi's Kaliurang route, or Sumatra's Dempo.

The scrapbook at Yoschi's (See "Cemara Lawang/Ngadisari" above) has the best information on hiking in the area. Check at the PHPA

(Forestry) offices around this National Park to find out about any recent seismic activity and the advisability of climbing Semeru as the gases belched from this crater can be hazardous. The rainy season also presents its own obstacles.

DAY 1: CEMARA LAWANG TO RANUPANI

Although it is the longest approach to climb Semeru, this is one of Java's superb treks. Count on around 5 hours for the 13 km hike to Ranupani—a pleasant walk through the Sea of Sands past Gunung Bromo and Kursi and the sheer walls of the Tengger caldera. You don't really need a guide, but pack one bottle of drinking water per person. An alternative is to pay around Rp12,000 and ride a horse.

From Cemara Lawang descend into the caldera and follow the marked trail to the left of Gunung Bromo. Some 1.5 km after entering the Sea of Sands the path joins a jeep-track. Follow the track to your right for about 3 km and watch for the large boulder on the left of the track before you reach a stand of trees.

Here a small path bears off to the left and winds up the steep caldera-wall, offering a short-cut to Ranupani which saves about 4 km. Alternately follow the more gently ascending jeep track to the top of the cauldron, where you come to a junction and a hut.

The track to the right leads to Ngadas and Malang. Take the left hand road to Ranupani. It's another 5 km to the start-off village but the track is good and descends all the way.

An alternative approach to Ranupani is from the Malang side using the "colt" up to Gubug Klakah and walking or hiring private transport from here 17 km on to Ranupani for around $10. A jeep and driver straight from Malang should be around $35. You also pay for the driver's meals along the way. Make sure he has made this trip before and knows how steep it gets. Only about 50 m behind Lake Ranu Pani (*sic*) is another, smaller lake worth visiting: Ranu Regulo.

RANUPANI

Ranupani is a *kampung* beside the cold foggy lakes of Ranupani and Ranu Regulo and is surrounded by mountains and extensive farmlands.

At the departure point to Semeru you will meet mountaineers from all over the world. For the latest information about climbing conditions and current moodiness of Semeru enquire at the PHPA office near Lake Ranu Pani at the other end of the village. Follow the road till you come to a T-junction, then turn right towards the lake.

On your left Just before the lake there's a *warung* and homestay which charges $2 for a double room. If you've brought a tent, pitch it at the campsite near the lake (ask at the PHPA). Alternatively stay overnight in a room at the PHPA-office, if a bus-load of climbers hasn't got there first. No bedding or meals, but in the morning you get a hot coffee. Dare-devils arriving without sleeping bag can rent one at the office: for just $3 it will save your life.

If you're alone and need a guide or porter, cook, or just company, ask for shopkeeper and guide Mr Kasimen. He charges $8 per day including his cooking skills—instant noodles three times a day. He lends pullovers too and has a *warung* if you need extra food. Noodles? If there's no room in the homestay or PHPA ask if you may stay at his house. Other guides here charge $5–10 per day, but bargain hard. PHPA guards also sometimes act as guides.

DAY 2: RANUPANI TO SEMERU BASE CAMP

Begin from the PHPA office. If you have opted not to hire a guide make sure you do not get lost in the extensive Tengger farmlands. Get the PHPA staff to explain the "get in" routes. During the dry season don't forget to ask if there's water at the Sumber Manis spring near Semeru.

There are two trails to Gunung Semeru. The "New Trail" climbs 2,400 m; and the "Ajek-Ajek-Trail" which is shorter but more tiring: you have to climb up the pass to a height of 2,800 m then descend again to 2,400 m. Instead of using this trail twice, take Ajek-Ajek on your return journey. You can stay overnight in a hut at Ranu Kumbolo (c. 13 km from Ranupani) but if you aim to hike straight to the Semeru base camp (a further 12 km) start at 7 am. Don't carry too much water up to Lake Kumbolo—one liter per person is sufficient.

The New Trail

Behind the PHPA-office take the trail to the right and follow it for about 15 minutes. Cross a bridge and continue to the right for about 150 m. Find the path at the foot of the hill to your left.

Follow it upwards. No more turnoffs confuse you, but prepare yourself for 2 hours crawling through a 1.5 m high green tunnel. Trees and bushes attack your backpack, making this walk rather uncomfortable for anybody taller than a midget. The path winds uphill and after about 4 hours you find yourself standing at the top of a ridge with a marvelous view of Ranu Kumbolo.

Rest and recoup some energy. Stock up with more drinking water (a minimum of 2 liters/person: boil it or use purification tablets). For the 12 km trek from Ranu Kumbolo to Arcopodho upper base camp count on another 4–5 hours.

From the hut at Kumbolo, climb up the small hill behind and descend to a plateau with alpine meadows and pine forest. After about 2.5 hours the pine forest thins and you enter a dusty grass plain with striking views of Semeru's cone.

To your right there is a canyon with a riverbed and a tiny waterfall, called Sumber Manis, the only water source near Mahameru. Climb down into the canyon, turn right and follow the riverbed for about 200 m. The waterfall is on the right. Take as much as you can carry.

Back on the plain follow the path to the right around the base of Gunung Kepolo. In 1 hour you reach the wooded base of Semeru's mighty cone and lower base camp: Kali Mati.

Now you know you're close to a volcano. Explosions cover both the trees and you with fine gray ash. Protect your camera: or expect expensive scrunching noises later.

If you're not too tired by now, climb on for another 1.5 hours to the upper base camp, Arcopodho, which lies just below the tree line at about 3,000 m. This will make the next morning marginally less terrible. Settle in for a chilly night, try to sleep. You're going to need all your energy.

DAY 3: TO THE SACRED PEAK

Before you start this hellish climb leave everything you don't need at the camp. Pack one bottle of drinking water and some energy snacks. Allow about 3 hours from Arcopodho to the peak. Leave the camp at 3 am if you're very fit (the less fit should begin around 1:30 am). Aim to be at the summit at sunrise, otherwise you'll freeze: it gets extremely cold when the wind is blowing.

The trail above the tree line is straight, tough and unremittingly steep. Your feet sink into fine, 20-cm deep ash, and for every four steps up you slide back two. It's an odd feeling, like climbing up and down at the same time. You'll reach the sacred peak after 3–4 hrs of sliding and crawling.

When the sun is out you can count on an incredible summit experience. All the mountains of eastern Java lie beneath you. On a clear day you can see as far as Bali. While enjoying the marvelous views you will suddenly be surprised by a strange rumbling that immediately turns into a terrifying thundering noise.

Roughly every half hour Semeru's dark throat belches a gas and ash explosion. Hot gas shoots into the sky with terrifying speed, building up a huge cloud shaped like a black cauliflower. Then 50 or more smoking lava bombs fall down from a height of 150 m, crashing into the fine ash and thundering down Semeru's steep flanks. To witness such an explosion close at hand is to switch off time and space and let pure awe take over. **WARNING**: stay a minimum 200 m away from Semeru's vent. The overly curious may well find themselves beneath a shower of lava chunks.

Leave the peak region by 11 am at the latest. Always be aware if the wind changes direction: this is very dangerous. Deadly gases from Semeru's vent then engulf both summits. Climbers unfamiliar with the mountain have become disoriented and died up here when this happens. If the weather becomes foggy or cloudy don't take the risk and turn back to Kali Mati. Only leave Semeru's summit in a Northerly direction: descending by any other route will end in disaster.

Just past Ranupani village there is a short cut down to the Sea of Sands: where the jeep track meets the rim of the Tengger caldera and turns left. Follow the track for another 200 m and find the path to your right.

It is best to take 3 days for this marathon, but fitter trekkers have done it in less. Allow for an extra day to rest your weary bones either at one of the lakes, at the Mata Kari Pura waterfall near Sukapura or on the balcony of your *losmen*.

— *Tom Otte/Bob Cowherd*

Java's Eastern Tip

See map, page 288.

Java's eastern tip, essentially the area east of Mount Bromo, has enormous potential for visitors. There are four important wildlife reserves: Baluran, South Banyuwangi (aka Alas Purwo), Ijen-Merapi and Meru Betiri, as well as great surfing beaches at Plengkung on the southeastern tip. This is an area nature lovers would do well to consider exploring for some time, for it remains largely untouched by the tourism boom, and retains an unsurpassed natural beauty. The ideal way to get around is to hire a 4-wheel-drive jeep: local public transport can be frustrating.

Pasir Putih

This isn't really a town but a strip of beach on the north coast with a handful of hotels and restaurants stretched along its length. And the sand isn't really white (as the name "white beach" implies) but dark gray. But on weekdays it's a quiet seaside getaway.

Pasir Putih is an hour and a half from Probolinggo by **public bus** (80¢) and 2 hours from Banyuwangi ($1). The entrance fee to the beach is 25¢. **Boat rentals** to see the reef cost $5 for a quick trip and $7.50 an hour for longer adventures. All hotels are near the beach but only the more expensive rooms open onto the sand.

Bhayangkara (51 rooms) ☎ 22/4 Panarukan. Rooms on the beach for $7.50 (fan) and $18 (AC).

Sido Muncul (33 rooms) ☎ 22/3 Panarukan. Pasir Putih's best bet. $5–10 with bath, $12 with fan. $15–26 for the good AC rooms.

Baluran National Park

Take a bus from Situbondo (55¢) or Ketapang Terminal (30¢) to Wonorejo, and the entrance and main office of the Baluran National Park (open 7 am–5 pm). Here you pay a $1 park fee and arrange transportation and accommodation.

To Bekol and the beach at Bama, round trip *ojek* is $3 and chartered *bemo* is $8. There's a campsite and a guesthouse at the gate or a dorm ($2 per bed) and bungalows ($4) at Bekol and bungalows for $2 at Bama. The rooms in Baluran are sometimes filled by groups so contact them in advance at Taman Nasional Baluran, Jl A Yani 108, Banyuwangi ☎ (0333) 41119.

Bondowoso

Telephone code is 0332.

A tidy town with tidy hotels near a beautiful National Park. A lot of competition in the budget range. Take a 2.5-hour bus ride from Probolinggo for $2, or a 1 hour (30¢) ride from Jember, to the Bondowoso terminal which is a 50¢ *becak* ride from the hotels and the *alun-alun*. Non-guests can use the Palm Hotel pool for 50¢.

Baru Jl RA Kartini 26 ☎ 21474. Best deal in town. Clean and cheap. $4 shared bath; $6 own bath.

Palm (62 rooms) Jl A Yani 32 ☎ 21505, 21201. A comfortable base camp for excursions into Ijen Crater. Has a pool, AC rooms, and restaurant. They can also arrange transportation into the park. $5 shared bath, $10 to $15 with bath and $22 to $44 with AC and hot water.

Wisma Kinanti (9 rooms) Jl Santawi 583A ☎ 41018. Funky two story sitting area. Clean. $3.25 S, $3.50 D shared bath and $3.75, $4.50 D private bath.

Go to **Depot Lezat** for *ayam Bali*, a spicy-sweet chicken and *nasi liwet*, five dishes with rice; **Restaurant Anugerah** for lots of food for little money.

Ijen Merapi Maelang Reserve

Kawah Ijen (Ijen Crater) is accessible from the west via a long road from Bondowoso, or from the east by taking a shorter drive and longer walk from Banyuwangi. Both routes go to Paltuding, the starting point for the 2.5 km, 1 hour climb. Even in the dry season, late morning clouds can obscure the view of Ijen, so stay nearby and start early enough to get to the crater rim by 8–9 am.

From Sasak Perot Terminal in Banyuwangi, take a *bemo* for the 1 to 2-hour drive up to Jambu (35¢) and pay 60¢ entrance fee. From here you must improvise. Either hitch a ride on a truck or charter a vehicle for the 24-km climb to Banyulinu: the end of the road. Other options are to charter a van and driver in Banyuwangi or charter a *bemo* at Sasak Perot Station for much less. From Banyulinu it's a 2-hour hike to Paltuding.

Bondowoso is a good base for trips onto the plateau. From here you can sometimes catch a *bemo* directly to Sempol for 40¢, or get on one heading for Situbondo and change at Wonosari.

If your funds are stretched, try the trucks which run from Bondowoso to Watu Capil, the last village before Kawah Ijen. They leave every morning from near Toko Hijau on Jl Wahid Hasyim, 300 m from Losmen Slamet. Departure times are extremely flexible: only rely on the answer from the driver himself, and make sure he's heading for Watu Capil direct. The cost is $1.10 for the 3-hour, 60 km journey. If you don't speak Indonesian, try the helpful advice of Mr Sujono, the owner of Toko Sentosa. His shop is near Toko Hijau and he speaks some German and English.

At the Sempol PHPA office, pay the 60¢ park fee and ride an *ojek* to Paltuding (around $2). Otherwise walk for 3 hours to Paltuding.

To get to Kawah Ijen early enough to enjoy the view try the rooms in and around Sempol. These aren't cheap and are arranged through the PHPA office in Sempol or by contacting PTP XXVI, Jl Gajah Mada 249, Jember. **Arabica Kalisat** has rooms for $12.50 economy and $25 standard; **Catimore Blawan** has rooms for $21 and two bungalows for $27 a night; **Robusta Malangsari** is $25; and **Wisma SK Jampit** has room for up to 50 guests for $4 a bed.

It's sometimes possible to share with the friendly staff of the PHPA hut just 4 km below the crater. Give a donation and bring extra food. If there's no room try the sulphur company hut at Pos 2, 1.5 km below the crater rim. The best time to visit is during the week. On weekends and holidays accommodation is scarce.

Jember

Telephone code is 0331.

Jember, set amid a lush agricultural region, is a 2-hour scenic bus ride ($1) from Banyuwangi.

Bandung Permai (70 rooms) Jl Hayam Waruk 38 ☎ 84528; fax: 81099. Well run. Has a big pool. $25 standard II, $31 standard I and $46 suite.

Losmen Widodo (32 rooms) Jl Suprapto 74 ☎ 86-350. The best deal in Jember. Fairly clean. $2.50 shared bath, $2.75 S and $3 D with bath, $3.75 S and $4 D with fan and open air showers.

Safari (30 rooms) Jl KHA Dahlan 7 ☎ 21058. Spotless. Great carved furniture in the sitting area. $5–8 (fan), $17 (AC) and $20–33 hot water & AC.

Seroja (25 rooms) Jl P Sudirman 2 ☎ 83905. Popular and often full. $5 to $7.50 shared bath, $11 to $12.50 with bath and fan.

Eat at **Mulyasari**, Jl Sultan Agung 24 for great *nasi gudeg* (rice with young jackfruit stew) or **Restaurant Jawa Timur** at Jl Gatot Subroto 10 which specializes in East Javanese dishes.

Watu Ulo Beach

The name translates as "Snake Stone" (*watu* means stone, *ulo* means snake) and the giant scaly rock which juts out of the ocean here gives this place its name. Your best bet is to stay at Wisnu Watu Ulo (see below) and explore this interesting area for a day or two.

Don't go straight to the popular beach by the rock itself, instead take the road 1km uphill towards **Papuma Beach**: a beautiful long stretch of sand which has purpose-built shady areas. Curiously, the beach here is pristine white, in contrast to the pitch black sand near Watu Ulo.

A short walk from Papuma Beach to the top of the hill brings you to a great spot for expansive views of the coastline and outlying islands.

From Jember, Watu Ulo is a 75¢ public (last trip at 3 pm), or $5 chartered, *bemo* ride. There is one humble hotel: **Wisnu Watu Ulo** (25 rooms, no phone) near the beach. Rooms $2.25–4 all with private bathrooms & fans.

Picturesque Mayangan Beach lies east of Watu Ulo: look out for a left turn some 2kms before Snake Rock. Rows of colourful Madurese fishing boats are moored here. Get there early to see the early morning arrival of the fleet.

Sukamade-Meru Betiri Reserve

You can take *bemo* from Banyuwangi as far as Pasanggaran for around $1.25 (3–4 hours) and charter a vehicle for around $10 for the last leg along very poor roads. Going back you can catch a ride on the Sukamade truck that leaves every morning at 6 am for 75¢ as far as Pasanggaran. Stay at the simple but friendly **Wisma Sukamade** for $8.25 a night including meals. From here to the beach to watch the turtles is a 5-kilometer $1.25 *ojek*, round trip.

Kalibaru

This small town, some 60 km east of Jember on the road to Banyuwangi, is of little significance except for the presence of one of the most comfortable and pleasant places to stay in East Java. This is the **Margo Utomo Hotel** ☎ (0333) 95001, just north of the train station. The rooms are spotless and comfortable with high ceilings in a fantastic garden setting surrounded by a plantation, the harvest of which is served in the dining room. Rooms are $25 D and $19 S including breakfast. Lunch and dinner cost $7 more. Trips to Ijen Crater and Sukamade are available. Trains leave every morning from Banyuwangi to Kalibaru for $1.50. A two-hour bus ride costs half the price and they run all day.

Banyuwangi

Telephone code is 0333.

The fabulously varied landscapes of eastern Java's national parks are well worth some time to explore. Buses arrive at **Ketapang Terminal** 8 km north of Banyuwangi at all times of night and day shuttling passengers by ferry across the narrow Bali Strait between Java and Bali.

There's a good **Tourist Information Center** at the south end of the terminal. To get to Banyuwangi from the terminal catch a *bemo* to Blambangan Station in town and either take another *bemo, becak* or walk to a hotel from there. Newer hotels offer the best deals.

Baru Jl Haryono 82–84 ☎ 21369. The new best bet in Banyuwangi. All rooms have private bathrooms with soap and hand towels. $3.50 S to $4.50 D economy and others from $8 S to $13 D.

Banyuwangi Beach Jl Raya Gatot Subroto Km 7, Ketapang ☎ 41090. Only so-so but less than 1 km south of Ketapang terminal. $7.50 fan; $12–14 AC.

Berlin Barat (34 rooms) Jl Haryono 93 ☎ 21323. Nice clean rooms around a courtyard. $3.25 S to $5 D with bath.

Ikhtiar Surya (39 rooms) Jl Gajah Mada 9 ☎ 210-63. New. Lots of cozy garden nooks with trees and water. A bit out of town. $6 Economy; $9 Standard with fan and TV; $14–18 First Class with AC; VIP rooms with a full fridge for $38.

Kumala (22 rooms) Jl A Yani 21B down the *gang* ☎ 61287. New. Very clean and reasonable. $5 S and $6.25 D with fan, $7.50 with bath, $10 with AC and $15 with hot water and refrigerator.

Wisma Blambangan (19 rooms) Jl Dr Wahidin 4, ☎ 21598. A long time Banyuwangi favorite. $3 S to $4.25 D shared bath. $6.50 S to $9.50 D with bath and fan, $10 to $12.50 with AC.

Eat at **Wina**, Jl Basuki Rakhmat (in front of the Blambangan Station) for good fish. Try the *ayam kecap* (a local chicken recipe) at **Rumah Makan Jawa Timur**, Jl Basuki Rakhmat 37.

Change money at **Bank Buana Indonesia** Jl A Yani 26 ☎ 41070. Open 8 am to 2 pm Mon to Fri, 8 am to 12:30 pm Sat. A good **travel agent** is Banyuwangi Tours and Travel Service at Jl KH Wahid Hasyim 42 ☎ 61720 offering package tours to the parks. You can also arrange a **car and driver** here for about $20 plus gas.

If you are chartering a *bemo* for the day from the Ketapang Terminal a reasonable price to get to Sukamade is $30 to $40. Anything less means they have probably never been there before and don't know any better. They may want to turn around half way or ask for more money later.

Alas Purwo National Park

See map, page 288.

From Banyuwangi, either take a car straight to Trianggulasi Beach, or public transportation from Blambangan Terminal, 5 kilometers south to Karang Inti Station (15¢) and change to a *bemo* to Kalipahit (50¢, 2 hours).

From Kalipahit hire an *ojek* for $1 to take you to Trianggulasi, stopping at the PHPA office on the way to pay your $1 park fee. From here it's a 15 km hike (about 3 hrs) to Plengkung Beach. Very basic quarters are available at Trianggulasi for $1.25 per person. Arrange this when you pay your park entrance fee. Bring food and water.

Plengkung Beach is considered one of the ten best surfing spots in Asia and the huts here are available only along with surfing trip packages from April to October. A 7-day trip is $400 and 3 days is $200 including food, lodging and the trip from Bali where most of the tours are arranged from. Also available in Banyuwangi with a $50 travel discount: PT Wanawisata Alamhayati, Jl Jaksa Agung Suprapto 152 ☎ 21485.

— Bob Cowherd/Tom Otte

Further Reading

The literature on Java, scholarly as well as popular, is copious. Below is a selection of the more readable and informative books in English mainly for the non-specialist. Many have been published or reprinted by Oxford University Press in Singapore and may be purchased either there (Changi airport has excellent bookshops) or Jakarta (try major hotel newsstands or Times Bookshop in Plaza Indonesia shopping center).

HISTORY

Abeyasekere, Susan (1985) *Jakarta: A History*. A good survey, strong on social history of 18th and 19th century Jakarta; available only in Singapore.

Anderson, B.R.O'G. (1972) *Java in a Time of Revolution: Occupation and Resistance 1944–46*. A compelling study by a leading scholar in the field.

Bellwood, Peter (1985) *Pre-history of the Indo-Malaysian Archipelago*. A detailed work that has revolutionized our view of Indonesian prehistory. By marshalling data from various fields, Bellwood traces the migrations of Austronesian peoples from mainland Asia via Taiwan and the Philippines to the islands of Indonesia and the Pacific.

Boxer, C.R. (1965) *The Dutch Seaborne Empire 1600-1800*. The story of Dutch empire-building and subsequent decay in Asia. A standard work that is available only in England.

Day, Clive (1904) *The Policy and Administration of the Dutch in Java*. A highly readable and polemical, if not always accurate, account of the social abuses of the 19th century Dutch "Cultivation System" (*Cultuurstelsel*) in Java. Available in an Oxford-in-Asia reprint. For the flip side of the coin, get a copy of *Java* or *How to Manage a Colony* (1861) by J.B. Money—an Englishman who was absolutely infatuated with the efficiently exploitative Dutch system. He urged that it be applied by the English in India. Also reprinted by Oxford.

Kahin, G. McT. (1952) *Nationalism and Revolution in Indonesia*. Fascinating eye-witness account of the revolution, by an American pioneer in the field of modern Indonesian studies.

Raffles, T. S. (1817) *The History of Java*. The first serious scholarly study published about the island and its people, this "history" contains fascinating tidbits of information on everything from food to antiquities to female comportment. Available in a costly Oxford reprint.

Ricklefs, M.C. (1974) *Jogjakarta under Sultan Mangkubumi 1749-1792: A History of the Division of Java*. An exciting, blow-by-blow narrative account of the convoluted battles and intrigues that resulted in the division of the Mataram kingdom and the founding of Yogyakarta at the middle of the 18th century. Based on Javanese and Dutch sources. A must for those interested in the *keraton* of Central Java. Available from Cambridge Univ. Press.

— (1981) *A History of Modern Indonesia c. 1300 to the Present*. A readable and succinct overview, much of it relating to Java. Rather heavy going for the lay reader, due to the many dates, names and toponyms cited, but a good reference work.

Schrieke, B.J.O. (1957) *Ruler and Realm in Early Java*. A fascinating reconstruction of such things as the early transportation network of Java, based largely on early Dutch descriptions.

THE ARTS

Becker, Judith (1980) *Traditional Music in Modern Java: Gamelan in a Changing Society*. An anthropological look at Javanese *gamelan*.

Bernet Kempers, A.J. (1959) *Ancient Indonesian Art*. A classic work by a former head of the Archaeological Service. Consists mainly of photos of the principal monuments, with brief but informative descriptions and diagrams. Unwieldy to carry around, but an essential companion for the temple nut.

Brandon, James (1967) *On Thrones of Gold: Three Javanese Shadow Plays*. Annotated, readable translations of three traditional Javanese *wayang kulit* stories or *lakon*.

Elliot, Inger McCabe (1984) *Batik: Fabled Cloth of Java*. Lavishly illustrated. A visual feast, with sections on regional *batik* styles.

Gittinger, Mattiebelle (1979) *Splendid Symbols: Textiles and Tradition in Indonesia*. The best overall survey of traditional textiles in Indonesia. Available in Singapore and Indonesia as an Oxford-in-Asia paperback reprint.

Holt, Claire (1967) *Art in Indonesia: continuities and change*. Still the best popular survey in English of traditional and modern Indonesian music, dance, wayang, painting and sculpture. Long out of print but available in many libraries.

Jessep, Helen (1990) *Court Arts of Indonesia*. Gorgeous book, prepared for Festival of Indonesia exhibition by the Asia Society. Includes photos and descriptions of some of the most sacred *pusaka* or royal heirlooms of Java. Gold crowns; *kris* scabbards studded with gems, etc.

Kunst, Jaap (1973) *Music in Java*. The standard, 2-volume work on the subject. Highly technical, but indispensible for the serious student.

Miksic, John (1990) *Borobudur: Golden Tales of the Buddhas*. An introduction to the world's largest Buddhist monument. Tells what is known of its complex architectural history and symbolism, and recounts the major stories contained in over 1,400

bas-relief panels on Borobudur. Lavishly illustrated; widely available in Singapore and Indonesia.
— (1990) *Old Javanese Gold.* Beautifully illustrated, with detailed descriptions of ancient Hindu-Javanese pieces collected in Java by a Singaporean businessman. Available only in Singapore.
Van Ness, Edward and **Sita Prawirohardjo** (1985) *Javanese Wayang Kulit.* A concise, popular introduction to the shadow play.

LITERATURE

Conrad, Joseph *Victory.* Part of this famous turn-of-the-century novel is set in Surabaya, with a number of memorable characters. Evokes the last days of the European merchantmen.
Koch, C.J. (1978) *The Year of Living Dangerously.* A somewhat kitschy romance set against the backdrop of the 1965 putsch, made into a feature film of the same name starring Mel Gibson and Sigourney Weaver. The title comes from Sukarno's prophetic phrase, *tahun vivere pericoloso.*
Lubis, Mochtar (1957) *Twilight in Djakarta.* The underside of Jakartan life during the down and out 1950s. The author was imprisoned by Sukarno for this and other works critical of the government.
Multatuli (Douwes Dekker, E.) (1860) *Max Havelaar, or the Coffee Auctions of the Dutch Trading Company.* A convoluted novel about a sensitive Dutch administrator stricken by a sense of guilt over the suffering of Javanese peasants under the "Cultivation System." The public outrage generated by this book in Holland was greatly responsible for a change in colonial policy ten years after its publication. Available in English from Univ of Mass. Press.
Nieuwenhuys, Rob (1982) *Mirror of the Indies: A History of Dutch Colonial Literature.* A survey of scores of literary works set in colonial Indonesia, several of which have been translated into English. Available from Univ. of Mass. Press.
Pigeaud, Th.G.Th. (1967) *Literature of Java.* 3 vols. An annotated catalog of Javanese manuscripts, mostly from Dutch collections. The first volume contains an introductory survey by "genres" of traditional Javanese literature.
Zoetmulder, P. (1974) *Kalangwan: A Survey of Old Javanese Literature.* A scholarly survey of the earliest works of Javanese literature.

LANGUAGE

Almatsier, A.M. (1974) *How to Master the Indonesian Language.* A handy teach-yourself guide. Widely available in Indonesia and cheap.
Barker, John (1976) *Practical Indonesian.* A traveler's phrase-book available in most hotel newsshops, giving you just enough Indonesian to get around on your own.
Echols, John and **Hassan Shadily** (1989) *An Indonesian-English Dictionary.* The best dictionary of its kind and the only one really worth consulting. Available in all major bookshops in Indonesia in an inexpensive, student paperback edition.
Uhlenbeck, E.M. (1964) *The Languages of Java and Madura.* A bibliography to linguistic studies of Javanese, now rather dated.

JAVANESE SOCIETY

Anderson, B.G.O'G. (1965) *Mythology and the Tolerance of the Javanese.* An analysis of Javanese character as seen through the mirror of the *wayang* shadow play.
Geertz, Clifford (1960) *The Religion of Java.* A thoroughly-documented work by one of America's best-known anthropologists, that has nevertheless been roundly criticized by a younger generation of scholars for vastly over-simplifying a very complex situation. Geertz's basic thesis is that the majority of Javanese peasants (*abangan*) are superstitious animists, while the aristocrats (*priyayis*) are more mystically inclined and the urban middle class (*santris*) tend to be orthodox Muslims.
— (1963) *Agricultural Involution.* Insightful study of 19th century economic and social stagnation in Java. An extension of earlier Dutch studies of a colonial "dual economy" which prevented Java from developing a class of Indigenous capitalists and urban enterpreneurs. One of the best things about the book is simply its description of wet-rice agriculture as an ecosystem.
Hefner, Robert (1985) *Hindu Javanese: Tengger Tradition and Islam.* A comprehensive anthropological study of religion in the Tengger region around Mt. Bromo in East Java.
Mulder, Niels (1978) *Mysticism and Everyday Life in Contemporary Java.* An analysis of the pervasive mystical and fatalistic attitude toward life on the part of the Javanese.

GEOGRAPHY, GUIDES AND TRAVELOGUES

Abdurachman, Paramita R. (1982) *Cerbon.* A useful little book on the history and arts of the Cirebon area. Text in both Indonesian and English, with many illustrations; sometimes available in Indonesian bookshops.
Bennett, Richard and Shila (1978) *Bandung and Beyond.* Useful guide, even if now quite outdated, to the more "adventurous" sights in West Java.
Dalton, Bill (1988) *Indonesia Handbook.* The first and most complete guide to the entire Indonesian archipelago. Lots of off-beat tips, but much of the hyped-up information has to be taken with a hefty pinch of salt. Recently up-dated, with a number of useful maps.
Heuken, Adolf (1982) *Historical sights of Jakarta.* A detailed guide to all places of historical interest in and around the nation's capital. A must for the serious visitor to Jakarta. Widely available.
Official Tourist Bureau, Weltevreden (1921) *Come To Java.* First travel guide to the island, in English. Fascinating as a historical document, on how people traveled in those days, where they stayed, etc.
Wallace, A.R. (1869) *The Malay Archipelago.* Famous travelogue by a contemporary of Darwin's, one of the greatest 19th century English naturalists. Contains vivid descriptions of Java as it was over a century ago: a wild island of pristine jungles inhabited by huge snakes, tigers, rhinos, etc.

About the Authors

Tim Behrend is a long-time student of Javanese literature and intellectual history. A native of Cleveland, Ohio, he first came to Indonesia in 1975 as a missionary for the Mormon Church. Since 1987, when he completed his Ph.D. in Javanese literary history at the Australian National University, he has been working as a Ford Foundation consultant on manuscript cataloguing and microfilming projects in Yogya and Jakarta. He resides in Jakarta.

Peter Bellwood is a Reader in Prehistory at The Australian National University, specializing on Southeast Asian and Pacific prehistory. His archaeological fieldwork have been in New Zealand, central Polynesia (Marquesas and Cook Islands), Indonesia (Talaud Islands) and Malaysia (Sabah). His books include *Man's Conquest of the Pacific* (1978), *Prehistory of the Indo-Malaysian Archipelago* (1985) and *The Polynesians* (1987).

Janet Boileau worked as a writer, editor and publisher in Jakarta since arriving from London in 1986. The author of innumerable articles on travel, business, culture and society in Indonesia, was also involved in feature films, documentaries and books. After two years of traveling, diving and filming in Indonesia, she is currently based in the capital.

Roggie Cale is a long-time student of Indonesian art and culture, having spent many years in Yogyakarta in the 1970s studying Javanese classical dance. The co-author of *Java: A Garden Continuum* now lives and works in Houston, Texas as a professional actor.

Simon Cook studied music at Cambridge University before moving to Holland, where he became interested in Indonesian culture and started playing Javanese *gamelan*. From 1985 to 1987 he taught Western music in Yogyakarta. He then embarked on graduate studies at SOAS, London University, specializing in Sundanese music and language. He now lives in Bandung.

Bob Cowherd is an architect whose attention was first drawn to Java while playing *gamelan* music in New York. Based in Solo since 1991, he is active in urban design, historic preservation and cultural tourism throughout Java and Bali and is an official advisor to the Keraton Surakarta.

Gary Crabb is a graduate of University of Michigan in applied linguistics and has been living abroad for over 15 years. A translator and writer of fiction, he is currently publisher-editor of *Bandung Banana Review*, a cross-cultural magazine.

Robert Cribb, an Australian, studied Indonesian history at the universities of Queensland and London. He worked as a specialist on Indonesia in Australia and the Netherlands. His research included such diverse topics as warlords and opium smuggling during Indonesia's revolution and the history of environmental protection in Indonesia. He is author of the *Historical Dictionary of Indonesia* (1990).

Peter Hadley was born in Perth, W. Australia. While studying for his B. Mus. (hons) in composition at the University of Western Australia he joined the university *gamelan* orchestra. During the Indian Ocean Arts Festivals of 1979 and 1984, when actual Indonesian musicians came to perform and teach in Perth, he became hooked on *gamelan*. He is currently studying *karawitan* at STSI Surakarta.

Sandra Hamid was born in Jakarta in 1962. She moved to Bali soon after finishing her degree at the Faculty of Social & Political Sciences of the University of Indonesia. She has also worked for an interior designer and the Bali Hyatt.

Robert Hefner and **Nancy Smith-Hefner**, anthropologist and linguist, are specialists of Javanese culture and reside in Boston, Massachusetts. Robert is Associate Professor of Anthropology at Boston University and the author of *Hindu Javanese: Tengger Tradition and Islam* (1985) and *The Political Economy of Mountain Java: An Interpretive History* (1991). Nancy is Assistant Professor of Linguistics at the University of Massachusetts and the author of numerous articles on women, language and religion in Java.

Derek Holmes was born in Kettering, England, in 1938, and graduated in geology at Bristol University in 1960. He has worked in the evaluation of land resources for agricultural development in Asia since 1963, and in Indonesia since 1974. He is also an ornithologist, and he is co-editor of *Kukila*, the bulletin of the Ornithological Society of Indonesia. He has authored two popular books on birds covering Java, Bali, Sumatra and Kalimantan.

Jan Hostetler has lived in Java for more than 7 years. She studied dance in Yogya, and while a student at Cornell University carried out dissertation research among young people in Jakarta. Currently she is Resident Director for the Cooperative Southeast Asian Program at IKIP Malang sponsored by the Council on International Educational Exchange.

Roy E. Jordaan is a graduate of Leiden University, where he obtained a Ph.D. with a thesis entitled *Folk-Medicine in Madura*. He is now living in Jakarta with his wife, Anke Niehof, and family. His most recent publications deal with the mid-9th century Loro Jonggrang temple complex at Prambanan.

Tim Kortschak was born in Melbourne, Australia, in 1963. After traveling extensively around Australia and Southeast Asia, he took an arts degree in the Department of Asian Area Studies and Languages at the University of Melbourne in 1988. Since then he has been living in Solo, Central Java, where he studies *pedalangan* at Solo's performing arts academy and privately with several *dalang* in the vicinity. He is interested in photography, billiards, writing and old motorbikes.

Ann Kumar was born in Melbourne, Australia, and studied history at the University of Melbourne and the Australian National University where she completed her Ph.D. She is currently Head of the Asian History Centre at ANU, where she teaches Indonesian history and contemporary politics. Current research interests are 19th century society, early history and Javanese influence outside Java.

Cécile Lomer was born in Paris and studied Arabic at Cambridge University. She is a translator and a writer especially interested in film media and has collaborated on several projects dealing with Indonesian wildlife. She has lived in Indonesia for four years, traveling extensively throughout the country.

John Miksic holds a doctorate in Southeast Asian history from Cornell University and is now a lecturer in history at National University of Singapore. He has spent many years conducting research in Indonesia under the sponsorship of the Ford Foundation and the Asian Cultural Council.

Anke Niehof studied cultural anthropology and demography, obtaining a Ph.D. at Leiden University in 1985 with a thesis entitled *Women and Fertility in Madura*. Presently she is in Jakarta as a consultant at the National Family Planning Coordinating Board, working on a project which supports income activities for family planning acceptors in three rural districts near Jakarta.

Dede Oetomo, a native of Pasuruan in East Java, came to Surabaya to attend high school in 1969 and has lived and worked there since, except for several years spent in Malang and 5 years at Cornell University, the latter to undertake graduate work in sociolinguistics and Southeast Asian studies. He is currently a lecturer in linguistics and anthropology at the Airlangga University.

Eric Oey attended Phillips Exeter Academy and has degrees in mathematics from Brown University and in Indonesian language and literature from the University of California at Berkeley. He studied for a year in Solo, Central Java, under a Fulbright grant in 1982-83.

Onghokham, whose special interest is the social history of Java, received a Ph.D. in history from Yale University. He lectured at the University of Indonesia from 1963–89. He contributes frequently to Indonesian newspapers and magazines, e.g.*Tempo, Kompas, Suara Pembaruan* and *Prisma*.

Tom Otte is a photographer/writer who has trekked extensively in the Rocky Mountains, the Andes, Asia and Europe. Drawn to Indonesia in 1989 by the country's 400 volcanoes, he returns regularly to work on his book *Climbing the Fire Mountain*.

Marc Perlman lived in Solo from 1984 to 1987 studying *karawitan*. In 1988-1990 he taught ethnomusicology at the University of North Sumatra, Medan, as a consultant to the Ford Foundation. Since 1989 he has been on the editorial board of the Indonesian Musicological Society. He is currently Program Notes Editor for the Festival of Indonesia.

Gottfried Roelcke graduated 1975 in geography from Hannover university, Germany. There, he befriended Indonesian students. He first visited the country in 1977 and has been a resident since 1982, working as technical adviser in Samarinda/East Kalimantan, Padang/West Sumatra, and now Bandung/West Java. He finds Indonesia a perfect place for his hobbies: hiking, photography and meeting nice people. He is currently working on a book on Bandung and the Parahyangan Highlands.

Laurie Sears is Assistant Professor of Southeast Asian History at the University of Washington in Seattle. She spent almost five years carrying out research in Central Java. Her work focuses on the interaction between Javanese oral and written literary traditions. She co-edited a volume entitled *The Boundaries of the Text: Epic Performances in South and Southeast Asia* (1991).

Amir Sidharta was born in Jakarta. After attending Oberlin College, Ohio, he received a B.A. in architecture from University of Michigan. He is keen on the traditional art and ancient architecture of Java and Bali. His photographs of Balinese antiquities appeared in an edition of Bernet Kempers' *Monumental Bali* (1991). Currently a Fulbright Scholar undertaking a M.A. degree in museum studies.

Holly Smith has a degree in journalism from Ohio State University. She has worked for various international newspapers and magazines and written three novels and a business textbook. As first "ambassador" for the Reproduction of Endangered Wildlife, she travels throughout Indonesia, pursuing projects on wildlife, culture and conservation.

Eric Summers, born in Australia, studied to be a veterinarian and worked in an airline office before coming to Indonesia in 1973 to begin a new career as a successful batik entrepreneur. He now divides his time between Jakarta, Yogya, Bali, Pekalongan, Singapore, Sydney, Semarang, Bangkok, Phuket, Koh Samui and anywhere else the Hash House Harriers happen to be running.

Joan Suyenaga first came to Indonesia in 1973 to study Javanese *gamelan*. Born in Hawaii, she studied both at the University of Hawaii (M.A., Anthropology) and in Java (*gamelan*, old Javanese literature). Presently residing in Yogya with her family, she does free-lance writing and translating.

Jennifer Thom has a M.A. in World Music from Wesleyan University. She has been in Indonesia for two years, studying language, then music and dance in Bali, and for the last year, music and dance in Solo towards her dissertation.

Roger Vetter, who teaches ethnomusicology at Grinnell College, was first introduced to Javanese performing arts in 1972. His interest in Javanese musical expression has been pursued through studying the performance practice of *gamelan* music both in Java and with Javanese musicians teaching in the U.S. To date, two albums of his field recordings have been released and several articles about Javanese music have been published. His dissertation, completed in 1986, is an extensive study of the musical life of the *keraton* of Yogyakarta.

Valeria Mau Vetter has been involved with Javanese performing arts since 1971. She spent extended periods of time in Central Java studying traditional Javanese dance, music, and *wayang golek* puppetry. She presently resides in Grinnell, Iowa, where she teaches Javanese dance and has directed several dance performances.

Index

Map Index